Contents at a Glance

D1543601

Windows® 7 Desktop Support and Administration

Real World Skills for MCITP Certification and Beyond

Darril Gibson

WILEY

Wiley Publishing, Inc.

Acquisitions Editor: Jeff Kellum
Development Editor: Gary Schwartz
Technical Editors: Troy McMillan and Rodney Fournier
Production Editor: Dassi Zeidel
Copy Editor: Linda Recktenwald
Editorial Manager: Pete Gaughan
Production Manager: Tim Tate
Vice President and Executive Group Publisher: Richard Swadley
Vice President and Publisher: Neil Edde
Media Project Manager 1: Laura Moss-Hollister
Media Associate Producer: Marilyn Hummel
Media Quality Assurance: Shawn Patrick
Book Designers: Judy Fung and Bill Gibson
Compositor: Craig Johnson, Happenstance Type-O-Rama
Proofreader: Publication Services, Inc.
Indexer: Ted Laux
Project Coordinator, Cover: Lynsey Stanford
Cover Designer: Ryan Sneed
Cover Image: Image Source / Jupiter Images

Copyright © 2010 by Wiley Publishing, Inc., Indianapolis, Indiana

Published simultaneously in Canada

ISBN: 978-0-470-59709-5

For general information on our other products and services or to obtain technical support, please contact our Customer Care Department within the U.S. at (877) 762-2974, outside the U.S. at (317) 572-3993 or fax (317) 572-4002.

Wiley also publishes its books in a variety of electronic formats. Some content that appears in print may not be available in electronic books.

Library of Congress Cataloging-in-Publication Data

Gibson, Darril.
  Windows 7 desktop support and administration : real world skills for MCITP certification and beyond / Darril Gibson.—1st ed.
    p. cm.
Summary: "A manual for Windows 7 desktop technicians and administrators It is estimated that 90 percent of the world's computers run Windows. Desktop technicians and administrators need this comprehensive manual to guide them through their daily work with Windows 7. While this Sybex guide is packed with information you'll need to know for the MCITP certification exam, it is equally valuable in real-world situations you will encounter on the job. Covers troubleshooting, hardware and software applications, large-scale desktop environment management, and planning and configuring the desktop infrastructure using Windows 7. Provides plenty of relevant information for those seeking MCITP certification, including full coverage of the exam objectives for both Desktop Support Technician and Desktop Administrator exams. Includes a CD with valuable study tools for the MCITP exams including video walkthroughs, flashcards, and two practice exams. Windows 7 Desktop Support and Administration provides knowledge that will be needed on certification exams and remains a valuable reference for support and administrative personnel on the job."—Provided by publisher.

ISBN: 978-0-470-59709-5 (pbk)
ISBN: 978-0-470-90079-6 (ebk)
ISBN: 978-0-470-90081-9 (ebk)
ISBN: 978-0-470-90080-2 (ebk)

  1. Electronic data processing personnel—Certification. 2. Microsoft software—Examinations—Study guides. 3. Microsoft Windows (Computer file) I. Title.
  QA76.3.G52693 2010
  005.4'46—dc22

                          2010019080

10 9 8 7

Dear Reader,

Thank you for choosing *Windows 7 Desktop Support and Administration: Real World Skills for MCITP Certification and Beyond*. This book is part of a family of premium-quality Sybex books, all of which are written by outstanding authors who combine practical experience with a gift for teaching.

Sybex was founded in 1976. More than 30 years later, we're still committed to producing consistently exceptional books. With each of our titles, we're working hard to set a new standard for the industry. From the paper we print on, to the authors we work with, our goal is to bring you the best books available.

I hope you see all that reflected in these pages. I'd be very interested to hear your comments and get your feedback on how we're doing. Feel free to let me know what you think about this or any other Sybex book by sending me an email at nedde@wiley.com. If you think you've found a technical error in this book, please visit http://sybex.custhelp.com. Customer feedback is critical to our efforts at Sybex.

Best regards,

Neil Edde
Vice President and Publisher
Sybex, an Imprint of Wiley

To Nimfa, my wife of over 18 years who also reminds me how much better life is when it is shared with a loved one. I'm looking forward to 18 more.

Acknowledgments

Books of this size and depth succeed because of the hard work put in by a full team of professionals. I'm grateful for all the hard work put in by several people at Sybex on this project. Gary Schwartz was a great developmental editor. He helped keep things on track and provided excellent editorial guidance. The technical editor, Troy McMillan, provided insightful input throughout the book. I appreciated the meticulous attention to detail provided by Dassi Zeidel, the production editor. Last, but certainly not least, I want to thank Jeff Kellum, the acquisitions editor, for having the faith in me to write another book for the Sybex brand.

About the Author

Darril Gibson   is the CEO of Security Consulting and Training, LLC. He has been a Microsoft Certified Trainer (MCT) for more than 10 years and has taught a wide variety of courses to both public and private clients. He has taught courses on MCSE (NT 4.0, Windows Server 2000, Windows Server 2003), MCITP (Windows Vista, Windows Server 2008, and SQL Server), MCSD (Visual Basic), networking fundamentals, and network security.

He currently holds many IT certifications, including MCT, MCSE, MCITP, Security+, CISSP, and ITIL Foundations v3.

Darril has authored, coauthored, or contributed on more than 10 IT books. These include books on Microsoft Windows Server 2008, SQL Server, Windows Vista, CompTIA's Security+, and risk management.

When not writing or teaching, he can often be found with his wife and two dogs at their country getaway. It's a little place on 20 acres where he spends a lot of time enjoying quiet country walks.

Contents

Table of Exercises

Introduction

Windows is the number 1 desktop operating system worldwide. With Windows XP close to the end of its successful lifetime and Windows Vista not fully embraced, Windows 7 is sure to be a huge success.

Microsoft has created several exams for Windows 7. These include the following:

- 70-680: Microsoft Certified Technology Specialist (MCTS): Windows 7, Configuration

- 70-685: Microsoft Certified Professional (Pro): Windows 7, Enterprise Desktop Administrator

- 70-686: Microsoft Certified Professional (Pro): Windows 7, Enterprise Desktop Support Technician

- 70-682: Microsoft Certified Professional (Pro): Upgrading to Windows 7 MCITP Enterprise Desktop Support Technician

You can view the objectives for each of these exams with the following links: http://www.microsoft.com/learning/en/us/exam.aspx?ID=70-680, http://www.microsoft.com/learning/en/us/exam.aspx?ID=70-682, http://www.microsoft.com/learning/en/us/Exam.aspx?ID=70-685, and http://www.microsoft.com/learning/en/us/Exam.aspx?ID=70-686.

If you pass the 70-680 exam, you'll earn the MCTS on Windows 7 Configuration certification. Two additional certifications are available:

- Microsoft Certified IT Professional (MCITP): Enterprise Desktop Support Technician 7

  To earn this certification, you must pass the 70-680 exam and the 70-685 exam.

- Microsoft Certified IT Professional (MCITP): Windows 7, Enterprise Desktop Administrator

  To earn this certification, you must pass the 70-680 exam and the 70-686 exam.

If you've previously earned either the Microsoft Certified Desktop Support Technician (MCDST) on Windows XP or the Enterprise Desktop Support Technician (EDST) certification on Windows Vista, you can take the 70-682 exam in place of both the 70-680 and the 70-686 exams.

Microsoft originally indicated that the MCITP Windows 7 Enterprise Desktop Support Technician certification would also require passing an HDI certification exam. That requirement has been dropped. You do not need to pass a third-party exam to earn either of the MCITP exams on Windows 7.

This book covers all of the objectives for the 70-685 and 70-686 exams. It doesn't include the more basic objectives for Windows 7 in the 70-680 exam.

Who Should Read This Book

This book was written for two primary audiences:

Administrators on the job   This book is primarily written for administrators who need to install, deploy, and support Windows 7. It's intended to be an on-the-job reference book to help real-world administrators support Windows 7 from a desktop administrator or desktop support technician perspective.

Exam takers   This book covers all of the objectives for the 70-685 and the 70-686 exams. If you're studying for either of these two exams, this book is an excellent supplement to other exam materials. It can help you master the objectives so that you will pass either of these exams the first time you take it.

What You Need

This book leads you through the paces of managing and supporting Windows 7. It includes many exercises that require you to have Windows 7 installed on your system.

Chapter 9, "Managing Windows 7 in a Domain," includes exercises that allow you to create a virtual environment using Windows Virtual PC (VPC). These exercises lead you through the process of installing Windows Server 2008 in the virtual environment and creating a virtual domain. Both VPC and a trial version of Windows Server 2008 can be downloaded for free. Your system will perform best if you have at least 4 GB of RAM installed.

What Is Covered in This Book

Windows 7 Desktop Support and Administration: Real World Skills and Knowledge for MCITP Certification and Beyond is organized to provide the knowledge you'll need to support Windows 7. It includes the following chapters:

Chapter 1: Planning for the Installation of Windows 7 covers some basics about the Windows 7 editions used in the enterprise. You'll learn how the User State Migration Tool can be used to ensure users have the same data and settings after an upgrade or migration as they did before the upgrade or migration. You'll also learn about different virtualization technologies including Windows XP Mode. This chapter closes with important details on licensing and activation including Multiple Activation Keys and the Key Management Service server.

Chapter 2: Automating the Deployment of Windows 7 covers the different types of images used to deploy Windows 7 using lite-touch and zero-touch installations. It includes details on how to use the Windows Automated Installation Kit and Windows Deployment Services to capture and deploy images. It also provides an overview on the Microsoft Deployment Toolkit.

Chapter 3: Using the Command Prompt and PowerShell covers the basics of the command prompt and the newer PowerShell. This is an invaluable chapter for administrators who aren't familiar with these tools but need to learn them to master important trouble-shooting and administrative skills.

Chapter 4: Managing the Life Cycle—Keeping Windows 7 Up to Date includes details on the different types of updates available for Windows 7 and how to keep systems up to date. You'll learn how to use free auditing tools such as the Microsoft Baseline Security Analyzer to check your systems. You'll also learn how to use Windows Server Update Services to automate the deployment of updates to clients on your network.

Chapter 5: Maintaining and Troubleshooting Windows 7 covers many of the common tools used to identify and resolve performance issues. It includes basic tools such as the Event Viewer, the new Action Center, the Services applet, and different power plans. It includes details on the new Windows Recovery Environment and how it can be used to resolve many common Windows 7 problems. This chapter closes with information on managing hardware in Windows 7 and troubleshooting boot issues.

Chapter 6: Configuring and Troubleshooting Application Issues includes details on requirements to install and configure software. If the application isn't supported on Windows 7, you can use one of several different virtual strategies including Windows XP Mode. The deployment of applications can be automated with Group Policy or System Center Configuration Manager. You'll also learn about various methods to identify and resolve software failure issues.

Chapter 7: Networking with Windows 7 includes details related to connecting a Windows 7 system in a network. These include basic connectivity in any enterprise and how names are resolved to IP addresses. You'll learn how to use the Network and Sharing Center to check and verify connectivity. You'll also learn how to troubleshoot network connectivity problems.

Chapter 8: Accessing Resources on a Network covers how resources are accessed in a network. This includes the basics of how you can connect to shared resources and how permissions can control who can connect. You'll also learn how to identify and resolve common network printer issues.

Chapter 9: Managing Windows 7 in a Domain shows you how Windows 7 functions in a domain. It includes exercises to help you create a virtual network of a domain controller and a Windows 7 client computer. You'll learn how to join a domain and basic differences between authentication and authorization. This chapter details how to identify and resolve logon issues and how different profiles are used. It ends with the basics on anti-malware software.

Chapter 10: Managing Windows 7 with Group Policy covers important concepts related to Group Policy. You'll learn about the scope of a GPO, the order of precedence, and how to configure advanced settings like Block Inheritance, Enforced, and Loopback Processing. You'll also see several of the Group Policy settings that you can use to control Windows 7 behavior in a domain.

Chapter 11: Managing Security in Windows 7 covers many of the important security capabilities that come with Windows 7. You'll learn about the improved User Account Control (UAC) feature and how you can modify its default behavior. You'll learn about many of the security policies that can be used to lock down any system including Windows 7 and the new Removable Storage Access Policy used to control removable devices. This chapter includes information on BitLocker, with a focus on how to recover keys needed to restore an enterprise user's data. It concludes with information on Windows Firewall.

Chapter 12: Supporting Mobile Windows 7 Users covers mobile and remote users. Windows 7 includes many security features that can help secure connections to wireless networks. It also includes support for several tunneling protocols used for virtual private networks (VPNs), including the newer IKEv2 tunneling protocol. You'll learn about DirectAcess, which can be used in place of VPNs. Last, this chapter covers BranchCache, which can improve performance for Windows 7 users in remote locations.

Chapter 13: Administering Internet Explorer covers Internet Explorer version 8 (IE 8). You'll learn about many of the new features including InPrivate Browsing. This chapter also covers many of the new and basic security features for IE 8. It closes with tips on troubleshooting different issues with IE 8.

Appendix A includes a mapping of all the 70-685 and 70-686 exam objectives to the chapter where the objective is covered. This appendix includes both the chapter and the section title for each objective.

Appendix B identifies the contents of the companion disk and how to use it.

The **Glossary** is a list of relevant terms covered in the book.

The companion CD is home to all the demo files, samples, and bonus resources mentioned in the book. See Appendix B for more details on the contents and how to access them.

How to Contact the Author

I welcome feedback from you about this book or about books you'd like to see from me in the future. You can reach me by writing to Darril@mcitpsuccess.com. For more information about my work, please visit my website at mcitpsuccess.com or search "Darril Gibson" on Amazon.com.

Sybex strives to keep you supplied with the latest tools and information you need for your work. Please check their website at www.sybex.com, where we'll post additional content and updates that supplement this book if the need arises. Enter *search terms* in the Search box (or type the book's ISBN—9780470597095), and click Go to get to the book's update page.

Chapter

1

Planning for the Installation of Windows 7

TOPICS COVERED IN THIS CHAPTER INCLUDE

- ✓ Choosing a Windows 7 edition
- ✓ Performing a local installation of Windows 7
- ✓ Designing User State Migration
- ✓ Considering virtualization
- ✓ Planning and managing client licensing and activation

One of the first steps you need to take when planning a migration to Windows 7 is choosing which edition of Windows 7 to deploy. For an enterprise, your choice is limited to Windows 7 Professional, Windows 7 Enterprise, or Windows 7 Ultimate. To make the right choice, you'll need to know what features are available in each edition.

Once you identify the edition you'll use, you need to come up with a migration plan. Because many organizations will be upgrading existing Windows XP computers to Windows 7, having a solid plan to migrate users' data is very important. The User State Migration Tool (USMT) can simplify this process for you with the use of `ScanState` and `LoadState`.

Although virtualization wasn't common on end users' desktops in the past, the new Windows XP Mode available in Windows 7 is sure to change this for many users. It's now possible for end users to run applications on a Windows 7 system in a transparent virtual instance of Windows XP.

Activation of Windows 7 can be done individually, with a Multiple Activation Key or with a Key Management Service server. Whereas home users will always use individual activation, you may need to use one of the other methods in larger or isolated enterprises.

Choosing a Windows 7 Edition

When planning a migration or tech refresh, a simple question to ask is what Windows 7 edition is needed. Windows 7 offers six editions, but you'll quickly whittle down the choice to just three for an enterprise because the first three are too basic for a work environment.

Microsoft lists this topic in some documentation as "Choosing a SKU (Stock Keeping Unit)." An SKU is the number associated with the bar code you see on just about any product these days.

These are the three basic editions that you won't see in an enterprise:

Windows 7 Starter   Some original equipment manufacturers (OEMs) preinstall this edition on specialized computers. It includes the fewest features, and it will not be available in 64-bit versions.

Windows 7 Home Basic   This is available only in certain countries referred to as emerging markets, and it includes very limited capabilities. It will not be available in the United States.

Windows 7 Home Premium   *Windows 7 Home Premium* is designed for home users. It includes the Windows Media Center, which can be used to record and play back TV shows or other media. It can also easily integrate on a home network with other devices such as Xbox gaming systems. Systems running this edition can't join a domain.

If you're a desktop support technician or desktop administrator working in an enterprise, you'll focus on the following three editions used in work environments:

Windows 7 Professional   *Windows 7 Professional* is intended for high-end home users and small-business users. It can join a domain, support a remote desktop, and run applications in a virtual environment using Windows XP Mode. It does lack some of the more advanced features.

Windows 7 Enterprise   The *Windows 7 Enterprise* edition is available only to organizations that have a Software Assurance contract with Microsoft and is purchased through a volume license. Home users won't have access to this, but businesses with as few as five PCs can purchase Software Assurance.

Some key features included in this edition are BitLocker, AppLocker, and BranchCache. Each of these will be explored in greater depth in later chapters. BitLocker (covered in Chapter 11, "Managing Security in Windows 7") can be used to protect data on both internal and external drives, including USB flash drives. AppLocker (covered in Chapter 6, "Configuring and Troubleshooting Application Issues") can be used to prevent unauthorized software from running. BranchCache (covered in Chapter 12, "Supporting Mobile Windows 7 Users") allows clients in remote locations to cache data used by others in the same location.

Windows 7 Ultimate   The *Windows 7 Ultimate* edition includes all of the features found in the Enterprise edition, and home users using a single license can purchase it instead of going through the Software Assurance program. Home users can upgrade to Windows 7 Ultimate from either Windows 7 Home Premium or Windows 7 Professional.

Windows 7 Ultimate doesn't include any "ultimate extras" as Windows Vista Ultimate did. These "extras" in Windows Vista were advertised to entice some users to purchase Windows Vista Ultimate. Instead of getting extras not available elsewhere, the reason to purchase Windows 7 Ultimate is to have the features found in the Enterprise edition, such as BitLocker, AppLocker, and BranchCache.

Table 1.1 shows a comparison of many of the features included in Windows 7 Professional, Windows 7 Enterprise, and Windows 7 Ultimate. Since there is very little difference between Enterprise and Ultimate, they are shown in the same column. Some of the features that are more relevant for desktop administrators working in an enterprise environment are covered after the table.

TABLE 1.1   Windows 7 versions and features

Feature	Windows 7 Professional	Windows 7 Enterprise and Ultimate
32-bit and 64-bit versions	Yes	Yes
AppLocker	No	Yes
Backup and Restore center	Yes	Yes
BitLocker Drive Encryption	No	Yes
BranchCache Distributed Cache	No	Yes
DirectAccess	No	Yes
Fast user switching	Yes	Yes
File and printer sharing connections	20	20
Home Group	Yes	Yes
Subsystem for UNIX-based applications	No	Yes
Virtual hard disk booting	No	Yes
Volume licensing keys	Yes	Enterprise only
Windows Aero	Yes	Yes
Windows Media Center	Yes	Yes
Windows XP Mode	Yes	Yes

x86 vs. x64

Windows 7 comes in both 32-bit (x86) and 64-bit (x64) editions. Let me state the obvious—you must have 64-bit hardware in order to install the 64-bit edition. It is also possible to install the 32-bit edition on 64-bit hardware.

The biggest benefit of using a 64-bit edition over a 32-bit edition is RAM (random access memory). With a 32-bit system, you're limited to addressing and using no more than 4 GB of RAM. But even that is limited. Because of the way that RAM is addressed and used in Windows operating systems, only about 3.3 GB of RAM is actually available when 4 GB is installed; the rest of the RAM is unused because of how address space is reserved.

However, Windows 7 Professional, Enterprise, and Ultimate all support as much as 192 GB of RAM on 64-bit systems. This gives you enough RAM to support multiple virtual environments hosted on a single system and also to support even the most demanding applications.

Years ago, many applications didn't run effectively on 64-bit editions of Windows because of various compatibility issues. However, the era of 64-bit systems has arrived. Many programs have both 32-bit and 64-bit versions, and those that don't have a separate 64-bit edition usually work on a 64-bit system without any problems.

AppLocker

AppLocker is a new feature in Windows 7 that can be used to control what software is allowed to run on individual PCs using either Local Security Policy (nondomain computer) or Group Policy in Active Directory. It can be used to restrict unauthorized software from running on systems.

Although software restriction policies existed in previous versions of Windows, AppLocker provides improvements that solve many of the problems with these software restriction policies. For example, a software restriction policy could be used to prevent an application from running. However, when some applications were updated, the software restriction policy no longer recognized the application and no longer restricted the application.

AppLocker uses a rule-based structure that an administrator can build to ensure that the policy doesn't need to be rewritten each time an application is updated. Group Policy and AppLocker will be covered in greater depth in Chapter 10, "Managing Windows 7 with Group Policy."

BitLocker

BitLocker Drive Encryption allows you to protect entire drives by encrypting them. This can be especially useful on disks in mobile computers when the data needs to be protected. When BitLocker is implemented, the entire drive is encrypted. It can be configured to unlock the drive automatically after the system verifies the drive is in the same computer or configured so that users enter a passphrase to unlock access to the drive.

The BitLocker to Go feature is new to Windows 7. BitLocker to Go can be used to encrypt and lock removable drives, including USB flash drives.

Both BitLocker and BitLocker to Go will be explored in greater depth in Chapter 11.

BranchCache

BranchCache is useful for clients in remote offices that access data over virtual private network (VPN) links. When data is stored on a Windows Server 2008 R2 server at the main office and BranchCache has been enabled, users in the remote office are able to store a cached copy of the data on their local computers. This is similar to Offline Folders, which has been available for many versions of Windows, but has a distinct difference. Data cached on one Windows 7 computer can now be shared with other Windows 7 users.

As an example, consider several users connected in a remote office over a very slow 56KB wide area network (WAN) link to the corporate office. Sally and Joe are users in the remote office, and their computers are connected to each other using 100MB network interface cards (NICs). Sally downloads an 8MB file from a Windows Server 2008 R2 server. Later, Joe wants to view the file and tries to access it from the same Windows Server 2008 R2 server. BranchCache verifies that Joe has permission to access the file, recognizes that the file is cached on Sally's computer, and recognizes that Sally's version is the most recent version. BranchCache then redirects Joe's computer to retrieve the file from Sally's computer instead of over the slow WAN link.

Users in remote offices can experience much greater speed when accessing commonly used files over the WAN link. However, only Windows 7 computers can take advantage of BranchCache. BranchCache will be explained in greater depth in Chapter 12.

Windows XP Mode

Windows XP Mode is a virtualization application that allows users to run a completely separate instance of Windows XP within Windows 7. This can be especially useful for applications that aren't compatible with Windows 7 but will run in Windows XP.

Applications installed in Windows XP Mode will appear on the user's Windows 7 Start menu. While they appear to run on the Windows 7 desktop, they are actually running in the virtual Windows XP Mode environment. Windows XP Mode is covered in more depth later in this chapter, including how to install it.

Software Assurance

Windows 7 Enterprise is available only to businesses that have purchased the Software Assurance program, so you may be interested in knowing a little about it. It's a Microsoft program offered to organizations that purchase licenses through a volume-licensing program. Volume licensing allows a company to purchase licenses in bulk at a discount instead of purchasing multiple individual copies.

Organizations that can purchase Software Assurance include businesses with as few as five employees, government entities, schools, and campuses. It is actually purchased through Microsoft partners, and the benefits are coordinated through Microsoft once they are activated. Benefits differ based on how many clients and licenses are purchased.

The benefits may include

- Free upgrades to newer versions of the software during the licensing period
- The option to spread payments over a longer period of time (as opposed to the initial cost of purchasing all the licenses)
- Training vouchers for Microsoft courses taught by Microsoft partners
- Access to e-learning courses
- 24x7 telephone and web support

Local Installation

It's possible that you'll need to install Windows 7 from the installation media at some point. You'll learn about Lite Touch Installation (LTI) and Zero Touch Installation (ZTI) in Chapter 2, "Automating the Deployment of Windows 7," but you may occasionally need to do a "heavy touch" installation. No, there's no acronym for heavy touch installation, mostly because you don't want to be doing it that often.

Installing one or two systems manually is no big deal, but if you have to install 5, 50, or more, you'll want to automate the process. For the most part, the installation of Windows 7 is straightforward with few surprises. The biggest challenge may come if you have to change partitions on the hard disk or add additional disk drivers.

Exercise 1.1 will walk you through the steps needed to install Windows 7 from the installation DVD.

EXERCISE 1.1

Installing Windows 7 from the Installation DVD

1. Place the Windows 7 installation DVD in the DVD drive and boot the system. After a moment, the Install Windows screen will appear, as shown in the following graphic.

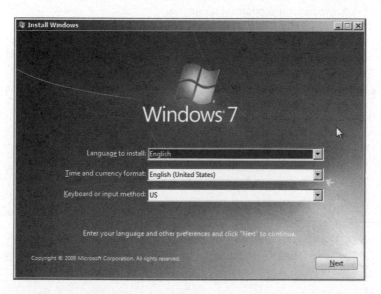

Although it looks like you have minimal choices here, you can press Shift+F10 to access the command line from this menu. In the "Creating a Bootable VHD" exercise later in this chapter, you'll access the command line to create and configure a VHD file.

EXERCISE 1.1   *(continued)*

2. Select the appropriate Language To Install, Time And Currency Format, and Keyboard Or Input Method, and click Next.

3. Click Install Now.

4. Review the license terms, and select I Accept The License Terms. Click Next.

5. Select Custom (Advanced) to install a new copy of Windows. If an existing version exists that can be upgraded to Windows 7, you can select Upgrade.

6. Select the partition where you want to install Windows.

    Notice that you can create additional partitions from this screen. However, if you start with anything other than a single precreated partition, Windows will create a partition labeled System Reserved of about 100 MB, as shown in the following graphic. This partition includes the Windows Recovery Environment (WinRE) and ensures that all Windows features can work correctly. Also, once it's created, you can't get rid of the partition without reinstalling the OS.

    If you don't want this partition added, you must format the entire drive as a single partition before starting the installation. You can do so by accessing the command prompt by pressing Alt+F10 at the Install Now page and using DiskPart. You can later shrink the volume to create additional partitions.

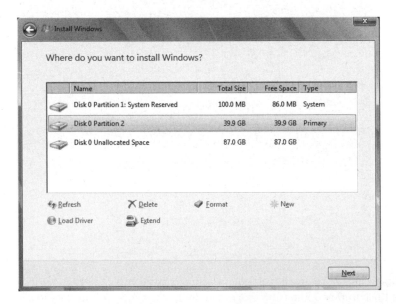

Notice that you can also delete, extend, and format partitions from this page. You can also load a driver from this page if your hard drive isn't recognized. Beware though— if you repartition the drive, you'll lose access to data that would normally be stored in the Windows.old folder after the installation. Once you have selected the partition, click Next.

7. The installation will take several minutes to complete, but it will be automated from this point.

8. When the installation completes and reboots, you will be prompted to type a user name, as shown in the following graphic. As you enter the user name, the computer name will be created by appending the user name with -*PC*. You can accept this computer name or type in a different computer name. Click Next once you're satisfied with the user name and computer name.

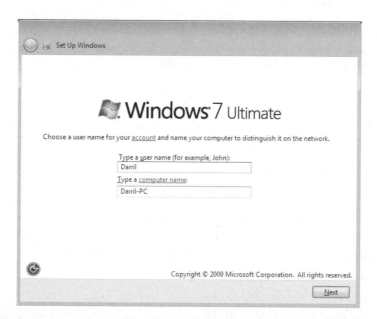

9. The Set A Password For Your Account page screen prompt will appear. This password is for the account you created in the previous step. You need to type in a password, retype the same password for confirmation, and type a password hint. Once you've entered this information, click Next.

10. Enter the product key for your edition of Windows on the Type Your Windows Product Key screen. The check box Automatically Activate Windows When I'm Online is checked by default. Leave it checked and click Next.

11. You'll be prompted to configure the computer for automatic updates. The Use Recommended Settings selection will automate the download and installation of updates, but you can choose Only Install Important Updates or set it to ask you later. Select one of the choices.

EXERCISE 1.1 *(continued)*

12. Choose your time zone on the time zone and clock screen. Make sure the time and date are accurate, and click Next.

13. Select Work Network as the computer's current location.

14. The Windows 7 desktop will appear. The installation is complete.

Designing User State Migration

The majority of Microsoft installed clients are Windows XP. Thus, if you're considering adding Windows 7, you probably have many Windows XP clients. Unfortunately, there isn't a direct upgrade path from Windows XP to Windows 7.

> If you can do a direct upgrade, you won't need to worry about migration. An upgrade will retain all of the installed applications and all of the user's data. An upgrade is still considered a risky operation, and it's possible that things can go wrong, so you should always have a backup of the user's data in case the worst happens.

If you've looked at the upgrade paths from earlier versions of Windows to Windows 7, you may have been a little surprised. There are very few upgrade choices. Some of the possible upgrade paths to versions likely to be used in the Enterprise are

- Vista Business to Windows 7 Professional, Enterprise, and Ultimate
- Vista Enterprise to Windows 7 Enterprise
- Vista Ultimate to Windows 7 Ultimate

If you're migrating other existing Windows clients, you probably won't be able to do an upgrade. This doesn't have to be as painful as it sounds. The User State Migration Toolkit has undergone significant changes and improvements and will make your job a lot easier.

USMT can be used in three types of migrations. Each one assumes that you have files and settings from a Windows XP, Windows Vista, or Windows 7 installation that you want to restore to a new installation of Windows 7.

In-place migration An in-place migration uses the same hardware for the old and new installations of Windows. Hard drive partitions are not modified, and files and settings from the previous installation are automatically retained in the Windows.old folder.

Wipe-and-load migration   A wipe-and-load migration uses the same hardware. However, partitions on the hard drive holding the original operating system need to be modified, which will prevent the Windows.old folder from being created during the new installation. Instead, you must use USMT before the installation to save the files and settings to a migration store from the previous installation. This migration store can then be restored to the new installation of Windows 7.

Side-by-side migration   A side-by-side migration uses two computers. You can use USMT to save the files and settings to a migration store from the original computer before it's decommissioned. You can then use USMT to restore the migration store to Windows 7 on the new computer.

In this section, you'll learn where to get the USMT, how to install it, and how to use it in each of the different types of migration.

User State Migration Toolkit

If you used the *User State Migration Toolkit (USMT)* from previous operating systems, you may not have been overjoyed by the performance. I know I wasn't. However, you'll find significant improvements in the USMT on Windows 7. In addition, the time required to perform a migration has been substantially reduced.

The User State Migration Toolkit is a part of the *Windows Automated Installation Kit (AIK)* for Windows 7. Older versions of the AIK exist, so you need to ensure you have the version specifically designed for Windows 7.

You can use the USMT to migrate data from Windows XP, Windows Vista, or Windows 7. It supports the following migration paths:

- Windows XP to Windows Vista
- Windows XP to Windows 7
- Windows Vista to Windows 7
- Windows 7 32-bit to Windows 7 64-bit

The Windows AIK is available as a free download from Microsoft's download site (www.microsoft.com/downloads) by searching for "Windows Automated Installation Kit (AIK) for Windows 7." This download is an .iso file, so you'll need to burn it to a DVD.

> Burning a CD or a DVD from an .iso file is built into Windows 7. Place the disk in the drive and then use Windows Explorer to browse to the .iso file. Right-click the file and select Burn Disc Image. Windows 7 will do the rest.

Once you download the Windows AIK for Windows 7 and burn the image to a DVD, insert the DVD into your computer's drive. You can then follow the steps in Exercise 1.2 to install the Windows AIK, which includes the USMT.

EXERCISE 1.2

Installing Windows AIK Including the USMT

1. If prompted after inserting the DVD, select Run The StartCD.exe. If not prompted, browse to the StartCD.exe file using Windows Explorer and double-click it to start Windows AIK. The installation screen appears, as shown in the following graphic.

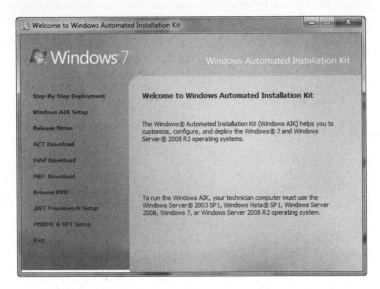

2. Select the Windows AIK Setup link on the left.

3. On the Welcome screen, click Next.

4. Review the license agreement, select I Agree, and click Next.

5. Accept the default installation folder of C:\Program Files\Windows AIK and the choice Install This For Everyone. Click Next.

6. On the Confirm Installation screen, click Next.

7. When the installation completes, click Close.

8. The Microsoft Windows AIK folder is available in the All Programs menu.

Once the Windows AIK is installed, you'll have several program links on the Start menu within the Microsoft Windows AIK Start menu folder. These include

Deployment Tools Command Prompt   This launches a command prompt at the C:\ Program Files\Windows AIK\Tools\PETools folder, which gives you access to many of the files used when creating a Windows Preinstallation Environment (Windows PE or WinPE).

Windows System Image Manager   This is used to create an unattend.txt text file that can be used to automate an installation and to open images.

Documentation   This provides links to several help files including the Unattended Windows Setup Reference, the Windows Automated Installation Kit, and the Windows PE User's Guide. Not all help files are available here. Notably for this chapter, the help file for the USMT isn't accessible here even though it was installed. The USMT help file is available in the C:\Program Files\Windows AIK\Docs\CHMs folder and is named WAIK.chm.

VAMT 1.2   The VAMT 1.2 folder includes a help file for the Volume Activation Management Tool (VAMT) and a link to launch the Volume Activation Management Tool.

You'll use more of these tools later in this chapter and in Chapter 2. For now, the focus is on the USMT tools ScanState and LoadState.

Performing In-Place Migration

When you do the installation of Windows on a computer running Windows XP, Windows Vista, or Windows 7, you can do a Custom (Advanced) installation. A message will appear similar to Figure 1.1, informing you that you can access files from the previous installation in a folder named Windows.old.

FIGURE 1.1   Windows installation notification

    Files from the previous installation will be gone if you do any advanced repartitioning of the existing hard drive. The Windows.old folder will be created only if you use the partition as it exists when the install is started.

Now all you have to do is get the data out of the Windows.old folder and back to the original location. You can spend hours cutting, pasting, and adjusting permissions, or you can automate the process with the User State Migration Tool.

Running ScanState and LoadState

Two important files that are added to your system with USMT are ScanState and LoadState. You can use these two files from the command prompt or in batch files to automatically examine your system and restore user accounts, files, and settings in a very short time.

ScanState   *ScanState* will collect files and settings from a previous installation or from the Windows.old folder. It will store these files and settings in a migration store.

LoadState   *LoadState* can read the files and settings from the migration store and restore them to the current computer.

> When you install the Windows AIK, it includes two folders for USMT: USMT\ x86\ and USMT\AMD64\. The x86 folder is for 32-bit systems, and the AMD64 folder is for 64-bit systems. While the AMD64 folder implies it's only for AMD 64-bit processors, you also use files within this folder for 64-bit Intel processors.

User profiles include a significant amount of data, including the desktop, document folders, Registry settings, and much more. When you use USMT for an in-place migration, it uses a hardlink migration store when the data is migrated from the Windows.old folder. This significantly reduces the time and space required to migrate all of this data. Instead of actually copying the data from one place to another on the hard drive, it just changes the links to where the data is located.

This is similar to what happens when you move a file from one location to another using drag and drop in Windows Explorer. For example, imagine a project on which you are working includes several files, so you decide to create a folder named Project and drag and drop all the files into that folder. The system doesn't create a brand-new copy of these files and then delete the originals. Instead, it just changes the file system links to these files so that they are now "located" in the Project folder.

Similarly, the hardlink migration feature in ScanState and LoadState will change the location of these files without having to copy all of the data. This can be significant if you're dealing with several GB of data.

It's fairly easy to put the ScanState and LoadState commands into a batch file that you can use to automate the migration of files and settings for multiple computers in your network. However, before automating ScanState and LoadState, it's good to know what the commands are doing.

The ScanState command is executed first. The following line shows how it may be executed to retrieve the migration data from the Windows.old folder. Note that even though it shows on more than one line in this book, you should enter it as a single command without any returns.

```
ScanState.exe c:\store /v:13 /o /c /hardlink /nocompress /efs:hardlink
  /i:MigApp.xml /i:MigDocs.xml /offlineWinDir:c:\windows.old\windows
```

I realize it's long, but the good news is that you don't need to modify it at all. Just copy it from the book, and it'll work for many common migrations. The following bullets break down the command:

- `ScanState` is the name of the command.
- `c:\store` is the location where the migration data will be stored.
- `/v:13` indicates the highest level of verbosity. It will provide a significant amount of output to the log that can be viewed later. The lowest level is 0, which logs only errors and warnings.
- `/o` causes it to overwrite an existing migration store (if one exists).
- `/c` tells `ScanState` to continue to run even if errors are encountered.
- `/hardlink` is used for in-place migrations to retrieve the data from the `Windows.old` folder. It requires the use of the `/nocompress` switch.
- `/nocompress` specifies that data is not compressed.
- `/efs:hardlink` specifies that encrypted file system (EFS) files will be moved using hardlink migration. The `/hardlink` switch must be used for this to succeed.
- `/i:MigApp.xml` specifies that the `MigApp.xml` file (which is included in the USMT folder) will be used to identify application settings to migrate.
- `/i:MigDocs.xml` specifies that the `MigDocs.xml` file (which is included in the USMT folder) will be used to identify document types to migrate.
- `/offlineWinDir:c:\windows.old\windows` is used to specify the location of the files from the original installation.

After the `ScanState` command is executed to capture the migration data, the `LoadState` command is executed to restore the migration data to the current installation.

When performing in-place migrations, you can enter the `LoadState` command with the following switches. Just as the `ScanState` command should be entered as a single line, the following `LoadState` command should be entered as a single line even though it spans more than one line in this book.

```
LoadState.exe c:\store /v:13 /c /lac:P@ssw0rd /lae /i:MigApp.xml
  /i:MigDocs.xml /sf /hardlink /nocompress
```

- `LoadState.exe` is the command.
- `c:\store` is the location of the migration store created by `ScanState`.
- `/v:13` indicates the highest level of verbosity. It will provide a significant amount of output to the log that can be viewed later. The lowest level is 0, which logs only errors and warnings.
- `/c` tells `ScanState` to continue to run even if errors are encountered.

- /lac:P@ssw0rd specifies that local accounts should be created if they don't already exist. If the /lac switch is not used, local accounts will not be migrated. The same password will be used for all migrated accounts, and if a password is not specified, the password will be empty. You should use caution if using the password in a batch file because it will be stored in clear text, and anyone with access to the batch file can read the password.

- /lae specifies that local accounts should be enabled. The /lac switch must be used to migrate the accounts. When it is used, all migrated accounts will be enabled.

- /i:MigApp.xml specifies that the MigApp.xml file (which is included in the USMT folder) will be used to identify application settings to migrate.

- /i:MigDocs.xml specifies that the MigDocs.xml file (which is included in the USMT folder) will be used to identify document types to migrate.

- /sf restores shell folder redirection if a user had previously used folder redirection on any of their user folders. For example, a user may have redirected the My Documents folder to be stored on a server share or on a different partition.

- /hardlink is used for in-place migrations to retrieve the data from the Windows.old folder. It requires the use of the /nocompress switch.

- /nocompress specifies that data is not compressed.

More details on both the ScanState and LoadState commands, including a full listing of all the switches, are included in the USMT.chm help file included with the Windows AIK. You can access this help file in the C:\ Program Files\Windows AIK\Docs\CHMs\ folder.

Exercise 1.3 will lead you through the process of creating a batch file and running it to migrate user data for in-place migrations. This assumes that the computer was running Windows XP, Windows Vista, or Windows 7 and that a clean installation of Windows 7 was then performed on the system. Data from the previous installation is stored in the Windows.old folder of the C: drive. Last, the Windows AIK for Windows 7 is also assumed to have been installed on this system.

EXERCISE 1.3

Running USMT in a Batch File

1. Launch Windows Explorer, and browse to the C: drive. Create a folder called **MyUSMT**.

2. Right-click within the folder, and select New ➢ Text Document. Press Enter to open the text document.

3. Type the following lines in the text document. Note that the ScanState and LoadState commands span two lines in this book, but they should be entered as a single command in the document.

    ```
    Cd "c:\Program Files\Windows AIK\Tools\USMT\x86"
    rem
    ScanState.exe c:\store /v:13 /o /c /hardlink /nocompress /efs:hardlink
      /i:MigApp.xml /i:MigDocs.xml /offlineWinDir:c:\windows.old\windows
    rem
    LoadState.exe c:\store /v:13 /c /lac:P@ssw0rd /lae /i:MigApp.xml
      /i:MigDocs.xml /sf /hardlink /nocompress
    ```

    The first command changes the directory to the . . .\USMT\x86 folder on the C: drive. If you are running a 64-bit system, you can substitute this with. . .\USMT\ amd64 instead. The rem lines are remark or comment lines I added to separate the ScanState and LoadState commands for easier readability.

4. Select File ➢ Save As.

5. Type in **usmt.bat** and click Save. By adding the .bat extension, you tell Notepad to save the file as a batch file (with a .bat extension) that can be executed instead of a text file (with a .txt extension). Close the file.

6. Click Start ➢ Accessories, right-click the command prompt, and select Run As Administrator. If prompted by User Account Control, click Yes to continue.

7. Type in the following command to change the directory to the C:\MyUSMT directory you created earlier:

    ```
    Cd \MyUSMT
    ```

8. Type in **usmt** and press Enter to run your batch file. This will take several minutes to complete, and the output will appear on the screen. When you've finished, the migration is complete.

9. Using Windows Explorer, browse to the C:\Program Files\Windows AIK\Tools\ USMT\x86 folder (or the C:\Program Files\Windows AIK\Tools\USMT\amd64 if you used that folder in your batch file. Locate and open the loadstate.log file and the scanstate.log file. With a verbosity level of 13 used in the commands, you'll see that a lot of data has been logged and can be reviewed to view the activity of both commands.

While the previous exercise had you create a batch file with the ScanState and LoadState commands, it is possible just to execute the commands at the command prompt. However, if you have created the batch file, you can create your own portable tool that can be easily executed on any system to perform an in-place migration.

Creating a Portable USMT Batch File

If desired, you can make your batch file a little more portable. Instead of installing the Windows AIK for Windows 7 on every computer that you are migrating, you can copy the appropriate files to a USB flash drive or CD. These files consume only about 50 MB.

You can then bring your USB flash drive or CD to any computer that has had an in-place migration, run the batch file, and the migration will be done in minutes.

 For more on this process, check out the TechNet article "Building a USB Drive to Store USMT 4.0 Files and Simple Commands." You can read it here: http://technet.microsoft.com/library/dd940094.aspx.

You'll still need to install the Windows AIK onto a Windows 7 computer. Once it's installed on any Windows 7 computer, you can use Windows Explorer to copy the USMT folder onto the portable media such as a USB flash drive.

- Browse to the C:\Program Files\Windows AIK\Tools\USMT folder.

- Right-click the USMT folder and select Copy.

- Insert a USB flash drive.

- Browse to the USB flash drive using Windows Explorer, right-click, and select Paste.

At this point, you'll have the entire contents of the USMT folder on the flash drive. This includes the USMT folder used for 64-bit systems (\USMT\amd64\) and the folder used for 32-bit systems (\USMT\x86).

Now you'll need to create a batch file that can be used on any system. The batch file used in the previous exercise can be used as a starting point, but it will need to be slightly modified.

The USMT files need to be copied to the C: drive on the system that is being migrated, so the first step in the batch file is to copy these files. This sounds simple enough, but it's impossible to tell what the letter of the USB drive will be when it's plugged in on any given system. That is, when you plug the USB into Sally's computer, the USB disk may be assigned the letter E:, but when you plug it into Joe's computer, it might be assigned the letter F:.

You can use the following If exist statement in the batch file to check to see if the USB flash drive is assigned the letter D:. It checks for the USMT folder at the root of D:. If it exists, it assumes this is the USB flash drive and copies the USMT folder from the flash drive to the Windows folder on the C: drive.

```
If exist D:\USMT\*.* XCopy /e /v /y C:\Windows\USMT\
```

The /e switch specifies that all directories should be copied—even empty ones. The /v switch is used to verify the files, and the /y switch is used to suppress prompting if any files are overwritten.

TIP   Chapter 3 covers the XCopy command and other elements of the command prompt in more depth.

Unfortunately, this works only if the USB flash drive is assigned the letter D:. It could be assigned other letters such as E:, F:, and so on. You can add multiple lines to your batch file to check for which letter is actually assigned to the USB flash drive. Simply copy and paste the following line, changing only the letter of the drive:

```
If exist E:\USMT\*.* XCopy /e /v /y C:\Windows\USMT\
If exist F:\USMT\*.* XCopy /e /v /y C:\Windows\USMT\
```

Once you have added the extra lines, the rest of the batch file becomes a little easier. You now know your USMT files exist in the C:\Windows\USMT\x86 and the C:\Windows\ USMT\AMD64 folders. You simply change to the appropriate directory and run the ScanState and LoadState commands.

For example, if you were migrating data to a 32-bit installation of Windows 7, you'd use the following batch file shown in Listing 1.1.

Listing 1.1: Batch file for 32-bit data migration

```
If exist D:\USMT\*.* XCopy /e /v /y C:\Windows\USMT\
If exist E:\USMT\*.* XCopy /e /v /y C:\Windows\USMT\
If exist F:\USMT\*.* XCopy /e /v /y C:\Windows\USMT\
If exist G:\USMT\*.* XCopy /e /v /y C:\Windows\USMT\
If exist H:\USMT\*.* XCopy /e /v /y C:\Windows\USMT\
If exist I:\USMT\*.* XCopy /e /v /y C:\Windows\USMT\
rem
Cd "c:\Windows\USMT\x86"
ScanState.exe c:\store /v:13 /o /c /hardlink /nocompress /efs:hardlink
  /i:MigApp.xml /i:MigDocs.xml /offlineWinDir:c:\windows.old\windows
LoadState.exe c:\store /v:13 /c /lac:P@ssw0rd /lae /i:MigApp.xml
  /i:MigDocs.xml /sf /hardlink /nocompress
```

This batch file checks to see if the USB drive has been assigned letters D: through I:, but if you want to check for all possible drive letters just copy an If exist line, paste it, and modify the letter in the new line. You can check for all drive letters up to Z: if desired.

You could save this file as usmt32.bat.

However, if you needed to run the migration on a 64-bit system, you could replace x86 with amd64 in the change directory line and save the file as usmt64.bat.

```
Cd "c:\Windows\USMT\amd64"
```

Wipe-and-Load Migration vs. Side-by-Side Migration

The majority of this section has covered an in-place migration. A common scenario is where a Windows XP system has the hardware to support Windows 7. Windows 7 is installed, and the user's data and settings are then migrated from the Windows.old folder.

However, there are some scenarios where the existing system needs to be wiped clean or completely replaced. In these scenarios, you can still use the USMT commands to capture the files and settings and then later restore them, but the process is a little different. The two possible scenarios are a wipe-and-load migration or a side-by-side migration.

Wipe-and-load migration   A wipe-and-load migration uses the same hardware but removes all data on the partitions. A simple example would be a system that has multiple partitions that aren't needed in Windows 7, so the drive is reconfigured as a single partition. Repartitioning the disk will result in the loss of all the data, so before this is done ScanState is run to capture all the files and settings. The ScanState data can be stored on a server, as shown in Figure 1.2, stored on an external USB drive, or even stored on a USB flash drive if the user doesn't have much data. After Windows 7 is installed, LoadState is executed to restore these settings from the server (or the external USB or flash drive). Figure 1.2 shows a wipe-and-load migration.

FIGURE 1.2   Wipe-and-load migration

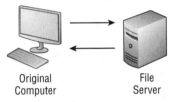

Original
Computer

File
Server

Side-by-side migration   In a side-by-side migration, a user has an older computer system that will be replaced. ScanState is run on the older system, and this older system is then decommissioned. The ScanState data can be stored on a server, as shown in Figure 1.2, stored on an external USB drive, or stored on a USB flash drive if the user doesn't have much data. A newer system with Windows 7 is provided, and LoadState is executed on it to restore the files and settings. Figure 1.3 shows a side-by-side migration.

FIGURE 1.3   Side-by-side migration

Original
Computer

File
Server

New
Computer

In both scenarios, the process is similar:

1. Run ScanState on the original computer, and store the files and settings externally, such as on a network share or an external USB drive. The ScanState version that comes with the Windows AIK for Windows 7 can be run on Windows XP, Windows Vista, and Windows 7 operating systems.

2. Install Windows 7. A wipe-and-load installation will install Windows 7 on the same computer, whereas a side-by-side installation will install Windows 7 on a separate computer.

3. Run LoadState on the Windows 7 system using the externally stored files and settings.

When ScanState is run for wipe-and-load and side-by-side migrations, the /offlineWinDir:c:\windows.old\windows switch is omitted. Instead of capturing the files and settings from the Windows.old folder, ScanState will retrieve the migration data from the actual system. In addition, instead of storing the results in the C:\Store folder, you could map a Universal Naming Convention (UNC) path to a share on a server or connect an external USB drive.

As an example, imagine that you have connected an external USB drive, and it is assigned the letter G:. The following ScanState command could be used:

```
ScanState.exe g:\store /v:13 /o /c /hardlink /nocompress /efs:hardlink
  /i:MigApp.xml /i:MigDocs.xml
```

The captured files and settings can be restored to the Windows 7 operating system with the following command. The only thing that will change is the letter of the drive where the \store folder is stored. For example, it may be G: on the original installation that had multiple partitions, but the external drive may be E: on a system that has Windows installed with only a single partition and a single DVD drive.

```
LoadState.exe e:\store /v:13 /c /lac:P@ssw0rd /lae /i:MigApp.xml
  /i:MigDocs.xml /sf /hardlink /nocompress
```

Determining Which User Data and Settings to Preserve

When running ScanState, you have some choices for which data and settings to preserve. The easiest choice is to accept the defaults, as we've done in this chapter. If your environment is typical and doesn't include any critical one-of-a-kind applications, this choice will meet most, if not all, of your needs. You can modify the defaults with the following files:

MigDocs.xml   This file includes rules used to find user documents on a computer. Some of the common file types identified in this document are .accdb, .ch3, .csv, .dif, .doc*, .dot*, .dqy, .iqy, .mcw, .mdb*, .mpp, .one*, .oqy, .or6, .pot*, .ppa, .pps*, .ppt*, .pre, .pst, .pub, .qdf, .qel, .qph, .qsd, .rqy, .rtf, .scd, .sh3, .slk, .txt, .vl*, .vsd, .wk*, .wpd, .wps, .wq1, .wri, .xl*, .xla, .xlb, and .xls*.

MigApps.xml   This file includes the rules used to migrate application settings. It will migrate many common applications published by Apple, Google, IBM, Intuit, Microsoft, and others.

MigUser.xml   This file includes rules that can be used to identify different elements of user profiles to include or exclude from the migration. By default, all users are migrated. This file is *not* used to specify which users to migrate.

Config.xml   The Config.xml file is optional and is created using the /genconfig switch with ScanState. It can be used specifically to exclude certain components or operating system settings from the migration.

> If you want to limit the users who are migrated, you can do so only from the command line. The /ui switch (user include) can be used to specify accounts with both ScanState and LoadState. When used, only the specified accounts will be migrated. You can't specify which users are migrated using any .xml files.

The User State Migration Tool (USMT) 4.0 User's Guide includes the article "What Does USMT Migrate?" which includes all the details of exactly what is migrated by default. This user guide is in the form of a help file named USMT.chm located in the C:\Program Files\Windows AIK\Docs\CHMs folder when the Windows AIK is installed.

Local vs. Remote Storage Considerations

When creating the migration store, you can use ScanState to store it locally or remotely. *Locally* means you're storing the migration store on a removable USB drive or on an internal drive for a side-by-side migration. *Remotely* means you're storing the migration data in a shared folder on a server in your network.

Storing data on a network share can be very convenient, but it can also result in a significantly slower migration process. A migration store can hold a large amount of data. With the size of files and the abundance of hard drive space, it would be easy for a user to accumulate 10 GB of data or more. If you're saving this to a network share over a 10Mbps or even a 100Mbps network connection, you'll be waiting awhile.

Not only will *you* be waiting, but users on the network may also find themselves waiting longer than normal. You should consider how storing the data on network shares affects the rest of the network. If the network is already busy and you begin moving gigabytes of storage over it, things may slow to a crawl and users will start complaining.

If your network infrastructure is reliably running with GB network interface cards, routers, and switches, you will probably be able to use network storage without any problem.

Securing Migrated Data

The amount of data included in a migration store can be considerable and, depending on the user's job responsibilities, the data can be sensitive. Any migration stores with sensitive data should be protected until they are used to restore the user's files and settings. They should be destroyed after the user's files and settings have been restored.

Sensitive data contained in the migration store could include the following:

- Classified information such as secret data
- Company secrets such as financial data, future product details, or plans for mergers
- Personally identifiable information (PII) on customers and employees, including names, addresses, phone numbers, social security numbers, and credit card information

At the very least, migration stores should be treated with the same level of protection as the original data. For example, if a user has secret data on her system, the migration store obtained from this system should be treated with the same level of protection used to protect the source data.

This becomes especially important when storing the data on external USB drives. Because these drives are highly portable, it's possible for an administrator to migrate secret data to an external USB drive and then use this migration store to restore the files and settings on a new computer. If the administrator stops there, the USB drive will still hold the secret data. If an educated user later comes across this USB drive and sees the migration store, he could run the `LoadState` command and restore all the data to his computer.

Destruction of the migration store can take several different forms depending on the type of data used. Some programs will erase the data and overwrite random patterns of 1s and 0s to ensure there isn't any data remaining on the drive that can be recovered.

Testing Designed Strategy

Once you've identified what strategy you'll use to migrate the user's data (in-place migration, wipe-and-load migration, or side-by-side migration), you should do some testing.

Except for the wipe-and-load migration, you'll have the original data that can be used to try to save the migration data over and over again. The in-place migration retains the original files and settings in the `Windows.old` folder, so if you're not happy with the results of either `ScanState` or `LoadState`, you can simply rerun the commands. Similarly, as long as you keep the original computer in a side-by-side migration, you can rerun both of the commands. However, you have only one chance to run `ScanState` with a wipe-and-load migration.

After testing and determining the best method, it's worth your time to document the procedure in a batch file that can easily be run without your having to struggle to remember the exact commands and the specific switches.

Virtualization Considerations

Virtual Desktop Infrastructure (VDI) has come a long way in the past few years. In short, VDI is the practice of hosting one or more virtual desktop operating systems on a desktop operating system. The desktop operating system is referred to as the host, and the virtual systems are referred to as virtual machines, virtual images, and sometimes just virtual applications.

As an example, you can run an instance of Windows 7 as the host operating system. Then, within the Windows 7 host, you can run other operating systems such as Windows XP, another virtual machine running Windows 7, and a third running Windows Server 2008.

With the cheap but abundant processing power built into desktop PCs, using VDI is now being seriously considered an alternative to Remote Desktop Services (RDS). Desktop PCs rarely use much of their processing power, and VDI applications and operating systems can provide distinct isolation from the host operating system.

 Remote Desktop Services (previously known as Terminal Services in Windows) can be configured on a server to allow users to run individual applications or entire desktops over a network. From the users' perspective, the application or desktop appears to be running on their individual system but is actually running on a server.

Microsoft introduced Windows Virtual PC (VPC) with Windows 7. This was previously known as *Microsoft Virtual PC* and was often used by administrators, technical trainers, and students. It's been available as a free download for years. If you've used Microsoft Virtual PC, you'll notice similarities with Windows Virtual PC, but the underlying technology provides some significant improvements.

VPC is not just for techies anymore. It can be installed and configured for regular users to run applications in virtual isolated environments using Windows XP Mode. It can be used to host applications running on other operating systems. It can even be used to host a dual-boot system using virtual hard disk files. You'll see all of this in this section.

Considering a VDI Environment

The choice between a complete physical environment and a hybrid physical and VDI environment requires considering several different elements related to how the VDI environment will be used. These include the following:

Existing hardware   There are several things to consider with existing hardware. First, if it's 32-bit, you're limited to no more than 4 GB of RAM, as discussed earlier. You're much better off if the hardware is 64-bit and has more than 4 GB of RAM.

Second, if the processor doesn't support virtualization, or the BIOS doesn't support virtualization, you won't be able to use Windows XP Mode. However, you can still use virtual machines.

Tradeoffs between physical and VDI environments   VDI environments require more resources. These include newer processors and more RAM. However, if the PC supports it, the environment may allow you to remove another PC. I've worked in some environments where users had to maintain two PCs—one to do most of their work and another for legacy applications. Two PCs cost more to maintain than one; this includes more electricity and more cooling power. Many companies consider VDI environments a "greener" alternative.

Network load considerations   Most PCs will have only a single network interface card (NIC). This NIC will be shared with the VDI machines. If the virtual machines are connected to the network and have a lot of network activity, you may want to consider upgrading the NIC.

Disk space   Windows XP Mode requires a minimum of 1.6 GB of disk space. If you start adding additional virtual machines, you'll find that they take significantly more. For example, a Windows Server 2008 virtual hard disk takes about 6 GB with an initial installation, and Windows 7 takes about the same. These are dynamically expanding disks, so as more is installed or added to the virtual systems, they will take more and more space.

This can be critical if the virtual hard disks are stored on the boot or system partition. If they are stored on one of these partitions, you should monitor disk space usage closely.

 Real World Scenario

Using Virtual PC for Mini Labs

I've been using Virtual PC (VPC) for many years to create virtual desktops and even virtual networks where I could test and learn different technologies.

As a simple example, when first learning Windows Server 2008 and Windows Vista, I was running Windows XP as my desktop operating system. I created two VPC images—one of Windows Server 2008 and another of Windows Vista. I was able to load these two systems, configure the server as a domain controller in a domain, and configure Windows Vista to join the domain. I now had a mini-network with a server and a client.

One of the greatest benefits of this virtual setup is that if I crashed the system, I could easily rebuild it and start over.

Similarly, that's what I've created for this book. While I'm running Windows 7 on my PCs, I also have a virtual network consisting of a virtual Windows Server 2008 server and another of a virtual Windows 7 client. With the knowledge you gain from this chapter, you can do the same thing.

Direct Connection vs. Brokered Connection

In the context of VDI, connections can either be direct or brokered. Direct would be directly within a virtual machine, and brokered would be indirectly through the virtual machine.

Direct connection   The user launches the virtual machine from within the host system, logs on to the virtual machine, and starts the application within the virtual machine.

Brokered connection   The user launches the application directly from the host machine. Even though it's running within the virtual machine, this is transparent to the user. Windows XP Mode (shown later in this chapter) uses a brokered connection, and this can be used with other virtual machines.

Imagine a user needs to launch an instance of an older application named LegacyApp. She can launch this in a direct connection or a brokered connection. In both instances, the application would be installed on a virtual machine, but the difference is in how it's delivered to the user. Brokered connections are easier for end users.

Determining a VHD Strategy

A cool feature available with Windows 7 is the ability to boot to a virtual hard drive (VHD). The VHD format has been used with Virtual PC for many years, but the abilities have been expanded significantly. This can be done only with Windows 7 or Windows Server 2008 R2, but it can be a useful feature.

Dual-boot environments allow you to boot to different operating systems. One of the challenges with traditional dual-boot environments is that you needed to ensure each operating system was installed on its own partition. If not, one OS could (and usually did) corrupt the other OS.

Now you can have multiple operating systems available on a single machine with a single partition. When you've finished with the operating system, simply delete the VHD file. You'll see how to create a bootable VHD later in this chapter.

The process creates a VHD file (with an extension of .vhd) at the root of C:. You can name the file whatever you want (the following exercise names it Windows7.vhd). The size of the file should be at least 20 GB and is expressed in MB. You can make it larger to accommodate more data and files: 10 GB is 10240, so 20 GB would be 20480, 30 GB 30720, and so on.

You can have the .vhd file either fixed or expandable. A 20GB fixed size will always take up 20 GB of space, while a 20GB expandable file will start at less than 100 MB and expand as data is added to the file. The fixed size is quicker since it doesn't need to expand dynamically, while the expandable size consumes only the space needed.

Exercise 1.4 shows how you can configure a system to boot to a virtual hard drive hosting Windows 7. In the exercise, the host system is running 64-bit Windows Vista and the installation DVD is 64-bit Windows 7.

EXERCISE 1.4

Creating a Bootable VHD

1. Turn on the Windows Vista system and place the Windows 7 installation DVD in the system. When the system starts, select the option to boot from the DVD.

2. When the initial installation screen appears prompting you to select a language, time and currency format, and keyboard or input method, press Shift+F10. This will launch a command-prompt window with the prompt

X:\Sources>

X: is mapped to the DVD drive, and it is pointed to the Sources folder in the drive.

3. At the command prompt, type **diskpart** and press Enter. After a moment, the command prompt will change to DISKPART> and your display will look similar to the following graphic.

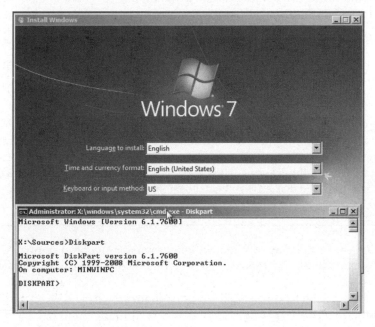

4. Type the following command, and press Enter to create a 40GB expandable virtual disk file.

Create vdisk file = c:\Windows7.vhd maximum=40960 type=expandable

You can name the .vhd file anything you want, enter a different maximum size, or omit the type=expandable statement to create a fixed-size file. If you choose a fixed size, it will take several minutes to complete and will show the progress. After the file is created, Diskpart will display the message "Diskpart successfully created the virtual disk file."

5. Type the following command and press Enter.

   `Select vdisk file=c:\Windows7.vhd`

   Diskpart will indicate it has successfully selected the virtual disk file.

6. Type the following command and press Enter:

   `Attach vdisk`

   Diskpart will indicate it has successfully attached the virtual disk file.

7. Type **Exit** and press Enter to exit Diskpart.

8. Type **Exit** and press Enter to exit the command-prompt window.

9. You will now see the Install Windows screen you saw before pressing Shift+F10. Make sure the correct language, time and currency, and keyboard or input method are selected and click Next.

10. Click the Install Now button.

11. Review the license terms, select the check box I Accept The License Terms, and click Next.

12. Click the Custom (Advanced) type of installation.

13. The Where Do You Want To Install Windows screen will appear with at least two disks showing. Below the physical disks and partitions, you will see the virtual disk file represented as a disk with a total size of 40 GB and free space of 40 GB (unless you created it as a different size). In my test system, it has one physical disk shown as Disk 0 and the .vhd disk as Disk 1 Unallocated Space. Select the virtual disk and click Next.

At this point, the installation of Windows will progress as would a normal Windows 7 installation. You can follow the exercise earlier in this chapter to install Windows 7 from the DVD if desired.

When it completes and reboots, you'll see a dual-boot screen. The Windows 7 choice will be first and, if you don't take any action, it will boot to the Windows 7 VHD file in 30 seconds. You can modify this behavior with bcdedit, which is covered in more depth in Chapter 5, "Maintaining and Troubleshooting Windows 7."

A warning may appear saying, "Windows cannot be installed to this disk. (Show Details)," indicating the hardware is not compatible. Don't believe it. Continue on. I've seen that message on two different systems, but the installation and operation worked without any problems I could identify.

Windows XP Mode

Windows XP Mode is a virtualization technology that addresses a specific problem that prevented many people from moving from Windows XP to Windows Vista. Many applications worked well in Windows XP but would not work in Windows Vista.

Interestingly, this problem prevented people from moving to Windows XP from Windows 2000 in the early XP days. It seems to be a common problem, but Windows XP Mode may be a definitive solution for those considering Windows 7.

Microsoft spent a lot of time and effort on Windows XP Mode, and from everything I've seen it looks like it'll be a success. It's not uncommon for Microsoft to use test topics to amplify the importance of features they've added. If you're preparing for the 70-685 and 70-686 Windows 7 exams, make sure you understand the benefits and requirements for Windows XP Mode.

Windows XP Mode is a virtual instance of Windows XP running within Windows 7. Applications that won't run in Windows 7 can be installed in this instance of Windows XP. However, Microsoft has engineered a great solution that doesn't require the user to launch Windows XP. When Windows XP Mode is configured, the user simply launches the legacy application from their Start menu, and it appears as though it's running just as any other application would run.

Although Windows XP Mode is free with Windows 7, there are some requirements you need to worry about. These include the following:

- The processor must be capable of hardware virtualization.
- Virtualization must be enabled in the BIOS.
- At least 1.6GB free hard drive space must be available.

If your system will support it, you can download and install Virtual PC for Windows 7 and then download and install Windows XP Mode for Windows 7.

Analyzing Your Existing Hardware Environment

Windows XP Mode originally required a processor that supports virtualization that needed to be enabled in the BIOS. However, Microsoft later released an update with KB 977206 that allows Windows XP Mode to work without hardware assisted virtualization (HAV). Intel refers to HAV as Intel VT, and AMD calls it AMD-V. Both companies include utilities you can download and run to determine if your processor has this capability.

Windows XP Mode works best if your processor supports virtualization. However, if the processor doesn't support virtualization or it isn't enabled in the BIOS, you can still use Windows XP Mode. Check out KB article 977206 at http://support.microsoft.com/kb/977206.

Figure 1.4 shows the Intel® Processor Identification Utility with the middle tab selected. Notice that the Intel(R) Virtualization Technology is listed as Yes, verifying that Windows XP Mode can be used on this system. This utility can be downloaded from Intel's website here:

`http://www.intel.com/support/processors/tools/piu/`

FIGURE 1.4   Intel® Processor Identification Utility

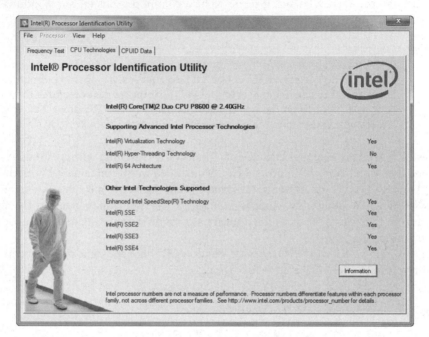

I have an older AMD system that doesn't support virtualization. After running the AMD Virtualization Compatibility Check Utility, the screen shown in Figure 1.5 appeared. This utility can be downloaded from AMD's support site at this address:

`http://support.amd.com/us/Processor_TechDownloads/AMD-V_Hyper-V_`
`Compatibility_Check_Utility_V2.zip`

FIGURE 1.5   AMD Virtualization Compatibility Check Utility

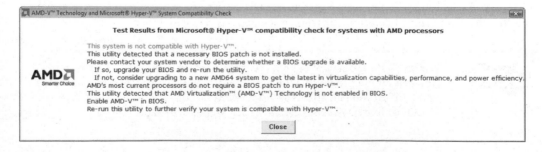

Next you'll need to enable the virtualization option in the BIOS. My experience is that this is not enabled by default, so you'll need to reboot your system, read the screen to see what key to use to enter BIOS, and then search for the virtualization option.

Many versions of BIOS are available, and there's no standard of how to access BIOS. Sometimes you're prompted to press F10, sometimes the Delete key, and at other times you're prompted just to press any key at the appropriate time. The only thing that is consistent is that a message will appear telling you what key to press to enter the setup mode that allows access to the system BIOS.

The virtualization setting can be called AMD-V or Intel VT or simply Virtualization Technology. Find the setting and enable it.

If the processor is capable, but the BIOS doesn't have the Virtualization Technology setting, it's possible you'll need to upgrade or flash the BIOS. Access the command prompt and enter **SystemInfo**. This takes a minute to complete, but it will list a significant amount of information about your system including the BIOS version. You can search the Internet using this information for a possible upgrade. Follow the manufacturer's instructions to complete this process.

Downloading the Software

Once you've verified your processor is capable and you've configured the BIOS, you can begin downloading the software needed for Windows XP Mode. You'll need at least 1.6 GB of free space. The space can be on any available partition.

The two files you'll need to download and install are as follows:

Windows Virtual PC   This is actually a Windows Update labeled as KB 958559. Both an x86 version (for 32-bit systems) and an x64 version (for 64-bit systems) exist. Make sure you install the one that's right for your system. This will require rebooting your system.

Windows XP Mode   This file is about 480 MB. It's a self-extracting executable that will add Windows XP Mode to your system and install the instance of Windows XP that can be used to run legacy applications. There is only one version of this file, and it will work for both 32-bit and 64-bit systems.

You can find both Windows Virtual PC and Windows XP Mode at Microsoft's download site at www.download.Microsoft.com. Search for "Windows Virtual PC" and "Windows XP Mode."

You'll need the version of Virtual PC designed to work with Windows 7 and Windows XP Mode. If you have an older version of Virtual PC, you'll need to uninstall it first. An easy way to see if you have a compatible version is by the name; if you're running a version called Windows Virtual PC, it'll work because Windows Virtual PC was released with Windows 7. If you're running a version named Microsoft Virtual PC, you'll need to uninstall it first.

Exercise 1.5 will walk you through the steps to install Windows Virtual PC and Windows XP Mode.

EXERCISE 1.5

Installing Windows Virtual PC and Windows XP Mode

1. Install Windows Virtual PC with the following steps:

    a. Launch Windows Explorer. Browse to where you downloaded Windows Virtual PC and double-click the executable. This actually installs update KB958559. If it is already installed, it will inform you that it is installed and you can continue with step 2.

    b. At the prompt to install the Windows software update, click Yes.

    c. Review the license terms and click I Accept. The installation will start and take a few minutes to complete.

    d. When the installation is complete, you'll be prompted to restart the computer. Click Restart Now.

2. Install Windows XP Mode with the following steps:

    a. Launch Windows Explorer. Browse to where you downloaded the Windows XP Mode file and double-click it.

    b. When prompted by the Security Warning to run the file, click Run.

    c. On the Welcome screen, click Next.

    d. If your C: drive has at 1.6 GB of free space, you can accept the default location of C:\Program Files\Windows XP Mode\ and click Next. Otherwise, choose another location.

    e. When prompted by User Account Control to continue, click Yes.

    f. The installation will complete, and the Setup Completed screen will appear. Leave Launch Windows XP Mode checked, and click Finish.

    g. Review the Windows XP Mode License Agreement. Click the check box I Accept The License Terms and click Next.

    h. You will be prompted to identify the installation folder and enter credentials for an XP Mode user account, as shown in the following graphic. Accept the default installation folder, and enter a password in the Password and Confirm Password text boxes. Make sure that the Remember Credentials (Recommended) check box is checked. Click Next.

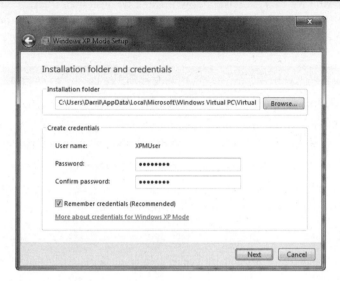

With Remember Credentials checked, users won't be prompted to enter credentials when using Windows XP Mode.

i.   Enable automatic updates by selecting Help Protect My Computer By Turning On Automatic Updates Now, and click Start Setup. It will take several minutes for the setup to complete. Once it completes, a window will open with the Windows XP Mode desktop.

Windows XP Mode is now installed on your system. However, it won't be of much use until you install some applications and configure them to run within your Windows 7 system. The next section leads you through this process.

Running Applications from Windows XP Mode

Although the previous exercise showed you how to install Windows XP Mode, the real value comes in using this to run applications in a virtual environment.

As an example, imagine that a user has a program she uses quite a bit, works well in Windows XP, but does not work at all in Windows 7. You can add Windows XP Mode to her Windows 7 desktop and then install the legacy application in the Windows XP Mode virtual environment.

This feature is most valuable for applications that work in Windows XP but not in Windows 7. However, you can install any application in Windows XP Mode that will work in Windows XP. The point of the exercise is not what you install but instead how it's accessed after it is installed.

Exercise 1.6 will lead you through the steps to make an application available to end users. As preparation for this exercise, I downloaded IrfanView (a freeware image viewer) created by Irfan Skiljan. However, you can use any program and, if you want to install another program, substitute your program where I refer to IrfanView in the exercise.

EXERCISE 1.6

Publishing Applications from Windows XP Mode

1. From the Windows 7 host machine, click Start ➤ All Programs ➤ Windows Virtual PC ➤ Windows Virtual PC. This will launch the Windows Virtual PC console.

2. Right-click the Windows XP Mode.vmcx file and select Settings.

3. Select Auto Publish, and verify that Auto Publish is set to Automatically Publish Virtual Applications, as shown in the following graphic.

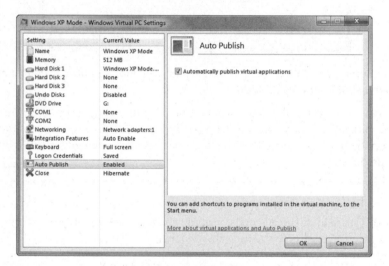

4. Click OK to close the Settings page, and then double-click the Windows XP Mode. vmcx file to start the Windows XP Mode VPC.

5. After Windows XP Mode starts, install the application you downloaded. Copy a shortcut for this program (many applications including IrfanView place a shortcut on the desktop that you can copy).

6. Right-click the Start menu within Windows XP, and select Explore All Users. This will open Windows Explorer in this folder:

    C:\Documents and Settings\All Users\Start Menu

7. Double-click Programs, and then paste the shortcut for the program that you installed into this folder. After a moment, this application will be available on your host system.

8. Click Windows 7 and select Start ➤ All Programs ➤ Windows Virtual PC ➤ Windows XP Mode Applications. You'll see that the program that you installed in Windows XP Mode is now available on the Windows 7 menu, as shown in the following graphic.

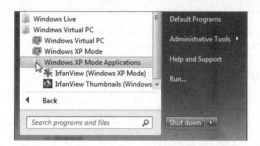

    While this shows how applications published from Windows XP Mode will appear, you can also publish applications from other Windows VPC programs. For example, if you install a virtual instance of Windows 7 and published an application from there, the published application will appear in a folder named Windows 7 Applications.

9. Try to launch the application by selecting Start ➤ All Programs ➤ Windows Virtual PC ➤ Windows XP Mode Applications ➤ IrfanView (Windows XP Mode). It will fail and inform you that you must close Windows XP Mode first.

10. Return to Windows XP Mode, and select Start ➤ Log Off. After you are logged off, select Action ➤ Close. This will cause Windows XP Mode to go into Hibernate mode.

11. Once the system finishes hibernating, try to start the program from the Windows 7 Start menu by selecting Start ➤ All Programs ➤ Windows Virtual PC ➤ Windows XP Mode Applications ➤ IrfanView (Windows XP Mode).

    Windows XP Mode will awaken from Hibernate mode, and the application will launch in its own window. Note that the full Windows XP desktop does not launch but only the application.

12. Browse to the Virtual PC console by clicking Start ➤ All Programs ➤ Windows Virtual PC ➤ Windows Virtual PC. You'll see that the Windows XP Mode VPC has a status of Running.

13. Close the IrfanView application.

14. Click Start ➤ All Programs ➤ Windows Virtual PC ➤ Windows XP Mode Applications. Right-click IrfanView PC, and select Copy to copy the shortcut to this program.

15. Access the Windows 7 desktop. Right-click and select Paste Shortcut to paste the program shortcut.

16. Double-click the shortcut on the desktop to launch it. You'll see that it launches the application just the same as it did from the Start menu.

This exercise shows you how easily you can integrate virtual applications into a user's desktop. Users don't have to know all the details of how the virtual applications are installed or how they work, and many end users don't want to know. They just want to be able to access an application when it's needed.

If an administrator configured the virtual application to run from a shortcut like this, the user will have very little indication that anything is different. They can still run their legacy application, and you are still able to migrate your older systems to Windows 7.

Using Windows XP Mode allows you to run legacy applications on a Windows 7 system easily. However, you can also use VPC to run other desktops that you create.

Running Applications from Other VPCs

The previous example showed you how to install applications in Windows XP Mode and make them available from the Windows 7 Start menu, but you aren't restricted to doing this with only Windows XP Mode.

Developers are notorious for crashing their systems. They develop applications and, during the test-and-debugging process, things sometimes go wrong. For example, an operating system that once worked now no longer works. Not only is the developer unable to continue the development of the application, but they can't even access email or do other day-to-day work. While you can't prevent a developer from crashing a development environment, you can isolate the problem by creating a virtual environment for development work.

You start with a regular Windows 7 desktop. You can then install another instance of Windows 7 in a virtual machine and install applications within the virtual machine. As long as the Auto Publish settings are set to Enabled, the applications will automatically appear on the host machine's Start menu for that PC once the shortcuts are copied to the Start menu on the virtual machine. Hibernate the VPC, and you can then launch the programs in the same manner as you did with Windows XP Mode.

The only pieces that are missing from this puzzle are the steps you need to take to create a Virtual PC image. Exercise 1.7 shows you the steps needed to create a virtual PC machine. You can then install an operating system within this virtual machine.

EXERCISE 1.7

Creating Other Virtual PC Machines

1. Launch the Virtual PC console by clicking Start ➢ All Programs ➢ Windows Virtual PC ➢ Windows Virtual PC.

2. Click Create Virtual Machine in the title bar.

3. Enter a name for your VPC in the Name text box. You can either accept the default location for the VPC or select another location. Your display will look similar to the following graphic. Click Next.

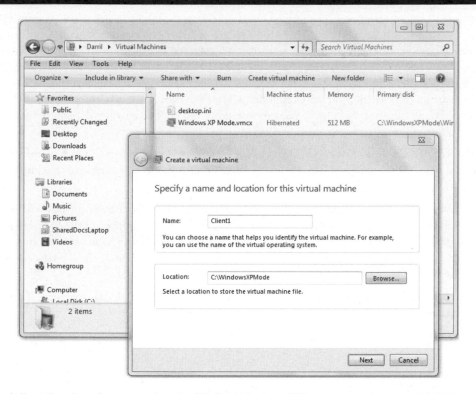

4. Adjust the size of memory for the PC. For Windows XP, you can get away with 512
    MB, but if you're running more applications, add more RAM. Similarly, you can start
    with 1 GB of RAM for Windows 7 and add more depending on the applications you're
    running. You can always adjust the RAM later when the virtual machine is turned
    off. Leave the networking check box enabled to Use Computer Network Connections
    unless you specifically don't want the VPC to have access to the network. Click Next.

5. The Add A Virtual Hard Disk page appears. Since this is a new VPC, accept the default
    of Create A Dynamically Expanding Virtual Hard Disk. Leave Enable Undo Disks
    unchecked and click Create.

    You'll be returned to the Virtual PC console. At this point, you have a Virtual PC
    image, although it's empty. The next step is to load an operating system into it.

6. Load the Windows installation DVD into the host system DVD drive.

7. Double-click the VPC image you just created to start it. It will boot from the DVD. At
    this point, follow the procedure to install the operating system. If you're installing
    Windows 7, you can use the installation steps from the exercise earlier in this chap-
    ter. If it's another operating system, use the steps for that OS.

Installing Integration Components

After installing an operating system using Virtual PC, you may notice that things aren't running as smoothly as you'd like them to be. For one thing, every time you click within a Virtual PC environment, your mouse gets trapped there. You can press Ctrl+Alt+left arrow to get it out, but it'd be a lot easier if your mouse moved in and out of this window just as it can do with other windows.

You can install the Integration Components after the operating system has been installed on the VPC. In addition to helping your mouse work a little better, they'll also give access to the following resources:

Clipboard You will be able to copy and paste data back and forth from the host operating system to the virtual machine. Data copied in one environment is available on the clipboard in the other environment.

Hard drives You'll have access to all of the hard drives on the host system from within the virtual machine. The drives appear as shares within Windows Explorer in the format of *X on ComputerName* where X is the actual drive letter and *ComputerName* is the name of the host computer. For example, if the host computer is named Client1, the C: drive would appear in Windows Explorer on the virtual machine as C on Client1.

Printers Printers available to the host system are available to the virtual machine. This allows you to print to a printer from the virtual machine.

USB devices USB devices plugged into the host system can be accessed from the virtual machine.

You can install the Integration Components by following the steps in Exercise 1.8.

EXERCISE 1.8

Installing Integration Components

1. With a Windows Virtual PC console open, click the Tools drop-down menu and select Install Integration Components. An AutoPlay box will pop up.

2. Click Run Setup.exe within the AutoPlay dialog box.

3. A Welcome page will appear. Click Next on the Welcome page, and click Yes when prompted by User Account Control. After a moment, the installation will complete.

4. Click Finish, and then click Yes to restart your computer.

   After you reboot and log onto the system, you'll find that your mouse now treats the VPC environment just like any other window, but you're not finished yet.

5. Select the Tools drop-down menu, and select Enable Integration Features. You'll be prompted to provide credentials that will be used on your system. Enter the user name and password you used when creating the VPC image, and click OK.

Windows Virtual PC Menu

The Windows Virtual PC interface is different from the Microsoft Virtual PC interface. As a matter of fact, it doesn't look like an interface at all. Instead, it looks like Windows Explorer with a couple extra menu items.

Figure 1.6 shows the Windows Virtual Machines console. It shows the virtual machines I have added to my system: one for Windows XP Mode, one Windows 7 client named Client1, and one Server 2008 system I'm using as a domain controller in the virtual environment.

FIGURE 1.6   Windows Virtual Machines console

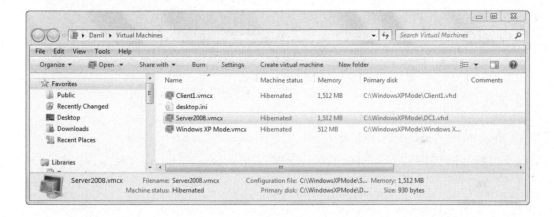

You can launch any virtual machine console from here by double-clicking it. You can also access the settings for any of the virtual machines by selecting the virtual machine and clicking Settings. Some settings can be manipulated while the system is running or hibernated. Other settings require you to shut down the virtual machine before you can modify them.

Once the virtual machine is launched, you'll see that it has a menu across the top, as shown in Figure 1.7. Figure 1.7 is a virtual instance of Windows 7 running within Windows Virtual PC. As you can see, there are four menu choices. Each one is explained in the following section.

FIGURE 1.7   Windows 7 launched within a Virtual PC machine

Action

The Action menu includes four choices:

View Full Screen   No surprise here. Selecting this option maximizes the VPC window to full screen. When set to full screen, a Title tab is pinned to the top of the window. This tab includes many of the same choices as the full menu. To the far right are icons reminiscent of minimize, maximize, and close icons but labeled as Switch To Your Computer Desktop, Exit Full Screen, and Close.

Sleep   Selecting Sleep puts the VPC into a power-saving sleep mode. Once Sleep is selected, the menu item changes to Wake Up. If you select Wake Up, the VPC will exit the sleep mode.

Restart   Selecting Restart forces a system restart. If you have programs running, you will be prompted that they are open, and you may lose work if you continue. You can click Force Restart or click Cancel to return to the desktop.

Close   The Close menu gives the choices Hibernate, Shut Down, or Turn Off. Hibernate will cause the current state to be saved—open windows and files remain open and, when you launch this VPC image again, everything is returned to the exact same state. Shut Down performs a logical shut down, and Turn Off simulates pressing the power button on the PC.

USB

The USB drop-down menu shows all the USB devices attached to your host system. As devices are added or removed from the host system, they will be added or removed from this menu.

Devices aren't automatically available in the VPC, though. If you want the device to be available, you need to select it from the menu, as shown in Figure 1.8. Devices that are attached to the VPC are removed from the host system.

FIGURE 1.8 Selecting USB devices in the Virtual PC

Once a device is attached to the VPC, you can release it by selecting it from the menu and choosing Release.

Tools

The Tools drop-down menu includes two choices: Integration Components and Settings.

Once you add and enable the Integration Components, you'll be able to work with VPC images in a more seamless manner. The mouse will easily move in and out of the VPC window, and you can easily cut and paste data from your host system into the VPC window.

If you select Settings, the VPC will launch a window similar to the one shown in Figure 1.9 that you can use to modify many of the environment settings for the VPC. Some settings (such as the Networking setting) can be configured while the VPC is running. Other settings (such as Memory) can be configured only when the VPC is turned off.

FIGURE 1.9 Windows Virtual PC Settings

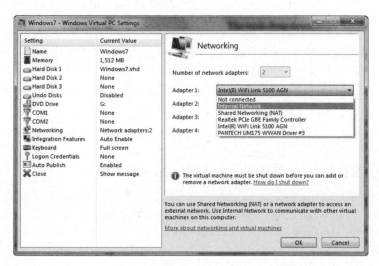

As an example, the network adapters will start as being configured to use the network adapters on your system. In the figure, the VPC network adapter is currently configured to share the WiFi network adapter connected to my system. It will have access to my system on a simulated network and can access the Internet.

However, if I select Not Connected, it will be completely isolated. If the VPC isn't fully protected with anti-malware software, this is one way to isolate it. In addition, I could select Internal Network. The VPC would be able to communicate with other VPCs that are active on my system but not the host machine or any systems external to the host machine.

Ctrl+Alt+Del

You can't press the Ctrl+Alt+Del keys on a virtual system because this key combination is always trapped by the host system. Windows Virtual PC provides the Ctrl+Alt+Del menu item that can be used to simulate pressing the Ctrl+Alt+Del keys on the virtual machine.

Figure 1.7 and Figure 1.8 shown earlier both show the Ctrl+Alt+Del menu item to the right of the Tools menu. Clicking this item on a virtual system is the same as pressing the keys on a nonvirtual system.

Windows Virtual PC does not support 64-bit operating systems. Since Windows Server 2008 R2 only comes in 64-bit versions, it won't run in VPC.

Planning and Managing Client Licensing and Activation

Software developers have been battling software counterfeiting (often called pirating or software piracy) since the very first operating system or application was sold. When it's easy to copy the software without paying for it, some people do just that.

Client licenses, product keys, and activation work together to help ensure that a software program that is being used is a valid copy. The goal is to make it more difficult for software counterfeiters to copy and sell the software to unsuspecting users while also making the process smooth for users who have purchased valid versions.

With this in mind, administrators have a responsibility to their company to help it develop sound licensing strategies and ensure they remain compliant with license agreements. You should understand the basics of client activation that can be implemented in an organization.

Licensing Strategy and Compliance

Windows 7 uses a product key and an *activation* process to help thwart counterfeiting. Figure 1.10 shows the product key screen from the installation process. You can still install Windows 7 without the product key by clicking Next on the installation screen, but it won't successfully activate without the key.

FIGURE 1.10   Entering the product key

Some product keys are designed for a single product, and some product keys are designed for multiple products. A Multiple Activation Key (MAK) uses a single key purchased for many clients. In larger organizations, MAKs or Key Management Service (KMS) servers could be used for activation, or a combination of the two can be used. MAK and KMS require a more complex license infrastructure and will be explored in greater depth later in this chapter.

Activation will ultimately be paired with the product key and your computer. The activation process collects information on the computer to uniquely identify it, but it does not collect any information on the user.

When installing Windows, you'll receive the prompt Automatically Activate Windows When I'm Online. If this box is checked, activation will be attempted three days after the user logs on the first time. If it is not checked, the user will be prompted to activate before the grace period expires.

Windows 7 Activation Grace Period

Windows 7 has a grace period of 30 days before it needs to be activated. During this time, users will see a pop-up reminding them they need to activate. This starts as a once-a-day pop-up four days after the installation and increases to as often as once an hour on day 30.

On day 31, a message will appear indicating that you must activate Windows to continue using all Windows features. A logical question is, "What features can't be used?" In past versions of Windows, Microsoft introduced a reduced-functionality mode where users can browse the Internet for one hour before having to log off and back on again.

At this writing, it appears as though everything in Windows 7 still works in this reduced-functionality mode. The desktop background goes black with text indicating the copy of Windows is not genuine. You can change the background, but it will change back within about an hour. Periodically, an Activation window appears, informing you the activation period has expired and prompting you to activate, buy a new product key online, retype your product key, or view other ways to activate.

On Windows Server 2008 R2 (the server companion to Windows 7), the server shuts down hourly after the activation period expires.

All of this can be frustrating when you use a system that isn't activated, but there is a simple solution—ensure the software is genuine and activate it.

You can activate Windows from the System page. Click Start, right-click Computer, and select Properties. If you scroll down to the bottom of the page, you'll see a Windows Activation menu similar to Figure 1.11.

FIGURE 1.11   Viewing the Windows Activation status

If your system is connected to the Internet, you can simply click this link. Your system will connect to Microsoft's servers, some information on your computer will be transferred back and forth, and a moment later you'll be notified that activation was successful. Microsoft stresses that the information transferred during the activation process can be used to identify your computer, but it does not include any information on the user.

Once the system is activated, the countdown to activate will be replaced with a message saying, "Windows is Activated." Windows activation is considered permanent, although Windows does periodically check to ensure that the system is the same.

Detecting Changes

Periodically, Windows 7 will verify that the copy of Windows is valid and is operating on the same system where it was originally installed. If significant changes are detected, the activation will be reversed and the system will need to be reactivated.

The most common scenario where this occurs is when imaging software such as Symantec's Ghost is used. It is possible to make an image copy or clone of a system and then use this cloned copy on other computers. The license for the original system wasn't purchased for the other computers, and Windows 7 will detect that the operating system that was activated on the original system is now located on a different computer. Once the change is detected, activation will be revoked and the client will need to be reactivated.

This can also occur if too many changes are made to the hardware of a system. For example, if the motherboard of a system is replaced, Windows 7 may assume it's been moved to a different computer. This can usually be resolved with a phone call to a Microsoft help center to obtain a new key.

Cloning systems can also result in duplicate security identifiers (SIDs). To prevent duplicate SIDs on a network, the Sysprep program is run before capturing the image. Sysprep *sanitizes* the system by removing unique information such as the computer name and SIDs. It also resets the licensing information used for activation, requiring computers receiving the image to be activated separately.

Software Manager Licensing Manager Tool

The Software Licensing Management Tool is a built-in Visual Basic script (slmgr.vbs) program that can be used for licensing and activation tasks. It includes several options that are entered as a switch. Some of the options directly relate to the clients (and are covered in this section), and some of the options directly relate to KMS (and are covered later in this chapter).

The slmgr tool must be run from an elevated command prompt. Click Start ➤ All Programs ➤ Accessories, right-click Command Prompt, and select Run As Administrator.

Many of the common slmgr switches are shown in the following sections. Some slmgr switches are more commonly used with the KMS server and are mentioned later in this chapter.

Reset Grace Period

You can extend the initial 30-day grace period using the slmgr /rearm command. In other words, if the 30-day grace period has expired, the background has gone black, and the reminder screens are coming up hourly, you can execute this command at the command prompt to give yourself another 30 days. This command can be executed three times.

> The Windows 7 activation limit can be extended to a total of 120 days. When the 30-day limit is reached, you can run `slmgr -rearm` from an administrator command prompt, which resets the activation limit for another 30 days. This command can be executed three times. Thus, if it is run at the end of each 30-day period, you'll get a total of 120 days.

Activate Windows

You can use `slmgr /ato` command to cause the system to activate right away. As a reminder, activation won't normally be done until three days after the user first logs on. If you are building computers that you'll move to an isolated environment without Internet access, you can use this command to force activation right away.

Display License Information

The `slmgr /dli` command can be used to display information on the license used for this system. When executed, it will show the name, description, a partial product key, and the license status of the current license. As an example, Figure 1.12 shows what it looks like on one of my systems:

FIGURE 1.12   Displaying license information

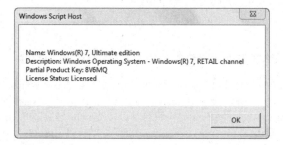

You can also execute it as `slmgr /dli all` to display information on all licenses on the system. Other licenses will indicate they are not in use and the status is Unlicensed.

Install Product Key

The `slmgr /ipk <Product Key>` command can be used to install a new product key. This can be useful if the system is configured to use a KMS but you want to switch it to use a MAK.

Display Detailed License Information

You can use the `slmgr /dlv` command to get more detailed information on the license. The result includes several identification numbers and certificate URLs. It will also show the status of the license and the remaining rearm count.

Expiration Data for Current License

The command `slmgr /xpr` can be used to indicate the expiration date for the current license. If the system has not been activated, this will indicate the date and time when the 30-day grace period expires.

If the license has been permanently activated, it will say, "The Machine is Permanently Activated." If the system has been activated by KMS, it will indicate the expiration of the KMS activation.

Volume Activation Methods

For smaller businesses, Windows 7 is purchased on an individual basis, and the clients are automatically activated three days after the installation. For larger enterprises, volume-activation methods are used to activate multiple clients with a single key. There are two methods of volume activation.

- *Multiple Activation Key (MAK)*
- *Key Management Service (KMS)*

KMS is used when the clients can't access the Internet and require the use of a KMS server. KMS requires significantly more administration than other methods of activation.

As an overview, Table 1.2 shows some of the comparisons between MAK activation and KMS server activation. It's important to realize that MAK keys and KMS keys are different. A MAK key can't be activated with a KMS server, and a KMS key won't be activated over the Internet.

TABLE 1.2   Comparing MAK and KMS

MAK	KMS
Activation is permanent.	Clients must connect to a KMS server periodically to renew activation.
Used when access to the Internet is possible (or manual phone method is desirable).	Used in isolated networks where Internet access is not possible (and manual activation via the phone is not desirable).
Can be used for any number of clients.	Requires a minimum of 5 servers, 25 clients, or a combination of 25 servers and clients.
Volume Activation Management Tool (VAMT) can be used with a MAK proxy.	Although a KMS server is used, it's not referred to as a proxy.
Supports clients duplicated from a single image.	Supports clients duplicated from a single image.

Microsoft has published the Volume Activation Planning Guide for Windows 7 and Windows 2008 R2. It includes some great explanations and a lot more detail on both the KMS and MAK processes. You can access it here: http://technet.microsoft.com/library/dd878528.aspx.

Multiple Activation Key

Large enterprises can purchase a Multiple Activation Key (MAK), which is a single key that can be used to activate many clients. For example, a company could purchase 100 licenses using a MAK. This single key is used for the image, and activation over the Internet is automatic.

A common method used to deploy the operating system to multiple computers is the use of imaging technologies. Chapter 2 will cover different imaging technologies, including Windows Deployment Services (WDS), in more depth. A single MAK is used and doesn't need to be reentered for each installation.

MAKs are purchased from Microsoft partners for a specific number of clients. They should be used only for these clients and no others.

If your clients cannot access the Internet, you can use a KMS server, as will be explained later in this chapter. You can also use the Volume Activation Management Tool with a MAK proxy to activate clients that can't access the Internet. The most common scenario where clients can't access the Internet is when they host or access sensitive data, and company policy specifically restricts them from accessing the Internet.

Volume Activation Management Tool

The Volume Activation Management Tool (VAMT) version 1.2 is part of the Microsoft Windows Automated Installation Kit for Windows 7, covered earlier in this chapter. It can be used to manage activation of Windows Vista, Windows 7, Windows Server 2008, and Windows Server 2008 R2.

You would use the VAMT if clients can't access the Internet or to manage MAK keys. The overall process to use VAMT is as follows:

1. Install VAMT on a host computer, which can be any Windows Vista, Windows 7, Windows Server 2008, or Windows Server 2008 R2 computer.

2. Configure the Windows Management Instrumentation (WMI) firewall exception on all clients (if not already configured and if the firewall is running).

3. Create a Computer Information List (CIL) as a group within VAMT.

4. Have VAMT collect license status information for clients in the CIL using WMI.

5. Add a MAK to the VAMT. The number of computers activated with the MAK is tracked by Microsoft, and you can query Microsoft to determine how many operating system activations are left using the MAK.

6. Install the MAK on the client computers and then activate them.

Figure 1.13 shows the VAMT with several computers added to a group named SecureNetwork. In the figure, one computer has already been activated with a retail (non-MAK) key. The other computers have not been activated yet.

FIGURE 1.13   Using VAMT to manage activation

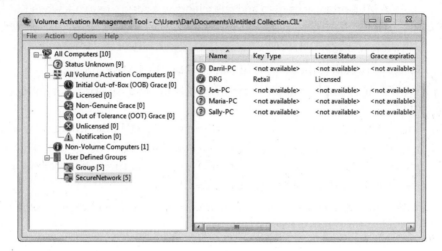

Inventory and Licensing Compliance Audits

The biggest benefit of using VAMT with MAK is the ability to inventory your licenses and help with licensing audits. A license audit is accomplished by identifying what software is installed and then comparing it to what software has been purchased.

Once you add MAKs to VAMT, you can access the Refresh Remaining Count command to query the Microsoft licensing site and identify exactly how many remaining activations exist for the MAK. This tells you both how many licenses are purchased for any MAK you add to VAMT and how many remain.

In large organizations, license audits will often be accomplished using advanced tools such as System Center Configuration Manager (SCCM).

Using a MAK Proxy

Although you can use VAMT to activate clients with a MAK, you may have noticed a problem for the computers working in an isolated network. By definition, the isolated network wouldn't have access to the Internet. On one hand, you would use VAMT for activation of computers in isolated networks, but on the other hand, the VAMT computer accesses both the network and the Internet, which would violate the security rules of ensuring the isolated network remains isolated.

Instead, you can use VAMT as a MAK proxy. One instance of VAMT is in the secure network and captures data from the secure computers. Another instance of VAMT is installed on a computer with access to the Internet. It acts as a proxy to connect to the

Microsoft licensing site, presents the data from the secure computers, and receives activation data. This activation data is then copied to the instance of VAMT in the secure environment.

> A MAK proxy is used to activate clients in a secure network when KMS is not being used. This would be common in secure networks with fewer than 5 servers or fewer than 25 clients.

The following steps outline the process of using VAMT as a MAK proxy:

1. Install VAMT on a computer in the secure network *and* in a network that has access to the Internet.

2. Perform the following steps on the computer hosting VAMT in the secure network:

   a. Collect the status of the computers in the secure network using VAMT. This data is referred to as a Computer Information List (CIL) and can be exported as a file.

   b. Copy the CIL to removable media such as a CD.

3. Transfer the removable media to the computer hosting VAMT with access to the Internet and complete the following steps:

   a. Import the CIL using VAMT.

   b. Use VAMT to connect to Microsoft and request Computer Identification numbers (CIDs) using this CIL.

   c. Export the CIL with the CIDs from Microsoft. Copy the new CIL to removable media.

4. Transfer the removable media holding the new CIL to the computer hosting the VAMT in the secure network and complete the following steps:

   a. Import the new CIL.

   b. Apply the new CIDs using MAK Proxy Activate.

While this process will work for networks of any size, there is an easier and more automated method for larger networks. In any isolated network with more than 5 servers, more than 25 clients, or a combination of more than 25 clients and servers, you can use the Key Management Service. MAK keys cannot be used with the Key Management Service, but instead KMS keys are used.

Key Management Service and Licensing Infrastructure

The Key Management Service is used for enterprises with a large number of clients in secure networks. Clients will access the KMS server for temporary activation instead of connecting to Microsoft's activation servers for permanent activation.

Two important concepts are worth repeating with KMS:

Activation is temporary.   Clients are not permanently activated. Instead, they must periodically connect to the KMS server to be reactivated. Temporary activation will last for 180 days.

KMS is used for a large number of clients.   Specifically, KMS can be used only if there are five or more servers or 25 or more clients and servers that need to be activated by KMS. If the numbers fall below this threshold, KMS will stop reactivating clients.

You can download KMS for free. Go to www.microsoft.com/downloads, and search for "Key Management Service." You can install it on Windows Server 2003, Windows Server 2008, or Windows Server 2008 R2.

If you're running a KMS server on a Windows Server 2008 server, you can update it to provide activation for Windows 7 and Windows Server 2008 R2. Knowledge Base article 968915 (http://support.microsoft.com/kb/968915) provides the information on this extension and links for the download.

 At this writing, there isn't a single download for KMS to support Windows 7 and Server 2008 R2. You must install the earlier version and then extend it using KB 968915. However, I expect it's just a matter of time before Microsoft releases a single-version download.

KMS Activation Terms

When discussing the Key Management Service (KMS), it helps first to understand the different terms associated with KMS. Once you grasp the terms, the process is much easier to understand. I've outlined many of the basic terms here:

KMS host   The server hosting the KMS service is commonly referred to as the KMS host.

KMS client   Clients configured to contact the KMS host are referred to as KMS clients.

DNS publication   A KMS host can publish Domain Name System (DNS) SRV records (server records) to the DNS server using dynamic DNS within a Microsoft domain. If DNS isn't configured to allow dynamic updates, the SRV records must be manually configured on the DNS server so that KMS clients can locate the KMS host.

Activation threshold   The minimum number of clients a network must have for KMS activation to work is referred to as the activation threshold. A network must have at least 5 servers for server activation to work or a combination of at least 25 servers and clients for client activation to work. The KMS host tracks this threshold, and if the threshold isn't reached or the number of clients falls below this threshold, it will no longer activate the clients. KMS clients that aren't activated because the activation threshold is not met will request activation every two hours.

Activation validity interval   After activation by a KMS host, KMS clients will remain activated for 180 days. If the KMS client has not connected to a KMS server within 180 days, the activation will be invalidated. Clients attempt to connect every seven days, and when they connect, this 180-day counter is reset.

Activation count   The current number of clients that are being activated by KMS is tracked using unique client machine identification designation (CMID) records. Clients attempt to contact the KMS server every seven days, and the KMS server renews this CMID when the client activates or reactivates. If the client doesn't renew within 30 days, the CMID is discarded and is no longer counted toward the activation threshold.

This is an important concept. Your network may have reached the threshold of 25, and then two systems are decommissioned or taken on the road by sales people. Within 30 days, the CMID for these two systems will be removed from the KMS host, and the count will be at 23. Clients will no longer be activated, and within seven days all 23 remaining systems will be trying to activate every two hours. Even though the clients will stay activated for 180 days, these failures will result in errors in the event logs. Once two new clients are added to the network, everything will normalize.

KMS Activation Process

The KMS activation process is ongoing, requiring the KMS clients to connect to the KMS host periodically. Before the process can start, an SRV record must exist in DNS so the clients can reach the KMS server.

Normally, dynamic update will be configured in DNS, which allows the KMS service on a KMS host to publish SRV records automatically to DNS. Once this is configured, no further steps are required. KMS clients then query DNS to locate the KMS host.

 DNS is a critical component of the KMS activation process. If KMS clients can't locate the KMS host because the SRV records aren't published in DNS, activation won't occur. If KMS was working and has stopped, DNS should be checked to ensure the KMS host record exists. These records will be in the _VLMCS._TCP folder on the DNS server.

Once the KMS client has located the KMS host, the following process is used to temporarily activate the client:

1. Every seven days, KMS clients query DNS for the IP of a KMS host.

2. KMS clients then try to renew their activation with KMS.

    a. If the activation fails, clients continue to try every two hours.

    b. If clients can't connect to the KMS host for 30 days, the record for the client in the activation count is deleted on the KMS server. If the activation count falls below the activation threshold, the KMS host will stop activating clients.

    c. If clients can't connect for 180 days, client activation expires.

3. If the client succeeds in reaching the KMS host, the activation will be renewed.

   a. Once the client is activated, the seven-day counter will be reset on the KMS client.

   b. The 180-day counter for the KMS client activation is renewed.

   c. The KMS host creates a new record for this client for the activation count (which is kept for 30 days). The original record is deleted.

4. Seven days after the client is temporarily activated, the process starts again.

Working with KMS

In order for the KMS to respond to activation requests, the firewall needs to be properly configured on the KMS server. If the Windows firewall is being used, the KMS Traffic exception can be enabled. If a third-party firewall is being used, you'll need to open port 1688.

In addition, you can use the Software Licensing Management Tool (`slmgr.vbs`) to configure and manage specific settings on the KMS server. Table 1.3 shows some of the common switches used with KMS.

TABLE 1.3   Slmgr switches used with KMS

Switch	Description
/sprt ####	Use this switch to change the default port number if necessary. The default port number is 1688.
/cdns	This will disable automatic DNS publishing by a KMS host. The SRV records must be manually created on DNS.
/cpri	This will reduce the priority of host processes. Use this if the KMS host needs more processing power for other server roles.
/spri	This returns the priority of host processes to normal on the KMS server.
/sai #	You can use this to change how often a KMS client tries to connect to a KMS if activation fails. The number is provided in minutes, and the default is 120 (two hours).
/sri #	This will change how often a KMS client contacts the KMS host to renew the activation. The number is provided in minutes, and the default is 10080 (seven days).
/dli	When executed on the KMS server, this provides the current activation count on the KMS server.
/skms	You can use this to set the name and the port of the KMS server for non-domain computers.

Virtualization Licensing

If your company is considering a Virtual Desktop Infrastructure (VDI) solution, you'll need to understand the licensing requirements. It's important to realize that licenses are needed for the virtual machines just as they are needed for a regular installation.

Virtual computers can be activated using MAK keys or KMS servers. In addition, Microsoft recently announced the Virtual Enterprise Centralized Desktop (VECD), which can be used specifically for VDI licensing. VECD allows an organization to license virtual copies of Windows client operating systems at a lower cost than a full version of the operating system. VECD uses a device-based subscription license and is available with two configurations:

- VECD for Software Assurance (SA), currently priced at $23/year
- VECD, currently priced at $110/device/year

Once VECD is purchased, you can deploy as many as four virtual desktops on any single system. This doesn't include the cost of the host operating system. The host operating system could be Windows 7, Windows Server 2008, Windows Server 2008 R2, or other operating systems.

VECD offers many benefits, including these:

- Rights to move virtual machines between systems for increased reliability
- Unlimited backup of virtual machines
- Ability to access up to four running VM instances per device
- Rights to access corporate desktops from home for a user who has already been licensed at work

Licensing of Microsoft products can easily get complicated, and pricing often changes. When you're looking at purchasing licenses, you should locate a Microsoft Licensing Specialist through a Microsoft partner.

Remember these two key points, however:

- No additional licenses are needed to use Windows XP Mode with the built-in Windows XP client.
- VECD includes licenses for up to four virtual machines.

Summary

In this chapter, you learned about the different editions of Windows 7 that will be used in an enterprise, including many of their different features and capabilities. Once Windows 7 is installed, you'll often have to migrate users' files and settings using an in-place, wipe-and-load, or side-by-side migration. USMT can help with all types of migrations.

Windows 7 supports a rich virtual desktop infrastructure including Windows XP Mode. Windows XP Mode can be used to run applications transparently in a virtual isolated Windows XP environment. You can also run full-blown operating systems in a virtual environment using Windows Virtual PC

Finally, you learned about the different tools used for activation and managing licensing. Windows 7 licenses can be purchased individually or in bulk using either MAK or KMS. The VAMT provides additional tools that can be used to manage licenses and activation.

Chapter Essentials

Choosing a Windows 7 edition   Know the features available in the different Windows 7 editions used in the enterprise. The three Windows 7 editions you'll see in an enterprise are Windows 7 Professional, Windows 7 Enterprise, and Windows 7 Ultimate. Windows 7 Enterprise is available only to organizations that purchase Software Assurance and includes additional features beyond Windows 7 Professional. Windows 7 Ultimate has all of the features of Windows 7 Enterprise but can be purchased without Software Assurance.

Performing a Local Windows 7 Installation   Know how to install Windows 7 from the DVD. While most of the deployments in large organizations will use automated methods, you should be able to install Windows 7 from the DVD and know what to do with issues that may appear.

Designing User State Migration   Be familiar with the User State Migration Tools (USMT) `ScanState` and `LoadState`. The USMT are part of the Windows Automated Installation Kit (Windows AIK) for Windows 7. The two most important tools are `ScanState` and `LoadState`. `ScanState` can collect user state data, including files and settings, and put it in a migration store. `LoadState` can then read the migration store and apply it to a new installation of Windows 7.

USMT can be used to migrate data using in-place migrations, wipe-and-load migrations, and side-by-side migrations. In-place migrations can be automated with a batch file that will retrieve data from the `Windows.old` folder created when Windows 7 is installed on a computer with a previous version of Windows.

Considering virtualization   Know how to use Windows XP Mode and Windows Virtual PC. Windows 7 introduces Windows Virtual PC. Entire operating systems can be hosted in Windows Virtual PC, and you can use Windows XP Mode to host specific applications. Applications hosted in Windows XP Mode can be launched from the Windows 7 Start menu or configured to start from shortcuts. Windows XP Mode works best when processor virtualization technologies are used, and virtualization is enabled in the BIOS. KB 977206 provides a workaround. Intel calls this Intel VT, and AMD calls this AMD-V.

Planning and managing client licensing and activation   Be familiar with different licensing and activation methods used in an enterprise. Windows clients should be activated within 30 days of installation. If access to the Internet is available, activation can be configured to occur automatically and will normally occur three days after the install. Large organizations can use a Multiple Activation Key (MAK), which is a single key that includes licenses for multiple clients.

If clients will never have access to the Internet, a Key Management Service (KMS) server can be used to activate clients. KMS requires a minimum of 5 servers or any combination of 25 clients and servers. Clients will periodically contact the KMS server to renew their activation. If you have fewer than 25 clients, you can use the Volume Activation Management Tool (VAMT) with a MAK proxy to activate the clients. The VAMT can also be used to identify how many licenses remain on a MAK.

Chapter 2

Automating the Deployment of Windows 7

TOPICS COVERED IN THIS CHAPTER INCLUDE

- ✓ Understanding and designing images
- ✓ Choosing a deployment strategy
- ✓ Imaging with the Windows Automated Installation Kit
- ✓ Deploying images with Windows Deployment Services
- ✓ Using the Microsoft Deployment Toolkit 2010

When preparing to deploy Windows 7, you should have a solid understanding of images and the different methods that can be used to capture, manage, update, and deploy the images. Microsoft provides several tools, and many of them have been updated specifically to support Windows 7. Images are stored in Microsoft's Windows Image (.wim) file format, and a .wim file can include a single image or multiple images.

Deployments are often categorized as using a heavy touch installation, a *Lite Touch Installation (LTI)*, or a *Zero Touch Installation (ZTI)* method. As clients are added in an enterprise, it becomes increasingly expensive to deploy them without automation. For example, in a Heavy Touch local installation, it may take four hours to complete a full installation. Multiply this by 1,000 clients, and the cost is quickly prohibitive. ZTIs are completely automated without any human interaction, and LTIs require minimal interaction.

The *Windows Automated Installation Kit (AIK)* was introduced in Chapter 1, "Planning for the Installation of Windows 7," and has two important tools used with imaging: ImageX and Deployment Image Servicing and Management (DISM). The tools are used together to capture, manage, and deploy images. Even when using other tools such as Windows Deployment Services for deployments, you can still use these tools for image maintenance.

Windows Deployment Services (WDS) is a free server role available with Windows Server 2008 and Windows Server 2008 R2. It can be used to automate the deployment of images to clients across an enterprise using multicasting, that is, sending a single image to multiple clients at the same time.

Last, the Microsoft Deployment Toolkit (MDT) 2010 includes additional tools that can be used to automate deployments. It can be combined with WDS to support LTIs, and it can be combined with *System Center Configuration Manager (SCCM)* to support ZTIs.

Understanding and Designing Images

Images are used to deploy Windows 7 to computers. All of the images are derived from the basic Windows Imaging (.wim) file type in Windows 7. This is the same .wim file type used in Windows Vista, Windows Server 2008, and Windows Server 2008 R2.

These images share many similarities no matter how they are deployed. You can deploy images using the following methods:

- DVD installation
- ImageX deployment

- Windows Deployment Services deployment
- System Center Configuration Manager deployment

Two primary image types are used:

Boot images   A *boot image* installs the Windows Preinstallation Environment (Windows PE, or WinPE). WinPE is used to provide a basic environment where a full installation can start. In installations before Windows Vista, installations began with a command-prompt mode, but now WinPE is used instead. The Windows 7 installation DVD includes a boot image (named boot.wim in the \Sources folder).

Install images   An *install image* includes a full operating system. The Windows 7 installation DVD includes the Windows 7 install images in the install.wim file. You can also create custom install images. A custom install image would include the operating system, applications, settings, and configuration.

Windows imaging files can contain more than one image. The Windows 7 installation DVD I have has four images contained within the install.wim file: the Home Basic edition, the Home Premium edition, the Professional edition, and the Ultimate edition. You can use ImageX with the /Info switch (as shown later in this section) to identify the images contained in a Windows image file.

It's important to realize the distinction between a .wim file and an image. An image is a full image of a bootable operating system, but it must be contained within a .wim file. Any .wim file can contain one or more images.

Images are stored in image files using compression and single-file technologies. Compression is easy enough to understand: The files are zipped or shrunk and can be uncompressed when needed.

Single-file technologies may be new to you, though. Files that are in more than one image are stored only once in the image file. For example, the Windows folder holds the regedit.exe file. If your .wim file includes four Windows 7 images, the regedit.exe file is stored only once as a resource that is available to each of the images. Space is saved by storing it once instead of four times.

Understanding Imaging

Imaging Windows 7 is the process of capturing an image on a single computer. This image can then be deployed to one or more other computers in the environment. This can be done with the Windows Automated Installation Kit (AIK) as shown in this section, with more automated tools such as Windows Deployment Services (shown later in this chapter), or with the more advanced enterprise application System Center Configuration Manager (SCCM).

Figure 2.1 shows the different computers involved in the imaging process when capturing and deploying images with the Windows AIK.

FIGURE 2.1   Computers involved in the imaging process with Windows AIK

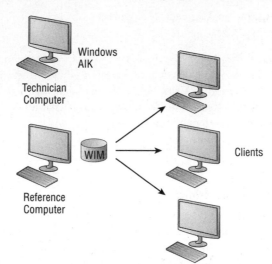

The technician's computer is the computer you use to do the preparation. You install the Windows AIK here and can use it to create bootable USBs, create bootable CDs, and do maintenance on images. You may also choose to store the images you've captured on this computer.

You capture an image from a reference computer. A reference computer has the operating system installed, applications installed, and any specific security or configuration settings desired.

Designing Images

When designing images for an enterprise, there are many different considerations. What you choose to do depends largely on your needs and on the capabilities of your organization.

A significant decision point is whether you have deployed System Center Configuration Manager. SCCM is an enterprise application that can be purchased, and it is the replacement for System Management Server (SMS). SCCM can be used to enhance significantly the administration and maintenance of an organization. From an imaging perspective, it can be used to deploy images, applications, updates, and other packages such as driver packages. Sounds great, right?

The challenge is that even though it is a solid product, not all organizations have it because it is not a free product. Furthermore, not all organizations have IT administrators who understand how to use it. A typical class to learn SCCM takes a full week.

On the other hand, there are several free tools that can be used. These include the Windows Automated Installation Kit, Windows Server Update Services (WSUS) to deploy updates, and Group Policy to deploy applications and settings.

If you have SCCM, use it. But if you don't and your company can't afford it, there are alternatives.

Real World Scenario

Using Images as Baselines

It's common for many companies to use an image as a baseline. At one organization where I worked, a single image was created to save time and money and to increase security.

This baseline image included the operating system, several Microsoft Office applications, anti-malware software, and some other software programs. The Local Security Policy was modified to ensure that the system met minimal security requirements at the first boot. Other configuration was completed to ensure that it matched the internal environment.

Desktop administrators had this image available on a DVD and could easily apply it to any computer. Two computer resellers also had a copy of this image, and new computers purchased from them included this image when they were received. Once the computer was booted with this image, it was joined to a domain, and Group Policy was used to fine-tune the image.

This saved both time and money. The desktop administrators didn't need to spend as much time with the computers because most of the time-consuming tasks were already completed. And because the same baseline was consistently applied, the systems started out much more secure than the default. In addition, the security state of these computers was well known and understood because they were all secured exactly the same way from the start.

Last, it reduced the cost of maintenance and troubleshooting. Since all the systems had the same configuration, desktop administrators were able to provide assistance quickly to any user without first trying to learn how the user's system was configured.

Understanding the Different Image Types

You create standard and custom images on reference computers. An organization can have a single standard image used as a baseline for all users; it can also have multiple custom images used for specific needs for different groups of users.

As an example, I work in a large organization with tens of thousands of users. A single standard image has been created and is used to deploy images to computers throughout the organization. While it has a significant amount of customization including additional applications, security, and other settings, it starts as only a baseline. Group Policy and SCCM are then used to deploy different applications and settings to users within the organization.

Standard image   A standard image is a single image used as a baseline for all computers. It includes customization such as additional applications, security, and other settings affecting features and components of the operating system. The enterprise then uses Group Policy, SCCM, and/or WSUS to deploy different settings, applications, and updates to users within the organization.

Custom image   Instead of a single image for everyone, it's possible for an organization to use different custom images for different target groups. For example, one custom image could be used for users in the Sales department, and another custom image could be used for users in the Accounting department. Even with custom images, it's common to use Group Policy to enforce settings and to use other tools to deploy updates.

Role-based image   A role-based image is just another type of custom image. Instead of creating images targeted to specific departments, they are created for users performing specific tasks. For example, an image could be created for graphic artists that includes all of the tools they need. It doesn't matter which department they work in; if that's their job or role, that's the image they receive.

Geographic and localization-based images   Very large organizations can span different countries supporting different languages and locales. Separate images can be created to support these different users. On a smaller scale, if needs are different for separate regions within the same company, it's possible to create different images for each of the regions.

Online vs. Offline Image Servicing

Images can be serviced either online or offline. An online image is booted into the operating system, and changes are made while it is running. This can be done before Sysprep is run, or it can be done in the Sysprep Audit Mode, which is presented in the next section.

An offline image is not running but instead is an image that is stored in a `.wim` file. The image can be extracted from the image file in a process referred to as *mounting the image*. Once it is extracted, files within the image can be modified and packages can be added. Common tools used to mount and modify images are `ImageX.exe` and `DISM.exe`, commonly referred to as ImageX and DISM.

After an offline image is modified, the changes can be saved back as an image contained within the original `.wim` file or stored in another `.wim` file. The image can then be deployed just as any other image.

Creating Images on Reference Computers

With any imaging process, the reference computers must be properly prepared. The overall steps involved in creating a reference computer for imaging are as follows:

Install the operating system   You can install the operating system using the installation DVD. Imaging tools we cover in this chapter can capture images from these operating systems: Windows XP, Windows Vista, Windows 7, Windows Server 2003, Windows Server 2008, and Windows Server 2008 R2.

Install desired applications   You can install any applications desired at this point. Installed applications will be available to users after the image is deployed. These include full-blown applications such as the Microsoft Office suite, simple applications such as Adobe Reader, Internet Explorer add-ons, and security applications such as antivirus software and host-based intrusion-detection systems.

Configure security settings   Although Windows 7 starts in a much more secure state than older Microsoft operating systems, you may want to tweak it for your own use. As a few examples, you can rename the administrator account, configure the firewall, and disable specific services.

Configure other desired settings   You can configure additional settings such as enabling or disabling features and components, modifying the desktop wallpaper, adding links to network shares and network printers, configuring logon or logoff scripts, and much more.

Test, test, test   Once the system has been configured, it should be well tested to ensure it meets the needs of the organization. While some modification of the image can be done after it's created, it's much easier to ensure that it has everything needed before capturing the image.

Run Sysprep   *Sysprep* will prepare the system for duplication. You can use it to remove computer-specific information such as the computer name and the computer security identifier (SID).

After these steps are completed, you can capture the image using ImageX or Windows Deployment Services.

Running Sysprep

The System Preparation (*Sysprep*) tool is a very important element of the imaging process. If an image is deployed to multiple computers with the same image without running Sysprep, these computers will have problems. A lot of information on a computer should be unique.

As a simple example, the SID will be the same on these computers if Sysprep isn't run. When more than one computer has the same SID in an environment, you end up troubleshooting a wide assortment of errors, none of which simply states "Duplicate SIDs identified." It's best to avoid these problems completely by running Sysprep.

The Sysprep.exe program is located in the Windows\System32\Sysprep folder. You can launch it from the command line or by double-clicking it to launch the graphical user interface (GUI).

Sysprep cannot be run on an upgraded version of Windows. In other words, if you were running Windows Vista and then upgraded to Windows 7, Sysprep would not run on this system. Instead, an information dialog box would appear saying, "You can only run Sysprep on a custom (clean) install version of Windows."

Figure 2.2 shows the GUI part of the Sysprep tool. It can also be launched from the command line.

FIGURE 2.2 Running the Sysprep GUI

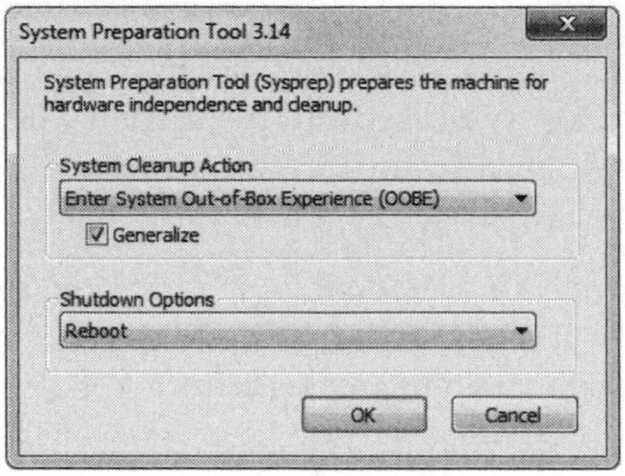

It includes two System Cleanup Actions and three Shutdown Options. The Generalize option is the most important check box for this GUI. When checked, it will remove system-specific information from the computer, which allows you to reuse the image on different computers.

The two System Cleanup Actions are Enter System Out-Of-Box Experience (OOBE) and Enter System Audit Mode. The three Shutdown Options are Reboot, Shutdown, and Quit.

Enter System Out-Of-Box Experience (OOBE)   When the system is turned on after using this option, it will mimic the first boot screens from an initial installation. The Windows Welcome program will run when it is booted to reinitialize settings on the computer. It's possible to automate this process with the use of an answer file.

Enter System Audit Mode   The system audit mode can be used by original equipment manufacturers, computer resellers, or enterprises for similar hardware. It allows a custom image to be saved and then booted into audit mode, where additional programs or updates can be added.

Using audit mode is also referred to as servicing an online image. It will run many of the initial setup tasks for a normal boot, but it bypasses the Windows Welcome phase, which speeds up the process considerably.

After a computer boots to audit mode, it will continue to boot to audit mode until you configure the computer to boot to the Windows Welcome phase by running Sysprep and selecting the Out-Of-Box Experience (OOBE) selection.

Quit   This will exit Sysprep after running without shutting down the system.

Reboot   As you'd guess, this reboots the system. Use it if you plan on either modifying settings in audit mode or immediately capturing the image.

Shutdown   This will power down the system after Sysprep is run.

When running Sysprep from the command prompt, you would generally use the following command:

```
C:\windows\system32\sysprep\sysprep /oobe /generalize /shutdown
```

The `/oobe` switch specifies the Out-Of-Box Experience, the `/generalize` switch causes unique information to be removed, and the `/shutdown` switch causes the system to shut down. The next time the system is turned on, the image should be captured using one of the available tools (such as ImageX or Windows Deployment Services). If the system boots normally without capturing the image, Sysprep will need to be run again before capturing the image.

You may want to use two additional switches when running Sysprep from the command prompt:

`/quiet`   This runs Sysprep without displaying any onscreen messages. It would be used if Sysprep was automated through a script.

`/unattend:answerfile`   This is used to specify the full path and name of an answer file to use when the system is rebooted. Windows 7 will use this answer file for an unattended installation. You can use the Windows System Image Manager (part of the Windows AIK) to create an answer file to use with `Sysprep`.

Choosing a Deployment Strategy

When considering the deployment of Windows 7 into your organization, you can choose from multiple methods. The method you choose is dependent on the number of clients in your organization, the number of IT professionals on staff, and their expertise.

Some Microsoft documentation states that the method you choose depends on whether you have dedicated IT staff. I'm going to assume all your staffs are dedicated, so I've changed this to IT professionals. (Or did they mean "dedicated" in some other way?)

If you support only 15 clients on a part-time basis, you probably won't be using any of the automated methods. On the other hand, if your organization has several thousand clients, it makes sense to take the time to learn the methods that can be used to automate the installation.

Installations are often referred to as High Touch, Lite Touch, and Zero Touch. It's worthwhile to compare the differences between these methods.

A Comparison of Installations

The more an IT professional has to touch an end user's computer, the higher the cost on a per-client basis. Because of this, as more computers are used in an organization, automated methods are needed to keep down the total cost of ownership.

You'll see recommended computer numbers in the following explanations. For example, an organization with fewer than 100 computers would use the High-Touch Installation with Retail Media method. These numbers are meant as guides only and to give you a point of reference. If your organization has 75 users and you want to use Lite Touch Installations, you certainly can. Similarly, an organization with 501 clients could choose any of the methods.

High Touch Installation with Retail Media   If an organization has fewer than 100 computers and doesn't have full-time IT professionals on staff, the local installation method can be used. Quite simply, a technician sits in front of each computer with the installation DVDs and installs the operating system and all the applications and then configures the computer for the end user.

High Touch Installation with Standard Image   If an organization has between 100 and 200 computers and has at least one full-time IT professional, it may choose an imaging solution to create and deploy images. The images can include applications and different configuration settings.

The Windows Automated Installation Kit includes tools, such as ImageX, that can be used to create bootable media. Bootable media can be used to capture and/or apply standard images.

In other words, an administrator could create a reference computer and then run Sysprep to prepare. The administrator would then boot using bootable media to the Windows Preinstallation Environment. Within WinPE, he can use ImageX to capture the image and store this image on a DVD or an external USB drive. He could later boot to another computer using bootable media to get to the WinPE and then use ImageX to apply the captured image to the clean computer. The detailed steps are covered later in this chapter.

Lite Touch Installation   Organizations with between 200 and 500 clients and a full-time IT staff may choose to use an LTI. LTI requires limited interaction at the beginning of the installation but is automated afterward.

In addition to the Windows AIK, Windows Deployment Services and the Microsoft Deployment Toolkit 2010 can be used for Lite Touch Installations.

When WDS is used, much of the process is automated. An end user (not necessarily an administrator) only needs to press the F12 key a couple of times, log on, and select an image. WDS then downloads the image. MDT 2010 can be used to add applications. WDS and MTD 2010 are covered in more depth later in this chapter.

Zero Touch Installation   Organizations with more than 500 clients and experts in deployment, networking, and Configuration Manager 2007 R2 products may choose ZTI installations. ZTI installations are fully automated without any human interaction.

While fully automated installations are quite valuable within an installation, I want to stress that there is an associated up-front cost. The System Center suite of products must be purchased, and then IT professionals often need to be sent to classes to learn how to use them. Last, there is a natural learning curve as the products are configured and tested. However, for large deployments, the up-front costs are considered an investment to reduce the long-term costs.

Deployment Tools Overview

Several different deployment tools are available. As an overview, the available tools are explained here:

Windows Automated Installation Kit   The Windows Automated Installation Kit is a free download that was introduced in Chapter 1 when the USMT was used. It also includes several other tools such as ImageX and DISM that can be used to capture, modify, and deploy images. The Windows AIK can be used in High Touch and Lite Touch Installations. A great strength is the ability to modify images after they have been captured.

Windows Deployment Services   Windows Deployment Services is a free server role that can be added to Windows Server 2008 or Windows Server 2008 R2. It is used in Lite Touch Installations requiring little interaction. Preboot Execution Environment (PXE)–compliant computers are used. Users need to press the F12 key twice, log on when prompted, and select an image. After that, the installation can be automated. A significant strength of WDS is the ability to multicast images. In other words, the WDS server can send a single image to multiple clients at the same time.

Microsoft Deployment Toolkit   The Microsoft Deployment Toolkit 2010 is a free product that can be downloaded and used in Lite Touch Installations and can also be combined with System Center tools in Zero Touch Installations. It includes the Deployment Workbench, which can be used to create task sequencers used in automating deployments.

System Center suite   The System Center suite of server products can be purchased to help a large organization manage clients and deployments. The server products available at this writing are as follows:

> **System Center Configuration Manager 2007 R2**   SCCM can be used to assess, deploy, and update servers, client computers, and devices. This is the primary tool that would be used for Zero Touch Installations. MDT 2010 can be integrated with SCCM.

> **System Center Operations Manager 2007**   SCOM is used for service management. It can be used to monitor the availability and performance of IT services throughout the network and provide alert capabilities. It is used to help identify problems and issues before they impact the performance of network services.

System Center Data Protection Manager 2007 SCDPM is used for Windows backup-and-recovery solutions. Users can store their data on a central server, and SCDPM can be used to provide a data backup-and-recovery solution for the file servers. It can also be used for application servers like Microsoft SQL Server or Microsoft Exchange Server.

System Center Virtual Machine Manager 2008 SCVMM is designed to be a central-ized server that can be used to configure and deploy virtual machines. It helps integrate virtual and physical environments and allows management from a central console.

System Center Essentials 2007 SCE is designed for midsize businesses of fewer than 500 clients and provides several of the tools included in the entire System Center suite in a single product.

In order to determine easily the best deployment strategy for your network, it's necessary to understand the capabilities of the available tools and how to use them. The rest of this chapter provides more details on these tools.

Imaging with the Windows Automated Installation Kit

The Windows Automated Installation Kit for Windows 7 was introduced in Chapter 1. Exercises within that chapter led you through the process of installing it and using the User State Migration Tool and the Volume Activation Management Tool contained within the Windows AIK.

 Multiple versions of the Windows AIK exist. Make sure you have the version for Windows 7. In addition, if you've installed a service pack on Windows 7, you should check to see if a newer version of the Windows AIK has been released. The Windows AIK can be found at Microsoft's download site at http://www.microsoft.com/downloads by searching for "Windows 7 AIK."

In this section, you'll learn how to use more of the tools to capture, deploy, and modify images. Using images for deployments is a primary method of automating deployments of Windows 7, and you have several tools available to help you. These include

- ImageX
- Deployment Image Servicing and Management
- Preinstallation environment tools
- Windows System Image Manager

ImageX

The ImageX command-line tool is part of the set of deployment tools installed when you install the Windows AIK. It can be used to capture, deploy, modify, and inspect images.

You can access the ImageX application via the Deployment Tools Command Prompt by selecting Start ➢ All Programs ➢ Microsoft Windows AIK ➢ Deployment Tools Command Prompt. When running ImageX within Windows 7, you'll need administrative permissions for most of the switches, so you should start it by right-clicking and selecting Run As Administrator.

One of the ways that ImageX is used is within the Windows Preinstallation Environment. You can create a bootable disk, such as a bootable USB disk or bootable CD, and copy the ImageX.exe program to the bootable media. You can then boot to a system with this bootable media and use ImageX to capture and/or deploy images. (An exercise later in this chapter will lead you through the process of creating PE-bootable media.)

ImageX can also be used on the technician's computer to manage .wim files. You can inspect .wim files to identify the images within it and extract the files within an image by mounting the image with ImageX. You can even modify these extracted files and save them back to the original image. You'll see how to do this in an exercise later in this chapter.

The following section covers many of the switches you'll use with ImageX to do common tasks. If you want to see a complete list of all the switches available with ImageX, check out the help article titled "ImageX Command-Line Options" in the Windows Automated Installation Kit User's Guide for Windows 7.

As you go through the following explanations, I strongly encourage you to execute all the commands you can. Although you may not have all the information necessary to capture or deploy an image yet, you should be able to execute ImageX with many of the other switches including /info, /mount, /unmount, and /dir.

Capturing Images

You can capture the image of a reference computer using the /capture switch. The reference computer must have had Sysprep run on it for this to work. You would then boot to the PE on the reference computer and run ImageX with the /capture switch.

This switch requires three parameters:

- The first parameter is the drive of the operating system (such as C:).

- Next you provide the path to the location where the image will be stored and the name of the image file. The specified folder must exist or the command will fail.

  - If the image file doesn't exist, it will be created.

- If the file does exist, it will be overwritten. If you want to add the image as an additional image within an existing .wim file, substitute the /capture switch with the /append switch.

- The last parameter is the name of the image.

In the following command, the image is being captured from the C: drive, stored in the Win7.wim image file in the C:\images folder, and named "Windows 7".

```
ImageX /capture c: c:\images\Win7.wim "Windows 7"
```

Deploying Images

You can deploy an image to a system with the /apply switch. This allows you to deploy an image that has been captured from a reference computer. You would boot to a system using bootable media and then use ImageX with the /apply switch to apply an image contained within a .wim file. The file could be available on the destination computer, on a USB drive, or via a network share.

The /apply switch needs three parameters:

- First, you need to provide the path and name of the .wim file.

- Next, you need to provide an image identifier to identify the image uniquely within the .wim file. Remember, any .wim file can hold multiple images. You can identify the image with the index number of the image or the image name. If the image is the first image in the .wim file, the index is 1.

- Last, you need to provide the drive (such as C: or D:) where the image will be deployed.

As an example, if you booted to the PE from a USB disc that included ImageX, you could use the following command to load the first image within the Win7.wim file to the C: drive.

```
ImageX /apply F:\Images\Win7.wim 1 C:
```

Viewing Information about an Image

A common question you may have about any .wim file is, "What's in there?" You can easily answer this question with the /info switch. It allows you to view detailed information about an existing image, including how many images are within the .wim file, the image index of each image, and other details on the image.

The result is displayed in XML format. Nodes are contained within < > symbols. For example, the image index is displayed as <IMAGE INDEX="1"> for the first image in the file and <IMAGE INDEX="4"> for the fourth image within the .wim file. The image index is valuable to have because you need to know it when deploying and mounting images.

As an example, the following output shows a partial printout after querying a .wim file with the /info switch. There are about 35 extra lines within the <IMAGE> node providing details such as when it was created, when it was last modified, and Windows version information. Execute the command against your `.wim` file to see all the results.

```
Available Image Choices:
------------------------
<WIM>
  <TOTALBYTES>185270805</TOTALBYTES>
  <IMAGE INDEX="1">
. . .
  </IMAGE>
</WIM>
```

The `/info` switch takes a single parameter—the path and name of the `.wim` file. For example, the following command will retrieve information from the `install.wim` file located on the installation DVD (where the installation DVD is assigned drive F:).

```
ImageX /info F:\sources\install.wim
```

Mounting Images

When you mount an image, it extracts all of the files for a specific image from a `.wim` file. You can compare this to unzipping a `.zip` file or extracting files from a Microsoft cabinet (`.cab`) file; the original `.zip` file and `.cab` file still exist, but now you have a new directory holding all of the files that were in the original files.

A mounted image is different from a zipped or cabinet file in that the system will track all mounted images, and they are not intended to stay mounted. Instead, you mount the image so that you can inspect, copy, and/or modify the files within the image. Once you've finished, you use the `/unmount` switch to unmount the image and delete all the extracted files.

If you mount an image with the `/mountrw` switch (notice the rw), you can modify the extracted files and save these changes back to the original image. If you mount an image with the `/mount` switch, changes to any files cannot be saved to the original image.

The `/mount` and `/mountrw` switches take three parameters:

- The first parameter is the path and the name of the `.wim` file.
- Next is the name or number of the image within the `.wim` file.
- Last, you provide a path to the location where you want to extract the image.

The following command will open the `install.wim` file (located in `\sources` on the installation DVD, which has been assigned the drive letter G: on my system), extract the first image (1), and store all the image files from this image into a folder named `C:\Win7Mount`. Try it.

```
ImageX /mount g:\sources\install.wim 1 C:\Win7Mount
```

If you want to make changes to the source image, change the `/mount` switch to `/mountrw`.

Unmounting Images

Mounted images can be unmounted using the /unmount switch. This will remove all of the files and folders of a mounted image. Images that have been mounted will take a considerable amount of space on your disk and are tracked by the operating system. A mounted image will still be available after a reboot. This includes the extracted files and also ImageX's ability to see the mounted image.

You should not delete the mounted image with Windows Explorer. While it is possible to delete all of the files and folders of the mounted image using Windows Explorer, ImageX will still try to track it and will generate errors until it is properly unmounted.

The /unmount switch accepts a single parameter—the mount path, or path to the mounted folder. For example, if the image was mounted in the C:\Win7Mount folder (as shown in the /mount explanation previously), you can use the following command to unmount it:

```
ImageX /unmount c:\Win7Mount
```

You can also view a list of all mounted images by using the /unmount switch without any parameters, like this:

```
ImageX /unmount
```

The output is provided in the following text. Notice both the Mount Path and the source Image File are identified. If the image was mounted with /mount, Mounted R/W will be a 0 (indicating read mode), and if the image was mounted with /mountrw, Mounted R/W will be a 1 (indicating read/write mode).

```
Listing all mounted images...
1.
 Mount Path ....:[c:\Images\Mount]
 Image File ....:[c:\Images\install.wim]
 Image Index ...:[1]
 Mounted R/W ...:[0]
```

Modifying Images

If you've mounted an image using the /mountrw switch, you can make modifications to the files and then save them back to the original image. This can be much quicker then re-creating a reference computer, running Sysprep again, and recapturing the image.

As a reminder, when you mount an image, it extracts all of the files for a specific image from a .wim file. You can now add files, delete files, and modify these files. A common reason to do this is to add driver files, but it's possible to add other files such as scripts or application packages.

When you've finished making changes, you can commit the changes to the image file with the /unmount /commit switches. If you try to use the /commit switch on an image that was mounted with the /mount switch, it will respond with an error.

When using the /unmount and /commit switches, you must provide only one parameter—the mount path. As an example, if an image was mounted to the C:\Win7Mount folder, the following command will commit the changes to the source .wim file that was used to mount the image.

```
ImageX /unmount /commit c:\Win7Mount
```

Creating New Modified Images

You may want to use an existing image as a baseline and create new images from this baseline. You can do so by using the /commit and /append switches. When doing this, you will not use the /unmount switch right away but will later unmount the mounted image after the new images have been created.

The process for this is as follows:

- Mount an image using the /mountrw switch.

- Modify the image as desired.

- Save the mounted image as a new image in a .wim file using the /commit and /append switches.

- Unmount the image (without using /commit).

The /append switch will add the image to an existing .wim file.

Deleting Images

You can delete images from a .wim file using the /delete switch. Obviously, you would want to delete an image only if you're sure you will never need it again. The .wim files don't include a Recycle Bin.

The /delete switch needs two parameters:

- The first parameter is the name and path to the .wim file.

- The second parameter is the index, or number of the image within the .wim file.

As an example, the following command will delete the second (2) image within the Win7.wim file stored in the C:\Images folder:

```
ImageX /delete c:\images\Win7.wim 2
```

Viewing a List of Files in an Image

If you just want to view a list of the files in an image without mounting it, you can do so with the /dir switch. The output will be extensive, so you may want to capture the results in a text file.

The /dir switch needs two parameters:

- The first parameter is the name and path to the .wim file.

- The second parameter is the index, or number of the image within the .wim file.

As an example, the following command will provide a list of files and folders within the first image of the Win7.wim file stored in the C:\Images folder.

```
ImageX /dir c:\images\Win7.wim 1
```

This can be an extensive list. If you want to direct the output to a text file, you can use the > redirector as follows:

```
ImageX /delete c:\images\Win7.wim 1 > Win7Dir.txt
```

Logging ImageX Results

Most of the ImageX commands can be used with the /logfile switch to create a log that you can use to view progress. The command-line output is minimal, but if you want additional results, just add the /logfile switch with the name of a log file in the format of *name.log*.

As an example, if you wanted to capture a log file to view the results of mounting an image, you could use the following command:

```
ImageX /mount g:\sources\install.wim 1 C:\Win7Mount /logfile mylog.log
```

Not all switches support the addition of the /logfile switch, but most do.

Splitting Image Files

If your .wim file is too big for the media where you want to store it, you can use the /split switch to split it into multiple read-only .swm (split .wim) files.

The /split switch needs two parameters:

- The first parameter is the name and path to the .wim file.

- The second parameter is the size in megabytes (MB) for each split file.

As an example, the following command will split the Win7.wim file into several 650MB files so that it can be stored on several CDs.

```
ImageX /split c:\images\Win.wim 650
```

The first .swm file will be named Win.swm, the next will be named Win2.swm, the next Win3.swm, and so on. Split .wim files can be deployed to a computer using the /apply and the /ref switches.

Several of these ImageX switches will be used later in this chapter. Another tool that you may find useful to service and manage images is the Deployment Image Servicing and Management tool.

Understanding the Deployment Image Servicing and Management Tool

The *Deployment Image Servicing and Management (DISM)* tool is also included in the Windows AIK for Windows 7. The primary benefit of DISM is its ability to modify the contents of an image hosted within a .wim file. This is referred to as offline servicing.

Earlier versions of the Windows AIK required the use of several tools including the Pkgmgr.exe, Intlcfg.exe, and PEimg.exe tools. The DISM tool provides all of the functionality for these tools in a single tool.

DISM is a command-line tool and includes a rich set of switches. If you understand how the ImageX command works with the images as described in the previous section, the DISM tool is easier to grasp. Interestingly, the DISM switches follow the verb-noun format used in Windows PowerShell. (Windows PowerShell is covered in greater depth in Chapter 3, "Using the Command Prompt and PowerShell".)

As an example, the *get* verb is combined with the *wiminfo* noun in the /get-wiminfo switch. With the verb-noun format, the switches become easy to figure out just by looking at them.

You can access the DISM application via the Deployment Tools Command Prompt by selecting Start ➢ All Programs ➢ Microsoft Windows AIK ➢ Deployment Tools Command Prompt. You'll need administrative permissions when running DISM, so you'll need to right-click the Deployment Tools Command Prompt and select Run As Administrator.

When any of the DISM switches needs to work with a .wim file, it is often specified with the /wimfile switch. The /wimfile switch takes the form of /wimfile:drivePath\filename. For example, an image named image.wim in the C:\images folder would be specified as

```
/wimfile:c:\images\image.wim
```

You'll see this used in many commands mentioned in this section. As an example, the /Get-WimInfo switch is used to get information about a .wim file with this full command:

```
DISM /Get-WimInfo /wimfile:c:\images\image.wim
```

Using DISM Get Commands

Many of the get switches are used to retrieve information. Table 2.1 shows some of the DISM get switches you're likely to use.

TABLE 2.1 DISM get switches

Switch	Description
/Get-Help	Displays help for DISM.
/Get-Wiminfo	Displays information on the images within a .wim file. `dism /get-wiminfo /wimfile:g:\sources \install.wim`
/Get-MountedWiminfo	Displays information on any images that have been mounted. This includes whether it is in read/write mode and the current status. `dism /get-mountedwiminfo`

Using DISM to Mount and Unmount Images

Images must be mounted before you can do any offline servicing. Although you saw earlier that you can use ImageX to mount and unmount images, you can also use DISM.

Table 2.2 shows some of the commands that can be used to mount, commit, and unmount images.

TABLE 2.2 DISM mount switches

Switch	Description
/Mount-Wim	Mounts an image to a specified directory. The format is `Dism /Mount-Wim /WimFile:C:\images\install.wim /index:1 /MountDir:C:\Mount /ReadOnly` The /ReadOnly switch is omitted to mount the image in read/write mode.
/Unmount-Wim	Unmounts the image. The /commit switch is used to write the changes to the image, and the /discard switch does not write the changes. `Dism /UnMount-Wim /MountDir:C:\Mount /commit`
/Commit-Wim	Commits the changes to the image but does not unmount the image. `Dism /commit Mount-Wim /MountDir:C:\Mount /commit`

Using DISM with Packages and Features

DISM can be used to install, remove, or update Windows packages to an image and manipulate installed features. Packages can be either cabinet (.cab) or Windows Update Stand-alone Installer (.msu) files and are used to distribute software updates, service packs, and language packs.

You can add many common packages to Windows PE images to extend the capabilities of the image depending on what is needed when the PE is booted. These include the following:

WinPE-HTA.cab   This installs HTML application support.

WinPE-Scripting.cab   This adds support for the Windows Scripting Host (WSH), which can be used to execute script files.

WinPE-WMI.cab   This installs support for Windows Management Instrumentation.

WinPE-WDS-Tools.cab   This installs the Windows Deployment Services tools package.

 When adding packages with DISM, the package names need to match the exact case of the package. For example, `WinPE-WDS-Tools.cab` will not work if entered as `winpe-wds-tools.cab`. However, the case doesn't matter for the DISM commands. For example, `DISM /GET-HELP` is interpreted the same as `Dism /Get-Help`.

You can also add packages to regular image files (not only the PE image files). For example, drivers and applications can be added as a package to an offline image.

Table 2.3 shows some of the DISM switches used to add and remove different elements to an image. Each of these switches is executed against a mounted image, so the `/image` switch must be used within the command.

TABLE 2.3   DISM package and feature switches

Switch	Description
/Add-Package	Use this to add a package to a mounted image.
	`Dism /image:C:\mount /Add-Package /PackagePath:C:\packages\package.cab`
/Remove-Package	Use this to remove a cabinet file package from a mounted image.
	`Dism /image:C:\mount /Remove-Package /PackagePath:C:\packages\package.cab`
/Get-Packages	This will display information about all packages in the mounted image.
	`Dism /image:C:\mount /Get-Packages`

TABLE 2.3   DISM package and feature switches *(continued)*

Switch	Description
/Get-Features	This will display a list of features that are enabled in the mounted image. Dism /Image:C:\mount /Get-Features
/Get-FeatureInfo	This will provide details on any specific feature. For example, the following command provides additional details on the installed games. The State property will be Enabled or Disabled. dism /image:c:\mount /Get-featureinfo /FeatureName:InboxGames
/Disable-feature	Features can be disabled using the /Disable-feature switch. The /FeatureName needs to be entered as shown in the Get-Features result. The following command will disable the default games on the image. dism /image:c:\mount /Disable-feature /FeatureName:InboxGames
/Enable-feature	Disabled features can be enabled using this switch. The following command will enable the default games on the image. dism /image:c:\mount /Enable-feature /FeatureName:InboxGames

Use Exercise 2.1 to explore the install.wim image on the installation DVD using DISM. This exercise assumes you have an installation DVD with install.wim installed in your DVD.

EXERCISE 2.1

Exploring an Image with DISM

1. Launch the Deployment Tools Command Prompt with administrative permissions. Select Start ➢ All Programs ➢ Microsoft Windows AIK, right-click the Deployment Tools Command Prompt, and select Run As Administrator.

2. If prompted by User Account Control, click Yes to continue.

3. Determine the drive letter where your installation DVD is installed. You will substitute this drive letter for each of the commands instead of the letter x.

4. View a listing of images in the `install.wim` file with the following command. Use the drive assigned to your DVD instead of the letter x.

```
dism /get-wiminfo /wimfile:x:\sources\install.wim
```

5. Create a directory to which you'll mount the folder with the following command:

```
md c:\mount
```

6. Mount the `install.wim` file in the `c:\mount` folder with the following command:

```
DISM /mount-wim /wimfile:x:\sources\install.wim /index:1 /mountDir:c:\mount
/ReadOnly
```

If you wanted to modify the image, you would omit the `/ReadOnly` switch.

7. View details on the mounted image with the following command:

```
DISM /Get-MountedWimInfo
```

8. View a list of the packages currently installed on the image with this command:

```
DISM /image:c:\mount /Get-Packages
```

Once you have mounted an image, you can refer to it using DISM with the `/image:path` switch. The path is the actual path where it was mounted. In the previous example, it was mounted to the `c:\mount` directory.

9. Retrieve a list of features available in the mounted image with the following command:

```
DISM /image:c:\mount /Get-features
```

10. Disable the games feature within the image with the following command:

```
DISM /image:c:\mount /Disable-feature /FeatureName:InboxGames
```

11. Verify that the current state of InboxGames has been changed to `disabled` with the following command:

```
DISM /image:c:\mount /Get-featureInfo /FeatureName:InboxGames
```

12. Unmount the image using the following command:

```
DISM /Unmount-Wim /mountdir:c:\mount /discard
```

Because the image was mounted in read-only mode, the changes cannot be committed. However, if the image was mounted in read/write mode, the `/commit` switch could be added to commit the changes to the image when it is unmounted.

If you want to see a more complete list of the switches available with the DISM command, check out the help articles titled "The Deployment Image Servicing and Management Command-Line Options" and "Take Inventory of an Image or Component" in the Windows Automated Installation Kit User's Guide for Windows 7.

Preinstallation Environment

The *Windows Preinstallation Environment (WinPE)* is used to begin the installation for Windows 7. This minimal operating system provides access to the tools needed to prepare a system and begin a full installation of Windows 7.

WinPE includes disk drive tools that can be used to partition and format them. A GUI allows you to partition hard drives as part of the process, and you can also press the Shift+F10 keys to launch the command prompt and use DiskPart, the command-line disk-partitioning tool. (DiskPart is covered in more depth in Chapter 5, "Maintaining and Troubleshooting Windows 7".) It also includes networking components that allow you to connect to a network share to download an image.

You can access WinPE from multiple boot methods:

- Booting to the installation DVD

- Performing a PXE boot and accessing a boot image from WDS

- Booting to media you've created, such as a bootable USB or bootable CD

Once the system has been booted to WinPE, the full installation can complete. If you've ever performed an installation of Windows 7, you've accessed the WinPE during that process.

It's also possible to boot to the Windows Recovery Environment (WinRE), which is a modified WinPE. However, instead of completing an installation, WinRE provides access to troubleshooting tools. The Windows Recovery Environment is covered in Chapter 5.

Creating a Bootable Media

You can create bootable media to load the WinPE environment on a USB flash drive or CD. Once you've booted into Windows PE, you could use ImageX to capture or deploy an image.

Bootable drives can be created for either 32-bit systems or 64-bit systems. A 32-bit bootable drive will be used when you are installing a 32-bit operating system, and a 64-bit system will be used when you are installing a 64-bit operating system.

In addition, it's possible to create a bootable drive to connect automatically to a Windows Deployment Services server. Normally, Preboot Execution Environment–compliant computers are used to connect to a WDS server, but for non-PXE computers, you can add a discover image to the bootable drive.

Two commands are used in this process that haven't been discussed previously:

CopyPE.cmd   CopyPE.cmd is a script file that creates three preinstallation folders in the specified folder that can be used to create your bootable media. You need to identify the hardware architecture (x86 or amd64) and the destination where you want the folders created. For example, to create the folders for a 32-bit system in the C:\MyPE folder, you'd use this command: CopyPE x86 c:\MyPE.

It will create the following three folders:

```
\winpe_x86
\winpe_x86\ISO
\winpe_x86\mount
```

OSCDImg   This command will create an .iso image using the contents of a folder. An .iso image can easily be burned to a CD. When used with the CopyPE script file, the CopyPE script file creates the \ISO folder. You can add additional files to this folder if desired and then use the OSCDImg command to create the .iso image. Once you have an .iso image, you can right-click it in Windows Explorer and select Burn To Disc.

 The following exercise will remove all existing data from the USB flash drive. Make sure you have backed up your data or use a drive that has no data on it.

You can use the Exercise 2.2 to create a bootable USB drive or CD for a 32-bit system. This exercise assumes you have downloaded and installed the Windows Automated Installation Kit for Windows 7 on a Windows 7 computer. Chapter 1 included exercises for the Windows AIK.

EXERCISE 2.2

Creating a Bootable USB Drive or CD

1. Launch the Deployment Tools Command Prompt with administrative permissions. Select Start ➢ All Programs ➢ Microsoft Windows AIK, right-click the Deployment Tools Command Prompt, and select Run As Administrator.

2. If prompted by User Account Control, click Yes to proceed.

3. Run the following command.

   CopyPE.cmd x86 c:\MyPE

   CopyPE.cmd is a script file that creates three folders in the specified folder (C:\MyPE).

   ```
   \Winpe_x86
   \Winpe_x86\ISO
   \Winpe_x86\Mount
   ```

To create this for a 64-bit system, use the following command instead:

CopyPE.cmd AMD64 c:\MyPE

It will create these three folders instead:

\Winpe_amd64
\Winpe_amd64\ISO
\Winpe_amd64\Mount

4. Copy the preinstallation image (Winpe.wim) file into the \ISO\sources folder, and rename it as **boot.wim** with the following command:

Copy c:\MyPE\Winpe.wim c:\MyPE\ISO\Sources\boot.wim

5. Add the ImageX application to the \iso folder with the following command:

copy "c:\program files\Windows AIK\Tools\x86\ImageX.exe" c:\MyPE\iso\

Although this step is optional, the ImageX application is valuable enough that you'll want it available for most deployments. To copy the ImageX application for a 64-bit environment, use the following command:

copy "c:\program files\Windows AIK\Tools\amd64\ImageX.exe" c:\MyPE\iso\

At this point, you have created the Windows Preinstallation Environment folder. You can create a bootable USB from this folder by following steps 6 and 7 and/or create a boot-able CD-ROM from this folder by following steps 8, 9, and 10.

6. Format your USB drive with DiskPart using the following commands:

a. Launch the command prompt with administrative permissions. If prompted by User Account Control, click Yes.

b. Type **DiskPart** and press Enter to access the Disk Partition tool.

c. Type **List Disk** to list all the disks on your system. You'll see a display similar to the following graphic. Identify the correct disk number for your flash drive. In the graphic, I have inserted a 16GB USB flash drive that is identified as Disk 2 with a size of 14 GB.

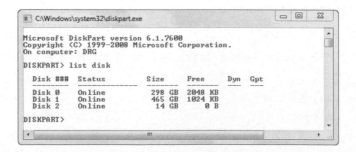

It's very important that you identify the correct drive. Otherwise, you may delete valuable data on another disk.

d. Enter the following commands to remove all of the data on the disk and prepare it. Substitute disk 2 with the actual disk number of your USB drive identified in the previous step.

```
Select disk 2
Clean
Create partition primary
Select partition 1
Active
Format quick fs=fat32
Assign
Exit
```

At this point, the drive will be formatted as a FAT32 disk and all data on the USB disk will be removed. When you press Enter after typing in Assign, Autoplay (if enabled on your system) will recognize the disk and prompt you to do something with the disk such as Open Folder To View Files.

7. Copy the entire c:\MyPE\ISO folder to the USB drive. You can use Windows Explorer or use the following command. Substitute the letter x in the command with the letter assigned to your USB drive.

```
Xcopy c:\MyPE\iso\*.* /e x:\
```

That's it. You now have a bootable USB drive.

8. To create a bootable CD-ROM, you'll need first to create an .iso image from the PE folders you've created. If it isn't still open, launch the Deployment Tools Command Prompt with administrative permissions. Enter the following command to create the PE .iso image.

```
oscdimg -n -bc:\MyPE\etfsboot.com c:\MyPE\ISO c:\MyPE\MyPE.iso
```

The oscdimg command creates an .iso file that can be burned to DVD. The –n switch specifies that long filenames are allowed. The –b switch specifies that a bootable CD is to be created (using etfsboot.com). Note that there is no space between –b and c:\MyPE\etfsboot.com. The c:\MyPE\ISO clause identifies the source folder to use when creating the image. Last, the c:\MyPE\MyPE.iso clause identifies the target file, or the name and location of the image that will ultimately be burned to CD.

9. Place a writeable CD into a CD burner.

10. Launch Windows Explorer and browse to the C:\MyPE folder. Right-click the MyPE.iso file, and select Burn Disc Image. Click Burn on the Windows Disc Image Burner window.

When it's done, you'll have a bootable CD.

Once you have a bootable USB or CD, you can boot any computer to it. You may need to adjust the BIOS to ensure that booting from the USB and/or CD is possible, but the media you've created in the previous exercise will work once the system is configured.

When you boot, the system will copy the contents of the media to a RAM disk and label it with the letter X. It will then load the Windows PE and open a command prompt as X:\ Windows\System32.

Once you have booted to WinPE, you can apply an image to the computer. As an example, I added a Windows 7 image file to my USB drive. After booting, I can use the ImageX application to apply the image on the USB drive to the computer.

My USB drive was assigned the drive letter F:, so I can use the following steps:

1. First, I need to change the context to the F: drive by typing **F:** and pressing Enter.

2. Next, I'll use the ImageX command with the /Apply switch to apply the image:

```
ImageX /apply Win7.wim 1 c:
```

The name of the image file is Win7.wim, and it has only a single image, so I used the number 1. I want the image applied to the C: drive, so I ended the command with the letter C.

While it may not be apparent, the images contained within the Win7.wim file can be custom images. In other words, I could have used a reference computer to install Windows 7, added applications to it, modified the security and other settings, and then prepared the image with Sysprep. I could then capture this image using the ImageX command with the /capture switch and copy the image to my USB drive.

System Image Manager

The *Windows System Image Manager* (SIM) is another tool available in the Windows AIK. It can be used to create unattended answer files.

Unattended answer files can be used to automate a Windows 7 installation. In short, a file is created and specified for the installation. Whenever the user is prompted to answer a question or make a choice, the installation process instead looks for the answer in the answer file. If the answer is in the file, the installation program uses this answer and continues without any user interaction.

Exercise 2.3 leads you through the steps to create an unattended answer file. The intent of this exercise isn't to show you how to create all answer files or even an answer file with all the possible settings. Instead, the goal is to let you see how the SIM can be used to create answer files.

This exercise assumes you have installed the Windows AIK and you have a Windows 7 Installation DVD (or at least the install.wim file from the installation DVD).

EXERCISE 2.3

Creating an Answer File with SIM

1. Launch the Windows SIM by clicking Start ➢ All Programs ➢ Microsoft Windows AIK ➢ Windows System Image Manager.

2. Select File ➢ New Answer File.

3. When prompted to open an image, click Yes. Browse to the `install.wim` file located in the \sources folder of the installation DVD.

4. Click the + symbol to open the Components section. Browse to the x86_Microsoft-Windows-Setup... section, and select the \DiskConfiguration\Disk\CreatePartitions\ CreatePartition selection. Right-click CreatePartition, and select Add Setting To Pass 1 WindowsPE, as shown in the following graphic.

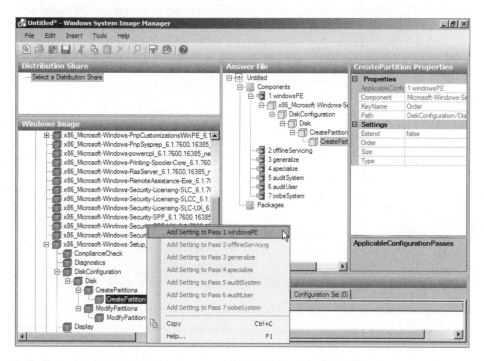

Note that your components may start with x64 instead of x86 if you're accessing a 64-bit image. The graphic also shows what the Answer File section in the middle pane will look like after the component has been added, not before.

EXERCISE 2.3 *(continued)*

5. Use the same procedure to add other Windows PE components to the answer file:

   - Microsoft-Windows-Setup...
     \Disk Configuration\Disk\ModifyPartitions\ModifyPartition
     right-click, and select Add Setting To Pass 1 WindowsPE.

   - Microsoft-Windows-Setup...
     \ImageInstall\OSImage\InstallTo
     right-click, and select Add Setting To Pass 1 WindowsPE.

6. Use the following steps to configure the answer file to wipe the disk clean automatically, create a new 40GB partition, format it with NTFS, assign it the letter *C* with the name Win7OS, and install the operating system on the first partition of the first drive.

   a. Select DiskConfiguration in the Answer File section and view the DiskConfiguration Properties section. Select the drop-down box next to WillShowUI and select OnError. Your display will look similar to the following graphic.

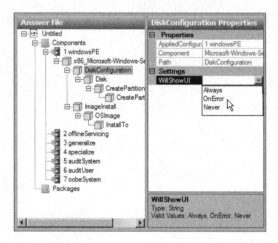

   b. Use the same procedure to modify the following settings in the Answer File section:

      - Microsoft-Windows-Setup...
        \DiskConfiguration\Disk:

      - Set the DiskID to 0.

      - Set WillWipeDisk to True.

      - Microsoft-Windows-Setup...
        \DiskConfiguration\Disk\CreatePartitions\Create Partition:

- Set Extend to False.

- Set Order to 1.

- Set Size to 40000.
  If you want a different size, change the number 40000 (for 40,000 MB or 40 GB) to a number of your choice.

- Set Type to Primary.

- Microsoft-Windows-Setup...
  \Disk Configuration\Disk\ModifyPartitions\ModifyPartition

- Set Active to True.

- Set Extend to False.

- Set Format to NTFS.

- Set Label to Win7OS.

- Set Letter to C.

- Set Order to 1.

- Set PartitionID to 1.

- Microsoft-Windows-Setup...
  \ImageInstall\OSImage

- Set WillShowUI to OnError.

- Microsoft-Windows-Setup...
  \ImageInstall\OSImage\InstallTo

- Set DiskID to 0.

- Set PartitionID to 1.

7. Select File ➤ Save Answer File As. Browse to a location on your system, name the file **Unattended**, and click Save to save the file. Notice that it is saved as an XML file.

8. Use Windows Explorer to browse to the location where you saved the file. Double-click the Unattended.xml file. This will open the unattended answer file in Internet Explorer so you can view it.

Although the Windows AIK includes many valuable tools that can help with deployments, if you're going to create and deploy images on a regular or recurring basis, you should consider WDS.

Deploying Images with Windows Deployment Services

Windows Deployment Services is a free service built into Windows Server 2008 and Windows Server 2008 R2. You can use it to easily capture, deploy, and manage images of clients. WDS has a few significant benefits.

It's free   If you're running Windows Server 2008 or Windows Server 2008 R2, you can simply add the WDS role and start using it.

It's automated   You can use it to automate the deployment of operating systems with very little user interaction. It can deploy images one at a time or multicast images to multiple clients at a time.

It supports multicasting   With multicasting, you can deploy a single image to multiple clients at the same time. In addition, clients don't need to connect at the same time. If a client connects late, WDS will start capturing the image in midstream, and when WDS finishes multicasting the image, it will start again to allow the late client to get the files that were missed at the beginning.

WDS is considered a Lite Touch deployment strategy. You don't have to interact much with it, but you will have to do some configuring. In this section, you'll learn about the following:

- WDS network requirements
- How images are deployed with WDS
- How to add and configure a WDS server

WDS Requirements

Although WDS is free, it needs to be operating within a Microsoft domain with an established network infrastructure. Your network must have the following elements:

Active Directory Domain Services   At least one server needs to have been promoted to a domain controller creating an *Active Directory Domain Services* domain. User accounts in the domain will be granted permissions to images served by WDS.

DNS   At least one server needs to be running the *Domain Name System (DNS)*. DNS is used primarily for name resolution of hostnames to IP addresses with host records. It uses server (SRV) records within a domain to locate servers running specific services such as domain controllers. DNS is required within a domain and is commonly installed on domain controllers.

DHCP   At least one server needs to be running the *Dynamic Host Configuration Protocol (DHCP)* service. DHCP provides TCP/IP configuration information such as an IP address, subnet mask, default gateway, and the address of a DNS server.

It is possible for a single server to host all these services. If you're building a test environment, it makes sense to use the same server for these three services and add the WDS role to it. However, in a production environment, you wouldn't typically host WDS on a domain controller, but you may choose to host the WDS role on the DHCP server.

Client Requirements (PXE Boot Method)

A *Preboot Execution Environment (PXE)* client can be booted to a network environment without any client operating system. PXE (pronounced "pixie") clients include a mini-program within the BIOS and can be configured to boot using the NIC.

When used with WDS, a PXE client can start without an operating system, connect to a WDS server, and allow a user to pick the image to download. WDS will be covered in greater depth later in this chapter.

The PXE boot method starts by the user pressing F12 on the PXE client after it is turned on. This starts a network boot process where it contacts a DHCP server, and then the user is prompted to press F12 again to start a network service boot process.

Once the WDS server is contacted, it will download the Windows PE so that the installation can continue.

Client Requirements (Discover Boot Method)

If your clients are not PXE compatible, you can still use them with WDS. Instead of the client booting from the NIC, you can use WDS to create discover images for non-PXE clients. These discover images can be used to boot to the Windows PE and then connect to the WDS server to download and install a full operating system image.

For non-PXE clients, you need only have a system that can support booting from the CD.

Deploying Images with WDS

Before digging too deep into the details of WDS, it's useful to understand the overall process. A PXE client can start as a bare metal box with no operating system, connect to a WDS server, and download an image. There's a lot going on when this happens, but the following figure and explanation clarify the process.

Figure 2.3 shows the overall process from start to finish. Refer to this figure as you're reading the steps in the following explanation.

FIGURE 2.3   PXE client connecting to WDS for an image

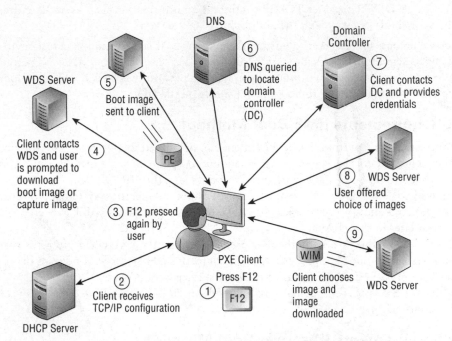

1. The user starts the process by pressing the F12 key on the PXE client computer.

2. This causes the client to broadcast DHCP discover messages looking for a DHCP server. A DHCP server responds with TCP/IP configuration information such as an IP address, subnet mask, default gateway, and address of a DNS server.

3. The user is prompted to press F12 again for a network service boot. If F12 is not pressed again, the system will boot normally. However, if F12 is pressed again, the client will contact the WDS server.

4. If the WDS server has both a boot image and a capture image, the user will be prompted to choose which one to download. Figure 2.4 shows the menu choice for a WDS server that has a boot image and a capture image. The user would choose the boot image.

FIGURE 2.4   Boot menu choice offered to PXE clients

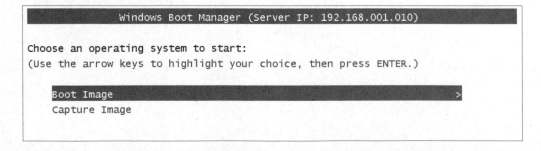

If the WDS server has only a boot image or has only a capture image, WDS will automatically download that image to the client.

 A capture image is used by WDS to capture the image on a computer and store the image on the WDS server. It would be used after Sysprep is run on a reference computer.

5. The boot image is sent to the client. This image is sometimes referred to as a Windows Preinstallation Environment image. The user is prompted to choose a Locale and Keyboard or Input method. The user selects the choices and clicks Next.

   The user is then prompted to log on with credentials for an account in the domain. The username must be entered as *domain\username* or as *username@domain* (also known as a universal principal name format).

6. A Domain Name System server is queried to locate a domain controller. Remember, DNS is required for WDS, and locating a domain controller in the user logon process is one of the key roles it plays for WDS. The client has the address of the DNS server from the DHCP lease it obtained earlier.

7. The domain controller includes Active Directory Domain Services, and the user-supplied credentials are checked against the domain controller. If the user account, domain name, or password is incorrect, the user will see an error and will have to enter the credentials again. When the user supplies valid credentials, the user is logged on and has the permissions for this domain account.

8. The user is offered a choice of images based on the permissions of the user's account. Images can be restricted to certain users or groups of users by modifying the permissions. If a user doesn't have permissions to download an image, it will not appear.

9. After a user chooses an image, it will be downloaded and installed on the client. The image could be a basic image (the default operating system) or a custom image. A custom image could include installed applications, modified settings, and much more.

   Now that you have an overall understanding of how WDS can be used to download images, let's dig into the details of how to add the WDS role and configure WDS to deploy images.

Adding and Configuring WDS

While none of the individual steps required to add a WDS server are difficult, there are nevertheless several steps. As a reminder, WDS is a free role that can be added to a Windows Server 2008 or Windows Server 2008 R2 server. If you have the server and your network includes a domain, DNS, and DHCP, you can add it.

These are the overall steps required to add a WDS server:

- Add the WDS role.
- Configure the WDS role.
- Add images to WDS.
- Restrict access to images with permissions.
- Deploy images with WDS.

> While this chapter covers adding the WDS role to a server to deploy images, it's beyond the scope of this book to walk through the configuration of the entire domain. If you're unsure how to create a test bed, check out *MCITP: Windows Server 2008 Server Administrator Study Guide*: (Exam 70-646) ISBN-10: 0470293152. It includes exercises to install Windows Server 2008, promote the server to a domain controller, and configure DNS and DHCP on the server. It also includes exercises to add and configure WDS on the same server.

Adding the WDS Role

While it's not a requirement, things work a little easier if you add your WDS server to the same server that is hosting the DHCP role. The wizard will automate the process of configuring the extra option needed by DHCP to inform PXE clients that the WDS server has been added.

You can use the Exercise 2.4 to add the WDS role to a Windows Server 2008 server. This exercise assumes you already have Active Directory Domain Services, DNS, and DHCP running on this server.

EXERCISE 2.4

Adding the WDS Role

1. Log on to your Windows Server 2008 server with an administrative account.

2. Launch Server Manager by clicking Start ➢ Administrative Tools ➢ Server Manager.

3. In Server Manager, select Roles ➢ Add Roles.

4. On the Before You Begin page, review the requirements and click Next.

5. On the Select Server Roles page, select the check box next to Windows Deployment Services. Your display will look similar to the following graphic. Click Next.

EXERCISE 2.4 *(continued)*

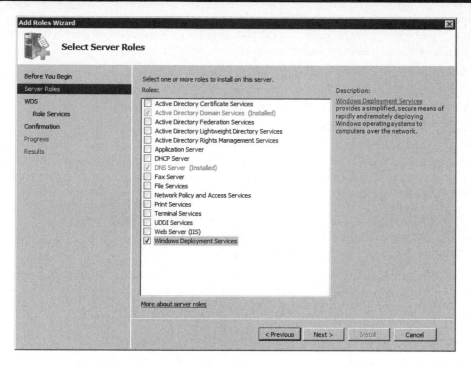

6. Review the information on the Overview Of Windows Deployment Services page, and click Next.

7. Verify that both the Deployment Server and the Transport Server services are selected on the Select Role Services page, and click Next.

8. Click Install on the Confirm Installation Selections page. The installation will complete after a few minutes. When it is complete, click Close.

At this point, you'll have the WDS role added, but it won't do anything until it is configured and images are added.

Configuring the WDS Role

Once WDS role has been installed, you need to configure it. A built-in wizard will lead you through the process, and you have only a couple of decision points.

The most important decision is related to DHCP. It's common for the DHCP server to be hosted on the same server as the WDS server. When DHCP is hosted on the same server (a recommended configuration), the WDS wizard will prompt you to configure two settings. Both of these settings are necessary so that booting PXE clients can find the DHCP server on the network and then find the WDS server.

Do Not Listen On Port 67   The DHCP server listens for DHCP Discover packets on UDP port 67 from DHCP clients. This setting ensures that the WDS server doesn't listen for these packets and interfere with the normal DHCP process.

Configure The DHCP With Option 60   DHCP option 60 is used to notify a booting PXE client that there is a listening PXE server on the network. Selecting the Do Not Listen On Port 67 option tells WDS not to listen on port 67 because the DHCP server is listening on this port. If the WDS server was not also a DHCP server, it would listen for WDS packets on port 67.

You will not see these prompts if DHCP is not on the same server.

You'll also need to decide if you want the WDS server to respond to clients right away or not. You'll be prompted to choose one of three choices:

Do Not Respond To Any Client Computer   You can leave it configured with this setting until you have completed the configuration of WDS. This will prevent the Windows Deployment Services from responding to any requests and ensure that images will not be deployed by WDS. This WDS setting doesn't affect the DHCP service if it's hosted on the same computer. The DHCP server will still respond to requests from clients for TCP/IP leases.

Respond Only To Known Client Computers   Clients must be prestaged, or added to Active Directory, before the image is deployed.

Respond To All (Known And Unknown) Client Computers   WDS will deploy images to clients that are prestaged and to clients that aren't prestaged.

Exercise 2.5 will lead you through the process of configuring the WDS server. It assumes that you have completed the previous exercise, which added the WDS role.

EXERCISE 2.5

Configuring the WDS Role

1. Launch WDS by clicking Start ➢ Administrative Tools ➢ Windows Deployment Services.

2. In Windows Deployment Services, select Servers. Select your server in Windows Deployment Services. At this point, your server has a yellow icon with an exclamation mark indicating that it hasn't been configured yet.

3. Right-click your server, and select Configure Server.

4. Review the information on the wizard's Welcome page and click Next.

5. Accept the default of C:\RemoteInstall on the Remote Installation Folder Location page. Ideally, you would select a partition that is not the same as the operating system. However, for a test environment, it's okay to use the same partition. Click Next.

   Note: If you choose the same partition as the operating system, you will receive a System Volume Warning. Read the warning, and click Yes to continue.

6. If DHCP is installed on this server, the wizard will guide you through the configuration of WDS and the DHCP server. If DHCP is not installed on the server, this DHCP option page will not appear.

   a. On the DHCP Option 60 page, review the information. Because your server is holding the role of a DHCP server, select both check boxes, as shown in the following graphic.

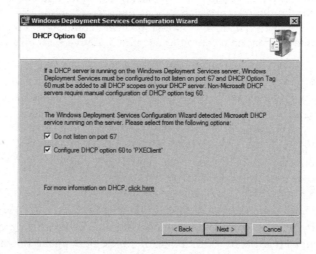

   b. Click Next.

7. On the PXE Server Initial Settings page, select Respond To All (Known And Unknown) Client Computers, as shown in the following graphic.

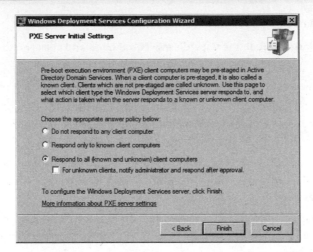

In a production environment, you may choose not to respond to any computers until everything is configured. You can also choose the second option (Respond To Only Known Client Computers), used if you prestage client computers. Prestaging a client computer is done by creating a computer account in Active Directory with the computer's GUID.

8. Click Next and then click Finish. After a moment, the configuration will complete. Uncheck the box Add Images To The Windows Deployment Server, and click Finish.

At this point, you have added and configured the WDS server. However, it doesn't include any images. The next section shows you how to add images to WDS.

Adding Images to WDS

You'll need to add both boot and install images to the WDS server. As a reminder, the boot image (contained in the `boot.wim` file) includes the Windows PE, which provides enough of an operating system so that the user can log on and pick an image to download. The install images (contained in the `install.wim` file) include images of full operating system versions.

The boot image can be used for three purposes:

Creating a boot image The boot image is the primary Windows PE image downloaded to PXE clients. Once the image is downloaded, the user at the PXE client is able to log in and select an available image.

Creating a capture image A capture image is created from a boot image that has been added to a WDS server. It is used to capture the image from a reference computer after Sysprep has been run.

Creating a discover image   A discover image is created from a boot image that has been added to a WDS server. The discover image is renamed as `boot.wim` and copied to the \ `sources` folder of bootable media. It can then be used to boot non-PXE clients. A discover image is created for a specific WDS server and automates the process of connecting to that WDS server; if the client can't reach the WDS server, the process will fail.

While it's not common to modify the boot image, you will often modify the install image. It's very common to create a reference computer, add applications, and modify the configuration of the computer for a custom install image. Once you've tested this image and you're satisfied with the configuration of the computer, you would run Sysprep and then capture the image.

Exercise 2.6 shows how to add a boot image, a capture image, and an install image to WDS. This exercise assumes you have completed the previous exercise that configured WDS.

EXERCISE 2.6

Adding Images to WDS

1.   Insert the Windows 7 installation DVD into your system's DVD drive. You will use the `boot.wim` and `install.wim` files located in the \sources folder of the DVD.

2.   If it's not already started, launch WDS by clicking Start ➢ Administrative Tools ➢ Windows Deployment Services.

3.   Use the following steps to add a boot image used to boot PXE clients.

    a.   In WDS, right-click the Boot Images folder and select Add Boot Image, as shown in the following graphic.

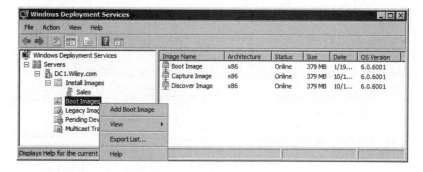

    The graphic shows the results after the boot, capture, and discover images have been added.

    b.   Browse to the \sources folder on the installation DVD, and select the boot.wim file. Click Open and then click Next.

    c.   Change the Image Name to Boot Image and change the Image Description to Use To Boot PXE Clients. Click Next.

    d.   Review the information on the Summary page and click Next.

    e.   When the image is added, click Finish.

4.   Use the following steps to create a capture image. This image can be used to capture images and store them on WDS so that they can be deployed to other clients.

    a.   Right-click the Boot Image created in the previous step and select Create Capture Boot Image.

    b.   Enter the following text:

        ▪   Image Name: Type in **Capture Image**.

        ▪   Image Description: Type in **Use to Capture Images from Sysprepped Clients**.

    c.   Click Browse. Browse to the root of C: and click New Folder. Name the folder **Images** and click Open. Enter **Capture** as the filename and click Open.

    d.   Click Next on the Capture Image Metadata page.

    e.   When the image is created, click Finish. While this creates the capture image, you'll notice that it hasn't been added to the WDS server.

    f.   Right-click the Boot Image folder, and select Add Boot Image.

    g.   Browse to the Images folder and select the image named Capture. Click Next.

    h.   Review the Image Name and Description, and click Next.

    i.   Review the information on the Summary page, and click Next.

    j.   When the image is added, click Finish.

5.   Use the following steps to create a discover image. This image can be used for non-PXE clients. Once created, it needs to be added to bootable PE media.

    a.   Right-click the boot image created in the previous step and select Create Discover Boot Image.

    b.   Enter the following text:

        ▪   Image Name: Type in **Discover Image**.

        ▪   Image Description: Type in **Use for Non-PXE Clients**.

    c.   Click Browse. Browse to the C:\Images folder. Enter **Discover** as the filename and click Open.

    d.   Click Browse For The Windows Deployment Server To Respond. Enter the name of your server, and click Check Names. Click OK.

EXERCISE 2.6   *(continued)*

e. Click Next on the Capture Image Metadata page.

f. When the image is created, click Finish.

g. You can use this image on any bootable media. Name the discover image **boot.wim** and replace the original boot.wim in the sources folder of the bootable media with this file. When you boot, it will automatically boot into Windows PE and connect to the WDS server.

6. Use the following steps to create an image group and add an install image to this group.

a. Select the Install Images folder under your server in the Windows Deployment Services console.

b. Right-click the folder, and select Add Image Group. Enter **Sales** and click OK. This creates an image group named Sales. You can add images to the group and restrict access to the group using permissions.

c. Right-click the Sales image group, and select Add Install Image, as shown in the following graphic.

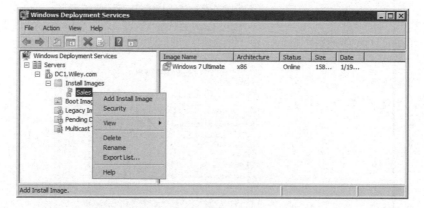

d. On the Image File page, click Browse. Browse to the \Sources folder on the installation DVD. Select the install.wim file and click Open. Click Next.

e. Review the images listed on the List Of Available Images. The images available will be dependent on your installation DVD. You can add them all, but to save yourself some time in this exercise, add only two. Deselect all the check boxes except two. Deselect the check box Use Default Name And Description For Each Of The Selected Images. Click Next.

f. If desired, change the Image Name and Image Description. Click Next.

g. Review the information on the Summary page and click Next. When the image is added, click Finish. This will take several minutes to complete.

At this point, you could boot a PXE client by pressing F12 to start the process and then pressing F12 again when prompted.

Restricting Access to Images with WDS

WDS includes a security component, allowing you to restrict who can receive images. As a reminder, users must have a domain account to be able to access install images on WDS. If users can't log in during the Windows PE stage, WDS won't provide access to any install images.

You can control who can receive specific images by modifying the permissions of the images or by placing images in image groups and modifying the permissions of the groups. Image groups and images are assigned standard NTFS permissions through WDS. Any permission assigned to an image group is inherited by all the images within the group.

By default, each image and image group assigns permissions to the Authenticated Users group. If you right-click an image or an image group, you'll see a display similar to Figure 2.5.

FIGURE 2.5   Viewing permissions of an image group in WDS

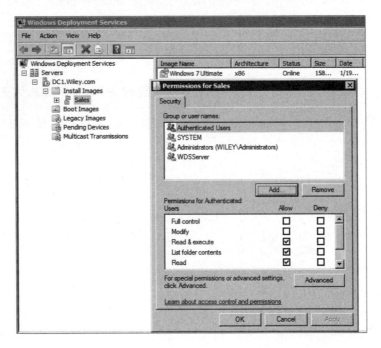

The WDS console shows the NTFS permissions and gives you access to modify the NTFS permissions. (NTFS permissions are described in greater depth in Chapter 9, "Managing Windows 7 in a Domain.") Any user who successfully logs in to Active

Directory is automatically added to the Authenticated Users group, so by default any user who logs in is automatically granted access to all images hosted on a WDS server unless the default permissions are modified.

If desired, you can remove the Authenticated Users group and add any other group. For example, your organization could have a group named G_Sales that includes all the users in the Sales department. You could add the G_Sales group and grant this group Read & Execute, List Folder Contents, and Read permission.

With the Authenticated Users group removed, only users in the G_Sales group will have access to the image. Other users won't even see the image offered to them during the WDS process.

Updating Images

Images that are served by a WDS server are the same types of images that are deployed using the Windows AIK, as discussed earlier. This allows you to use tools such as ImageX and DISM to perform maintenance on the images. However, you do have a couple of extra steps to perform first.

Disable the image　Before you can perform maintenance on an image, you must disable it. You can do so by right-clicking the image within WDS and selecting Disable.

Export the image　Next, you need to export the image by right-clicking the image in WDS and selecting Export. Browse to a location where you can copy the image, and click Save. This creates a copy of the .wim file that can be manipulated.

Modify the image　Access the exported image and make any modifications necessary. You can view and modify the image file using tools within the Windows AIK. ImageX and DISM (presented earlier in this chapter) are the tools you'll probably use most often. As an example, you might use DISM to add driver packages to the image. You can also copy files to the image. Once you've completed the modifications, you must commit the changes using either ImageX or DISM, depending on which tool you used to mount it.

Add the image back to WDS　You can overwrite the original image by right-clicking it and selecting Replace Image. Or, if you want to retain the original image, you can right-click the image group and select Add Image. Follow the same procedure as described earlier to add an image. You need to enable the original image by right-clicking it and selecting Enable.

Deploying Images with WDS

You have several considerations when deploying images with WDS. A primary consideration is the type of transmissions you'll use, such as unicast, multicast, auto-cast, and scheduled-cast. You'll also need to decide when the images are deployed.

If you're using WDS to deploy only single images, the choices are clear. You'll simply use unicast transmissions and deploy the images when needed. However, if you're using WDS to deploy images to many different clients, you'll need to know the different choices to help you plan more efficiently.

> Multicast transmissions are a significant benefit of WDS. When multicast transmissions are enabled, the WDS server can transmit a single image to multiple clients at the same time. On the other hand, if only unicast transmissions are used, a separate copy of the image is transmitted for each client, which can consume a lot more bandwidth. The Transport Server service (added when the WDS role was installed) is needed to support multicasting.

Transmitting Images

Images can be sent as unicast or multicast transmissions. If you've completed the exercises so far in this chapter, the WDS server is configured to send unicast transmissions. Multicast transmissions require a couple of extra steps. As a comparison, the operations of unicast and multicast transmissions are explained here:

Unicast transmissions A single image is sent to a single client. No additional configuration is necessary. If the PXE client is able to connect to the WDS server and the user has a domain account with permissions for an image, it can be selected and downloaded.

Multicast transmissions A single image is sent to multiple clients. This is useful if the same image is being deployed to multiple clients, and it takes significantly less bandwidth than multiple unicast transmissions. A multicast transmission must be created on the WDS server and configured before it will work. Multicast transmissions require the Transport Server service, which is installed when the WDS role is added.

As an example, imagine you need to deploy Windows 7 Ultimate to 10 clients. If you used 10 unicast transmissions at the same time, the WDS server would try to send 10 different images to these clients. Each transmission would be competing with the others for network bandwidth, and each would be consuming additional resources on the server.

However, if you configured a multicast transmission, you could deploy a single image to all 10 clients simultaneously. Only a single image is being sent over the network and being processed by the server.

A neat feature of multicast transmissions is that clients can even join the transmission late and still receive the entire image. In other words, imagine that 9 clients connected and the transmission started. Later, the 10th client connects. It will start receiving the transmission at whatever stage it joins. When the transmission completes for the other 9 clients, the 10th client would receive the beginning of the transmission up to the point where it started.

Transmissions can also be configured as either auto-cast or scheduled-cast. Figure 2.6 shows the wizard screen used to choose the multicast transmission type.

FIGURE 2.6   Choosing the multicast transmission type in WDS

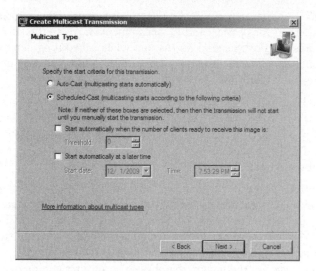

Auto-cast transmissions   An *auto-cast transmission* will start automatically when a client connects. If an image is being transmitted to 10 clients, it will start as soon as the first client connects. Additional clients that connect will begin capturing the data when they connect, and when the full image has been transmitted, it will start again at the beginning, allowing the late clients to receive what they missed.

Scheduled-cast transmissions   A *scheduled-cast transmission* can start based on three criteria. A threshold (such as 10 clients) can be set, and when the threshold is reached, the transmission starts. A specific time can be set, and the transmission will start when the time arrives. If neither of these choices is selected, an administrator must manually start it by right-clicking the multicast transmission and selecting Start after the clients connect.

Staggering Deployments

When deploying images with WDS, you should consider staggering the deployments. In other words, perform the deployments in stages where a percentage of the computers are deployed at different times.

One of the primary benefits of staggering deployments is that you can apply lessons learned from early stages to later stages. No matter how much you test and plan, the production environment has a way of throwing in unforeseen issues. These issues can be identified and resolved in early stages and then mitigated in the later stages.

Staggered deployments also help you address scheduling and network load issues:

Scheduling concerns   An important point to remember is that computers are meant to be tools to help users do their jobs easier, and IT departments have an integral goal of helping users to use these tools. Part of this goal means that when scheduling deployments, users' needs should be heavily considered. It's very common for deployments to occur after hours to minimize the impact on end users.

Network load considerations   Another important consideration is the load the deployment will have on the network. Again, deployments are frequently done after hours to minimize the impact the deployment has on the network. Images are often several GB in size, and custom images could easily be close to 10 GB. Even in the best networks, transmitting a file this large will affect other operations.

Because of the different considerations associated with deploying images, some organizations deploy images in isolated networks. For example, an IT department may set up a single server running Active Directory, DNS, and DHCP and hosting WDS. It could be configured in a single subnet network, and when a client needs an image, an administrator plugs the computer into this isolated network and downloads the image.

Once the computer receives the image, the physical computer can be deployed to the end user. A primary consideration when doing this type of deployment is the user's data. As a reminder, Chapter 1 covered using the USMT tools to perform a side-by-side migration.

Capturing Images with WDS

Once WDS is configured and a capture image has been added, you can use WDS to capture images in addition to deploying images. You can use this process to capture an image immediately after creating your reference computer and running Sysprep to prepare it.

One of the earlier exercises led you through the process of adding a capture image onto the WDS server. This is a Windows PE that is used to capture an image from a reference computer.

As a reminder, the reference computer is a computer configured specifically to be captured as an image. You would first install the operating system, add applications, and then configure any other desired settings. Once you're satisfied it is configured as desired, you would run Sysprep on it to remove the computer-specific information from the computer.

When the system is rebooted, you can use the PXE boot process to connect to the WDS server and capture the image. Figure 2.7 shows the overall process of capturing an image from a reference computer. It is similar to the process of deploying an image up to step 4. Refer to this figure as you're reading the steps in the following explanation.

FIGURE 2.7   Using WDS to capture a computer from a PXE client

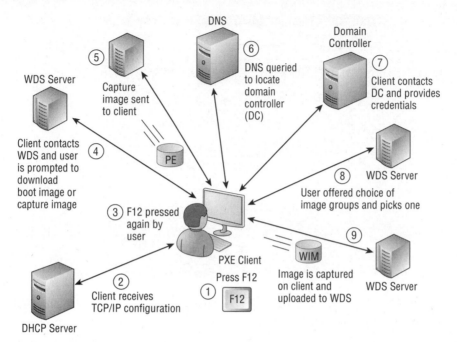

1. The user starts the process by pressing the F12 key on the PXE client computer.

2. This causes the client to broadcast DHCP discover messages looking for a DHCP server. A DHCP server responds with TCP/IP configuration information such as an IP address, subnet mask, default gateway, and address of a DNS server.

3. The user is prompted to press F12 again for a network service boot. If F12 is not pressed again, the system will boot normally. However, if F12 is pressed again, the client will contact the WDS server.

4. If the WDS server has both a boot image and a capture image, you will be prompted to choose which one to download. You would choose the capture image.

5. The capture image is sent to the client. This image is a Windows Preinstallation Environment image with additional elements that allow it to capture an image. This will launch the Windows Deployment Services Image Capture Wizard. Follow these steps for the wizard.

    a. Click Next on the Welcome page, and the Image Capture Source page will appear, as shown in Figure 2.8.

FIGURE 2.8   Identifying the source of the image to capture

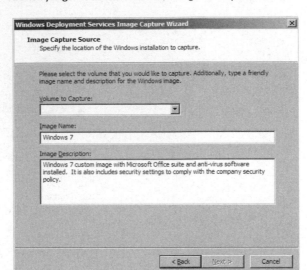

b.   Select the Volume To Capture; this is normally C:. Enter an Image Name and an Image Description and click Next.

If a drive letter doesn't appear under the Volume To Capture selection, it usually indicates that the system wasn't Sysprepped. Less often, it could mean that the system has not been activated and has been Sysprepped and/or rearmed three times.

c.   On the Image Capture Description page, click Browse. Create a folder and give it a name such as **Images**. Double-click the folder. Give the capture image file a name such as **Win7** and select Save.

d.   It's possible to click Finish here. The image will be captured and saved on the local drive. You can then copy the image as desired.
The following steps will be used to upload the image to the WDS server.

e.   Select the check box Upload Images To WDS Server. Enter the name of the server and click Connect.

f.   You will be prompted to log on with credentials for an account in the domain. The username must be entered as *domain\username* or as *username@domain* (also known as a universal principal name format).

6.   A Domain Name Service server is queried to locate a domain controller. Remember, the DNS server is required for WDS, and this is one of the key roles it plays. The client has the address of the DNS server from the DHCP lease it obtained earlier.

7. The supplied credentials are checked against Active Directory. These credentials are used to provide access to specific image groups.

8. You can now select one of the image groups on the server based on the permissions of the logged-in user. Select an image group from here and click Finish.

9. The image is captured and stored on the C: drive. After the capture completes, the image will be uploaded to the WDS server.

Note that this process is imaging the C: drive and is storing the image on the C: drive. This is not a typo. It really works. The imaging process takes an inventory of the files and folders before the process starts and adds all of them to the image. Since the created image isn't created before the process starts, it is not included in this list.

Once the process completes, you can reboot your computer and access the C:\Images folder. You'll see the captured image as a .wim file located here. If you selected the check box to store the image on the WDS server, it will also have been uploaded and available there.

Using the Microsoft Deployment Toolkit 2010

The *Microsoft Deployment Toolkit (MDT) 2010* can be used capture and deploy images for both Lite Touch Installations and Zero Touch Installations. It is used with WDS for LTI and with SCCM for ZTI.

The Microsoft Deployment Toolkit (MDT) 2008 and Business Desktop Deployment (BDD) 2007 were touted by Microsoft as tools to automate the deployment of Windows Vista. However, I never really saw these tools take off. The MDT 2010 is an upgrade to these tools. With the improvements and the expected popularity of Windows 7, I expect that MDT may be more widely used than it was in the past. Either way though, you should understand the capabilities for the 70-686 exam.

One of the primary tools you'll use with MDT is the Deployment Workbench. It's installed with MDT 2010, and it includes the ability to create deployment shares, add images, create task sequences, and more.

Task sequences are an important element of MDT 2010. You use these to identify all of the steps of an installation, and they can include steps to add applications, drivers, or just about anything you might need within an application. However, instead of including these extras within the image, they are referenced and available on the deployment share created with MDT 2010.

MDT 2010 refers to images as thin images, thick images, and hybrid images.

Thin image   A *thin image* is a basic Windows installation with very little customization. Applications, updates, and settings are then deployed and configured using other network tools such as through Group Policy, SCCM, and WSUS. This reduces the size and complexity of the images, making the imaging solution easier to maintain.

Thick image   A *thick image* is customized with applications, device drivers, and updates. Creating thick images increases the need to have multiple custom images because it's harder to create a one-size-fits-all solution.

Hybrid image   Just as it sounds, a *hybrid image* is a cross between a thin and a thick image. It can include additional applications, but instead of including the applications in the image, a MDT 2010 task sequence includes references to them on a network share (referred to as the deployment share by MDT 2010). Applications are deployed from network shares, and scripts can be used to identify which applications to deploy to which clients.

Just as you'd run Windows Deployment Services from a server, MDT 2010 is intended to be run from a server. In other words, it should be installed on a server. If you're using it with WDS, install it on the WDS server. If you're using it with SCCM, install it on the SCCM server.

MDT 2010 requires Windows PowerShell to run. This is installed by default in Windows Server 2008 R2, but if you're installing MDT 2010 on Windows Server 2008, you'll need to add the Windows PowerShell feature through Server Manager.

MDT 2010 is a free download. You can get it by accessing Microsoft's download site (www.microsoft.com/downloads) and searching for "Microsoft Deployment Toolkit (MDT) 2010." It comes in both x86 (32-bit) and x64 (64-bit) versions. Download the version to match the server where you'll install it.

After installing MDT 2010, you'll need to complete these big-picture steps. Most of this work is done within the Deployment Workbench.

Create a deployment share   The Deployment Workbench is used to create a deployment share. This is a folder shared as a network share, and the Deployment Workbench builds the underlying structure and adds several different scripts and other files used for deployments. When complete, this share will include all the resources needed to build and modify an image, including the operating system source files, any desired applications, device drivers, and packages.

Add operating system files to the deployment share   Operating system files are added to the deployment share using the Deployment Workbench. Older operating systems are added by copying the source files (such as the i386 folder for Windows XP and Server 2003). Windows Vista, Windows 7, and newer operating systems are added by adding the .wim files. The Deployment Workbench has the capability to extract all of the individual images from the .wim file and make them available for deployments.

Create a task sequence   A *task sequence* is used to define a specific set of steps that need to be run during an installation. Several task sequence templates are available, and this makes this process much quicker. As an example, the Standard Client Task Sequence template includes about 50 individual tasks organized in phases from Initialization to State Restore. Task sequences are associated with an unattended.xml file and an operating system image.

Update the deployment share   When the deployment share is updated, it updates the boot image and boot image settings used for deployments. A wizard leads you through this process, and it will create multiple files that can be used to create bootable media.

When creating deployment shares and images, you need to match the architecture for the entire process. In other words, if you're using a 64-bit edition image, other elements must also be 64-bit. However, both editions of MDT 2010 (32-bit and 64-bit) can work with both types of images. You just need to ensure that the x86 edition is installed on a 32-bit OS and the x64 edition is installed on a 64-bit OS.

Installing MDT 2010

Exercise 2.7 leads you through the process of installing MDT 2010.

EXERCISE 2.7

Installing the Microsoft Deployment Toolkit 2010

1. Browse to the location where you downloaded the MDT .msi installer file and double-click it. When prompted to run the file, click Run.

2. The Microsoft Deployment Toolkit Setup Wizard will begin. Click Next.

3. Review the license agreement, select I Accept The Terms In The License Agreement, and click Next.

4. Accept the default Custom Setup selection, which will install the entire MDT on your system, and click Next.

5. Click Install. If prompted by User Account Control, click Yes. When the wizard completes, click Finish.

At this point, a Microsoft Deployment Toolkit folder will be added to the All Programs menu. It will include the following items:

Configure ConfigMgr Integration   If you're using MDT with SCCM, you need to run this tool to integrate the features of MDT into SCCM. It will copy the appropriate files to the Configuration Manager server. It will also add Windows Management Instrumentation classes for the custom actions that are possible with MDT.

Deployment Workbench   This is the primary tool you'll use to assist with deployments. It includes a full set of tools and documentation used to automate deployments.

Microsoft Deployment Toolkit Documentation   This launches the Microsoft Deployment Toolkit Documentation Library, which is a help file.

Release Notes   This help file includes information on the usage of MDT. If you used MDT 2008 or BDD 2007 and have installed MDT 2010 on the same system that held the previous editions, you should read this document thoroughly because of known issues with the older versions.

Remove WDS PXE Filter   If you used MDT 2008 and installed the PXE filter with it, it should be removed. This menu item allows you to launch a wizard to remove it. If you've never installed MDT 2008 on the computer where you're installing MDT 2010, you won't need this tool.

With MDT 2010 installed, you can now start creating the pieces for a deployment. The first step is to create a deployment share using the Deployment Workbench.

Creating a MDT 2010 Deployment Share

The deployment share is a shared folder created on the server. The Deployment Workbench does most of this under the hood, so you don't really see what is occurring.

Chapter 8, "Accessing Resources on a Network," will cover the details of accessing resources on a network in more detail, but in short, a share can be accessed over the network using a Universal Naming Convention (UNC) path. A UNC path is formatted as \\serverName\ShareName. Exercise 2.8 creates a share named DeploymentShare$ on a server that is used to share the C:\DeploymentShare folder.

The $ symbol will hide this share to prevent users from accidentally stumbling onto it, but if the path name is known and permissions have been assigned, users will be able to connect even if it is hidden. If the server name is WDS1, the UNC path is \\WDS1\DeploymentShare$.

EXERCISE 2.8

Creating a Deployment Share

1.   Launch the MDT Deployment Workbench by clicking Start ➢ All Programs ➢ Microsoft Deployment Toolkit ➢ Deployment Workbench.

2.   Right-click Deployment Shares, and select New Deployment Share.

EXERCISE 2.8   *(continued)*

3. Accept the default Path of C:\DeploymentShare and click Next.

4. The default Share Name is DeploymentShare$. Click Next.

5. Click Next to accept the default Deployment Share Description.

6. On the Allow Image Capture page, leave the selection Ask If An Image Should Be Captured checked. Click Next.

7. Leave the selection Ask User To Set The Local Administrator Password unchecked. This will prevent users from accessing the local administrator account. Click Next.

8. Leave the selection Ask User For A Product Key unchecked and click Next.

9. Review the information on the Summary page and click Next. When complete, click Finish.

10. Click the plus sign to open the deployment share you just created. It will look similar to the following graphic.

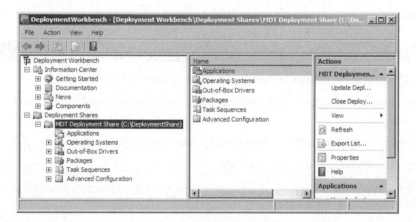

11. Launch Windows Explorer and browse through the C:\DeploymentShare folder. You'll see that it includes several folders, and some of the folders (such as the Scripts folder) have files within them.

Leave the Deployment Workbench open to complete the next exercise.

Adding Operating System Files to the Deployment Share

Once you create the deployment share in MDT 2010, you'll need to add at least an operating system before anything can be deployed. When you launch the wizard to import operating systems, it will give you the following choices:

Source Files For operating systems before Windows Vista and Windows Server 2008, the operating system was deployed using a source directory, often labeled I386. You can add the entire source directory to the deployment share, which will include the source files.

Custom Image File Any .wim file can be added here. Although the wizard labels it as a custom image file, you can import the install.wim standard image file on the installation DVD and use it as a thin image if desired. If the .wim file includes multiple images, all of the images will be imported. After the images are imported, individual images can be deleted.

Windows Deployment Services Image File Any images that have been captured using WDS can be imported to MDT 2010.

You add Windows 7 to the Operating Systems folder by adding the .wim file. Exercise 2.9 will lead you through the process of adding Windows 7 to the deployment share.

EXERCISE 2.9

Adding Windows 7 Image Files to the Deployment Share

1. Select Operating Systems in the deployment share that you created in the previous exercise.

2. Right-click Operating Systems, and select Import Operating System.

3. Select Custom Image File and click Next.

4. Insert the Windows 7 installation DVD, and browse to the \Sources folder. Select the install.wim file and click Next.

5. Accept the default of Setup And Sysprep Files Are Not Needed and click Next.

6. Change the Destination Directory Name to Windows 7 Images and click Next.

7. Review the Summary page and click Next. The Progress page will appear and display progress as the images are imported into the MDT folder.

8. When the import completes, click Finish. Your display will look similar to the following graphic:

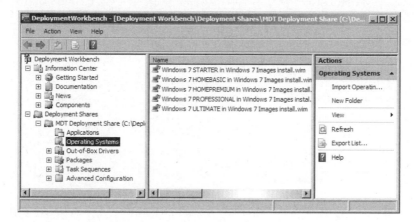

9. Use Windows Explorer to browse to C:\DeploymentShare\Operating Systems\ Windows 7 Images. You'll see the install.wim file and a language configuration file (lang.ini).

Leave the Deployment Workbench open to complete the next exercise.

In addition to adding images, you can add applications, drivers, and other packages to the deployment share. Any applications that are added to the share can be selected during the installation.

After adding the image (and any optional applications, drivers, or other packages), you'll need to add a task sequence to specify the order of the installation.

Creating a Task Sequence

A task sequence is a component that you add to the deployment share. It is formulated as an XML file but, unless you really want to, you never have to look at the XML file. Instead, the Deployment Workbench leads you through the process of creating it.

The task sequence provides a list of tasks that are performed in a specific order to complete the installation. As an example, Figure 2.9 shows the validation phase of a task sequence with the Validate task selected. This task validates that the system has a minimum amount of memory and minimum processor speed. It can also be configured to check that a minimum amount of disk space is available and even verify that the system that is being overwritten is either a client or a server.

FIGURE 2.9   Viewing the Validate task in a task sequence

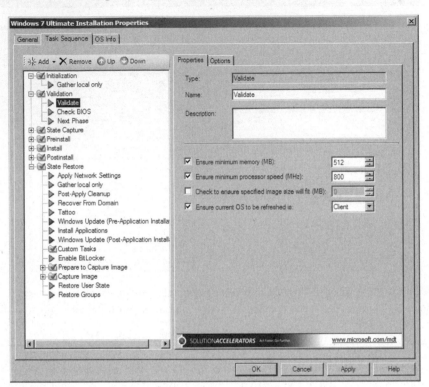

Several task sequence templates are available. Each of these templates is created with underlying XML files provided by Microsoft. These are the available templates:

- Sysprep and Capture
- Standard Client Task Sequence
- Standard Client Replace Task Sequence
- Custom Task Sequence
- Lite-Touch OEM Task Sequence
- Standard Server Task Sequence
- Post OS Installation Task Sequence

Each template includes a predefined group of steps organized in phases. When one task completes, control is passed on to the next task until the operation completes.

As an example, Figure 2.10 shows part of the Standard Client Task Sequence that will be created in the next exercise. This is a typical task sequence, and as you can see, it can include a significant number of steps.

FIGURE 2.10   Viewing the properties of a task within a task sequence

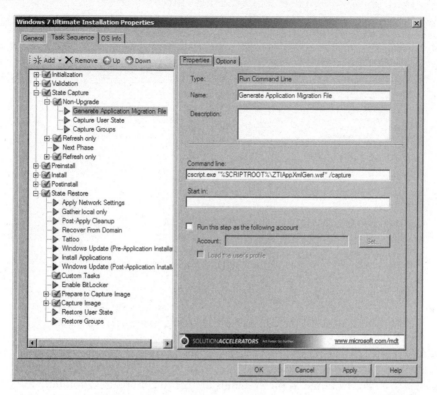

In the figure, the State Capture and State Restore phases are opened and the Generate Application Migration File step is selected. Notice that the command-line command is calling one of the scripts that were created when the deployment share was added to the Deployment Workbench. Again, all of this is part of the template. The State Capture phase will automatically capture migration data (if any exists) on the computer, and later the Restore User State phase will automatically restore migration data.

Every step also has options, as shown in Figure 2.11. You can use the Disable This Step option to disable an option temporarily. As you're testing an image, you may want to try omitting a step or two. Instead of deleting the step, you can disable it, and if things don't work as you expected, you can easily add the step back by simply enabling it. Disabled steps have a dimmed icon.

FIGURE 2.11 Viewing the options of a task within a task sequence

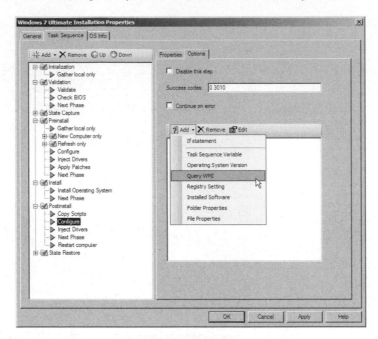

In addition, you can modify the response to errors. Normally, an error condition will cause the deployment to fail. However, you may want to ensure the installation continues even if a step fails. For example, if the system is unable to get updates, you may want to allow it to continue and have the updates applied after the installation completes. You can also add advanced task sequence conditions, as shown in the drop-down box.

Exercise 2.10 will lead you through the process of creating a task sequence. This exercise assumes the previous exercise was completed, which added Windows 7 images to the deployment share.

EXERCISE 2.10

Creating a Task Sequence

1. Right-click Task Sequences and select New Task Sequence.

2. Enter **Win7ThinImage** as the task sequence ID. Enter **Windows 7 Ultimate Installation** as the Task Sequence Name. Users will see this during the installation. You can also add comments in the Task Sequence Comments section. Users will also see this text during the installation.

3. Accept the default of Standard Client Task Sequence and click Next.

4. Select the Windows 7 Ultimate image from the Windows 7 Images install.wim operating system. This was added to the Deployment Workbench in an earlier exercise. Click Next.

EXERCISE 2.10 *(continued)*

5. On the Specify A Product Key page, select Do Not Specify A Product Key At This Time and click Next.

6. Enter the name of your organization (or **Home Sweet Home**) on the OS Settings page. Enter **bing.com** (or another website address) as the Internet Explorer home page. Click Next.

7. Enter **P@ssw0rd** in the Administrator Password and Confirm Administrator Password text boxes. Click Next.

8. Review the information on the Summary page and click Next. When the operation completes, click Finish.

Leave the Deployment Workbench open to complete the next exercise.

Once a task sequence has been created, it can be modified. You can right-click the task sequence within the Deployment Workbench and select Properties to view the details of the task sequence.

You can add additional tasks to a task sequence, as shown in Figure 2.12. Notice that there are several different groups of tasks. Each group has additional tasks that can be selected.

FIGURE 2.12   Adding additional tasks to a task sequence

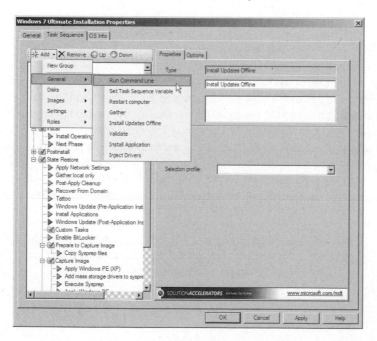

In the figure, the Run Command Line task is selected. This allows you to run any command including batch files and scripts. The old scripting mantra comes to mind—if you can imagine it, you can do it with a script. You have very few limitations.

You can also remove tasks with the Remove button and modify the order of tasks using the Up and Down arrows.

Creating Windows PE Images by Updating the Deployment Share

Once the deployment share has been created, you need to create the Windows PE images. The process is referred to as updating the deployment share. Exercise 2.11 will lead you through this process.

EXERCISE 2.11

Updating the Deployment Share

1. Right-click the MDT deployment share, and select Update Deployment Share.

2. Review the information on the Options page, and accept the default of Optimize The Boot Image Updating Process. Click Next.

3. On the Summary page, click Next.

When complete, the following image files will have been created in the Boot folder of the deployment share:

- `Lite Touch Windows PE.wim`

- `LiteTouchPE_platform.iso`

You can then use these files to deploy images to systems. As an example, you could burn the `.iso` image to a CD and use it to boot a system. This is easily done in Windows 7 by right-clicking the `.iso` file in Windows Explorer and selecting Burn Disc Image.

You can also rename the `Lite Touch Windows PE.wim` file to `boot.wim` and copy it to the `sources` folder of the same bootable USB drive you created earlier in this chapter. When you boot it, you'll see that the `Lite Touch Windows PE.wim` file is just another form of Windows PE.

When you boot to this media, it will start Windows PE, and ultimately you'll see a display similar to Figure 2.13. From here you can select Run The Deployment Wizard.

 If you follow this Deployment Wizard and click Begin at the end of it, it will partition your system and you will lose all data on the system. Make sure you have saved all of your data before clicking Begin.

FIGURE 2.13   Booting to the MDT Deployment Wizard

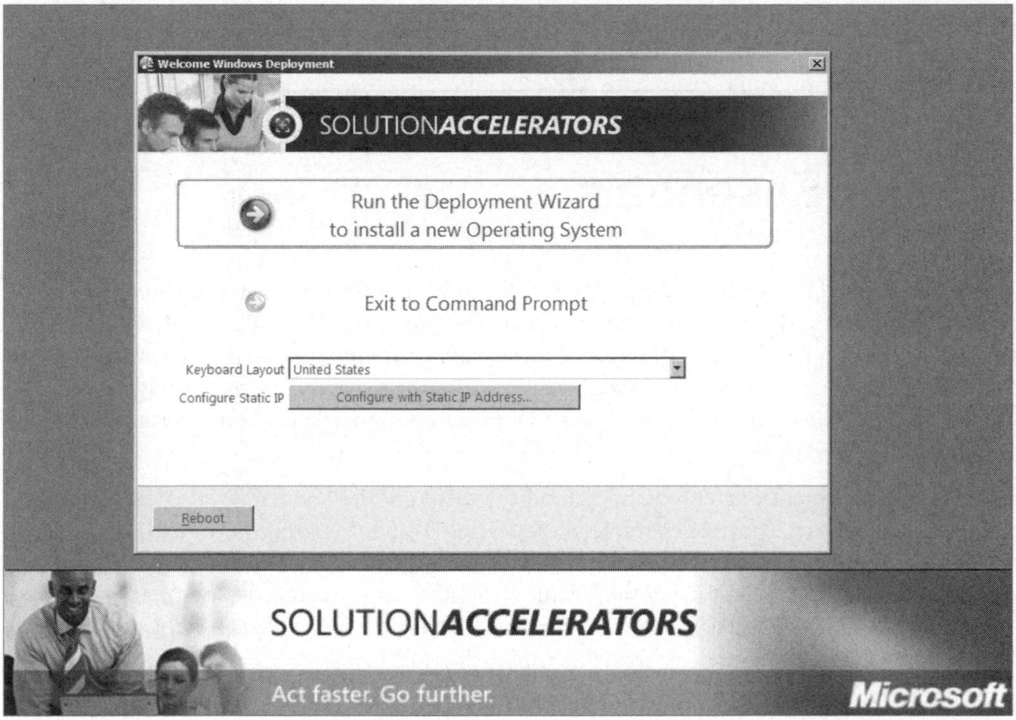

After clicking Run The Deployment Wizard, you'll be prompted to enter domain credentials, pick a task sequence, and select several other options from the wizard. You can reduce the manual choices by modifying the answer files as much as desired. After you've answered the last question for the wizard, you can select Begin to start the installation.

This section didn't make you an expert on MDT 2010. Instead, the goal was to install it, touch it, and become aware of some of its capabilities. If your organization can benefit from using MDT 2010, dig in deeper. One source of additional information is the Windows 7 Resource Kit, which covers MDT 2010 in several chapters.

Summary

In this chapter, you learned about the many different ways that Windows 7 can be deployed, ranging from High Touch completely manual installations to Lite Touch partly automated installations, to Zero Touch completely automated installations. Windows 7 is deployed using images, and images can easily be modified, captured, and deployed.

Several tools are available to use, and most of them are free. The Windows AIK includes ImageX and DISM, which can be used to service images offline. Windows Deployment Services can be used to multicast a single image to multiple clients, and MDT can be used to provide automation to image deployment. While SCCM isn't free, for larger organizations it can be used in conjunction with MDT to automate installations fully.

Chapter Essentials

Understanding and designing images   Be familiar with the different types of images used for deployments. Windows 7 images are contained within .wim files and include boot images that boot to the Windows PE and install images that include the full operating system. Install images can be customized offline and online. After an online image is customized, Sysprep must be run on the image to remove computer-specific information and prepare it to be captured.

Choosing a deployment strategy   Understand the different deployment strategies available. Deployment strategies are characterized as High Touch Installation, Lite Touch Installation, and Zero Touch Installation. A High Touch Installation includes installing from the installation DVD or using the Windows AIK to capture and deploy images. An LTI uses WDS and MDT 2010 to automate most of the installation. MDT 2010 can be used with SCCM to automate deployments fully using a ZTI.

Imaging with the Windows Automated Installation Kit   Be familiar with the Windows AIK. The Windows AIK includes two important tools used to create, manage, and deploy images: ImageX and DISM. ImageX can be used to capture, modify, and deploy images. DISM can be used to modify images, including adding application packages, adding driver packages, or modifying the availability of features in the image using more advanced tools.

Deploying images with Windows Deployment Services   Know how to capture and deploy images with WDS. WDS is a free server role available with Microsoft Windows Server 2008 and Windows Server 2008 R2. It can be used to multicast a single image to multiple clients in an organization. Clients should be PXE–compliant, meaning they can initiate a network service boot by pressing F12. Noncompliant systems can boot using a modified boot image known as a discover image. WDS operates in an Active Directory Domain Services domain and requires DNS and DHCP.

Using the Microsoft Deployment Toolkit 2010   Be familiar with MDT and the use of task sequences. MDT 2010 includes tools that can be used to combine forces with WDS for an LTI or SCCM for a ZTI. The primary tool is the Deployment Workbench, which is used to create deployment shares. Deployment shares include an operating system image and can include applications, additional files, and any extras needed on the image. Task sequences are created within the MDT to specify all of the tasks that must be executed and their specific order. Task sequences can be modified within the Deployment Workbench.

Chapter

3

Using the Command Prompt and PowerShell

TOPICS COVERED IN THIS CHAPTER INCLUDE

- ✓ Using the Windows command prompt

- ✓ Using Windows PowerShell and the PowerShell Integrated Scripting Editor (ISE)

I often say that the difference between a good administrator and a great administrator is the ability to script. Good administrators can get the job done. Great administrators can get the job done more efficiently, in less time, and often have the time to do much more. Their secret is the ability to script.

Hence, if scripting is the secret, how do you learn scripting? The answer quite simply is to start.

You can start by creating batch files, as we'll do here, or start by creating PowerShell scripts, as we'll also do here, or jump right into more advanced Visual Basic scripts using the Windows Management Instrumentation (WMI), but whichever method you choose, start.

The goal of this chapter isn't to make you an expert scripter but instead to give you a taste of scripting and help you see that you can use both the command prompt and PowerShell. As you'll see, the individual pieces aren't that difficult to master. You'll be creating basic scripts that you can schedule to run automatically or run when you need to automate a task. After you master the basics, you'll be prepared to master a little more. Then you'll find other pros wondering how you accomplish so much, so quickly. If you share your secret of scripting, they'll soon be asking you how they can learn to script.

Smile and say, "Start."

Using the Windows Command Prompt

Many older administrators cut their teeth on the old DOS prompt that preceded Windows. They moved from the DOS prompt to the Windows graphical user interface, only to realize that many things can be accomplished only from the command prompt. While the command prompt may look out of fashion to some, it is indeed an integral tool to accomplish many basic and advanced administrative tasks.

PowerShell (a souped-up command prompt) was introduced in Windows Vista and Windows Server 2008, and it has been significantly enhanced with version 2.0 in Windows 7 and Windows Server 2008 R2. Windows Server 2008 and Windows Server 2008 R2 include Server Core editions that are Windows operating systems without the GUI—everything is done from the command prompt.

In short, the *command prompt* is not going away. It's stronger than ever. One of the biggest reasons is that anything that can be executed at the command prompt can be scripted, and anything that can be scripted can be scheduled or programmed to respond to specific events.

In this section, you'll learn some basics related to the command prompt and some basic commands, and then you'll create some basic scripts in the form of batch files. Remember though, this small section won't tell you everything about the command prompt.

Launching the Command Prompt

This is a participative sport. You can't just read about it—you really need to get your hands on the keyboard and execute these commands to see how they work. Start by launching the command prompt. In Windows 7, you can launch it using one of these two methods:

- Click Start ➢ All Programs ➢ Accessories ➢ Command Prompt.
- Click Start, type **CMD** in the Search text box, and press Enter.

> By default, the command prompt will launch without administrative permissions. However, some commands need to be executed with administrative permissions. For these, right-click the Command Prompt link or the cmd.exe executable that shows when you use the Search text box, and select Run As Administrator.

It starts with white text on a black screen, though you can modify it if you desire. After launching the command prompt, right-click the title bar, select Properties, and then select the Colors tab. You'll see a dialog box similar to Figure 3.1.

FIGURE 3.1   Modifying the display of the command prompt

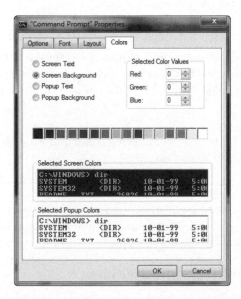

The screen background is black by default, but you can modify it to a white background by clicking the white block. Select Screen Text, and click the black block.

In addition to modifying the colors, you can modify the font from the Font tab. You can select one of only three fonts, but you can choose one of many sizes. I often modify the fonts when doing demonstrations in the classroom so students can easily see the commands—even from the cheap seats.

Command Prompt Basics

First, let's cover some basics when using the command prompt. These basics apply if you're using basic commands, using advanced commands, or using the commands in scripts. In addition, many of these same basics apply to PowerShell commands.

Help Is Always Available

You can find help for just about any command by typing in the command with either /? or /Help. In other words, to get help on the Shutdown command, you can enter either Shutdown /? or Shutdown /Help at the command prompt. Also, many commands have help available by typing in Help and then the command. For the Shutdown command, you can enter Help Shutdown.

Windows 7 help includes several help topics files and links to online resources. Click Start, select Help And Support, type in **Command Reference Overview,** and click Search Help (or press Enter). The Command Reference Overview help article includes a short intro and links for many online articles, including help topics for about 200 individual commands that can be executed at the command prompt.

Spelling Counts

At some point in the future, computers will do what we want them to do, not what we ask them to do. For now, they interpret our commands quite literally. As an example, if I wanted to start the Print Spooler service, I would enter this command:

```
Sc start spooler
```

However, if I accidentally entered the following command instead (Sx instead of Sc), the command prompt would give a syntax error:

```
Sx start spooler
```

The error indicates the command is not recognized, because it is trying to execute a command called Sx, which doesn't exist. When things don't work, it's worth your time to read the error message. It will often point you in the right direction.

Commands Are Modified with Switches

A switch is identified with either a / symbol or a - symbol. The / symbol was used often in older DOS commands, and the - symbol was common in UNIX and UNIX derivatives. However, at this point, most commands will accept either switch.

Each command has a specific set of switches that are accepted and can be identified when the command is entered with the /? switch.

As a simple example, you can use the DIR command to view the contents of the current directory (by typing DIR and pressing Enter). You can modify the command to view all the files in the current directory that start with IP (using DIR IP*). It can be modified to look for any file that starts with IP* in any subdirectories with the following command that adds the /S switch.

```
DIR IP* /S
```

Commands Are Not Case Sensitive

Most command-prompt commands are not case sensitive. In other words, a command is interpreted the same if it's entered as all uppercase, all lowercase, or a mixture of both uppercase and lowercase. As an example, the SET command allows you to view many different environment variables for your system. You would see the same result if you entered it as SET, SeT, set, or even sET.

It's extremely rare, but occasionally you'll run across a parameter used within a command-prompt command that needs to be a specific case. When this true, it will be stressed.

Commands Can Use Wildcards

A *wildcard* is a character that can take the place of other characters. They are often used for search and copy operations. The command prompt includes two wildcard characters: the asterisk (*) and the question mark (?).

The * symbol will look for any instance of zero or more characters in the place of the * symbol. As an example, if you want to know if you have any TXT files (with the .txt extension) in the current directory, you can use the following command:

```
Dir *.txt
```

Similarly, if you want a listing of all files that start with App and end with .exe, you can use this command:

```
Dir App*.exe
```

Note that it will include a file named App.exe, if it exists, in addition to any files that that have letters after App.

The ? wildcard will take the place of a single character. It isn't used as often, but you can use it if you're looking for something more specific. For example, if you were looking for any files that had an extension of .ex and any third character, you could use this command:

```
Dir *.ex?
```

It would not include any files that ended with .ex without a third character in the extension. In other words, the ? wildcard specifies that a single character must exist for a match to occur. This is different from the * symbol, which will match for zero or more characters.

Strings with Spaces Need Quotes

Many commands will accept parameters, and when the parameters include spaces, the parameter usually needs to be enclosed in quotes.

As an example, the Net Shell command (*netsh*) can be used to configure a lot of networking settings, including the properties for the network interface card (NIC). The default name for the wired network interface card is *Local Area Connection*. If you want to set the DNS IP address to 10.10.0.10 using `netsh`, you could use the following command:

```
netsh interface ipv4 set DNSServer "Local Area Connection" static 10.10.0.10
```

In this example, the name of the NIC is expected after the `DNSServer` parameter. Since `"Local Area Connection"` is enclosed in quotes, it's interpreted as the name of the NIC.

However, the following command (without the quotes) would be interpreted quite differently:

```
netsh interface ipv4 set DNSServer Local Area Connection static 10.10.0.10
```

In this example, `Local` would be interpreted as the name of the NIC and the `netsh` command would then try to interpret `Area` as a separate command. Since `netsh` doesn't have an `Area` command, the entire command would fail.

You can occasionally get away without using the quotes. For example, if you're at the root of C (C:\) and want to change to the `Program Files` folder (which has a space), the following command will work:

```
CD Program Files
```

This is only because the `CD` command has been programmed to accept it, but that wasn't always the case. You could also enter this command as

```
CD "Program Files"
```

DOSKEY Saves Typing

DOSKEY is a utility that is constantly running in the background of the command prompt and can be very valuable—if you know how to use it. Every time you enter a command in a command prompt session, it is recorded by `DOSKEY` and it can be recalled.

As an example, imagine you're testing connectivity with a server using the following `ping` command:

```
Ping DC1.Training.MCITPSuccess.com
```

You could execute the command and then realize the NIC wasn't configured correctly, or the host cache needed to be cleared with `IPConfig /FlushDNS`, or something else needed to be done. After resolving the issue, you want to execute the command again. Instead of typing it in from scratch, simply use the up arrow to recall it, press Enter, and you've executed it again (without typing it again).

The up arrow can be used to retrieve any previous command that you've entered in this session (up to the limit of the buffer, which is rather large). This can be valuable when you're entering very long commands or even short commands if you use the hunt-and-peck method of typing.

Typos are also common at the command line. However, you don't have to retype the entire command. You can use the up arrow instead to recall the command and then use the left and right arrows to position the cursor where you want to modify the text. Make your corrections, press Enter, and the corrected command executes.

You can also use the F7 key to display a pop-up window that shows a history window. It includes all of the commands you've entered in the current session. You can then use the up or down arrow to select the desired command.

DOSKEY is a command-prompt utility itself, and it includes some commands you can use. For example, if you want to view all the commands that have been entered in the current session, enter DOSKEY/History.

By default, the system includes a buffer size of 50 commands. If you need more, you can modify the buffer size. For example, the following command changes the buffer to 99:

```
DOSKEY /Listsize=99
```

System Variables Identify the Environment

Many *system variables* are available within Windows 7, and you'll see these often when using the command prompt and Windows PowerShell. They are useful in identifying specific information about the environment, without actually knowing the current environment. As a simple example, every computer has a computer name, but the computer names are different. However, the system variable %computername% holds the value of the local computer's computer name.

System variables are easy to identify. They always start and end with a percent symbol (%). An easy way to view the value of any variable is by using the echo command in the following format:

```
Echo %variableName%
```

Table 3.1 shows many of the commonly used system variables and their value.

TABLE 3.1 Some commonly used system variables

Variable	Value
%windir% %systemroot%	Both %windir% and %systemroot% identify the folder where Windows was installed, typically C:\Windows.
%systemdrive%	The folder where the system boot files are located, typically C:\.

TABLE 3.1   Some commonly used system variables *(continued)*

Variable	Value
%computername%	The name of the local computer.
%username%	The name of the user logged on to this session.
%date%	Holds the value of the current date in the format ddd mm/dd/yyyy. The first three letters are an abbreviation of the day such as Mon, Tue, Wed, and so on. The remaining format is all numbers with mm for the month, dd for the day, and yyyy for the year.
%time%	Holds the value of the current time in a 24-hour format as hh.mm.ss.ms.
%errorlevel%	Indicates whether the previous command resulted in an error. If it didn't have an error, the value is 0.
%ProgramFiles%	Points to the location of the Program Files folder, which is normally C:\Program Files.
%Public%	The location of the Public folder, typically C:\Users\Public.

Commands Use Paths

When you execute commands from the command prompt, the system needs to know where to find the command. It first tries to execute it in the current path and then looks for it in predefined paths. A path identifies a location on the hard drive.

As an example, when you first launch the command prompt, it will start in the C:\Users\%username% path by default, where %username% will be replaced with the username you're logged on with. (If you launch it with Run As Administrator, it will start in the c:\%windir%\System32 folder.) If you execute a command (such as IPConfig), it will look for it in the current folder first. If it isn't located in the current folder, it will search the folders identified in the predefined paths. If the command isn't located in any of the known paths, you'll see an error. For example, if you type x and press Enter, you'll see this error:

```
'x' is not recognized as an internal or external command, operable program or batch file.
```

Documentation commonly uses the terms *folders* and *directories* interchangeably. In the early DOS days, they were almost always called directories. When the Windows GUI came out, they were referred to as folders because the icon looks like a folder. It matched a metaphor users could easily understand; that is, files were placed in folders in the real world and they are placed in folders in Windows. However, there is no difference between a folder and a directory; both terms mean the same thing.

If the system didn't have predefined paths, it would search only the current folder, and commands would be a lot harder to enter and execute. However, the system starts with several predefined paths. On my system, this path includes all of these directories:

- `C:\Windows\system32`
- `C:\Windows`
- `C:\Windows\System32\Wbem`
- `C:\Windows\System32\WindowsPowerShell\v1.0\`
- `C:\Windows\System32\Windows System Resource Manager\bin`
- `C:\Windows\idmu\com`

You can execute the `PATH` or the `SET PATH` command to view the predefined path for your system. Some applications will modify the path, and you can also modify the path yourself.

Identifying Executables

When you execute the `SET PATH` statement, you also see something else valuable: a list of file types that are known to be executables. Some files can be executed or run, while others are simply data files used by executables.

So what is an executable? It is any file that can be run. For example, you can run the `ipconfig.exe` file because it's an executable. If a file named `IPConfig.txt` existed, it could not be executed. The extension `.exe` identifies the first file as an executable, whereas the extension `.txt` identifies the second file as a text file.

Known executables are defined by the system variable `PATHEXT` (path extension). The path extensions, or file extensions, known to be executables are listed as on my system: `.COM`, `.EXE`, `.BAT`, `.CMD`, `.VBS`, `.VBE`, `.JS`, `.JSE`, `.WSF`, `.WSH`, and `.MSC`.

So when you execute the `IPConfig` command, it searches for a file that starts with `IPConfig` and ends with one of the identified known executable extensions. Since `IPConfig` ends with `.EXE`, the `IPconfig.EXE` command is located and executed.

Modifying the Path to Executables

If you need to modify the known paths of the system, you can do so with either the `SET PATH` statement or via the GUI. As an example, you may have an executable in the `C:\App` path, and you may want this path included in the `Path` variable. You can use one of these methods.

SET PATH Command

Before modifying the path, take a look at what it currently is with the following command:

```
SET PATH
```

You can use the `SET PATH` statement to modify the path to include the `C:\App` folder with the following command.

```
SET PATH = C:\App
```

After you modify the path, view the current path by executing SET PATH again. You'll notice that there are two paths currently set—the original default path and another PATH = C:\App path that you just created, as shown in code Listing 3.1 and Listing 3.2. Listing 3.1 is what appears before executing the Set Path = C:\App statement. Listing 3.2 shows what appears after executing the statement.

Listing 3.1: Output of the Set Path statement

```
Path=C:\Windows\system32;C:\Windows;
C:\Windows\System32\Wbem;
c:\Program Files (x86)\Microsoft SQL Server\90\Tools\binn\;
C:\Windows\System32\WindowsPowerShell\v1.0\;
C:\Windows\System32\Windows System Resource Manager\bin;
C:\Windows\idmu\common;C:\Program Files\Windows Imaging\
PATHEXT=.COM;.EXE;.BAT;.CMD;.VBS;.VBE;.JS;.JSE;.WSF;.WSH;.MSC
```

Listing 3.2: Output of the Set Path statement after appending the path

```
Path=C:\Windows\system32;C:\Windows;
C:\Windows\System32\Wbem;
c:\Program Files (x86)\Microsoft SQL Server\90\Tools\binn\;
C:\Windows\System32\WindowsPowerShell\v1.0\;
C:\Windows\System32\Windows System Resource Manager\bin;
C:\Windows\idmu\common;C:\Program Files\Windows Imaging\
PATH = C:\App
PATHEXT=.COM;.EXE;.BAT;.CMD;.VBS;.VBE;.JS;.JSE;.WSF;.WSH;.MSC
```

This behavior of the set path statement is different in Windows 7 than it was in previous versions of Windows. In previous versions, if you used the Set Path = C:\App statement, it would overwrite the previous path and only C:\App would be included in the path. However, when you execute the Set Path statement in Windows 7, it appends, not replaces, the current path.

This modified path will be modified for only the current session. In other words, if you exit the command-prompt window, launch it again, and enter SET PATH, you'll see only the original system default path.

Modifying the Path with the GUI

The path can also be modified by modifying the system variables in the GUI, as shown in Exercise 3.1.

EXERCISE 3.1

Modifying the Path System Variable

1. Click Start, right-click Computer, and select Properties.

2. Select Advanced System Settings.

3. Click the Environment Variables button.

4. Scroll to the Path in the System Variables pane. Select Path and click Edit.

5. Scroll to the end of the text in the Variable Value text box.

    Warning: Make sure you separate each path with a semicolon. If the semicolon is omitted, the path will be interpreted as a part of the previous path and the previous path will no longer be accessible.

6. Enter a semicolon (;) and then the path you want added, as shown in the following graphic. Click OK to dismiss all of the windows.

7. If you launch the command prompt, you'll see that the new path has been appended to the system path.

Changing the Current Path with CD

As I mentioned earlier, when you open the command prompt, the default path is C:\ Users\%username%, with %username% being replaced with your actual user name. For example, if I logged on with a user name of Darril, the default path would be c:\Users\Darril.

You can change the path with the CD command (short for change directory).

- CD \ will take you to the root of the current drive.

- CD .. will take you up one folder.

- CD folderName will take you into the folder specified as long as the folder is in the current folder.
- CD \1st folder\2nd folder\3rd folder will take you to the third folder, as long as the path is valid.

Use Exercise 3.2 to see this in action.

EXERCISE 3.2

Using the CD Command

1. Launch a command prompt and note the current path. Unless you launched it using Run As Administrator, it will point to a directory with your name in the C:\Users directory.

2. Type **CD** .. (CD, space, and two dots), and press Enter. This will take you up one folder to the C:\Users folder.

3. Type **CD** \ and press Enter. This will take to you the root of C:\.

4. Type in **Dir** and press Enter to view the contents of the root.

5. Type the following command to change the directory to the windows\sytem32 folder:

   CD \windows\system32

   Note that the backslash (\) before windows causes the path to start from the root of the C:\ drive.

6. Type in **DIR** and press Enter to view the contents of this folder.

7. Press the up arrow twice to recall the CD \ command, and press Enter. You'll be returned to the root.

8. Enter the following command to change to the system32 folder using the windows variable.

   CD %windir%\system32

Changing the Current Path with Windows Explorer

A neat feature that's available with the command prompt is the ability to use drag and drop from Windows Explorer to copy the path. It doesn't change the directory, but you can use it to make things a lot easier.

This feature is not available when you run the command prompt using Run As Administrator. Exercise 3.3 shows how this can be useful.

EXERCISE 3.3

Using Drag and Drop with the Command Prompt

1. If a command prompt is not already open, launch a command prompt.

2. Launch Windows Explorer and browse to the Libraries\Documents\My Documents folder.

3. Position Windows Explorer and the Command Prompt window side by side.

3. Click My Documents in Windows Explorer, drag it to the Command Prompt window, and release it. You'll notice that the path is now displayed in the window. Your display will be similar to the following graphic.

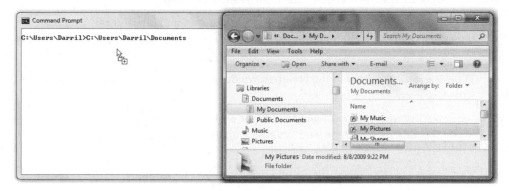

4. In the figure, the user name is Darril, so the default path of Darril's Libraries starts as C:\Users\Darril and the actual path to the Libraries\Documents\My Documents folder is C:\Users\Darril\Documents. When the My Documents folder is dragged and dropped into the Command Prompt window, the path is typed out. However, you're not finished yet.

5. Use the left arrow (or the Home key) to position your cursor to the left of all the text. Type **CD** and a space to modify the command, and press Enter. Your path will be changed to the equivalent of the My Documents folder.

The previous exercise showed how you can easily change the path using Windows Explorer, but you can also launch the command prompt to any folder's location from Windows Explorer. Press the Shift key, right-click the folder, and select Open Command Window Here. The command prompt will be launched with the directory set at the same folder as Windows Explorer.

Copy and Paste with the Command Prompt

At first glance it looks like you can't copy and paste to or from the command prompt. It doesn't work exactly as it does in Windows, causing a lot of people to assume you can't, but it is possible.

You can actually copy and paste by default, but enabling the QuickEdit mode makes it a little easier. This can be valuable when you are testing commands that you want to paste into a script file. Exercise 3.4 shows how copy and paste works from the command prompt, how to enable QuickEdit mode, and its benefits.

EXERCISE 3.4

Using Copy and Paste from the Command Prompt

1. Open a Command Prompt window, type in **Notepad**, and press Enter. This will launch an instance of Notepad that you'll use to copy and paste text to and from the Command Prompt window.

2. Type in **ping localhost** in the Notepad window. Press Ctrl+A to select the text and Ctrl+C to copy it.

3. Click in the Command Prompt window. Right-click and select Paste. You'll see the command pasted into the Command Prompt window. Press Enter and the command will execute.

4. Right-click the command prompt title bar and select Edit ➢ Mark.

5. Use your mouse to highlight the output from the ping command. When the text has been highlighted, press Enter to copy it to the clipboard.

6. Click in Notepad and press Ctrl+V to paste the output into the text file.

7. Enable QuickEdit Mode with these steps:

    a. Right-click the title bar and select Properties. The Options tab is selected by default.

    b. Select the check box next to QuickEdit Mode, as shown in the following graphic. Click OK.

EXERCISE 3.4   *(continued)*

8. Now you can select text within the Command Prompt window without selecting Mark. Simply use the mouse to select the text and press Enter. The following graphic shows how text can be selected by highlighting it and using the menu to select Edit ➢ Copy. It also shows the shortcut Enter, or you can simply press the Enter key.

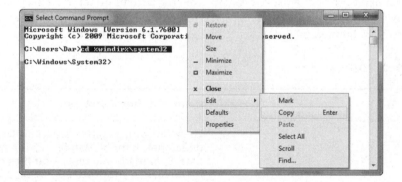

Capturing the Output

It's common to need to capture the output of commands executed at the command prompt. This can easily be done by redirecting the output to a text file using the > symbol.

As an example, you may want to document the current status of all of the services in a text file so that you can review them later. The command to view a list of all the currently running services is

```
sc query
```

If you execute this at the command prompt, you'll see that it quickly scrolls off the screen. However, you can redirect the output to a text file by modifying the command to this:

```
sc query > SvsStat.txt
```

You can then view the file in Notepad with the following command:

```
notepad SvsStat.txt
```

Of course, you can also redirect the file to any location by including the path in the filename. The following command creates and stores the file in the C:\Data folder:

```
sc query > C:\Data\SvsStat.txt
```

A Sampling of Commands

The following sections provide an introduction to some of the things you can do at the command prompt. They are by no means all the commands that you'll come across. As you read through these, I strongly encourage you to try out each of the commands at the command prompt.

Several notable commands are missing from this list because they are covered in other chapters. For example, in the networking chapter we'll touch on tools like Ping and IPConfig.

Dir

The DIR command provides a list of contents from the current directory. This is an easy way to view a list of files in this directory, and it also includes a list of directories in the current directory. Some commonly used switches are shown in Table 3.2.

TABLE 3.2   DIR switches

Switch	Comments and Examples
/A:x	Lists files with specific attributes. Use D for directories, H for hidden files, S for system files, R for read-only files, A for files ready for archiving, I for files not indexed, and L for reparse points. (A reparse point is an NTFS extended object, such as a mount point, which looks like a folder but points to another drive.)
	DIR /A:H shows hidden files.

TABLE 3.2   DIR switches *(continued)*

Switch	Comments and Examples
/S	Displays files in subdirectories within the current directory. DIR *.exe /S lists all the executables in the current directory or any subdirectories.
/W	Displays the contents in a wide format that is sometimes easier to read. DIR /W
/P	Pauses the output if it scrolls for more than a page.

Copy

The Copy command can be used to copy files from the command prompt. When the Copy command is used, the original file is not modified and a new file is created. It has the following format:

```
Copy sourceFile destinationFile
```

Both the sourceFile and the destinationFile can include a path statement. If the path is omitted, the current path is used. If the file is being copied to a different path, the destinationFile name can be omitted and the name will be the same.

As an example, you can copy a file named test.txt to a file named test2.txt in the current directory with this command:

```
Copy test.txt test2.txt
```

If the test.txt file exists in a folder named Docs on the C: drive and you want to copy it to the C:\Data folder keeping the original name, use this command:

```
Copy C:\docs\test.txt c:\data
```

You can also use wildcards with Copy commands. For example, if you wanted to copy all of the files from the C:\Data folder to the C:\Archive folder, you could use this command:

```
Copy C:\data\*.* c:\archive\
```

As explained earlier, the asterisk (*) wildcard can be used in place of zero or more characters. When you use *.*, it will include all files in the folder.

Similarly, if you were already in the C:\Archive folder, you could use the following command, omitting the destination. All of the files would be copied from the source folder and copied into the current folder.

```
Copy C:\data\*.*
```

XCopy

One of the problems with the Copy command is that it can't copy subdirectories. XCopy can copy subdirectories, and that's one of the primary reasons why it's used.

The format of the XCopy command is similar to that of the Copy command:

```
xCopy sourceFile destinationFile
```

Some of the common switches used with XCopy are listed in Table 3.3.

TABLE 3.3   XCopy switches

Switch	Comments
/S	Copies both directories and subdirectories except empty ones. The following command copies all of the files and subdirectories from the current folder to the C:\Archive folder. XCopy *.* c:\Archive\ /S
/E	Copies both directories and subdirectories, including empty ones. The following command copies all of the files and subdirectories from the current folder to the C:\Archive folder. XCopy *.* c:\Archive\ /E
/Y /-Y	/Y suppresses prompting to confirm you want to overwrite files. This can be useful in scripts. XCopy *.* c:\Archive\ /S /Y /-Y turns prompting back on.
/C	Continues copying even if errors occur. XCopy *.* c:\Archive\ /S /C
/Q	Quiet mode. Does not display files while copying. XCopy *.* c:\Archive\ /S /Q

SET

The SET command was used earlier to show and modify the path, but it can be used to view and/or modify many of the environment variables. Entering SET with no parameters will show many of the system variables and their current value:

SET

Listing 3.3 shows the output of the Set command on my computer.

Listing 3.3: Output of the Set command

```
ALLUSERSPROFILE=C:\ProgramData
APPDATA=C:\Users\Darril\AppData\Roaming
CommonProgramFiles=C:\Program Files\Common Files
CommonProgramFiles(x86)=C:\Program Files (x86)\Common Files
CommonProgramW6432=C:\Program Files\Common Files
COMPUTERNAME=DRG
ComSpec=C:\Windows\system32\cmd.exe
FP_NO_HOST_CHECK=NO
HOMEDRIVE=C:
HOMEPATH=\Users\Darril
LOCALAPPDATA=C:\Users\Darril\AppData\Local
LOGONSERVER=\\DRG
NUMBER_OF_PROCESSORS=2
OS=Windows_NT
Path=C:\Windows\system32;C:\Windows;C:\Windows\System32\Wbem;↵
c:\Program Files (x86)\Microsoft SQL Server\90\Tools\binn\;↵
C:\Windows\System32  \WindowsPowerShell\v1.0\;↵
C:\Windows\System32\Windows System Resource Manager\bin;↵
C:\Windows\idmu\common
PATHEXT=.COM;.EXE;.BAT;.CMD;.VBS;.VBE;.JS;.JSE;.WSF;.WSH;.MSC

PROCESSOR_ARCHITECTURE=AMD64
PROCESSOR_IDENTIFIER=Intel64 Family 6 Model 23 Stepping 6, GenuineIntel
PROCESSOR_LEVEL=6
PROCESSOR_REVISION=1706
ProgramData=C:\ProgramData
ProgramFiles=C:\Program Files
ProgramFiles(x86)=C:\Program Files (x86)
ProgramW6432=C:\Program Files
PROMPT=$P$G
PSModulePath=C:\Windows\system32\WindowsPowerShell\v1.0\Modules\
```

```
PUBLIC=C:\Users\Public
SESSIONNAME=Console
SystemDrive=C:
SystemRoot=C:\Windows
TEMP=C:\Users\Darril\AppData\Local\Temp
TMP=C:\Users\Darril\AppData\Local\Temp
USERDOMAIN=DRG
USERNAME=Darril
USERPROFILE=C:\Users\Darril
VS80COMNTOOLS=C:\Program Files (x86)\Microsoft Visual Studio 8\Common7\Tools\
windir=C:\Windows
```

You can narrow the search by using the first letter of the variable in which you're interested. For example, to see all the variables that start with the letter C, you can use the following command:

```
SET C
```

NET USE

The NET command includes several subcommands, but one of the most basic and frequently used NET commands is NET USE. The NET USE command can be used to connect to shares on remote computers. It does this by mapping an unused drive letter (such as Z:) to a Universal Naming Convention (UNC) path of \\ServerName\ShareName.

In other words, if you have a server named Srv1 that has a share named Data, you can use the UNC path of \\Srv1\Data. Use the following command to map this UNC path to the Z: drive:

```
Net Use Z:  \\Srv1\Data
```

Now you can change the drive name to Z: by simply typing Z: and pressing Enter, and you'll have access to the UNC path from the command prompt. You can copy files to or from the Z: drive (as long as you have permission).

When you've finished, you should return the environment to normal and delete the mapping. The following command will do so:

```
Net Use Z: /delete
```

SystemInfo

The SystemInfo command will output a significant amount of information on the system. This can be very valuable when troubleshooting a system because it gives you a lot of information at a glance. It can quickly tell you things like these and more:

- Hostname
- Operating system name, edition, and version

- When it was installed and when it was last booted
- Details on the hardware such as BIOS version, number, and type of processors and how much RAM is installed
- Names of hotfixes that have been installed

Listing 3.4 shows the output of this command on my system.

Listing 3.4: Output of the SystemInfo command

```
Host Name:                   DRG
OS Name:                     Microsoft Windows 7 Ultimate
OS Version:                  6.1.7600 N/A Build 7600
OS Manufacturer:             Microsoft Corporation
OS Configuration:            Standalone Workstation
OS Build Type:               Multiprocessor Free
Registered Owner:            Darril Gibson
Registered Organization:     SYO-201.com
Product ID:                  00426-065-0543977-86656
Original Install Date:       8/9/2009, 4:42:31 AM
System Boot Time:            9/21/2009, 12:46:35 PM
System Manufacturer:         Hewlett-Packard
System Model:                HP Pavilion dv7 Notebook PC
System Type:                 x64-based PC
Processor(s):                1 Processor(s) Installed.
                             [01]: Intel64 Family 6 Model 23
     Stepping 6 GenuineIntel ~2401 Mhz
BIOS Version:                Hewlett-Packard F.26, 2/6/2009
Windows Directory:           C:\Windows
System Directory:            C:\Windows\system32
Boot Device:                 \Device\HarddiskVolume1
System Locale:               en-us;English (United States)
Input Locale:                en-us;English (United States)
Time Zone:                   (UTC-05:00) Eastern Time (US & Canada)
Total Physical Memory:       6,111 MB
Available Physical Memory:   969 MB
Virtual Memory: Max Size:    13,799 MB
Virtual Memory: Available:   8,529 MB
Virtual Memory: In Use:      5,270 MB
Page File Location(s):       C:\pagefile.sys
Domain:                      WORKGROUP
Logon Server:                \\DRG
Hotfix(s):                   3 Hotfix(s) Installed.
```

```
                              [01]: KB958559
                              [02]: KB972636
                              [03]: KB973874
Network Card(s):              1 NIC(s) Installed.
                              [01]: Intel(R) PRO/100 VE Network Connection
                                    Connection Name: Local Area Connection
                                    DHCP Enabled:    Yes
                                    DHCP Server:     192.168.1.1
                                    IP address(es)
                              [01]: 192.168.1.103
                              [02]: fe80::bd37:44ef:a2c5:47d2
```

As with any command, you can send the output of this command to a text file using the redirection symbol, like this:

```
Systeminfo > SystemInfo.txt
```

DriverQuery

The DriverQuery command can be used to list all of the installed device drivers. The drivers are listed with their name, the type of driver, and when they were installed. The basic syntax is

```
DriveryQuery
```

That seems simple enough, but if you do it, you'll notice that there are so many drivers listed that if fills the screen buffer, and you can't even scroll back to where the DriverQuery command was entered. However, you can get around this in a couple of ways.

Use the | More command. The symbol before the word More is called pipe, so it's read as "pipe more" or sometimes referred to as pipelining. Pipelining allows you to combine two commands and have the output of one as the input to another in this case. The symbol is usually located above the Enter key and is typed by using Shift+backslash (\). Enter it like this:

```
DriverQuery | More
```

The More command will display a screen at a time. You can press the spacebar to get another screen or press the Enter key to get the next line.

You can modify the screen buffer size as a second method to ensure you can view all of the data provided by the command. Right-click the title bar of the command prompt and select Properties. Select the Layout tab. Change the Screen Buffer Size Height value to **9999** and click OK.

Also, just as you saw with the SystemInfo command, you can redirect the output to a text file.

Echo

`Echo` can be used to display text on the screen. You can use this to provide some type of information to the user from a batch file. The basic syntax is

```
Echo Your Message
```

When included in a batch file, this command will display in entirety and then display the message, all of which can be a little distracting. As an example, if a batch file has the `Echo Hello` line, it will output the following text:

```
Echo Hello
Hello
```

You can easily turn off the first line (`Echo Hello`) with the `Echo off` command. Even the `Echo Off` command can be suppressed by adding the at symbol, like this:

```
@Echo off
```

If you want to display a blank line, add a period after `Echo` without any spaces, like this:

```
Echo.
```

To put all of this together, you can use the following code in a batch file. The first line suppresses the echo (including the command that suppresses echo), and the second line outputs the message "Hello." The third line creates a blank line, and the last line outputs another message.

```
@Echo off
Echo Hello
Echo.
Echo Let's get started
```

When this batch file is executed, it will output the following three lines (with the middle line blank).

```
Hello

Let's get started
```

Advanced Shell Commands

Several advanced shell commands are beyond the scope of this chapter, but I want to mention them. Shell commands generally allow you to enter the command completely from the command prompt or enter the shell.

A shell command has several layers. As an example, the Net Shell (`netsh`) command is entered by typing `netsh`. Once launched, it will change the command prompt to `netsh>`.

You can then enter ? to see all the available commands. Type in `interface` and press Enter, and you're in a different layer of `netsh` identified as `netsh interface>`. Another request for help with the ? symbol will show a completely different set of commands that can be executed here.

When working with shell commands, you'll often be trying to achieve a specific objective and following detailed steps, such as through a Microsoft Knowledge Base article. In other words, you probably won't ever master all of the shell commands, but instead you will occasionally use them to perform specific tasks.

You can also enter the full `netsh` command from the command line without entering the actual shell program. For example, the following command can be executed from the command prompt, and it will set the IP address to 10.10.5.100 with a subnet mask of 255.255.255.0 and a default gateway of 10.10.5.1. Although the command spans two lines in this book, you should enter it as a single line at the command prompt:

```
netsh interface ipv4 set address name="Local Area Connection" static
  10.10.5.100 255.255.255.0 10.10.5.1
```

 Real World Scenario

Automating IPv4 Settings with a Script

I once needed to change the address of the DNS server for about 50 non-DHCP clients in the network. Yes, I could have accessed the NIC, then the IPv4 properties, and so on for each system, but I knew that if I could just launch a batch file, it would be much easier and quicker.

After some experimentation, I found this command (executed as a single line from the command prompt) would work:

```
netsh interface ipv4 set DNSServer "Local Area Connection"
  static 10.10.0.10
```

I created a batch file with this single command in it and then configured the batch file to run as a logon script. (Chapter 5, "Maintaining and Troubleshooting Windows 7," will cover logon scripts in more depth.) I asked the users to log off and then back on, and I was done.

Some of the other common shell commands you may come across are these:

Wmic   This allows you to perform advanced Windows Management Instrumentation (WMI) queries from the command line. WMI is very rich and robust, and if you dig into scripting more, you'll find you can do quite a bit with it. It's intertwined with many products that use WMI queries to learn details about systems remotely. WMIC allows you to execute WMI queries from the command line. As a simple example, the qfe command (short for Quick Fix Engineering) will retrieve a listing of all updates installed on the system and is executed using WMIC qfe. You'll see this in action in the batch file section.

 WMI is used both to retrieve and set information on computers. As an example, you can create scripts to set the power-setting values on computers remotely using the Win32_PowerSetting class or remotely activate a specific power plan using the Win32_Plan.Activate() method.

NTDSUtil   The New Technology Directory Services Utility (**NTDSUtil**) is often used to maintain Active Directory. You can use it to restore Active Directory, change the directory services restore mode administrator password, or seize single master operations roles held by domain controllers. While Active Directory maintenance is often left to domain administrators, you may come across it in your travels if your desktops are in a domain.

Creating a Batch File

A *batch file* is a listing of one or more command-prompt commands within a text file. When the batch file is called or executed, the commands are executed. The best way to understand this is to do it. While there are sophisticated text editors you can use, Notepad will work.

Exercise 3.5 shows the steps used to create a simple batch file, and then it builds on the simple batch to add extra capabilities. Ultimately, you'll end up with a batch file that can create a list of patches installed on the system and that can copy the file to a share on another computer.

EXERCISE 3.5

Creating a Batch File

1. Launch the command prompt.

2. Type **Notepad ListPatches.bat** and press Enter. Notepad will launch, and because a file named ListPatches.bat doesn't exist, you'll be prompted to create it. Click Yes.

   Note that the file will be created in the same directory in which the Command Prompt window was launched.

3. Type in the following text in Notepad:

   ```
   Echo Off
   Echo Hello %username%. Today is %date%.
   ```

   Press Ctrl+S to save the file, but don't close it.

4. Return to the command prompt, type **ListPatches**, and press Enter. Notice that since the batch file is considered one of the executable types, it is automatically located and executed. You'll see a greeting with today's date. This is okay but not very useful.

5. Access Notepad, and type in the following text after your first two lines:

```
Wmic qfe > %computerName%patches.txt
```

This will create a list of updates currently installed on this system and store the updates in the file named computerNamepatches.txt, where the computer name will be different for each computer where it is executed. Press Ctrl+S to save the file.

6. Return to the command prompt, press the up arrow, and press Enter to execute the batch file again. Notice that it almost seems as though it's the same as before. A greeting appears, it pauses for a second or two, and then the command prompt returns.

7. Provide some user feedback by adding the following lines to the batch file:

```
Echo A list of patches is stored in the %computername%patches.txt file.
```

Press Ctrl+S to save the file.

8. Access the command prompt, press the up arrow to retrieve the last command, and press Enter to view the difference. Notice that instead of %computername%, your actual computer name is used.

9. You could also open the file for the user by adding this command to the batch file:

```
Notepad %computername%patches.txt
```

If you add this to the batch file to test it, make sure you remove it before moving on.

10. Last, if you wanted to copy it to a network share (such as a central computer that will hold files from multiple computers), you could use the NET USE command. For this set of commands, I'm assuming I have a share named Patches on a server named Srv1 that I can access in the network and I have permissions to copy the file. I'm accessing it using the \\Srv1\Patches UNC path. You can use any server (or another Windows 7 box) and any share that has appropriate permissions.

```
Net Use Z:  /delete
Net use z: \\SRV1\Patches
Copy %computerName%Patches.txt Z:
net use Z: /delete
```

11. The first command ensures that the Z: drive isn't already mapped to something else. The next command maps the Z: drive to the UNC path using the \\serverName\ shareName format. The third line copies the file to the Z: drive using the Copy command, and the fourth line returns the environment to normal.

Now that the file is created, it can be configured to execute automatically based on a schedule. Windows 7 includes the built-in *Task Scheduler* that can be used to schedule tasks.

 Real World Scenario

Preparing a Classroom

At my current job, I teach several different courses. The various courses require different student materials. Since I'm never sure what previous students might have done, I always refresh the files before each class.

Walking around the room with my USB and touching as many as 18 student computers could easily take an hour or so. However, I've created scripts to load these materials onto the systems for the different courses. I simply turn on the student computers and launch my script from the instructor computer. A few minutes later, I verify that the script ran successfully and I'm done.

The script ensures that the process is always exactly the same for each student. It also saves me a lot of time and effort.

Scheduling a Batch File

Once a batch file is created, it can be scheduled to run at any time. Exercise 3.6 shows how the batch file (ListPatches.bat) created in the previous exercise can be scheduled. This exercise assumes the \\srv1\Patches share exists as mentioned in the previous exercise.

EXERCISE 3.6

Scheduling a Batch File

1. Launch Windows Explorer, and create a folder named **Scripts** in the C: drive.

2. Copy the ListPatches.bat file created in the previous exercise to the C:\Scripts folder.

3. Launch the Task Scheduler by clicking Start, typing **Task** in the search box, and selecting Task Scheduler from the search results. You can also access the Task Scheduler from the Administrative Tools menu.

4. When Task Scheduler launches, select Create Basic Task from the Action pane on the right of the window.

5. Name the task **Document Patches** and put in a description if desired. Click Next.

6. On the Trigger page, select Weekly and click Next.

7. Select Thursday and set the time to 3:00 PM to cause the script to run every Thursday afternoon at 3:00. Click Next.

8. On the Action page, select Start A Program and click Next.

9. Browse to C:\Scripts and select the ListPatches.bat file you copied to this location earlier. Click Next.

10. Select the check box "Open the Properties dialog for this task when I click Finish" and then click Finish.

11. The Properties page will appear with the General tab selected. Click the Change User Or Group button.

12. Enter **System** as the user and click OK. This will cause the script to run using the System account instead of your account. Your display will look similar to the following graphic. Click OK.

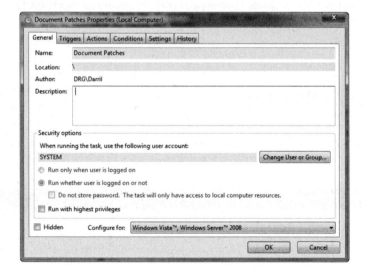

13. Test your task using the following steps:

   a. Select Task Scheduler Library within the Task Scheduler, and locate your task.

   b. Right-click your task and select Run. Notice that you won't get any feedback indicating success or failure of the task.

   c. Select the History tab of the task in the middle pane. It should show that the task completed with a time stamp.

   d. Browse to the Patches share. Verify that the file has been copied to this share.

Note that you can use this script on as many computers as you like within your network to document the patches that are currently installed. If you need to verify that a certain patch has been installed on a certain computer, it's as simple as accessing the share and opening the text file to get your answer.

Of course, that's a lot of steps to create the task on all of your computers. If only there was a way to automate this process. How about a script? Exercise 3.7 shows how you can automate the process of adding this scheduled task to other computers.

EXERCISE 3.7

Creating Scheduled Tasks with a Script

1. If Task Scheduler isn't open, open it and access the Document Patches task you created in the previous exercise.

2. Right-click the task and select Export. Browse to the C:\Scripts folder, and name the file **DocumentPatches.xml**.

3. Create a batch file named **CreateTask.bat** in the C:\Scripts folder using Notepad. Enter the following text as a single line in Notepad:

    ```
    Schtasks /create /tn NewDocPatches /xml c:\Scripts\DocumentPatches.xml
    ```

    This uses the command-line program Schtasks. The /create switch specifies that you are creating a task. The /tn switch is required to name the task, and although I named it NewDocPatches, you can give it any name desired. The /xml switch specifies that the task will be created from an XML file and the full path of the .xml file is used.

4. Launch a Command Prompt window with administrator permissions (right-click Command Prompt and select Run As Administrator).

5. Change the path to the C:\Scripts folder with the CD command:

    ```
    CD \Scripts
    ```

6. Type **CreateTask** and press Enter.

7. Return to Task Scheduler, and you'll see that this additional task has been created on your system. Feel free to delete the task by right-clicking it and selecting Delete.

This batch file can be run on any system where you want the task added. Chapters 5 and 10, "Managing Windows 7 with Group Policy," cover Group Policy in depth. You'll see how Group Policy can be used to configure a script to run on all of your computers without ever touching them. In other words, you could configure this task to run on all of the computers in your enterprise using Group Policy.

Just a Glimpse

Remember, this chapter is not intended to make you an expert on the command prompt. There's no way it can. Entire books are written on the command prompt, and there's no way this half of a chapter can hold the entire contents of a book.

Just as the angel (Don Cheadle) tells Nicholas Cage in *Family Man*, this is "just a glimpse." It provides you with a glimpse of the possibilities. What you do with this glimpse is up to you.

> Now that you have a taste of the some of the things that you can do from the command prompt, you may want to do more. Microsoft maintains an excellent page named "Command-line Reference A-Z" that you can access to view here: http://technet.microsoft.com/library/cc778084.aspx

Using Windows PowerShell and the PowerShell ISE

Windows PowerShell is an extensible version of the command prompt. It is integrated with the Microsoft .NET Framework, which gives it extensive capabilities well beyond the command prompt. Windows 7 comes with Windows PowerShell 2.0 installed (the same version that's installed on Windows Server 2008 R2).

The PowerShell commands can be used to perform and automate many administrative tasks such as managing services, managing event logs, modifying the Registry, and interacting with Windows Management Instrumentation. PowerShell was designed with scripting in mind, so you'll find that you can create elegant scripts that can automate many of your administrative tasks.

One of the challenges with PowerShell is that it is so rich in capabilities and features that it can be intimidating. However, you can start using it without understanding everything about it. You can learn as you go.

> You'll get the most out of this section if you're able to launch PowerShell, execute the commands, and see them in action. You can launch Power-Shell normally or with administrative permissions. To launch it with administrative permissions, you'd right-click and select Run As Administrator. However, I strongly recommend that you launch it normally unless you need specifically to use administrative permissions (such as when you need to change the execution policy, as shown later in this chapter).

Just as the command prompt has its own environment, PowerShell too has its own environment. It also has a distinctive look and feel. Launch it and see for yourself by clicking Start ➢ All Programs ➢ Accessories ➢ Windows PowerShell ➢ Windows PowerShell.

While the look and feel are a little different, you can right-click the title bar and have access to the same menu as the command prompt. You can also copy and paste to and from the PowerShell window and enable QuickEdit mode, so this is a little easier. Copy and paste works exactly the same as shown with the command prompt earlier in this chapter.

In addition to the Windows PowerShell, you'll see the *Windows PowerShell ISE*, which is the Integrated Scripting Environment (ISE). If you're running a 64-bit system, you'll see the following four choices:

- Windows PowerShell (x86)
- Windows PowerShell ISE (x86)
- Windows PowerShell
- Windows PowerShell IS

I haven't run across any issues using the 64-bit Windows PowerShell and ISE for all my scripts, but if you need to step down to the 32-bit version, you can.

Windows PowerShell ISE

The Windows PowerShell Integrated Scripting Environment can be used just as easily as the Windows PowerShell prompt, but it gives you a lot more capabilities. Figure 3.2 shows the PowerShell ISE.

FIGURE 3.2   Windows PowerShell ISE

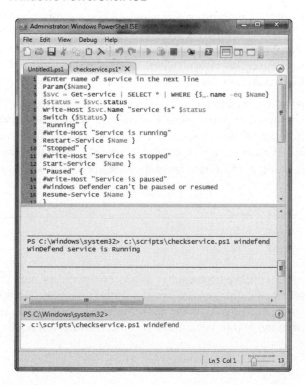

You can see that it has a familiar menu across the top just like any other Windows application. Below the menu are several icons. As with other applications, you can hover your mouse over the icon to see the name. The most common icons you'll use are Save, Run Script, and Run Selection. The Run Script icon is the right-arrow icon, and if you highlight any text, the icon next to it will be enabled so that you execute the text that you've highlighted.

The middle pane shows the output of the script. The bottom pane is the PowerShell prompt. Any commands you can enter at the PowerShell prompt can also be entered at the prompt in the bottom pane. You can even save the script you're writing and execute it using the full path and name from this prompt.

At the bottom right, you'll notice some status that can be very useful. Right now, I have the cursor at the beginning of line 5, and the status shows it at "Ln5 Col 1." Sometimes, an error message will indicate there's an error at "line 43, col 17." Using the ISE, it's easy to determine exactly what the error refers to by using this status information.

Last, you can easily zoom in to make the text bigger or smaller. Currently, it's set at 13, but you can move the pointer at the bottom of the screen to the right to increase the size or to the left to decrease the size. As you play around with PowerShell, feel free to use either the PowerShell interface or the PowerShell ISE.

PowerShell Commands

PowerShell includes three types of commands that can be executed or scripted:

Cmdlets   PowerShell *cmdlets* are built-in commands. They are different from command-prompt commands in that they are tightly integrated with Microsoft's .NET Framework, providing a much richer set of capabilities. You can think of them as mini-programs. Many cmdlets can accept parameters and return values. Values can be displayed, assigned to variables, or passed to other cmdlets or functions.

As an example, the `Get-Command` cmdlet will retrieve a list of all PowerShell commands. You can modify the command with parameters to alter the results. For example, the following three commands can be used to retrieve a list of only the cmdlets, only the aliases, and only the functions. In these examples, the `Get-Command` cmdlet is being used with the `-CommandType` switch, and `cmdlet`, `alias`, and `function` are the parameters passed to the `Get-Command` cmdlet.

```
Get-Command -CommandType cmdlet
Get-Command -CommandType alias
Get-Command -CommandType function
```

Aliases   An *alias* is another name for a cmdlet. Many command-prompt commands have been rewritten as PowerShell commands. While the actual PowerShell command is different from the command-prompt command, many aliases have been created so that you enter the command-prompt command and it will launch the PowerShell command.

As an example, the CD command-prompt command is used to change the current directory. The PowerShell cmdlet is Set-Location, but CD is recognized as an alias for Set-Location.

Try it. These two commands achieve the same result of changing the current path to the root of the C: drive:

```
CD \
Set-Location \
```

All command-prompt commands have not been rewritten. If you enter a command such as path, which works at the command prompt, you'll see it doesn't work here. You can enter the Get-Alias command to get a list of all the aliases supported within PowerShell.

In addition, some longer cmdlets have been rewritten as aliases. As an example, the Get-WMIObject cmdlet has an alias of gwmi.

Functions   A *function* is a type of command that you can run within PowerShell or PowerShell scripts. They are very similar to cmdlets. They can accept parameters and can return values that are displayed, assigned to variables, or passed to other functions or cmdlets.

A commonly used function is the Help function, which provides help on PowerShell topics and concepts. When executed without a parameter, it provides one set of information. When a valid PowerShell command is added as a parameter (such as Help Get-Command), it provides specific help on the command. Another function that is commonly used is the drive letter (such as C:, D:, and so on). It will change the current PowerShell prompt location to the named drive. You can also create your own functions.

Any of these commands can be executed from the PowerShell prompt or embedded into PowerShell scripts. Also, many server applications (such as Internet Information Services (IIS), Exchange Server 2007, and Exchange Server 2010) are heavily intertwined with PowerShell commands. In other words, what you learn here on Windows 7 will be useful when you're managing servers.

Verbs and Nouns

PowerShell cmdlets are composed of verbs and nouns in the format of verb-noun with the dash (-) separating the two. You may remember from your English classes that verbs denote action and nouns are things. Common PowerShell verbs are Get, Set, and Test. You can combine them with nouns to get information on objects or to set properties on objects.

Earlier, you saw the Set-Location cmdlet that is similar to the command-prompt change directory command (CD). Set is the verb and Location is the noun. Similarly, Get-Service uses the verb Get to retrieve information on services, and Out-File uses the verb Out to send information to a file.

If you can remember Get, Set, and Test, you're halfway there because PowerShell will give you a lot of clues. Try this. Type in **Get-** and then press the Tab key. PowerShell will display each of the legal commands that can be executed starting with Get- (from Get-ACL to Get-WSMan-Instance).

You can do the same thing with the Set and Test verbs. Type in **Set-** and press Tab to see all of the objects (nouns) that can have properties set: Set-ACL to Set-ManQuickConfig. If you type in Test-, you'll be able to tab through the choices from Test-ComputerSecureChannel through Test-WSMan.

Functions don't necessarily follow the verb-noun format but instead are just commands. For example, the E: function will set the current drive to E: by actually calling the Set-Location cmdlet using the parameter E:. However, the Clear-Host function does use a verb-noun format to indicate the host screen (the noun) is being cleared (the verb).

Sending Output to a Text File

Many times you'll want the output of the PowerShell command to be written to a file instead of the screen. This can be especially useful when you're creating documentation. While learning, you may want to send the output of some of these commands so you can read them later. There are two ways to do this.

The first is the same method used with the command prompt using the redirection symbol (>). For example, if you want to send a list of all aliases to a text file named PSAlias.txt and then open the text file, you could use these commands:

```
Get-Alias > PSAlias.txt
Notepad PSAlias.txt
```

PowerShell also uses the Out-File cmdlet to send the output to a file. If you wanted to send a listing of services and their current status to a file, you could use the Get-Service cmdlet and the Out-File cmdlet in the same line.

Just as pipelining can be used at the command line, it can be used in PowerShell. When you want the output of one PowerShell command to be used as the input to another command on the same line, you would separate the commands with the pipe symbol (|), which is typically Shift+backslash (\) on most keyboards. The following shows how this is done:

```
Get-Service | Out-File Service.txt
Notepad Service.txt
```

Of course, if you wanted to save the file to a different location, you could include the full path. For example, you could save the file in the Data folder on the C: drive with this command:

```
Get-Service | Out-File C:\Data\Service.txt
```

PowerShell Syntax

Many of the rules that apply to the command prompt also apply to PowerShell. As a reminder, here are some of these rules:

- Spelling counts.
- Commands are not case sensitive.

- Commands are modified with switches.
- Spaces usually need to be enclosed in quotes.
- Help is always available.
- DOSKEY saves typing.

Although these items are the same, there are a couple of other items you should know about PowerShell. These include variables, comparison operators, and command separators (such as parentheses, brackets, and braces) which are all covered in the following sections.

Variables Created with a $ Symbol

Many times, you'll need to create a variable that will be used to store information and later retrieve information. This can be as simple as loading a number (such as 5) into a variable, like this:

```
$num = 5
```

Variables can be used to create a pointer to an object. For example, the following variable is used to store a pointer to an instance of the calculator program (named `calc.exe`):

```
$calc = get-wmiobject -query↵
 "select * from win32_process where name = 'calc.exe'"
```

 NOTE　Even though the previous code is shown on two lines, it would be entered on a single line.

You can also use variables to hold collections of information. Collections can hold several similar items. As an example, the following command will load a list of all the event logs into the variable named $Log and store them as a collection:

```
$Log = Get-EventLog -list
```

Once the collection is created, data about any of the items stored in the collection can be retrieved.

Comparison Operators

You can use many comparison operators to specify or identify a condition. Comparison operators compare two values to determine whether a condition exists. Most comparison operators return True if the condition exists and a False if it doesn't exist.

As a simple example, imagine a variable called $num had a value of 100. The comparison $num -eq 100 would be evaluated as True, while $num -eq 5 would be evaluated as False.

Comparisons don't have to be numbers. They can also be text; however, when comparing text data, the text string needs to be enclosed in quotes. For example, if you wanted to know if a variable named $str has a value of "MCITP," you'd use this comparison:

```
$str -eq "MCITP"
```

String comparisons are case insensitive by default. In other words, both of these would evaluate to True:

```
$str -eq "mcitp"
$str -eq "MCITP"
```

However, if you want the comparison to be case sensitive, you can add the letter c to the operator switch, like this:

```
$str -ceq "True"
```

Table 3.4 lists some of the commonly used comparison operators. You can enter these at the command line to see the result. For example, to see how the -eq command works, you could populate the variable $num with 5 and then use the variable in a comparison like this:

```
$num = 5
$num -eq 100
```

PowerShell will return False.

TABLE 3.4 Comparison operators

Operator	Description
-eq	Equals, as in $x -eq 100 or $x -eq "y"
-ne	Not equal, as in $x -ne 100 or $x -ne "y"
-gt	Greater than, as in $x -gt 100
-ge	Greater than or equal to, as in $x -ge 100
-lt	Less than, as in $x -lt 100
-le	Less than or equal to, as in $x -le 100
-like	Compares strings using the wildcard character * and returns True if a match is found. The wildcard character can be used at the beginning, middle, or end to look for specific matches. If a variable named $str holds the string "MCITP Windows 7," then all of the following comparisons will return True: $str -like "MCITP*" $str -like "*Win*" $str -like "*7"
-notlike	Compares strings using the wildcard character * and returns True if the match is not found.

You'll see comparison operators used in many different ways. For example, they are used in cmdlet switches when a comparison is needed and in IF statements when you're scripting.

Parentheses, Brackets, and Braces

PowerShell commands can include parentheses (( )), brackets ([ ]), and braces ({ }). Braces are also referred to as "curly brackets" and even "funky brackets" by some. Each is interpreted differently within PowerShell.

Parentheses ( )   Parentheses are commonly used to provide arguments. For example, when a script needs to accept a parameter, you can use `Param($input)`. Here the `$input` is identified as an argument for the `Param` command.

> The terms *parameter* and *argument* are often used interchangeably. On one level, they are the same thing; but there is a subtle difference between the two. A parameter is provided as input to a piece of code, and an argument is what is provided. The value is the same but the perspective is different. A parameter is passed in, and the value of this parameter is used as an argument within the code.

Brackets [ ]   Brackets are used for various purposes. You'll see them used when accessing arrays, when using `-like` comparisons, and with some parameters. As an example, the following command uses them to indicate the output should include only names that start with a letter:

```
Get-wmiObject Win32_ComputerSystem | Format-List [a-z]*
```

Braces { }   Braces are used to enclose a portion of code within a statement that is interpreted as a block of code. You'll see them in condition statements (like `ForEach` seen later in the chapter). The following example shows how braces are used to separate the block in the `Where` clause in a single line of code:

```
Get-service | Select * | Where {$_.name -eq $Name}
```

The point here is not that you need to memorize when these characters need to be used. Instead, the goal is to let you know that all three could be used and, when you're executing code and writing scripts, to recognize each. If you replace curly braces with parentheses when you type in your own code, you'll find things simply don't work.

Running PowerShell Scripts

Creating and running PowerShell scripts has a couple of hurdles that can stop you in your tracks if you don't know what they are. They aren't hard to overcome as long as you recognize them. The two issues are

- PowerShell Execution Policy
- Path usage in PowerShell

These issues are explained in the following sections.

PowerShell Execution Policy

Microsoft has embraced a secure-by-default mindset, and this is reflected in the *PowerShell Execution Policy*. This policy has several settings that you can modify to allow or disallow the execution of different types of scripts.

If you don't modify the policy, you'll find that each attempt to execute a PowerShell script will result in an error that says, "The execution of scripts is disabled on this system." This message is telling you that the Execution Policy is set to Restricted, the default setting. There are several possible settings for the Execution Policy:

Restricted The Restricted setting prevents any scripts from being executed and is the default setting. You can still execute individual PowerShell commands.

RemoteSigned It's common to change the Execution Policy to RemoteSigned. This will let you execute any scripts on your local system but will prevent scripts that don't have a digital signature from being executed remotely, such as over an Internet connection.

Signed scripts have a digital signature added to them, which is associated with a code-signing certificate from a trusted publisher. The idea is that if a script is signed with a certificate, you can identify the writer. Since malicious scriptwriters don't want to be known or identified, they won't sign their scripts.

AllSigned This is a little more secure than RemoteSigned. While RemoteSigned will allow the execution of unsigned local scripts, AllSigned will not allow the execution of any unsigned scripts. All scripts must be signed.

Unrestricted Just as it sounds, Unrestricted allows the execution of any scripts. This setting will warn you before running scripts that are downloaded from the Internet.

Bypass This is similar to Unrestricted in that it allows the execution of any scripts; however, it does not give any warnings. This would be used when an application is using scripts, and it wouldn't be able to respond to any warnings.

You can use the following script to determine the current setting for the Execution Policy:

```
Get-ExecutionPolicy
```

You can change the policy using the `Set-ExecutionPolicy` cmdlet with the name of the policy. You must be running Windows PowerShell with administrative permissions to change the Execution Policy. Exercise 3.8 shows how to change the Execution Policy.

EXERCISE 3.8

Changing the Execution Policy

1. Click Start ➢ All Programs ➢ Accessories ➢ Windows PowerShell, right-click Windows PowerShell, and select Run As Administrator.

You may notice that this defaults to a different location. Instead of your user name folder, it defaults to `C:\Windows\System32`.

2. Enter the following command:

    ```
    Set-ExecutionPolicy RemoteSigned
    ```

3. When prompted, type **Y** and press Enter.

4. Enter the following command to verify the policy is changed:

    ```
    Get-ExecutionPolicy
    ```

5. Close the Administrator Windows PowerShell window. If desired, open Windows PowerShell as a regular user.

Looping

Any programming language has the ability to loop through code. This allows it to perform the same action repeatedly without the programmer having to write the code repeatedly.

You'll run across several looping commands in scripts. They are very often used to loop through collections, which are explained in the next section. In each of these looping commands, the code that is executed is included in the curly brackets.

The ForEach command is commonly used in PowerShell in the following format:

```
ForEach (Item in a collection) {
    Code to execute
}
```

You'll see the ForEach loop used in this chapter.

Another looping command that is commonly used is the Do While loop. It will execute code as long as (or while) a condition is met. The format is

```
Do {
    Code to execute
}
While (condition is true)
```

Here's a simple example of how a Do While loop could be used to execute code. It creates a variable named $counter and populates it with the number 0. It then outputs the value using the Write-Host line, increments the counter using $counter++, and then checks the value in the While line.

```
$counter = 0
Do {
Write-Host "Value is" $counter
$counter++
}
While ($counter -lt 5)
```

The output of the code will be five lines that look like this:

```
Value is 0
Value is 1
Value is 2
Value is 3
Value is 4
```

Collections

A collection is a type of an array used to hold information on objects.

Imagine that you have a bucket, and you've placed 10 marbles in the bucket. These marbles are objects and very likely they are different. Some may be clear and others cloudy, some steel and others glass, some small and others large. You get the idea. Each of these marbles has specific properties that can be used to describe it.

Now if you created a spreadsheet, you could list each of the marbles and their associated properties. Later, if you wanted information on a specific marble, you could access the spreadsheet and retrieve the information. In this context, the data in the spreadsheet is the collection that represents the actual objects.

Similarly, with PowerShell you can create a collection of information on objects. You can then use code to loop through the collection.

As an example, consider this code:

```
$colLog = get-EventLog -list
```

The Get-EventLog -list will list information on the EventLogs on a system in five columns: Max(K), Retain, OverflowAction, Entries, and Log. The $colLog = will store the result of the command in the variable named $colLog. While the get-EventLog command will retrieve many logs, imagine there are only five. The collection would look like Table 3.5.

TABLE 3.5 A Collection of Logs

Max(K)	Retain	OverFlowAction	Entries	Log
20,480	0	OverwriteAsNeeded	46,266	Application
20,480	0	OverwriteAsNeeded	53,635	System
20,480	7	OverwriteOlder	2,345	Security
15,360	0	OverwriteAsNeeded	1,206	Session
15,360	0	OverwriteAsNeeded	453	Windows PowerShell

Data stored in the collection can be accessed and retrieved, and it is commonly done so using a ForEach command. As an example, the following script will store the data in a collection and then loop through the collection to retrieve it:

```
$colLog = get-EventLog -list
ForEach ($Item in $colLog) {
Write-Output $Item
}
```

This is actually no different than just executing the Get-EventLog -List command. However, the real strength of the collection is that you can manipulate it. If you were interested in only some of the columns, you could pick and choose what is displayed.

Imagine that all you really want to know is the log name and its size. These two columns have headers of Log and Max(K) (though Max(K) is identified as MaximumKilobytes). Each item in the collection can be identified using these names. Because the script uses $Item as the variable name to hold the collection, the columns would be identified as $Item.Property. In other words, $Item.Log retrieves the log name and $Item.MaximumKilobytes retrieves the Max(K) value.

```
$colLog = get-EventLog -list
ForEach ($Item in $ColLog) {
Write-Output $Item.Log, $Item.MaximumKilobytes
}
```

However, this is pretty messy. Instead of outputting the data as a table, it sends each item on a single line. You'll see later in the chapter how this can be cleaned up using the -f formatting switch.

Creating a PowerShell Script

With the basics out of the way, it's time to walk through the creation of some basic scripts using the Windows PowerShell Integrated Scripting environment. Exercise 3.9 assumes you have modified the Execution Policy so that scripts can be run.

EXERCISE 3.9

Creating and Running a PowerShell Script

1. Launch the Windows PowerShell ISE.

2. Click in the top pane (labeled Untitled1.ps1), type in the following text, and press Enter:

   ```
   Get-EventLog -List
   ```

   Notice the command doesn't execute when you press Enter but instead starts a line 2.

EXERCISE 3.9 *(continued)*

3. Click the green button to run the script. You can also press F5. You'll see the result displayed in the middle pane. If there is a syntax error, you'll see a red text error instead of black text as the output.

   If you do see a red error message, look for these characters: <<<<. They will often point to the specific string of text that is causing the problem.

4. Click the Save icon on the menu (or press Ctrl+S). Browse to a folder named C:\ Scripts (create it if you need to), and change Untitled to **LogInfo** to save the script as C:\Scripts\LogInfo.ps1.

5. Move your cursor to the bottom of the screen, type **C:\Scripts\LogInfo.ps1**, and press Enter. The script will execute.

6. Change the current location to the script file with this command:

   Set-Location C:\Scripts.

7. Try to run the script with this command (it will fail):

   LogInfo.ps1

   Even though the script is in the current path, PowerShell needs a hint to find it.

8. Press the up arrow, and modify the last command so it looks like this:

   .\LogInfo.ps1

   The .\ characters tell PowerShell the script is in the current path.

At this point, you've created and executed a PowerShell script. If it's the first time, feel free to yell out, "Woo hoo!" However, you may want to create a script that has a little more value.

Exercise 3.10 shows how the ForEach loop can be used to loop through a collection.

EXERCISE 3.10

Modifying a Script Using a ForEach Loop

1. Click File ➢ New to create a blank area to work with a new script.

2. Enter the following text, and press F5 to execute it.

   get-service | select-object name, status

   This lists all the services on the system by name and their current status (such as running or stopped).

3. Instead of outputting this data to the screen, you can store it in a collection. The following command will store the result in a collection named $colService. Notice that you don't have to retype the entire command, but instead you just add $colService = to the beginning of the line:

```
$colService = Get-service | select-object
    name, status
```

4. Now add a ForEach loop to loop through the collection. The loop will check each service stored in the collection and then use the Write-Host cmdlet to display only the services with a status equal to "running".

```
ForEach ($item in $colService)  {
    If ($item.status -eq "running")
    {write-host $item.name}
}
```

Similarly, you could use the same method to list all the services that are stopped by simply changing "running" to "stopped" in the script.

While this example does show how a ForEach loop can be used to loop through a collection, it's not the only way to get a list of running services. As with most scripts, there's more than one way to get what you need. For example, the following one-liner could also be used to get a list of running services:

```
Get-Service | Select name, status |  where {$_.status -eq "running"}
```

Documenting Scripts

It's worth your time to spend a few minutes documenting your scripts. You can do it while you're creating the scripts or spend a couple of minutes when you've finished, but in either case it'll save you some headaches later. Documentation is done by adding comment lines, which start with a # character in PowerShell (or by using REM, short for remarks, in batch files).

When you write a good script, it'll automate a job for you, and you may not have to touch it again for six months. I don't know about you, but if I haven't touched something in six months, I just don't remember it as well. However, by adding a few lines here and there, I'm quickly able to remember what I did and why I did it.

Documentation in scripts starts with a few lines at the beginning that could be like this:

```
#Script written Sep 2009 by Darril Gibson
#Purpose. Checks status of service.
#Expects Display Name of service
# as a parameter ($Name)
```

Notes can also be embedded within the script. This is often done when the script includes large blocks of code. These notes are easy to add while you're writing and debugging the script and don't need to be complex.

Using PowerShell Commands

Instead of giving you a laundry list of all the commands, my goal instead is to use the limited space in this chapter to give you some examples of commands you may find useful. I also hope to give you some information that will easily translate to other commands to allow you to expand your knowledge. You'll see some other PowerShell commands in other areas of this book.

When you're ready to learn more, you can pick up one of the complete books on PowerShell or visit the TechNet Script Center Gallery (`http://gallery.technet.microsoft.com/ScriptCenter`) for more commands and scripts.

> Microsoft hosts a site titled "Hey, Scripting Guy!" where you can find a wealth of information, tutorials, and examples of different types of scripts, including PowerShell scripts. There are actually two scripting guys (Ed Wilson and Craig Liebendorfer). You can find their column and archives here: `http://www.microsoft.com/technet/scriptcenter/resources/qanda/all.mspx`.

If you want to create your own list of all the commands and document them in text files you can review periodically, try these commands:

```
Get-Command -CommandType cmdlet | Out-File cmdlets.txt
Get-Command -CommandType alias | Out-File alias.txt
Get-Command -CommandType function | Out-File function.txt
Get-Command | Out-File Commands.txt
```

As a reminder, you don't need to type in everything when entering PowerShell commands. PowerShell will give you some help. As an example, the first command in the previous list could be typed in like this:

- First, type in only **Get-Co** and then press the Tab key twice to see the command:

  ```
  Get-Command
  ```

- Press the spacebar, enter the dash (-) symbol, type in **C**, and press the Tab key to see it become

  ```
  Get-Command -CommandType
  ```

- Press the spacebar, type in **cmdlet**, the pipe symbol (|), **Out-F**, and press the Tab key once to get

  ```
  Get-Command -CommandType cmdlet | Out-File
  ```

- Last, type in the name of the file as **cmdlets.txt**.

Getting Help on PowerShell

You'll find a rich set of help available to you within PowerShell. What I've found is that many people are uneasy about using the help provided from the command prompt or PowerShell. However, this help has become much richer in recent years.

If you overlook it, you'll be missing a lot. Here are some of the commands you can use to retrieve the available help:

Help or Get-Help   This will display generic help information on how to execute help commands and their results. Both Help and Get-Help will work.

Get-Help commandName   You can request help on any PowerShell command by simply typing in Help and the command name. The command can be a cmdlet, a function, or an alias.

When you request help for an alias, it provides help on the associated cmdlets. As an example, if you type in Get-Help dir, it will return help on the Get-Children cmdlet since dir is an alias for Get-Children.

Get-Help commandName -examples   Examples are only a few keystrokes away just by adding the -examples switch to your Get-Help request. For example, you can use the following command to see examples with descriptions of the Get-Service command. There are several pages, so adding the More command will allow you to view a page at a time. Press the spacebar to scroll to the next page.
```
Get-Help Get-Service -Examples | More
```

Get-Help commandName -detailed   The -detailed switch can be used to provide more detailed help than the basic help command. It will include examples.

Get-Help commandName -full   The -full switch provides all of the available help on the topic. This will often provide more information on parameters used within the command.

Many help files are available from PowerShell that provide more information about specific topics and are referred to as "about" topics. For example, if you want information on the pipelines command, you can enter Help about_pipelines. To see a full listing of all of these "about" topics, enter help about.

Using WMI_Cmdlets

Windows Management Instrumentation is used on many administrator applications to automate the process of retrieving information on computers or taking action on computers.

As a simple example, different applications are used to deploy updates to clients, but they often first checked to see if the update has already been deployed. WMI is used to query the computer to determine if the update is deployed. Applications such as Windows Server Update Services (WSUS), Microsoft Systems Management Server (SMS), and System Center Configuration Manager (SCCM) all use WMI regularly.

PowerShell includes a full set of WMI cmdlets that can be used to retrieve information on systems just as they do on applications. One of the challenges with these is that there is so much that can be done that it's easy to get overwhelmed by the complexity. However, if you understand how a few of them work, you'll easily be able to use the concepts you've learned and branch off in different directions.

First, when querying WMI objects, you need to include an extra parameter that includes the class and the name of the object that you want to query. As an example, the Win32_ Share class includes the name of the class (Win32) and the name of the object type (Share).

Classes and objects sometimes confuse people. You can think of a class as a blueprint, similar to a blueprint for a house. You can't live in a blueprint. Similarly, a class isn't an actual object but the definition for an object. When a folder is shared, it's viewed by WMI as a share object, and the Win32_Share class can be used to query information on this share object.

 There are too many classes in the Win32 Class family to list here. However, if you want to see a full list, check out this link: http://msdn.microsoft.com/library/aa394084.aspx.

Win32 classes are the primary classes used to query and work with Windows-based operating systems. There are hundreds of objects in this class, but here's a small sampling: Win32_Account, Win32_BIOS, Win32_ComputerSystem, Win32_SystemEvent, Win32_CurrentTime, Win32_DiskQuota, Win32_Group, Win32_LogicalDisk, Win32_ NetworkAdapter, Win32_NTEventLogFile, Win32_OperatingSystem, Win32_Printer, Win32_ Process, Win32_Service, and Win32_Session.

A logical question is, "What do each of these do?" The simplest answer is, "Ask PowerShell with a query."

Getting Details on an Object

You can query information from any of these classes with the Get-wmiObject cmdlet. This command will provide basic information on the queried object and looks like this for the Win32_ComputerSystem class.

```
Get-wmiObject Win32_ComputerSystem
```

The output on one of my systems is

```
Domain               : WORKGROUP
Manufacturer         : Dell Inc.
Model                : Dell DM051
Name                 : DARRIL-PC
PrimaryOwnerName     : Darril
TotalPhysicalMemory  : 3756154880
```

The Get-wmiObject cmdlet has its own alias of gwmi. Instead of typing in the entire command, you can substitute it with gwmi whenever desired. For example, the following two commands are interpreted the same:

```
Get-wmiObject Win32_ComputerSystem
gwmi Win32_ComputerSystem
```

You can use the same command for any Win32 class to see what type of information is provided.

You can also modify what information is provided. For example, by adding the Format-List cmdlet, you'll see significantly more detail on the queried object. Instead of just a few commonly used properties, it will list all of the properties:

```
Get-wmiObject Win32_ComputerSystem | Format-List *
```

If you execute these commands, you may notice that some of the properties start with two underscores (such as __Genus, __Class, and so on). These are used by the system and are referred to as system classes. If you want to eliminate them, you can use the following command to list properties that start with a letter:

```
Get-wmiObject Win32_ComputerSystem | Format-List [a-z]*
```

Querying Information on Specific Objects

If you tried to retrieve information on some of the other Win32 classes, you may have been a little overwhelmed by the results, especially if you included the | Format-List cmdlet. For example, if you queried the Win32_Service class (using Get-wmiObject Win32_Service), it would have scrolled through several screens. This is because it's querying every instance of the object on your system.

If you query the Win32_Computersystem class, it retrieves only information on your system. However, the Win32_Service class will query information on every single instance of a service on your system.

Many times, instead of retrieving all of the information about all the objects, you may want only information on a specific object. As an example, here's how you can use the -query switch to retrieve information about a specific service.

Imagine that you only want to see if the Windows Defender (`WinDefend`) service is running. You can use this query:

```
Get-WmiObject -query "Select * From Win32_service Where name ='WinDefend'"
```

The `Select` statement in the query starts by saying that you want to retrieve all columns (using the * as a wildcard). Next, it identifies the class `Win32_Service` as the source in the `From` clause. Last, it uses a `Where` clause to identify the name of the service. You should be aware of a couple of rules here:

- The entire `Select` statement must be enclosed in double quotes.

- String data used in comparisons must be enclosed in single quotes (as in `'WinDefend'`).

- The `Select` statement uses symbols (such as = for equals) for comparison operators instead of the comparison switches used in PowerShell commands (such as `-eq` for equals).

You may be wondering how I knew that the Windows Defender service is named `WinDefend`. Well I didn't, but I knew a couple of ways to determine the name. If I knew the common name was Windows Defender, I could have used the PowerShell command `Get-Service "Windows Defender"` to display the status, name, and DisplayName to see this result:

```
Status    Name        DisplayName
------    ----        -----------
Running   WinDefend   Windows Defender
```

Or, I could have looked in the Services applet and identified the service name on the General tab, as shown in Figure 3.3.

FIGURE 3.3   Viewing the service name in the Services applet

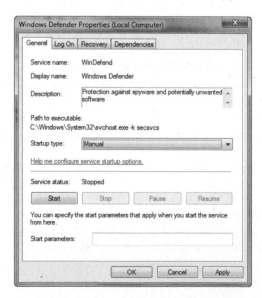

Similarly, you may be interested in knowing if the Windows Defender service is running on a remote computer named WS23. You could use this command:

```
Get-WmiObject -query↵
  "select * from Win32_service where name ='WinDefend'" -computername WS23
```

> Even though the previous code is shown on two lines, it would be entered on a single line.

The only extra that is added is the -computername switch and the name of the remote computer. If you don't have another computer to query right now, you can query your own system. Type **hostname** and press Enter to determine the name of your system, and substitute WS23 with your system's name.

> While you can query your local computer without invoking administrator rights, you must have local administrator rights on remote computers that you want to query using WMI. If you don't have local admin rights, access will be denied.

Killing Applications with Win32_process

You may come across an application that occasionally causes a problem and needs to be terminated. You can do so with the Remove_WmiObject cmdlet. However, before you terminate the application, you'll need to identify it in a variable.

Exercise 3.11 shows how this cmdlet can be used to terminate an application.

EXERCISE 3.11

Using the Remove_WmiObject

1. Launch an instance of PowerShell.

2. Type **calc** and press Enter to launch an instance of the calculator.

3. Return the focus to PowerShell and enter the following line:

   ```
   $calc = get-wmiobject -query "select * from win32_process where name = 'calc.exe'"
   ```

   This line identifies the process running the calculator application and stores this information in the variable $calc.

4. Enter the following command to retrieve the handle to the application, and then terminate the application with the Remove-Wmi-Object cmdlet:

   ```
   $calc | Remove-WmiObject
   ```

Formatting Output with the -f Format Operator

The -f format operator is a neat tool you can use to control how output is displayed in a script. Using the -f operator, you first identify the column format and then identify what will be in the column. The basic format is

```
"{0,jp} {1,jp}" -f $Item.itemx, $Item.y
```

The format of all of the columns is enclosed in the quotes, with each individual column enclosed in braces. The first column is 0, the second column is 1, and so on. Within the column definition, you specify whether it should be right or left justified and the number of characters the column should have. For right justification, the number is positive (such as 30); for left justification, the number is negative (such as -30).

As an example, if you want the first column to be left justified with 30 characters and the second column to be right justified with 15 characters, you'd use this to define the columns:

```
"{0,-30} {1,15}"
```

Earlier in the chapter, you saw this code create a collection of the event logs and then loop through them using a ForEach loop, like this:

```
$colLog = get-EventLog -list
ForEach ($Item in $ColLog) {
Write-Output $Item.Log, $Item.MaximumKilobytes
}
```

However, the output wasn't pretty. You can use the -f format operator to identify how the columns should be formatted. The full script would then look like this:

```
$colLog = get-EventLog -list
ForEach ($Item in $ColLog) {
"{0,-30} {1,15}" -f $Item.Log, $Item.MaximumKilobytes
}
```

Notice that with the -f operator, you don't need to include the Write-Output clause. Listing 3.5 shows the output on my system.

Listing 3.5: Output using the -f operator

```
Application                        20480
DFS Replication                    15168
HardwareEvents                     20480
Internet Explorer                    512
Key Management Service             20480
Media Center                        8192
```

```
ODiag                        16384
OSession                     16384
Security                       512
System                       20480
Windows PowerShell           15360
```

You can use the -f format operator to format as many columns as desired.

 If you want to explore the -f format operator more, check out this comprehensive blog by Thomas Lee: http://tfl09.blogspot.com/2007/11/formatting-with-powershell.html

Filtering the Output with the Where-Object Command

There are times when you don't want to see all the data, but instead you wish to see only a subset of the data that meets a certain condition. You could use the Where-Object command (which has an alias of Where) to filter the result.

In the following code, the Where clause is used to retrieve a list of only the logs that have a Max(K) value greater than 15168. Notice the use of $_. The first command, Get-EventLog, creates a collection of event logs that is then piped to the Where clause. The $_ refers to this collection, and a period can then be added to reference any of the properties of the objects in the collection.

```
Get-EventLog -list | Where {$_.MaximumKilobytes -gt 15168}
```

Notice that the entire condition is enclosed in braces ({ }).

Similarly, here's a method you can use to list only services that start with the letter *S* using the -like operator. Notice that the asterisk (*) is used as the wildcard, and the string you're searching for must be in double quotes:

```
Get-Service | Select name, service, status |  where {$_.name -like "S*"}
```

Using the IF statement

Occasionally, you'll want to check for a specific condition and, if the condition is met, execute some code. You can use the IF statement. The basic syntax of the IF statement is

```
If (condition 1)
  { execute code }
Elseif  (condition 2)
  { execute code }
Else
  { execute code }
```

The `Where-Object` filter could be rewritten using a ForEach loop with an IF clause, like this:

```
$colLog = get-EventLog -list
ForEach ($Item in $ColLog) {
If ($Item.MaximumKilobytes -gt 15168) {
"{0,-30} {1,15}" -f $Item.Log, $Item.MaximumKilobytes }
}
```

The collection of logs is stored in the `$colLog` variable. The `ForEach` loop loops through each log in the collection and includes an IF statement. Notice that the IF statement has a condition (enclosed in parentheses), and the statement (or statements) to execute when the condition is true is enclosed in a set of curly braces ({ }).

When using the IF statement, you can include as many statements as desired within the curly braces. When the condition is met, all the statements in the curly braces will be executed.

The following code checks to see the status of the `eventlog` service and includes the `Elseif` and `Else` clauses. If the service is running, it outputs `"Running"`. If the service is not running, it checks to see if it is stopped and, if so, outputs `"Stopped"`. If it's not running or stopped, it'll output a line indicating the service is not running or stopped (indicating it is paused).

```
$service = Get-Service |
 Select name, service, status |  where {$_.name -like "eventlog"}
If ($service.status = "Running")
{Write-Host "Running"}
Elseif ($service.status = "Stopped" )
{Write-Host "Stopped"}
Else
{Write-Host "Service not stopped or running"}
```

Using the Switch Statement

While the IF statement is useful when choosing between one or two options, when you start choosing between many options, it becomes very cumbersome with all of the IF ELSEIF ELSE clauses. A solution is the `Switch` statement, which is very valuable when you want to take one of many possible choices.

If you've done programming with other scripting or compiled languages, you may have run across the Case statement. If you know the Case statement, you know the `Switch` statement—just by another name. The `Switch` statement in PowerShell works just like the Case statement in other languages.

The Switch statement uses the value of a variable to determine which action to take. The basic syntax is

```
$switchVar
Switch ($switchVar) {
Value1 {"action for this value"}
Value2 {"action for this value"}
Value3 {"action for this value"}
}
```

Exercise 3.12 walks through an example of the Switch statement using the PowerShell ISE. This example will show you how to determine the state of a service and then take different actions based on the state.

EXERCISE 3.12

Using the Switch Statement

1. Launch an instance of the PowerShell ISE.

2. Enter the following command in the top pane, and press F5 to execute it. Note that you can use the Tab key to save some typing, just as you can in PowerShell.

    ```
    $Name = "WinDefend"
    Get-service | Select * | Where {$_.name -eq $Name }
    ```

    This will return the details on the Windows Defender service.

3. Now modify the command to populate the $svc variable with the results as a collection by adding $svc = to the beginning of the command. It will look like this:

    ```
    $svc = Get-service | Select * | Where {$_.name -eq $Name }
    ```

4. Next, create a variable named $status and populate it with the status of Windows Defender (which is stored in the $svc collection as $svc.status) with this line. If desired, you can use the Write-host command to show you the status and execute the entire script.

    ```
    $status = $svc.status
    Write-Host $svc.Name "Service is" $status
    ```

5. Next, create the Switch statement using the $Status variable.

    ```
    Switch ($Status)  {
    "Running" {Write-Host "Service is running"}
    "Stopped" {Write-Host "Service is stopped"}
    "Paused"{Write-Host "Service is paused"}
    }
    ```

6. Execute the script. You may not want the first Write-Host line to execute, so you can "comment it out" by placing the # symbol at the beginning of the line. Why would you comment it out and not delete it? You may want to easily add it in later for debugging purposes, and it is easier to delete the # character than it is to type in the whole line again. Your display will look similar to the following graphic.

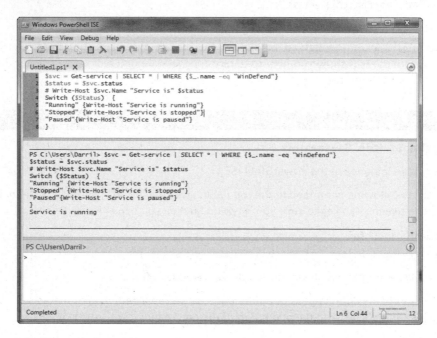

7. Instead of just displaying the status, you may want to take an action. For example, if it's stopped, you can start it by adding this line in the "Stopped" section:

```
Start-Service $Name
```

8. You can also run only part of your script in the ISE. Use your mouse to highlight only the following part of the first line in the top of the ISE:

```
Get-service | Select * | Where {$_.name -eq $Name
```

You can click the Run Selection icon (next to the Run Script icon) or press the F8 key to run only the highlighted text.

9. At this point you should save the script. Click the Save icon. Browse to C:\Scripts and save it as **CheckService.ps1**.

10. Execute the script file using the bottom pane of the ISE by typing the following and pressing Enter:

```
c:\scripts\CheckService.ps1
```

Script Reusability

You may be wondering why I used the variable $Name in the script used in the previous exercise. After all, instead of these two lines:

```
$Name = "WinDefend"
Get-service | Select * | Where {$_.name -eq $Name }
```

I could have used just this line:

```
Get-service | Select * | Where {$_.name -eq "WinDefend }
```

The reason is for script reusability. Although this code was written for the Windows Defender service, it can easily be used for any service. The only thing that needs to change is the name of the service.

For example, if I wanted to use this for a different service, such as the Print Spooler service, I'd just need to identify the name of the Print Spooler service (Spooler) and put it in place of "WinDefend" in the $Name = "WinDefend" line as $Name = "Spooler".

It's even possible to use the Param command to allow the script to accept a parameter. In other words, I can name my script CheckService and program it to accept the name of a service as Param($svc). I could check the Windows Defender service with the command CheckService WinDefend or the Print Spooler service with the command CheckService Spooler.

To put it all together, I added a couple of extra touches to this script. This script checks to see if the service is running, and if so, it restarts it (which can sometimes be useful for services that hang, like the Print Spooler service). If the service is stopped, it will be started. If it is paused, it'll be resumed.

Listing 3.6 shows it in full.

Listing 3.6: Check status of service

```
#Script written Sep 2009 by Darril Gibson
#Purpose. Checks status of service.
# Restarts if running, starts if stopped,
# and resumes if paused.
#Expects Display Name of service
# as a parameter ($Name)
Param($Name)
$svc = Get-service | Select * | Where {$_.name -eq $Name}
$status = $svc.status
# Write-Host $svc.Name "service is" $status
Switch ($Status) {
"Running" {Restart-Service $Name }
"Stopped" { Start-Service  $Name }
"Paused" {
#Windows Defender can't be paused or resumed
Resume-Service $Name }
}
```

Notice the use of the `Param` command. Instead of hard-coding the name of the service, it accepts a parameter (such as `WinDefend` or `Spooler`). The `Param` command must be the very first executable line (comments can precede it). You would execute the script from PowerShell as

```
c:\scripts\CheckService.ps1 WinDefend
```

The script can also be called from other programs including Task Scheduler, as was shown with a batch file earlier in the chapter.

However, you'll find that this script won't work completely unless you run it with elevated permissions. For example, if the Windows Defender service is running, the script will try to restart it but can't because it doesn't have permissions. Instead, launch the script from a PowerShell window with elevated permissions by selecting Run As Administrator or execute it with the System account when executed from a program such as Task Scheduler.

Well, that's a taste of Windows PowerShell. Don't expect to walk away with a full understanding of everything that can be done with PowerShell. However, if you come across any PowerShell commands or scripts, they should make a little more sense to you.

Summary

In this chapter, you learned about both the command prompt and Windows PowerShell. There are many similarities between the two, and both are heavily used by administrators. The biggest reason why people take the time learn these tools is so that they can write or modify scripts.

Anything that can be executed from the command line can be scripted. Anything that can be scripted can be automated through tools such as the Task Scheduler. Once you get comfortable with some scripting and start writing your own scripts, you'll realize that there are very few limitations on what you can do.

Chapter Essentials

Using the Windows command prompt Be familiar with the command prompt. The command prompt is a separate interface from the typical Windows GUI where commands are typed at the command prompt. Many commands exist that can be used to perform a wide array of tasks.

Know how to cut and paste to and from the Command Prompt window. Typical shortcuts of Ctrl+C (copy) and Ctrl+V (paste) don't work in the command prompt, but instead you can access the Edit menu by right-clicking the title bar.

Know how to create a batch file. Any command that can be entered at the command prompt can be put into a basic script file called a batch file. Batch files end with a .bat extension and can be executed. When the batch file is executed, all the commands in the batch file will be executed.

Be familiar with how to schedule a task, including how to schedule a script. Any executable file (including batch and script files) can be scheduled to run at certain times using the Task Scheduler. Once a script file has been created and scheduled, the task becomes fully automated.

Using Windows Windows PowerShell and the PowerShell ISE   Know how to launch and use Windows PowerShell. Windows PowerShell is an extension of the command prompt. It's integrated into the Microsoft .NET Framework and provides access to significantly more capabilities. PowerShell commands take the form of a verb-noun such as Get-Alias, which gets (the verb) a listing of each alias command (the noun). Three common verbs are Get, Set, and Test. By entering the verb and a dash (such as Get-), you can tab through all available nouns that can be combined with the verb to form cmdlets.

Use Windows PowerShell to get basic help. A significant amount of help is available. Get-Help retrieves generic information. Get-Help Command retrieves information on any specific command. The -examples, -detailed, and -full switches can be added to provide additional help for any command.

Know how to launch and use the Windows PowerShell ISE. Windows 7 includes a full-featured integrated scripting environment called the Windows PowerShell ISE. It can be used to create, debug, test, and execute scripts.

Be familiar with the PowerShell Execution Policy and what you must do to execute scripts. Scripts won't run by default in Windows 7. Instead, you must first modify the Execution Policy. The Execution Policy is set to Restricted by default and will prevent any scripts from being executed. It's common to change this to RemoteSigned, so that local scripts can be executed. However, remote scripts cannot be executed unless they are signed.

Be familiar with basic PowerShell scripts. PowerShell scripts include many features of other scripting languages, including variables, looping, and the ability to accept parameters. When executing scripts, the full path should be used. Scripts in the current path need either the full path or .\ preceding the script name.

Chapter

4

Managing the Life Cycle— Keeping Windows 7 Up to Date

TOPICS COVERED IN THIS CHAPTER INCLUDE

- ✓ Keeping Windows up to date
- ✓ Choosing an update tool
- ✓ Using MBSA for security audits
- ✓ Using Windows Server Update Services

Once you have Windows 7 installed and running in the enterprise, you'll need to keep it up to date. Thankfully, several tools are available to manage updates in the enterprise. Updates include additions to both the operating system and the applications that are issued after the release of such products.

The first decision is which tool to use. For small enterprises with fewer than 50 users, you can use Automatic Updates to download and install updates automatically on all the clients. For larger enterprises with a limited budget, you can use Windows Server Update Services (WSUS). Or, if your organization has the resources, it can purchase the enterprise application System Center Configuration Manager (SCCM), which can be used to schedule the deployment of updates.

The Microsoft Baseline Security Analyzer (MBSA) is a powerful tool that can be used to audit the security of clients in the enterprise, including the deployment of updates. MBSACLI is the command-line equivalent of MBSA that can be scripted and scheduled to automate the auditing process.

WSUS is a popular free product that can be installed on a server to manage updates in the enterprise centrally, and you're likely to see this in most enterprises. You'll learn how to install it in this chapter, and once WSUS is installed, you can review, approve, and deploy updates to computers with just a few clicks.

Keeping Windows Up to Date

Although Chapter 1, "Planning for the Installation of Windows 7," and Chapter 2, "Automating the Deployment of Windows 7," covered deploying Windows 7 and handling migrations, this marks only the beginning of the life cycle. You'll also need to keep the systems up to date. Keeping a system up to date includes updating the operating system and the software applications.

Updates are additions to the system or software that are issued after the official release. A critical use of updates is to distribute patches for security issues. Ideally, software wouldn't have any bugs or be vulnerable to any type of security breaches, but the truth is that software is inherently insecure.

You keep Windows secure by keeping it up to date. Updates related to security are labeled as *security updates* and also as Important updates. Microsoft releases security updates on the second Tuesday of each month (commonly called Patch Tuesday) and occasionally releases urgent updates at other times (commonly called out-of-cycle updates).

Security updates often include the number of a Knowledge Base article (such as KB 958559) that includes amplifying information.

 Knowledge Base articles are available on Microsoft sites via the Internet. You can usually locate the page by searching on "KB" followed by the number of the article. For example, search on "KB 958559" to locate and read that article.

Here are some of the other common uses of updates:

- Patches and fixes for the operating system
- Patches and fixes for applications
- Driver updates
- Language packs

 Windows 7 updates include updates for both the operating system and applications. Early versions of Windows included only updates for the Windows operating system, and updates for applications were obtained separately. Windows 7 updates are now used to update applications such as Microsoft Office. This eliminates the need to manage updates for applications separately.

Updates are displayed as Important, Recommended, and Optional by the Windows Update client. These categories are set by Microsoft when the updates are released, and each can be configured with different deployment choices.

Important updates   *Important updates* are security related and designed to protect your PC from security or privacy threats. As an example, if a known bug is discovered that can be exploited by an attacker, a patch would be written to plug the hole. When the patch is applied as an update, the attacker can no longer use this method to exploit your system.

Recommended updates   *Recommended updates* are performance related and designed to help improve the operation of your computer. As an example, if a bug is discovered that causes an application to hang or crash when a user takes specific actions, a patch would be written to resolve the problem and released as a recommended update. Alternatively, if a driver is created to improve the performance of hardware, it would be released as a recommended update.

Optional updates   *Optional updates* are free additional software programs that you might like to have on your system. They aren't related to security or the performance of your computer but instead add capabilities. Once these optional updates are installed on your computer, they may be updated using either important or recommended updates if needed. If they aren't installed on your computer, you won't be prompted to download other updates related to them.

Deploying Updates

Three primary methods are available to keep Windows 7 up to date in an enterprise:

Automatic Update   Clients individually connect to *Microsoft Update* for updates. For small organizations of up to 50 clients, the *Automatic Update* method is often used. It doesn't require any additional servers to support it. It's common to use Group Policy to configure the settings for updates to ensure that all clients are configured to download and install the updates automatically. However, this method does not give administrators the ability to approve or decline updates.

Windows Server Update Services   *Windows Server Updates Services (WSUS)* is a free server product available from Microsoft. A central server is used to download updates, and all clients can receive their updates from this server instead of Microsoft Update. This saves bandwidth because updates are downloaded only once for an organization, and it also gives administrators control over what updates are approved and deployed to clients. WSUS is installed on a server product (not Windows 7), and it is relatively easy to get up and running.

WSUS is widely used, and installing it on a server is explained later in this chapter, along with some basics associated with using WSUS in an enterprise.

System Center Configuration Manager   *System Center Configuration Manager (SCCM)* is a specialized enterprise server application that must be purchased (similar to how Microsoft Exchange or Microsoft SQL Server is a separate enterprise application that must be purchased). It provides a lot more control to the administrator, including not only what updates are applied to which clients but also exactly when these updates are deployed. Large enterprises use SCCM to have more control over deployed updates. One of the deciding factors on using SCCM is whether the IT staff has expertise with SCCM or the training funds to get the staff up to speed on its use.

When preparing for the 70-686 exam, you should be aware of the capabilities of SCCM related to delivering updates to clients. You aren't expected to be an expert on it, but you should be aware of it. One of the primary benefits of SCCM over WSUS related to updates is the ability to schedule when updates are delivered.

Auditing Updates

In addition to deploying updates, you occasionally need to audit systems for updates. Auditing a system for updates allows you to verify that updates are installed on the system.

WSUS and SCCM both have the ability to audit systems for updates. However, if you're not using WSUS or SCCM to deploy the updates, you can use the *Microsoft Baseline Security Analyzer (MBSA)*. MBSA includes both a GUI and a command-line interface (*MBSACLI*) tool.

In addition to checking for updates, MBSA can be used to check several other security issues on a system. MBSA is covered in more depth later in this chapter.

Deploying Service Packs and Rollups

When you are installing a new computer, you don't necessarily want to install all of the updates individually. This can be both time and labor intensive. Instead, you'd install either a service pack and/or an update rollup to bring the computer close to being up to date. You'd then apply all the updates that were released since the service pack or update rollup was released.

Service pack   A comprehensive update to the system that includes all of the critical updates, security updates, and update rollups since either the last service pack (SP) or the operating system was released.

Update rollup   A significant number of updates released since the last service pack or the operating system was released. It is a cumulative set of critical updates, security updates, hotfixes, and other updates. Update rollups are usually targeted at specific products. For example, an update rollup may be released for Microsoft Office, but it wouldn't include updates for other software.

 Service packs and update rollups are usually well tested because the updates have been in place for a while. This means that there is less risk of a service pack or an update rollup causing a problem than there may be from the initial release of another update.

Service packs and update rollups are characterized as either cumulative or incremental.

Cumulative   A cumulative SP includes all the previous service packs. For example, if SP3 includes the contents of SP1 and SP2, it is considered a cumulative SP. Update rollups have been consistently released as cumulative, but that could change.

Incremental   An incremental SP includes only the updates since the last service pack. This requires you to install the previous SP before you can install the newer SP.

Microsoft has done both incremental and cumulative service packs. As an example, Windows XP SP2 was cumulative, but Windows XP SP3 was incremental. When deploying service packs, you should be aware of whether it is cumulative and can be deployed alone or incrementally and needs the previous service packs to be installed first.

Windows Update Client

Windows 7 includes the *Windows Update client* that is responsible for installing updates. The Windows Update client works the same way no matter where the updates are coming from (Microsoft Update site or internal server).

The Windows Update service is the primary service used to detect, download, and install updates used to keep Windows 7 and other applications up to date. This service should always be running. The Windows Update Agent is used by applications like WSUS and SCCM to interact with this service.

You can access the Windows Update client by selecting Start ➤ All Programs ➤ Windows Update. Your display will look similar to Figure 4.1.

FIGURE 4.1   Launching Windows Update

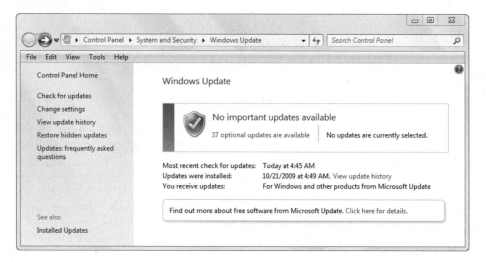

This page shows at a glance the current status of updates on a system, including whether updates are available, when they were installed, and how updates are received. The figure shows that updates are received from Microsoft Update. If the computer was within a network that used WSUS or SCCM, it would instead state that updates are Managed By Your System Administrator.

Windows 7 clients should normally check for updates once a day, so the date shown for the Most Recent Check For Updates should be today or yesterday. If it isn't, it indicates a problem.

Although Windows Update automatically checks for updates based on the settings, it is possible to check for updates manually at any time by clicking the Check For Updates link on the Windows Update screen. Windows Update will then attempt to connect to the designated source for updates. This could be Microsoft Update, WSUS, or SCCM. If updates are available, it will indicate the type of updates available and how many are available.

Microsoft Update Standalone Packages (MSU Files)

Windows 7 updates are released as MSU files (named with an `.msu` extension). These files aren't executables, but if you double-click one, it will be installed using the Windows Update Standalone Installer (`wusa.exe`).

It's worthwhile to understand the format of the naming convention used with MSU files. They are formatted as *WindowsVersion*-KB*number*-v*Number*-*platform*.

- For Windows 7, the Windows version is 6.1. Windows Vista is version 6. (This common version number of 6 with Windows Vista and Windows 7 is used for compatibility checks. If an application is compatible with Windows Vista, it is compatible with Windows 7.)

- The KB number lists the associated Knowledge Base number for the update, such as KB958559.

- If an update is released a second time, the version number will be included (such as v2 or v3). For the first version, this is typically omitted.

- The platform can be either x86 or x64, indicating the architecture.

As an example, the initial Windows 7 update related to KB958559 for 64-bit systems is called `Windows6.1-KB958559-x64.msu`.

These updates can be scripted using the WUSA command as follows:

```
Wusa Windows6.1-KB958559-x64.msu
```

Viewing Windows Update Settings

If you launch Windows Update, you can view and modify the settings by clicking the Change Settings link on the left side of the window. Figure 4.2 shows the settings page for Windows Update.

FIGURE 4.2 Viewing Windows Update settings

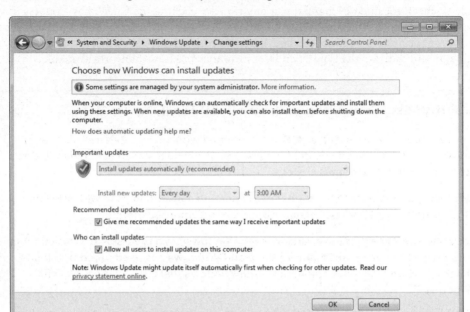

This page includes several important settings, starting with Important Updates, used to identify how and when they are installed. If you select the drop-down box under Important Updates, you'll see several choices:

Install Updates Automatically (Recommended)   Windows will periodically check for updates and will download them in the background. Updates will be installed on the computer based on the schedule, with 3:00 AM daily being the default.

Download Updates, But Let Me Choose Whether To Install Them   Updates will be downloaded in the background, and a text bubble will occasionally appear when updates have been downloaded and installed. The user must manually install them. This allows users to take more control over when the updates are installed but also risks that updates are never installed. From an administrator's point of view, you can't depend on users to perform core security steps, but you must instead take control of the process whenever possible.

Check For Updates, But Let Me Choose Whether To Download And Install Them
Windows Update will periodically check for updates in the background, and a text bubble will occasionally appear when updates are available for download. This is useful when clients are connected through slow connections, such as a dial-up link, but will rarely be used in an enterprise.

Never Check For Updates (Not Recommended)   A computer that is not kept up to date will soon be an unsecured computer. It's just a matter of time before a bug is discovered and can be exploited. About the only reason to select this setting is if the computer is completely isolated and cannot receive updates from any source.

You can allow recommended updates to be installed on the same schedule as the important updates by checking the box Give Me Recommended Updates The Same Way I Receive Important Updates, as shown previously in Figure 4.2.

If you want only administrators to be able to install updates manually, you can uncheck the box Allow All Users To Install Updates On This Computer. When this box is checked, any logged-on user can install updates.

 Two additional selections are available to home users or clients that are not joined to a domain. They are Microsoft Update and Software Notifications.

All of these settings can be controlled using *Group Policy*. If the settings are dimmed, it indicates that they have been set by Group Policy and cannot be modified or configured by the user. In addition, a message will appear in the window that says Some Settings Are Managed By Your System Administrator.

A WSUS exercise later in this chapter will show how to configure some of these Group Policy settings.

Installing, Hiding, and Restoring Updates

If you don't have updates set to install automatically, or you want to install optional updates, you can install them manually. When updates are available, a link exists on the Windows Update page that you can click to access the page to install them.

Figure 4.3 shows a list of updates that can be selected to install on a system. In the figure, I have selected the check box next to the nVidia -Display - NVIDIA GeForce 9600M GT driver update. To install this update, I'd simply select the check box and click OK to begin the installation.

In addition, updates can be hidden from this page. Let's say that I decided that I'll never master the Bulgarian language, so I won't need the Bulgarian language pack on my system. I can right-click it (as shown in the previous figure) and select Hide Update. The update will be gone the next time I return to this page.

But what if I change my mind and decide that I do want the Bulgarian Language Pack update that I hid? It's not gone for good. The main page of the Windows Update page includes the link Restore Hidden Updates. After you click this link, a display similar to Figure 4.4 will appear.

To restore the Bulgarian Language Pack update, select the check box for it and click Restore.

FIGURE 4.3 Installing and hiding updates

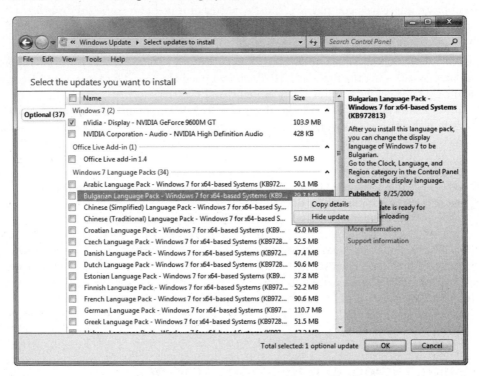

FIGURE 4.4 Restoring a hidden update

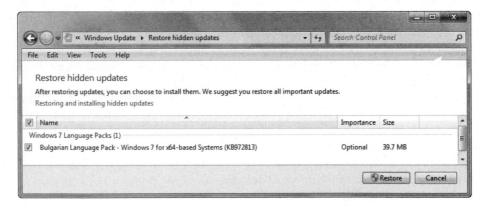

Viewing Update History

You can view a list of all updates that have been deployed to your computer by clicking the View *Update History* link on the Windows Update page.

The update history report includes the common name, the status (Successful or Failed) of the update installation, the importance (Important, Recommended, or Optional), and the date it was installed. You can double-click any update to view additional information.

Figure 4.5 shows the update history for one of my computers. I also double-clicked Security Update For Windows 7 For x64-Based Systems (KB975467) to view additional details on this update.

FIGURE 4.5   Viewing details of an update from the Review Your Update History page

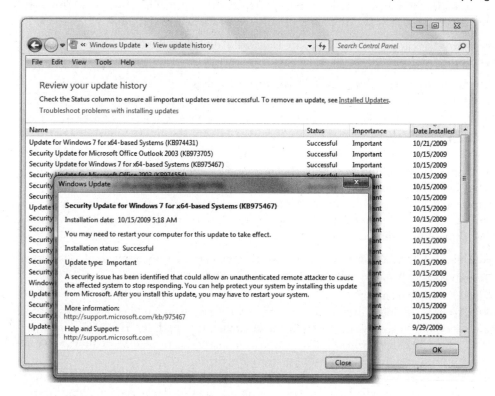

This is a simple but effective method to verify that an update has been deployed to a system.

Choosing an Update Tool

As mentioned previously, there are three methods you can use to update Windows: automatic update, WSUS, or SCCM. With automatic update, clients receive updates directly from the Microsoft Update site. With WSUS and SCCM, clients receive their updates from a server.

Each method has pros and cons to consider:

Network bandwidth   The amount of bandwidth used to download updates from the Internet is an important consideration. If you have five clients and each of them downloads their updates from the Microsoft Update site, it's no big deal. However, if you have 500 clients downloading their updates from the Internet, it's significant. If you have more than 50 clients, you should seriously consider using one of the server solutions.

With both WSUS and SCCM, the update is downloaded from the Internet once to the server, and then it is deployed to the clients from this internal server.

Ability to test updates   Unfortunately, when an update is released to fix one problem, it occasionally creates another problem. If you're using automatic updates, they will be automatically deployed when Microsoft deploys them and you won't have an opportunity to test them. However, if you use WSUS or SCCM, you have the ability to test updates before deploying them.

Limited application of updates   Sometimes an update will cause problems for specific systems but not others. For example, your organization's computers could be 50 percent Dell, 50 percent HP. If testing shows that the update causes detrimental effects for one manufacturer but not the other, you wouldn't want to deploy the updates to all of them. Both WSUS and SCCM allow you to limit the updates to specific computers or specific groups of computers.

Scheduling updates   You may want to schedule when updates are applied. SCCM provides much more granular control over the scheduling of updates.

What does all this mean? If your organization has fewer than 50 clients, you may choose to use automatic updates. Even with fewer than 50 clients, you could choose to use WSUS to gain more administrative control over the deployment of updates. If your organization has more than 50 clients, you will likely choose either WSUS or SCCM to limit the Internet bandwidth used and to gain more administrative control.

WSUS is free, and many administrators can often learn it on the job. SCCM is an enterprise application that must be purchased and often requires additional training for administrators to learn and master it. Small to midsize organizations often use WSUS, whereas larger organizations usually use SCCM.

Testing Updates

The worst thing that can happen when an update is applied is that the system crashes or goes into an endless boot/reboot cycle. Less severe problems may result in an incompatibility with other applications. Software that once worked suddenly doesn't.

Obviously, the goal of an update isn't to cause problems, but it's not uncommon for the fix of one problem to result in the creation of another problem. If this happens to one or two clients, it's inconvenient because you need to take steps to restore them. However, if this happens to 500 or 5,000 clients, it can impact the organization's ability to do business.

Because of this, updates should be tested. Many organizations won't even apply updates until the update goes through an official change-management process. A change-management process allows a change to be submitted and reviewed by different experts within the organization. When change-management processes aren't used, changes to one system often affect other elements in the organization.

Testing an update means that it is applied to a system that is similar to the actual system where it will be deployed. This includes the same hardware and software. After the update is applied to the test system, the system is rebooted and put through the paces to ensure that it still operates as well as it did before the update. If testing shows that the update doesn't have any detrimental effects, it can be approved for deployment.

 Real World Scenario

Change Management on the Job

Stringent change-management procedures are being adopted by more and more IT organizations. These are often based on the Information Technology Infrastructure Library (ITIL) or Microsoft's adoption of ITIL with the Microsoft Operations Framework (MOF).

The goal of change-management processes is to ensure that changes to one system or setting don't adversely affect other systems or settings. It might seem obvious that administrators don't want to take down a network while fixing another problem, but that's exactly what has sometimes happened.

At an organization where I worked, someone took down a significant portion of a network by changing a setting on a printer connected to a server. Specifically, he changed the manually assigned IP address. Unfortunately, he used an IP address that was the same as the DNS server on the network. Suddenly, DNS no longer worked. Name resolution (resolving names to IP addresses) didn't work, and users couldn't connect to servers. Users couldn't log on to the network. Email wouldn't work. The list went on and on.

It sounds silly. Someone troubleshooting a printer took down the network. However, when the IT shop was suddenly faced with a serious outage, *silly* wasn't one of the words used. If the IP address change had been submitted as a change request, it would have quickly been identified as an incorrect address, and the whole scenario would have been avoided.

While this is an extreme example of a change resulting in unwanted problems, it does help illustrate the importance of a change-management process.

Using MBSA for Security Audits

The Microsoft Baseline Security Analyzer (MBSA) is one of the tools you can use to audit security on systems in your network. It checks for updates and for various security vulnerabilities.

> One of the core principles of hardening any computer is keeping it up to date. If a computer isn't up to date with security updates, it can be vulnerable to any attack that exploits the vulnerabilities that the updates are trying to resolve.

Figure 4.6 shows the first screen you'll see when launching the MBSA. Although the title bar shows it as version 2.1, the introductory text states that it includes support for Windows 7, indicating that it is version 2.1.1.

FIGURE 4.6   MBSA 2.1.1

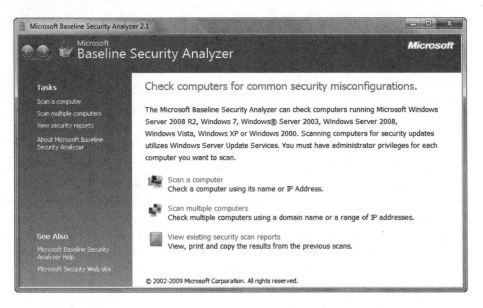

MBSA 2.1.1 was released to support Windows 7 clients. It can run on and scan any of the following clients:

- Windows 2000
- Windows XP
- Windows Vista

- Windows Server 2003

- Windows Server 2003 R2

- Windows Server 2008

- Windows Server 2008 R2

After you've run at least a single report, the View Existing Security Scan Reports link will be enabled, allowing you to view past reports. If you click this link, it'll provide a list of all the reports that have been run. This list includes the computer name, the IP address, the overall assessment of the scan, and the date when it was run.

Picking Computers to Scan

You can run MBSA against a single computer or multiple computers in a network. When you choose to scan a single computer, you'll see a screen similar to Figure 4.7. You can identify the computer to scan based on the computer name or its IP address.

FIGURE 4.7   Picking a single computer to scan

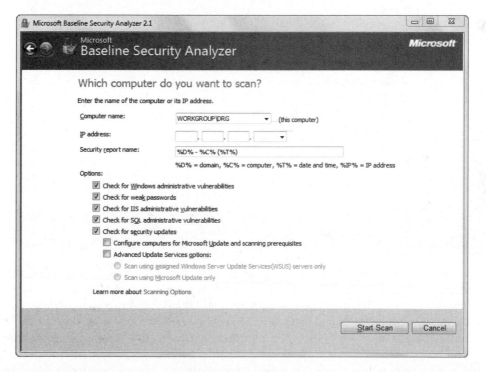

You'll need administrative access to scan any computers using MBSA, so if you're scanning remote computers, you should be logged on with an account that is in the remote computer's Administrators group.

When running MBSA in a domain, you should use a domain account that is added to the Administrators group of the desktop computers. Most organizations create a group that is automatically added to the local Administrators group on desktop computers that desktop support personnel manage.

If you instead click the Scan Multiple Computers link of MBSA, you'll see a display similar to Figure 4.8. You can choose to scan all the computers in a domain or all the computers in a range of IP addresses.

FIGURE 4.8   Selecting multiple computers to scan

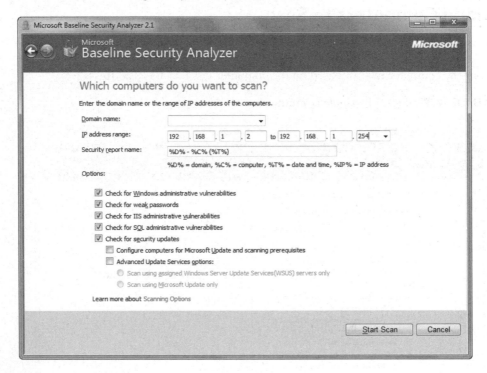

In the figure, I added the IP address range of 192.168.1.2 to 192.168.1.254 to scan all the computers in this subnet. I omitted 192.168.1.1 because it is the address of the router in this network and not a Microsoft computer. MBSA will then connect to the specified computers and inspect them for installed updates and other security issues.

When MBSA is run, it will first connect to a Microsoft website to download the MBSA detection catalog (wsusscn2.cab). This catalog includes information about all available updates and security vulnerabilities. It is used to compare the existing updates and configurations on individual clients with a list of security updates that have been released along with known vulnerabilities. If the catalog has already been downloaded, MBSA will check to be sure it is up to date.

You can download the wsusscn2.cab catalog directly from Microsoft's site using this link: http://go.microsoft.com/fwlink/?linkid=76054. This file can then be centrally located and used with the /catalog switch when using MBSACLI (the command-line equivalent of MBSA).

The previous version of the cabinet file was named wsusscan.cab and is still available. However, wsusscan.cab has not been updated since March 2007 and doesn't include updates and security vulnerabilities since then. You need to use the wsusscn2.cab file to ensure that you are checking against the most recent data.

Vulnerability Checks

MBSA will scan computers for several security issues. It uses Windows Management Instrumentation queries to inspect the system for the following vulnerabilities:

Check for Windows Administrative Vulnerabilities   MBSA inspects the system for basic security issues such as whether more than one user is a member of the Administrators group, the Guest account is enabled (it should be disabled), NTFS is used on all the drives, and any folders are being shared.

Check for Weak Passwords   MBSA checks for blank or weak passwords on each local account on the system. A strong password will have at least eight characters and use a combination of at least three of the four character types (uppercase, lowercase, numbers, and symbols).

Check for IIS Administrative Vulnerabilities   This check looks for vulnerabilities in Internet Information Services (IIS) versions 5.0, 5.1, and 6.0. It also checks to see whether the IIS Lockdown Tool has been run on these versions. If IIS is not installed on the scanned system, this check is skipped.

Check for SQL Administrative Vulnerabilities   This check looks for vulnerabilities in both SQL Server instances and the Microsoft Data Engine (MSDE) that is installed on any scanned computers. If SQL Server or MSDE is not installed on the system, this check is skipped.

Check for Security Updates   This check scans all systems to determine whether all current security updates are installed. It uses the same technology that is used by WSUS and SCCM to scan the computers. However, if your network is not using WSUS or SCCM, this is a valuable tool to determine easily whether clients are up to date. A green check indicates that no missing security updates were identified. Missing updates are marked with a red X, and missing service packs or update rollups are marked with a yellow X.

The easiest way to verify that *unmanaged* clients have installed updates is by using MBSA. Clients managed by WSUS or SCCM will be checked using those tools, but if clients aren't being managed by WSUS or SCCM, they can be checked with MBSA.

The security updates check gives you several additional options, including these:

Configure Computers for Microsoft Update And Scanning Prerequisites   If a client doesn't have the Windows Update Agent installed, it can't be scanned. However, selecting this setting allows you to install the Windows Update Agent and other prerequisites automatically on the target computers so that they can be scanned.

Advanced Update Services Options   Two additional update services options are available for clients that are configured to receive updates from WSUS servers. If your environment is not using WSUS, these settings won't be used.

> **Scan Using Assigned Windows Server Update Services (WSUS) Servers Only**   This option can be used in an environment where WSUS is being used. It will scan only computers that are configured to receive updates from WSUS servers.

> **Scan Using Microsoft Update Only**   This option allows you to compare clients against the list of updates available from Microsoft instead of the list of updates that have been approved on the WSUS server.

MBSA provides a report on the findings for each scan. Reports include information on any issues that are found and also provide instructions on how to fix any of the issues.

Figure 4.9 shows a sample report with the Windows Scan Results showing. If you look at the vertical scroll bar on the right side of the window, you can see that there is a lot more to this report.

FIGURE 4.9   Viewing the MBSA report

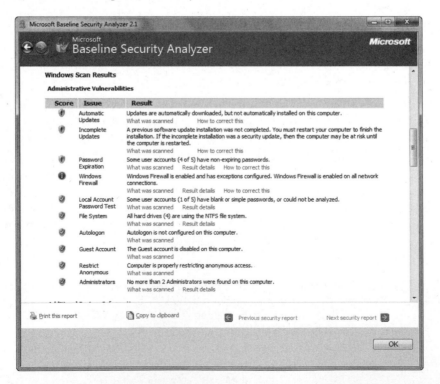

The report shows three different icons referred to as risk scores. The orange shield icon with an exclamation mark generally indicates that action is required to secure your system. You may also find a red shield icon, which indicates a severe risk.

Orange shield with exclamation mark   This indicates a risk that should be addressed. In the figure, it shows that automatic updates are not set to be installed automatically (requiring user action), an update is not complete and is pending a reboot, and four out of five accounts have non-expiring passwords.

Blue circle with exclamation mark   This generally indicates a best practice and not necessarily a security issue. An exception for a firewall allows certain traffic through. The firewall should be enabled and that's the most important setting, but it is often acceptable and even necessary to enable exceptions.

Green shield with check mark   This indicates that MBSA checked for the vulnerability and found the system compliant.

Red shield with an X   This indicates a known security update, service pack, or update rollup is not installed. In addition, if Automatic Updates is completely disabled, it will show up with a red shield.

By clicking Result Details in the report for any of the issues, you can see additional data that can tell you what to do. As an example, Figure 4.10 shows the result details for the issue related to user accounts having non-expiring passwords.

FIGURE 4.10   Viewing report details from MBSA

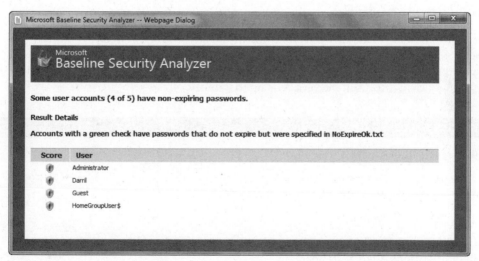

You can drill into the details of any of the report issues and determine exactly what the problem is and how to resolve it.

Installing MBSA

MBSA is a free download available at Microsoft's download site (www.microsoft.com/downloads) by searching for "MBSA 2.1.1." You should download at least version 2.1.1 to support Windows 7. Versions exist for both x86 (32-bit) and x64 (64-bit) systems. Once you download a version, you can follow Exercise 4.1 to install it.

EXERCISE 4.1

Installing the MBSA

1. Browse to where you've downloaded the MBSA, double-click it, and click Run.

2. If prompted by User Account Control, click Yes to continue. Review the information on the Welcome page and click Next.

3. Review the license agreement, select I Accept the License Agreement, and click Next.

4. Accept the default destination folder and click Next.

5. Click Install on the Start Installation page.

6. When the installation completes, click OK.

Running the MBSA

Once you've downloaded the MBSA onto your system, you can run it, as explained in Exercise 4.2. The first time it is run, it may take some time to connect to Microsoft's site to download the wsusscn2.cab file, which includes the catalog of security update information. Later, it only checks to see if the version is up to date.

EXERCISE 4.2

Running the MBSA GUI

1. Click Start ➢ All Programs ➢ Microsoft Baseline Security Analyzer to launch MBSA. If prompted by User Account Control, click Yes to continue.

2. Click Scan a Computer.

3. It will default to the selection of your computer. Review the options, and accept the default settings. Click Start Scan.

4. After a moment, the scan will complete and the report will appear. Review the report, and investigate any issues that are reported.

Running the MBSACLI

When you install the MBSA, the MBSA command-line interface (MBSACLI) will also be installed. The great strength of the MBSACLI is the same as with any command-line tool: It can be scripted, and anything that can be scripted can be scheduled.

> Chapter 3, "Using the Command Prompt and PowerShell," covered some basics on the command prompt and scripting. Any commands that can be executed from the command prompt can be created as a batch file, and batch files can be scheduled to run automatically using the Task Scheduler.

As an example, you could create a batch file to run MBSACLI on all the computers in your domain or on all the computers within a specific subnet. You can then schedule this batch file to run every Sunday night. When you come in to work on Monday, you'll only need to check it. If you want to get fancier, you can include a script to send the output to your email address or the email address of a group of administrators.

MBSACLI Location

The `Mbsacli.exe` file is located in the `\Program Files\Microsoft Security Baseline Analyzer 2\` folder when MBSA is installed. You need to specify this path when executing MBSACLI.

Just as MBSA must be run with administrative permissions, MBSACLI also needs administrative permissions. When running the command from the command prompt, launch it with administrative permissions by right-clicking Command Prompt and selecting Run as Administrator.

As a simple way to see MBSACLI in action, you can execute the following command:

```
"C:\Program files\Microsoft Baseline Security Analyzer 2\mbsacli" ↵
/target localhost
```

> Even though the previous code is shown on two lines it should be entered on a single line.

Since the path and command contain spaces, they must be enclosed in quotes. The `/target` switch is used to identify the computer to check. `Localhost` is resolved to the computer from where it's run using the host file (located at `C:\Windows\System32\Drivers\etc\`).

> The `/target` switch is useful when running MBSACLI against a remote computer. However, it can be omitted. If MBSACLI is run without the `/target` switch, MBSACLI will run on the local computer.

Some of the common switches used with MBSACLI are shown in Table 4.1. As with any command-prompt tool, you can redirect the output to a text file using the redirect symbol (>). For example, the following command runs the same report as shown in the previous command but redirects it to a text file named mbsacli.txt.

```
"C:\Program files\Microsoft Baseline Security Analyzer 2\mbsacli" ↵
/target localhost > mbsacli.txt
```

Even though the previous code is shown on two lines it should be entered on a single line.

TABLE 4.1 MBSACLI switches

Switch	Description
/target	Use this to identify the target computer where MBSACLI will run. You can specify the target as a hostname or an IP address. Mbsacli /target 192.168.1.10
/r	Use this to specify a range of IP addresses. Both the beginning IP address and the ending IP address are specified. Mbsacli /r 192.168.1.10–192.168.1.20
/listfile	You can create a file with a list of computers or a list of IP addresses and then direct MBSACLI to run the command against all the computers in the list. The following command assumes a file named computers.txt exists in the current directory. Mbsacli /listfile computers.txt
/d	Use this to specify the domain name in which to run MBSACLI against all computers in the domain. The domain name needs to be expressed as a NETBIOS name (single name). For example, if the domain name is wiley.com, it should be expressed as wiley, not wiley.com. Mbsacli /d wiley
/n	You can use the /n option to exclude specific tests. Valid options are OS, SQL, IIS, Updates, and Password. You can exclude more than one option by adding the + with no spaces. The following command will run the check on the local system and exclude the SQL and IIS checks. Mbsacli /target localhost /n SQL+IIS
/nd	This switch can be used to tell MBSACLI to not download any updates from the Internet. It will just use the current version of the cabinet files.

TABLE 4.1   MBSACLI switches *(continued)*

Switch	Description
/wa	This specifies that only results that have been approved on the WSUS server should be checked. Append this switch to commands that scan the domain or a range of IP addresses.
/wi	This specifies that all updates should be checked even if not approved by the WSUS server. Append this switch to commands that scan the domain or a range of IP addresses.
/u	You can specify a specific user name to use to perform the scan.
/p	When specifying a user name, you must also provide a password with the /p switch.
/catalog filename	You can specify the location of the wsusscn2.cab file using the catalog switch. This is useful if you've downloaded the cabinet file and stored it in a central location (such as a share on a server) and mapped the share. Mbsacli /catalog z:\wsusscn2.cab
/nvc	The no-version-check switch will prevent MBSA from checking to see if a newer version is available. It is often used with the /catalog switch. Mbsacli /catalog z:wsusscn2.cab /nvc
/ia	This switch will update any prerequisite Windows Update Agent components during a scan and is also often used with the /catalog switch. Mbsacli /catalog z:wsusscn2.cab /nvc /ia
/l	This shows a list of reports available on this system. The output list includes Computer Name, IP Address, Assessment, and Report Name columns. The Report Name column can be used to identify report names that are needed for other list switches such as the /lr and /ld switches. Mbsacli /l
/ls	This shows a list of reports available from the most recent scan. Mbsacli /ls
/lr	This displays an overview of a specific report. The report name must be used and can be determined with the /l switch. Mbsacli /lr reportName
/ld	This displays a detailed output from a specific report. The report name must be used and can be determined with the /l switch. Mbsacli /ld reportName

Microsoft has created a free download that includes several sample scripts you can use to accelerate your learning and use of the MBSACLI. The current version is called `mbsa2samples.exe` and can be located on Microsoft's download site (www.microsoft.com/downloads) by searching for "MBSA scripts." Just be aware that any script that references the `wsusscan.cab` file needs to be modified to use the `wsusscn2.cab` file (or the `wsusscn2.cab` file needs to be renamed as `wsusscan.cab`). The older `wsusscan.cab` file has not been updated since March 2007.

Running in an Isolated Environment

It is possible to run MBSACLI in an isolated environment that doesn't have access to the Internet. For example, you may be running Windows 7 in a VPC machine used for testing, or you may have an entire network that is completely isolated from the Internet for security reasons. When running MBSACLI in an isolated environment, you'll need to take a couple of extra steps:

- Download an up-to-date version of the `wsusscn2.cab` file from `http://go.microsoft.com/fwlink/?linkid=76054`.

- Download an up-to-date version of the `wuredist.cab` file from `go.microsoft.com/fwlink/?LinkId=84399`.

- Copy the `wuredist.cab` file to the `%systemroot%\Users\username\AppData\Local\Microsoft\MBSA\2.1.1\Cache` folder.

If the `wuredist.cab` file is not copied to the appropriate folder, MBSACLI will return the following error: `The catalog file (Wuredist.Cab) is damaged or an invalid catalog.` Once these steps are taken, you can then run MBSACLI with the `/catalog` switch to point to the location of the file. It's also common to include the `/nvc`, `/nd`, and `/ia` switches. Assuming the `wsusscn2.cab` file is located in the `c:\mbsa` folder, you could use the following commands. The first command changes the directory to where MBSACLI is located, and the second runs it with the appropriate switches for an isolated environment.

```
CD "C:\Program files\Microsoft Baseline Security Analyzer 2\mbsacli"
Mbsacli /catalog C:\mbsa\wsusscn2.cab /ia /nvc /nd
```

Using Windows Server Update Services

Windows Server Update Services is a free download you can install on a Windows server. It's used as a central location to download, approve, and deploy updates.

When preparing for the 70-686 exam, you should have a solid understanding of WSUS. Microsoft has spent of a lot of time and energy creating and improving WSUS over the years, and it's used by enterprises of all sizes. Being free is good, but it's also easy to learn and works very well.

Figure 4.11 shows a typical configuration using WSUS in an enterprise. In the figure, the WSUS server retrieves updates from the Microsoft update site and all clients receive their updates from the WSUS server.

FIGURE 4.11 Using WSUS in an enterprise

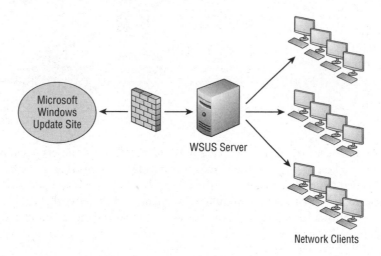

An administrator chooses which updates to download to WSUS. Once the updates have been downloaded, they can be tested, approved, and deployed to clients. WSUS allows you to organize computers in groups, so it's possible to approve an update for one group of computers but not another group.

Although Figure 4.11 shows only 12 network clients, your network could have many more. In a large network, you may even choose to use multiple WSUS servers.

Figure 4.12 shows a typical configuration when multiple WSUS servers are used. A single WSUS server is used to download updates from the Microsoft update site and is referred to as the *upstream server*. WSUS servers that receive updates from the upstream server are referred to as *downstream servers*. Downstream WSUS servers retrieve the updates from this server, and administrators of each downstream server can then choose to approve and deploy updates to their clients based on their needs.

FIGURE 4.12 Using WSUS in an enterprise

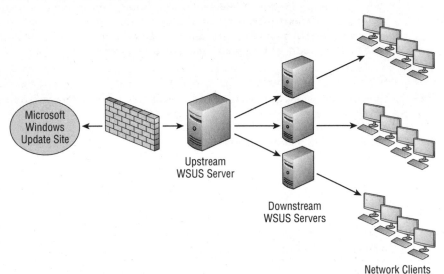

This is useful in a large but decentralized environment where administrators in different locations need to make decisions on the management of the systems that are different from what may be needed in another location of the enterprise. In other words, an administrator of one downstream server can deploy an update to clients in her network, while an administrator for another downstream server can wait until further testing is completed before deploying updates to his network.

WSUS Updates

WSUS can receive and deploy a wide range of updates. This includes updates for operating systems, applications, and enterprise applications.

Operating systems　All Microsoft operating systems, from Windows 2000 through Windows 7 and Windows Server 2008 R2, are supported.

Applications　A full range of Microsoft applications, including Microsoft Office, Microsoft Works, Microsoft Live, Silverlight, Expression, Report Viewer, Visual Studio, and much more, are supported.

Application server products　Microsoft server products, such as Microsoft Exchange, Microsoft SQL Server, Internet Security and Acceleration Server, Host Integration Server, System Center Configuration Management Server, Windows Small Business Server, and more, are supported.

WSUS Requirements

WSUS is installed on a server such as Windows Server 2003 R2, Windows Server 2008, or Windows Server 2008 R2. To support Windows 7 clients, you'll need at least WSUS 3.0 with SP2 or later.

Other requirements are as follows:

Server roles   WSUS requires both the Application Server and the Web Server (IIS) roles installed. Internet Information Services (IIS) is Microsoft's web server product, and it is installed when the Web Server (IIS) role is installed. These roles should be added prior to adding WSUS. IIS 6.0 or later is required.

Disk space   You should have at least 8 GB of available disk space. WSUS will need at least 6 GB to store updates downloaded from the Microsoft Update site. If you're short of disk space, it is possible to store the updates on the Microsoft Update site, but the overall performance will be slower. An additional 2 GB of disk space is need to house the Windows Internal Database that will be used to store the WSUS data, but it's also possible to use an existing SQL Server and store the database on that server.

Downloaded files   You'll need to download the following two files: WSUS 3.0 and the Microsoft Report Viewer Redistributable 2008. Both are available as free downloads from Microsoft's download site (www.microsoft.com/downloads). Search for "WSUS 3" and "Report Viewer Redistributable 2008" to locate each item.

Both x86 and x64 versions are available for WSUS, so download the version you need based on where you'll install it. For example, if you're installing it on a 64-bit server, download the x64 version. The Report Viewer has only a single edition that works on both x86 and x64 servers.

Installing, Configuring, and Using WSUS

Once you've reviewed the requirements and prerequisites, you can begin the installation of WSUS, configure clients to use WSUS, approve updates for deployment, and verify that updates have been deployed by viewing WSUS reports. The following sections will lead you through the entire process.

Adding the Application Server and Web Server (IIS) Roles

Exercise 4.3 will lead you through the process of adding the Application Server and Web Server (IIS) roles on a server. This server must be running at least Windows Server 2008.

EXERCISE 4.3

Adding the Application Server and Web Server (IIS) Roles

1.   Launch Server Manager in Windows Server 2008 by clicking Start ➢ Administrative Tools ➢ Server Manager.

2.   Click Roles in Server Manager, and select Add Roles.

3.   When the Before You Begin page appears, click Next.

4.   Select the check box next to Application Server. When you do, a dialog box appears, as shown in the following graphic. Click the Add Required Features button.

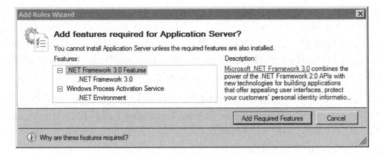

5.   Select the check box next to Web Server (IIS) and click Next.

6.   Review the information on the Introduction To Application Server page, and click Next.

7.   The Application Server Foundation Role Service is selected by default. Click Next.

8.   Review the information on the Introduction To Web Server (IIS) page, and click Next.

9.   Several role services are selected by default. You'll need to add the following additional role services:

   a.   In the Application Development section, select ASP .NET. This will cause a dialog box to appear, prompting you to add additional services. Click the Add Required Role Services button.

   b.   In the Security section, select Windows Authentication.

   c.   In the Performance section, select Dynamic Content Compression.

   d.   In the Management Tools section, select IIS 6 Management Compatibility, which automatically selects the other four IIS 6 compatibility settings.

   Your display will look similar to the following graphic. Click Next.

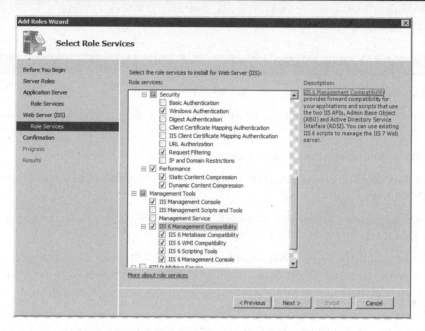

10. Review the information on the Confirmation page and click Install.

11. This will take a few minutes to complete. When it is done, review the results and click Close.

Installing the Report Viewer

WSUS uses the Report Viewer to display reports. This is not installed by default but instead must be installed separately. Exercise 4.4 leads you through the steps to install the Microsoft Report Viewer 2008 Redistributable file. This exercise assumes you have already downloaded the file from the www.microsoft.com/downloads site.

EXERCISE 4.4

Installing the Report Viewer

1. Browse to the location where you stored the Report Viewer install application. Double-click it to launch it.

2. When the Welcome page appears, click Next.

3. Review the License Terms page, select I Have Read and Accept the License Terms, and click Install.

4. When the setup completes, click Finish.

Installing WSUS

With the prerequisites out of the way, you can now install WSUS. Exercise 4.5 will lead you through these steps.

EXERCISE 4.5

Installing WSUS

1. Locate the WSUS application you've downloaded, and double-click it to begin the installation.

2. When the wizard's Welcome page appears, click Next.

3. Make sure that Full Server Installation Including Administration Console is selected, and click Next.

4. Review the License Agreement. Select I Accept the Terms of the License Agreement, and click Next.

5. Accept the defaults on the Select Update Source page. This will set the C:\WSUS folder to be used to store the updates. Alternatively, you can browse to a different location to store the updates. Click Next.

6. Review the options on the Database Options page. Accept the default Install Windows Internal Database On This Computer in the C:\WSUS folder. Click Next.

7. On the Web Site Selection page, accept the default Use the Existing IIS Default Web Site (Recommended) option, as shown in the following graphic.

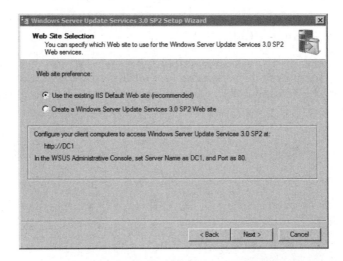

This graphic has some important information under the selections. It identifies how you should configure the client computers to access Windows Server Update Services using `http://servername`. I have installed it on a server named DC1, so the address is `http://DC1`. Port 80 is the default port used for HTTP.

8. Review the information on the Ready to Install page. Notice that it also identifies the path for the Client Self Update Site as `http://serverName/selfupdate`. Click Next to begin the installation.

9. After several minutes, the installation will complete. Click Finish.

10. The Windows Server Update Services Configuration Wizard will launch automatically.

11. Review the information on the Before You Begin page and click Next.

12. Review the information on the Microsoft Update Improvement Program page and click Next.

13. On the Choose Upstream Server page, accept the default Synchronize From Microsoft Update, as shown in the following graphic, and click Next.

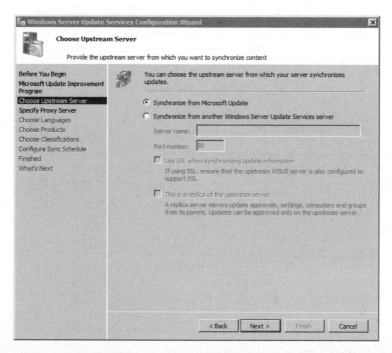

If you were using both upstream and downstream servers, you'd configure the downstream servers to obtain their updates from the upstream server, and the upstream servers would obtain their updates from the Microsoft Update site.

14. If your network uses a proxy server, specify the details in the Specify Proxy Server page. Click Next.

15. The Connect to Upstream Server page will appear. Since this is the only WSUS server, the Windows Update server is considered the upstream server. Make sure that your server has Internet connectivity, and click Start Connecting. This process will take several minutes to complete. When it completes (the progress bar will reach the far right-hand side), click Next.

16. On the Choose Languages page, select your language and click Next.

17. Review the information on the Choose Products page. By default, Office updates and Windows updates are included. You can select or deselect any updates desired. Click Next.

18. Review the information on the Choose Classifications page. The following graphic shows the default selections, but you can choose other classifications to download. Click Next.

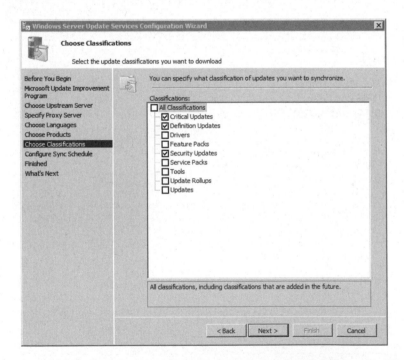

19. On the Set Synch Schedule page, accept the default Synchronize Manually. Click Next.

EXERCISE 4.5 *(continued)*

20. Review the information on the Finished page. The Launch The Windows Server Update Services Administration Console and Begin Initial Synchronization Server selections are both checked by default. Click Next.

21. Review the information on the What's Next page and click Finish. Note that when WSUS connects with the Microsoft Update site at this point, it does not download the updates but instead downloads an XML file that describes the updates. Once the updates are approved, they are downloaded to the WSUS server and are available to deploy to clients.

22. WSUS will launch. Expand by the server by clicking the plus (+) sign. Select Updates in the Update Services console, and you'll see a display similar to the following graphic.

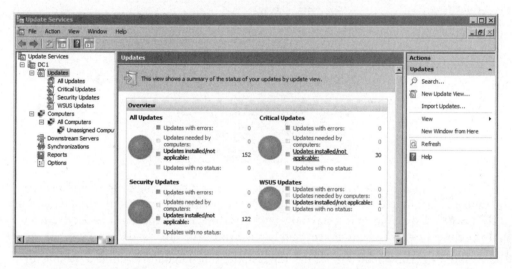

23. At this point, WSUS is successfully installed, and other network components can be configured to ensure your clients get their updates from this WSUS server.

Configuring Group Policy Settings for WSUS

Group Policy will be covered in greater depth in Chapter 10, "Managing Windows 7 with Group Policy," but in short, you can configure any single setting one time with Group Policy and have it apply to all the clients in a site, domain, or organizational unit (OU). If you want all the clients to receive their updates from your WSUS server, you can configure the clients with Group Policy. You can either create a new Group Policy object (GPO) or modify an existing one.

The Group Policy node that is configured is Computer Configuration ➤ Policies ➤ Administrative Templates ➤ Windows Components ➤ Windows Update. Figure 4.13 shows the GPO setting that can be manipulated to configure clients for Automatic Updates. Once the setting is set to Enabled, you can select one of four settings from the Configure Automatic Updating drop-down box.

FIGURE 4.13   Group Policy Settings for Automatic Updates

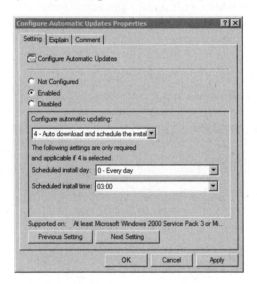

The choices available from the Configure Automatic Updating drop-down box are numbered 2 through 5. If Configure Automatic Updates is set to Disabled, updates must be downloaded and installed manually, and this value is 1 (which isn't selectable from the drop-down box). The four choices numbered 2 through 5 are as follows:

2 – Notify for Download and Notify for Install   When updates become available for download, an icon appears in the status area of the taskbar to inform the user that updates are available, but the update is not automatically downloaded. This can be used for clients located in remote sites who need to connect to the WSUS server over a slow wide area network connection. However, it has an inherent risk because it depends on the user to download and install the updates.

3 – Auto Download and Notify for Install   This is the default setting when this Group Policy setting is enabled, but it is not the best setting. The update is downloaded based on the schedule but not installed. An icon appears in the status area that the user can click to initiate the installation. Just as with the previous option, it has an inherent risk because it depends on the user to take action to install the updates.

4 – Auto Download and Schedule the Install   When using WSUS, this is the commonly used setting. The update is automatically downloaded to the client, and the installation of the update is scheduled. By default, the scheduled install occurs every day at 3:00 AM, though you can change the day and time setting.

5 – Allow Local Admin To Choose Setting   This option allows a local administrator to select one these options. However, the local administrator cannot disable Automatic Updates. In other words, Automatic Updates will be scheduled, but the local administrator can choose whether the update is automatically downloaded and/or automatically installed via the Windows Update console.

Figure 4.14 shows the Specify Intranet Microsoft Update Service Location Properties setting. You'd use this to configure the clients to use the WSUS server for updates instead of getting updates from the Windows Update site. In my network, I have configured a server named DC1 as the only WSUS server, so the address is `http://dc1`, and I have set this address for the update server and the statistics server.

FIGURE 4.14   Configuring the address of the WSUS server

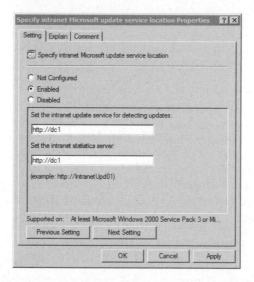

The *WSUS statistics server* is a single WSUS server that collects information from all WSUS-managed clients in the enterprise.

If your environment has multiple WSUS servers, you can direct some clients to use one WSUS server with one GPO and direct other clients to use other WSUS servers with other GPOs. However, a central WSUS server would still be used for overall statistics in the enterprise, so the intranet statistics server setting would be the same for all clients in the enterprise.

You can also configure how often clients check to see if updates are available. Figure 4.15 shows the Automatic Updates Detection Frequency with an interval of 20 hours selected. This time isn't specific but is instead randomized around the number entered.

FIGURE 4.15   Configuring the Automatic Updates Detection Frequency GPO setting

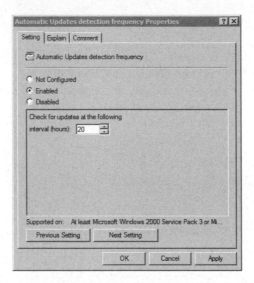

The actual time when a client is checked is a random number between 80 percent of the given number and 120 percent of the number. With the number at 20, the client would check at some point between 16 hours (20 × 0.80) and 24 hours (20 × 1.2) after the last check. The default setting is 22, causing clients to check for updates at random intervals of between about 17.6 and 26.4 hours. Other Group Policy settings exist that can be manipulated, but these are the common ones.

Creating a GPO to Configure Clients to Use WSUS

Exercise 4.6 shows how to configure Group Policy for all the clients in the domain to use your WSUS server for updates. This exercise assumes you have added the WSUS server and know the name of the server where you installed it.

EXERCISE 4.6

Configuring Clients to Use WSUS with Group Policy

1. Launch the Group Policy Management Console by clicking Start ➢ Administrative Tools ➢ Group Policy Management.

EXERCISE 4.6   *(continued)*

2. Browse to your domain. Right-click the domain, and select Create A GPO In This Domain, and Link It Here, as shown in the following graphic:

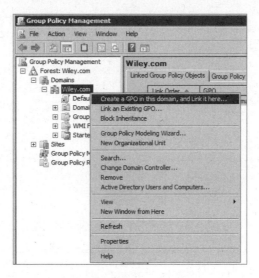

3. Type **WSUS** as the name of the new GPO and click OK.

4. Right-click the WSUS GPO and select Edit.

5. Select Computer Configuration, and browse to the following GPO setting: Policies ➢ Administrative Templates ➢ Windows Components ➢ Windows Update.

6. Select the Configure Automatic Updates selection. Select Enabled. Select the 4—Auto Download and Schedule the Install From the Configure Automatic Updating selection. Click Next Setting.

7. On the Specify Intranet Microsoft Update Service Location setting page, select Enabled and type **http://***ServerName* (where *ServerName* is the name of the server where you installed WSUS). Click Next Setting.

8. On the Automatic Updates Detection Frequency setting page, select Enabled, and change Interval Hours to 20. Click OK. At this point, your display will look similar to the following graphic.

EXERCISE 4.6 *(continued)*

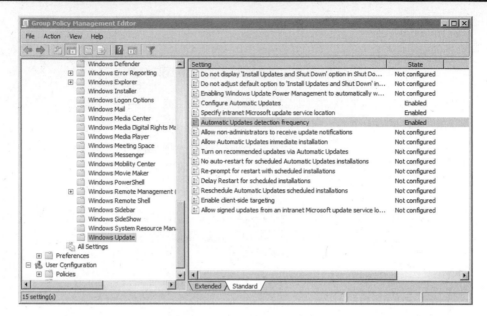

9. Close the Group Policy Management Editor and the Group Policy Management Console.

Verifying That Clients Are Using GPO Settings for WSUS

Group Policy will be applied to clients every 90 to 120 minutes by default. You can wait two hours and check to see if it has been applied, or you can use the `gpupdate /force` command from the command prompt to force an immediate refresh of Group Policy. I suggest using the command if you're trying to verify the update.

After the GPO has been applied, you can verify that the clients are using the WSUS server. Exercise 4.7 shows how to run the `gpupdate /force` command and then verify that clients are configured to their updates from the WSUS server.

EXERCISE 4.7

Verifying That Clients Are Using the WSUS Server for Updates

1. Log on to a Windows 7 client in the domain that is affected by this Group Policy.

2. Force Group Policy to be updated with the following steps:

    a. Launch a command prompt.

    b. Type the following command and press Enter.

    ```
    gpupdate /force
    ```

EXERCISE 4.7   *(continued)*

After a moment, you'll receive two messages indicating that both the User Policy and Computer Policy have been updated. Close the command-prompt window.

3. Click Start ➢ All Programs ➢ Windows Update. Your display will look similar to the following graphic.

Notice that the You Receive Updates setting is now set to Managed by Your System Administrator. If WSUS wasn't being used, this setting would instead display For Windows and Other Products from Microsoft Update, as shown earlier in the chapter.

If you want the client to connect to the WSUS server immediately and check for updates, you can enter the following command at the command prompt:

```
wuauclt /detectnow
```

However, if no updates have been approved by the WSUS server, nothing will be downloaded.

Verifying That Clients Are Using GPO Settings with GPResult

You can also verify that clients are using the WSUS server from the command prompt. Launch a command prompt, and execute the following two commands:

```
Gpresult /v > gpr.txt
Notepad gpr.txt
```

Gpresult /v shows the result of applied Group Policies. The /v switch provides the results in verbose mode (lots of words), and > gpr.txt redirects the output to a text file named `gpr.txt`. You can then open the file in Notepad with `Notepad gpr.txt`, which can then be easily browsed and searched.

If you created a new policy and named it WSUS, it will be displayed in the Computer Settings section under the Applied Group Policy Objects heading as follows:

```
Applied Group Policy Objects
----------------------------
     Default Domain Policy
     WSUS
     Local Group Policy
```

In addition, the Administrative Templates section will have several settings related to updates but aren't in simple English. The easiest thing to decipher here is the `UseWUServer` Registry key. It has a value of 1, indicating that a WSUS server is designated.

```
GPO: WSUS
KeyName:    Software\Policies\Microsoft\Windows\WindowsUpdate\AU\UseWUServer
Value:      1, 0, 0, 0
State:      Enabled
```

Not so easy to decipher is that the server is designated as `http://DC1` using ASCII characters. Each character is separated with a 0 or an ASCII null character.

```
GPO: WSUS
KeyName:    Software\Policies\Microsoft\Windows\WindowsUpdate\WUServer
Value:      104, 0, 116, 0, 116, 0, 112, 0, 58, 0, 47, 0, 47, 0,
            100, 0, 99, 0, 49, 0, 0, 0
State:      Enabled
```

ASCII 104 is *h*, ASCII 116 is *t*, ASCII 112 is *p*, and so on.

Creating Computer Groups on WSUS

A significant improvement of WSUS over earlier versions is the ability to approve updates for specific groups of computers. In other words, you can choose to approve updates for one group of computers but not others.

In order to support this with WSUS, you create computer groups and then move the computers into the appropriate group. Exercise 4.8 shows how this is done.

EXERCISE 4.8

Creating Computer Groups

1. If WSUS is not launched, start WSUS on the server by clicking Start ≻ Administrative Tools ≻ Windows Server Update Services.

2. Click the plus (+) symbol next to Computers to open it. Select All Computers. Change the Status drop-down box to Any and click Refresh. This will show a list of all computers known by the WSUS server. At the very least, the name of the WSUS server should be here.

3. Right-click All Computers, and select Add Computer Group.

4. Type in **Servers** as the Name and click Add.

5. Select Unassigned Computers. Right-click the server name and select Change Membership.

6. Select the Servers group and click OK.

7. Select the Servers group. Select Any from the Status drop-down box, and click Refresh.

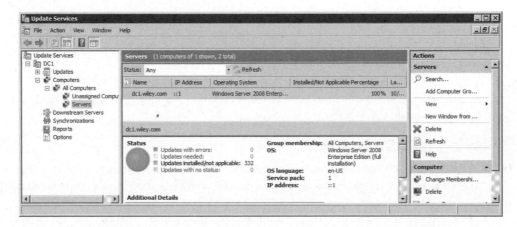

You will see the single server you've added in the Servers group. In the graphic, you may notice that there are two computers, though only one is shown in the Servers group. In my small network, I have a Windows 7 computer that is still in the Unassigned Computers group.

Approving Updates in WSUS

At this point, WSUS is configured to receive and deploy updates. In addition, clients in the domain are configured through Group Policy to receive updates from the WSUS server. However, updates will not be deployed to the clients automatically, and they aren't even downloaded to the WSUS server automatically.

Instead, an administrator must take several steps to deploy updates. These steps are as follows:

- Locate the update in the WSUS console.

- Right-click the update and select Approve.

- Select either the All Computers group or individual computer groups where the update should be deployed.

- Right-click the computer group(s), select Approved for Install, and click OK.

If desired, you can configure auto-approval rules for WSUS. This allows you to identify updates that should be automatically approved based on a classification, a product, or a deadline (in days) when the update should be automatically approved.

Once an update is approved, it will be scheduled for download from Microsoft's website to the WSUS server. When the client checks in with the WSUS server, it will see that the server has the new update, and the client will download and install it (unless the GPO settings were configured to handle the update differently).

Updates are downloaded to the WSUS server when the server synchronizes with the Microsoft website. Synchronization can be done manually, or a synchronization schedule can be created using the WSUS Options page.

Viewing WSUS Reports

WSUS includes a rich set of reporting capabilities. You can create summary and detailed reports based on updates or based on computers and also view reports of synchronization results.

Figure 4.16 shows the report for a Windows 7 PC managed by WSUS. The report was created by right-clicking the computer and selecting Status Report. The first page provides summary data, and the following pages list all of the updates, their approval status, and their installation status.

If you select the Reports node, it allows you to create reports on all of the updates and all of the computers. It also includes the ability to create the reports in a tabular format, which can easily be displayed in a Microsoft Excel worksheet. All of the reports can also be saved in a PDF format if desired.

WSUS is feature rich, especially considering that it's a free product. It provides administrators with any easy-to-learn and easy-to-use tool that gives them better administrative control over updates in the enterprise.

FIGURE 4.16 Viewing a WSUS report for a client

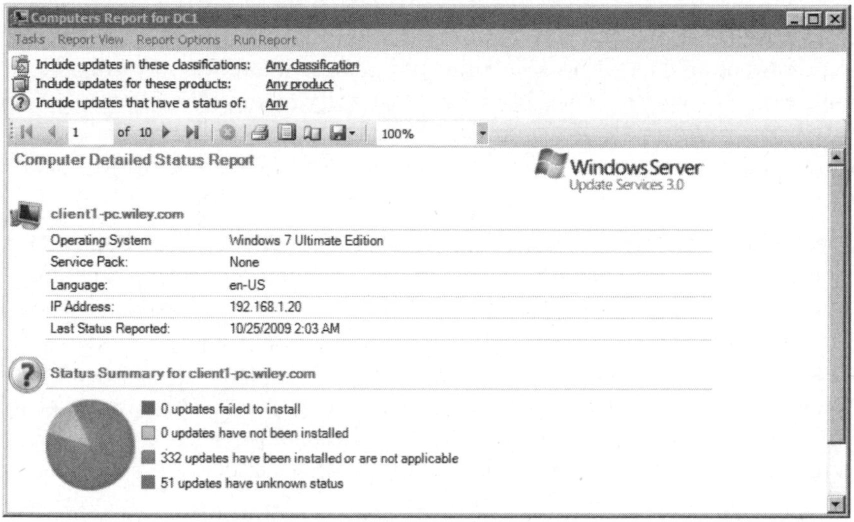

While this section covered some of the basics of WSUS, the goal was to help you realize the benefits of using it. The goal wasn't to teach you everything you need to know about WSUS but instead to help you get started. If it's the right product for you and your enterprise, you can start with what you've learned here. But you need to realize that there's more to WSUS than what we've covered here.

Summary

In this chapter, you learned about the different methods that can be used to deploy updates to Windows 7 clients. You also learned how they can be audited to verify they are being updated.

You have three choices when deciding on how the clients will be updated. Automatic Updates is often used in smaller networks of 50 or fewer clients and doesn't require any administrative intervention after it is set up. Windows Server Update Services is a free server product used in medium and large organizations. Larger organizations that can afford to purchase an enterprise application can use System Center Configuration Manager (SCCM).

The Microsoft Baseline Security Analyzer (MBSA) and its command-line equivalent (MBSACLI) can be used to audit security settings for clients in the enterprise. Among other security checks, it can verify whether clients are receiving updates.

Windows Server Update Services (WSUS) is a popular product that can be used to manage updates on the network centrally. You learned how to prepare a server with the prerequisites, install WSUS, configure it, and approve and deploy updates.

Chapter Essentials

Keeping Windows up to date   Know the value of updates. Windows operating systems and applications need to be updated regularly with patches, fixes, and other updates. As bugs, vulnerabilities, and performance issues are discovered, Microsoft releases these updates to help keep the operating systems and applications secure and running at their peak performance.

Choosing an update tool   Know the available tools and where they're used. Smaller networks of about 50 or fewer clients will typically use Automatic Updates to download and deploy updates to clients automatically. This requires very little administrative work, but it also doesn't give much administrative control. Windows Server Update Services (WSUS) is a free product that can be installed on a server to improve the network bandwidth utilization and allow administrators to approve and deploy updates for specific groups of computers. System Center Configuration Manager (SCCM) is an enterprise application that can be purchased to automate deployment of updates. SCCM allows updates to be scheduled. All of the choices can be enhanced with Group Policy.

Using MBSA for security audits   Be familiar with the Microsoft Baseline Security Analyzer (MBSA) and MBSACLI. MBSA is a GUI application that can be used to audit systems for security issues, including whether the systems have updates installed. MBSA is provided as a free download from Microsoft and when installed includes MBSACLI, which is the command-line equivalent of MBSA. You can create batch files using the MBSACLI and schedule them to run regularly to automate the auditing process.

Using Windows Server Update Services   Understand the capabilities and uses of WSUS. WSUS is a popular free product that can be used to take control of updates in an enterprise. WSUS 3.0 SP2 or later is needed to support Windows 7 clients. Prior to installation, it requires Internet Information Services (IIS) and the Microsoft Report Viewer to be installed. Once WSUS is installed, updates can be approved on the WSUS server and deployed to clients in the network. Clients are typically configured with Group Policy settings to ensure that they receive their updates from the WSUS server.

Chapter

5

Maintaining and Troubleshooting Windows 7

TOPICS COVERED IN THIS CHAPTER INCLUDE

- ✓ Identifying and resolving performance issues
- ✓ Using the Windows Recovery Environment
- ✓ Managing hardware in Windows 7
- ✓ Troubleshooting boot issues

In a perfect world, you'll never have to worry about trouble-shooting Windows 7. However, it's a complex operating system, and changes in one place often result in problems elsewhere. As the operating system is modified, updated, reconfigured, and exposed to endless security threats, things go wrong.

Your first line of defense is built-in tools such as Event Viewer, the Action Center, the Services applet, and Power Options to monitor your system and help identify issues before they become problems.

The Windows Recovery Environment (WinRE) is a modified Windows PE that can be used to recover from several different recovery scenarios. The System Repair feature in the WinRE is a very robust tool that can recover from a wide range of system failures. You can also apply system restore points, reapply images, run memory diagnostics, and access the command prompt from the WinRE.

You also have several tools that can be used to manage basic hardware components. These include memory diagnostics, Check Disk (chkdsk), Disk Defragmenter, and Device Manager, all of which can be used to check and manage memory, manage and maintain hard drives, and manage other devices.

The last section in this chapter provides details on the different phases of the boot process. When the boot process is interrupted, you may want to access some of the tools from the Advanced Boot Options page, such as Repair Your Computer and the different Safe Modes.

You'll learn about all of these tools in this chapter.

Identifying and Resolving Performance Issues

When a system starts having problems, you want to figure out the source of the problem as quickly as possible. One of the ways to get a head start on that goal is to become familiar with the tools you have available for troubleshooting.

In this section, you'll learn about the following tools:

- Event Viewer
- Action Center
- Services
- Power Options

Analyzing Logs with Event Viewer

One of the most important tools you always have available to you on Windows 7 is *Event Viewer*. Events are constantly logged to various logs on Windows 7, and when you know what logs to look at, you can quickly determine the problem.

Windows 7 is constantly logging events on the health and performance of your system, and you can easily query one of many logs to retrieve valuable information. The primary logs you'll monitor when working with Windows 7 are these:

System   The System log records Windows system component events. This includes components such as drivers, services, and Windows-based processes.

Application   The Application log contains events related to applications or programs. As an example, antivirus application events are typically logged in the Application log. Program developers have the choice of which log to use when recording events, so it is possible for an application developer to log an event in the System log instead.

Security   The Security log records security-related events such as logon attempts and auditing. When auditing is enabled, it can be used to record auditable events such as anytime a user accesses a resource. Auditing can also record if someone attempted to access a resource but failed because of not having permissions. Auditing will be covered in more detail in Chapter 11, "Managing Security in Windows 7."

Setup   The Setup log is used to record events related to application installations.

The Forwarded Events log is used if an event subscription is created. A single computer can subscribe to events that are forwarded from multiple other computers.

Event Viewer looks the same on Windows 7 as it does on Windows Vista, Windows Server 2008, and Windows Server 2008 R2. Many of the available logs are much more valuable on a server than they are on a desktop computer. Desktop administrators often focus on only the Application and System logs for troubleshooting and on the Security log when investigating security events.

Figure 5.1 shows the Event Viewer in Windows 7. The Event Viewer is one of the Administrative Tools and can be accessed by multiple methods. One way is by clicking Start ➢ Control Panel, typing **Event Viewer** in the Search box, and pressing Enter. You can then select View Event Logs under Administrative Tools.

There are several items of interest in the figure. The left pane shows the different logs that you can select. Our focus in this chapter is on the Windows logs, especially the System and Application logs. The System log is selected in the figure. The top of the center pane includes summary information on the events for the selected log. The event that is selected is displayed in the bottom of the center pane.

FIGURE 5.1   Viewing the Application log in Event Viewer

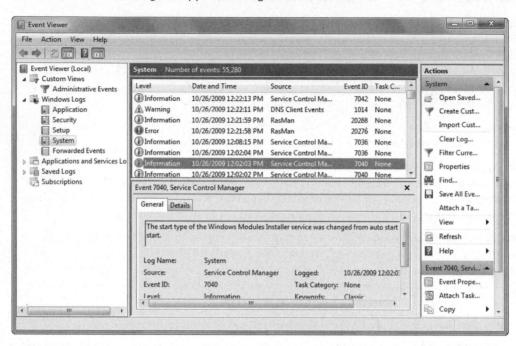

Logs are displayed based on the Date And Time value, with newest log entries showing first. However, you can click any of the headings to sort the logs by a different order. For example, you could click the Event ID header, and the logs would be resorted based on the number of the Event ID.

Events are classified based on a severity level. Four severity-level types can be logged in the System, Application, and Setup logs:

Information severity-level events   Information events are logged when a change to an application or component has occurred. For example, if a service is stopped or started, it will be logged here.

Information events have an icon of a blue *i* in a white circle.

Warning severity-level events   Warning events indicate that something has occurred that may impact a service or result in a more serious problem if the event is not addressed. Errors are usually preceded by warnings.

Warning events have an icon of a black exclamation point (!) in a yellow triangle.

Error severity-level events   An error event indicates that a problem has occurred. Errors can impact the functionality of the application or component that triggered the event. For example, if a service tried to start but a condition prevented it from starting, an error event would be logged.

Error events have an icon of a white exclamation point (!) in a red circle.

Critical severity-level events   Critical events indicate that a failure has occurred and the application or component that triggered the event cannot recover.

Critical events have an icon of a white *X* in a red circle.

You can double-click any event in the Event Viewer to see additional details on the event. Figure 5.2 shows the details of an event logged after Windows Explorer hung on a system, requiring it to be stopped via Task Manager.

FIGURE 5.2   Viewing the details of an application error event

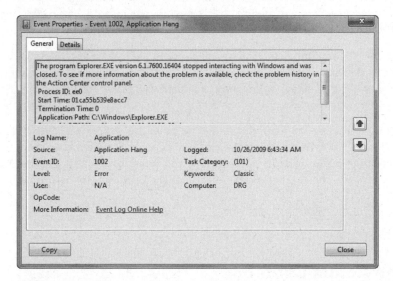

Events include details such as what, when, and where and, in the case of security events, also identify the user performing the event. If an error or a warning event occurs on a regular basis, it indicates a problem that needs to be addressed. If the event occurs only once, you may be able to ignore the event.

An Application Hang source indicates that the application would not respond and had to be forcibly terminated using Task Manager.

The Details tab is more useful to the developers of the application or component than to the administrators. As an administrator, you'll find all the information you need on the General tab. A valuable feature is the Copy button, which allows you to copy the details of the event easily to the Clipboard so that you can paste them into another document.

Real World Scenario

Don't Even Call Me Until You've Checked the Logs!

Interestingly, the Event Viewer seems to be overlooked by a lot of newer administrators. At one place where I was doing some work, a senior administrator shared the following story with me.

He was called at home for help. He quickly recognized the problem based on the symptoms and thought that the technician calling him should also have recognized the problem. He asked if there were any errors in the System log, because he was certain these errors would verify the problem.

However, he soon realized the technician hadn't checked the logs at all. He (not so mildly) expressed some irritation that the technician chose to call him without doing what he considered a very basic troubleshooting step of gathering data on the error. He then told the technician to go back and check the logs and not to call back until he had done so.

He's since adopted this as a standard question if he's ever asked for help: "What do you see in Event Viewer?" He's asking the technicians this question to help train them to use it. He's also asking this question to help himself by receiving fewer calls at home. Many times a little analysis of the log entries will lead the technician right to the problem and the solution.

Using the Action Center

The *Action Center* provides a central location to view alerts and take actions. Messages in the Action Center provide insight into the system's security, reliability, and stability. When the Action Center has issues that can be resolved by taking specific actions, a little white flag appears in the notification area of Windows 7.

    The notification area is on the far right of the taskbar. It includes several notification icons such as the Clock, Volume, Network, Power, and Action Center. Any of these icons can be enabled or disabled by right-clicking the notification area and selecting Properties.

Figure 5.3 shows the Action Center on a Windows 7 system. It includes several issues that the Action Center suggests should be investigated.

FIGURE 5.3   Viewing messages in the Action Center

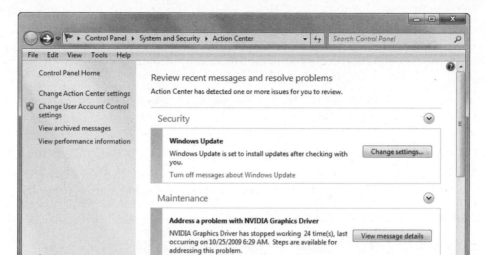

Not all Action Center messages need action. As an example, the Security section is reminding me that I have Windows Update set to download the updates automatically, but I must choose when to install them. Since this is contrary to the recommendations, it's included in the Action Center. It is possible to turn off messages about Windows Update, but that will turn off all messages about Windows Update, not only this notification.

On the other hand, it also shows I have issues with an NVIDIA graphics driver that has stopped working 24 times. When I click View Message Details, it does an Internet query and gives me a list of possible solutions, such as checking for driver updates through the Microsoft Update site or other methods.

The NVIDIA driver occasionally fails when the system is waking up from hibernate, forcing a reboot. The Action Center has detected the failure and identified the problem as a driver issue. Unfortunately, there doesn't seem to be a driver update for it just yet. Since Windows 7 has been officially released for just a couple of days as I write this, I'm willing to be patient.

The Action Center has two areas where different messages can be displayed: Security and Maintenance.

Security   The Security section provides security-related messages. It can provide messages on network firewall, Windows Update, virus protection, spyware and unwanted software protection, Internet security settings, User Account Control, and Network Access Protection.

Maintenance   The Maintenance section provides messages related to backups, checking for updates, and system maintenance settings.

Changing Action Center Settings

It's possible to turn on or off various Action Center messages. If you click the Change Action Center Settings link in the Action Center, a display similar to Figure 5.4 appears.

FIGURE 5.4   Modifying Action Center settings

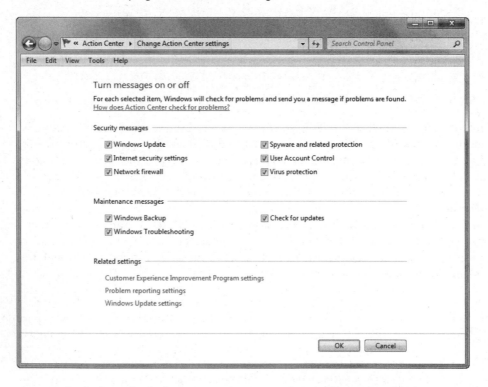

You can check or uncheck the boxes to turn on or turn off messages for that category. For example, if you wanted to keep your system configured to download updates automatically but you choose when to install them, and you don't want to be notified of your choice, uncheck the Windows Update selection.

The Related Settings section at the bottom of the figure has three links. The Windows Update Settings link provides another path to the Change Settings page for Windows Update, which was covered in depth in Chapter 4, "Managing the Life Cycle—Keeping Windows 7 Up to Date." However, the other two topics have not been covered.

Customer Experience Improvement Program Settings

This program collects information about the computer hardware and how Windows is being used, but it does not collect any information that can be used to identify or contact the user personally. It also periodically downloads a file that can be used to collect information about problems experienced on the system.

By using this method, Microsoft is able to identify how people are using Windows. This information can then be used to identify ways Windows can be improved or enhanced.

You have two choices when you click this link:

- Yes, I Want To Participate In The Program
- No, I Don't Want To Participate In The Program

Problem Reporting Settings

The Problem Reporting Settings are directly related to *Windows Error Reporting (WER)*. WER is used to report issues to Microsoft from individual computers. When a problem event occurs, WER can be invoked to collect and report information on the error.

WER is most commonly invoked when an unresponsive application is terminated using Task Manager. If authorized, information on the error is sent to Microsoft servers that collect the data. Once Microsoft is aware of an error that is causing problems for end users, they begin looking for a solution.

WER is especially useful for emerging threats. If thousands of computers start having the same issue that WER reports, Microsoft is able to collect data quickly on the issue and respond with a solution in a much more timely fashion.

The solution may require a patch that is written and released as an update, or investigation may show that the problem is due to a set of circumstances that the user can control. Once a solution is identified, Microsoft's response to the WER message indicates that a solution is available. In addition, if the Action Center is configured to receive the solutions, the solutions will appear in the Action Center, prompting the user take action.

Figure 5.5 shows the four choices for WER, with the recommended setting selected.

FIGURE 5.5 Configuring problem reporting in the Action Center

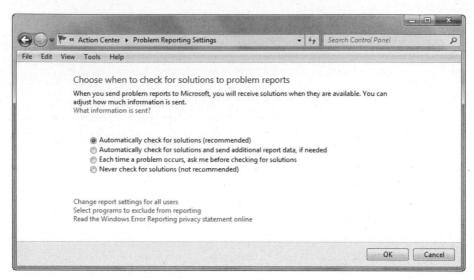

When WER is configured as shown, problems are automatically reported to Microsoft. When solutions are identified, they will appear in the Action Center.

Changing User Account Control Settings

User Account Control (UAC) is used to prevent malicious software (malware) or other potentially harmful programs from making unauthorized changes to your computer. The challenge is determining the difference between an authorized change and an unauthorized change.

If a user is using a system and that system becomes infected with malware, the malware can assume the permissions and rights of the user. If the user has sufficient rights to make system-level changes, the malware has those same rights. With elevated rights and permissions, the malware can quickly embed itself deep into the system and start its mischief.

Windows Vista introduced UAC to detect when changes were occurring to the system and to ask users if they initiated the action. If the action was initiated by malware, it could be stopped. However, one of the complaints about UAC with Windows Vista is that users were prompted too frequently to confirm their actions.

Windows 7 has improved UAC. One significant change is that Windows 7 can differentiate between changes made by a user and changes made by an application. By default, UAC in Windows 7 notifies the user only when an application attempts to make a change.

Protected Admin and Standard User Accounts

The Protected Admin (PA) is the default type of account for the first account in a system. The PA runs with two sets of permissions. One set of permissions is regular permissions used to do regular work. The other set of permissions is full administrator permissions and is used only when allowed by UAC.

Anytime a user with a PA account attempts to do something requiring administrator permissions, such as a system-level change, the system recognizes it's a PA account and can prompt the user to approve the use of the elevated permissions.

A standard user is any local user account created after the first account. Standard user accounts can do a lot without extra permissions, but standard users are prompted to provide different credentials if they try to perform a system-level change.

Balancing Security

When it comes to security, it's often difficult to find the right balance that ensures an acceptable level of security while also allowing an acceptable level of usability to the end user. You probably know that the only way to ensure a computer is 100 percent secure is never to take it out of the box. As soon as you plug it in, you start accepting some risk.

On the other hand, a computer without any security at all may be very easy to use but won't be secure. What's important—usability or security? The answer is that both are important, so when computers are deployed they are done so with a balance of security and usability. However, that balance isn't the same for everyone.

If a computer houses highly classified data, security is much more important than usability. On the other hand, a computer used by administrative staff for day-to-day tasks doesn't need the same level of security.

Selecting the UAC Level

Figure 5.6 shows the User Account Control Settings page that can be accessed from the Action Center with the default selected. There are four choices available:

Always Notify   This is the most secure setting. Any system-level change results in a UAC prompt. It doesn't matter whether the change was initiated by the user or by a program. This setting is recommended if a user routinely installs new software or visits risky or unfamiliar websites. The desktop is switched to a secure desktop mode (the user will see it dimmed) until the UAC prompt is approved or denied.

Secure desktop mode is used to prevent malware from mimicking the UAC prompt. When dimmed by UAC, nothing else can be done until the UAC query is answered.

FIGURE 5.6   Configuring User Account Control

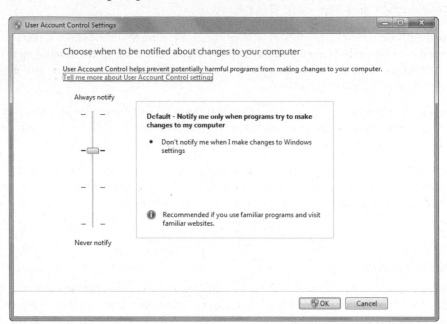

Notify Me Only When Programs Try To Make Changes To My Computer   This setting will notify the user when a program attempts to make changes to a computer that requires administrator permissions. When this occurs, the desktop will be dimmed. Changes made by the user do not result in notification. This is the default setting.

Notify Me Only When Programs Try To Make Changes To My Computer (Do Not Dim My Desktop)   This is the same as the previous setting but does not use the secure desktop setting. Since the desktop is not dimmed, malware may be able to spoof or otherwise interfere with the appearance of the UAC dialog box.

Never Notify   This is the least-secure setting. Any changes made by the user or a computer will be allowed without any notification.

Configuring Services

Services are started when the system starts and before a user logs on. Any Windows system today includes multiple services that are performing a wide assortment of tasks behind the scenes. As an example, the Windows Firewall service starts when Windows starts and will quietly monitor all the traffic, allowing and blocking traffic based on the rules of the service.

In contrast, applications are launched by users after the user logs on. For example, a user may launch the Internet Explorer application to access the Internet.

Accessing Services

The primary tool used to access services is the *Services console*. You can launch it by clicking Start ➢ Administrative Tools ➢ Services.

> You can add the Administrative Tools menu to the Windows 7 Start menu if it's not already showing. Right-click the Start button and select Properties. With the Start Menu tab selected, click Customize. Scroll to the bottom of the Customize Start Menu section and locate the System Administrative Tools section. Select Display On The All Programs Menu And The Start Menu, and click OK twice.

Figure 5.7 shows the Services console highlighting the Windows Firewall service (started). The console allows you easily to see an overview of the services. Two important columns to which you should pay attention are Status and Startup Type. In the figure, the Windows Firewall service is selected. You can see that the service is started and the startup type is set to Automatic.

FIGURE 5.7   Viewing the Services console with the Windows Firewall service selected

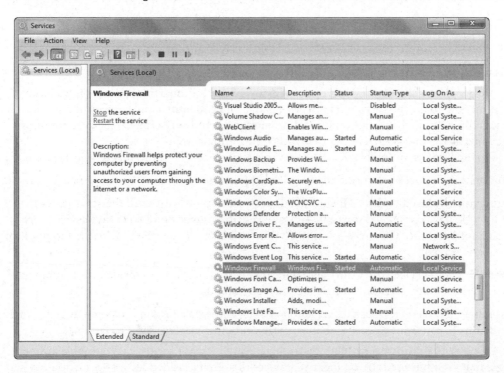

When you select a service, the Extended view gives action links and a description. Since the Windows Firewall service is running, you can use the action links to stop or restart the service.

As with most consoles in Windows 7, you can click any of the headings to reorder the display. The display is sorted in alphabetical order by the service name by default. If you click the Name heading, it reorders the services in reverse order, starting with the Ws. You could also click the Status heading and quickly sort it by the services that are started or by any heading, depending on what you're looking for.

Configuring Services Settings

Each service has several properties and settings that can be viewed and manipulated. To access these properties, you can right-click the service and select Properties.

 You may notice that some context menus (right-click menus) include a bolded item. This indicates the default selection if the item is double-clicked. For example, the Properties selection is bolded when you right-click a service in the Services console. If you double-click the service, the Properties page will appear.

Each service has four tabs that include different properties and settings that can be manipulated.

Viewing the General Tab of a Service

Figure 5.8 shows the General tab of the Windows Search Properties page. It shows basic information about the service. The Service Name value identifies the name of the service that is often used when using command-prompt commands or scripts. The Description is the same as the one shown in the Extended view of the service.

Startup Type is an important setting on this page. It can be set to one of four types:

Automatic   Services set to Automatic will start when the operating system starts.

Automatic (Delayed Start)   This setting directs a service to wait until the services set to Automatic have completed starting. This reduces the contention of so many services competing for hardware resources at the same time and also reduces the time needed to boot to the logon screen.

Manual   The service won't start automatically but will respond to service start commands such as through the Net Start or the SC Start commands.

Disabled   The service doesn't start automatically and won't respond to commands to start manually. If you want to ensure that a service cannot be started, set it to Disabled.

One way to optimize a system's performance and increase security is to disable any services that aren't needed. If you identify services that aren't needed for a system, you can set them to Disabled from this page.

FIGURE 5.8   Viewing the General tab of a service

It's also possible to set the startup type of services using Group Policy. Group Policy will be covered in more depth in Chapter 10, "Managing Windows 7 with Group Policy," but in short you can choose to enable or disable a service for all computers in the domain or all users in an organizational unit using a Group Policy object.

Figure 5.9 shows the default domain policy opened to the Computer Configuration ➢ Policies ➢ Windows Settings ➢ Security Settings ➢ System Services node. The Windows Error Reporting Service selection has been opened, and the Define This Policy Setting and Automatic startup options have been selected. This will ensure the service is enabled and automatically started for all clients in the domain.

FIGURE 5.9   Configuring the startup type for a service via Group Policy

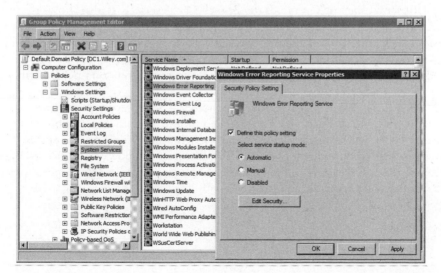

Similarly, you could set a policy to ensure a service is disabled for all clients in the domain. When settings are managed by a GPO, they become dimmed and unchangeable on clients affected by the GPO.

Viewing the Log On Tab of a Service

Services must run with some type of permissions, and the permissions are determined by the account used to start the service. One of three built-in local accounts is typically used to start most services, and it's also possible to configure a service to run using a local or domain account you've created.

These are the three built-in local are accounts:

Local System   Most services use the Local System account, which grants them rights and permissions to perform their designated tasks on the local system. An additional check box can be selected to allow the service also to interact with the desktop. The Print Spooler service is one of the few services that has this selection checked.

Local Service   This account is used for services that need fewer rights and permissions than the Local System service.

Security in Windows services has been improved through an internal Microsoft process referred to as Windows Service Hardening. Whenever possible, services are configured to use the Local Service or Network Service accounts to limit the rights and permissions of a service. This is a change from operating systems before Windows Vista, which would often use the Local System account by default.

Network Service   This account is used for services that need fewer rights and permissions than the Local System service but need access to network resources. As an example, the BranchCache and DNS Client services are configured to use the Network Service account.

Figure 5.10 shows the Log On tab of the Branch Cache service. It also shows the extra screens that would be selected to use a different account.

To select a different service account, you'd select Browse, click the Advanced button, click Find Now, and select one of the accounts displayed in the Search Results. When adding the Local Service or Network Service account, you don't need to enter a password.

Notice that you can also select a regular user account. Some server applications require the creation of a user account that will be assigned specific permissions and be used to start a specific service. However, this is rarely needed on Windows 7 desktop computers.

Managed service accounts are a new feature available in Windows 7 and Windows Server 2008 R2. This is a special class of domain account that can be created for applications that need to be started with service accounts.

FIGURE 5.10   Viewing the Log On tab of a service

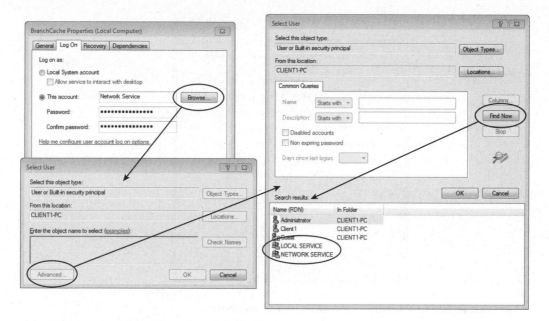

In the past, regular domain user accounts were created to start services and were referred to as service accounts. Passwords either needed to be changed regularly on these accounts to prevent them from being locked out, or security could be weakened to ensure passwords never expired on these accounts.

However, you can now create a single managed-service account for a computer and use it to run services on the system. The passwords for these accounts will be reset automatically, so passwords don't need to be managed for a managed service account. Managed serviced accounts work only on Windows 7 or newer desktops and Windows Server 2008 R2 or newer servers.

> Managed-service accounts are available in Windows 7 and Windows Server 2008 R2. A significant feature of a managed service account is that passwords are reset automatically, removing the need to manage passwords manually for service accounts. For more information, check out this Tech-Net article: http://technet.microsoft.com/library/dd367859.aspx.

Viewing the Recovery Tab of a Service

The Recovery tab of any service allows you configure actions to take if the service fails. Figure 5.11 shows the Recovery tab with several actions configured.

FIGURE 5.11   Viewing the Recovery tab of a service

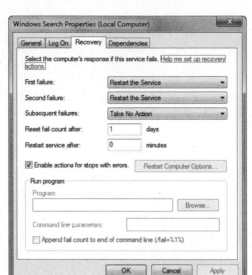

The actions you can select if a service fails are as follows:

Restart The Service   This attempts to start the service again if it fails.

Run A Program   The program can be any executable including a script or batch file. The program is specified in the Run Program section.

Restart The Computer   If you select Restart The Computer, you can also configure restart options. This allows you to select the time to wait (in minutes) before restarting and have the computer send a message to other computers before restarting.

Viewing the Dependencies Tab of a Service

The Dependencies tab shows two lists. If you plan to modify the start state of a service, you should check the dependencies. This is especially true if you change the start state to Disabled.

This Service Depends On The Following System Components   This list shows services and components that this service depends on to run. If the listed services or components are not running, the service will usually not even start.

The Following System Components Depend On This Service   The second list identifies services that depend on this service. If this service is not running and can't be started, services in the list will not be able to start.

Using Service Control to Manipulate Services

Services can be queried, started, stopped, and manipulated from the command line using the *Service Control (SC)* command. SC communicates with the Service Controller and the installed services, and it allows you to perform most of the actions from the command prompt that you can do from the Services console.

Remember, the value of using any command-line commands is that they can be scripted. SC commands can be added to any batch file to manipulate services.

As an example, if you want to start the fax service, you can use the following command:

SC start fax

Table 5.1 shows some of the common SC commands you can use to query and manipulate services, with examples of how the command could be used.

TABLE 5.1   SC commands

Command	Description
SC query	Retrieves a listing of running services, or if a service name is included, it will retrieve details on the named service. SC query SC query defragsvc
SC queryex	Retrieves a listing of running services with extended details. If a service name is included, it will retrieve extended details on the named service. SC queryex SC queryex defragsvc
SC query type= all	Can be used to provide a list of all services. Notice that a space must be added after the = sign. SC query type= all
SC stop	Stops a service. The service name must be provided. SC stop defragsvc
SC start	Starts a service. The service name must be provided. SC start defragsvc
SC pause	Pauses a running service. The service name must be provided. SC pause defragsvc
SC continue	Continues a paused service. The service name must be provided. SC continue defragsvc

If you want to see more of the commands that can be used with the Service Control command, check out this TechNet library article: http://technet.microsoft.com/library/cc754599.aspx.

Managing Power Settings

As the cost of energy continues to rise, power conservation has become more important to companies concerned about the bottom line. Windows 7 includes access to many power settings that can be configured to help PCs conserve power.

Individual components can be placed into low-power states, and the entire computer can be put to sleep without completely powering it off. You can access the majority of the settings from the Power Options page in Control Panel. Click Start ➢ Control Panel. Select Hardware And Sound ➢ Power Options. You'll see a display similar to Figure 5.12.

FIGURE 5.12   Power Options page in Control Panel

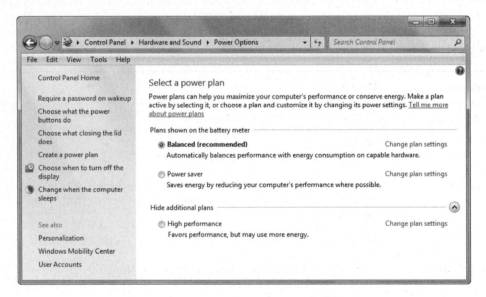

In the figure, the High Performance plan is showing, but this is not displayed by default. By default, this space will have a text link labeled Show Additional Plans instead of Hide Additional Plans. If you click the text, the additional plan will show.

Powercfg is a neat tool you can use to analyze and configure power settings on a computer. As an example, you can use the following command to analyze the current power settings and performance of a Windows 7 computer: powercfg -energy -output power.html. You can then enter power.html to view the report.

Understanding Low-Power States

Windows 7 supports three low-power states:

Sleep   When the computer is in *sleep* mode, most of the components will not draw any power, but the memory and processor will still consume some power. Enough power is provided to the memory to ensure that the contents of memory are not lost and that the processor has enough power to check occasionally for use action such as pressing a key. When a key is pressed on the keyboard, the computer wakes up fully.

If the system senses that the battery power is low on a laptop computer, it will automatically put the laptop into hibernate mode.

Hibernate   *Hibernate* is primarily used for laptops. It takes the entire contents of memory and stores them on the hard drive. When the data is stored on the hard drive, the system will completely power down and not use any power. This works even if a user has open applications and open documents. For example, you could have a Microsoft Word document open when the system hibernates. Later, when you turn it back on, Microsoft Word will open with your document just as it was when the system hibernated.

Hybrid Sleep   *Hybrid sleep* mode is similar to the hibernate mode used on laptops but remains powered on. The current state of the computer is retained in memory with enough power provided to keep the memory refreshed. In addition, the contents of memory are stored on the hard drive. If a power failure occurs, the system can resume as if it was hibernated. If a power failure doesn't occur and the user takes an action such as pressing a key, the system will resume as if waking from sleep mode. Hybrid sleep mode is intended to be used on desktop PCs.

You can choose one of the low-power states from the Start menu, or you can configure a system to enter these states based on different actions. Figure 5.13 shows how you can select either Sleep or Hibernate on a laptop computer from the Start menu.

FIGURE 5.13   Choosing Sleep or Hibernate from the Start menu

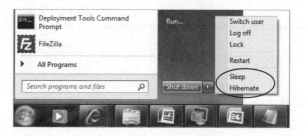

    Available power settings are dependent on the capabilities of your system and whether the capabilities are enabled in the system BIOS.

You can also configure your system to go into one of these states when the power button is pressed, when the sleep button is pressed (if the system has a sleep button), or when the lid of a laptop is closed.

Figure 5.14 shows the System Settings page that you can access from the Control Panel ➢ Hardware And Sound ➢ Power Options page. In the figure, I've selected the drop-down box for When I Close the Lid when the system is Plugged In. These same options are available for any of the choices.

FIGURE 5.14 Choosing a response for different power actions on a laptop computer

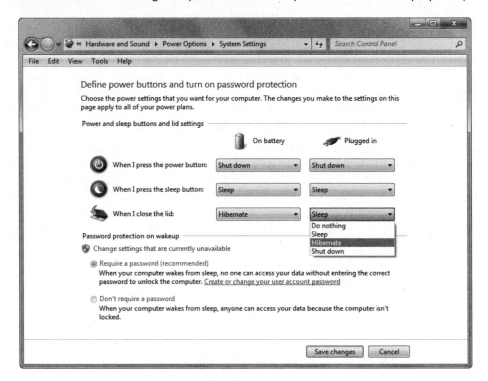

For a desktop PC, the On Battery settings and the When I Close The Lid settings are not available.

Understanding Power Plans

A power plan is a collection of individual settings that can be configured for individual components of a computer. While the low-power states like sleep and hibernate affect the entire computer, these power settings affect specific components such as the display or hard drive.

Three power plans exist on the system. The two plans that are shown by default are designed to help you maximize the performance of the system while also conserving energy; the High Performance plan is hidden by default.

Balanced (Recommended)   This is the default setting for a system that is plugged in, and it will meet the needs of most systems. It provides high performance for the system while it is being used, and it will automatically invoke different power settings when the computer is not being used.

Power Saver   The Power Saver plan uses reduced power all the time to conserve energy. This is a good choice for a laptop that will be on battery power for an extended period of time.

High Performance   The High Performance plan is used to provide maximum performance without considering energy conservation. This plan could be used if a system has extra uses such as sharing a printer or sharing files.

The settings for these plans can be manipulated individually by clicking Change Plan Settings. Figure 5.15 shows the basic settings for the Balanced plan.

FIGURE 5.15   Viewing the power settings for the Balanced power plan

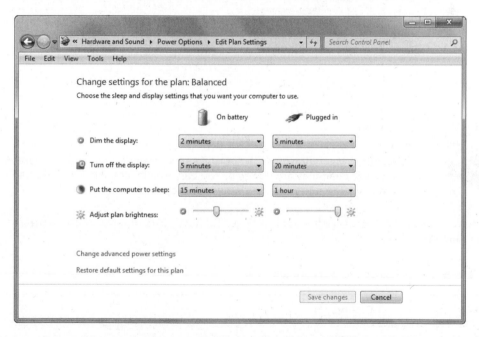

Notice that you can configure different power savings for a laptop when it is plugged in and when it is on battery power. The Adjust Plan Brightness setting uses a slider bar. By sliding it to the right, the brightness becomes full. Slide it to the left to make it dimmer. This setting is probably the one that users will notice the most.

Changing Advanced Power Settings

You can also click the Change Advanced Power Settings link to access advanced power settings for any of the individual plans. These settings allow you to access settings for disk drives, USB settings, and more.

Figure 5.16 shows the Advanced Settings page for the Balanced power plan and also indicates that the Balanced plan is active.

FIGURE 5.16   Viewing the Advanced Settings page for the Balanced power plan

 Settings that require advanced permissions often don't appear, and when they do appear, they are dimmed. You can enable all the settings by clicking the link Change Settings That Are Currently Unavailable.

You can configure several settings on this page. Table 5.2 lists of many of the settings and comments.

TABLE 5.2   Advanced power settings

Setting	Comments
Require A Password On Wakeup	This requires the user to provide credentials when the system wakes up from sleep or hibernate mode.
Hard Disk	You can configure the hard disk to turn off after a specific amount of time (such as 20 minutes) to conserve power.

TABLE 5.2   Advanced power settings *(continued)*

Setting	Comments
Desktop Background Settings	Slide shows can be configured to run (Available) or not (Paused). For example, you can configure this as Paused on battery power to reduce power consumed by the disk, video, and processor.
Wireless Adapter Settings	Adapters can be configured for Maximum Performance, Low Power Saving, Medium Power Saving, and Maximum Power Saving modes. This affects the power used for wireless transmissions, but it can also affect the ability to connect to wireless networks.
Sleep	The different low-power modes can be configured here, such as automatically putting the computer to sleep after 15 minutes when on battery or after 30 minutes when plugged in. You can also configure the system to awaken for timed events.
USB Settings	You can enable the Selective Suspend setting, which allows the USB hub to suspend individual ports selectively (such the port for a hard disk but not the hub for the mouse or keyboard).
Power Buttons And Lid	You can specify actions for closing the lid, pressing the power, or pressing the sleep button.
PCI Express	You can configure power settings for PCI Express devices. You can turn Link State Power Management off or select Maximum Power Savings or Minimum Power Savings.
Processor Power Management	These settings allow you to configure thresholds for power consumed by the processor.
Display	You can configure when a display is dimmed and when it is turned off. You can also configure the brightness in percentages here.
Multimedia Settings	If the computer is used to share media or play video, you can configure when it is allowed to sleep and the power plan to use when it is running.
Battery	You can configure thresholds and actions for different battery power levels. For example, the system can provide a low-battery warning when it reaches a low battery level (configured at 10 percent) and go into hibernate when it reaches a critical battery level (configured at 5 percent).

As long as we're talking about power, you may be interested in how you can modify the default behavior of the Shut Down button available from the Start menu. Right-click the Shut Down button and select Properties. You can reconfigure the Power Button Action to Switch User, Log Off, Lock, Restart, Sleep, or Hibernate.

Configuring Wake On LAN

Most systems include Wake On LAN or Remote Wake-up capabilities. This allows the system to go into a low-power mode such as sleep but awaken in response to a special data packet, referred to as a Magic Packet. Network administrators use this to schedule remote administration while still allowing the system to use the lower power modes.

In order for system to listen for and respond to Magic Packets, the motherboard, BIOS, network adapter, and adapter driver must all support it. When all of the pieces are available, you can configure it in the properties of the NIC via Device Manager. Most NICs include a Power Management tab where Wake On LAN can be enabled.

Using Windows RE

The *Windows Recovery Environment (WinRE)* includes several tools that can be used to troubleshoot and recover a system. The *WinRE* is an extension of the Windows preinstallation environment (PE) covered in Chapter 2, "Automating the Deployment of Windows 7."

You can access the WinRE using the following methods:

- Pressing F8 when booting to a Windows 7 installation
- Booting with an installation DVD
- Using bootable WinRE media

Once you boot into WinRE, you'll have access to the following tools:

- Startup Repair Tool
- System Restore
- System Image Recovery
- Windows Memory Diagnostic
- Command Prompt

The methods to access the WinRE and the available tools are described in the following sections.

Accessing the WinRE

The primary method you'll use to access the WinRE is by pressing the F8 key when the system is booted. WinRE is automatically included in the installation of Windows 7.

However, if the system is corrupt, you can also access it using the installation DVD or by creating your own bootable WinRE CD or USB disk.

Accessing the WinRE with F8

The WinRE environment is included in the installation and, if the installation hasn't been corrupted, it can be accessed by pressing the F8 key on boot. This will display the Advanced Boot Options screen, as shown in Figure 5.17.

FIGURE 5.17   Accessing the Advanced Boot Options

```
                          Advanced Boot Options

Choose Advanced Options for: Windows 7
(Use the arrow keys to highlight your choice.)

    Repair Your Computer

    Safe Mode
    Safe Mode with Networking
    Safe Mode with Command Prompt

    Enable Boot Logging
    Enable low-resolution video (640x480)
    Last Known Good Configuration (advanced)
    Directory Services Restore Mode
    Debugging Mode
    Disable automatic restart on system failure
    Disable Driver Signature Enforcement

    Start Windows Normally

Description: View a list of system recovery tools you can use to repair
            startup problems, run diagnostics, or restore your system.

ENTER=Choose                                          ESC=Cancel
```

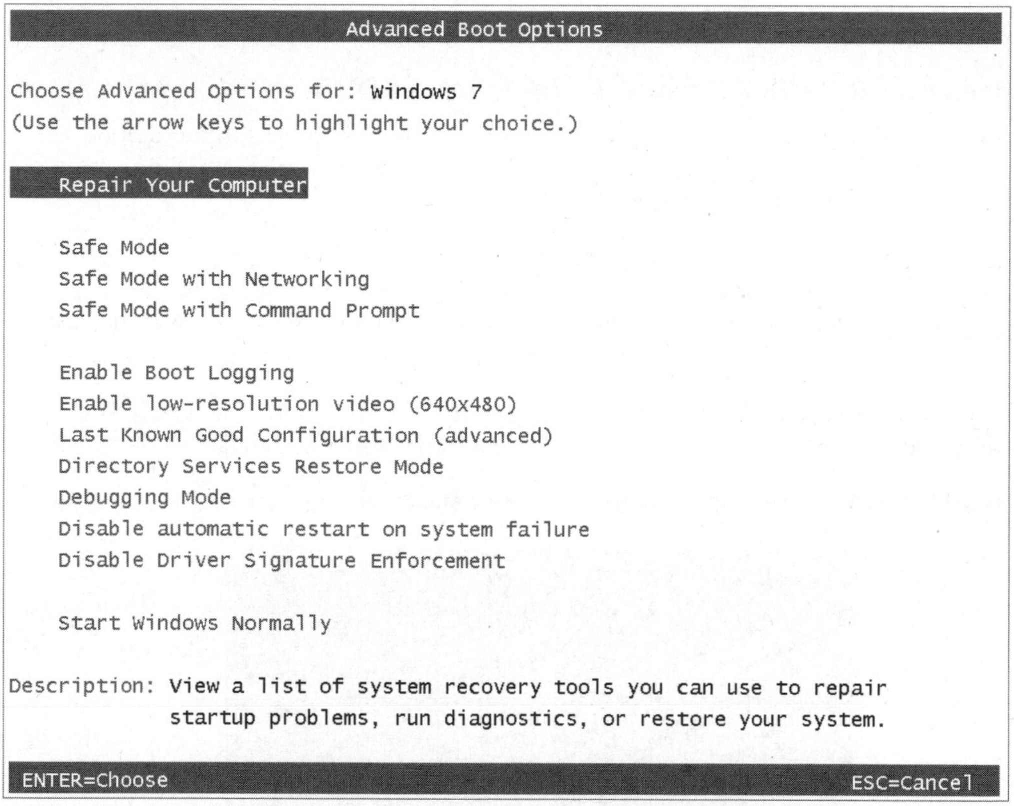

The Repair Your Computer option is the first selection, and it will launch the WinRE. You can also access the different Safe Mode options and some other troubleshooting tools from this screen. Exercise 5.1 shows how to access the WinRE with the F8 key.

EXERCISE 5.1

Accessing the WinRE on Boot

1. Reboot the Windows 7 computer, and press F8 as it starts. You need to press this key right away. If the Windows screen appears, it's too late, and you'll need to reboot and try again.

2. When the Advanced Boot Options page appears, select Repair Your Computer and press Enter.

3. Select your keyboard type and click Next.

4. Enter a valid user name and password and click OK.

5. The System Recovery Options page will appear.

Accessing the WinRE from the Installation DVD

If the installation is corrupt and you can't access the WinRE from the Advanced Boot Options screen, you can use the installation DVD. Place the installation DVD in the system, and boot to it as if you were installing Windows 7.

 WARNING You need to use an installation DVD that matches the architecture of the system you're checking. If the installed system is 64-bit, for example, you'll need to use a 64-bit installation DVD.

You'll first be prompted to choose a language. After you click Next, the Install Now page appears, as shown in Figure 5.18. Select Repair Your Computer to launch the WinRE.

FIGURE 5.18 Accessing the WinRE from the installation DVD

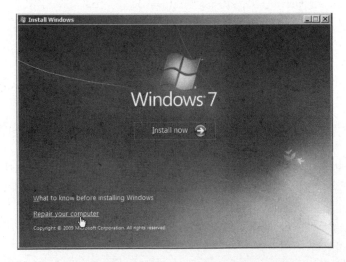

Creating Bootable Media to Access the WinRE

You can also create your own bootable media to access the WinRE. Although this is a little more advanced, it will give you easy access to the WinRE so that you can troubleshoot problems when the installation won't start.

If you created a bootable WinPE disk (as done in Chapter 2), you have only a few more steps to create a WinRE disk. The WinRE.wim image file is embedded in the install.wim file on the installation DVD and can be extracted. After extracting it, you can rename it to boot.wim and use it instead of the boot.wim used on a bootable WinPE disk.

Exercise 5.2 shows how to create a bootable USB disk or CD that will boot to the WinRE. This exercise assumes you've installed the Windows Automated Installation Kit from Chapter 2, have created a bootable PE environment in Exercise 2.2, and have access to an installation DVD.

EXERCISE 5.2

Creating a Bootable Windows RE USB or CD

1. Launch the Deployment Tools Command Prompt with administrative permissions. Select Start ➤ All Programs ➤ Microsoft Windows AIK, right-click the Deployment Tools Command Prompt, and select Run As Administrator.

2. If prompted by User Account Control, click Yes to proceed.

3. Create the folders that will store the Windows 7 mounted image with the following command:

   ```
   MD c:\Win7Mount
   ```

4. Extract one of the Windows 7 images from the install.wim file on the installation DVD with the following steps:

   a. Insert the Windows 7 installation DVD in the DVD drive, and determine the drive letter assigned to the DVD. You can find this by launching Windows Explorer and browsing to the DVD.

   The following step assumes the letter is D:, but your system may assign a different letter.

   b. Mount an image from the install.wim file with the following command. The install.wim file is located in the Sources folder of the installation DVD and contains multiple images. This command will mount the first image. This will take a few minutes to complete.

   ```
   ImageX /mount d:\sources\install.wim 1 C:\Win7Mount
   ```

   At this point, the C:\Win7Mount folder includes all the files of a Windows installation.

5. Extract the Windows RE image using the following steps:

    a. Use the following command to create the folder that will hold the `WinRE.wim` file that is in the mounted Windows 7 image.

        `MD C:\WinRE`

    b. Copy the `WinRE.wim` file from the mounted Windows 7 image with the following command:

        `Copy c:\Win7Mount\Windows\System32\Recovery\WinRE.wim c:\WinRE`

    c. At this point, you've finished with the mounted image, so unmount it with the following command:

        `ImageX /unmount c:\Win7Mount`

        This will remove all of the files from this folder.

6. Verify that you have a MyPE folder on your C: drive (from Exercise 2.2 in Chapter 2). If not, complete Exercise 2.2.

7. Make a copy of the MyPE folder named MyRE with the following command:

    `Xcopy c:\MyPE /s c:\MyRE`

    This will create a copy of the folders including the `iso` folder. The `iso` folder includes all of the required files and folders for the WinPE, and you can modify it slightly to use it as a WinRE.

8. You'll need to overwrite the `boot.wim` file in the `iso` folder with the `WinRE.wim` file you extracted from the installation image in step 5. Execute the following command:

    `Copy c:\WinRE\WinRE.wim c:\MyRE\iso\sources\boot.wim`

    When prompted to overwrite `boot.wim`, type **Y** and press Enter.

    At this point, you have created the Windows Recovery Environment (WinRE) folder. You can create a bootable USB drive by following steps 9 and 10 and create a bootable CD-ROM by following steps 11 through 13. These steps are very similar to the steps you used to create bootable media for Windows PE in Exercise 2.2.

9. Format your USB drive with DiskPart using the following commands:

    a. Launch the command prompt with administrative permissions. If prompted by User Account Control, click Yes.

    b. Type **DiskPart**, and press Enter to access the Disk Partition tool.

c. Type **List Disk** to list all the disks on your system. Identify the correct disk number for your flash drive. You'll use this disk number when executing the Select Disk command.

It's very important that you identify the correct drive. Otherwise, you may delete valuable data on another disk.

d. Enter the following commands to prepare this disk. Replace disk 2 with the actual disk number of your USB drive identified in the previous step.

```
Select disk 2
Clean
Create partition primary
Select partition 1
Active
Format quick fs=fat32
Assign
Exit
```

At this point, the drive will be formatted as a FAT32 disk and all the data on the USB disk will be removed. When you press Enter after typing in Assign, AutoPlay will recognize the disk and prompt you (assuming AutoPlay is enabled on your system). Select Open Folder To View Files.

10. Copy the contents of the entire c:\MyRE\ISO folder to the root of the USB drive. You can use Windows Explorer or the following command. Replace the letter x in the command with the letter assigned to your USB drive.

```
Xcopy c:\MyRE\iso\*.* /e x:\
```

That's it. You now have a USB drive configured with bootable WinRE.

11. To create a bootable CD-ROM, you'll need first to create an .iso image from the WinRE folders you've created. If it is not still open, launch the Deployment Tools Command Prompt with administrative permissions. Enter the following command on a single line to create the WinRE .iso image from the MyRE\iso folder.

```
oscdimg -n -bc:\MyRE\etfsboot.com c:\MyRE\iso c:\MyRE\MyRE.iso
```

The oscdimg command creates an .iso file that can be burned to DVD. The -n switch specifies that long filenames are allowed. The -b switch specifies that a bootable CD is to be created using (using etfsboot.com). Note that there is no space between -b and c:\MyRE. The c:\MyRE\iso clause identifies the Source folder to use when creating the image. Finally, the c:\MyRE\MyRE.iso clause identifies the target file, or the name and location of the image file that ultimately will be burned to CD.

EXERCISE 5.2 *(continued)*

12. Place a writeable CD into the system's CD burner.

13. Launch Windows Explorer, and browse to the C:\MyPE folder. Right-click the MyRE.iso file, and select Burn Disc Image. Click Burn on the Windows Disc Image Burner window.

This image allows you to boot to the Windows Recovery Environment just as you could from the installation DVD. You'll be prompted to select a keyboard, and the WinRE will then search for any installed operating system. Once you select the operating system, the System Recovery Options screen will launch.

Using the WinRE

Once you boot to the WinRE, it will search your system for Windows installations. You'll have three choices from here:

Use Recovery Tools That Can Help Fix Problems Starting Windows   You select an operating system from the list of choices, and you can select this option. It will then launch the System Recovery Options screen.

Restore Your Computer Using A System Image You Created Earlier   If you have a system image, you can choose this to restore the previous image.

Load Drivers   If your operating system isn't shown because additional drivers need to be loaded, you can select Load Drivers to load them.

The most common choice is to launch the WinRE by accepting the defaults (Use Recovery Tools with the Windows 7 installation) and click Next. This will launch the System Recovery Options screen, as shown in Figure 5.19.

FIGURE 5.19   System Recovery Options in the WinRE

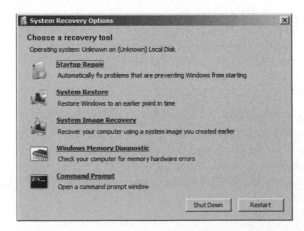

The following sections cover the details of these tools, including how to use them.

Startup Repair Tool

The *Startup Repair* tool can automatically resolve many startup problems. It can also be launched manually. It will inspect the system for a wide assortment of problems that can prevent Windows 7 from starting, and it can implement solutions for them with very little user interaction. This includes repairing or replacing system and configuration files, solving disk problems, and launching System Restore to return the system to a previous state.

If the system fails to start, Windows 7 will usually boot into this tool automatically. It provides a few prompts for the user and will then resolve the problems it locates. While it's not guaranteed to fix everything, it will fix many problems and should be your first choice in most situations.

Exercise 5.3 shows how the Startup Repair tool can be used. You can use this exercise on a healthy system without any detrimental effects. It will report that it can't resolve the problem, but that's because it won't find a problem to resolve.

EXERCISE 5.3

Performing a Startup Repair

1. Boot into the System Recovery Options menu using one of the available choices.

2. Click Startup Repair.

3. The Startup Repair process will check your system for problems. If any problems are identified, they will automatically be repaired. This process may automatically reboot your computer.

4. You may be prompted to perform a System Restore. If this prompt appears, you can choose Restore or Cancel. Click Cancel to allow the Startup Repair process to complete without a System Restore.

5. When the process is complete, you can view diagnostic and repair details.

6. Click Finish. This will return you to the Choose A Recovery Tool page, where you can choose another tool or choose Shut Down or Restart.

System Restore

System Restore allows the system to be restored to a previous state. If you've used System Restore in Windows XP or Windows Vista, this will be familiar to you. System Restore does not affect any documents, pictures, or other user data. It affects only system files by applying a restore point created previously.

Restore points are automatically created on a regular basis as a part of Windows system protection. Windows creates a file that includes system files and settings. When a restore point is applied, all of the system files and settings included in the restore point are applied to return the system to its previous state.

Restore points are captured at the following times by default:

- When an application or update is installed or updated
- When a driver is installed or updated
- Automatically every seven days if not created from other installs or updates
- When manually created by the user by clicking Create on the System Protection tab of the System Properties page

Figure 5.20 shows the System Protection settings for a Windows 7 system. You can access this screen by clicking Start, right-clicking Computer, and selecting Properties. Select System Protection to access the System Protection tab of the System Properties page. If you click the Configure button, you can modify the Restore Settings.

FIGURE 5.20   System Recovery Options in the WinRE

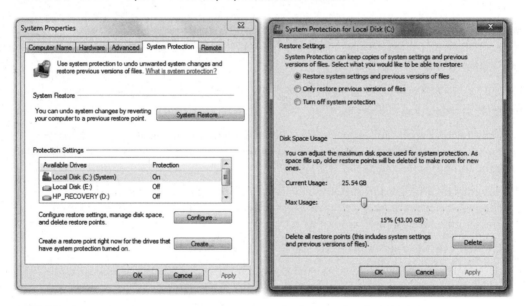

Notice that Restore Settings has three choices:

Restore System Settings And Previous Versions Of Files   This must be enabled for restore points to be created. If any other settings are selected, restore points are not available. This requires a minimum of 300 MB of disk space.

Only Restore Previous Versions Of Files   This will allow previous versions of files to be restored. Previous versions of files are stored on a per-drive basis. By default, the drive where Windows is installed (normally C:) would be enabled, but previous versions for other drives is not available unless enabled on those drives. The Previous Versions feature is explained later in this chapter.

Turn Off System Protection   Neither restore points nor previous versions of files are available. You can select this if you are running out of disk space, but it is not recommended. You'll lose the ability to restore your system to a previous restore point if this option is selected.

> System Restore is a valuable tool if an update causes problems for a system. As an example, an early update to Windows 7 caused some systems to go into an endless reboot cycle, and this was the recommended fix. For the systems that had restore points disabled, the solution was much more complex.

Before applying a restore point, it is possible to identify the programs that are affected. When you select the restore point, you can click the Scan Affected Programs link. This will help you identify specifically what programs or drivers might be deleted or the programs or drivers that might be restored to their previous state.

Performing a System Restore

Exercise 5.4 shows how you can select the System Restore option from the WinRE to apply a restore point. This will restore your system to the state it was in at the time when the restore point was created, but it will not affect any data files.

EXERCISE 5.4

Performing a System Restore from WinRE

1. Boot into the System Recovery Options menu using one of the available choices.

2. Click System Restore.

3. The Restore System Files And Settings page will appear. Review the information on this screen and click Next.

4. A list of restore points will appear. This list includes the date and time of the restore point, a description, and the type (such as Update, Critical Update, Install, and so on). System Restore automatically recommends the most recent restore. Older restore points are hidden but can be seen by selecting the check box Show More Restore Points. Choose the desired restore point and click Next.

5. The Confirm Your Restore Point page will appear. Review the information and click Finish.

6. The System Restore will begin. Once the System Restore is complete, a dialog box will appear indicating that the system has been restored, and you will be prompted to restart the computer.

7. Click Restart to restart your computer.

8. When the system restarts, a System Restore dialog box will appear indicating the system has been restored successfully, with a date and time of the restore point.

Applying a Restore Point Online

You can also apply restore points when your system is up and operational. For example, if you installed an application, driver, or update that is causing problems, but you can boot into the system, you can apply a restore point without using the WinRE

Follow the steps in Exercise 5.5 to access only system restore points.

EXERCISE 5.5

Applying a Restore Point from Windows 7

1. Click Start, right-click Computer, and select Properties.

2. Select System Protection. The System Properties page will appear with the System Protection tab selected.

3. Click System Restore.

4. Review the information on the Restore System Files And Settings page, and click Next.

5. Select the check box Show More Restore Points. Your display will look similar to the following graphic.

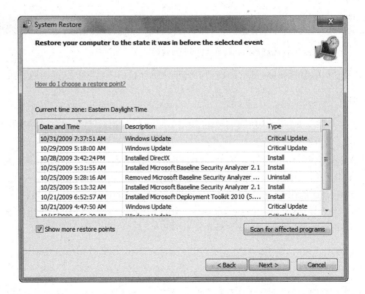

6. Select a restore point and click Next.

7. Review the information on the confirmation page and click Finish. After the restore point is applied, the computer will restart.

Using Previous Versions

System Protection includes both restore points and previous versions of files. When *Previous Versions* is enabled (and it is by default), you can restore a modified file to a previous version of the file.

As an example, I often use a Microsoft Excel worksheet as a template to create invoices. When I need to create an invoice, I open the template and begin the invoice. I should rename this template and save it with a new invoice name, but occasionally I forget and overwrite the original template. With Previous Versions, I can restore the original template even if I don't have a backup of the file.

Figure 5.21 shows the Previous Versions tab selected. You can access this page by right-clicking the file in Windows Explorer and selecting Restore Previous Versions.

FIGURE 5.21   Accessing Previous Versions for a file

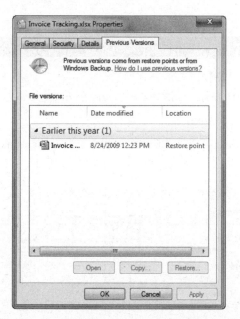

You can select the previous version of the file and then select one of the following choices:

Open   This will open the file so you can inspect it. You can then save it with a different name.

Copy   This will create a new file as a copy of the previous version.

Restore   This will overwrite any changes made to the file and restore the current file to the state of the previous version.

System Image Recovery

This should be used only as a last resort. It will perform a complete restore of the system hard disk from another image. You'll need an image of the system, and only the files available on that image will be available for this installation.

You should ensure you have a backup of any files before using this method. Although data files may be moved to the Windows.old folder, if any changes are made to the system partition during the reimaging, the Windows.old folder will no longer be available.

Windows Memory Diagnostic

The *Windows Memory Diagnostic* will check both your installed RAM and the processor cache memory. This test is the easiest and most effective way to check your memory. If you suspect you have a memory problem, or just want to check it, you can use Exercise 5.6 to walk you through the steps.

EXERCISE 5.6

Running the Memory Test

1. Boot into the System Recovery Options menu using one of the available choices.

2. Click Windows Memory Diagnostic.

3. Select Restart Now And Check For Problems (Recommended), as shown in the following graphic.

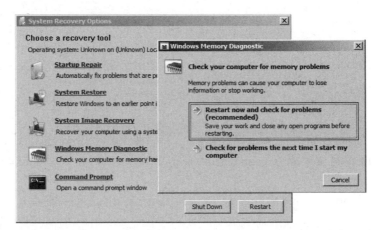

4. The system will restart and automatically boot into the memory test.

5. When the computer restarts, press F1 to access the options for the test. You can change the test from Standard to either Basic or Extended and disable the Cache test. You can also change the number of passes it will run (enter 0 for an infinite number of passes). If you change options, press F10 to apply them. You can cancel the change by pressing the Escape key.

EXERCISE 5.6   *(continued)*

6. The system will run through two passes of memory tests by default. As it runs, it will report any memory problems it finds. Ideally, the status will remain as No Problems Have Been Detected Yet.

7. Once the test completes, the system will automatically restart.

8. When the system restarts and you log on, the results will be displayed.

Command Prompt

You can also access the command prompt from the WinRE. While you can access many of the normal command-prompt commands, you'll have access to some extra tools in the WinRE command prompt. The two extra tools that you might want to explore are these:

- Bootrec
- Bcdedit

Although these tools are available, I want to stress that the majority of the repair actions that you can do manually with them are done automatically using the Startup Repair process. Unless you want to slow down the process to identify exactly what happened, use the Startup Repair process as the first step.

These tools allow you to edit the *boot configuration data (BCD)* store. The BCD replaced the boot.ini file, which was used in Windows XP and earlier versions of Windows.

Using Bootrec

The Bootrec command can be used to repair critical disk structures such as boot records and partition information.

If you used the Recovery Console in Windows XP, you may be wondering how to get to it in Windows 7. You can't. It's not available. However, some of the common commands used in the Recovery Console can be executed using Bootrec.

The Bootrec command has four switches you can use:

/FixMbr   The Bootrec /FixMbr command will write the master boot record of the system partition using a master boot record compatible with Windows 7. It does not overwrite the existing partition table. This can be useful if malware or a hardware problem corrupted the master boot record.

This command is similar to the Fixmbr command used in the Recovery Console.

/FixBoot   The Bootrec /FixBoot command will write a new boot sector onto the system partition using a boot sector that is compatible with Windows 7.

This command is similar to the Fixboot command used in the Recovery Console.

/ScanOS   The Bootrec /ScanOS command will scan all partitions on the computer and display any entries that are not currently in the boot configuration data store. You can then use the BCDEdit command to add the other entries.

/RebuildBCD   The Bootrec /RebuildBCD command will scan all partitions on the computer and allow you to choose which installation to add to the BCD store.

This command is similar to the bootcfg command used in the Recovery Console.

Using BCDedit

The *BCDEdit* command can be used to view and make low-level modifications to the boot configuration data store. The BCD is a store of data that you can think of as a mini-database. It's used when Windows starts up to identify the location of operating system files and, if multiple operating system files are on the system, which one to use by default. While it's possible to make changes to the BCD with BCDedit, you'll use the GUI tools like System Configuration to configure the store more often than you'll actually use BCDedit.

In Windows XP and earlier versions of Windows, the boot.ini file was used to specify different startup settings. The boot.ini has been completely replaced with the BCD store.

You can list (or enumerate) the contents of the BCD store using the bcdedit /enum command from the command prompt. You'll see something similar to the output in Listing 5.1.

Listing 5.1: Viewing the boot configuration data

```
Windows Boot Manager
--------------------
identifier              {bootmgr}
device                  partition=C:
description             Windows Boot Manager
locale                  en-US
inherit                 {globalsettings}
default                 {current}
resumeobject            {a12c4258-897e-11de-9279-001372e62895}
displayorder            {current}
toolsdisplayorder       {memdiag}
timeout                 30


Windows Boot Loader
-------------------
identifier              {current}
device                  partition=C:
path                    \Windows\system32\winload.exe
description             Windows 7
locale                  en-US
inherit                 {bootloadersettings}
recoverysequence        {a12c425a-897e-11de-9279-001372e62895}
recoveryenabled         Yes
```

```
osdevice            partition=C:
systemroot          \Windows
resumeobject        {a12c4258-897e-11de-9279-001372e62895}
nx                  OptIn
```

This information is used during the startup process. The system first loads the Windows Boot Manager using the BCD store to locate it, and it then calls the Windows Boot Loader to load Windows 7.

Managing Hardware in Windows 7

Hardware management is an important element of any operating system, including Windows 7. The two most important hardware components are memory and disks, but you'll occasionally have to consider BIOS and use the Device Manager to troubleshoot other hardware components.

Managing Memory

The processor can't access any data until it is placed in memory, and the amount of memory you have will directly impact the speed of your system. Generally, the more memory you have, the better your system will perform.

However, the architecture will limit the amount of memory available to your system. Figure 5.22 shows a screenshot of a 32-bit edition of Windows 7 installed on a 64-bit system that has 8 GB of random access memory (RAM).

FIGURE 5.22   Viewing system information including available memory

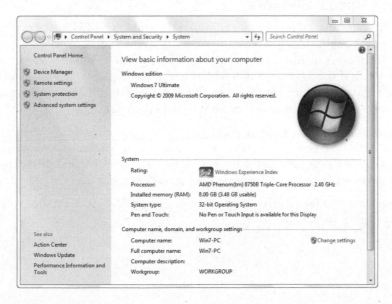

The amount of unusable RAM on any Windows 7 system can vary depending on the hardware installed. One system may not use any more than 3.2 GB of RAM, while another may use only 3.48 GB of RAM.

Even though Windows 7 recognizes that the system has 8 GB of RAM installed, it can use only 3.48 GB of this RAM. The rest of the RAM is wasted for two reasons:

- A 32-bit system can address only 4 GB of RAM.
- Some of this 32-bit address space is reserved for system devices.

In the system shown in Figure 5.22, it's reserving a little over 500 MB of addressable space for the system devices. The rest of the RAM is simply not being used.

Understanding Virtual Memory

Computer users have wanted more RAM virtually ever since computers were created. It doesn't matter how much they have; they want more. One solution that was implemented early in the history of computers is *virtual memory*.

Virtual memory is hard drive space used to mimic physical RAM when the physical RAM is running low. A processor can't access the data stored in virtual memory on the hard drive space but instead must move it to physical RAM. When the system needs to access data that is stored on the drive, other data in the physical RAM is moved onto the hard drive, and the requested data is swapped back to RAM.

Data is swapped back and forth between the hard drive and physical RAM in 64KB blocks. A 64KB block is also referred to as a *page*. So this entire process is often referred to as *paging* or *swapping*. The file on the disk is referred to as the *paging file,* and it is treated by Windows 7 as virtual memory.

Optimizing Virtual Memory

You can optimize the virtual memory by adjusting the amount of disk space used by Windows 7 for the paging file. The recommended size of the paging file is 1.5 times the physical RAM. In other words, if you have 2 GB of RAM, the recommended size for the paging file is 3 GB; if you have 6 GB of RAM, the recommended size is 9 GB; and so on.

Windows 7 manages the paging file by default, and you generally don't need to configure it. There are two reasons why you may need to modify these settings:

Minimize contention with the C: drive   The paging file is stored on the C: drive, which is typically also the boot and system partition. The operating system heavily uses the boot and system partition, so by moving the paging file to a different physical drive, you can minimize contention of regular operating system activity and paging.

Minimize space used on the C: drive   If you are running out of space on the C: drive, you can move the paging file another drive.

> In Windows XP and previous operating systems, if you moved the pag-
> ing file to a partition other than %systemroot%, you lost the capability to
> capture a kernel memory dump file. In Windows Vista and newer operat-
> ing systems, you can move the paging file to other drives without losing
> functionality. However, you'll need to modify the registry by adding the
> DedicatedDumpFile key and modifying some other values. This article
> shows the steps: http://support.microsoft.com/kb/969028.

Figure 5.23 shows the Virtual Memory settings page. In the figure, the Automatically
Manage Paging File Size For All Drives option is selected. This is the default selection when
Windows 7 is installed.

FIGURE 5.23   Viewing Virtual Memory settings

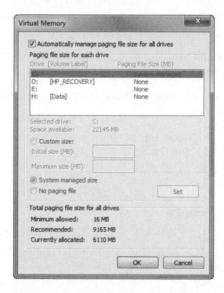

The bottom of the screen shows information on paging file sizes, including the minimum
allowed, recommended size, and currently allocated. Exercise 5.7 shows you how to access
this page and modify the settings.

Viewing the Virtual Memory Settings

1.   Click Start, right-click Computer, and select Properties.

2.   Select Advanced System Settings. The System Properties page will appear with the
Advanced tab showing.

3.   In the Performance section, click the Settings button.

4. Select the Advanced tab of the Performance Options page. Notice the Virtual Memory section on this page. It will identify the currently allocated paging file size for all drives in MB.

5. Click the Change button to access the Virtual Memory page.

6. Note the current state of the check box for Automatically Manage Paging File Size For All Drives. It is selected by default. Deselect this check box to reconfigure the paging file. This will allow you to change the settings manually.

7. If you have more than one partition, you can use the following steps to add a paging file to the other partition and manipulate it.

   a. Select another partition and click Custom Size. Enter a number equal to 1.5 times the physical RAM in the Initial Size and the Maximum Size text boxes. Click Set, and it will configure the paging file always to be the same size.

   b. Select System Managed Size and click Set. Notice Paging File Size is now changed to System Managed.

   c. If you want the paging file removed from any partition, select the drive, select No Paging File, and click Set.

   d. A message will appear indicating that the changes you've made will not take effect until you reboot. Click OK.

Diagnosing Memory Issues

Memory problems very often cause stop screens. A stop screen is sometimes referred to as a Blue Screen of Death (BSOD), but these stop errors aren't really that bad. Yes, your system is stopping because of a critical error, but it isn't usually dead. The error can be read, and you can get it operational again.

The blue screen includes a stop error with a hexadecimal code. For example, a stop error of 0x50 indicates a possible memory error. If you receive this error (or other errors indicating memory problems), you should access the recovery screen and run memory diagnostics, as shown earlier.

You may also find a system that doesn't have enough memory. A common symptom of a system that doesn't have enough memory is excessive paging. The symptom that the user will see and hear is disk thrashing. The LED on the drive is constantly blinking, and the disk can be heard working its little sectors off. With all this activity swapping data back and forth between RAM and the hard drive, the system is painfully slow.

If you experience disk thrashing, you should first check for disk fragmentation (covered later in this chapter). If the system is not fragmented, the system needs more memory for the work the user is performing.

Managing Disks

Disk drives can often cause problems on any system, and you should be aware of some basic tools that you can use to resolve basic drive issues. By keeping the disk drives running optimally, you can often increase the reliability of the system.

The primary tools you'll use to manage disks are these:

- Check Disk
- Disk Defragmenter
- Diskpart

Identifying Bad Sectors

You can select the Check Now button on the Tools tab to launch the Check Disk program. This program can check for file errors on any drive and also check the drive for bad sectors. NTFS will usually locate and repair problems with files on its own, but it cannot identify bad sectors.

Check Disk can be launched via Windows Explorer by right-clicking any drive, selecting Properties, and selecting the Tools tab. When you click Check Now, the Check Disk dialog box will appear, as shown in Figure 5.24. Scan For And Attempt Recovery Of Bad Sectors is not selected by default, but when this is checked, Check Disk will test the disk sectors.

FIGURE 5.24   Checking a drive for file system errors and bad sectors

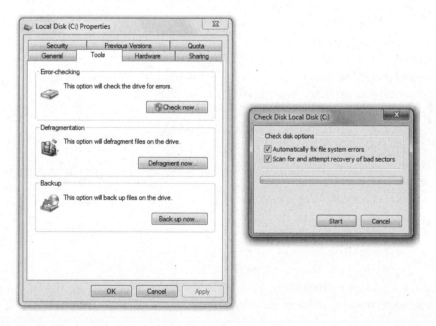

When you click Start, the system will first check to see if the drive is currently being used. The check can't be done on the system or boot partition in Windows immediately. If you try to run it on the boot or system partition, it will prompt you to schedule a disk check, and the check will be done on the next boot.

If the drive is currently being used but is not the boot or system partition, the systems will prompt you to dismount the drive. You can click Force A Dismount, and the check will then start.

When the scan completes, a dialog box appears indicating whether any problems were found. It starts as a small dialog box, but if you click the See Details link, you can view the complete results of the scan. The results will be similar to Listing 5.2.

Listing 5.2: Output of Check Disk utility

```
Volume label is Windows7.

CHKDSK is verifying files (stage 1 of 5)...
  448 file records processed.
File verification completed.
  0 large file records processed.
  0 bad file records processed.
  0 EA records processed.
  0 reparse records processed.
CHKDSK is verifying indexes (stage 2 of 5)...
  528 index entries processed.
Index verification completed.
  0 unindexed files scanned.
  0 unindexed files recovered.
CHKDSK is verifying security descriptors (stage 3 of 5)...
  448 file SDs/SIDs processed.
Security descriptor verification completed.
  41 data files processed.
CHKDSK is verifying Usn Journal...
  15592 USN bytes processed.
Usn Journal verification completed.
CHKDSK is verifying file data (stage 4 of 5)...
  432 files processed.
File data verification completed.
CHKDSK is verifying free space (stage 5 of 5)...
  361873 free clusters processed.
Free space verification is complete.
```

```
Windows has checked the file system and found no problems.

  11968511 KB total disk space.
  10457488 KB in 349 files.
       140 KB in 42 indexes.
         0 KB in bad sectors.
     63391 KB in use by the system.
     61904 KB occupied by the log file.
   1447492 KB available on disk.


      4096 bytes in each allocation unit.
   2992127 total allocation units on disk.
    361873 allocation units available on disk.
```

You can run the same CHKDSK command from the command prompt. This includes the command prompt accessible within Windows, the WinRE, or the WinPE. When running CHKDSK from the command prompt, you would use the following command:

```
CHKDSK x: /f /r
```

CHKDSK is the command. The x: is substituted for the drive letter that you want to check and repair, the /f switch directs it to fix or repair all errors it locates, and the /r switch directs it to check the disk sectors.

Defragmenting a Drive

Drives become fragmented when the files that are written to a system cannot be stored in a contiguous location. Imagine a 10-page report. If you printed this report as 10 separate pages, you could staple them together and it would be a contiguous report.

However, if you had 10 drawers, but you had room in each drawer for only one piece of paper, you could store the report in these 10 drawers. Now when you need to read the report, you'd first have to retrieve it from the 10 drawers. It would take extra time to retrieve the report before you could actually read it.

Similarly, when files are written to the system, there is sometimes limited space to store an entire file in a single location. Instead, pieces of the file are stored in different locations, and when it's read, the different pieces are put together. When this occurs too often, the entire drive is referred to as fragmented.

Drives that are excessively fragmented are often subject to disk thrashing. You can hear the drive constantly whirring and buzzing, but the performance seems excessively slow. If you do hear disk thrashing, you should check the drives to see if they are fragmented. If not, disk thrashing usually indicates the system doesn't have enough memory.

Defragmenting a drive is the process of rearranging the files so that more of them are stored in contiguous locations.

Figure 5.25 shows the *Disk Defragmenter* tool. You can access this by right-clicking a drive in Windows Explorer, selecting Properties, selecting the Tools tab, and then clicking Defragment Now.

FIGURE 5.25   Viewing the Disk Defragmenter tool

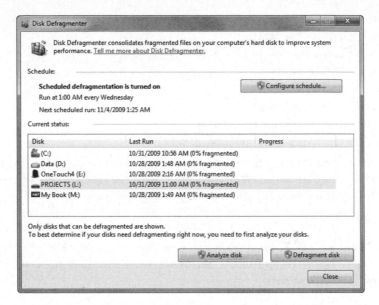

Notice that this screen includes a Last Run column. Not only does this verify that defragmentation was run (and when), but it also shows the current percentage of the disk that is fragmented.

Defragmentation is automatically scheduled to occur every week on drives that are connected to your computer. If you add additional drives, such as an external USB drive, these extra drives will automatically be added to the schedule. As long as the schedules are not modified, fragmentation is rarely a problem.

Running DiskPart

One of the command-line tools you may use to manage disks is *DiskPart*. The DiskPart command is primarily used to partition disks for advanced tasks. As an example, DiskPart was used in Chapter 2 and earlier in this chapter to prepare a USB disk to become bootable.

Another time to use DiskPart is when the partition of a system disk can't be cleared using the normal GUI tools in the Disk Management snap-in. Disk Management can be added as a stand-alone snap-in to a Microsoft Management Console (MMC) or accessed via Computer Management.

As an example, one of the systems I upgraded had a built-in RAID-1 (mirror) that I wanted to break up. Instead of a single RAID-1 partition made up of the two drives, I wanted to use one drive for the operating system and have the second drive available for data.

Although I was able to break the mirror, Disk Management didn't allow me to repartition the second drive that I wanted to use for data. The partition was identified as an OEM partition, and Disk Management wouldn't even let me delete it.

Instead, I launched the command prompt, accessed DiskPart, and was able to delete the partition using the /override option and ultimately reformat the entire disk.

One of the important things to remember when using DiskPart is that you first must select the disk and then select the partition. You can use the LIST DISK command to identify what disks are available. After you select one using SELECT DISK # (where # is the disk number), you can then use LIST PARTITION to list the available partitions and select the partition you want to manipulate. We followed these steps when creating a bootable USB drive earlier in this chapter and in Chapter 2.

Managing BIOS

Every PC today has a basic input/output system (BIOS). It's built into the motherboard and usually as some type of erasable programmable read-only memory (EPROM).

BIOS is needed to help the processor locate the basic components of a system and find the hard drive. Once the hard drive is located, a Windows 7 system will use the BCD store to start the boot process and ultimately load Windows 7.

The BIOS program includes many different settings that can be manipulated to modify how some of the hardware is used. A common reason to go into the BIOS is to change the boot order or enable the system to boot from different components. For example, a system may not be configured to boot from the DVD drive, a USB drive, or the NIC. The BIOS would include settings that can enable these selections and to change the boot order.

Just as any other program can be upgraded, the BIOS can be upgraded too. If an update is available for your BIOS, you can download the update from the manufacturer and apply it to your system. This is commonly referred to as flashing the BIOS.

The common reason to flash your BIOS is that a capability is not available in the current program. For example, a processor may have the virtualization capability available, but the BIOS may not have the ability to enable virtualization. If a newer version of the BIOS is available, you can download it, flash your BIOS, and you'll have the capability.

Managing Devices

Beyond memory and the disks, you may need to manage and troubleshoot issues with other devices installed on a system. The process of installing devices is often automated using the driver store, but if you need to do any manual intervention, the primary tool you'll use is Device Manager.

Devices are installed in two steps: staging and installation.

Staging   During the staging step, all of the driver files are staged in the *driver store*. Drivers can be staged at any time (even if the device is not present in the system). The driver store is located at %systemroot%\ system32\DriverStore.

Installation   The Plug and Play (PnP) process detects the new device and installs the driver from the driver store. If the driver is not in the store, Windows Update is checked and the driver is downloaded, staged, and then installed. If PnP detects the device but can't find a driver, the Add New Hardware Wizard will launch.

When installing drivers from third-party sources (such as the installation CD provided with the hardware), the drivers will be added to the driver store and then installed.

Although Windows 7 will check Windows Update for drivers not in the driver store by default, this can be modified. Figure 5.26 shows the default Device Installation Settings page. You can get to this page by right-clicking Computer, selecting Properties, selecting the Hardware tab, and clicking the Device Installation Settings button.

FIGURE 5.26   Automating driver downloads

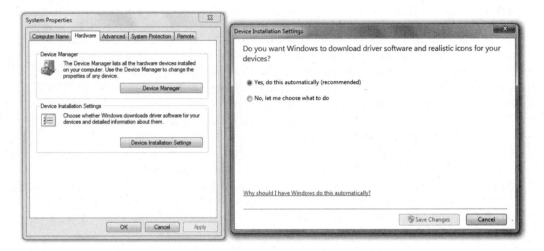

This feature also downloads icons of your hardware devices that you see in the Devices And Printers page. Although this setting will allow drivers to be downloaded automatically when a new device is initially added to your system, it will not update the drivers for installed devices if drivers later become available.

The primary tool you'll use to manage devices and device drivers, including updating drivers for existing devices, is the Device Manager tool.

Using Device Manager

You can easily use *Device Manager* to check on the status of devices installed on the system and for updating device drivers. In this section, you'll learn about Device Manager, rolling back drivers, and signed or trusted drivers.

You can access Device Manager using several different methods. For example, you can click Start ➢ Control Panel and enter **Devices** in the Control Panel search text box. Several links will appear. Click any of them labeled Device Manager.

Figure 5.27 shows Device Manager with the Realtek PCIe network interface card in the Network Adapters section disabled. This shows how easy it is to identify problems with Device Manager. If there are issues with any devices in Device Manager, the related sections will be expanded and the devices will have an extra icon.

FIGURE 5.27   Viewing Device Manager

In the figure, the Realtek NIC has a small down-arrow icon to indicate it is disabled. When the device is disabled, the Disable choice changes to Enable, and it can be enabled again by right-clicking it and selecting Enable.

If you suspect a device is causing problems in your system, you can use Device Manager to disable it. This ensures it isn't using any resources.

Device Manager will display a warning icon if there are any issues with the device. A common problem with devices is related to the driver, and a warning icon usually indicates the driver should be reinstalled.

Understanding Signed Drivers

Microsoft has a process in place that verifies device drivers. Drivers are submitted by manufacturers to the *Windows Hardware Quality Labs (WHQL)*. WHQL performs a series of compatibility tests on the driver, and if the driver passes the tests, the driver is signed and is referred to as a *signed driver* or a trusted driver.

WHQL issues a certificate and associates the certificate with the driver. The certificate provides the signature for the driver and assures you that it has been tested and verified by Microsoft. Signed drivers are then made available via the Windows Update site.

Hardware developers can sign their drivers without submitting them to WHQL. A certificate is purchased from a Certificate Authority (CA) and associated with the driver. If the CA is trusted by the end user, the driver is considered trusted. This provides proof that the driver being installed has not been corrupted with malware.

Although signed drivers will help ensure a more stable system, unsigned drivers can also be used in a system. An unsigned driver could have been created by a reputable company, but it could also have been created or modified by an attacker who wants to infect a system. Only members of the Local Administrators group can install an unsigned or untrusted driver.

If the driver lacks a valid signature or the driver has been altered, Windows 7 displays a warning prompt indicating that the file does not have a valid digital signature, and an administrator must approve the installation. Only administrators can approve the installation of an untrusted driver.

In versions of Windows before Windows Vista, you could configure a driver-signing policy to block the installation of unsigned drivers, warn that the driver is unsigned, or ignore the warning. Windows 7 supports only the Warn option, so each time an unsigned driver is being installed, Windows will always warn that it is untrusted.

The File Signature Verification tool (`sigverif.exe`) can be used to scan your system and identify any unsigned drivers in it. You can start it by clicking Start, typing **sigverif** in the Search box, and pressing Enter. Click Start, and it will scan the drivers in your system.

Figure 5.28 shows the results of running the File Signature Verification tool. It identified four unsigned files on this system. These are nVidia graphics files. Again, just because a file is not signed doesn't mean it isn't valid, but only that it doesn't include a digital signature from a trusted certificate authority.

FIGURE 5.28 Running the File Signature Verification tool

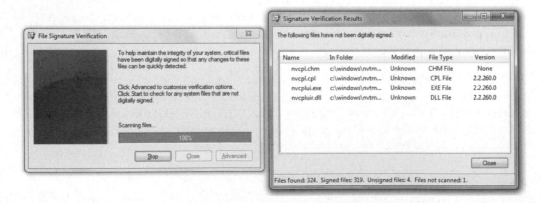

Signed driver files are also prevented from being infected. If the driver becomes infected with malware, it will no longer match the data in the certificate, and the signature will be recognized as invalid.

If there aren't any unsigned drivers, sigverif will return a dialog box that indicates that all your files have been scanned and verified as digitally signed. Sigverif will also create a log located in your Documents folder named `sigverif.txt` that you can review at any time. It lists all the files that have been scanned.

Updating a Driver

Drivers are often updated by the manufacturer because of bugs or to add capabilities. Manufacturers then submit them to WHQL for verification, and ultimately they are released on the Windows Update site.

You can update the drivers from Windows Update using the following steps:

1. Right-click the device in Device Manager, and select Update Driver Software.

2. Select Search Automatically For Updated Driver Software.

3. The Windows Update site will be contacted. If an updated driver is available, it will be downloaded, and you'll be led through the process to update it.

If the driver has not completed the WHQL process, you can download it from the manufacturer. Often, a manufacturer will include a self-extracting executable that you can launch to complete the installation.

Other times, you'll download the driver and extract it to location on your system. You can then update drivers using Device Manager with the following steps:

1. Right-click the device in Device Manager, and select Update Driver Software.

2. Select Browse My Computer For Driver Software.

3. Click Browse to browse to where you extracted the driver files, and click Next.

4. The wizard will locate the driver and lead you through the process of installing it.

If the driver is not signed, you'll see a warning dialog box indicating it isn't signed and asking if you want to continue.

Rolling Back a Driver in Device Manager

If you've updated a driver and found that it's an incorrect driver or that it's causing problems on the system, you can roll back the driver. This will uninstall the current driver and reinstall the previous driver.

You can roll back only to the previous driver. If you update driver 1 to driver 2 and then update driver 2 to driver 3, the best you can do is roll back to driver 2. You cannot roll back two versions of a driver. As a best practice, if you install a driver that isn't what you want, you should roll it back before installing another one. This allows you always to get back to the original driver.

Figure 5.29 shows the properties of a driver that has been updated. You can access this page by right-clicking the device in Device Manager and selecting Properties. If a driver hasn't been updated, the Roll Back Driver button is dimmed and cannot be selected.

FIGURE 5.29   Viewing the driver properties

To roll back the driver, click the Roll Back Driver button. You'll be prompted with an Are You Sure dialog box, and when you click Yes, the current driver will be removed and the previous driver will be installed.

Troubleshooting Boot Issues

If Windows 7 won't start, it's not very useful. Thankfully, you have several tools you can use to help troubleshoot different boot issues. You've already read about the most valuable tool, Startup Repair in the WinRE. However, you do have some other tools available.

Understanding the Boot Phases

When troubleshooting boot issues, it's important to understand the different phases of the boot process for Windows 7. With an understanding of the different phases, you'll have a better idea of what method to use to resolve the problem. The different phases are

- Power On Self Test
- Initial startup phase

- Windows Boot Manager phase
- Windows Boot Loader phase
- Kernel-loading phase
- Logon phase

Power On Self Test (POST)

During the POST phase, the computer starts the BIOS program and checks the functionality of basic devices such as the processor, memory, and video. If the system fails here, it is hardware related and not affected by Windows 7 at all.

Initial Startup Phase

After POST, the BIOS directs the system to boot from a device such as a CD, NIC, USB, or hard drive. The system locates the Windows Boot Manager program from the data in the BCD store and begins the boot process.

If this phase fails, you'll receive the following error:

```
Non-system disk or disk error
Replace and press any key when ready
```

This indicates the BCD store could not be located. Verify that you're booting from a device that holds the BCD store.

 Some computers use an Extensible Firmware Interface (EFI), which is a replacement for the BIOS. EFI uses a boot menu that allows users to choose from different operating systems installed on a system. When Windows 7 is installed on an EFI system, it will modify the EFI menu to load the Windows 7 Boot Manager program automatically after a two-second delay.

Windows Boot Manager Phase

Windows Boot Manager is used to read the BCD store and launch the Windows Boot Loader program. It has a built-in delay that allows you to press a key to access different menus.

If you press any key during this phase, the Boot Manager menu will appear, as shown in Figure 5.30. From this menu, you can boot to Windows 7, press F8 to access the Advanced Boot Options page, or select the Windows Memory Diagnostic (which is the same memory diagnostic available in WinRE described earlier in this chapter).

It's possible to install more than one operating system on a single computer. If other operating systems have been installed, this menu will allow the user to choose different operating systems.

You can also press the F8 key instead of any key, and the Advanced Boot Options screen will appear, bypassing the Windows Boot Manager menu. The Advanced Boot Options screen includes the Repair Your Computer choice (discussed earlier in this chapter), the Safe Modes, and some other options discussed in the next section.

FIGURE 5.30   Accessing the Windows Boot Manager menu

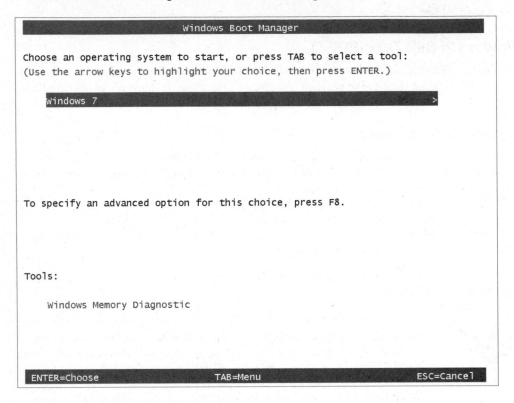

```
                        Windows Boot Manager

Choose an operating system to start, or press TAB to select a tool:
(Use the arrow keys to highlight your choice, then press ENTER.)

    Windows 7                                                      >




To specify an advanced option for this choice, press F8.



Tools:

    Windows Memory Diagnostic




ENTER=Choose                    TAB=Menu                ESC=Cancel
```

If different operating systems are installed on the same system, they should be installed on separate partitions. In addition, newer operating systems should be installed after older operating systems to avoid corrupting the first installation. As an example, if you install Windows 7 on a system and then later install Windows XP on the system, the Windows XP installation will corrupt the boot process for Windows 7, and you won't be able to boot into Windows 7 until the problem has been resolved. A Startup Repair from the WinRE will resolve this problem.

Windows Boot Loader Phase

After the Boot Manager phase, the Windows Boot Loader phase begins. This phase will load several components that are used to boot the operating system in the kernel-loading phase. It does not start the components but instead only loads them. The following components are loaded in this phase:

- Operating system kernel program: `ntoskrn1.exe`
- Hardware Abstraction Layer (HAL): `hal.dll`
- System Registry hive: `(system32\Config\System)`
- Services and device drivers configured to start automatically

Paging is enabled in this phase to give the system access to virtual memory if needed.

Kernel-Loading Phase

The Windows Boot Loader phase passes control to the kernel-loading phase once it is complete. All the components that were loaded during the Boot Loader phase are started at this time.

This includes all the services and device drivers configured to start automatically. At this stage, both services and device drivers are handled the same and are generically referred to as services. The start types of these services are prioritized, with critical services starting first and less-critical services configured with a delayed start to give time for the critical services to start.

If things go wrong in the boot phase, they often go wrong here. But if the system crashes during this phase, Windows 7 will usually recognize the crash and automatically launch a Startup Repair on the reboot. Figure 5.31 shows this in action. Windows 7 recognized the system couldn't restart and launched Startup Repair. If the Startup Repair doesn't start automatically, you can launch the WinRE and initiate a Startup Repair.

FIGURE 5.31 Startup Repair trying to resolve a problem automatically

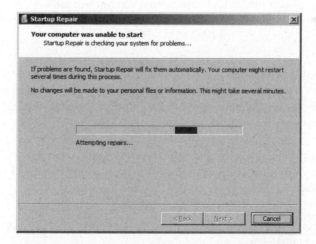

For some problems, you'll see a stop error instead—the so-called Blue Screen of Death. Don't overlook the obvious; that is, read the text on the screen. There seems to be

something about these blue screens that paralyzes a lot of people, and they don't recognize that there is valuable information on these screens. Often the text will give you insight into exactly what the problem is, and at other times you can search the Internet for additional information on the stop code.

If the stop error indicates the problem is related to a device or driver you just installed, you can select Last Known Good Configuration (Advanced) from the Advanced Boot Options menu discussed in the next section.

Logon Phase

Once the kernel-loading phase has completed, the `Winlogon.exe` program starts. The logon screen appears, or if the computer is in a domain, the Ctrl+Alt+Delete message appears, prompting users to press these keys to log on.

After a user logs on, the system is considered to have booted successfully. If a user is not able to log on, it could be due to an application or process configured to start when the user logs on. You can boot into Safe Mode and reconfigure the application or process.

Using Advanced Boot Options

The *Advanced Boot Options* page includes several choices that you can use to trouble-shoot, and if the system won't boot, this is often a good place to start. You access the Advanced Boot Options page by pressing F8 as the system boots or by pressing any key during the Boot Manager phase and then pressing F8.

Figure 5.32 shows the Advanced Boot Options menu with one of the Safe Modes selected.

We discussed the Repair Your Computer choice earlier, and it is first in this menu for a reason—it is often your first choice to resolve a problem with a system that won't boot. Select this option to launch the WinRE, and select Startup Repair.

For some other problems, you may want to use the other options available in this menu.

Safe Modes

The Advanced Boot Options menu includes three Safe Modes. Safe Mode is used to boot a system with only the core drivers and services running. The idea is that one of the drivers or services is causing the system to misbehave, so by accessing Safe Mode, you can start the system without the errant driver or service.

Safe Mode is often valuable when troubleshooting malicious software (malware) issues. Often malware will protect itself when the operating system is fully loaded, and it prevents critical malware files from being deleted. You can usually delete these files in Safe Mode manually or run other malware scans.

Three Safe Modes are available:

Safe Mode   Only the basic files, drivers, and services are loaded. This includes drivers for the mouse, keyboard, disk drives, and basic video.

Safe Mode With Networking   This is the same as Safe Mode, except that it includes the extra drivers and services necessary to access network resources.

Safe Mode With Command Prompt   This is Safe Mode without the GUI. You have access only to the command prompt. It does not include networking resources.

FIGURE 5.32   Accessing the Advanced Boot Options menu

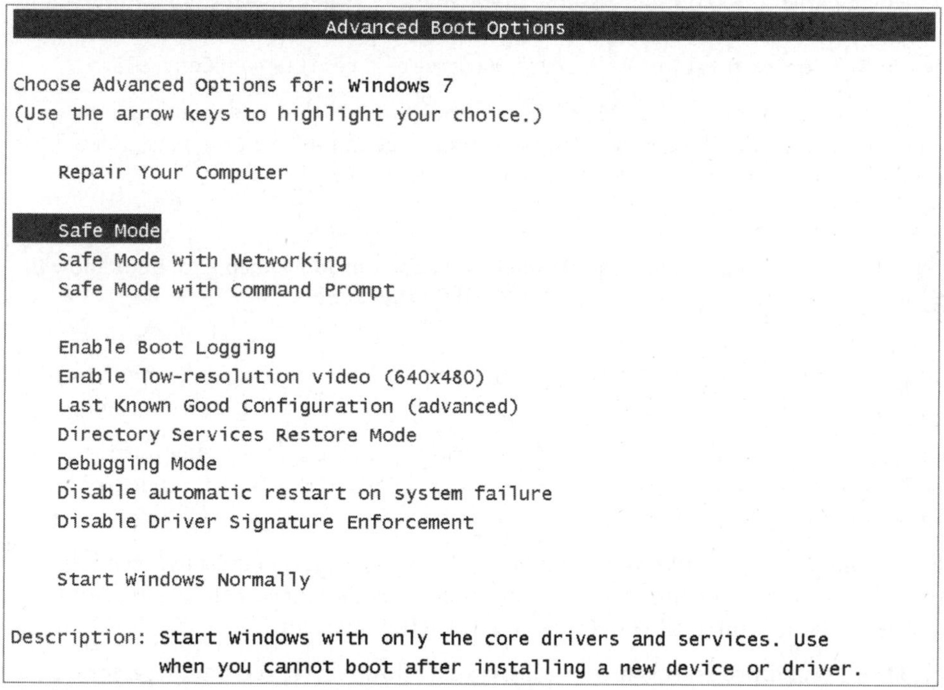

```
                      Advanced Boot Options

Choose Advanced Options for: Windows 7
(Use the arrow keys to highlight your choice.)


    Repair Your Computer

    Safe Mode
    Safe Mode with Networking
    Safe Mode with Command Prompt

    Enable Boot Logging
    Enable low-resolution video (640x480)
    Last Known Good Configuration (advanced)
    Directory Services Restore Mode
    Debugging Mode
    Disable automatic restart on system failure
    Disable Driver Signature Enforcement

    Start Windows Normally

Description: Start Windows with only the core drivers and services. Use
            when you cannot boot after installing a new device or driver.
```

Other Boot Options

Several other boot options are available from the Advanced Boot options screen:

Enable Boot Logging   This will create a running log of the boot process. The log name is ntbtlog.txt, and it is stored in the Windows folder. You can use this if you suspect a specific driver or service is causing the system to blue screen. Enable this, reboot the system, and then after the system crashes, you can boot into Safe Mode to view the log. One of the last services or drivers listed in the log is likely the problem.

Enable Low-Resolution Video (640X480)   This loads the current video driver but set to a low-resolution mode. Regular Safe Mode uses only the base video driver. It's possible for some video drivers to be set to a resolution that causes them to blink out after they've been configured and confirmed. The obvious solution is to reset the resolution, but if you can't access the display, you can't reconfigure the resolution. You can select this mode to access the current video driver set to a low resolution and then reconfigure the resolution.

Last Known Good Configuration (Advanced)   The *Last Known Good Configuration* is recorded in the Registry when the system successfully boots. A successful boot is defined as someone being able to log on successfully. If you made changes to a system and then find it crashes or blue screens on reboot before anyone has logged on, you can select this and restore the Registry settings for HKEY_Local_Machine\System\CurrentControlSet.

A key part of understanding the Last Known Good choice is that you can't use it after someone has successfully logged on. If someone has logged on, you now have a new Last Known Good Configuration that is recorded in the Registry.

Logging in with Safe Mode is not considered a successful boot and will not overwrite the Last Known Good Configuration.

Directory Services Restore Mode   This applies only to servers running Active Directory Domain Services (domain controllers). It would not be used on a Windows 7 computer.

Debugging Mode   Debugging Mode is used for advanced troubleshooting purposes. It allows Microsoft personnel to connect to the computer and determine the cause of a problem but would rarely be used on a desktop PC.

Disable Automatic Restart On System Failure   If your system is caught in an endless reboot cycle where it never completes the boot but instead restarts, you can use this to change the configuration until you're able to resolve the problem.

Disable Driver Signature Enforcement   This setting allows drivers containing improper signatures to be loaded. If a driver has an invalid or missing digital signature that is preventing the successful boot of Windows 7, you can use this to boot normally and resolve the problem.

Using MSConfig

The *System Configuration* utility (MSConfig) is a useful tool that can be used to modify different system configuration settings, boot options, and startup options. You can access it by clicking Start, typing **msconfig** in the Search box, and pressing Enter. It's also available in the Administrator Tools section of the Control Panel. MSConfig has several tabs that can be manipulated.

Figure 5.33 shows the General tab of the System Configuration utility. You can modify the start of the system. Normal Startup is the default. If you select Diagnostic Startup, it will start Windows with basic services and drivers only so that you can rule out basic

Windows files as the source of a problem. Selective Startup allows you pick and choose which drivers and services will start.

FIGURE 5.33 System Configuration General tab

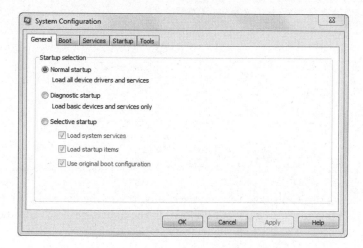

You can modify which services and applications start from the Services and Startup tabs. Each service and application that is installed and configured to start automatically is checked. When you uncheck any of the blocks in Services or Startup, the Startup Selection will change from Normal Startup to Selective Startup.

 Using a Selective Startup can sometimes be helpful when troubleshooting malware. If the malware won't allow itself to be deinstalled while it's running or won't stop, you can deselect the problem application or service in the Services or Startup tab and reboot the system. The system will run normally without the malware.

Figure 5.34 shows the Boot tab of System Configuration with the Advanced Options. You can use this to choose one of the Safe Modes without pressing the F8 key to access the Advanced Boot Options. The Make All Boot Settings Permanent selection will result in the current settings being configured as a Normal Startup in the BCD store.

If you click the Advanced Options button, the BOOT Advanced Options page will open. You can limit the number of processors or the amount of memory used on the next boot. You can use this to narrow down suspect hardware or simulate the operation of the system with less hardware.

The last tab is the Tools tab. This is actually a pretty cool addition to the MSConfig utility. It provides quick links to several very useful tools.

FIGURE 5.34 System Configuration Boot tab

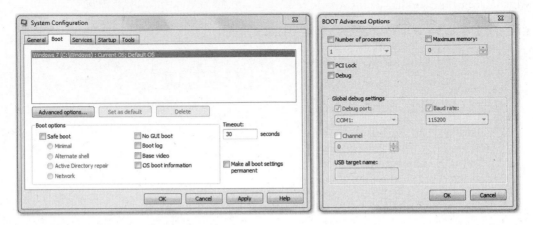

Figure 5.35 shows the Tools tab. You can select any tool in the list and click the Launch button to start it. Some tools, like IPConfig shown in the figure, have advanced options that can be selected.

FIGURE 5.35 System Configuration Tools tab

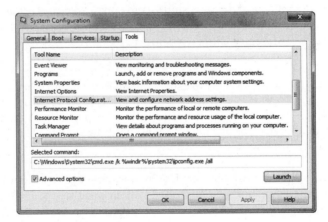

You can consider this a great list of tools that you should know both for on-the-job use and for preparing for Windows 7 certification exams. Start at the top and go through the entire list until you're familiar with each tool, its purpose, and how to use it. This tab includes links to the following tools:

- About Windows
- Change UAC Settings
- Action Center

- Windows Troubleshooting
- Computer Management
- System Information
- Event Viewer
- Programs
- System Properties
- Internet Options
- Internet Protocol Configuration (IPConfig)
- Performance Monitor
- Resource Monitor
- Task Manager
- Command Prompt
- Registry Editor
- Remote Assistance
- System Restore

Startup and Recovery Options

Another way the BCD store can be modified is from the Startup And Recovery options page. You can access this page by selecting the Advanced tab of the System Properties page. The Startup And Recovery options page is shown in Figure 5.36.

FIGURE 5.36   Startup And Recovery options

The System Startup section is most useful if you have a dual-boot or multiboot configuration, where your system has more than one operating system installed, allowing you to boot to different operating systems at different times. Here you can modify which operating system will load by default. You can also modify how long to wait before loading the default operating system.

The recovery mode setting will apply only if your system is in recovery mode. Depending on the recovery procedure occurring, the user may be given a choice, or the system may launch into a single recovery option.

Setting the time to 0 seconds for any of these options will result in the default choice launching without giving the user an option.

System Failure settings are at the bottom of this page. The available choices are as follows:

Write An Event To The System Log   This allows you to use the Event Viewer later to view the details of the event.

Automatically Restart   When this option is checked, the system will attempt to reboot if a fatal error causes it to crash before the boot completes.

Write Debugging Information   You can select None, Small Memory Dump (128 KB), or Kernel Memory Dump. The default location and filename are shown (`c:\memory.dmp`), but they can be modified. In order to create this dump file, you need to have two things in place: The paging file must be located on the same drive as the operating system, and this drive must have enough space to hold the dump file. The dump file can be as large as 50 percent of the physical RAM, so if you have 6 GB of RAM, the target drive must have at least 3 GB of free space. You can modify the default behavior of the dump file by modifying the registry. This KB article shows how: `http://support.microsoft.com/kb/969028`.

Summary

Windows 7 includes several tools that are designed to help your system stay healthy and running smoothly. The System Repair tool is the most valuable when failures prevent the system from booting, and it can automatically correct many problems with very little user interaction.

You also have several tools that you can use to monitor and adjust your system, such as Event Viewer and Services. Occasionally things go wrong, and you need to do some more aggressive troubleshooting. In this chapter, you learned about many of the tools available to do both minor and major troubleshooting of Windows 7.

Chapter Essentials

Identifying and resolving performance issues   Know the capabilities of basic tools such as Event Viewer and the Services console. They can be used to identify and troubleshoot many of the basic problems that occur with Windows 7. As problems are identified by the system, the Action Center will report those issues and recommend solutions.

Using the Windows Recovery Environment   Be familiar with the WinRE. It includes several tools that can be used to troubleshoot critical problems with Windows 7. The most valuable tool is the System Repair tool, but other tools include System Restore (which allows you to apply restore points and return your system to a previous state), System Image Recovery (which allows you to restore your system to a previous image), and memory diagnostics.

Managing hardware in Windows 7   Know the tools used to manage and monitor hardware. Windows 7 includes several tools used to manage and monitor memory and hard disks. The memory paging file is automatically configured, and the Disk Defragmenter runs regularly by default. However, you may need to check occasionally for bad sectors on the system with the Check Disk (chkdsk) tool or manage devices with Device Manager.

Troubleshooting boot issues   Be familiar with tools that can troubleshoot the boot process. If the system fails to start, the Startup Repair process will often detect and correct the problems on its own. However, occasionally you'll need to take some extra steps. The Advanced Boot Options page is accessed by pressing F8 on boot and gives you access to several of the Safe Modes in addition to the WinRE by selecting the Repair Your Computer option.

Chapter

6

Configuring and Troubleshooting Application Issues

TOPICS COVERED IN THIS CHAPTER INCLUDE

✓ **Installing and configuring software**

✓ **Designing a delivery strategy**

✓ **Designing a deployment strategy**

✓ **Identifying and resolving software failure issues**

Installing software is relatively easy for most applications. You locate the installation package, double-click the setup file, and you're in business. However, there are a few things to consider such as administrator permissions, licensing, and the use of digitally signed files. In addition, you can use Windows Features to enable and disable different features of some software.

The delivery strategy identifies how the software is delivered to the user. If the software is not compatible with Windows 7, you can use one of the virtualization strategies to deliver the application. Windows XP Mode and Virtual PC are virtualization strategies that allow the application to run on the same system. Remote Desktop Services and Application Virtualization allow the application to be delivered from a server.

If the application will be installed on Windows 7, there are different ways to deploy it. You can use the manual method for one or two systems. However, if the application needs to be deployed to multiple systems, you'll want to automate it. You can choose between Group Policy and Systems Center Configuration Manager.

When the software doesn't run as advertised, some basic troubleshooting is required. Many applications allow you to repair the installation from the Control Panel. If the software still refuses to run, you can use the Application Compatibility Wizard. This allows Windows 7 to mimic the settings from an earlier operating system.

Installing and Configuring Software

When you get right down to it, a computer is useless without software. The hardware allows it to host an operating system. The operating system allows it to run software or applications. The applications are needed to make the box productive.

Although some applications are installed by default on Windows 7, such as Internet Explorer and Windows Media Player, most users need more. These applications need to be installed.

Applications are distributed in one of the following formats:

Msi   This is a Windows installer (`.msi`) package file. It uses the Windows Installer engine to complete the installation. Windows Installer was previously known as Microsoft Installer. Microsoft recommends the use of installer packages for third-party applications.

Msu   This is a Microsoft update (`.msu`) package. It is installed using the Windows Update Stand-alone Installer.

Exe   This is an executable file. It is sometimes used by developers to check the environment before calling the installer package. For example, an application may require a specific version of the .NET Framework. The `.exe` file can be used to check to see if the framework exists, and if not, it can then install it. After the prerequisites are checked and installed, the `.msi` file is called to install the application.

Installing applications on a local system is straightforward. You browse to the file, double-click it, and the installation begins. If Autorun is enabled on your system, you may just need to put in the CD and click the prompt to start the installation.

However, there are some other items to consider when installing and configuring software:

- Installation permissions
- Licensing restrictions
- Digital signing
- Enabling and disabling features

Installation Permissions

Administrative permissions are required to install software. If a user is logged on as a regular user, the prompt shown in Figure 6.1 will appear at some point during the installation. As long as the user can provide credentials for an account with local administrative permissions, the installation will continue.

FIGURE 6.1   UAC prompt for administrative credentials

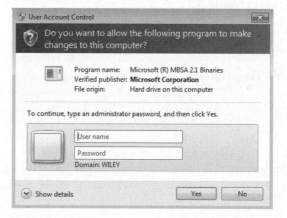

    Administrative permissions are also required to uninstall an application.

User Account Control (UAC) is covered in greater depth in Chapter 11, "Managing Security in Windows 7." The default settings prompt users for credentials. However, if an administrator is logged on, UAC will prompt the administrator to continue.

UAC uses two access tokens when a user is logged on with administrative permissions. One token is as a regular user and the other token is as an administrator. A regular user access token is used for most activities. When advanced privileges are needed, UAC prompts the user before using the access token with administrative permissions.

Licensing Restrictions

Almost any software you purchase or install has a software license associated with it. This is also called an end-user license agreement (EULA).

Figure 6.2 shows the EULA for the Microsoft Baseline Security Analyzer tool. Almost all software requires you to indicate that you accept the license agreement before the installation will continue. This is often done by changing the selection to indicate you accept it, as shown in the figure.

FIGURE 6.2   End-user license agreement

It's common for a EULA legally to restrict the installation of the software to a single system. Some EULAs grant you the right to install it on multiple systems. A EULA typically applies to the application and any subsequent updates to the application.

Digital Signing

Software applications can be sophisticated. The magic that is possible very often approaches the "wow" factor.

However, many attackers can also write some sophisticated applications. The damage that they inflict on a system or your personal finances can also approach the "wow" factor, though not in a good way. If you've ever been infected with malware, you may have substituted "wow" with another word or two.

One of the ways that you can protect yourself and systems on your network is to ensure that software is digitally signed before installing it. *Digitally signed software* provides verification that the software has been published by a specific company.

As an example, Figure 6.3 shows the UAC prompt for software that was released by Microsoft. Microsoft Corporation is listed as the Verified Publisher.

FIGURE 6.3   Verification that software is digitally signed by a known company

 If the software is digitally signed but the publisher can't be verified, the Verified Publisher will be listed as Unknown.

If this software does something wrong or malicious to your system, you know who wrote it. You can go back to the company for a resolution. Digitally signed software provides authentication and integrity.

Authentication   This allows anyone who uses the software to verify the origin. The digital signature proves who created the original file. This step requires that the certificate be obtained from a trusted certificate authority.

Integrity   This ensures that the software hasn't been modified after it was signed. For example, if a virus infected the installation file, the digital signature would no longer match. As long as the signature is valid, you know the file has not been modified.

Digital signatures require the support of a *Public Key Infrastructure (PKI)*. A PKI issues certificates, including certificates used for digital signatures. In addition, PKIs use public and private key pairs for the certificates.

Private key   Anything encrypted with a private key can be decrypted only with the corresponding public key. The private key always stays private.

Public key   Anything encrypted with a public key can be decrypted only with the corresponding private key. The public key is freely shared and included in a certificate.

Public/private key pair   These are pairs. Anything encrypted using a key from one public/private key pair can't be decrypted with a key from another public/private key pair.

Figure 6.4 shows how a digital signature is created for a file. The first step is to create a hash of the file. A hash is simply a number. It's created by performing a calculation (a hashing algorithm) on a string of data such as a message or a file. The hash is then encrypted with a private key. The original file is then packaged with the encrypted hash and the certificate holding the public key.

FIGURE 6.4 Creating a digital signature

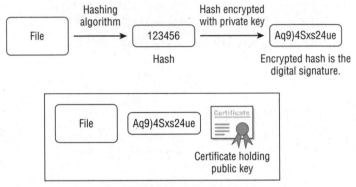

Digitally signed file

 A hash will always be the same when it is calculated on an unchanged file. As long as the data is not changed, the hash will always be the same. This verifies integrity of the data.

Remember, this public key is matched to the private key that encrypted the hash. In other words, because the hash was encrypted with the private key, only the matching public key can decrypt it. Figure 6.5 shows how this digitally signed file is later used with the installation file in a three-step process.

1. In the first step, the hash is calculated on the installation file. For this example, imagine that the file has been infected with malware. It has been modified. Since the file is different, the calculated hash is also different (642531 instead of 123456).

2. In the second step, the encrypted hash is decrypted using the public key. This gives the original hash of 123456.

3. The last step compares the two. If the hashes are the same, the file has maintained integrity. However, if the hashes are different, the file is no longer the same. The installation reports a problem and installation is not recommended.

 Digital signatures can also be used for driver files, macros, and scripts.

FIGURE 6.5   Verifying the digital signature

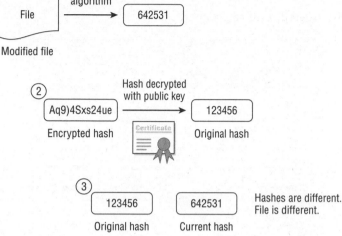

What if the malware writer wants to get creative? There are two possibilities. The first one won't work, but the second one has a chance of success.

Providing a different hash   Instead of only modifying the file, what if the malware also creates a new hash and encrypts it? This will fail. The encrypted hash must be encrypted with the private key in order to be decrypted with the public key that is included in the digital signature. However, the private key is kept private and isn't available. If the encrypted hash is replaced with other data, the public key won't be able to decrypt it and the installation will report a problem. At that point the installation is not recommended.

Providing a different digital signature   What if the malware writer creates and provides a certificate for the infected file? In this situation, the writer does not purchase a certificate but, instead, creates one. Needless to say, this certificate doesn't identify the actual creator of the malware. A new hash is created and encrypted with the private key. The new digital signature includes the infected file, the new hash, and the new certificate. The certificate includes the matching public key. When the installation starts, a problem won't be discovered unless the certificate is verified.

You may be saying, "Wait a minute. I thought the certificate provides authentication." It does, but only if the certificate can be verified.

To overcome this vulnerability, you need to ensure that the publisher can be verified. The certificate used to sign software should come from a *trusted certificate authority* (CA). A commercial CA will verify the identity of anyone who purchases a certificate. If you trust the CA, you automatically trust any certificates issued from the CA.

This is similar to a driver's license issued from a department of motor vehicles (DMV). Since a merchant trusts the DMV when you present your driver's license to make a purchase, they will also trust the validity of the driver's license.

Figure 6.6 shows a partial list of the Trusted Root Certification Authorities store. If a software company purchases a certificate from the VeriSign Commercial Software Publishers CA, that software certificate will be trusted because the CA is trusted.

FIGURE 6.6   Trusted certificate authority store

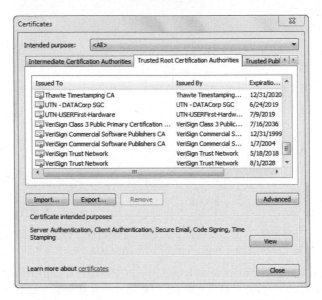

On the other hand, if the attacker created a certificate authority to issue certificates, it would not be listed in the Trusted Root Certification Authorities store. The attacker's certificates could not be verified.

You can view the Trusted Root Certification Authorities store from Internet Explorer. Launch Internet Explorer and then select Tools ➢ Internet Options. Select the Content tab ➢ Certificates ➢ Trusted Root Certification Authorities.

It's possible to add additional certificates to the Trusted Root Certification Authorities store. For example, you can add certificates to employee computers for internal certification authorities.

Enabling and Disabling Features

When you first install Windows 7, not all of the features are added by default. In addition, some of the features that are installed can be removed. You can use the *Windows Features* tool to add or remove features.

Chapter 2, "Automating the Deployment of Windows 7," covered details on how features can be added and removed from an image using the DISM tool.

Figure 6.7 shows the Windows Features screen expanded to show all of the available features. You can access this from the Control Panel ➢ Programs ➢ Programs And Features ➢ Turn Windows Features On And Off link.

FIGURE 6.7   Turning Windows features on or off

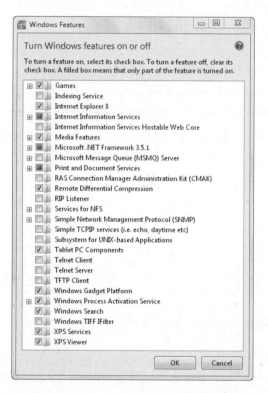

You can add additional features to this menu. For example, in Chapter 10, "Managing Windows 7 with Group Policy," you'll see how to install the Remote Server Administration Tools (RSAT). You can then use the Windows Features tool to add the desired administrative tools to your system.

Exercise 6.1 shows how to use Windows Features to add or remove the Games feature. You can use these steps to add or remove any features on the menu.

EXERCISE 6.1

Disabling the Games Feature

1. Click Start ➢ Control Panel.

2. Type **Features** in the Control Panel Search box located in the upper-right corner.

3. Click Programs And Features. Note that this is populated with all of the installed applications. You can use this page to uninstall applications by selecting an application and clicking Uninstall.

4. Click Turn Windows Features On Or Off.

5. On the Windows Features screen, deselect the check box for Games if it is selected. If it's already deselected, you can select it to add Games. Click OK.

    After a moment, Windows Features will complete and the window will close.

Chapter 10 covers how to configure and apply Group Policy. However, there are a few Group Policy settings worth mentioning here. These settings apply to both Windows Vista and Windows 7.

You can access Local Group Policy by adding the Group Policy Object Editor snap-in for the local computer to an MMC. An easier way is to click Start, type **Group** in the Start Search text box, and select Edit Group Policy.

 The settings available in Group Policy can be applied at the site, domain, or OU level, and those available in Local Group Policy apply to a single computer. The path for a domain Group Policy starts with User Configuration ➢ Policies ➢ Administrative Templates. The path for Local Group Policy starts with User Configuration ➢ Administrative Templates.

Hide Windows Features   This setting removes access to Windows Features. This prevents users from adding or removing any features. This setting is located in the Administrative Templates ➢ Control Panel ➢ Programs node.

Hide Programs And Features Page   With this setting enabled, users won't be able to access the Programs And Features page at all. This also prevents them from uninstalling programs, viewing installed updates, and uninstalling updates. This setting is located in the Administrative Templates ➢ Control Panel ➢ Programs node.

Hide The Programs Control Panel   This option removes the Programs link in Control Panel and all programs within the Programs link. It includes Programs, Default Programs, and Desktop Gadgets. This setting is located in the Administrative Templates ➢ Control Panel ➢ Programs node.

Designing a Delivery Strategy

A delivery strategy identifies how the application is delivered to the user. The primary method of delivery is to install it on the user's computer. When the user wants to run the program, it is launched from the Start menu.

However, there are several other methods of delivery available. These additional methods use different types of virtualization techniques. Virtualization techniques include the following:

- Windows XP Mode
- Virtual PC
- Remote Desktop Services
- Application Virtualization

Windows XP Mode

Windows XP Mode was covered extensively in Chapter 1, "Planning for the Installation of Windows 7." Chapter 1 included exercises to install and use Windows XP. As a reminder, Windows XP Mode can be used for any applications that aren't compatible with Windows 7. It is a full Windows XP operating system in a virtual environment.

After adding Windows XP Mode, you can install applications in the Windows XP Mode VPC. Applications will appear and can be launched from the Windows 7 Start menu without starting the Windows XP Mode VPC. From the user's perspective, it looks just as if it's running in Windows 7.

If an application is not compatible with Windows 7, this will often be your first choice as an alternative. It doesn't require any additional servers on the network. However, Windows XP Mode does work best if the hardware supports virtualization. You can install the update from KB 977206 (http://support.microsoft.com/kb/977206) as a workaround.

Virtual PC

If the PC hardware doesn't support virtualization and you don't want to use the workaround, you can still use Microsoft Virtual PC (VPC) on the system. With VPC, you can install another operating system (such as Windows XP) in the Virtual PC and then install the application within the VPC.

Microsoft Virtual PC is available as a free download. It is the precursor to Windows Virtual PC. Windows XP Mode must use Windows Virtual PC.

The drawback is that the user must launch VPC and then launch the application within the VPC image. Although this will work, the extra steps can sometimes confuse the end user. VPC also requires more RAM and processing power.

Remote Desktop Services

Remote Desktop Services (RDS) can be used to deliver applications to users. The application is hosted on a server configured as an RDS Session Host server. Users can then connect to the server and run applications remotely.

Remote Desktop Services was previously known as Terminal Services. It was renamed in Windows Server 2008 R2.

Figure 6.8 shows how RDS can be used in a network. In the figure, three clients are using RDS. The clients can be running Windows 7, Windows XP, or just about any operating system. They need only network connectivity to the RDS Session Host server.

FIGURE 6.8   RDS used in a network

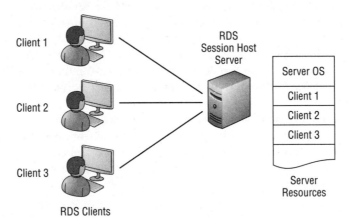

The server can host full desktops or individual applications.

Full desktops   The client could be running Windows XP and then connect to the server to launch a Windows 7 desktop. The Windows 7 desktop will operate within a window on the client's system.

Applications   A single application can be run on the server. RemoteApp applications can be hosted on an RDS Session Host server. Clients can then start the application from their Start menu, from a desktop icon, or from a web page depending on how the RemoteApp application is configured. The application runs in a window on the user's desktop and has the look and feel of a locally run program.

Application Virtualization

Applications can also be streamed to a user's desktop on demand similar to how audio and video can be streamed to the client. Microsoft's Application Virtualization server (App-V server) can be used to stream applications to SoftGrid clients. App-V was previously known as Microsoft SoftGrid.

Figure 6.9 shows how an App-V server works in a network. The client has the Microsoft Application Virtualization for Desktops tool, which is also known as the SoftGrid client. The client requests the application.

FIGURE 6.9   Application virtualization

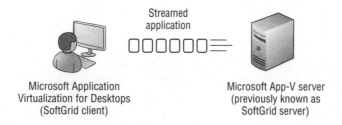

Microsoft Application
Virtualization for Desktops
(SoftGrid client)

Microsoft App-V server
(previously known as
SoftGrid server)

The App-V server then sends the application in streamed chunks. Depending on the activity of the user, different chunks of the application will be sent. The SoftGrid client formats the streamed application and presents it to the user.

Although applications can be very large, most users don't access all of the features. For example, Word has many different capabilities related to formatting, translating, and more. These capabilities will be streamed to users who need them but not sent to users who don't.

Designing a Deployment Strategy

One of the things to consider when an application needs to be installed on several systems is how you will install it. If you're installing it on a single system, the obvious choice is to install it directly. Pop the CD in, run setup, and you're finished.

However, if you need to install it on multiple systems, you'll probably want to automate the installation. This allows you to deploy the installation over the network. There are two primary issues to address when automating the installation:

- Identifying deployment concerns
- Choosing a deployment method

Identifying Deployment Concerns

When you decide that you want to deploy applications to computers over the network, you'll need to consider several other issues. By identifying your needs and concerns in these areas, it'll be easier to decide on the deployment method.

> The primary two choices you have to deploy an application are Group Policy or System Center Configuration Manager. SCCM provides additional capabilities with scheduling and staggering deployments that aren't available to Group Policy.

The deployment concerns are these:

- Application packages
- Network considerations
- Scheduling considerations
- Client requirements

Application Packages

Applications must be packaged as .msi files in order to deploy them over the network using Group Policy or System Center Configuration Manager. If the application isn't already packaged as an .msi file, there are some methods you can use to package it.

You can also apply *transforms* (.mst) to .msi package files. A transform can be used to modify how the default installation is done for an .msi package. As an example, the default installation of Word may install the English dictionary. You may also want the Spanish dictionary included. You could create a transform as an .mst file and deploy the package with this transform.

Network Considerations

The biggest consideration with the network is available bandwidth. This is a comparison of the size of the network pipe and how much bandwidth is used on your network.

For example, you could have a 100Mbs network infrastructure without much usage. This would give you high available bandwidth. If you wanted to deploy applications over this network, you would probably be able to do so without impacting its performance.

On the other hand, you could have a 1Gbs network with high usage. Even though the network starts with a wider pipe, if it's already close to peak capacity, you may impact the performance of the network by deploying various applications.

Scheduling Considerations

You can often overcome any problems with a slow network by deploying the applications during off-peak hours. In other words, the network could be at peak capacity during working hours but have a lot of capacity during non-work hours.

You can also choose to stagger the deployments. Instead of pushing out the application to 1,000 clients at the same time, you could deploy the application in phases.

SCCM allows you to schedule and stagger the deployments. Group Policy doesn't have a scheduling deployment choice. However, you can also stagger the deployment with Group Policy by linking the Group Policy object to Organizational Units one at a time. For example, you can link the GPO to the Sales OU on Monday, link the GPO to the HR OU on Tuesday, and so on.

Client Requirements

When deploying applications to clients, you can first audit the systems to ensure that they meet prerequisites and minimum requirements.

Scripts using Windows Management Instrumentation (WMI) can be used to identify the current status of any system. You can check for available disk space, the amount of memory, the version of the operating system, and much more. You can use these results to identify which computers should receive the applications.

Group Policy includes the ability to use WMI filters with a GPO. As long as the requirements in the WMI filter are met, the application will be deployed.

Similarly, SCCM allows systems to be inventoried to determine if they meet certain requirements. SCCM also uses WMI queries.

Choosing a Deployment Method

The two primary methods of deploying software are Group Policy and SCCM. Group Policy is free and can be used in any Windows domain hosting Windows 2000 servers or newer. SCCM is a server product that must be purchased. However, SCCM offers greater flexibility in scheduling the deployments.

Other less-used choices are as follows:

Scripts   If you can write a script to deploy the application, the script can be scheduled to run with Group Policy. Chapter 10 shows how you can schedule a script to run when a user logs on or when a computer starts up. The script could be configured to check to see if the software is installed. If it is installed, the script will stop. If it isn't installed, the script could install it.

Deploy manually from a central server   It's also possible to store the software package on a central server share. Users or administrators could then connect to the share using the UNC path of \\ServerName\ShareName.

Group Policy

You can use Group Policy to deploy applications. Group Policy can be used as long as your network is hosting a domain. The steps to deploy an application are covered in more depth in Chapter 10.

When deploying applications, you'll deploy them by assigning or publishing.

Assigning   An application can be assigned to a user or to a computer. When assigned to a computer, it is installed the next time the computer is booted. When assigned to a user, it is available on the Start menu. The first time the user selects it from the Start menu, it is installed.

Publishing   An application can be published only to a user, not to a computer. When published, it is available to be installed by the user via the Control Panel ➢ Programs menu.

When an application is assigned or published to users, it can also be installed when a user attempts to open a file that requires the application (called document invocation). In other words, a user may have Microsoft PowerPoint 2007 assigned, but it has never been installed. If the user receives a file with the `.pptx` extension and double-clicks it to open it, Microsoft PowerPoint 2007 will then be installed.

System Center Configuration Manager

System Center Configuration Manager (SCCM) is a server product that can be purchased. It can be used to install software on computers and much more. For example, it can be also used to deploy full images and deploy updates to clients.

> The primary tradeoff between Group Policy and SCCM is cost. Group Policy is free. SCCM is a server product that must be purchased. Also, because of the richness of SCCM, it takes some time and training for administrators to get up to speed on SCCM.

One of the significant benefits of using SCCM is that you can schedule the deployments. As mentioned before, this can be useful if the network infrastructure is close to peak capacity. The amount of bandwidth needed to install some applications can be extensive. If software is installed during peak usage of the network, the installation could interfere with normal operations.

With SCCM, you can schedule the deployments to occur during off-peak times. It also allows you to stagger the deployments so that they occur at different times.

Real World Scenario

SCCM vs. Available Operating System Tools

Most of what you can do with SCCM you can also do with available tools in Windows Server 2008 or Windows Server 2008 R2. However, SCCM provides additional features for each of these capabilities.

For example, Group Policy is a built-in tool that can be used to deploy applications. SCCM gives additional features such as scheduling and staggering deployments.

Windows Server Update Services (WSUS) is a free Microsoft product that can be used to control how updates are downloaded and deployed to clients. SCCM provides better control of these updates and how the clients can be audited.

Windows Deployment Services (WDS) is a free server role that can be added to capture and deploy full operating system images to clients. SCCM can be used to improve these deployments so that they are Zero Touch Installations (ZTI).

When evaluating the choice to add SCCM, it's important to realize that it does provide these extra benefits.

Identifying and Resolving Software Failure Issues

It would be nice if every time you installed an application it worked perfectly. Then again, if that happened, there'd be less of a need for desktop administrators to troubleshoot and repair the failures.

Here are some of the actions you can take and tools you have available to help troubleshoot problems:

- Checking and repairing installations
- Checking the logs
- Problem Steps Recorder
- Checking the application in Safe Mode

Checking and Repairing Installations

If an application isn't working as expected, you can use some of the tools in the Programs area of Control Panel to check them. Using these tools, you can verify that an application is installed, often verify the version, and sometimes change or repair the installation.

Figure 6.10 shows the *Programs and Features applet* open. If you select any program available on this screen, you'll be able to select Uninstall to remove it from the system. However, some systems have additional features. In the figure, Microsoft Office Live Add-in 1.3 is selected. The program has two additional choices: Change and Repair.

FIGURE 6.10 Programs and Features

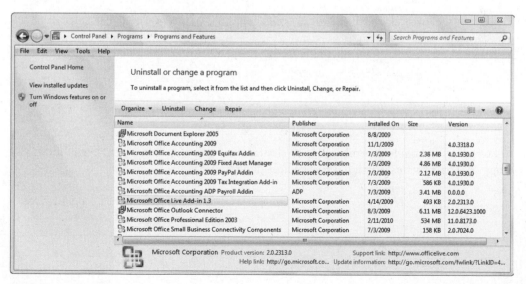

Notice that the version number is listed on the far right of the display. This depends on the developer entering the appropriate data. In the figure, the version is blank for one application and listed as 0.0.0.0 for another one.

Change　When you select Change, the setup program will run. Depending on how the developer created this, you may be able modify the installation by adding or removing components. Other times, selecting Change only gives you the opportunity to repair or uninstall the application.

Repair　This allows the application to check for missing or corrupt files, Registry keys, and other key elements needed to run the program. Selecting this choice can often repair an application that is not running correctly.

 If the Repair choice isn't available, you can still uninstall and reinstall the application. This will work similarly to a repair but will take longer.

Figure 6.11 shows the screen for an application after Change has been selected. The Modify choice is highlighted. If selected for this application, it will allow you to add and remove features.

FIGURE 6.11　Modifying, repairing, or removing an application

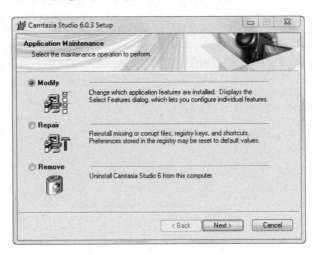

The choices available depend on the developer. If a developer didn't include methods to change or repair the installation, these choices don't appear.

> ### 🌐 Real World Scenario
>
> #### Repair Malware Infections
>
> Because the Repair feature checks for missing and corrupt files, it can repair some malware infections.
>
> Not too long ago, I ran across a Windows 7 system that had been infected by a virus. After I updated the virus signatures, removed the malware, and had a clean virus scan, I started checking the operation of the computer. I realized that a couple of the applications in Microsoft Office 2007 weren't working.
>
> I tried the Repair feature, and the problem was quickly resolved. It was quite a bit easier than removing Microsoft Office and reinstalling it from scratch.

Exercise 6.2 shows the steps you can take to check or repair an installation.

EXERCISE 6.2

Checking and Repairing an Installation

1. Click Start ➤ Control Panel.

2. Type **Programs** in the Control Panel Search box located in the upper-right corner.

3. Click Uninstall A Program.

4. Select various applications in this list. Notice how the commands on the toolbar change for different applications. The available choices include Uninstall, Uninstall/Change, Change, and Repair.

5. Locate an application that has Change listed. Select Change and view the choices. Click Cancel.

When you select Uninstall or Repair, you'll often be given just one confirmation screen. Once you confirm the action, it will continue until it is complete.

Checking the Logs

Chapter 5, "Maintaining and Troubleshooting Windows 7," included information on Event Viewer. The Application log is one of the primary sources you can look at to troubleshoot problems with applications.

The log entries are created by the application developer. There are times when these logs can be very useful, but there are also times when they can be somewhat cryptic. However, even if the entry is cryptic, plugging the recorded error data into your favorite Internet search engine may turn up the solution.

There are additional Microsoft logs that you can view related to applications. Microsoft or the application developer may direct you to look at these logs for specific instances, so it's good to know where they are. Figure 6.12 shows Event Viewer expanded to show the relevant logs.

FIGURE 6.12 Viewing Application logs in Event Viewer

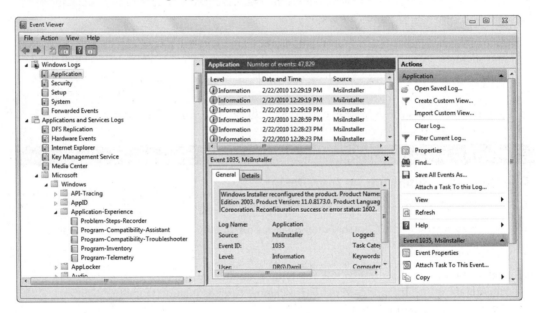

The extra logs are in the Applications and Services Logs ➢ Microsoft ➢ Windows ➢ Application-Experience section. These extra logs are as follows:

- Problem-Steps-Recorder

- Program-Compatibility-Assistant

- Program-Compatibility-Troubleshooter

- Program-Inventory

- Program-Telemetry

These logs may be empty if the features haven't been used.

Problem Steps Recorder

A neat new feature available with Windows 7 is the *Problem Steps Recorder*. Users can use this to record the actual steps they take to run or use an application. This can be very useful for users who have trouble articulating the actions they took. Users often take many steps but aren't aware of the importance of each step they take. They may omit these steps when explaining the problem.

When the Problem Steps Recorder runs, it records all of the steps the user takes and takes screen shots of their actions. The result is an archive format HTML document with an .mhtml extension. This single document includes all of the text and images recorded by the user. It is compressed as a zip file.

The user can then email the zip file to a help desk administrator for review. The administrator can open the zip file and view the document.

Figure 6.13 shows the Problem Steps Recorder. Exercise 6.3 shows how to launch and use it.

FIGURE 6.13   Problem Steps Recorder

EXERCISE 6.3

Using the Problem Steps Recorder

1. Click Start ➢ Control Panel.

2. Type **Problem** in the Control Panel Search box located in the upper-right corner.

3. Click Record Steps To Reproduce A Problem.

4. Click Start Record. If you're currently running any applications as an administrator, a warning dialog box will appear. Review it and click OK.

5. Launch the command line.

6. Enter IPConfig /all at the command line and press Enter.

7. Click Add Comment on the Problem Steps Recorder. Type **IPConfig results** and click OK.

8. Click Stop Record on the Problem Steps Recorder.

9. Browse to a location where you want to save the file. Enter a filename such as **App-Problem** and click Save.

10. Use Windows Explorer to browse to where you saved the file. Notice that an end user can right-click this document and select Send To ➢ Mail Recipient to send the file as an attachment for an email.

EXERCISE 6.3   (continued)

11. Right-click the file and select Extract All. Ensure Show Extracted Files When Complete is checked. Click Extract. (You can alternatively click the zip file if you simply want to view it.)

12. Double-click the .mhtml document to open it. This will open the file in Internet Explorer. Review the document.

13. Close all open windows.

Checking Whether an Application Runs in Safe Mode

Safe Mode can sometimes be useful when troubleshooting applications. You can use Safe Mode to uninstall an application that caused problems with the normal operation of the system or to see if the application will run in Safe Mode.

Windows Safe Modes were covered in Chapter 5. As a reminder, Safe Mode starts Windows with a limited set of files and drivers. You can start Windows 7 in Safe Mode by pressing the F8 key when you turn on your system. Pressing F8 will bring you to the Advanced Options screen, which includes several Safe Mode choices.

There's a short time between the startup of the system and when the splash screen appears. If you miss it, you'll need to reboot the system and start again. After the system starts, it's okay to press the F8 key repeatedly until the Advanced Options screen appears.

If you installed an application and now find that Windows 7 is no longer working properly, there could be an incompatibility with the application and Windows 7. You can boot into Safe Mode and uninstall the application using Programs and Features via the Control Panel, as shown earlier. You can also perform a System Restore from within Safe Mode if necessary.

It's also possible that you're able to boot into Windows 7, but problems appear when you launch the application. If you can launch the application in Safe Mode, you can eliminate the default settings and basic device drivers as possible causes.

Managing Application Compatibility

Some applications will run fine but not in Windows 7. The most common reason why an application won't run in Windows 7 is the extra security that comes with Windows 7. Other compatibility issues arise because of how the application interacts with the hardware.

You have two primary choices when you're faced with a compatibility issue:

- Use the Application Compatibility tools.
- Run the application in a previous version of Windows.

Application Compatibility

Windows 7 allows you to run applications in *Application Compatibility mode*. As an example, I have an old game that I occasionally like to run—Risk II. Unfortunately, it is supported only in Windows XP.

After installing the application, I can right-click it on the Start menu and select Properties. Figure 6.14 shows the different application compatibility selections that can be selected.

FIGURE 6.14 Application compatibility

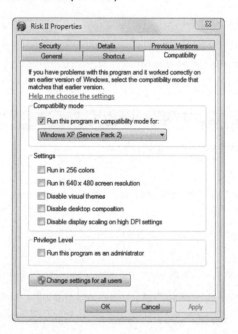

 The Privilege Level setting Run This Program As An Administrator can be used for older applications that require elevated privileges. Although older applications didn't require administrative permissions, it was common for developers to program them to need such elevated permissions. This causes conflicts with UAC. Checking this box can resolve the problem for the application.

In the figure, the application is using the Windows XP (Service Pack 2) selection. Windows 7 emulates the settings of the older operating system when the application is run. Other operating system selections are as follows:

- Windows 95
- Windows 98/ME
- Windows NT 4.0 (Service Pack 5)
- Windows 2000
- Windows XP (Service Pack 3)
- Windows Server 2003 (Service Pack 1)
- Windows Server 2008 (Service Pack 1)
- Windows Vista
- Windows Vista (Service Pack 1)
- Windows Vista (Service Pack 2)

You can also use the Program Compatibility Wizard to configure an application to run with the settings of a previous version of Windows. Exercise 6.4 shows how this is done.

EXERCISE 6.4

Using the Program Compatibility Wizard

1. Click Start ➢ Control Panel.

2. Type **Compatibility** in the Control Panel Search box located in the upper-right corner.

3. Click Run Programs Made For Previous Versions Of Windows to launch the Program Compatibility Wizard.

4. Click Next. The wizard will attempt to detect any issues with the system.

5. After a moment, it will complete scanning your system and will provide a list of programs.

   a. If the program is in the list, you can select it and click Next.

   b. If it's not in the list, you can select Not Listed. Click Next. Either enter the application's full path or click Browse to browse to the application. Click Next.

6. The Program Compatibility Wizard will recommend settings for the application. Click Try Recommended Settings.

7. On the Test Compatibility Settings For The Program screen, click Start The Program. Determine whether the program is working correctly.

8. Click Next.

   a. If the application works, select Yes, Save These Settings For This Program.

EXERCISE 6.4   *(continued)*

> **b.** If the application doesn't work, you can click No, Try Again Using Different Settings. This will display a window similar to the following graphic.

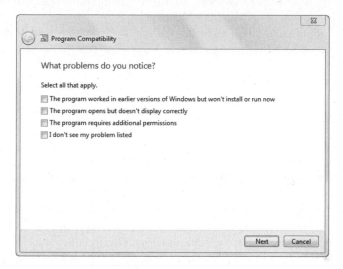

> **c.** You can experiment with these settings by checking one or more of the boxes and trying the program again.
>
> **d.** Once you've identified settings that work, click Yes, Save These Settings For This Program. These settings will automatically be used each time the application starts in the future.

9. You can always view the application compatibility settings by right-clicking the shortcut, selecting Properties, and clicking the Compatibility tab.

Running the Application in a Previous Version of Windows

Instead of using the application compatibility settings, you can run the application in an actual previous version of Windows. There are several ways to do this.

The most extreme solution is to give the user two computers. The user can run one computer with Windows 7 and another computer for the problematic application. However, this is not desirable for most companies.

You can virtualize the application as mentioned previously. As a reminder, you have the following choices:

- Windows XP Mode
- Windows VPC
- Remote Desktop Services
- Application Virtualization

As a comparison, Windows XP Mode is the cheapest, most seamless solution. For just a few computers, this is likely the first choice. As a reminder, it works best with hardware virtualization, but KB 977206 provides a workaround.

Windows VPC can be the second choice if you need the incompatible application to run on only a few computers. You can use VPC to install a compatible operating system and then install the application in this Virtual PC image.

If you need to support more than a few computers, you can go to one of the server solutions. Remote Desktop Services and Application Virtualization are the two server solutions currently available.

Summary

In this chapter, you learned about various issues related to software. Most software can be installed directly on Windows 7. If there are any compatibility issues, several solutions are available to resolve them.

It's possible to run the software using one of several virtualization methods. These include Windows XP Mode, Virtual PC, Remote Desktop Services, and Application Virtualization.

If you need to deploy software to multiple systems, Group Policy and SCCM can both be used. Group Policy is free and available in any domain. SCCM is a server product that must be purchased, but it provides several more capabilities such as the ability to schedule and stagger deployments.

You also have several tools available for troubleshooting. Many software installations allow you to repair the installation from Control Panel. In addition, the Application Compatibility Wizard can be used to allow Windows 7 to mimic a previous operating system.

Chapter Essentials

Installing and configuring software   Know the requirements for installing software. Local administrative permissions are required to install software packages, and software packages come in .msi or .msu formats. Files should be digitally signed by a trusted publisher to be assured of their safety. Features can often be enabled or disabled by using Windows Features in Control Panel.

Designing a delivery strategy   Be aware of the different methods of delivering software. Most software will be installed directly on the Windows 7 system. It's also possible to use virtualization techniques. Windows XP Mode can be used if the hardware supports hardware virtualization. Virtual PC can be used if the hardware doesn't support hardware virtualization. Remote Desktop Services and Application Virtualization are two server methods that can be used to deliver software applications.

Designing a deployment strategy   Know the different methods that can be used to automate deployments of applications. Group Policy is a free method that can be used in any domain. SCCM can be used if more control is needed. SCCM allows you to schedule and stagger the deployments.

Identifying and resolving software failure issues   Be aware of the different tools available for troubleshooting. Some applications can be repaired from Control Panel. Logs may provide insight into problems with an application. You should know how to use the Application Compatibility Wizard.

Chapter 7

Networking with Windows 7

TOPICS COVERED IN THIS CHAPTER INCLUDE

- ✓ Understanding network connectivity in an enterprise
- ✓ Resolving names to IP addresses
- ✓ Using the Network and Sharing Center
- ✓ Troubleshooting network connectivity problems

The majority of Windows 7 computers will be connected to a network, especially in enterprises. When connected to the network, computers can access and share resources. In addition, the network provides access to the Internet and email, which have become integral tools in the workplace.

This chapter lays a foundation for many of the basics related to networking. It covers IP addressing, assigning TCP/IP configuration information manually, using DHCP for dynamic configuration, and name resolution.

Basic tools covered in this chapter are Ping, IPConfig, and NSLookup. You'll also learn about the Network and Sharing Center that was introduced in Windows Vista. While all of these are basic tools, they are invaluable when troubleshooting network connectivity problems.

Understanding Network Connectivity in an Enterprise

Before digging into the details of networking topics, it's worthwhile to review the basics of networking within an enterprise. Windows products have long used the Transmission Control Protocol/Internet Protocol suite (commonly called TCP/IP), and Windows 7 is no exception. The Internet is based on TCP/IP, and computers today need access to the Internet.

The concepts are pretty much the same with Windows 7 as they were with Windows XP and Windows Vista. If you've been working with networked clients for awhile, you can probably skim over this material. However, it does lay a foundation for the rest of the chapter and for Chapter 8, "Accessing Resources on a Network."

Figure 7.1 shows several components of a typical network. You should understand the purpose and use of each of these components.

DHCP   A *Dynamic Host Configuration Protocol (DHCP)* server issues TCP/IP configuration information to users. This includes an IP address, subnet mask, address of the DNS server, address of the default gateway, and more.

DNS   The primary purpose of the *Domain Name System (DNS)* server is to resolve hostnames to IP addresses. The client sends the name of a host on the network, and the server responds with the IP address. It can also do reverse lookups (resolving the IP address to a name) with pointer (PTR) records and locate domain controllers with server (SRV) records.

FIGURE 7.1   Components of a typical network

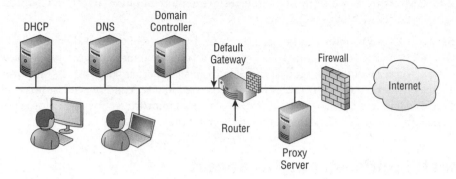

WINS   A *Windows Internet Name Service (WINS)* server is used to resolve NetBIOS names to IP addresses. The use of NetBIOS names is significantly reduced in current Microsoft networks (and is not shown in Figure 7.1), but they may still be used by legacy applications, requiring the use of a WINS server in a network.

Domain Controller   A domain controller (DC) hosts Active Directory Domain Services (AD DS) in a Microsoft domain. AD DS holds objects (such as users, computers, and groups) that can be centrally managed and administered. Users and computers must have an account in AD DS to be able to log on to the domain and use domain resources. DNS is required for clients to locate DCs on the network.

Default Gateway   A *default gateway* identifies the default path out of the subnet. All of the computers in the drawing to the left of the default gateway are on the same subnet, and their path to the Internet is through the default gateway. The default gateway is also referred to as the near side of a router, and it is specifically identified by the IP address assigned to the network interface connected to the subnet.

 A router is often assigned the first hostname in a network. This isn't required, but this standard is often followed in many networks. As an example, if the network ID is 192.168.1.0 (with a subnet mask of 255.255.255.0), the default gateway is often assigned 192.168.1.1.

Router   A router is a hardware device that routes data from one subnet to another. The router in the diagram has two network interfaces; one is the default gateway for the Internet network, and the other is the connection to the DMZ. Routers have filtering capabilities that allow them to restrict what traffic can be passed through the router. These filtering capabilities provide the router with firewall characteristics.

Firewall   A *firewall* is designed to filter traffic so that only specific traffic is allowed into or out of a network. A firewall starts with basic router-filtering capabilities but can be much more sophisticated in how the traffic can be examined and filtered. The two firewalls shown in the diagram (to the left and right of the proxy server) are a combination of hardware and software. Host-based firewalls can be installed on any system and are referred to as software-based firewalls. Firewalls are explored in more depth in Chapter 11, "Managing Security in Windows 7."

Proxy Server   A *proxy server* can be used to access Internet resources. When it's used in a network, all clients would be configured to submit Internet requests to the proxy server, and the proxy server would then request the data from the Internet. Proxies can improve the performance of Internet access by caching data requested by users and providing this cached data when it's requested by another user. Proxies can also improve security or enforce business policies by preventing users from going to specific sites.

Unicast, Multicast, and Broadcast

IP traffic travels from host to host in networks using unicast, multicast, or broadcast methods. You'll see these terms throughout the chapter and even elsewhere in the book. It's worthwhile defining them to ensure they are clear to you.

Unicast   Data travels from one computer to another computer. A unicast message will be processed only by the host with the destination IP address.

Multicast   Data travels from one computer to multiple computers. This was mentioned and stressed as one of the benefits of Windows Deployment Services (WDS) in Chapter 2, "Automating the Deployment of Windows 7." WDS is able to multicast a single image to multiple computers at the same time. In contrast, if WDS did this as unicast, it would have to send a separate copy of the image over the network for each client.

Broadcast   Data travels from one computer to all computers in the subnet. Each computer that receives the packet will process it and determine whether it needs to take action with the packet. Broadcast traffic is not passed through the router.

Using IPConfig

The *IPConfig* command is a familiar command to many people, but it has some extra capabilities that are sometimes overlooked. Just as with most command-prompt commands, it can be executed alone or with switches to modify what it does.

IPConfig and IPConfig /all are two commands commonly used to check the TCP/IP configuration of a system. IPConfig will provide the output shown in Listing 7.1.

Listing 7.1: IPConfig output

```
Windows IP Configuration
Ethernet adapter Local Area Connection:
    Connection-specific DNS Suffix  . :
    IPv4 Address. . . . . . . . . . . : 192.168.1.15
    Subnet Mask . . . . . . . . . . . : 255.255.255.0
    Default Gateway . . . . . . . . . : 192.168.1.1
```

The IPconfig /all command will show much more information, starting with the host-name. Listing 7.2 shows the partial output of IPConfig /all for a system that is receiving TCP/IP configuration from a DHCP server. The output of only one adapter is shown, but depending on the configuration, you may see more data on your system.

Listing 7.2: IPConfig /all output

```
C:\>ipconfig /all

Windows IP Configuration

    Host Name . . . . . . . . . . . . : Darril-PC
    Primary Dns Suffix  . . . . . . . :
    Node Type . . . . . . . . . . . . : Hybrid
    IP Routing Enabled. . . . . . . . : No
    WINS Proxy Enabled. . . . . . . . : No
    DNS Suffix Search List. . . . . . : Wiley.com

Ethernet adapter Local Area Connection:

    Connection-specific DNS Suffix  . : Wiley.com
    Description . . . . . . . . . . . : Realtek RTL8168C(P)/8111C(P)
                                        Family PCI-EGBE NIC #2
    Physical Address. . . . . . . . . : 00-23-5A-33-C4-CA
    DHCP Enabled. . . . . . . . . . . : Yes
    Autoconfiguration Enabled . . . . : Yes
    IPv4 Address. . . . . . . . . . . : 192.168.1.50(Preferred)
    Subnet Mask . . . . . . . . . . . : 255.255.255.0
    Lease Obtained. . . . . . . . . . : Tuesday, November 28, 2009 9:59:44 AM
    Lease Expires . . . . . . . . . . : Monday, December 4, 2009 9:59:43 AM
    Default Gateway . . . . . . . . . : 192.168.1.1
    DHCP Server . . . . . . . . . . . : 192.168.1.10
    DNS Servers . . . . . . . . . . . : 192.168.1.10
    NetBIOS over Tcpip. . . . . . . . : Enabled
```

Notice that DHCP Enabled is set to Yes, indicating it is a DHCP client. In addition, it shows the IP address of the DHCP server, the DNS server, and the default gateway. The lease length for DHCP servers hosted on Windows Server 2008 is often set for either six days or eight days, and the output shows when the lease was obtained and when it expires.

Table 7.1 shows the switches available with the IPConfig command.

TABLE 7.1   IPConfig command switches

Switch	Comments
/?	Displays help.
/All	Displays the full configuration information for the client.
/Release	Releases the DHCP assigned IPv4 address for the adapter, giving it an address of 0.0.0.0. This does not have any effect on adapters with statically assigned addresses.
/Release6	Releases the DHCP assigned IPv6 address for the adapter. This does not have any effect on adapters with statically assigned addresses.
/Renew	Requests a new IPv4 DHCP lease for the adapter from a DHCP server. If a DHCP server is not available, an APIPA address (169.254.y.z) will be assigned. This does not have any effect on adapters with statically assigned addresses.
/Renew6	Requests a new IPv6 DHCP lease for the adapter. If a DHCP server does not respond, a link-local address with a prefix of FE80 is assigned. This does not have any effect on adapters with statically assigned addresses.
/DisplayDNS	Displays the contents of the host cache. Each time a name is resolved by DNS, the name resolution information is placed in cache.
/FlushDNS	Purges the contents of the hostname cache. Names in cache from the Hosts file will always remain in cache.

Understanding the DHCP Lease

You'll almost always find at least one DHCP server used within an enterprise. It automates the process of assigning TCP/IP configuration, and once it's configured, it takes very little management to keep it running. A single DHCP server can handle as many 10,000 clients, though when you have that many clients, you'd usually add another DHCP server for redundancy and fault tolerance.

When a DHCP client turns on, four packets are exchanged over the network between the DHCP client and the DHCP server. This is often referred to as the DORA process because of the names of the IP packets: D for Discover, O for Offer, R for Request, and A for Acknowledge.

Consider Figure 7.2. In the figure, a single DHCP server is being used to serve three subnets. When the client in subnet C turns on, it will start the DHCP process by broadcasting the Discover packet, and the DHCP server in subnet A will respond.

FIGURE 7.2   Using DHCP on a network

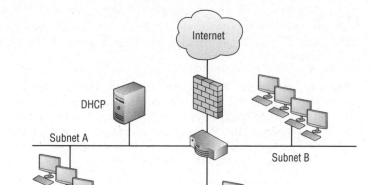

Discover   When the DHCP client turns on, it will broadcast a DHCPDiscover packet. It's asking, "Are there any DHCP servers out there?"

Offer   When a DHCP server receives a DHCPDiscover packet, it will respond by broadcasting a DHCPOffer. This offer includes a DHCP lease, which includes the TCP/IP configuration for the client. If multiple DHCP servers are on the network, each one can respond with an offer.

Request   The client sends a DHCPRequest in response to the first DHCPOffer it receives. In essence, it says, "Thank you; I'll take that lease." A DHCP lease is typically configured to last eight days on a network. If a second DHCP server sent an offer but did not receive a request, the offer will expire and the IP address will still be available to be issued.

Acknowledge   When the DHCP server receives the request, it allocates the lease to ensure the IP address is not issued to any other clients and responds with the DHCPACK (Acknowledge) packet.

After 50 percent of the lease length has expired, the client requests a renewal of the lease from the DHCP server. For example, if the lease length is set to eight days, the client will try to renew the lease after four days. If the DHCP server doesn't respond, the client will continue to request a renewal until 87.5 percent of the lease length has expired (after seven days for an eight-day lease). After 87.5 percent, the client will repeat the DORA process every 5 minutes looking for any DHCP server. At 100 percent, the client will assign itself an IP address in the range of 169.254.y.z /16.

Understanding DHCP Scopes

DHCP servers are typically configured with multiple DHCP scopes. Each *DHCP scope* typically refers to a subnet, though it is possible to have more than one scope for a subnet. In addition, the DHCP server can configure different TCP/IP options for individual scopes.

When preparing for the 70-685 exam, you won't be expected to configure the DHCP server, but you should understand how the scopes relate to the network. This is especially important when troubleshooting name resolution issues related to DNS. You should understand how the address for DNS is obtained when DHCP is used and how DHCP clients may use the default gateway to reach the DNS server.

As an example, consider Figure 7.3. This shows three subnets served by a single DHCP server. One router routes packets between the subnets and to the Internet via the firewall. This router has three network adapters, and each adapter is configured with an IP address (identified as the default gateway) for the subnet.

FIGURE 7.3   Using DHCP on a network

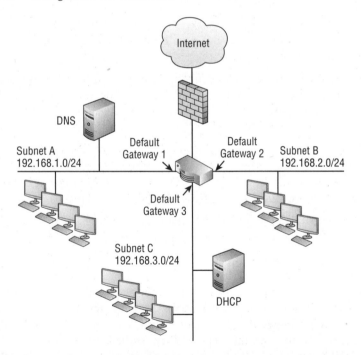

In addition, the network has a single DNS server located in subnet A. The options in the DHCP server can be set up to configure clients in all three subnets using three different scopes.

Figure 7.4 shows the DHCP console configured for the network shown in Figure 7.3. In the figure, the options for the Subnet A scope are shown. The 003 Router option is for the default gateway. The DNS server has an IP address of 192.168.1.10, and the domain name is Wiley.com.

FIGURE 7.4 The DHCP console showing three scopes and options

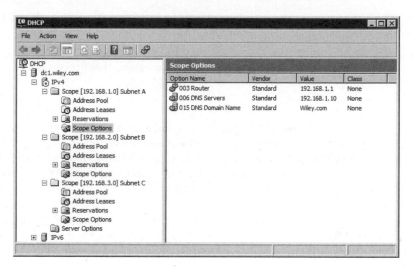

You may notice that the icon for the option for the 003 Router is a little different from the 006 DNS Servers and 015 DNS Domain Name options. The Router option is configured at the scope level and applies only to clients connecting from Subnet A. However, the 006 DNS Servers and 015 DNS Domain Name options are server-level options and apply to all clients served by this DHCP server. Server-level options are configured once for the server and apply to all scopes.

It's also possible to issue the addresses for multiple DNS servers to clients. The first DNS server would be used as the preferred DNS server, and others would be designated as alternate DNS servers. Alternate DNS Servers are queried only if the preferred DNS server does not respond.

DCHP and RFC 1542

If you know a little about networking, you may have been thinking, "Wait a minute! Broadcasts can't go through the router," as you read through the DHCP DORA process. You're absolutely correct. However, DHCP broadcasts are special broadcasts, and the router is configured to allow them on most internal networks. Either that or a DHCP server, or a DHCP relay agent, must be placed on every subnet. It's much more common to configure the router to pass the DHCP broadcasts.

RFC 1542 (Request For Comments 1542) is a TCP/IP standards document that specifies that DHCP broadcasts are to use UDP ports 67 and 68. Furthermore, routers that are RFC 1542 compliant can be configured to allow these DCHP broadcasts through UDP ports 67 and 68.

If you look back at Figure 7.2 and Figure7.3, the router would be configured to allow DHCP broadcasts through UDP ports 67 and 68 on the network interfaces connected to Subnet A, Subnet B, and Subnet C. It would not allow these broadcasts from the network interface connected to the Internet via the firewall.

APIPA

What if the DHCP server doesn't answer, or what if the DHCP lease expires? Well, TCP/IP has an app for that.

Automatic Private IP Addressing (APIPA) is used to configure clients with addresses in a special range when the DHCP server doesn't respond. The range of addresses is 169.254.0.1 through 169.245.255.254, with a subnet mask of 255.255.0.0.

> If you receive an APIPA address, you know that the DHCP client was unable to locate a DHCP server. You don't necessarily know why. The DHCP server may be down, the router may be down or misconfigured, or there may be some other network problem. However, you know that the DHCP server couldn't be reached or didn't respond.

As mentioned previously, you can use the IPConfig /all command at the command prompt to view the current TCP/IP configuration. Figure 7.5 shows what this looks like when the DHCP server can't be reached and an APIPA address is assigned.

FIGURE 7.5   Identifying an APIPA address

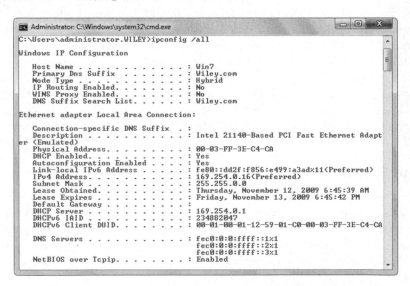

Several line items shown in the figure are worth mentioning here:

DHCP Enabled   The Yes setting indicates that it is configured as a DHCP client.

Autoconfiguration Enabled   The Yes setting indicates that APIPA is enabled. This is enabled by default but can be disabled with a Registry modification.

IPv4 Address   An address in the 169.254.0.0/24 range indicates an APIPA address. Because it is configured as a DCHP client and an address of 169.254.0.16 is assigned, it clearly indicates the DHCP server couldn't be reached or didn't respond.

DHCP Server   A DHCP address of 169.254.0.1 also indicates that this is an APIPA-assigned address. If a DHCP server was reached, this would show the IP address of the DHCP server, and a DHCP server would never be assigned an address in the APIPA range.

> The TCP/IP configuration of a client with an APIPA address will never include an address of a DNS server or a default gateway. A client that has been assigned an APIPA address can communicate with other clients that have APIPA addresses in the same subnet but will not be able to communicate with any clients in other subnets.

Understanding the IP Addresses

The IPv4 address has two important components: the network ID and the host ID. The network ID identifies the subnet the client is on, and the host ID is a unique address on the subnet. The subnet mask identifies which portion of the IP address is the network ID and which portion is the host ID.

> Subnetting can be more complex than the description given previously, and instead of dealing with just 255 or 0 in the subnet mask, you could have different numbers like 128, 192, and so on. However, for the purpose of the 70-685 exam and this explanation, we are keeping it simple.

You should easily be able to determine the network ID when you see an IP address and a subnet mask. Moreover, you should be able to determine when these are misconfigured for clients on a network.

Determining the Network ID

As an example, consider the following IP address and subnet mask:

192.168.1.10
255.255.255.0

Both the IP address and the subnet mask use dotted decimal format, with four decimal numbers separated by dots. To determine the subnet portion of the IP address, look for the 255s in the subnet mask. Because the first three numbers in the subnet mask are 255, the first three numbers in the IP address are the network ID.

192.168.1.x

255.255.255.x

> Under the hood, each decimal number is represented by 8 bits. 192 is represented by 1100 0000, 168 is represented by 1010 1000, and 1 is represented by 0000 0001. Because of this, when the numbers are shown in binary, they are referred to as octets.

The network ID is expressed with all four numbers, and the trailing numbers are always set as 0. For example, the previous network ID would be expressed as 192.168.1.0.

Can you identify the network ID for the following IP address and subnet mask?

10.80.1.5

255.0.0.0

Because only the first number in the subnet mask is a 255, only the first number in the IP address is in the network ID. The network ID is 10.0.0.0.

Classful IP Addressing

You may occasionally see IP addresses identified as classful addresses represented without a subnet mask. There are three primary classes you may run across: Class A, Class B, and Class C.

When a classful address is used, you automatically know what the subnet mask is, and you can then identify the network ID.

Class A   The first number in a Class A address is between 1 and 126, and the subnet mask is 255.0.0.0. For example, an IP address of 10.1.2.3 has a first number of 10, and since 10 is between 1 and 126, the subnet mask is 255.0.0.0 and the network ID is 10.0.0.0.

Class B   The first number is between 128 and 191 and the subnet mask is 255.255.0.0.

For example, an IP address of 172.1.2.3 has a first number of 172, which is between 128 and 191, so the subnet mask is 255.255.0.0 and the network ID is 172.1.0.0.

Class C   The first number is between 192 and 223 and the subnet mask is 255.255.255.0.

For example, an IP address of 192.1.2.3 has a first number of 192, which is between 192 and 223, so the subnet mask is 255.255.255.0 and the network ID is 192.1.2.0.

> Where's 127? You may have noticed that Class A ends at 126 and Class B starts at 128. Technically, Class A addresses include the 127.x.y.z range, but this entire range is used for testing, so it is not used.

The biggest benefit of using classful IP addresses in documentation is that the subnet mask can be omitted. However, it's important to realize that the rules of classful IP addresses can be broken. For example, an administrator can specify an IP address of 10.1.2.3 with a subnet mask of 255.255.255.0. In this case, the network ID is 10.1.2.0.

If you see an IP address that is identified as classful, you can use the first number of the IP address to determine the subnet mask and the network ID. However, if you see an IP address with a subnet mask, you would use the subnet mask regardless of the first number in the IP address.

Identifying Misconfigured Clients

All assigned IP addresses within a single subnet must have the same network ID. If not, they will not be able to communicate with other clients on the subnet. In addition, each client must be configured with the correct default gateway or it will not be able to communicate outside the network.

Consider Figure 7.6. Each client (numbered 1 through 6) has an assigned IP address (IP), subnet mask (SM), and default gateway (DG). Can you tell what's wrong with this picture? (The network interfaces on the router are configured correctly.)

FIGURE 7.6   A misconfigured network

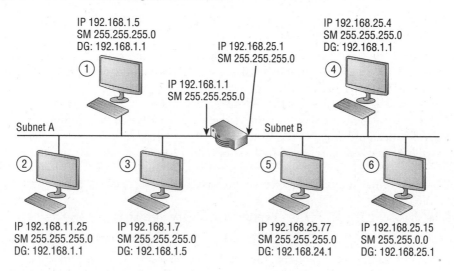

Client 1   This client is configured correctly. The network ID is 192.168.1.0.

Client 2   This client is configured with an incorrect IP address. The third decimal is 11 but must be a 1 to have the same network ID of 192.168.1.0 as other clients in the subnet. It currently has a network ID of 192.168.11.0. This client will not be able to communicate with any other clients on the network.

Client 3 This client is configured with an incorrect default gateway. The near side of the router has an IP address of 192.168.1.1, so the default gateway should be 192.168.1.1. This client will be able to communicate with other clients in Subnet A that have the same network ID (only client 1 in the figure), but it will not be able to communicate with any clients on Subnet B.

Client 4 This client is configured with an incorrect default gateway. The near side of the router has an IP address of 192.168.25.1, so the default gateway should be 192.168.25.1, not 192.168.1.1. This client will be able to communicate with other clients in Subnet B that have the same network ID (only client 5 in the figure), but it will not be able to communicate with any clients on Subnet A.

Client 5 This client is configured with an incorrect default gateway. The near side of the router has an IP address of 192.168.25.1, so the default gateway should be 192.168.25.1, not 192.168.24.1. This client will be able to communicate with other clients in Subnet B that have the same network ID (only client 4 in the figure), but it will not be able to communicate with any clients on Subnet A.

Client 6 This client is configured with an incorrect subnet mask. The third decimal is 0 but should be 255, resulting in a network ID of 192.168.0.0 instead of 192.168.25.0. This client will not be able to communicate with any other clients on the network.

Understanding CIDR Notation

You may occasionally see IP addresses expressed with a slash and a number at the end, like this: 192.168.1.5/24. This is referred to as Classless Inter-Domain Routing (CIDR) notation, and the number after the slash (/) represents the number of bits in the subnet mask.

Each IPv4 address and each subnet mask are represented by 32 bits (32 1s and 0s). However, when working with Windows interfaces, we normally use the decimal format of the IP address instead of listing all the 1s and 0s.

When a subnet mask is represented in dotted decimal format, it has four octets separated by dots, such as 255.255.255.0. If you look under the hood though, the subnet mask is represented in binary format and each octet is represented by 8 bits (such as 1 1 1 1 1 1 1 1 or 0 0 0 0 0 0 0 0).

A subnet mask of 255.255.255.0 is expressed in binary format as

1 1 1 1 1 1 1 1 . 1 1 1 1 1 1 1 1 . 1 1 1 1 1 1 1 1 . 0 0 0 0 0 0 0 0 .

Each string of 8 binary 1s represents the decimal number 255. A subnet mask of 255.255.255.0 has three strings of 8 binary 1s, with a total of 24 1s (3 * 8 = 24). CIDR notation uses the number of 1s in the subnet mask to express the value. Instead of the traditional method of expressing the subnet mask as 255.255.255.0, it can be expressed as /24.

Similarly, an address of 10.80.5.2/8 would have a subnet mask of 255.0.0.0. The /8 indicates only the first 8 bits of the subnet mask are 1s. In other words, the subnet mask in binary format is

1 1 1 1 1 1 1 1 . 0 0 0 0 0 0 0 0 . 0 0 0 0 0 0 0 0 . 0 0 0 0 0 0 0 0 .

Private IP Ranges

IP addresses are either public (on the Internet) or private. The Internet Assigned Numbers Authority (IANA) has designated several IP address ranges as private, and they will never be used on the Internet. These private IP address ranges are as follows:

- 10.0.0.1 through 1.255.255.255.254 (available IP addresses: 16,777,214)

- 172.16.0.1 through 172.31.255.255 (available IP addresses: 1,048,574)

- 192.168.0.1 through 192.168.255.254 (available IP addresses: 65,534)

Although the same public IP address can't be used by more than one host on the Internet, the same private IP addresses can be used by different private companies. For example, Acme could use the same IP address in the 192.168.1.0/24 range as Zycom uses. Since the addresses are private within each company, there is no conflict.

A Few Words on IPv6

IPv6 has arrived—on the Internet anyway. While it's spreading rapidly on the Internet, you may not see it being used as much on internal networks. Still, you should be aware of some of the basics of IPv6.

IPv6 does not support NetBIOS names. If your network is still using Net-BIOS names and WINS servers, you will not be able to migrate to an IPv6-only network. However, IPv4 and IPv6 can coexist, so it is possible to support NetBIOS with IPv4 but use IPv6.

As background, the move to IPv6 was driven largely because the Internet was running out of available IP addresses. IPv4 uses 32 bits (2^{32}), and it could *only* address about 4 billion clients. However, IPv4 wasted a lot of addresses, so we didn't really have 4 billion IP addresses that could be used.

IPv6 uses 128 bits (2^{128}), which is almost incomprehensible. Instead of having a total of 4 billion IP addresses on the entire Internet, it allows for more than 4 billion IP addresses for every person alive today (currently estimated at about 6.8 billion people).

Both IPv4 and IPv6 can coexist on the same network, and they are currently doing so on the Internet. While private networks can also support both IPv4 and IPv6 at the same time, there doesn't seem to be a quick move to do so. The servers that interact with the Internet need to use both IPv4 and IPv6, but most internal networks don't need IPv6 yet.

A simple reason why IPv6 isn't needed is that private networks aren't running out of IP addresses. The three private IP address ranges can be used to meet the needs of any organization on the planet.

An IPv6 address is expressed in hexadecimal. A hexadecimal character can be 0 through 9 and A through F, and it represents four binary bits. Because the IPv6 address has 128 bits, it is represented by 32 hexadecimal characters (128/4). These hexadecimal characters are represented in eight groups of four separated by a colon. As an example, the following is an IPv6 address:

2000 : 0001 : 4137 : 9E50 : 006C : 229E : B43A : 21E5

IPv6 Prefixes

There's no such thing as a subnet mask for IPv6. IPv6 uses an implicit 64-bit address prefix for any addresses assigned to network interfaces. However, there are some exceptions. IPv6 uses several unique prefixes to identify different types of addresses.

Global unicast   The address prefix is 2000::/3. A global unicast address is globally routable over the Internet. It uniquely identifies a single host on the Internet, and it can be thought of as similar to an IPv4 address.

Link-local unicast   The address prefix is FE80::/8. A *link-local address* is used within a private network and is not recognized outside the enterprise. Link-local addresses are assigned using autoconfiguration similar to IPv4 APIPA addresses. These are used when a DHCP server is not available.

Unique local unicast   The address prefix is FD00::. A unique local unicast address is an address assigned within a private network. This has been defined in RFC 4193, and it is intended to be used instead of site-local addresses.

Site-local addresses (with a prefix of FEC0::/7) were deprecated in September 2004 by RFC 3879. Unique local unicast addresses are used instead.

Configuring a Network Interface Card

One of the first steps to ensure a system has connectivity is to verify the TCP/IP configuration. You can check the TCP/IP configuration from the command line (using IPConfig) and configure it by accessing the properties of the network adapter.

IPConfig /all will provide a lot more information, as shown and discussed earlier in this chapter. If the system has the wrong address, you can configure the network adapter directly to assign a statically assigned IP address, or it can be configured to receive the IP address from a DHCP server.

Figure 7.7 shows a NIC configured with a statically assigned IP address. The IP address, subnet mask, default gateway, and DNS server addresses are all entered manually. Alternatively, you could select the Obtain An IP Address Automatically check box, indicating that the information is being obtained from DHCP.

FIGURE 7.7   Configuring the NIC

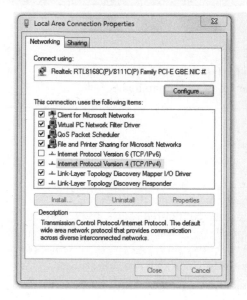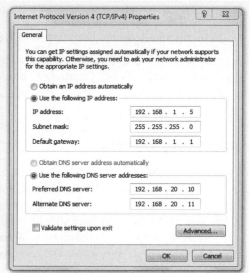

It's more common to use DHCP in an enterprise. Statically assigning the TCP/IP configuration information requires more administrative effort, which directly translates into more cost.

Exercise 7.1 shows how to configure a wired NIC.

EXERCISE 7.1

Configuring a Network Interface Card

1. Launch Control Panel by clicking Start ➤ Control Panel.

2. Click View Network Status And Tasks in the Network And Internet section. This will launch the Network and Sharing Center.

3. Click Local Area Connection in the Connect Or Disconnect section of the Network and Sharing Center.

4. On the Local Area Connection Status page, click Properties.

5. Select Internet Protocol Version 4 (TCP/IPv4), and click the Properties button.

6. Use the following information to configure a static IP address:

    a. If the IP address is configured as Obtain An IP Address Automatically, select Use The Following IP Address.

    b. Enter the IP address and subnet mask assigned to the client.

EXERCISE 7.1 *(continued)*

    c. Enter the IP address of the default gateway.

    d. Enter the IP address of the preferred DNS server.

7. To configure the client to obtain an IP address from DHCP, select Obtain An IP Address Automatically and Obtain DNS Server Address Automatically.

Using Proxy Servers

Proxy servers were mentioned briefly earlier in the chapter. It's common for an enterprise to use a proxy server to improve the performance of clients accessing the Internet.

When a *proxy server* is used, user computers must be configured to use it. Consider Figure 7.8. The proxy server is configured to accept all web-based requests from the clients and forward these requests on the Internet. When the proxy server receives a response from the Internet-based server, it forwards the response to the client that sent the request.

FIGURE 7.8 Using a proxy server in a network

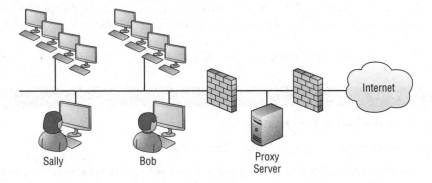

 Microsoft's Internet Security Accelerator (ISA) server application product can be used as a proxy server, a firewall, or both. The next version is known as Microsoft Forefront Threat Management Gateway 2010.

As an example, if Sally needed to access Microsoft's TechNet site to do some research or download an article, Sally's request would go through the proxy server.

Proxy servers provide two important benefits:

Caching Data retrieved from the Internet is cached on the server and can be served from cache if requested by another user. For example, if Bob later needed to view the same content from TechNet that Sally recently viewed, the proxy server wouldn't need to retrieve the content via the Internet again. Instead, the data Bob requested can be returned from cache.

Content filtering   Sites can be filtered to restrict users from visiting certain sites. As an example, a company may not want employees to access any gambling sites. The proxy server can be configured with the addresses of blocked sites, and users who try to access these sites will be blocked using URL filtering. Proxy servers can also filter out malware.

An enterprise may subscribe to a list of sites based on categories such as gambling. These URL lists are regularly updated by the company selling the subscription. This provides the enterprise with an easy method of ensuring employees' web-browsing habits using company resources comply with company policies.

Figure 7.9 shows where Internet Explorer is commonly configured to use a proxy server. This can be configured locally or via Group Policy.

FIGURE 7.9   Configuration of a proxy server

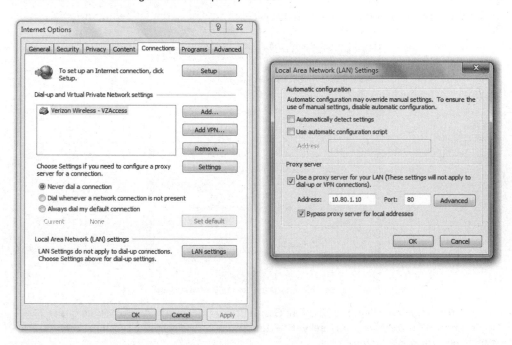

When setting this via Group Policy, use the User Configuration ➤ Policies ➤ Windows Settings ➤ Internet Explorer Maintenance ➤ Connection node. This node includes proxy settings that can be configured with the proxy server address.

Exercise 7.2 shows how you can configure Internet Explorer to use a proxy server on individual systems.

EXERCISE 7.2

Configuring Internet Explorer to Use a Proxy Server

1. Launch Internet Explorer.

2. Select Tools ➢ Internet Options. Tools is a drop-down menu on the far right of the Internet Explorer command bar.

3. Select the Connections tab.

4. Click the LAN Settings button.

5. Select the Use A Proxy Server For Your LAN check box. Enter the IP address for the proxy server. Some proxy servers listen on port 80, whereas others listen on port 8080, and it's possible to configure the proxy server to listen on other ports. Enter the proper port number for your proxy server.

6. Click the Advanced button. Your display will look similar to the following graphic.

Notice that you can select the Use The Same Proxy Server For All Protocols check box. It's common for a single proxy server to handle the Internet traffic for all protocols, so this is commonly selected.

7. If you don't want the proxy server used for specific sites, you can enter the domain names in the bottom text box separated by semicolons. In the graphic, the proxy server is configured with an exception so that it is not used for sites with wiley.com in the address.

Resolving Names to IP Addresses

Name resolution is used on networks to resolve names to IP addresses. You and I use names and words to communicate, but computers use numbers.

If I ask you the IP address of bing.com, you probably don't know it. However, if I ask you the name of Microsoft's online search engine, you probably know the name Bing.com, and that's all you need to know. When you enter Bing.com into a web browser, it is resolved to an IP address and the IP address is used for connectivity.

There are seven methods of resolving names. Three are used primarily, with hostnames used on the Internet and internal networks. Three are found on internal Microsoft networks using NetBIOS names.

Hostnames and NetBIOS names can also be resolved using a seventh method: broadcasts. Broadcasts are usually used as a last resort to help minimize broadcast traffic on a network. The client broadcasts the name onto the network, and if the host with that name is on the network, it will respond with the IP address. Remember though, broadcasts do not cross routers, so the broadcast name resolution method is good only for the same subnet.

Name resolution methods are tied to two types of names:

Hostnames   A *host name* can be up to 255 characters in length and is the only type of name used on the Internet. When a hostname is combined with a domain name, it becomes a fully qualified domain name (FQDN). For example, a Windows 7 PC named Client1 in the domain wiley.com has an FQDN of Client1.wiley.com. Hostnames are primarily resolved by DNS servers.

NetBIOS names   A *NetBIOS name* has 15 readable characters, with the 16th byte identifying a service running on the system. The use of NetBIOS names has been significantly reduced in networks in favor of hostnames, but they are still being used by older applications. Since NetBIOS names are not supported in IPv6, this usage will eventually disappear. NetBIOS names are primarily resolved by WINS servers.

Hostname Resolution Methods

While DNS is the primary method used to resolve hostnames, it's not the only method. There are three primary methods used to resolve hostnames:

DNS   DNS servers answer queries for name resolution of hostnames. When queried with a name, the DNS server returns the IP address. DNS servers are typically configured with addresses of other DNS servers. If the queried DNS server does not know the IP address, it will forward the name resolution request to other DNS servers to determine the IP address. This forwarding occurs on internal networks and on the Internet.

> You can easily check which DNS server is assigned to a client with the IPConfig /All command.

Hosts file   The *Hosts file* is located in the %windir%\System32\Drivers\etc folder. Entries in the Hosts file are automatically placed into the host cache. Malware sometimes modifies the Hosts file to prevent a client from accessing specific websites. For example, a bogus entry could be placed in the file for Microsoft's update site, and the client would no longer be able to get updates.

Host cache   Once a name is resolved by DNS, the result is placed in the *host cache* (also called the DNS cache, which is a little misleading because this cache also holds entries from the Hosts file). You can view the host cache with the IPConfig /DisplayDNS command.

> You can remove host cache entries from cache using the IPConfig /FlushDNS command. This will remove all entries that were cached from a DNS query, but it will not remove entries placed in cache from the Hosts file.

Exercise 7.3 shows how to view the different name resolution methods. This exercise assumes you have connectivity with the Internet.

EXERCISE 7.3

Using Hostname Resolution Methods

1. Launch a command prompt.

2. Enter the following command to resolve a name using DNS:

   Ping msn.com

   The first line should be something like this:

   Pinging msn.com [207.68.172.246] with 32 bytes of data:

   The IP address verifies that name resolution is working. It's very likely that msn.com will block the ping, so it will result in Request Timed Out errors. However, you can still use this method to verify name resolution with DNS.

3. Enter the following command to view the host cache entries:

   IPConfig /displayDNS

   You'll see that the address of msn.com is included in this result with other data from the answering DNS server. Time To Live indicates how long (in seconds) the entry will remain in cache.

```
-----------------------------------------
Record Name . . . . . : msn.com
Record Type . . . . . : 1
Time To Live  . . . . : 247
Data Length . . . . . : 4
Section . . . . . . . : Answer
A (Host) Record . . . : 207.68.172.246
```

4. Enter the following command to clear the host cache of all DNS entries:

   `IPConfig /flushDNS`

5. Enter the following command to view the host cache entries again:

   `IPConfig /displayDNS`

   You'll see that the address of msn.com is no longer shown. The only entries showing are those derived from the Hosts file.

6. Enter the following command to open the Hosts file:

   `notepad %windir%\System32\Drivers\etc\hosts`

7. Scroll to the bottom of the Hosts file, and add the following entry:

   `192.168.1.77        msn.com`

8. Press Ctrl+S to save the file.

9. Enter the following command to view the host cache entries again:

   `IPConfig /displayDNS`

   You'll see that the address of msn.com is now in cache. Even if you enter the `IPConfig /FlushDNS` command, the entry will remain in cache.

10. Enter the following command to try to ping msn.com:

    `Ping msn.com`

    The first line should be something like this:

    `Pinging msn.com [192.168.1.77] with 32 bytes of data:`

    Notice that this is not the valid address of msn.com, but instead it reflects the entry you entered in the Hosts file. With this entry in the Hosts file, the client will never be able to access the actual msn.com site.

11. Delete the msn.com entry in the Hosts file, and save the Hosts file in its original configuration.

NetBIOS Name Resolution Methods

NetBIOS names can be resolved using three methods. These methods are different from the primary methods used to resolve hostnames. However, if a hostname can't be resolved using the primary hostname resolution methods, you can attempt the NetBIOS name resolution methods.

These are the primary methods used to resolve NetBIOS names:

WINS   WINS servers will answer name resolution queries for NetBIOS names. When queried with a name, the WINS server returns the IP address. Whereas DNS servers can be configured to query other DNS servers to resolve a name, WINS servers cannot query other WINS servers.

LMHosts file   The LMHosts file is located in the `%windir%\System32\Drivers\etc` folder.

NetBIOS cache   Once a name is resolved by WINS, the result is placed in the NetBIOS cache. You can view the NetBIOS cache with the `NBTStat /c` command.

The use of NetBIOS names in networks is significantly reduced today.

Using NSLookup

Although the `IPConfig` and `Ping` commands can very often be useful when troubleshooting name resolution issues, there are times when you'll want to query the DNS server directly to get detailed information. The *NSLookup* tool is a command-prompt utility that you can use to get specific information from a DNS server.

NSLookup uses the DNS server IP address that is either manually assigned to the network adapter or received by the DHCP server. Because of this, you don't have to identify the IP address of the DNS server when using NSLookup.

As an example, you may want to check to see if DNS can resolve the name of a file server (FS1) to an IP address. Listing 7.3 shows how the `NSLookup` command can be used. The line numbers are shown for explanation purposes. Line 1 is the command, and lines 2–6 show the results.

Listing 7.3: Using NSLookup

```
1 C:\>nslookup fs1
2 Server:  dc1.wiley.com
3 Address:  192.168.1.10
4
5 Name:    fs1.Wiley.com
6 Address:  192.168.1.21
```

Lines 2 and 3 identify the DNS server (by name and IP address), resolving the name. The client knows the IP address of the DNS server and uses a reverse lookup to identify the name of the DNS server. Lines 5 and 6 provide the result of the query. This shows definitively that the DNS server (hosted on DC1) can resolve the server named FS1 to an IP address of 192.168.1.21.

If the DNS server did not have a record for the name and couldn't resolve it, you'd see something like Listing 7.4.

Listing 7.4: Verifying a DNS record doesn't exist with NSLookup

```
1 C:\>nslookup fs25
2 Server:  dc1.wiley.com
3 Address:  192.168.1.10
4
5 *** dc1.wiley.com can't find fs25: Non-existent domain
```

Notice that lines 2 and 3 stay the same because the same DNS server is providing the answer. However, these first two lines are dependent on the DNS server having a reverse lookup zone and a PTR record for the DNS server in the zone. Because reverse lookup zones are optional, you often won't see them.

As an example, Listing 7.5 shows what you'll see if the DNS server (DC1) doesn't have a PTR record in DNS.

Listing 7.5: Using NSLookup without a PTR record

```
1 C:\>nslookup fs1
2 Server:  Unknown
3 Address:  192.168.1.10
4
5 Name:    fs1.Wiley.com
6 Address:  192.168.1.21
```

Line 2 shows that the DNS server couldn't be identified (because the PTR record is deleted). However, it's important to note that FS1 is still successfully resolved.

If the DNS server doesn't have a reverse lookup zone, it will still work, though the result looks like something is drastically wrong. Listing 7.6 shows the result when the reverse lookup zone doesn't exist.

Listing 7.6: Using NSLookup without a reverse lookup zone

```
1 C:\>nslookup fs1
2 DNS request timed out.
3    timeout was 2 seconds.
4 Server:  UnKnown
```

```
5 Address:  192.168.1.10
6
7 Name:    fs1.Wiley.com
8 Address:  192.168.1.21
```

When looking at lines 2 and 3, you may think that DNS isn't responding, but all this is saying is that it timed out when it tried to do a reverse lookup of 192.168.1.10 to determine the name.

Note that lines 7 and 8 still provide the result of the name resolution request. In other words, even though you see the message stating "DNS request timed out," the DNS server still resolved the hostname to an IP address.

What if the DNS server is not responding at all? This could happen if the DNS server is down or the DNS service is not running on the server. Listing 7.7 shows the result when NSLookup is used to query a server with the DNS service stopped.

Listing 7.7: Using NSLookup with an unreachable DNS server

```
1 C:\>nslookup fs1
2 DNS request timed out.
3     timeout was 2 seconds.
4 Server:  UnKnown
5 Address:  192.168.1.10
6
7 DNS request timed out.
8     timeout was 2 seconds.
9 DNS request timed out.
10     timeout was 2 seconds.
11 *** Request to UnKnown timed-out
```

Line 5 shows the IP address that the client is using as the DNS server. The rest of the information indicates the DNS server is not responding at all. At this point, you should check that this is a valid IP address for the DNS server and verify that it is operational.

Using the Network and Sharing Center

A user may not be able to access the Internet with Internet Explorer and may complain that "the Internet is down," but as a technician you know there are lots of pieces between the user's system and the Internet. One of those pieces is much more likely to be the problem rather than the entire Internet.

If a system is not communicating with other hosts, it's important to check the TCP/IP connectivity and configuration information. A primary tool you can use to start checking TCP/IP is the *Network and Sharing Center*, shown in Figure 7.10.

FIGURE 7.10   Network and Sharing Center

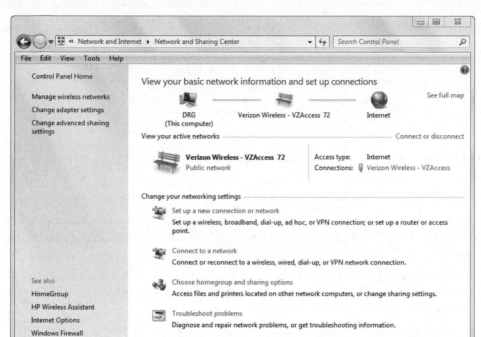

You can access the Network and Sharing Center via the Control Panel ➢ Network And Internet group. You can quickly determine a lot about the connection from this page:

- The computer name is DRG.

- The computer is connected to a network. If the connection had a problem, there would be a yellow triangle or a red X on the line connecting the computer to the network (see Figure 7.11).

- The known network name is Verizon Wireless – VZAccess 72. Networks can be identified as public or private. The icon of a park bench is used to represent a public network.

- The computer is connected to the Internet. If it wasn't connected to the Internet, it would have a red X between the network and the Internet. In addition, the Internet icon would be dimmed if the Internet wasn't accessible.

The View Your Active Networks section also shows that the connection is a public network. You can click the Public Network link and change this to Home Network or Work Network (both of which are considered private).

Figure 7.11 shows the icons for a different computer that has connectivity problems with an unknown network and is not connected to the Internet. Notice that this connection is listed as the Local Area Connection. This is the default name for a wired network interface card.

FIGURE 7.11   Bad connections shown in the Network and Sharing Center

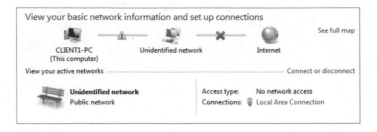

The left panel of the Network and Sharing Center includes several links that can be used to configure networking:

Control Panel Home   This will return you to the main page of the Control Panel.

Manage Wireless Networks   If the computer has wireless capabilities, this link appears. It can be used to add and configure wireless profiles. Wireless settings will be covered in more depth in Chapter 12, "Supporting Mobile Windows 7 Users."

Change Adapter Settings   This link gives access to all of the network adapters and connections on the system. This includes wired adapters, wireless adapters, and virtual private network connections if they've been added to the system.

Change Advanced Sharing Settings   Advanced sharing settings are used to configure different profiles such as a public or private profile (used for home or work).

Public vs. Private Networks

The first time Windows 7 connects to a network, the system will determine the type of network or will prompt the user to identify the type of network. In general, a network is identified as either Public or Private, and it can also be identified as Domain.

Public   A public network is one that is in a public place, such as in an airport or coffee shop. When the network type is identified as Public, Windows Firewall is configured to protect the client by refusing unsolicited connections. A user can connect to the Internet to retrieve email or Internet pages because these connections are solicited by the user. Anytime a computer has a public IP address, Public should be selected as the network type.

Private   A private network is one that is private for the user. For example, a corporate network or a home network is commonly configured with the Private network type. Security on the Windows Firewall is relaxed to improve usability within the network. Private networks are typically protected with a router and a firewall placed between the user and the Internet, and they can be labeled as Home or Work.

Domain   If a computer is a member of a domain and authenticates with a domain controller, it will be put into a Domain network location. This is similar to a private network where Windows Firewall is relaxed to improve usability within the network.

Two important networking elements are automatically set up when a computer is configured as a Public, Private, or Domain network type: Windows Firewall exceptions and Network Discovery.

Network Discovery

Network Discovery is used to simplify the process of configuring and connecting network-connected systems and devices. It is enabled by default in private (nondomain) networks and can be enabled in a domain network with Group Policy. It should remain disabled in public networks to prevent clients from connecting to the system and accessing resources.

Several protocols work together to enable the Network Discovery feature. The Function Discovery Provider Host service and Web Services Dynamic Discovery service are both used by Windows 7 to locate other Windows Vista or Windows 7 clients on the same subnet. The Simple Service Discovery Protocol is then used to identify devices that support these protocols.

Network Discovery is limited to the same subnet. The Network Discovery messages are not passed by routers, so any clients on different subnets will not be located or discovered using Network Discovery.

As an example, Media Center Extender Devices (such as Microsoft's Xbox 360) use the Network Discovery protocol. When the Xbox 360 is on the same subnet and Network Discovery is enabled, clients can easily connect and use all of the features available, such as watching movies in one room from the Xbox 360 in another room.

Network Discovery is automatically configured for the different types of networks as follows:

Public   Network Discovery is disabled by default. This prevents other clients in a public network from seeing or discovering the Windows 7 client.

Private (home or work)   Network Discovery is enabled by default in private network types. This is useful in home networks and small-office networks where users share resources with others, and it allows the clients to easily discover each other.

Domain   Network Discovery is disabled by default in domain networks, but it can be enabled with Group Policy.

When Network Discovery is enabled, the system can also create a Network Map. The Network Map identifies all of the discoverable clients on the network that have Network Discovery enabled. If the network has a path to the Internet, this path will also be displayed in the map.

Two protocols must be running to support the Network Map feature. Both can be enabled on the network adapter property page. They are

- Link-Layer Topology Discovery Mapper I/O Driver
- Link-Layer Topology Discovery Responder

The Link-Layer Topology Discovery Mapper service is also used by Network Discovery. This service is set to Manual and is started when needed by Network Discovery. If the service is set to Disabled, the Network Mapping feature will fail.

Windows Firewall Exceptions

Windows Firewall will be explored in more depth in Chapter 11 but, in general, Windows Firewall uses different rules to allow or block traffic.

Most firewalls are configured with an implicit deny policy, where all traffic is blocked except for some specific exceptions. Exceptions are identified with rules that specifically identify what traffic is allowed.

Windows Firewall is configured as follows for the different network types:

Public   All unrequested incoming traffic is blocked. Exceptions can be created to allow specific traffic if desired. Clients will still receive requested traffic. For example, if a user accesses msnbc.com using a web browser, the msnbc.com web page will be displayed.

Private (home or work)   The firewall is configured to allow connections with other clients in the network. Computers can share resources that are accessible by others, assuming they have the correct permissions.

Domain   The firewall is configured similarly to a private network. Network administrators may need to configure other exceptions via Group Policy to allow specific traffic within the network, depending on the applications used in the domain.

Network List Manager Policies

Network List Manager Policies are included as part of the Group Policy and Local Security Policy settings. These settings affect how networks are identified (public or private) by the system when the user is not prompted to select a network type.

Although Group Policy is covered in more depth in Chapter 10, "Managing Windows 7 with Group Policy," the Network List Manager Policies are important to understand when troubleshooting system connectivity. If the system is set to Public and you can't change it, you might like to know why.

Figure 7.12 shows the Local Security Policy console with Network List Manager Policies selected. You can access this console by clicking Start, typing **Secpol.msc**, and pressing Enter, or by selecting Local Security Policy from the Administrative Tools menu.

Network types you may see here are as follows:

Unidentified Networks   An unidentified network is one that can't be identified because of a network issue or a lack of identifiable characteristics.

Identifying Networks   This is a temporary state of a network until it has been identified or Windows 7 has determined it cannot identify it.

All Networks   This includes settings for all networks whether they are identified or not.

Named Networks   A named network is usually a wireless network. Figure 7.12 shows the name of the Verizon Wireless – VZAccess 72 network because the system is currently connected to that wireless network.

FIGURE 7.12   Network List Manager Policies

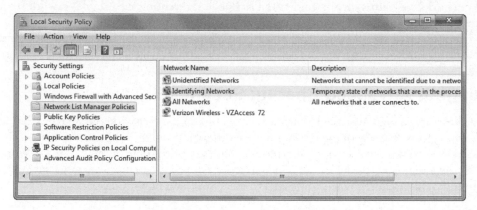

If a network is set to Public, preventing any external connectivity or the use of Network Discovery, and you can't modify the settings, you should check the Network List Manager Policies. These may be controlled by a GPO in a domain or by the local security policy in a workgroup.

When troubleshooting issues, you should focus on the properties of the Unidentified Networks and All Networks settings. The properties are shown in Figure 7.13.

FIGURE 7.13   Unidentified Networks and All Networks settings

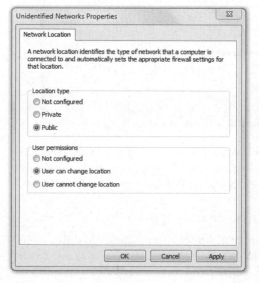

When the Unidentified Networks settings are configured, they can ensure that unidentified networks are automatically configured as Public (preventing the use of Network Discovery and outside connections). The user permissions can also be configured so that users cannot change the location type. It's also possible to prevent the user from modifying any of the network settings from the All Networks Properties page.

Changing Advanced Sharing Settings

If you click the Change Advanced Sharing Settings link in the Network and Sharing Center, you'll have access to many of the settings for the different profiles (Public or Private).

Figure 7.14 shows the Advanced Sharing Settings page with some of the Home Or Work settings. As a reminder, the Home Or Work selections are considered private, and the Public selection should be chosen when connected to a network in a public place.

FIGURE 7.14   Advanced Sharing Settings

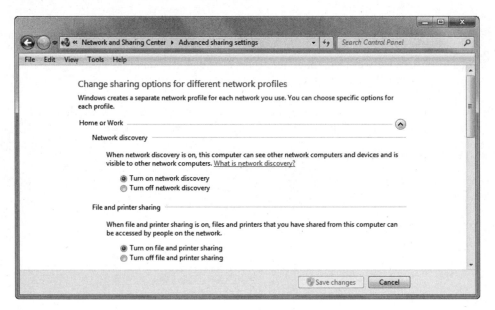

You can access the following settings from this page. Once a setting is selected and configured, it will apply to all network connections using this profile. For example, if you disable the Home Or Work setting for Network Discovery, Network Discovery will be disabled for all private network connections.

The following settings can be configured on this page:

Network Discovery   When enabled, other computers can see this computer and this computer can see other computers. This is turned on by default for private networks and turned off for public networks.

File And Printer Sharing   When turned on, files and printers shared on this computer can be accessed over the network by other users. This is turned off by default for private networks and public networks.

Public Folder Sharing   This allows other people to access files in the public folders. This is turned off by default for private networks and public networks.

Media Streaming   When enabled, media files (such as pictures, music, and videos) stored on this computer can be accessed. This is off by default on both private and public networks.

File Sharing Connections   This uses stronger 128-bit encryption to protect file-sharing connections, but you can weaken security to use 40- or 56-bit encryption for devices if necessary.

Troubleshooting Network Connectivity Problems

The symptoms a user may see and report when a computer has connectivity problems can be wild and varied: "the server is down," "email doesn't work," or "this program doesn't work." When troubleshooting connectivity, you need to go back to basics.

Basic network troubleshooting often starts with using the IPConfig command to check TCP/IP configuration and continues with the Ping command to check connectivity. IPConfig was discussed in greater depth earlier in this chapter, but remember, you can determine several valuable pieces of information using IPConfig when troubleshooting, including the following:

IP address and subnet mask   An address of 169.254.y.z. should jump right out at you as an APIPA address. For some reason, the client can't reach a DHCP server.

Source of IP address   If DHCP Enabled is set to Yes, then you'll also see the IP address of the DHCP server. If DHCP Enabled is set to No, you won't see a DHCP address. If the DHCP address is set to 169.254.0.1, the address is assigned by APIPA.

Default gateway   The default gateway should be on the same subnet. When TCP/IP is manually configured, this can sometimes be configured incorrectly through simple typos.

DNS address   The DNS server is usually on a different subnet and can often be used to check connectivity with a host on a different subnet by pinging the IP address of the DNS server. This address is also used by NSLookup.

Armed with the information from IPConfig, you can check connectivity with other systems using basic troubleshooting steps such as these:

- Verifying hardware and cabling
- Using Ping to test connectivity and determine the scope of the problem
- Verifying that name resolution is working

Verifying Hardware and Cabling

If IPConfig doesn't list the network adapter or lists Media State as Media Disconnected, check the hardware. The NIC needs to be enabled, operating correctly, and connected to the network. Figure 7.15 shows some basic symptoms you may see from IPConfig if the NIC is disconnected.

FIGURE 7.15 Symptoms when the NIC is disconnected

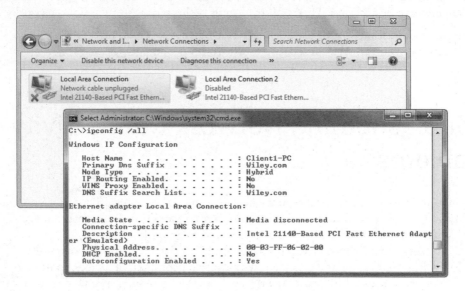

 When the NIC isn't connected, the network icon in the Notification area displays a red X icon. If you hover your mouse over this icon, the tooltip will display Not Connected - No Connections Are Available.

This Network Connections page is pretty clear with a red X and the message "Network Cable Unplugged." IPConfig shows the Media State as Media Disconnected, but normally you won't see a Media State line in IPConfig.

The cable could be unplugged at the NIC, at the network device (hub, switch, or router), or at one of the connections between the NIC and the network device, such as at a wall connection. When the cable is plugged in correctly, you should see a link light. However, if other symptoms show it's not connected, the link light will be missing.

A quick check to determine whether the problem is internal to the computer or external is to swap the cables. Find another computer close by that's working and showing a good link light on the NIC, and swap the cables. If the original faulty computer is still faulty, the problem is in the computer. If the original faulty computer now has a link light and shows that the NIC is connected, the problem is in the original cabling or a distant device.

If the hardware is not the problem, using Ping to check connectivity is a logical step to take after using IPConfig.

Exercise 7.4 shows how to verify and diagnose the network adapter. You can use these steps to reset the network adapter. Resetting the network adapter can often resolve some problems related to the NIC.

EXERCISE 7.4

Verifying and Diagnosing the Network Adapter

1. Access the Network and Sharing Center by clicking Control Panel and selecting View Network Status And Tasks in the Network And Internet section.

2. Right-click the adapter and select Status. You'll see a page similar to the following graphic.

You can use this page to determine the speed and connectivity status of the adapter. In the graphic, you can tell it has Internet access using IPv4, has been operational for more than three days, and has a speed of 100 Mbps.

3. Click the Details button. This will show you information similar to what you can see with the IPConfig /all command. Click Close.

4. Click the Diagnose button. The Windows Network Diagnostics page will appear and diagnostics will begin. These diagnostics run several checks and provide different results depending on what the diagnostics determine. If Internet access isn't detected, the adapter is reset, which will often resolve problems. Other times, a specific problem will be detected, and you may be prompted to apply the fix.

Using Ping

Ping is a basic but invaluable troubleshooting tool. You've probably used it at some point, and I mentioned it previously in this chapter. It sends out echo request packets and returns echo reply packets using the Internet Control Message Protocol (ICMP). If you receive the packets back, you know that the other host is up and operational. You should also know what the Ping responses mean when the host is not up and operational.

> **NOTE** Ping was invented by Michael Muus, who named it after the sound that sonar makes when it hits another object and is reflected back. It sends packets out to a target host, which are then reflected back to the sending host (if the target host is operational), similar to how sonar sends sound waves out and measures the sound waves that are reflected back.

ICMP is very often used in malware attacks, so it's common for firewalls to block Ping messages. In other words, if you don't receive a response from Ping, you can't assume the other host is down.

You can ping an IP address or a hostname. When a hostname is used in the Ping command (as shown in Listing 7.8), the name is resolved to an IP address. Ping normally sends out four echo request packets and receives four echo reply packets in return.

Listing 7.8: Using Ping to check connectivity

```
C:\>ping darril-pc
Pinging darril-pc [192.168.1.101] with 32 bytes of data:
Reply from 192.168.1.101: bytes=32 time=1ms TTL=128
Reply from 192.168.1.101: bytes=32 time=1ms TTL=128
Reply from 192.168.1.101: bytes=32 time=1ms TTL=128
Reply from 192.168.1.101: bytes=32 time=1ms TTL=128
Ping statistics for 192.168.1.101:
    Packets: Sent = 4, Received = 4, Lost = 0 (0% loss),
Approximate round trip times in milli-seconds:
    Minimum = 1ms, Maximum = 1ms, Average = 1ms
```

Here are some of the common error messages you'll see when using the Ping command:

Request Timed Out   The echo request did not receive an echo reply. This could be because the target was not operational, a firewall on the host blocked the traffic, or network problems between the source and target prevented the Ping packets from reaching the target or source. If the network policy of the target is set to Public, the firewall will be configured to block pings, and you'll receive this message even though the system is up and operational.

Ping Request Could Not Find Host   The name could not be resolved to an IP address. If you know the IP address and can successfully ping the IP address but not the name, it indicates a name resolution problem. This often points to a DNS issue in a Microsoft network but could be caused by other name resolution methods.

Destination Host Unreachable This message often indicates TCP/IP is not configured with the proper default gateway on either the source or destination computer. It could also indicate a problem with a router configured as the default gateway for either of the computers. Finally, it could be something as simple as an incorrect IP address or incorrect subnet mask on either end.

Normally, Ping will send out only four echo request packets, but you may occasionally want Ping to continue sending the messages while you troubleshoot. The -t switch is used to start a Ping loop, as in the following command:

```
Ping -t 192.168.1.1
```

Ping will continue sending messages until you press the Ctrl+C to interrupt the process.

Using Ping to Determine Scope of the Problem

From a basic troubleshooting perspective, you should quickly try to determine the scope of the problem. After all, if the problem is affecting the entire network, you don't need to spend much time troubleshooting a single system.

Consider Figure 7.16. Bob normally prints to a shared printer on Sally's computer, but for some reason it isn't working anymore. What should be done?

FIGURE 7.16 Troubleshooting a network problem

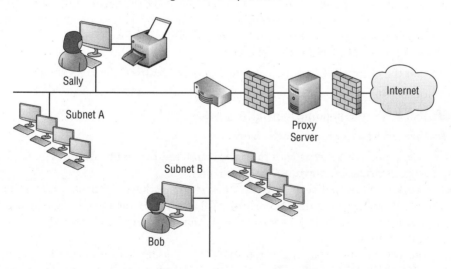

 It's important to remember that Windows Firewall can block packets. If the Windows 7 computer is using a public network profile that blocks all incoming requests, Ping will fail. However, this doesn't mean the client is down.

Here are some steps that you can take using Ping to narrow down the scope of the problem

Ping Sally's computer by IP address   You can do this to verify connectivity with Sally's computer.

Ping Sally's computer by name   You can do this to verify name resolution. When Ping is used to check connectivity with a hostname, it first resolves the name to an IP address. If the name can't be resolved, Ping will reply, "Ping request could not find host." If name resolution works, the first line of the Ping packet identifies the IP address.

Ping the IP address of the default gateway   This is the near side of the router. If you can't get successful pings to the default gateway, you have either a TCP/IP configuration problem on the local system or a problem with the router. However, if the router has a problem, more than just a single person will be complaining.

Ping the local IP address and the loopback address   If you can't successfully ping the local IP address or the loopback address (127.0.0.1), it indicates you have a problem with TCP/IP itself or a hardware problem with the NIC. You can try to reset the NIC or do a cold boot by completely shutting down the computer and restarting it.

Troubleshooting and Resolving Name Resolution Issues

If you can successfully ping the IP address of a client but you can't successfully ping the name, the problem is related to name resolution. In a Microsoft network today, this usually indicates a problem with DNS but could be a problem with the Hosts file.

Some basic steps to take include the following:

- Verify that the client is configured with the correct IP address of a DNS server.
- Verify that DNS is operational and reachable.
- Verify that DNS is responding to name requests.
- Verify that DNS has a record for the name.

You can accomplish these steps with the basic command-prompt tools of IPConfig, Ping, and NSLookup, as discussed previously in the chapter.

If recent work was accomplished on DNS, the system may have either incorrect TCP/IP configuration information or stale DNS records. You can renew the DHCP lease by using IPConfig /release and IPConfig /renew to verify that the client is configured with current DHCP information.

In addition, you can use IPConfig /DisplayDNS to view the records currently in cache. You can use IPConfig /FlushDNS to remove existing records and ensure only new records are used.

If records remain after flushing the DNS cache, check the Hosts file at %windir%\ System32\Drivers\etc. Malware sometimes modifies this file to prevent access to specific servers.

Summary

In this chapter you learned about many of the basics of networking with Windows 7 clients. TCP/IP is used in Microsoft networks, and for the most part, TCP/IP works the same in Microsoft networks as it does in other networks.

The majority of Windows 7 clients in an enterprise receive TCP/IP configuration via DHCP. You learned how the DHCP lease is generated and some of the obvious symptoms that indicate something is wrong with the DHCP lease (such as a 169.254.y.z address).

Name resolution resolves computer names to IP addresses. DNS is the primary method used, and three tools that are very valuable when troubleshooting DNS and other networking issues are Ping, IPConfig, and NSLookup.

The Network and Sharing Center is a central console you can use to quickly identify connectivity in a Windows 7 client. It also allows you to determine whether the network type is identified as Public or Private. When configured as Public, Network Discovery is disabled, and the Windows Firewall will block all unsolicited incoming connections.

Chapter Essentials

Understanding network connectivity in an enterprise   Understand the capabilities of the IPConfig command. This includes using /All to view full details including DHCP and DNS addresses, /FlushDNS to flush the DNS cache, /DisplayDNS to show the DNS cache, and /Release and /Renew to renew the DHCP lease.

Be familiar with the purpose and use of DHCP in a network. DHCP dynamically assigns the IP address, subnet mask, default gateway, and address of DNS servers in most networks. If a DHCP client can't reach a DHCP server, it will assign itself an address in the 169.254.y.z range without a default gateway or DNS server.

Resolving names to IP addresses   Understand how names are resolved to IP addresses in a network. Although the focus in a Microsoft network is on DNS, you should be aware of the other six methods of name resolution (Hosts file, host cache, WINS, LMHosts file, NetBIOS cache, and broadcast).

Using the Network and Sharing Center   Be familiar with the tools available in the Network and Sharing Center. You should especially be aware of the differences in public and private network types and how they impact Network Discovery and the Windows Firewall.

Troubleshooting network connectivity problems   Know how to use NSLookup to check for records on DNS and the ability of DNS to respond to queries. NSLookup can be a valuable tool to check DNS, especially when firewalls are used to block ICMP traffic.

Be familiar with the use of Ping to check connectivity. You should also know what some of the error messages mean, such as "Request Timed Out" (indicating the client is not up or the firewall is blocking traffic), "Ping Request Could Not Find Host" (indicating a problem with name resolution), and "Destination Host Unreachable" (indicating a problem with the default gateway configuration).

Chapter

8

Accessing Resources on a Network

TOPICS COVERED IN THIS CHAPTER INCLUDE

✓ **Accessing network resources**

✓ **Understanding permissions**

✓ **Identifying and resolving network printer issues**

Networks include resources such as shared folders and printers that are accessed by users throughout the enterprise. In addition to making the resources available, you'll also need to ensure that users have the appropriate permissions to access the resources.

Chapter 7, "Networking with Windows 7," laid a foundation for basic networking. This chapter goes a step further with the file and print resources. You'll learn how to share the resources and how to point to shared resources, and you'll review the important details of how permissions affect access to the network resources. You'll also learn some basics on troubleshooting network printer issues.

Accessing Network Resources

One of the great strengths of any local area network is the ability to share resources over the network. The two primary resources that can be shared are folders and printers. A shared folder is also referred to as a *share,* and it includes files that are to be shared among different users.

Files and printers can be shared on Windows desktop systems (including Windows 7), but within an enterprise files are more commonly shared on servers. For example, a Windows Server 2008 or 2008 R2 server could be configured as a file server to host files shared by users in the network. Users connect to the shared folders and access the files.

When files are hosted on a central server, they are much easier for administrators to back up. It's almost impossible for an administrator to back up all of the data on end-user systems, but if the data is centrally located, it's relatively easy to schedule regular backups.

The *Universal Naming Convention (UNC)* format is commonly used to point to and connect to network resources. The UNC is composed of a server name and a shared folder or server name and a shared printer in the format \\ServerName\ShareName. For example, if a server named DC1 hosts a shared folder named Data, the UNC path is \\DC1\Data.

Pointing to Network Resources

There are two primary ways to connect to shares from Windows 7. You can use the Start Search box to point to the resource or map a drive to point to the resource using Windows Explorer. The method you choose depends on how often you plan to connect.

The first method uses the UNC path in the Start Search box in Windows 7. If you pause after entering \\ServerName\, the system will attempt to connect to the server and will then show all the available shares on the servers, as shown in Figure 8.1. In this figure, the server name is DC1, and it includes several shares that can be accessed by the users.

FIGURE 8.1   Connecting to a server to identify available shares

At this point, any of the shares could be selected, or the rest of the UNC path could be entered. Shares can be hidden by appending the $ sign to the share name. If the share is hidden, it won't appear in the share list, but users can still connect to it if they know the share name. For example, a share named Project$ is available on DC1 but is not shown in Figure 8.1. However, a user could still connect by entering \\DC1\Project$.

Using the UNC path is useful if you plan on connecting to the share only once or twice. However, if you plan on connecting to the share on a regular basis, you can map a drive letter to the UNC path.

Windows Explorer in Windows 7 includes the Map Network Drive link on the toolbar that you can click to display the Map Network Drive window, as shown in Figure 8.2. In the figure, the UNC path \\DC1\ProjectData is being mapped to drive letter Y:.

FIGURE 8.2   Mapping a drive

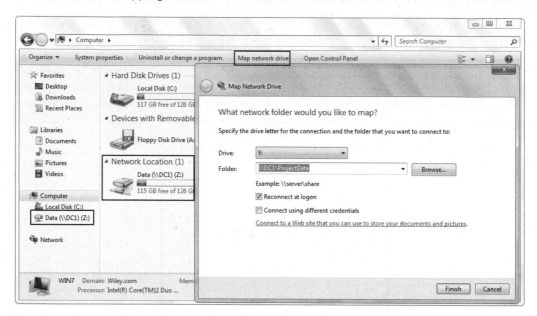

 TIP   The Map Network Drive link in Windows Explorer appears only when Computer is selected in the left pane. If a drive or folder is selected, the Map Network Drive link disappears.

You can select any unused drive letter and then enter any valid UNC path in the Folder text box. If you want the mapped network drive to remain even after the system reboots or users log off, select the check box next to Reconnect At Logon.

Figure 8.2 also shows how a mapped drive appears after it has been mapped. In the far left pane within the Computer node, the \\DC1\Data UNC path has been mapped to the Z: drive. The same path is also shown as a Network Location in the figure.

Creating Shares on Windows 7

You can also create shares on Windows 7 systems. This can be useful if users want to share data among themselves without requiring a server to host the data. Before data can be shared, the system needs to be configured to enable shared folders.

Chapter 7 presented some of the basics of networking and included a section on using the Network and Sharing Center. If the computer is in a private location (such as in a home or work environment), the network can be set either to Private or Domain, and folder sharing can then be enabled.

Figure 8.3 shows the Advanced Sharing Settings, which can be accessed via the Network and Sharing Center. You can access the Network and Sharing Center from Control Panel ➢ Network And Internet and then access the screen in Figure 8.3 by clicking Change Advanced Sharing Settings in the Network and Sharing Center.

FIGURE 8.3   Advanced Sharing Settings

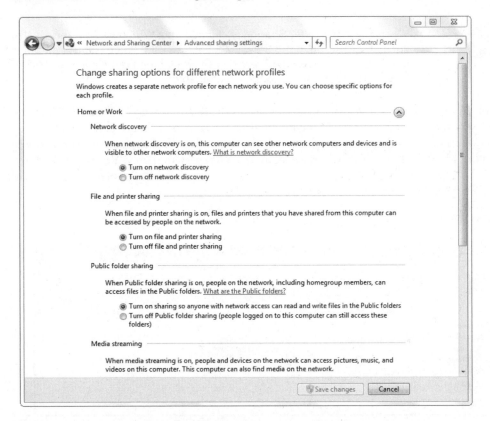

Two settings are directly related to sharing folders in an enterprise:

File And Printer Sharing   This setting must be turned on to allow any type of file and printer sharing on the computer. When turned on, the Windows Firewall exceptions are configured to allow other clients to connect to the system.

If this setting is turned off, Public Folder Sharing will not work even if Public Sharing is turned on. This setting also allows users to share individual folders on their system.

Public Folder Sharing   This setting can be used to enable sharing of the *Public folder* (as long as File And Printer Sharing is enabled). The Public folder is in the C:\Users\ folder, which is shared as Users. The Users\Public folder includes these subfolders: Public Documents, Public Downloads, Public Music, Public Pictures, Public Recorded TV, and Public Videos. When this setting is enabled, users can copy data they want to share directly into the related folder so that it is accessible to other users.

An important consideration of the Public **folder is that you can't control who can access it. Either everyone can access it equally when Public Folder Sharing is turned on, or no users can access it when it is turned off.**

When File And Printer Sharing is enabled on a Windows 7 system, it also adds an exception to the firewall that allows ICMP Echo Requests—pings. In other words, when the firewall is enabled, pinging the client will fail when File And Printer Sharing is not enabled.

In Windows Vista, the Public folder appears as the Public share. However, in Windows 7, the Users share appears instead of the Public share, as shown in Figure 8.4. (This figure also shows an additional share named MyShare.) Clients can double-click the Users share to access the Public folder. In other words, for a Windows Vista system named Vista1, the Public folder is accessed with \\Vista1\Public. For a Windows 7 system named Win7, the path to the Public folder is \\Win7\Users\Public.

FIGURE 8.4   Shares available when Public Folder Sharing is turned on

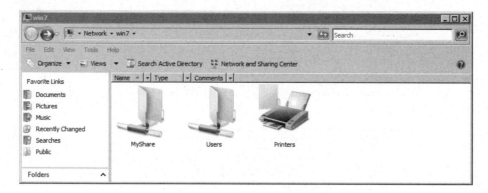

Within a workgroup, the Password Protected Sharing and HomeGroup Connections settings can also be used to control access to the computer. The Password Protected Sharing option restricts access to shared folders to only users with user accounts on the computer; however, this setting is not available when the computer joins the domain. The HomeGroup Connections settings are not available when the computer is in Domain mode but can be used when the computer is in a small private network.

Exercise 8.1 shows how you can enable sharing on a Windows 7 computer and create a share.

| EXERCISE 8.1 |

Enabling File Sharing and Creating Shares

1. Access Control Panel by clicking Start ➢ Control Panel.

2. Click View Network Status And Tasks to access the Network and Sharing Center.

3. Click Change Advanced Sharing Settings.

4. Scroll down to File And Printer Sharing, and select Turn On File And Printer Sharing.

5. Select Public Folder Sharing, and select Turn On Sharing So Anyone With Network Access Can Read And Write Files In The Public Folders.

6. Click Save Changes.

7. Launch Windows Explorer by clicking Start ➢ Computer. Browse to the C: drive.

8. Click New Folder, and name the folder **MyShare**.

9. Select the MyShare folder, and click Share With from the toolbar on Windows Explorer. Select Specific People, as shown in the following graphic.

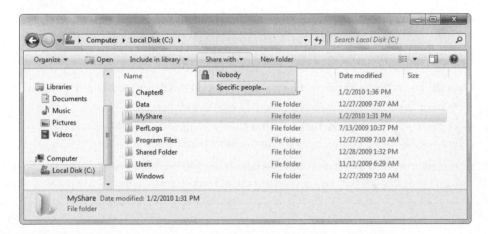

10. You can add additional users and grant specific permissions from here. Type **Everyone** in the text box and click Add. The default permission is Read, but you can change this if desired. Click Share.

11. Review the information on the Your Folder Is Shared screen, and click Done. At this point, you could access the share from another system in the network using the \\computerName\MyShare UNC format.

12. Click New Folder, and name the folder **HiddenShare**.

13. Right-click the HiddenShare folder and select Properties. Select the Sharing tab.

14. Click Advanced Sharing. Select Share This Folder, and name the share **HiddenShare$**. Click Permissions. Your display will look like the following graphic.

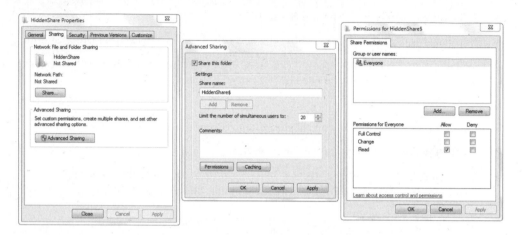

Notice that Everyone is granted Read permission by default. You can add or remove users and modify permissions as desired on this screen.

15. Click OK on the Permissions dialog box. Click OK on the Advanced Sharing dialog box, and click Close on the HiddenShare Properties page.

16. Click Start and type **\\LocalHost** in the Search Programs and Files text box. The Users and MyShare shares appear, but the hidden share is not shown.

17. Complete the entry to \\LocalHost\HiddenShare$ in the Search Programs And Files box and press Enter. You will connect to the hidden share.

Working with Printers on Windows 7

The primary tool you'll use to manage printers on Windows 7 is the *Devices and Printers* applet. This is available from the Start menu (below the link to Control Panel), and it can also be accessed from Control Panel within the Hardware And Sound category.

Figure 8.5 shows the Devices and Printers applet with Printers And Faxes showing. If a printer is selected, additional menu items appear on the toolbar. In addition, the context menu (accessed by right-clicking the printer) shows several other choices.

TIP If the link to Devices and Printers is not on the Start menu, you can add it. Right-click Start and select Properties. Click Customize and select the Devices And Printers check box in the Customize Start Menu dialog box. Click OK twice, and Devices and Printers will be on the Start menu.

FIGURE 8.5   Devices and Printers

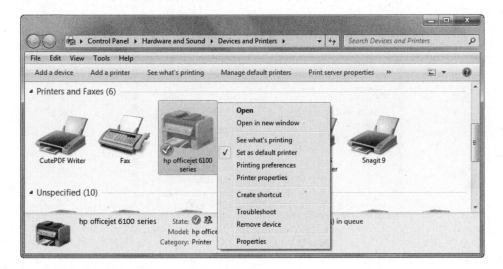

Some context menu choices are worth mentioning:

Set As Default Printer   When this is checked, the printer is the default printer for all print jobs. Although this will be the default selection, most applications allow you to change the printer when you actually send the print job.

Printing Preferences   You can set different preferences for the printer such as print quality (draft or best quality), page orientation (landscape or portrait), color options, and more, depending on the characteristics of the printer. These choices will be different for different printer brands and models.

Properties   This provides a limited amount of read-only information on the printer.

Printer Properties   This is the primary page you'll access to manipulate a printer's properties. Figure 8.6 shows the Properties page for a printer. The General tab can be used to print a test page, the Security tab is used to manipulate permissions, the Sharing tab is used to share the printer, and the Ports tab is used to add and manipulate ports. The Advanced tab is used for advanced configuration settings such as updating the driver or setting print priorities or print schedules.

FIGURE 8.6 Printer Properties

See What's Printing

The See What's Printing link on the Devices and Printers menu allows you to view the print queue for the printer that is selected. If you have sent print jobs to a printer but the jobs aren't printing, you can view the queue from here.

Jobs in the queue can be paused, restarted, or cancelled by right-clicking the job and accessing the context menu. This can be useful if a job gets hung up in the queue.

Manage Default Printers

Windows 7 provides a tool that allows you to set different default printers when a computer is attached to a different network. Figure 8.7 shows the screen that appears when Manage Default Printers is selected from the toolbar in Devices and Printers.

 The Manage Default Printers choice appears only on mobile computers when the computer has more than one network connection. It does not appear on desktop systems.

This can be useful for users with mobile computers that connect to different networks. As shown in the figure, when the system connects to the network named HomeSweetHome (a wireless connection), it will default to the HP Officejet 6100 printer. When connected using the Verizon Wireless air card, it will use the CutePDF Writer as the default printer.

FIGURE 8.7   Manage Default Printers for mobile computers

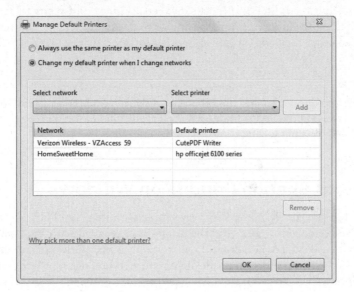

Print Server Properties

If you share printers on a Windows 7 system, it will behave as a print server and you can manipulate Print Server Properties. Manipulating server properties is commonly done on an actual print server in an enterprise, but if Windows 7 is being used in a small office or home office, it can be used to host multiple printers.

 If a Windows 7 computer is used as a print server, it is limited to no more than 20 concurrent connections. This is an increase. Windows XP and previous desktop systems could support only 10 concurrent connections.

The Print Server Properties screen allows you to change settings for all printers on the same computer. It includes five tabs:

Forms   The Forms tab shows the different form sizes (such as letter size or legal size) that are supported by printers on the system. You can also create additional forms from this tab.

Ports   The Ports tab allows you to manipulate the ports such as serial, parallel, or TCP/IP address ports. These are added when a printer is added, but you can also delete ports from this tab.

Drivers   The Drivers tab can be used to add and remove drivers; however, drivers are commonly manipulated using Printer Properties.

Security   Server permissions can be assigned here. By default, administrators are assigned all permissions, and the Everyone group is assigned the Print permission.

Advanced   The most important element here is the location of the Spool folder. By default the Spool folder is located in the C:\Windows\System32\Spool\Printers folder. If the drive is filling up with a high volume of print jobs and/or is causing excessive fragmentation on the drive, you can move the Spool folder to another location by just typing in the new location on this tab.

You should ensure the print queue doesn't include any print jobs before moving the Spool folder. Any print jobs held in the queue will be lost when a new path for the Spool folder is entered.

Installing and Sharing Printers on Windows 7

Installing a local printer on Windows 7 is very simple with Plug and Play. Most printers today use USB connections, and after the printer is connected with the USB cable, the printer is automatically added. Windows 7 will attempt to install the correct driver from the driver store, or if the driver is not in the driver store, it will attempt to download the driver using Windows Update. You can also install the driver using the installation media that came with the printer.

Drivers can be updated manually from the Advanced tab of the Printer Properties if necessary. Figure 8.8 shows the wizard that appears after clicking New Driver. If the driver is in the driver store, it will appear as a Printer Driver Selection. If not, you can try to use Windows Update to download an updated driver. Finally, you can download a driver from the manufacturer, select Have Disk, and browse to the location where it was downloaded.

FIGURE 8.8   Updating the printer driver

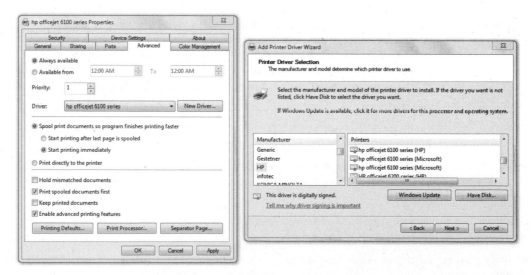

If the printer uses a network, wireless, Bluetooth, serial, or parallel port, you'll have to install it manually using either the installation media that came with the printer or the Devices and Printers applet. Selecting Add Printer from the toolbar of Devices and Printers will launch a wizard that can be used to add non-USB printers. When you click Add Printer, you'll see the following two choices:

Add A Local Printer   This is used for non-USB printers that are connected directly to the Windows 7 system or can be reached with a TCP/IP address.

Add A Network, Wireless, Or Bluetooth Printer   This choice is used to connect to wireless printers or network printers that are shared by other systems and can also be used for printers that have their own IP address.

The Add Printer Wizard will prompt you to share the printer. After the printer has been added, you change the selection using the Sharing tab of the Printer Properties page, as shown in Figure 8.9.

FIGURE 8.9   Sharing a printer

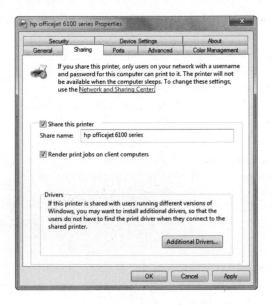

You can also add additional drivers from this page to support users running different architectures, such as 32-bit or 64-bit systems.

Print drivers have been simplified in recent years. As long as the end-user computers are running Windows 2000 or greater, you only need to add Type 3 – User Mode drivers. Type 3 – User Mode drivers come in three versions:

- Itanium Type 3 – User Mode (for Itanium-based systems)

- x64 Type 3 – User Mode (for x64 or 64-bit systems)

- x86 Type 3 – User Mode (for x86 or 32-bit systems)

Type 2 drivers are for systems older than Windows 2000.

Connecting to a Shared Printer

A common task with printers in an enterprise will be to connect to a shared printer that is hosted by another computer such as a print server. You'll need to know the name of the print server, and it's also helpful to know the name of the shared printer.

Exercise 8.2 shows how to add a shared printer to a Windows 7 system.

EXERCISE 8.2

Connecting to a Shared Printer

1. Launch Control Panel, and click View Devices And Printers in the Hardware And Sound category.

2. Click Add A Printer to start the Add Printer Wizard.

3. Click Add A Network, Wireless, Or Bluetooth Printer. The wizard will use Network Discovery to locate any printers on the same network. If you have a printer shared on your system, it will locate and list it using the UNC path. Network Discovery cannot locate printers on different subnets.

4. Select The Printer That I Want Isn't Listed. You can now browse for a printer using Windows Explorer, enter the UNC path of the printer if it's shared by another computer, or add the printer using the TCP/IP address if it isn't being shared by another computer. Select A Shared Printer By Name is selected by default, allowing you to enter a UNC path.

5. Enter the name of the server in the UNC format (\\servername\) and, when you type the last slash, the shared printers for the server will appear. You can either select one of the shared printers or enter the full UNC path of the shared printer. Your display will look similar to the graphic shown here. Click Next.

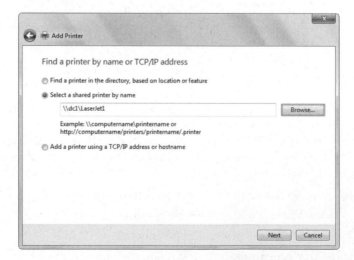

If the printer doesn't exist or the server can't be contacted, the wizard will generate an error. However, if the connection succeeds, the correct drivers will automatically be downloaded and the printer will be added.

6. After the driver is downloaded and the printer is installed, click Next.

7. The last page will indicate you've successfully added the printer. You can print a test page and set the new printer as a default printer from here. Click Finish.

Understanding Permissions

Permissions are used to control who can access objects such as files, folders, shares, and printers. They also control the level of access that is granted. For example, a user may be granted permission to read a file or be granted permission to print to a printer.

Authentication and authorization go hand in hand, but they aren't the same thing. When a user logs on with credentials, the user is authenticated. However, just because a user can log on doesn't mean the user is authorized to access everything on a system or in a network. Permissions are used to provide the appropriate level of authorization or access for specific users or groups to specific resources and functions.

We cover three categories of resources in this chapter that can have permissions assigned. The types of permissions that can be assigned are as follows:

NTFS   New Technology File System (NTFS) permissions are used to control access to files and folders on local systems.

Share   Share permissions are used to control access to shared folders when they are accessed over the network.

Printer   Printer permissions are used to control who can print and manage printers.

 Active Directory objects such as Organizational Units (OUs) are also resources that can have permissions assigned. Active Directory object permissions aren't covered in this book, but many of the same principles of other permissions apply to Active Directory object permissions.

Permissions can be assigned as either Allow or Deny. As an example, Figure 8.10 shows NTFS permissions assigned for a user named Sally. Sally is assigned Allow for Read, Read & Execute, and List Folder Contents. She is also assigned Deny for Write. Sally will be able to read the files in the folder, but she won't be able to alter the files or create new ones.

FIGURE 8.10   Assigning Allow and Deny permissions

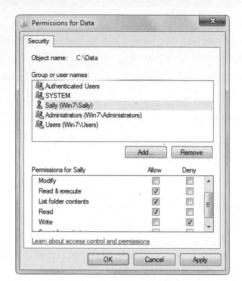

This brings up three important points related to permissions for any of the objects:

Permissions are cumulative   Users can be granted multiple permissions based on group membership. For example, if a user is granted read access as a member of the Users group and granted Write access as a member of the G_Sales group, the user is granted both read and write access.

Permissions use an implicit deny philosophy   If permissions are not explicitly granted, permissions are denied. In other words, if Bob is not granted any permission on a file or folder, his access is denied.

Deny takes precedence   If there is ever a conflict where a user is granted Allow and Deny to the same permission, Deny wins and takes precedence. In other words, if Sally is a member of the Administrators group and is granted Full Control access to the folder, but her account is assigned Deny Write access to the folder, she will not be able to make any changes that require the Write permissions. Deny takes precedence.

Each of these three types of permissions (NTFS, Share, and Printer) depends on the use of security identifiers to identify users and also uses Discretionary Access Control Lists to assign permissions.

SIDs and DACLs

In Windows operating systems, every user and group are identified with a *security identifier (SID)*. This SID is assigned when the user or group is created, and the SIDs are unique within the domain and forest.

When a user logs on, the system creates a token that includes the user's SID. In addition, the SID for each group of which the user is a member is added to the token.

> Although the operating system uses the SIDs, you'll hardly ever see them. Instead, the operating system does internal lookups to identify the user or group name identified by the SID and displays the name instead of the SID. Occasionally, when the system is low on hardware resources or has a problem looking up the SID, you'll see the SID instead of the user or group. A domain SID starts with S-1-5-21- followed by other numbers that are unique in the domain.

Every object has a security descriptor called a *Discretionary Access Control List (DACL)*. The DACL is a list of Access Control Entries, and each *Access Control Entry (ACE)* includes the SID of a user or group and the permissions assigned to the user or group. When a user tries to access an object, the object's DACL is compared to the user's token to determine whether the user should be granted access.

As an example, Figure 8.11 shows the Security tab for a folder on an NTFS drive. This is actually a list of several ACEs that make up the DACL. In the figure, Sally's account is selected, and you can see the specific permissions that she's been assigned. Sally's entry is a single ACE within the DACL.

You can access the Security tab for any file or folder from Windows Explorer. Right-click the file or folder, select Properties, and then select the Security tab. You can select any of the users or groups to determine the specific permissions assigned.

FIGURE 8.11   NTFS Security

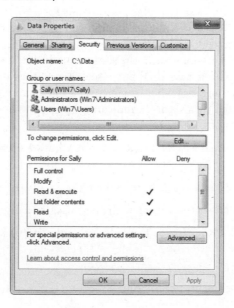

> Users listed in the DACL follow the format of computer\user or domain\user. If the computer name is Win7, a local user named Sally is identified as Win7\Sally. A domain user named Bob from a domain named Wiley.com would be listed as Wiley\Bob. Groups listed in the DACL follow the same format of computer\group or domain\group.

NTFS

The New Technology File System (*NTFS*) is the standard file system used by Microsoft since the NT operating systems, although it has been steadily improving over the years. The primary benefit of NTFS is more flexibility in assigning permissions to control access. It also allows for assigning different permissions to a folder and to the files within the folder. Many functions of the Windows operating system are allowed only NTFS partitions or volumes.

NTFS permissions are assigned to files and folders on an NTFS drive to control what users can do with files and folders. They are typically presented as basic permissions, which are easier to understand by most end users, but there are 13 granular or advanced permissions. The basic permissions map to the granular permissions. For example, the basic Read permission maps to four granular permissions.

NTFS Granular Permissions

It's important to understand what the 13 granular permissions are and how they work before you see how they work together in the basic NTFS permissions.

Figure 8.12 shows some of these granular permissions for a folder named Data. You can access this page from Windows Explorer by first right-clicking the folder and selecting Properties. Then click Advanced ➢ Change Permissions ➢ Edit.

Although most of the permissions mean the same thing if they are assigned to a file or a folder, some of the permissions have dual purposes; that is, they mean one thing when assigned to a file and something else when assigned to a folder. In Figure 8.12, several of the permissions are separated by a slash (/), indicating the permission has a dual purpose.

The 13 granular permissions are as follows:

List Folder / Read Data   When assigned to a folder, it allows a user to view the contents of the folder.

When assigned to a file, it allows a user to read the file.

Read Permissions   This allows a user to view the permissions assigned to the file or folder.

Read Attributes   Attributes (such as read-only or hidden) can be viewed by the user when this permission is assigned.

Read Extended Attributes   Extended attributes (such as the compression or encryption attributes) can be viewed with this permission.

FIGURE 8.12   Viewing advanced NTFS permissions

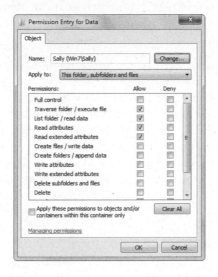

Traverse Folder / Execute File   Traverse Folder applies only to folders and allows a user to navigate to a child folder even if they don't have access to a parent folder. For example, if a user has Full Control access to `C:\Parent\Child` but does not have any access to `C:\Parent`, the Traverse Folder permission allows the user to go across (or traverse) the file structure to reach the destination folder.

Execute File applies only to files and allows a user to execute or run a program.

Create Files / Write Data   Create Files applies only to folders, and it allows a user to add new files to a folder.

Write Data applies only to files, and it allows a user to modify the data within the file.

Create Folders / Append Data   Create Folders applies only to folders, and it allows a user to add folders within a folder.

Append Data applies only to files, and it allows a user to add data to the end of the file.

Write Attributes   This permission allows a user to modify the attributes (such as read-only or hidden) of a file or folder.

Write Extended Attributes   This permission allows a user to modify the extended attributes (such as compression or encryption) of a file or folder.

Delete   Delete allows a user to delete a file or folder.

Delete Subfolders and Files   Users with this permission can delete subfolders and files even if they don't have the Delete permission on the subfolder or file.

Change Permissions   This permission allows a user to modify the existing permissions of a file or folder. An owner of a file or folder can always modify the permissions of the file or folder in Windows operating systems.

Take Ownership   This allows a user to take ownership of a file or folder. Once ownership is taken, the permissions can be changed. Administrators can always take ownership of files and folders.

Full Control   This grants all of the preceding permissions to a file or folder.

The *Change Permissions* and *Take Ownership* permissions deserve a special mention. Imagine a user named Darril was working on a project with multiple files stored in a folder named `Project`. Darril is the only user who has any permission to this folder, and then a wonderful thing happens—Darril wins the lottery! Woo-Hoo!

You're not sure where Darril is, but he's not at work anymore, and no one can access the `Project` folder. However, an administrator can take ownership of the file and then change the permissions so that other users can access the files and folders.

It's also possible to assign ownership to files and folders within Windows 7, which wasn't possible in Windows XP and previous versions of Windows. You'll see how to do this in an activity later in this chapter.

NTFS Basic Permissions

The NTFS basic permissions are designed to be simpler for regular users to use. When a user wants to allow someone else access to a file, they simply grant Read, and other required permissions are automatically assigned.

Several of these permissions encompass other permissions. For example, Read & Execute includes the Read permission and Modify includes Read & Execute and Read permissions. Figure 8.13 shows the relationships among these permissions.

FIGURE 8.13   Relationships among permissions

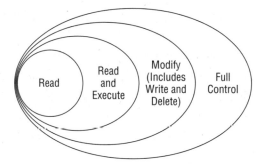

These are the basic permissions:

Read   Users granted Read permission can view the contents of a file or folder. Read includes the following granular permissions: Read Attributes, Read Extended Attributes, and Read Data permissions.

Read & Execute   Users granted the Read & Execute permission have all of the Read permissions, and they can also run or execute programs.

Read & Execute includes the granular permissions assigned to Read and also the Execute File granular permission.

List Folder Contents   List Folder Contents allows a user to view the files and folders within a folder.

This permission includes the following granular permissions: Read Attributes, Read Extended Attributes, List Folder, and Traverse Folder.

Write   Users can create new files and folders, and they can also make changes to existing files and folders.

Write includes the following granular permissions: Create Files/Write Data, Create Folders/ Append Data, Write Attributes, and Write Extended Attributes. Notice that Write does not include any of the Read permissions (such as Read Data, Read, and so on).

Modify   When granted the Modify permission to a file or a folder, a user can read, execute, write, and delete files and folders. The primary addition is the ability to delete files and folders.

Modify includes all of the granular permissions included with Read, Read & Execute, and Write, and it adds the Delete permission. It does not include the Delete Subfolders And Files permission.

Full Control   Full Control grants all of the 13 granular permissions. Full Control is the only basic permission that includes the Delete Subfolders And Files, Change Permissions, and Take Ownership permissions.

Exercise 8.3 shows how to view basic NTFS permissions on a Windows 7 system.

EXERCISE 8.3

Viewing Basic NTFS Permissions

1. Launch Windows Explorer by clicking Start ➢ Computer.

2. Double-click the C: drive to select it. Click New Folder. Rename the folder **Chapter8**.

3. Right-click Chapter8 and select Properties. Select the Security tab. The existence of a Security tab verifies that the drive is NTFS. You can view the permissions assigned to users and groups on this screen, but it will not allow you to modify the permissions.

4. Click Edit. Click Add to access the Select Users or Groups dialog box.

5. Click Advanced on the Select Users or Groups dialog box, and click Find Now to list all of the user accounts on the Windows 7 system. Select a user and click OK. Click OK again.

6. Notice that by default, the user is granted Read, Read & Execute, and List Folder Contents permissions. You can modify the defaults if desired. Click OK.

7. Back on the Security tab of the Chapter8 Properties page, click OK. Click OK again to close the Properties page.

Exercise 8.4 shows how to view granular NTFS permissions on a Windows 7 system, view the owner, and assign ownership to a different user. This exercise assumes the Chapter8 folder was created in the previous exercise. If you didn't complete the previous exercise, just create a folder named Chapter8.

EXERCISE 8.4

Viewing Granular Permissions and Owners

1. If it is not already open, launch Windows Explorer by clicking Start ➤ Computer.

2. Double-click the C: drive to select it. Right-click the Chapter8 folder and select Properties.

3. Select the Security tab and click Advanced. Click Change Permissions.

4. Select the Users group and click Edit. Notice that some permissions are checked but dimmed. This indicates the permissions are inherited and can't be changed unless inheritance is modified. You'll see how to change inheritance later in this chapter.

5. Click Allow Full Control and notice how Allow is selected for all the permissions. Click Cancel on the Object page. Click Cancel on the Permissions page.

6. Select the Owner tab. This shows the current owner and lists users or groups that can be designated as the new owner. If you logged on with an account in the Administrators group, it will list the Administrators group as the current owner.

7. Click Edit. On the Owner page, click Other Users Or Groups. You can enter the name of any local user, or if the computer is in a domain, you can enter the name of a domain user. For this exercise, enter **Guest** and click OK. Your display will look similar to the following graphic. Click OK.

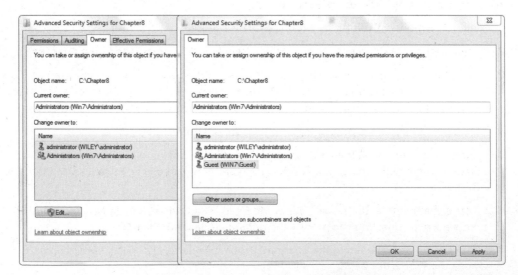

8. A dialog box will appear indicating that if you just took ownership of the object, you'll need to close and reopen the properties before changing the permissions. Review the information and click OK.

9. Back on the Owner tab of the Advanced Security Settings screen, notice that the current owner is now listed as the user you just selected. Click OK. Click OK again to close the Chapter 8 Properties page.

Sometimes you want to know a user's effective NTFS permissions for a file or folder. You could first list all of the user's group memberships and then check to see what permissions are assigned to each group and the user to identify the cumulative permissions. Alternatively, you can use the Effective Permissions tab of the Advanced Security Settings screen, as shown in Figure 8.14. After selecting the Effective Permissions tab, click Select to enter the user or group you want to check. In the figure, the user account for Alice is entered and the effective permissions for Alice are checked.

You can't change the permission from the Effective Permissions tab, but you can easily determine the NTFS permissions. Effective permissions include only NTFS permissions; they do not include Share permissions.

FIGURE 8.14   Identifying Effective Permissions for a user or group

NTFS Permission Inheritance

Permissions are normally inherited from parent folders to child folders. In other words, if a folder is created within another folder, the child folder inherits all of the permissions assigned to the parent folder. Inherited permissions are dimmed and can't be changed.

As long as *permission inheritance* is enabled, new permissions applied to the parent folder will apply to objects within the folder. For example, if you grant Full Control to a folder named Sales to a group named G_Sales, all files in the Sales folder will inherit the same permissions.

However, you can disable permission inheritance. Figure 8.15 shows the permission screen after the Include Inheritable Permissions From This Object's Parent check box is deselected. This setting is normally checked. When you uncheck the box, the Windows Security dialog box appears, giving you three choices.

FIGURE 8.15   Disabling permission inheritance

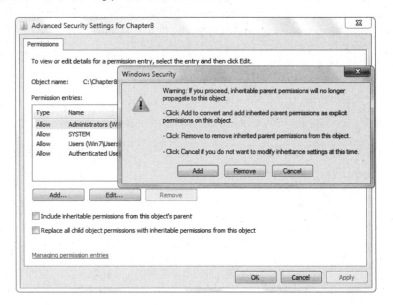

The three choices are as follows:

Add   Clicking Add will cause all inherited permissions to become explicitly assigned permissions. The benefit of selecting Add is that the permissions aren't changed, but they can now be modified because they are explicitly assigned instead of inherited.

Remove   Clicking Remove removes all the inherited permissions. It does not remove any explicitly assigned permissions.

Cancel   Clicking Cancel allows you to exit without making any changes.

Figure 8.15 also shows another selection at the bottom of the screen: Replace All Child Object Permissions With Inheritable Permissions From This Object. You can think of this as a reset switch. Imagine that some files within a folder have explicitly assigned permissions that are different from those of other files in the folder. If you select this check box and apply it, all the explicitly defined permissions will disappear, and only the inherited permissions will remain.

Exercise 8.5 shows how inheritance works and how it can be modified.

EXERCISE 8.5

Viewing and Modifying Inheritance

1. Launch Windows Explorer by clicking Start ➤ Computer.

2. Double-click the C: drive to select it. Click New Folder. Rename the folder **Parent**.

3. Double-click Parent. Click New Folder and name the new folder **Child**.

4. Double-click Child. Right-click within the Child folder, and select New Text Document.

5. Select the new text document, and press Ctrl+C to copy it. Press Ctrl+V to make a copy of the text document.

6. Right-click a text document and select Properties. Select the Security tab. Click Edit. Notice that the permissions are all dimmed, indicating they are inherited and can't be modified. Click Cancel twice.

7. Click Back to access the contents of the Parent folder. Right-click the Child folder and select Properties.

8. Select the Security tab. Click Edit. Click Add.

9. In the Select Users Or Groups box, type **Guest** and click OK.

10. Select Full Control to grant the Guest account full control to the Child folder. Click OK. Click OK again.

11. Double-click Child. Right-click the text document named New Text Document and select Properties. Select the Security tab. You'll see that the file has inherited Full Control permissions for the Guest account.

12. Click Advanced. Click Change Permissions. Deselect the Include Inheritable Permissions From This Object's Parent check box.

13. On the dialog box that appears, click Add. Click OK on the Permissions dialog box. Click OK on the Advanced Security Settings page. You'll see that all of the permissions are explicitly assigned and can now be changed. Click OK.

14. Return to the root of the C: drive. Right-click Parent and select Properties. Select the Security tab.

15. Click Advanced and click Change Permissions. Select the Replace All Child Object Permissions With Inheritable Permissions From This Object check box. This will reset the original permissions and reverse your changes. Click OK.

16. Review the dialog box that appears, and click Yes to continue. Click OK twice to return to Windows Explorer.

17. Return to the `Child` folder. Right-click the New Text Document and select Properties. Select the Security tab. Notice that all of the changes you previously made have been reset to only the permissions applied to the `Parent` folder.

18. Close all open windows.

Share Permissions

Folders can be shared on any computer by creating a share. Within an enterprise, file servers (such as Windows Server 2008 or Windows Server 2008 R2) are commonly used to share folders, but it's also possible to share folders on a Windows 7 system. However, the Share permissions are the same on both clients and servers.

Compared to NTFS permissions, Share permissions are much simpler. There are only three permissions, but they take different names depending on how you access them. Figure 8.16 shows the traditional way Share permissions are identified, and Figure 8.17 shows the way Share permissions are assigned with Permission Levels.

FIGURE 8.16   Traditional Share Permissions

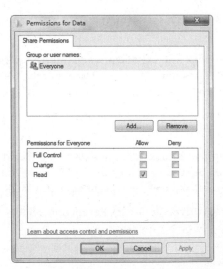

FIGURE 8.17   Share Permissions using Permission Levels

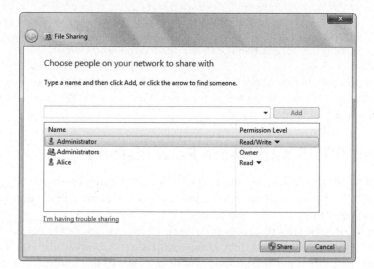

In Windows XP and older operating systems, the Share permissions were listed as Read, Change, or Full Control. In Windows 7, the interface guides you to assign Permission Levels of Read, Read/Write, or Full Control. Table 8.1 shows the Share permissions and Permission Levels, including the level of access granted for each.

TABLE 8.1   Share Permissions and Permission Levels

Share Permission	Permission Level	Access
Read	Read Also known as Reader	Users can view the files and folders, view data within files, and run any executable files.
Change	Read/Write Also known as Contributor	Users have Read permission and can also add files and subfolders, change data in files, and delete subfolders and files.
Full Control	Owner Can also have co-owners	Users have all Read and Change permissions and can also change the permissions for any NTFS files and folders.

In Windows Vista and Windows Server 2008, the Permission Levels were known as Reader, Contributor, Owner, and Co-owner roles. In Windows 7, these permissions levels aren't assigned as roles but instead are assigned using the permissions of Read, Read/Write, and Owner.

It's important to realize that Share permissions apply to shared folders only when they are accessed over the network. If the folder is accessed locally with Windows Explorer, the Share permissions do not apply at all.

Combining NTFS and Share Permissions

When a share is accessed over the network, the NTFS and Share permissions interact. This is a common source of confusion for many administrators until they understand exactly how the permissions interact.

As an example, if Sally tries to access a file named `Project.docx` over the network but is denied access, she'll be asking for help. If she requires access to this file, you'll need to determine what her current permissions are and what needs to be changed to grant her access. For our example, imagine that Sally is a member of the G_Sales and G_Marketing groups and the following permissions are assigned:

- **NTFS permissions** G_Sales is granted Read and G_Marketing is granted Modify.
- **Share permissions** G_Sales is granted Read and G_Marketing is granted Full Control.

Groups are commonly prefixed with letters to identify the scope of the group. For example, a global group is often identified with a prefix of G_, and a domain local group is often identified with a prefix of DL_.

The simplest way to determine the resulting permissions is by using a three-step process:

1. **Determine the effective NTFS permissions.** NTFS permissions are cumulative, so the effective NTFS permissions are determined by combining all of the assigned NTFS permissions. Because Sally is in both the G_Sales and G_Marketing groups, she is granted both Read and Modify.

   Modify includes Read, so her cumulative NTFS permission is Modify.

2. **Determine the effective Share permissions.** Share permissions are cumulative, so the effective Share permissions are determined by combining all of the assigned Share permissions. Because Sally is in both the G_Sales and G_Marketing groups, she is granted both Read and Full Control.

   Full Control includes Read, so her cumulative Share permission is Full Control.

3. **Determine the most restrictive permissions.** The resulting permission is the most restrictive permission (the permission that provides the least access) between the effective NTFS and the effective Share permissions. The effective NTFS permission is Modify, and the effective Share permission is Full Control.

Modify is more restrictive than Full Control, so the resulting permission when the share is accessed over the network is Modify.

 The most common reason why people become confused with this is that they try to do all three steps at the same time. However, if you separate the process into three distinct steps, you can reach the correct result without confusion.

As another example, imagine that Bob is a member of the G_Supply and G_Production groups, and the following permissions are assigned to a folder named Data, which is also shared from a Windows 7 system:

- **NTFS permissions**   G_Supply is granted Read and G_Production is granted Full Control.

- **Share permissions**   G_Supply is granted Read and Administrators is granted Full Control.

Can you determine Bob's permissions when he accesses the share? Can you determine Bob's permissions when he accesses the Data folder on the Windows 7 system?

1. **Determine the effective NTFS permissions.** Because Bob is in both the G_Supply and G_Production groups, he is granted both Read and Full Control.

Full Control includes Read, so his cumulative NTFS permission is Full Control.

2. **Determine the effective Share permissions.** Because Bob is in the G_Supply group he is granted Read. He is not in the Administrators group, so he is not granted the permissions from that group.

Bob has Read permission on the share.

3. **Determine the most restrictive permissions.** The effective NTFS permission is Full Control and the effective Share permission is Read.

Read is more restrictive than Full Control, so the resulting permission when the share is accessed over the network is Read.

However, if Bob accesses the folder on the local Windows 7 system, share permissions will not apply; only NTFS permissions will apply. Bob will have Full Control permissions if he accesses the Data folder locally on the Windows 7 system.

Here's one more example. Imagine that Alice is a member of the G_HR and G_Legal groups, and the following permissions are assigned:

- **NTFS permissions**   G_HR is granted Full Control and G_Legal is granted Modify. Alice is assigned Deny Full Control.

- **Share permissions**   G_HR is granted Modify and G_Legal is granted Read.

1. **Determine the effective NTFS permissions.** Because Alice is in both the G_HR and G_Legal groups, she would be granted both Full Control and Modify. However, Alice is specifically denied Full Control, and because there's a conflict, Deny takes precedence.

   Alice's effective NTFS permission is Deny Full Control.

2. **Determine the effective Share permissions.** Because Alice is in the G_HR and G_Legal groups, she is granted Modify and Read.

   Modify includes Read, so the effective Share permission is Modify.

3. **Determine the most restrictive permissions.** Deny Full Control is more restrictive than Modify, so the resulting permission for Alice is Deny Full Control.

Printer Permissions

Printer permissions apply when a printer is shared. There are three basic printer permissions and three special permissions. Figure 8.18 shows the basic permissions for a printer.

FIGURE 8.18   Printer permissions

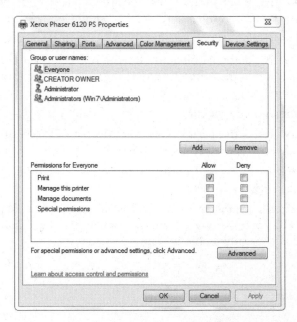

Print   Users granted this permission can print to the printer. By default, the Everyone group is granted Allow Print permissions when a printer is added.

Manage Documents   Users with Manage Documents permission can pause, cancel, and restart print jobs for any user. In organizations where multiple users share a single printer, a responsible user may be granted Manage Documents permission so that they can pause, restart, and cancel print jobs that any user has sent to the printer.

By default, the Creator Owner group is granted Manage Documents permission. Any user who sends a print job to a printer is identified as the Creator Owner for that print job, allowing the user to manage the print job.

Manage This Printer   Users with the Manage This Printer permission can modify any of the properties for the printer including ports used, drivers installed, and permissions assigned. Users with this permission can also restart the Printer Spooler service, which is sometimes useful when print jobs become hung up in the print queue and can't be cancelled or deleted.

The Printer Spooler service can be restarted from the Services applet available via the Administrative Tools menu or from a command prompt with administrative permissions with the following commands: SC Stop Spooler and SC Start Spooler, or Net Stop Spooler and Net Start Spooler.

Figure 8.19 shows the three basic permissions and the three special permissions for a printer with the three basic permissions.

FIGURE 8.19   Special printer permissions

Read Permissions Users granted this permission can read the assigned permissions. The Everyone group is granted Read Permissions when the printer is shared in addition to the Print permission.

Change Permissions Any user granted Manage This Printer permission is also granted the Change Permissions permission. This allows them to change permissions for other users. This permission is automatically granted to the Administrators group.

Take Ownership Any user granted Manage This Printer is also granted the Take Ownership permission. This permission allows a user to take ownership of a printer. As the owner, the user is able to modify permissions. This permission is automatically granted to the Administrators group.

Identifying and Resolving Network Printer Issues

It's rare to have a single printer for every user; rather, printers are shared on the network. When the printer fails, you'll need to be able to identify the source of the problem to allow all of the users to begin printing again. Network printer problems can be categorized as one of the following:

- Printer issues

- Server issues

- Network issues

First of all, it's important to realize that printers can be shared from computers or servers, placed directly on the network and managed by a print server, or placed directly on the network and not managed by a print server. However the printer is available, though, it's still referred to as a network printer. Consider Figure 8.20, which includes four printers configured differently.

FIGURE 8.20 Printers on a network

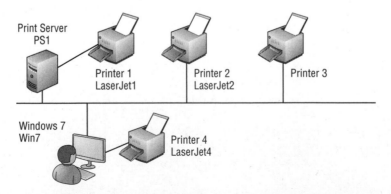

Printer 1 is named LaserJet1 and is connected directly to a print server. This could be via a USB port or some other type of connection. Users will send print jobs to Printer 1 via PS1, and the UNC path is \\PS1\LaserJet1.

The print server can also be configured to share printers on the network. Printer 2 is connected to the network using a NIC with an IP address. If PS1 were configured as the print server for this printer, the UNC path would be \\PS1\LaserJet2.

Printer 3 is connected to the network using a NIC with an IP address just like Printer 2. However, Printer 3 is not managed by the print server. If users need to connect to Printer 3, they need to know the IP address of the printer and configure it using the IP address. This printer doesn't enjoy any of the benefits of print servers.

Finally, Printer 4 is connected directly to the Windows 7 computer (named Win7) and shared from this computer. For the user on this computer, it's a local printer. However, if the printer is shared on the Windows 7 system, other users can send print jobs to Printer 4 via Win7, and the UNC path is \\Win7\LaserJet4.

One of the benefits of using print servers is that print drivers need to be managed only on the server. The correct driver is first placed on the server. When the printer is first added to the end user's computer, the correct driver is automatically downloaded. The driver can be changed or upgraded on the server, and it will automatically be downloaded to the client the next time the client connects.

The use of print servers becomes a choice between cost and convenience for some companies. If print servers are used, it is very convenient for the users and administrators. However, a print server adds to the load and management requirements for the server and can directly result in increased costs.

Printer Issues

If a user can't print to a printer, it's worth taking the time to ensure the printer is working properly. Most printers have power-on self-tests that can diagnose most problems. Just looking at the printer may indicate the problem.

Common problems with printers that can result in a user's request for help are these:

- Printer not turned on

- Printer not online

- Printer out of paper

Yes, these are simple problems, but it pays off to check the simple things first. It's embarrassing enough for a user to learn the problem was that the printer wasn't turned on. It would be even more so for a seasoned tech to spend an hour troubleshooting only to learn that the problem was the power switch.

Once you've eliminated the simple problems, you can do another simple check to determine whether the problem is with the printer or somewhere else, such as another user's system. Print to it from another system. If you succeed, there's no need to troubleshoot the printer anymore. The problem lies elsewhere. If it fails, the problem may be with the printer.

Hardware Failure

One of the simplest checks for a printer is to print a test page. You can do this by clicking the Print Test Page button from the General tab of the Printer Properties page, as shown in Figure 8.21.

FIGURE 8.21   Printing a test page from the Printer Properties

Most printer devices can also print test pages if you manipulate the menu of the printer or hold down specific keys when the printer is powered on. The process is different for different printers, and the printer manual will explain how it's done for your printer.

If the test page works, the printing hardware of the printer is good. If you can print a test page using the local console but you can't print a test page by clicking the Print Test Page button in the Printer Properties page, the problem is likely a network issue related to connectivity between the printer and computer.

Driver Issues

When a driver is installed for a printer, it will often do some checks and inform you if the driver is incompatible. However, it is still possible to install an incompatible driver for a printer.

The most common symptom of an incompatible driver is garbled output. You can also get garbled output from a loose connection to the printer, so you should check the connection first. However, if the connection is good and the output is garbled, you should update the driver.

You can change the driver from the Advanced tab of the printer properties. Click the New Driver button, and follow the wizard.

Network Issues

Network issues affect the ability of clients to connect to network or shared printers. Basic network troubleshooting (as covered in Chapter 7) comes into play here to troubleshoot network issues.

If it's a networked printer, check to see if you can ping the IP address of the printer. If this is unsuccessful, check to ensure that the networked printer has the same TCP/IP configuration. Many printers allow you to print the current configuration using a console menu. If it's been changed, identify the reason why it was changed, and then either change the printer or alter the client's configuration to use the printer's new IP address.

If the printer is shared from a print server, you'll need to check connectivity from the client to the print server and then check connectivity from the server to the printer. Again, you should follow basic network troubleshooting steps for each of the paths.

Server Issues

If the server has a problem, you should be able to narrow down the source by doing the following big-picture checks:

- Ensure the server is up and online.
- Ensure the server has connectivity on the network.
- Ensure the printer is configured correctly on the server.
- Ensure the server has connectivity with the printer.

Once you resolve the issues in these areas, the server should work successfully as a print server.

Summary

In this chapter, you learned how resources can be shared and accessed over the network. Both folders and printers are commonly shared so that multiple users can access them. The Universal Naming Convention uses the format of \\ServerName\ShareName, and it is used to access both shared folders and shared printers.

Permissions are used to control who can access shared resources and how much access they are granted. Shared folders use both Share permissions and NTFS permissions.

Individually, Share permissions and NTFS permissions are cumulative, granting the user the combination of all permissions granted. However, when Share permissions and NTFS permissions are combined, the user is granted only the most restrictive permission.

When troubleshooting network printer issues, you should first try to isolate the problem as a printer issue, a network issue, or a server issue. Once the problem is isolated to one of these categories, it becomes much easier to resolve.

Chapter Essentials

Assigning network resources   Know that the Universal Naming Convention (UNC) is formatted as **\\ServerName\ShareName**. Shares can be connected to directly using the Start Search box, or drives can be mapped to the UNC path using Windows Explorer.

Be familiar with the Devices and Printers applet and the Printer Properties pages. The Devices and Printers applet is the primary tool used to work with printers. You can add printers and manipulate printer properties from this tool. The majority of the administration for a shared printer is done through the Printer Properties pages.

Know how to connect to a shared printer. You can connect to shared printers using the Add Printer Wizard in the Devices and Printers applet. When connecting to a shared printer, the UNC path is used in the format \\ServerName\ShareName, just as it's used when connecting to a share. This tool can also be used to connect to network printers and wireless printers.

Understanding permissions   Understand the NTFS and Share permissions and especially how they interact. NTFS permissions are available on any NTFS drive, and Share permissions are available on any shared folder. Individually, the permissions are cumulative, but when NTFS and Share permissions are combined, the user is granted only the most restrictive permission between the two. If Deny Permission is assigned, Deny always takes precedence.

Know the purposes of the three basic printer permissions. When a printer is shared, the Everyone group is granted Print permission, which allows users to print. The Manage Documents permission can be granted to a responsible person in the workplace and allows the user to pause, restart, or cancel any user's documents for a printer. The Manage Printer permission is granted to administrators by default and effectively gives them full control over the printer.

Identifying and resolving network printer issues   Be familiar with basic network printer troubleshooting. When troubleshooting network printer issues, it's easiest to identify first whether the problem is related to the printer, the network, or the server and to troubleshoot from there.

Chapter

9

Managing Windows 7 in a Domain

TOPICS COVERED IN THIS CHAPTER INCLUDE

- ✓ Joining a domain
- ✓ Using authentication and authorization
- ✓ Identifying and resolving logon issues
- ✓ Understanding user profiles
- ✓ Running anti-malware software

If you work with a network that has more than 10 computers, it's probably in a Windows domain. It's important to understand some basics of how Windows 7 operates in a domain.

This chapter will lead you through the steps to create a domain in a virtual environment that you can use as a test bed. You can use this test bed to join a Windows 7 computer to a domain, create user accounts and groups in the domain, and view some of the symptoms of logon failures. You'll learn about standard, roaming, mandatory, and super-mandatory profiles. Last, anti-malware software is covered briefly.

Joining a Domain

When Windows 7 is first installed, it is a member of a workgroup by default. Workgroups are used in small offices, home offices, and home networks to allow users to share resources among themselves.

However, networks of more than 10 users implement domains. A domain is easier to manage and provides better security than a workgroup. One important benefit of a domain is that it provides single sign-on capabilities. In a domain, each user has one account that they can use to log on to almost any computer in the domain. In a workgroup, users need a separate account for each computer.

A Windows domain includes at least one server acting as a domain controller and hosting *Active Directory Domain Services* (AD DS). Desktop computers (such as Windows 7 computers) are then joined to the domain so that users can access the domain resources.

AD DS includes objects such as users, computers, and groups. In order for a user to log on to the domain, the user needs a user account. In addition, the user must log on to a computer that is joined to the domain. If the computer isn't a member of the domain, the user won't be able to log on even if the user has a domain account.

That being said, it's important to know how to join a computer to a domain. In the following section, you'll have an opportunity to create a virtual test environment that includes a single domain controller hosting a domain. You can then use this to join a Windows 7 computer to the domain. This test bed will also be useful for exploring Group Policy in the next chapter.

Creating a Test Bed

A test environment (or test bed) can be used for testing, learning, experimenting, and practicing. It includes one or more systems that can be completely isolated, connected to each other, and in some instances given limited connectivity to the live network. A virtual test bed is one or more virtual systems created in a virtual environment such as Microsoft Virtual PC or Windows Virtual PC.

Figure 9.1 shows a virtual network hosted on Windows 7. It includes two virtual systems—one running Active Directory as a domain controller and one running Windows 7 as a client in the domain. If you're running Windows 7, this is relatively easy to set up using the exercises in this chapter.

FIGURE 9.1   Virtual network hosted on Windows 7

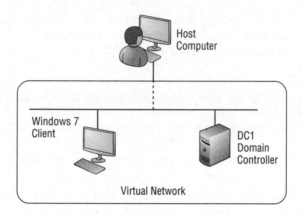

Windows 7 can run both Microsoft Virtual PC and Windows Virtual PC. Either of these products can be used to create a test bed on your local Windows 7 system. As a reminder, Microsoft Virtual PC is the older product run on Windows XP and Windows Vista. Windows Virtual PC (VPC) is the newer product that can also host Windows XP Mode to run virtualized applications.

Your system should have at least 3 GB of RAM for satisfactory performance. You can use 1 GB (1024 MB) for the virtual server running Windows Server 2008, 1 GB for the virtual desktop running Windows 7, and 1 GB for the host operating system. If necessary, you can use as little as 512 MB for Windows Server 2008 VPC, though the performance will be slow.

More RAM is always better. I'm running a 64-bit system with 6 GB of RAM, so I have given each of the VPCs 1.5 GB (1536 MB), leaving 3 GB for the host.

Chapter 1, "Planning for the Installation of Windows 7," included several exercises you can use to help build a test bed.

- Exercise 1.1 included the steps to install Windows 7 on a system. These steps can also be used to install Windows 7 on a Virtual PC if needed.

- Exercise 1.5 covered installing Windows Virtual PC and Windows XP Mode. XP Mode isn't needed for the virtual environment, so you can skip that if desired.

- Exercise 1.7 covered creating other Virtual PC machines. This can be used to create VPC for Windows Server 2008 and another VPC for Windows 7.

In this chapter, we'll build on those skills to create a virtual network that includes a domain controller and a Windows 7 system.

Creating a Domain

A domain includes a server running Active Directory Domain Services. The domain controller could be running Windows 2000 Server or Windows Server 2003, but it's more likely you'll be working with Windows Server 2008 and Windows Server 2008 R2 servers in your domain today. For the virtual network created in this chapter, you'll use Windows Server 2008.

You can download a trial edition of Windows Server 2008 from Microsoft's download site (www.Microsoft.com/downloads) by searching on "Windows Server 2008 Enterprise Eval." You need to download the x86-based version (32-bit).

 Windows Virtual PC and Microsoft Virtual PC do not support x64-based operating systems. You can run VPC on a 64-bit host, but you can only add x86-based operating systems as virtual machines to VPC.

Before starting Exercise 9.1, you should have accomplished the following steps on your Windows 7 system:

- Install Windows Virtual PC on the system. Exercise 1.5 can be used as a guide.

- Create a VPC machine named DC1 with at least 512 MB of RAM (1536 MB if possible), networking deselected, and a dynamically expanding virtual hard disk. Exercise 1.7 can be used as a guide. Note that this step doesn't install Windows Server 2008 but only creates the VPC.

- Obtain an evaluation copy of Windows Server 2008 Enterprise edition. An .iso image can be downloaded from www.Microsoft.com/downloads and burned to a DVD.

EXERCISE 9.1

Installing Windows Server 2008 on VPC

1. Start Windows Virtual PC by clicking Start ➤ All Programs ➤ Windows Virtual PC ➤ Windows Virtual PC.

2. Insert the Windows Server 2008 Enterprise Edition DVD in the DVD drive.

3. Start the DC1 VPC machine by double-clicking it. It will automatically begin booting from the DVD. If necessary, you can click the Ctrl+Alt+Del selection on the VPC menu to force a boot cycle.

4. When the Install Windows screen appears, select your language, time and currency, and keyboard. Click Next. Click Install Now.

5. The Type Your Product Key For Activation screen will appear. Deselect the Automatically Activate Windows When I'm Online check box. Click Next. When prompted again to enter your product key, click No.

6. Select Windows Server 2008 Enterprise (Full Installation). Select I Have Selected The Edition Of Windows That I Purchased, and click Next.

7. Review the software license terms and select I Accept The License Terms. Click Next.

8. Click Custom (Advanced) to start the installation.

9. Select Disk 0 Unallocated Space and click Next. The installation will begin at this point.

10. While the installation is running, select Tools ➢ Settings from the Windows Virtual PC menu. You will need to hold down the Ctrl+Alt+right-arrow keys to allow your mouse to escape the VPC window.

11. Select Networking. Adapter 1 should be listed as Not Connected. Change this to Internal Network, as shown in the following graphic. Click OK. This will allow the virtual systems to connect to each other but not with the network or Internet.

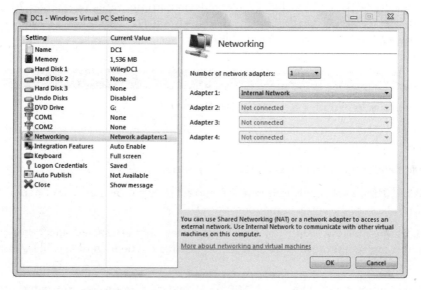

12. The installation process will complete after several minutes, and the VPC will reboot. When prompted to change the password, click OK.

13. Enter **P@ssw0rd** in the New Password and Confirm Password text boxes. Press Enter or click the right arrow. When prompted that the password has been changed, click OK.

14. When the desktop appears, the Initial Configuration Tasks screen will start. Use the Ctrl+Alt+right-arrow keys to allow your mouse to escape the VPC window. Select Tools ➢ Install Integration Components from the Windows Virtual PC menu. Review the information in the dialog box, and click Continue.

15. If the installer doesn't start automatically, click Start ➢ Computer. Double-click the DVD drive and double-click Setup.

16. Review the information on the Welcome page, and click Next.

17. When installation completes, click Finish. When prompted to restart the computer, click Yes.

This evaluation edition is a fully functional copy of Windows Server 2008 edition, but the evaluation period expires after 60 days. You can renew this evaluation period up to three times for a total of 240 days by entering the following command at the command prompt with elevated permissions:

```
Slmgr.vbs -rearm
```

KB article 948472, which includes full details on rearming Windows Server 2008, can be viewed here: http://support.microsoft.com/kb/948472.

Exercise 9.2 shows how to configure a Windows Server 2008 server.

EXERCISE 9.2

Configuring a Windows Server 2008 Server

1. Start DC1 created in Exercise 9.1, and log on with the Administrator account and a password of P@ssw0rd.

2. The Initial Configuration Tasks screen will appear.

3. Click Set Time Zone. If the time zone is incorrect for your location, click Change Time Zone and select the correct time zone. Click OK twice.

4. Click Configure Networking. Right-click Local Area Connection and select Properties. Deselect Internet Protocol Version 6 (TCP/IPv6). It's not needed for a small virtual network.

5. Select Internet Protocol Version 4 (TCP/IPv4), and click Properties. You can configure any TCP/IP settings desired, but exercises in this book assume the following settings are being used:

- IP Address: 192.168.1.10

- Subnet Mask: 255.255.255.0

- Preferred DNS Server: 192.168.1.10

Your display will look similar to the following graphic.

EXERCISE 9.2   *(continued)*

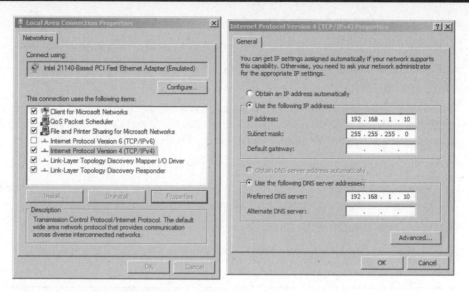

Click OK. Click Close. Close Network Connections.

6. On the Initial Configuration Tasks screen, click Provide Computer Name And Domain. Click Change. Type in **DC1** as the Computer Name and click OK.

7. When prompted that you'll need to restart your computer, click OK. Click Close and click Restart Now.

The system is now configured as a virtual Windows Server 2008 server. The next step is to promote it to a domain controller as the first domain controller in a domain, as shown in Exercise 9.3.

Domain names need to have at least two parts such as Microsoft.com or Wiley.com. However, they don't need to have a legal top-level domain name such as .com, .org, or .net. You can use a test bed domain name of test.bed if desired. For examples in the book, I'm using wiley.com as the domain name.

EXERCISE 9.3

Promoting a Server to a Domain Controller

1. Start DC1 and log on with the Administrator account.

2. Click Start, type **DCPromo** in the Start Search box, and press Enter.

3. After a moment, the DCPromo Wizard will start. Click Next.

4. Click Next on the Operating System Compatibility screen.

EXERCISE 9.3   *(continued)*

5. Select Create A New Domain In A New Forest, and click Next.

6. Enter a fully qualified domain name for the domain, such as wiley.com. Click Next.

7. Select Windows Server 2008 from the drop-down menu as the Forest Functional Level. Click Next.

8. The Additional Domain Controller Options page will appear. It will have DNS Server and Global Catalog both selected. Leave them selected and click Next. A warning will appear because DNS hasn't been created yet. This is normal. Click Yes to continue.

9. Accept the default locations for Active Directory files, and click Next.

10. Type **P@ssw0rd** in the Password and Confirm Password text boxes for the Directory Services Restore Mode Administrator Password. Click Next.

11. Review the information on the Summary screen, and click Next.

12. Select Reboot On Completion. Active Directory will be installed and the server will reboot.

To complete your virtual network, you'll also need to add a Windows 7 VPC machine.

- Create a VPC machine named Win7 with at least 1024 MB of RAM (1536 MB if your system has enough RAM), networking deselected, and a dynamically expanding virtual hard disk. You can use Exercise 1.7 as a guide.

- Install Windows 7 on the VPC. You can use Exercise 1.1 as a guide.

Configure the networking for the Windows 7 VPC machine using the following settings. You can use Exercise 1.7 as a guide if necessary.

- IP Address: 192.168.1.5

- Subnet Mask: 255.255.255.0

- Preferred DNS Server: 192.168.1.10

Joining the Domain

Once you've created a domain by promoting a server to a domain controller, you can add the Windows 7 client to the domain. Adding a Windows 7 client will result in the following:

- A computer object will be created in the domain.

- A password will be established for the computer to authenticate in the domain. This password will automatically be changed periodically.

- Users will be able to log on using a domain account and access domain resources.

- Group Policy objects will be applied to the computer and to users logging on to the computer.

Exercise 9.4 shows how to join a Windows 7 computer to a domain. If you're using the virtual network, both the domain controller and the Windows 7 client need to be running. It's critical that the Windows 7 client can reach the DNS server that is running on the domain controller. The Windows 7 VPC should have the Preferred DNS address configured with the address of the domain controller (192.168.1.10 if you're using the settings in this chapter).

EXERCISE 9.4

Joining Windows 7 to a Domain

1. Start Windows 7 and log on.

2. Click Start, right-click Computer, and select Properties.

3. Click Advanced System Settings. Select the Computer Name tab.

4. Click Change.

5. On the Computer Name/Domain Changes page, select Domain and enter the name of the domain. Click OK. You'll be prompted to enter the credentials for an account in the domain that has permission to join the domain. Your display will look similar to the following graphic.

6. Enter the credentials of a user account that has permission to join the domain (such as the Administrator account), and click OK. After a moment, a dialog box will appear welcoming you to the domain. Click OK.

7. You'll be prompted that you must restart the computer to apply the changes. Click OK.

8. Click Close. When prompted to restart the computer, click Restart Now.

At this point, you have a virtual network that includes a domain controller and a Windows 7 server that has been joined to the domain.

Authentication vs. Authorization

Two important security principles in use within a domain are *authentication* and *authorization*. In short, authentication is used to identify a user, and authorization is used to control access of the user.

As an example, if Joe is given a domain account, he can log on with that account. He uses it for authentication. However, just because Joe can log on doesn't mean he's automatically granted access to all the resources in the domain. Instead, his account is granted access to specific resources based on his needs and what he's authorized to access.

Authentication

Authentication is used to prove a user's identity. In general, there are three factors of authentication:

Something you know   This can be implemented with domain user accounts that have specific user names and passwords. As long as users know their user name and password, they are able to use these credentials for authentication.

Something you have   Smart cards are being used more and more today. A smart card is a credit card–sized card that can be inserted into a reader (often as part of the keyboard). Users insert the card and usually enter a personal identification number (PIN) for authentication. Within a domain, the smart card is associated with a domain user account.

Something you are   Biometrics can be used to prove a user's identity. Fingerprint readers can be found on more and more mobile computers today. Once configured, a user authenticates with their finger on the fingerprint reader. Other biometric methods include retinal scanners and hand scanners.

Multifactor authentication involves using more than one authentication factor. For example, a smart card is considered something you have, whereas a PIN or password is something you know, so when a smart card is used with a PIN, it is considered multifactor authentication.

Authorization

Users are granted rights and permissions based on the user accounts that authenticate them. If users log on with the local administrator account, they are able to perform any action and access any of the resources on the system.

Rights and *permissions* are different but often clumped together. In short, rights identify what a user can *do* on a system and permissions identify the resources a user can *access*.

Figure 9.2 shows the User Rights Assignment page from the Local Security Policy. It includes several actions that a user can be authorized to perform on a system, such as logging on locally, backing up files and directories, and changing the system time.

FIGURE 9.2   User Rights Assignments in Local Security Policy

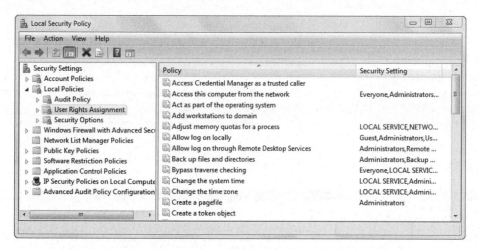

You can access the Local Security Policy from the Administrative Tools menu. The User Rights Assignment node is also available in Group Policy objects.

Chapter 8, "Accessing Resources on a Network," covered NTFS permissions, share permissions, and printer permissions in depth. As an example, when a user is granted the Full Control NTFS permission on a folder, they can access any of the files in the folder.

Built-in Groups

Although rights and permissions can be assigned to individual user accounts, they are much more commonly assigned to groups. If a user is a member of a group, and the group is granted specific rights and permissions, the user also has those rights and permissions.

Windows 7 and Windows domains both include many built-in groups. Figure 9.3 shows the built-in groups on a local system, and Figure 9.4 shows some of the built-in groups in a domain. These groups have been assigned specific rights and permissions to perform actions on systems and within domains.

FIGURE 9.3 Groups on a Windows 7 system

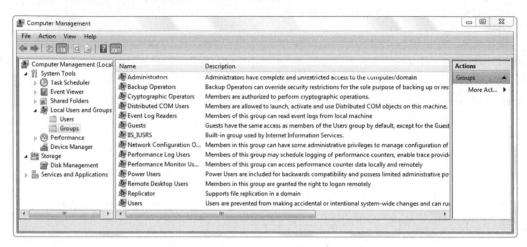

FIGURE 9.4 Built-in groups in a domain

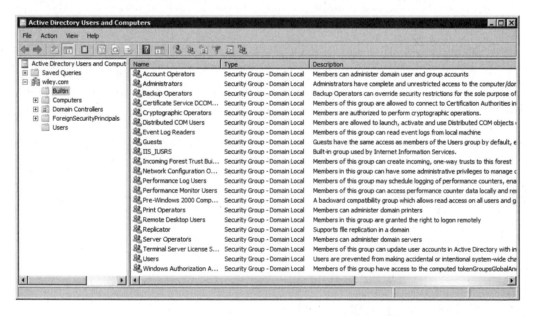

You can access the Computer Management console to view local built-in groups via the Administrative Tools menu or by clicking Start, right-clicking Computer, and selecting

Manage. You view domain built-in groups via the Active Directory Users and Computers console on a domain controller found in the Administrative Tools menu. There is a Builtin container, but additional built-in groups exist in the Users container.

Some of these groups deserve special mention:

Administrators (local) Members of the *Administrators* group on local computers (including Windows 7 computers) can do anything on that computer. The local administrator account is a member of this group, and the first account created on a Windows 7 computer when it is installed is a member of this group.

Administrators (domain) Members of the domain Administrators group have complete and unrestricted access to computers in the domain. The domain administrator account, the Domain Admins group, and the Enterprise Admins group are all members of the domain Administrators group by default.

Domain Admins Users in the *Domain Admins* group can do anything in the domain. This group is automatically added to the local Administrators group for every computer in the domain. It's also added to the domain Administrators group.

Enterprise Admins Users in the *Enterprise Admins* group can do anything in the forest. A forest is a group of one or more domains, and users in this group have permissions to add, remove, and administer all of the domains in the forest. This group is a member of the domain Administrators group for every domain in the forest.

Power Users Power Users is a local group added for backward compatibility. It was used on older operating systems to give a user additional permissions without putting the user in the Administrators group.

Server Operator This is a special group on domain controllers. It grants members rights and permissions to administer the domain controller without granting them any permission in the domain.

Backup Operators This group grants members the ability to back up and restore files.

Organizing Users with Groups

It's also possible to create additional groups to meet specific needs. This is rarely done on local Windows 7 systems alone, but it's often done in a domain to organize users and easily grant specific rights and permissions.

As an example, consider Figure 9.5. Sally, Bob, and Alice are all in the Sales department. A group named G_Sales is created to organize the users, and each user account is then placed in the G_Sales group. Now imagine that the users in the group need access to the SalesData Share hosted on FS1.

FIGURE 9.5   Organizing users with a group

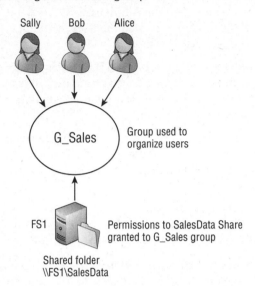

Instead of granting the same permissions to the individual accounts, the permissions to the SalesData Share are granted to the group. Because the users are members of the group, they have the same permissions as the group.

While it takes a little planning initially to design and create the groups, it eases the administration burden in the long run. For example, imagine that you originally granted Read permission to a share, but later wanted to change this to Modify for all the users in the Sales department. If a group is created and permissions are assigned to the group, you make the change once and you're done. However, if you originally assigned the permissions to each user, you'd have to modify the permissions for each user.

Groups are also useful even if only one user is a member. For example, imagine that an HR department has only one employee, Maria. On the surface, it may seem easier to assign all the permissions to Maria's account. However, what do you do if Maria is transferred or promoted within the company and someone else needs to take over?

If the permissions are assigned to the individual user, then they all have to be modified to remove Maria's access and grant the new employee's access. However, if a group was created and all the permissions were assigned to the group, you'd simply need to add the new employee's account to the group and remove Maria's account.

Group Scope and Group Type

Groups created in a domain have both a group scope and a group type. Figure 9.6 shows the screen used to create a new group. You can access this in Active Directory Users and Computers by right-clicking a container and selecting New ➢ Group.

FIGURE 9.6   Creating a new group in a domain

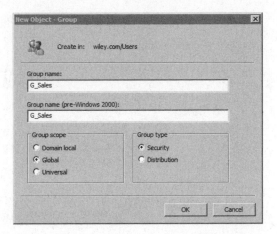

The three group scopes are global, domain local, and universal:

Global   *Global groups* are commonly used to organize users (such as all the users in the Sales department with a group named G_Sales). Global groups can also contain other global groups.

Domain local   *Domain local groups* are sometimes used in administrative models in larger domains. A domain local group commonly identifies assigned permissions to specific resources. As an example, the DL_Print_ClrLaserPrinter group could be used to identify a group that is assigned print permission for a color laser printer. A domain local group typically contains one or more global groups and can also contain universal groups.

Universal   Universal groups are used in multiple-domain environments. They can contain global groups from any domain and can be added to domain local groups in any domain.

A commonly used naming convention is to begin the group name with the group scope. G_Sales is easily identified as a global group used to organize the users in the Sales group. Similarly, it's common to include the permissions and resources in the domain local group. DL_Print_ClrLaser-Printer identifies it as a domain local group used to grant print permission for a color laser printer.

The two group types are distribution and security:

Distribution   A *distribution group* is used for email only. It cannot be assigned permissions.

Security   A *security group* can be assigned permissions or used as a distribution group.

In larger domains where both global and domain local groups are used, a common strategy known as A G DL P is used. Figure 9.7 shows an example of A G DL P.

FIGURE 9.7 A G DL P administrative model used in larger domains

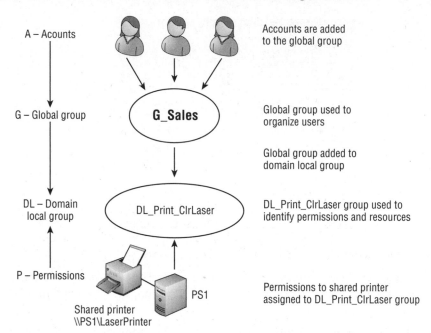

When A G DL P is used, accounts (A) are added to global groups (G). Global groups are added to domain local (DL) groups, and permissions (P) are assigned to domain local groups.

The direction of the arrows in the figure also helps to identify what can be added to a group. The arrow goes down from the accounts, indicating they can be added to global groups or domain local groups. The arrow also goes down from the global group, indicating it can be added to a domain local group.

However, a global group can't be added to a user (which admittedly sounds silly), and a local group can't be added to a global group; both of these examples go against the arrow.

The arrow goes up from permissions. Permissions can be assigned to accounts or any type of group, but it's a good practice to assign permissions to groups whenever possible. When you begin assigning permissions directly to users, administration becomes more difficult.

The benefits of using domain local groups are realized only in larger domains where administrators want to manage permissions for some resources more closely. Most organizations use a simpler model of AGP (shown earlier in Figure 9.5) where accounts (A) are placed into global (G) groups and permissions (P) are assigned to the global groups.

Exercise 9.5 walks through the process of creating users and groups in a domain.

EXERCISE 9.5

Creating Users and Groups in a Domain

1. Start the domain controller and log on.

2. Launch Active Directory Users and Computers by clicking Start ➢ Administrative Tools ➢ Active Directory Users And Computers.

3. If necessary, expand the domain to view the Users container. Right-click the Users container and select New ➢ Group.

4. Enter the name of the group in the Group Name text box (such as G_Sales). Global is selected as the Group Scope and Security is selected as the Group Type by default, but you can change these if needed. Click OK.

5. Create a user account in the domain with these steps:

   a. Right-click Users and select New ➢ User.

   b. Enter the First Name, Last Name, and User Logon Name. The User Logon Name must be unique in the domain, and it's common to use a combination of the user's First Name and Last Name. Your display will look similar to the following graphic. Click Next.

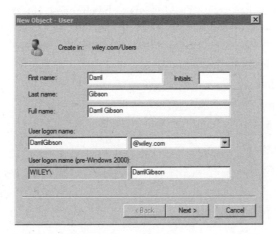

   c. Enter a password such as P@ssw0rd in the Password and Confirm Password text boxes. Click Next and then click Finish.

6. Right-click the user account you just created, and select Properties.

7.   Select the Member Of tab. You'll see that the user is a member of the Domain Users group. Click Add.

8.   Enter **G_Sales** and click OK. (You can also click Advanced and then Find Now to search or browse for objects in Active Directory.)

9.   Click OK on the User Properties page. The user is now a member of the G_Sales group, and any permissions assigned to this group will apply to the user.

Identifying and Resolving Logon Issues

Users must be able to log on to a domain to access domain resources. Thus, if they cannot log on, it quickly becomes a critical issue for the user. You'll need to be able to identify and resolve the problem as quickly as possible.

Many of the items just require looking at the symptoms. That may seem obvious, but for some end users an error message just indicates that things aren't working, even if a message clearly says the password has expired and needs to be changed. If it's the first time the user has seen the message, it's translated simply as "it's broken."

Here are some of the items to consider when troubleshooting logon issues:

- Hardware versus network problems
- Using cached credentials
- Password expiration
- Determining logon context
- Logon hours compliance
- Time synchronization

Hardware vs. Network

If a user is unable to log on to a system using a domain account, one of the first things to do is to ensure that the computer is operational and has connectivity. This can be done by logging on to the local computer using the local administrator account. If you can't log on locally, there's no need to troubleshoot the network—the problem is in the local machine.

Once you log on locally, you can do basic connectivity checks to ensure the client has an IP address on the network and has connectivity with other systems on the network. IPConfig and Ping are two basic command-line tools that were covered in Chapter 7, "Networking with Windows 7," that can help you quickly verify connectivity.

Using Cached Credentials

Windows 7 will cache the domain credentials of up to 10 users who have logged on to a system. These *cached credentials* are stored in an encrypted format in a secure area of the Registry, and they can be used by Windows 7 if a domain controller is not available to authenticate a user.

Consider a user named Sally who has a mobile computer. When she's at work, her mobile computer is connected to the domain and she uses her domain account to log on. Her credentials are then cached onto her system. Sally then goes on a business trip. While at the airport, she can still log on to her mobile computer using the same domain account even though a domain controller isn't reachable.

This works the same way in a network if a domain controller is unreachable. The network could have problems preventing the user from accessing a domain controller, but the user can still log on using a domain account. There is no indication to the user that cached credentials are being used, other than the logon seems to take a little longer and network connectivity is prevented after the user is logged on.

Figure 9.8 shows how the Network and Sharing Center appears when a user is logged on with cached credentials. Notice the warning icon between the computer and the network.

FIGURE 9.8   Connectivity affected by cached credentials

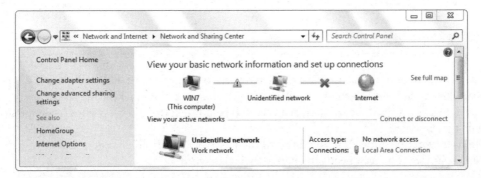

Users cannot access any domain resources when authenticated with cached credentials. If a user tries to access a network share, print to a network printer, or use any other network resources that require valid credentials, the attempt will fail with cached credentials.

The reasoning is that the user has not been authenticated by Active Directory, and it's possible the account has been disabled or deleted. Until the account can be authenticated with Active Directory for this session, access is not granted.

When Windows 7 is logged on with cached credentials, it will periodically try to connect to the domain controller and authenticate normally. If the domain controller comes back online or the network is repaired so that the domain controller can be reached, the user's credentials will be authenticated and the user will have access to network resources as normal.

Password Expiration

If a user uses the same password for a long period of time, the possibility of the password being discovered and used by an attacker increases. In a domain, Group Policy is commonly used to force users to change their password on a regular basis.

Group Policy will be covered in more depth in Chapter 10, "Managing Windows 7 with Group Policy," but in short, Group Policy allows you to configure a setting one time and have it apply to all users or computers equally. The Default Domain Policy is created when the domain is created, and it includes several settings for the Password Policy, as shown in Figure 9.9 with Password Policy selected.

FIGURE 9.9   Password Policy

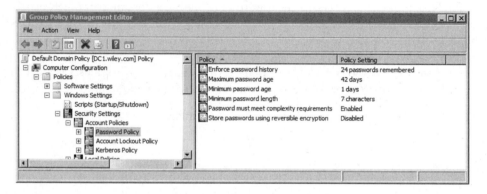

When the default policy is used, users are required to change their password every 42 days. Users are given reminders to change their password when it is close to expiring. If the user ignores the warning until the last day, the user will be notified that the password has expired and must be changed.

The user won't be allowed to log on until the password has been changed. Luckily, the solution is simple. The user needs to change their password.

Determining Logon Context

Users can log on to the local computer using a local account, or they can log on to the domain using a domain account. Which account a user logs on with determines the logon context, and if a user logs on with a local account, access to domain resources will be limited to permissions granted to the local account.

As an example, imagine that Sally has a domain account in the Wiley.com domain named Sally (Wiley\Sally) and a local computer account on a computer named Win7 (Win7\Sally). She could be granted full control for a share using the Wiley\Sally account but no access using her Win7\Sally account.

Accounts are commonly listed in the format domain\account or computer\account. If it is a domain account, the NetBIOS name of the domain (Wiley if the domain is named Wiley.com) is used. If it is a local computer account, the name of the computer is used.

If you've verified that Wiley\Sally has full control to the share but she is being denied access, you should check the logon context. One way to do so is by pressing Ctrl+Alt+Del to access the Ctrl+Alt+Del menu. You can then select Change A Password to access the screen shown in Figure 9.10.

FIGURE 9.10   Checking logon context

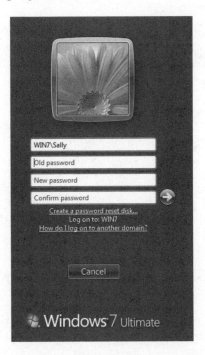

In the figure, you can see that the account is identified as Win7\Sally, indicating that she is logged on using the local account. If it was the domain account, it would be listed as Wiley\Sally.

You can also use the whoami command from the command line. This will return the username in the format of domain\username for a domain account or computer\username for a local account. The whoami /all command will also list SIDs, group memberships, and privileges for the account.

Logon Hours Compliance

By default, users are granted permissions to log on to computers at any hour of the day, any day of the week. However, you can modify the properties of a user account to restrict logon hours.

Figure 9.11 shows the screen used to change the logon hours. You can access this from Active Directory Users and Computers by right-clicking the user account and selecting Properties. In the figure, the logon hours have been changed to allow a user to log on only between 5:00 AM and 8:00 PM.

FIGURE 9.11   Setting logon hours

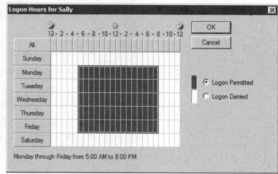

If a user tries to log on outside of the logon hours, the following message will appear: `Your account has time restrictions that prevent you from logging on at this time. Please try again later`.

Users will not be logged off if the logon time passes, and if they are connected to any network resources, they won't be disconnected. However, they won't be able to make any new connections.

As an example, imagine that logon times for Sally are set to 5:00 AM to 8:00 PM. One night she stays late working on a critical report stored on a network share. As the clock ticks past 8:00 PM, she is still able to continue working on the report and save it to the network share. However, if she tries to connect to another network resource, she'll see a message like the one shown in Figure 9.12.

FIGURE 9.12   Denied access to a resource after hours

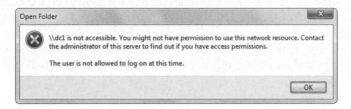

 Real World Scenario

Restricting Computer Access

By default, users can log on to any computer in the domain except for domain controllers. This can be modified for individual accounts by clicking the Log On To button in the user Properties screen (shown earlier in Figure 9.11). If you enable this feature and add computers, users will be able to log on only to the added computers and no others.

It is also possible to prevent users from logging on to member servers (nondomain controllers) in the domain. Group Policy objects (GPOs) can be created and applied to ensure that only specific groups (such as IT administrators) are authorized to log on to servers. This provides an added layer of security for the servers.

Time Synchronization

Active Directory Domain Services uses *Kerberos* as the primary authentication protocol within the domain, and Kerberos requires all computers to be set to within five minutes of each other. If not, the trust relationship with the machine account is lost.

When a computer first authenticates in a domain, it is issued a ticket-granting ticket (TGT) from a Key Distribution Center (KDC). Then when the computer wants to access any resources, it presents the TGT and requests a ticket for the resource. However, if a computer is more than five minutes out of sync, the KDC will no longer issue tickets and the computer will not be able to access resources.

Computers within a domain are synchronized as shown in Figure 9.13. One domain controller holds the role of a primary domain controller (PDC) emulator. It is commonly configured to synchronize with an external time source.

All domain controllers get their time from the PDC emulator. Then when a domain computer is turned on and authenticates with a domain controller, the client synchronizes its time with the domain controller.

This works great as long as a user doesn't change the time on their computer. If a user does change their time (or date) so that it is more than five minutes off, the computer will effectively be kicked off the domain, at least until it's rebooted and synchronizes with a domain controller.

When the system time is changed and the system is kicked off the network, it's sometimes challenging to identify why. However, this is a great example of how rebooting a system often clears up the problems.

FIGURE 9.13   Time synchronization in a domain

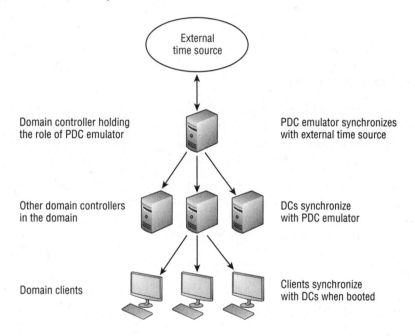

Understanding User Profiles

A *user profile* is a set of data that is used to re-create the user's environment each time a user logs on. It includes several folders such as Contacts, Cookies, Desktop, Downloads, Favorites, and more. It also includes user-specific Registry settings.

As an example, Bob could use a Windows 7 system and have it configured with a left-hand mouse, the Windows 7 Landscapes theme, a weather gadget on his desktop, and several drives mapped to network shares he uses regularly. Each time Bob logs on, these settings are re-created from his profile. Sally could use the same computer with a different user account. She can reconfigure all of these settings, and they will be re-created from her profile each time she logs on, without affecting the settings for Bob.

Windows 7 profiles are stored in the %systemroot%\Users folder by default. The Users folder includes the standard profiles of any user who has ever logged on to the system and also the *All Users profile* and the *Default User profile.*

All Users   The All Users profile holds settings that affect all users. As an example, when you install an application, you are often prompted to choose to allow all users access to the program. When you select All Users, the application modifies the All Users profile, ensuring the application is available to any user who logs on to the system.

Default User   This profile is used when a user first logs on to a system. Windows 7 will copy the Default User profile to a new folder named with the user's logon name. If Bob logs on, a folder is created named Bob and includes all the data from the Default User profile. This new profile is used to re-create the same environment for the user each time Bob logs on.

There are many differences in how profiles are implemented in Windows XP and Windows 7. The changes occurred between Windows XP and Windows Vista. For example, in Windows XP the profile was located under the %systemroot\Documents And Settings\ folder. This was changed to %systemroot%\Users\ in Windows Vista and Windows 7.

If you look in the %systemroot%\Users folder, you won't see the Default User folder, but it's there—it's just hidden. By default, the only folders that a user will see in the %systemroot%\Users\ folder are the Public folder and the profile folders of any users who have logged on. There are many hidden and system-protected folders that don't show by default, and you can follow these steps to show them:

1.   Launch Windows Explorer and browse to the %systemroot%\Users\ folder.

2.   Click Organize ➢ Folder And Search Options.

3.   Select the View tab.

4.   Select Show Hidden Files And Folders.

5.   Deselect Hide Protected Operating System Files. When prompted, if you're sure you want to display these files, click Yes. Click OK.

You will now see the All Users folder, the Default User folder, and some other folders.

Standard Profiles

Profiles stored in the %systemroot%\Users\username folder are referred to as local user profiles or standard profiles. The profile includes several folders and a Registry hive. Many of the folders and data are system files and hidden by default.

Figure 9.14 shows the user profile with hidden and system files showing.

FIGURE 9.14   User profile folder

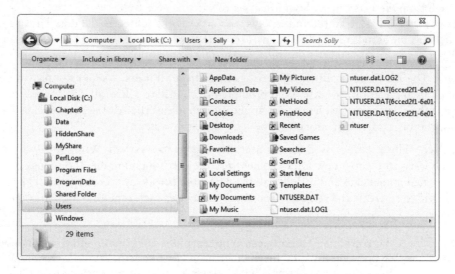

Folders   The folders hold data and settings needed by the user. These include desktop icons and shortcuts, links and shortcuts to other folders, startup applications, and more.

Registry hive   The HKEY_CURRENT_USER portion of the Registry holds user-defined settings for the desktop, applications, printers, and more. These are stored in a file named ntuser.dat.

Roaming Profiles

Local user profiles work great if a user logs on to the same system all the time. However, in some organizations users may frequently log on to different systems. Mapped network drives, shortcuts on the desktop, and other elements of the user's profile are often useful if they're available to a user no matter where the user logs on. *Roaming profiles* can be implemented to ensure the same profile is available to a user no matter which computer is used.

Figure 9.15 shows how roaming profiles are used. A folder is shared on a server that is available to the user on the network, and the user's account is then configured to use this share for the profile.

When the user logs on to a computer, the profile is retrieved from the network share and copied onto the local computer. If the user makes any changes, these changes are copied up to the roaming profile on the network share. If a user then moves to a different computer and logs on, the profile is copied down to the different computer.

FIGURE 9.15   Using roaming profiles in a domain

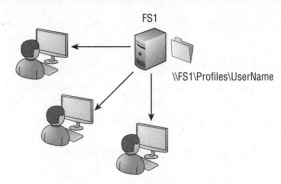

Roaming profiles can be implemented only in a domain. The two steps used to create a roaming profile are as follows:

1. Create a share on a server.   This share needs to be accessible to users using the UNC path (\\ServerName\ShareName). If more than one user will use this share, the Authenticated Users group should be granted Full Control. It's not necessary to create the folder for each user because this can be created automatically.

2. Modify the domain user account.   The Profile tab of the user account Properties page includes a Profile Path text box. The UNC path to the share is added here and appended with the %UserName% variable, giving a full path of \\ServerName\ShareName\%UserName%. When the user logs on, a folder will be created within the share with the appropriate permissions for the user to access the folder.

Exercise 9.6 demonstrates how to implement roaming profiles.

EXERCISE 9.6

Implementing Roaming Profiles

1. Start the domain controller and log on.

2. Create a shared folder to store the user profiles with the following steps:

    a. Start Windows Explorer by clicking Start ➤ Computer.

    b. Double-click the C: drive. Right-click the main Windows pane and click New ➤ Folder. Name the folder **Profiles** or another name that matches your company's needs.

    c. Select Share from the Windows Explorer toolbar.

    d. Type **Authenticated Users** in the text box, and click Add. (You can also click Find And Search and use the Active Directory search tool to locate any group.) Change Reader to **Contributor**.

    e. Click Share. Click Done.

3. Launch Active Directory Users and Computers by clicking Start ➤ Administrative Tools ➤ Active Directory Users And Computers.

4. Locate a user account. Right-click the user account and click Properties.

5. Select the Profile tab. Enter the UNC path to the share in the Profile Path text box, as shown in the following graphic. For my test bed, I created the Profiles share on DC1, so the full path is \\DC1\Profiles\%UserName%. Click OK.

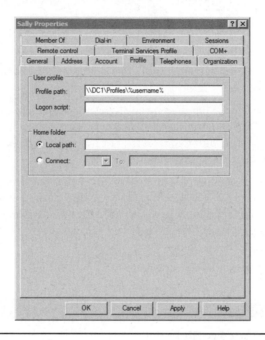

If you look in the Profiles folder now, you won't see anything. However, the next time the user logs on, a folder will be created for the user in the UNC path. Figure 9.16 shows an example of what this looks like for a user. Notice that since the %UserName% variable was used, the folder was created using the user name. The V2 indicates to the operating system that this roaming profile is using the newer format of profiles that was implemented with Windows Vista.

The operating system also configures the NTFS permissions for the folder. The user and the system both have full control of the folder, but no other users are granted any access to the data in the folder.

FIGURE 9.16   Roaming profiles created for a user

Mandatory Profiles

A *mandatory profile* is a roaming profile that is configured as read-only. Users will use this profile as a roaming profile, but any changes made by the user will not be saved. The primary reason to create mandatory profiles is so that users have a consistent profile.

It is possible for enthusiastic users to modify the standard profile in such a way that it adversely affects the system. This results in a call to the help desk and troubleshooting by a technician. Some companies have had one too many of these calls and have decided to use mandatory profiles to prevent these problems.

As a reminder, here's how the roaming profile works. The user logs on, the profile is retrieved from the server where it's stored, and then the profile is copied down to the local computer. When the user logs off, any changes to the profile are copied back up to the server where the roaming profile is stored.

The only difference between a roaming profile and a mandatory profile is that the changes are never copied back up to the server when the user logs off. The user can still make changes to the local profile. However, because these changes aren't saved to the server, the next time the user logs on, the mandatory profile will be copied from the server down to the client, overwriting any changes the user may have made.

There are three primary steps involved in creating a mandatory user profile:

1.   Create a profile with the desired settings on a Windows 7 system. Copy it to a network share.

2.   Rename `ntuser.dat` to **`ntuser.man`**. This is a hidden system file, so you'll need to modify the Windows Explorer view to show hidden files and show system files. The steps to do this are listed in the "Understanding User Profiles" section in this chapter.

3.   Configure accounts to use the mandatory roaming user profile. This is similar to Exercise 9.6, which showed how to create a roaming user profile, except the `%username%` variable isn't used. Instead, all users will use the UNC path of `\\ServerName\ShareName`.

You can set the profile path for multiple users at the same time in Active Directory Users and Computers. Use either the Shift key or the Ctrl key to select multiple user accounts. After you've selected all of the accounts, right-click one of them, select Properties, and then select the Profile tab, as shown in Figure 9.17.

FIGURE 9.17   Modifying profiles for multiple users at the same time

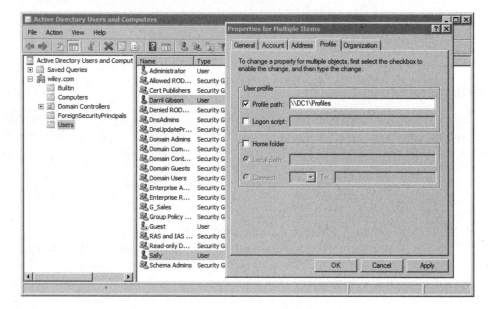

It's also possible to set a mandatory profile for many users using Group Policy. This will be covered in Chapter 10.

Super-Mandatory User Profiles

Windows 7 also supports *super-mandatory profiles*. A super-mandatory user profile is similar to a mandatory roaming user profile with one important addition. If network or server problems prevent the user from downloading the mandatory profile, the user is unable to log on.

With a regular mandatory user profile, the user is still able to log on even if the mandatory user profile is unavailable. As a reminder, when a roaming profile is used, it copies the profile to the local system. If a user has previously logged on to a system and has a copy of the profile on the system, Windows 7 will use this if the share for the roaming profile is unavailable.

If you want to ensure that users are not allowed to log on unless the mandatory profile is downloaded, you can configure the profile to be a super-mandatory user profile. A profile is created as a super-mandatory profile by renaming the profile folder with a `.man` extension.

 You should use super-mandatory user profiles only when the network is reliable. If network problems prevent users from accessing the share where the profile is stored, users will be prevented from logging on at all.

As a reminder, to create a mandatory roaming profile, the `ntuser.dat` file (located at the root of the profile) is renamed to `ntuser.man`. This may be stored in a network share identified as `\\DC1\Profiles`.

If you want the profile to be a super-mandatory profile, you could name the share `Profiles.man` so that it's accessed using a UNC path of `\\DC1\Profiles.man`. In addition to appending the share with `.man`, you also need to ensure that the client is configured to access the share using the full UNC path, including `.man` (`\\DC1\Profiles.man`).

Modifying the Default User Profile

If you want new users to have consistent settings that are different from the default, you can modify the Default User profile. However, this process isn't as simple as it sounds or as simple as it was in Windows XP.

In Windows XP, you typically followed these steps to modify the default user profile:

1. Create an account and log on. (This creates a profile for this account from the Default User profile.) You would typically create another administrator account so that you would have permission to make the changes.

2. Modify the desired settings to modify the profile of the account. When all of the settings have been modified, log off.

3. Log on with the regular administrator account. Access the Profiles page (from the Advanced tab of System Properties), and copy the new profile over the top of the Default User profile.

However, this causes problems in Windows 7 (and actually caused some problems in Windows XP). It is no longer the recommended method and isn't even possible. Figure 9.18 shows the User Profiles page for a Windows 7 system.

If you select any profile except the Default Profile, the Copy To button is disabled. You're not able to copy an existing profile over the top of the Default Profile in Windows 7 using this screen.

FIGURE 9.18　Viewing user profiles in Windows 7

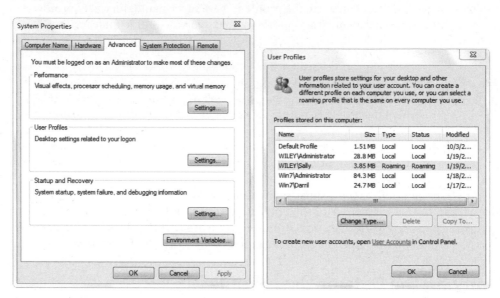

Instead, the recommended method is to use the Windows System Image Manager tool (available in the Windows Automated Installation Kit), which was covered in Chapter 1 and the Sysprep tool that was covered in Chapter 2, "Automating the Deployment of Windows 7." The overall steps are as follows:

1. Log on with any account that you want to use as the default. The account will need administrative permissions, and you can use the Administrator account if desired.

2. Modify the desired settings to modify the profile of the account.

3. Create an `unattend.xml` file using Windows System Image Manager.

4. Add or modify the `CopyProfile` parameter so that it reads as follows:
   `<CopyProfile>true</CopyProfile>`.

   This will cause the currently logged-on user settings to be copied to the Default User profile when Sysprep is run.

5. Run Sysprep on the system with the following command:

   `sysprep.exe /generalize /unattend: unattend.xml`

   If the `unattend.xml` file is located in a different directory, you'll need to include the full path.

It's important to realize that even though you are copying the profile settings of the Administrator account, you are not copying the rights and permissions. Rights and permissions are not stored in the profile, so copying the administrator's profile to the Default User profile does not give all new users full administrative permissions.

If you need to customize the Default User profile, check out Microsoft's Knowledge Base article 973289, which provides more in-depth details on these steps. You can find it here: http://support.microsoft.com/kb/973289.

Configuring Settings with Scripts

It's also possible to configure many of the settings using scripts. Some basic scripting was covered in Chapter 3, "Using the Command Prompt and PowerShell." You can configure the scripts to run for an individual user within a domain by modifying the properties of the user account.

As an example, imagine that someone within your company created a PowerShell script that can configure system settings for a Windows 7 computer. You are now asked to ensure it always runs when a user logs on. You could create a share on a server, place the script within the share, and then configure the user account.

Figure 9.19 shows the Profile tab of a user Properties screen. The Logon Script text box will accept the UNC path of a script. In the figure, the script is stored in the Scripts share on the FS1 server (\\FS1\Scripts) and is named Logon.ps1.

FIGURE 9.19   Configuring a logon script for a single user

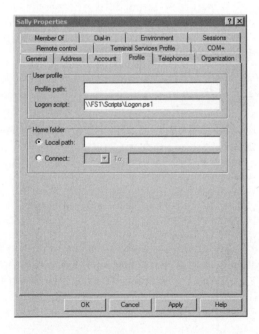

If you want the script to run for many users, you can use Group Policy. Group Policy allows you to run scripts when a computer starts up or shuts down and when a user logs on or logs off. You'll learn more about Group Policy in the next chapter.

Anti-Malware Software

An essential requirement for any computer that has access to the Internet today is the use of anti-malware software. Attackers are constantly creating new methods and techniques to infect your system with malicious software (*malware*).

Years ago, malware was less focused. It would sometimes wait until a specific day and pop up a relatively harmless message like "Legalize Marijuana." Other malware would delete data or corrupt the hard drive. However, malware is much more focused today. Attackers want money and data.

Most malware today has the specific goal of gaining information about you or your organization. The information about you may be used to steal your identity, impersonate you, or hack into your online bank accounts. The number of people who have lost money from Internet-based attacks continues to grow. Other times, corporate or governmental espionage is used to gain secrets. Malware is commonly used to exploit weaknesses and unpatched vulnerabilities in systems.

Chapter 4, "Managing the Lifecycle—Keeping Windows 7 Up to Date," covered the importance of keeping systems patched and some methods used to do so. In addition to keeping systems patched, anti-malware software is also needed. Anti-malware falls into two primary categories.

Anti-spyware   *Anti-spyware software* is intended to protect against spyware. Spyware is software that can install itself or run on your computer without your knowledge or consent. It often is used to monitor your online activities, collect personally identifiable information, and report this back to the attacker.

Antivirus   *Antivirus software* is intended to protect against viruses, worms, Trojan horses, rootkits, and other malware. Many current antivirus software products also protect against spyware.

Malware is identified through definitions. Each piece of malware has a specific signature similar to a fingerprint that can be used to identify it using anti-malware software. Just as it's important to keep systems up to date, it's also important to keep anti-malware definitions up to date.

Windows Defender

Windows Defender is built into Windows 7 and is designed to protect against spyware. It's configured to run automatically in the background and protect the system against spyware. You can launch Windows Defender by clicking Start, typing **Defender** in the Start Search box, and pressing Enter.

Windows Defender provides two types of protection:

Real-time protection   Windows Defender alerts you when spyware attempts to install itself or run on your computer without your consent. It also alerts you when programs attempt to change important settings.

Scanning protection   You can launch Windows Defender at any time to perform an on-demand scan to check your system for spyware. It is also configured to scan your system automatically on a regular basis.

When scanning the computer you can do a quick scan, a custom scan, or a full scan. A quick scan scans the most likely places on your hard disk where spyware is likely to be found. A custom scan allows you to pick which drives and folders you want to scan. A full scan checks all files on the hard drive and all currently running programs. Not only does a full scan take longer, but it can also affect the performance of the system as it is running.

Figure 9.20 shows the options for Windows Defender. You can access this page by clicking Tools on the toolbar and selecting Options in the Tools And Settings page. Notice that Automatically Scan My Computer (Recommended) is checked. This enables Windows Defender.

Check For Updated Definitions Before Scanning is also checked by default. This ensures that Windows Defender is kept up to date.

FIGURE 9.20   Windows Defender options

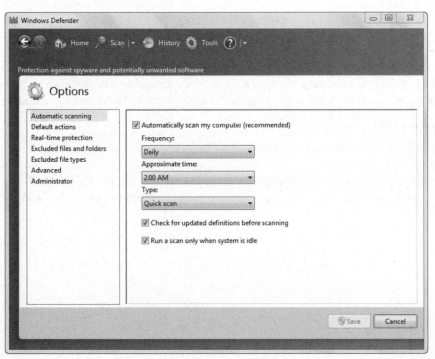

Third-Party Anti-malware Software

Most companies purchase third-party antivirus or anti-malware software. Two of the major companies that sell third-party antivirus software are McAfee and Symantec.

Both of these companies sell corporate editions of the software that can be centrally managed from a server. This server can deploy the software to the clients, verify that scans are being run regularly, and keep the software up to date with current definitions.

Windows 7 verifies that antivirus software is installed, running, and up to date. If antivirus software that meets all of these conditions isn't detected, the Action Center will report it as a discrepancy. The Action Center was covered in more depth in Chapter 5, "Maintaining and Troubleshooting Windows 7."

Summary

In this chapter, you had an opportunity to create a Windows Server 2008 domain in a virtual environment that can be used as a test bed. After creating the virtual environment, you learned how to join a Windows 7 computer to a domain.

Authentication is used to verify the identity of a user, and authorization is then used to grant the user access to resources. User accounts are created using Active Directory Users and Computers. Built-in groups and administrator-created groups are commonly used in the domain to streamline the process of granting access.

User profiles ensure that users have the same environment each time they log on. Standard profiles are stored locally in the `%systemroot%\Users` folder. Roaming profiles are stored on a central server and can be used when a user logs on to any system in the domain. Mandatory profiles are roaming profiles that can't be changed and are created by renaming `ntuser.dat` to `ntuser.man`. Super-mandatory user profiles are created by renaming the shared folder with a `.man` extension.

Windows Server 2008 brings many new features and benefits that will drive a lot of migrations to the new operating system. In this chapter, many of these new additions were presented.

Anti-malware software is as important in a domain as it is for a home or small-office computer. It includes both anti-spyware software (such as Windows Defender) and antivirus software.

Chapter Essentials

Joining a domain   Know how to join a computer to a domain. Users must have a user account to log into the domain. Additionally, the user must use a computer that is a member of the domain.

Using authentication and authorization   Understand the difference between authentication and authorization. A user provides credentials such as a username and password to authenticate on the domain. Users can then be granted authorization based on permissions to access resources.

Identifying and resolving logon issues   Know some of the basics related to troubleshooting logon issues. Understand how cached credentials can be used. Know how to determine the logon context using tools such as whoami. Be aware of how a user will be stopped from logging in to an account at certain times if logon restrictions are used.

Understanding user profiles   Be aware of the different types of user profiles. You should know that profiles are created the first time a user logs on. A standard profile is stored on the local system. A roaming profile is stored on a central server and can be used by a user no matter which computer they log onto. Mandatory profiles start as a roaming profile but it can't be modified. The ntuser.dat file is renamed to ntuser.man.

Running anti-malware software   Be aware of the dangers of viruses, worms, and other malicious software (malware). Windows Defender is a free product in Windows 7 and can be used to combat spyware. Other third party anti-malware software should also be installed on your system.

Chapter

10

Managing Windows 7 with Group Policy

TOPICS COVERED IN THIS CHAPTER INCLUDE

✓ Group Policy and the GPMC

✓ Group Policy settings

Group Policy is one of the primary tools you have available to manage users and computers within a domain. It doesn't matter how many users or computers you have, you can manage all of them with a single Group Policy object (GPO).

When learning about Group Policy, it's important to understand how different GPOs are applied. A GPO can be linked to a site, domain, or OU, and where it's linked determines its scope. When multiple GPOs are applied, the settings are merged. To determine what settings apply, you need to understand the order of precedence with multiple GPOs. Because there are too many GPO settings to cover them all in a single chapter of this book, you will learn about a few of them here.

Group Policy and the GPMC

Group Policy is a group of technologies that allows administrators within a domain to configure a setting one time and have it apply to multiple users or computers. Group Policy settings can be configured using the *Local Computer Policy* or using the *Group Policy Management console* (GPMC) in a domain.

As a comparison, Figure 10.1 shows the Local Computer Policy for a Windows 7 computer, and Figure 10.2 shows the *Default Domain Policy* for a domain. There are some important differences.

FIGURE 10.1 Local Computer Policy for a single computer

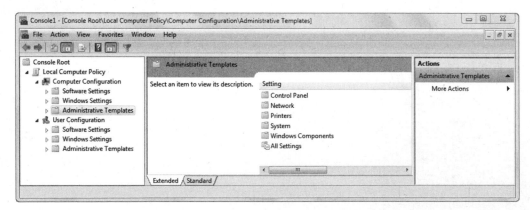

FIGURE 10.2 Default Domain Policy for the entire domain

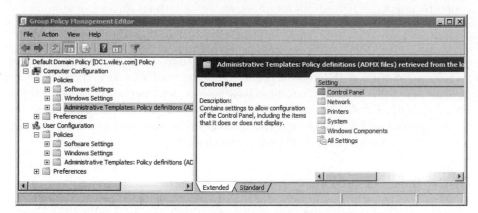

First, the Local Computer Policy affects only the local machine. If only the Local Computer Policy is used, each individual computer must be modified. The Default Domain Policy affects all users and computers in the domain. Other *Group Policy objects (GPOs)* can be created in a domain that will affect all the user accounts and computer accounts in a site or all the accounts in an Organizational Unit (OU).

> When you create a reference computer that will be used as an image, the Local Computer Policy is useful to configure settings that will be the same in all deployed images.

Second, domain policy includes policies and preferences. Any settings in the Policies node are enforced and cannot be changed by users once the settings are applied. Settings in the Preferences node are set but aren't enforced. In other words, users can override the settings in the Preferences node.

Group Policy settings are organized in the following nodes:

Software Settings This node can be used to deploy software to clients. Software deployed with Group Policy can be automatically installed on computers or installed based on a user's action. For example, a Group Policy–deployed application can appear on a user's Start menu and be installed when the user first selects it or deployed to a computer and installed the next time the computer restarts.

Windows Settings This node includes Security Settings and Scripts for the computer and also Folder Redirection and Internet Explorer Maintenance for the user. Scripts can be configured to run when the computer starts or stops and when a user logs on or logs off. Security settings will be explored further in Chapter 11, "Managing Security in Windows 7."

Administrative Templates   This node includes a large assortment of settings that can be used to modify and manage the user's environment. These settings directly modify the Registry of the client computers.

There are literally thousands of Group Policy settings. One of the first things to grasp is that you'll never learn them all. What you should concentrate on first is how Group Policy works. Then, as you work with Group Policy, you'll be exposed to more and more settings.

The good news is that most of the settings have built-in documentation. When you find the setting in the GPMC, you also find the documentation. In addition, there's a built-in search feature that makes it easier to find Group Policy settings in the Administrative Templates node. You'll see how to use the search feature later in this chapter.

Enabling a GPO Setting

Most GPO settings have one of three options that can be applied: Not Configured, Enabled, and Disabled. Figure 10.3 shows an example of an Administrative template setting that can be used to set the roaming profile for all users.

FIGURE 10.3   GPO setting to set roaming profiles for all users

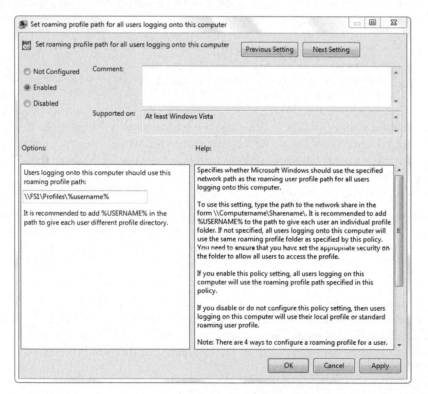

Not Configured   Not Configured simply means that the setting hasn't been set. If this setting isn't configured by any other GPOs, the user will be able to modify the setting on the local computer.

Enabled   When a setting is enabled, it will be applied, and if the setting has additional options, they can be configured when it is enabled. For example, in Figure 10.3, the roaming profile path is set as \\FS1\Profiles\%username%.

Disabled   When a setting is disabled, it prevents any options for this GPO from being applied. As an example, if a previously applied GPO has enabled the setting, the Disabled setting will prevent the previously applied GPO from taking effect.

Exercise 10.1 walks through the steps of viewing the Local Computer Policy and enabling a setting.

EXERCISE 10.1

Viewing the Local Computer Policy and Enabling a Setting

1. Launch the Group Policy Editor for the Local Computer Policy by clicking Start, typing **Group** in the Search text box, and clicking Edit Group Policy. Alternatively, you can create an MMC using these steps:

   a. Click Start, type **MMC** in the Start Search box, and press Enter. If User Account Control prompts you to continue, click Yes.

   b. Click File ➢ Add/Remove Snap-in.

   c. Select Group Policy Object Editor and click Add.

   d. The Welcome to the Group Policy Wizard appears, with Local Computer selected as the Group Policy object. Click Finish. Click OK.

2. Expand Local Computer Policy. You'll see a Computer Configuration node and a User Configuration node. Browse to the Computer Configuration ➢ Windows Settings ➢ Security Settings node. This node includes many of the security settings, including Account Policies and Local Policies.

3. Browse to the Computer Configuration ➢ Administrative Templates ➢ System ➢ User Profiles node. This node includes several settings that can be used to configure profiles for users.

4. Browse to the Computer Configuration ➢ Administrative Templates ➢ System node. This includes several nodes that can be used to control different functions of the operating system. Feel free to browse around to different nodes. As long as you don't enable any settings, nothing will be modified.

5. Select the User Configuration ➢ Administrative Templates ➢ Start Menu And Taskbar node. Double-click Remove Games Link From Start Menu. Click Enabled. Your display will look similar to the following graphic. Click OK.

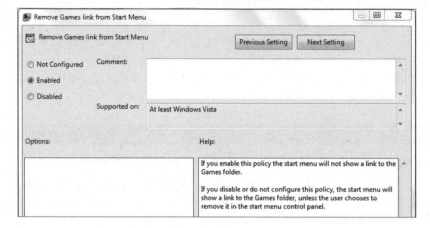

6. Click Start. You'll notice that the Games link is no longer on the Start menu. Note that this doesn't actually remove the games. If Chess Titans is installed, you can still type in Chess in the Start Search text box to access the Chess game.

7. Return to the Local Group Policy Editor. Double-click Remove Games Link From Start Menu. Click Not Configured and click OK.

8. Click Start. You'll notice that the Games link has reappeared on the Start menu.

Applying Multiple GPOs

It's possible for multiple GPOs in a domain to apply to any individual user account or computer account. When that occurs, the settings are merged.

If the GPO settings are different, all the settings are applied. For example, one GPO could be used to configure all computers to download and install updates automatically, and another GPO could configure all computers to use roaming profiles. These two settings are different and do not conflict with each other, so both settings will apply.

However, if any of the same GPO settings are used with different parameters, there's a conflict. As an example, one GPO could configure clients automatically to download updates and notify clients when they are ready to be installed, and another GPO could configure clients automatically to download updates and install them without user intervention. This is a conflict.

When there's a conflict, the last GPO applied wins. This is an important phrase—*the last GPO applied wins*. It will help you understand many of the scenarios with GPOs.

There are some exceptions to the "last GPO applied wins" rule. These include using the Enforced option and Loopback Processing. Both of these exceptions will be covered later in this chapter.

As an example, imagine that Local Computer Policy is configured on a reference computer, as shown in Figure 10.4. Updates will automatically be downloaded and the user will be prompted to install the updates. Windows Deployment Services (WDS) can be used to capture the image of the reference computer and then deploy the image to 100 clients in the domain.

FIGURE 10.4   Local Computer Policy used for Automatic Updates

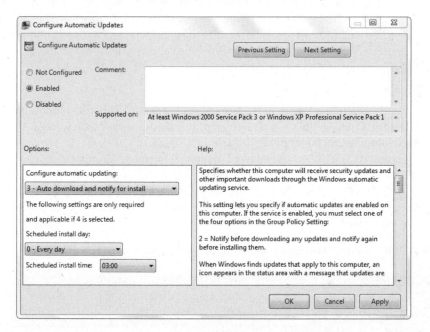

Unfortunately, users are not installing these updates when they're being notified that the updates are ready to be installed. You could configure the Default Domain Policy with option 4—Auto Download And Schedule The Install. Now there's a conflict. The Local Computer Policy says one thing, and the Default Domain Policy says something else. The Default Domain Policy wins because it was applied after the Local Computer Policy.

Only Group Policy settings that are set to Enabled or Disabled are evaluated when Group Policy is applied. If the setting is set to Not Configured in one GPO but set to Enabled in another GPO, this is not considered a conflict. The setting that is set to Enabled is applied.

GPO Scope

The *GPO scope* refers to where it is applied. A Local Computer Policy applies to only a single GPO, but other GPOs can apply to many users and computers in the organization.

GPOs can be created and linked to sites, domains, and OUs. Where a GPO is linked determines which users and computers will have the GPO settings applied. Any users or computers within the scope of a GPO will inherit the settings of the GPO. If a user or computer is within the scope of multiple GPOs, it will inherit the settings of all the GPOs.

> Even though a user or computer object within the scope of multiple GPOs will inherit the settings of all GPOs, all the settings won't necessarily apply. You'll see later in this chapter how conflicts are handled. In general, if there is a conflict with any settings, the last setting applied wins. This default behavior can be modified using different advanced GPO settings, which are also covered later in this chapter.

Domain Scope

GPOs linked to the domain apply to all accounts in the domain. When a domain is first created, the Default Domain Policy is also created. It includes some basic settings that apply to all user and computer accounts in the domain.

Consider Figure 10.5. It shows the Active Directory Users and Computers console in the Wiley.com domain. There are multiple OUs (Domain Controllers, Servers, Sales, and IT) and containers within the OUs. The East and West OUs are children of the Sales OU, but all of the other OUs and containers are on the same level and don't have a parent/child relationship with each other.

FIGURE 10.5   Active Directory Users and Computers showing OUs and containers

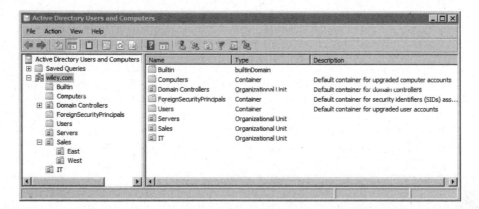

The Default Domain Policy applies to any accounts that are in any of the OUs or containers in the domain. This includes the Users and Computers container and any accounts in child OUs. Another way of saying this is that GPO settings applied at the domain level are inherited by all the OUs and containers in the domain.

> A container looks similar to a folder in Active Directory Users and Computers. The Computers container is the default location for new computers that join the domain, and the Users container holds the Administrator user account and some groups. OUs have an additional icon within the folder, and the only default OU in a domain is the Domain Controllers OU. All other OUs are created by an administrator.

GPOs are not inherited between domains. In other words, if a forest has a root domain of Wiley.com and a child domain named Propubs.Wiley.com, any GPOs applied to the Wiley.com domain are not inherited by the Propubs.Wiley.com domain.

OU Scope

GPOs linked directly to an OU have a scope of that OU. All of the GPO settings apply to accounts in that OU. In addition, any child OUs inherit the settings of GPOs applied to the parent OU.

As an example, consider Figure 10.6, which shows the Group Policy Management console (GPMC) with the Domain Controllers OU selected. The *Default Domain Controllers Policy* is linked to the Domain Controllers OU and listed right below it in the figure. Both are created when the domain is created. Domain controllers are automatically added to the Domain Controllers OU, so this GPO applies to the domain controllers in the domain (as long as they aren't removed from the Domain Controllers OU).

FIGURE 10.6   Group Policy Management console showing OUs

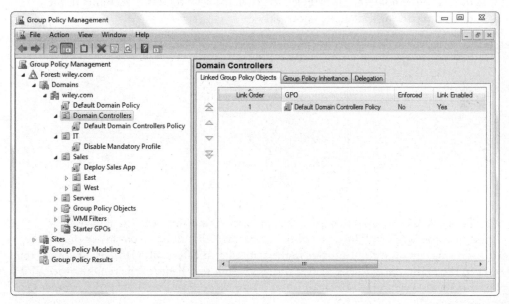

Two additional GPOs have also been created. The Disable Mandatory Profile GPO is linked to the IT OU and applies only to users and computers in the IT OU. The Deploy Sales App GPO is linked to the Sales OU. The East and West OUs are both children of the Sales OU, so the Deploy Sales App GPO applies to all accounts in the Sales OU, the East OU, and the West OU.

You can see the hierarchical relationships among the domain, OUs, and child OUs in the GPMC. The OUs and containers are indented to show they are children of the domain. The East and West OUs are indented to show they are children of the Sales OU. Child OUs inherit GPO settings from the parent.

The Default Domain Controllers Policy does not apply to any users in the IT, Sales, or Servers OUs because these are all peers. Similarly, the Disable Mandatory Profile GPO applies to accounts in the IT OU but does not apply to accounts in any other OUs or containers.

Site Scope

A site is a group of well-connected computers or subnets used for multiple-location environments. As an example, imagine a company with a main location in one city and a branch office in another city. Individually, each location is well connected using 1Gbs local area networks. However, the locations are connected to each other using a T1 line at about 1.544 Mbs. Although a T1 line is not bad for a WAN link, it has only about 1.5 percent of the bandwidth available within the LAN.

Now the organization wants to deploy Microsoft Office to clients using Group Policy. Figure 10.7 shows an ineffective method of deploying the application with a single GPO (GPO1) linked to the domain. This single GPO would apply to all the accounts in the domain (including all the accounts in both sites).

FIGURE 10.7   Using a single GPO to apply settings to different sites

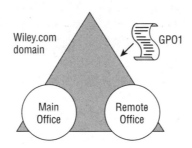

When a single GPO is used to deploy the application to both sites, it will have to be deployed over the WAN link for some of the clients, which will be much slower than if the application was deployed from a server in the same site. If Microsoft Office is deployed from a server in the main office, it will go over the WAN link for clients in the remote office. If it's deployed from a server in the remote office, it'll have to go over the WAN link for users in the main office.

Instead, two separate GPOs (GPO2 and GPO3) can be used, as shown in Figure 10.8. GPO2 can deploy the application from a server in the main office to users in the main office. GPO3 can deploy the application from a server in the remote office to users in the remote office.

FIGURE 10.8   Deploying an application to two sites using two GPOs

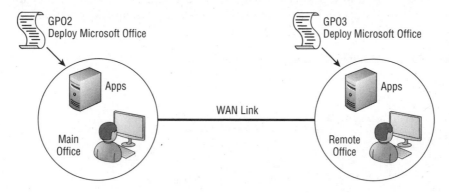

 While it isn't efficient to use a single GPO to deploy applications to multiple sites, it is efficient to deploy settings to multiple sites with a single GPO. For example, if you want to configure computers to use automatic updates, it isn't necessary to create separate GPOs if the organization has multiple sites.

GPO Order of Precedence

Since the last GPO applied wins, it's important to understand the order in which GPOs are applied. This is also known as the order of precedence, and the order is Local Computer Policy followed by site, domain, and OU GPOs.

Local Computer Policy   This is applied first. Within a domain, the Local Computer Policy is always overwritten if there is any conflict.

Site Group Policy   Site GPOs are applied after the Local Computer Policy. If there any conflicts, settings in the site GPO take precedence.

Domain Group Policy   Any GPOs that are applied at the domain level override the Local Computer Policy and any site GPOs (if they exist). The Default Domain Policy is automatically created in a domain when the domain is created. It's also possible to create other domain GPOs at the domain level.

Organizational Unit Group Policy GPOs can be created and applied to OUs. When this is done, an OU GPO overrides any GPOs applied at the local, site, or domain levels. If child OUs are created and GPOs are applied to the child OUs, the GPOs applied to the child OUs are applied after parent OUs and take precedence.

As an example, consider Figure 10.9, which shows a domain with multiple OUs and multiple GPOs. Look at these GPOs to see if you can determine the effective policy for users who have their accounts in different OUs. The relevant Group Policy settings are explained in the following bullets.

FIGURE 10.9 Multiple GPOs applied at multiple levels

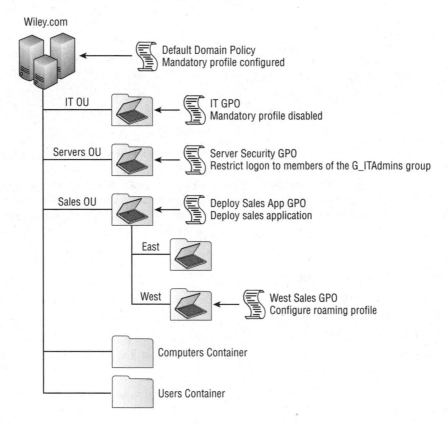

 In Figure 10.9, the IT OU, Servers OU, Sales OU, and Computers and Users containers are all considered peers; they are on the same level directly under the domain. The East and West OUs are children of the Sales OU.

- **Default Domain Policy.** Among other settings, this GPO has set a roaming profile path for all users that is configured as a mandatory profile by renaming the `ntuser.dat` file to `ntuser.man`. This setting is in the Computer Configuration ➢ Policies ➢ Administrative Templates ➢ System ➢ User Profiles node as Set Roaming Profile Path For All Users Logging Onto This Computer.

- **Server Security GPO.** This GPO has modified the Allow Logon Locally user right to allow only members of the Administrators or G_ITAdmins group this right. Normally, users can log on to any server in the domain except for domain controllers. This setting is in the Computer Configuration ➢ Windows Settings ➢ Security Settings ➢ Local Policies ➢ User Rights Assignment node.

- **Deploy Sales App GPO.** This GPO will be used to deploy a Sales User application to users. This setting is in the User Configuration ➢ Policies ➢ Software Settings ➢ Software Installation node.

- **West Sales GPO.** This GPO has set a roaming profile path for all users.

Consider the following scenarios, and see if you can determine the results based on the GPOs shown in Figure 10.9.

1. If a user logs on using an account in the IT OU, what kind of user profiles will be used?

2. Who can log on to servers placed in the IT OU?

3. Who can log on to servers placed in the Servers OU?

4. Who will receive the Sales application?

5. If a user logs on using an account in the West OU, what kind of user profiles will be used?

Here are the results with a short explanation of how the policy is applied.

1. Local user profiles will be used. Both the Default Domain Policy and the IT GPO are applied. The Default Domain policy configures a mandatory roaming profile, but the IT GPO disables roaming profiles. This is a conflict and the last GPO applied wins. Since the IT GPO is applied after the domain GPO, the IT GPO is the winning GPO.

2. Any user in the domain can log on to servers placed in the IT OU. By default, users can log on to any computer in the domain except for domain controllers. This is not being modified by Group Policy for this OU.

3. Only members of G_ITAdmins group can log on to these servers. The Server Security GPO is restricting this right to this group. The G_ITAdmins group would need to be created if it doesn't exist. Then any users or groups (such as administrators in the IT department and domain administrators) would be added to this group.

4. All the users in the Sales OU, the East OU, and the West OU will receive the Sales application. The GPO deploying this application is linked to the Sales OU. Since the East and West OUs are children of the Sales OU, they inherit the settings from this GPO.

5. Roaming profiles will be used (but not mandatory roaming profiles) by users in the West OU. The Default Domain Policy sets mandatory profiles, but it is overridden by the West Sales GPO.

RSAT and the Group Policy Management Console

The *Remote Server Administration Tools (RSAT)* for Windows 7 can be installed on a Windows 7 computer to enable IT administrators to manage roles and features on servers in the domain. Windows Server 2003, Windows Server 2008, and Windows Server 2008 R2 servers can all be managed using RSAT.

> There are different versions of RSAT for Windows Vista and Windows 7. The Windows 7 version includes the ability to manage up to Windows Server 2008 R2, whereas the Windows Vista version includes only the ability to manage roles and features up to Windows Server 2008.

RSAT includes the Group Policy Management console, which is the primary tool used to manage Group Policy. The GPMC is automatically installed on a domain controller when it is promoted. However, additional settings are available on a Windows 7 and Windows Server 2008 R2 GPMC that you won't see on the GPMC installed on Windows Server 2008.

After installing RSAT on a Windows 7 computer, you enable the desired features via Control Panel. Figure 10.10 shows the Windows Features dialog box with all of the Remote Server Administration Tools. In the figure, only Group Policy Management Tools are added, but as you can see there are many more tools you can add.

FIGURE 10.10 Adding RSAT features to Windows 7

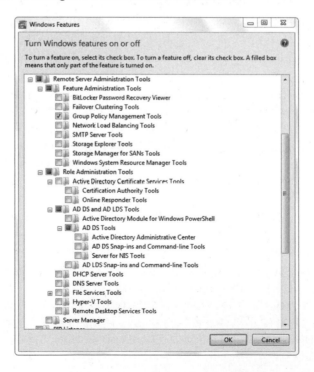

You can download RSAT for free from Microsoft's download site (`http://www.Microsoft.com/downloads`) by searching on "RSAT Windows 7." Both 32-bit and 64-bit versions are available. The 32-bit version includes the x86 prefix, and the 64-bit version includes the amd64 prefix. You should download the version to match the architecture of your Windows 7 system.

After downloading RSAT, you can follow the steps in Exercise 10.2 to install it on a Windows 7 system and enable the GPMC. While this activity adds only the GPMC, you can easily install additional features from the Windows Features dialog box.

EXERCISE 10.2

Installing Remote Server Administration Tools

1. Launch Windows Explorer and locate the RSAT file you downloaded. Double-click the file to open it.

2. When prompted to install an update (KB958830), click Yes to continue.

3. Review the license terms, and select I Accept.

4. When the installation completes, click Close. Microsoft Help will launch with information on RSAT.

5. Click Start ➤ Control Panel ➤ Programs. Click Turn Windows Features On Or Off.

6. Expand the Remote Server Administration Tools, and select Group Policy Management Tools. If desired, select additional tools to install. Click OK.

   After a moment, the installation will complete. The Group Policy Management console will be available via the Administrative Tools menu.

7. Launch the GPMC using one of two methods.

   a. Click Start, type **Group** in the Start Search box, and press Enter.

   b. If Administrative Tools is on the Start menu, click Start ➤ Administrative Tools ➤ Group Policy Management.

 You can add the Administrative Tools menu to the Start menu with the following steps. Right-click Start and select Properties. Click Customize from the Start Menu tab. Scroll down to the bottom, and select Display On The All Programs Menu And The Start Menu. Click OK twice.

As long as you're logged on to a domain account with permissions to at least read Group Policy in the domain, you'll be able to launch and view the Group Policy Management console. Members of the domain Administrators, Domain Admins, and Enterprise Admins groups will be able to create and apply GPOs.

Exercise 10.3 shows how to navigate the GPMC and a GPO.

EXERCISE 10.3

Navigating the GPMC and a GPO

1. Launch Group Policy Management by clicking Start ➤ Control Panel. Enter **Admin** in the Control Panel Search text box and select Administrative Tools. Double-click Group Policy Management.

2. Expand Forest ➤ Domains and your domain. Right beneath your domain name, you'll see the Default Domain Policy. This policy applies to all users and computers in the domain.

3. Expand Domain Controllers. You'll see the Default Domain Controllers Policy. This policy applies to the Domain Controllers OU. Because only domain controllers should be in the Domain Controllers OU, this policy will typically be applied only to domain controllers.

4. With Domain Controllers selected, select the Group Policy Inheritance tab in the main window. Your display will look similar to the following graphic. You can see that this OU has two GPOs that will apply. The Default Domain Controllers Policy is directly linked to the OU, and the Default Domain Policy is inherited.

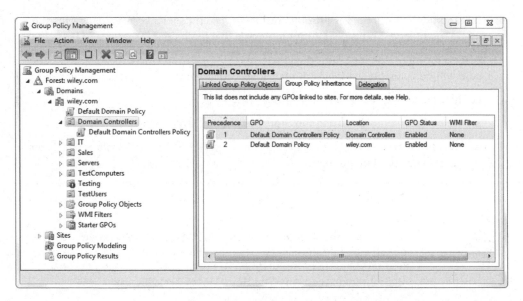

The Precedence column identifies which GPO takes precedence. Because the Default Domain Controllers Policy is applied after the Default Domain Policy, the Default Domain Controllers Policy takes precedence and has a Precedence value of 1.

5. Expand any of the OUs by clicking the plus (+) sign. If a GPO is linked to the OU, it will show, but all OUs won't have GPOs directly linked.

6. Expand Group Policy Objects. You'll see the Default Domain Controllers Policy, the Default Domain Policy, and any other GPOs that have been added after the domain was created.

7. Right-click Group Policy Objects and select New. You can name the GPO whatever you like, such as Practice GPO. Click OK. Note that while this GPO is created, it's not linked to a site, domain, or OU, so it will not apply to any clients.

8. Right-click the GPO and select Edit. This launches the Group Policy in the Group Policy Management Editor. You can browse through the settings the same way you can browse through the Local Computer Policy.

User vs. Computer Settings

As you've seen, Group Policy objects have two primary nodes:

Computer Configuration This node includes settings that apply to computers, no matter which user is logged on. These settings apply only if the computer is in the scope of the GPO.

User Configuration This node includes settings that apply to a user, no matter which computer the user logs on to. These settings apply only if the user is in the scope of the GPO.

On the surface, the settings that apply are simple to understand. Computer settings apply to computers, and user settings apply to users. However, there are a couple of subtleties that sometimes elude administrators.

It's common for a user object and a computer object to be in the same OU. But if the objects are in different containers, the settings are applied differently. For example, look at Figure 10.11. The User account for Joe is in the IT OU, and he's logging on to a computer in the Sales OU. The Sales OU has a GPO named NoGames that has enabled Remove Games Link From The Start Menu in the User Configuration node. This setting is located in the User Configuration ➤ Policies ➤ Administrative Templates ➤ Start Menu And Taskbar node.

Because Joe's user account is in the IT OU, the User Configuration settings on the Sales OU GPO don't apply to his account. The link to the Games menu will remain on his computer.

On the other hand, if Sally logs on to the same computer, the Games link will be removed because her user account is in the Sales OU.

FIGURE 10.11 User and Computer objects in different OUs

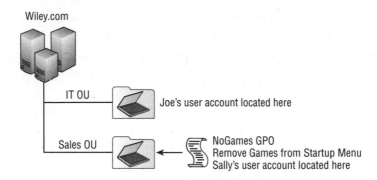

Exercise 10.4 demonstrates how Group Policy works when the user object is in one OU and the computer object is in another OU. It also demonstrates how you can reverse the default behavior using loopback processing.

If there are any conflicting settings between the User Configuration and the Computer Configuration nodes, the User Configuration settings will take precedence. To make this clear, it's important to know when GPOs are applied, and then you can use the simple rule of the last GPO applied wins.

Computer GPOs applied When the computer first boots, the computer account retrieves all applied GPOs. If there are any conflicts with any of these settings, the last setting applied wins. The logon screen appears when Group Policy has been applied.

In addition, the computer will check for updates or changes to computer Group Policy settings every 90–120 minutes (90 minutes with a random offset of 30 minutes).

User GPOs applied When a user first logs on, all the GPO settings that apply to the user are retrieved. If there are any conflicts with any of these settings, the last setting applied wins. If there are any conflicts with the computer settings, the user settings win. The desktop appears when Group Policy has been applied.

In addition, a system will check for updates or changes to user Group Policy settings every 90–120 minutes (90 minutes with a random offset of 30 minutes).

You can improve performance of Group Policy by disabling either the User or Computer Configuration settings. For example, if there aren't any computer settings in a GPO, you can right click over the policy in the Group Policy Editor, select Properties, and then select the Disable Computer Configuration Settings checkbox.

Forcing Group Policy Updates

When testing Group Policy changes, you usually don't want to wait for the default refresh time. In other words, when you modify a GPO, you don't want to wait 90 to 120 minutes to see if the setting has been applied as you configured it. Instead, you can use the *GPUpdate* command from the command line.

GPUpdate is commonly used to reapply all GPO settings for the currently logged-on user and computer. Many of the common switches used with GPUpdate are listed in Table 10.1.

TABLE 10.1   GPUpdate switches

Switch and Example	Comments
/Force GPUpdate /Force	Reapplies all Group Policy settings.
/Target GPUpdate /Target: Computer GPUpdate /Target: User	Instead of reapplying both user and computer Group Policy settings, you can apply only the computer or user settings.
/Logoff GPUpdate /Logoff	Causes a logoff after the Group Policy settings have been updated if the settings require a logon to be applied. This is good for some settings that are processed only when the user logs on, such as Software Installation and Folder Redirection settings. It has no effect if GPO settings do not require a logon to be applied.
/Boot GPUpdate /Boot	Causes a computer restart after the Group Policy settings are applied if the settings require a restart to be applied. This is good for some settings that are processed only when the computer starts, such as Software Installation settings. It has no effect if GPO settings do not require a reboot to be applied.

When using GPUpdate to update all GPO settings, it's best to use the /force command. Although documentation indicates that GPUpdate without the /force command will retrieve GPO settings that have changed, the results aren't consistent in practice. However, when you use the GPUpdate /force command, it will consistently update all of the settings.

Advanced Group Policy Settings

Occasionally, you may need to modify the default Group Policy behavior as applied to users and computers within the domain. When necessary, you can use the following four settings for some special circumstances.

- Block Inheritance
- Enforced
- Loopback Processing
- Filtering

Use of these settings should be the exception. In other words, their usage should be minimal. Group Policy can be complex on its own, but when you start modifying the default behavior with these exceptions, it can make the environment even more complex and harder to maintain.

Block Inheritance

It's possible to block the inheritance of all GPOs for an OU. For example, you could create an OU for testing purposes and decide that you don't want to allow GPOs from the domain or parent OUs to apply. You can enable the *Block Inheritance* setting on the OU, as shown in Figure 10.12. In the figure, block inheritance has been enabled on the Testing OU.

FIGURE 10.12 Blocking inheritance of GPOs

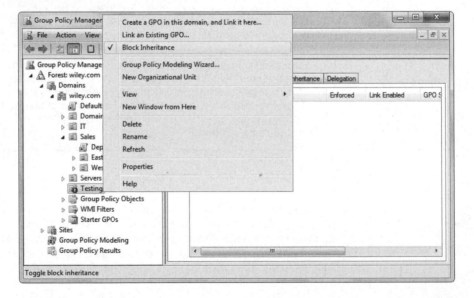

You can enable block inheritance by right-clicking the OU and selecting Block Inheritance. Once this is set, there will be an icon of an exclamation point in a blue circle to indicate block inheritance is enabled.

When using block inheritance, there are two important points to remember:

- You can block inheritance only at an OU. You can't block inheritance of a GPO.
- All GPOs are blocked. You can't pick and choose which GPO to block.

Enforced

Very often you'll want to configure settings and ensure that they are not overwritten or blocked. Normally, the last GPO applied wins, but you can use the Enforced setting to override this default behavior. In other words, if the *enforced* GPO is the first one applied and other GPOs have conflicting settings, the GPO with the Enforced setting will always win. In addition, if any OUs have the Block Inheritance setting enabled, the GPO configured with the Enforced setting will not be blocked.

As an example, you may have configured different security settings in the Default Domain Policy that you want to ensure are applied to all users and computers in the domain. You don't want the settings overwritten by conflicting GPOs or by the Block Inheritance setting on an OU.

Figure 10.13 shows the Default Domain Policy GPO set to Enforced. This setting is enabled by right-clicking the GPO and selecting Enforced. A GPO that has the Enforced setting will have an icon of a lock to indicate that Enforced is enabled.

FIGURE 10.13   Configuring Enforced on a GPO

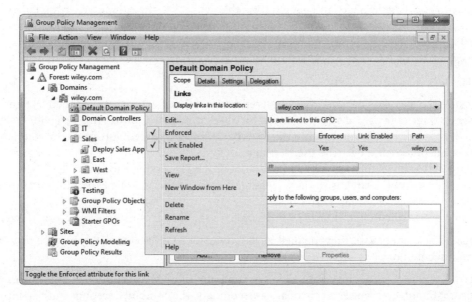

Real World Scenario

Configuring Enforced on the Default Domain Policy

The Enforced setting is often configured on the Default Domain Policy or another domain policy that administrators want to ensure is applied to all objects in the domain. This prevents administrators who have been delegated permissions at the OU level from blocking the domain-level policy.

In some larger enterprises, rights and permissions are often delegated to administrators to manage different OUs. When this is done, different IT professionals are granted full control at the OU, but they are not granted permissions at the domain level.

For example, an organization could have several departments such as Sales, Marketing, HR, and IT. Full control can be granted to a group of administrators to the Sales OU but no permissions at the domain level or to the other OUs.

Full control also includes the ability to block inheritance. This allows these administrators to block domain policies. While this may be acceptable for some policies, settings enforced on a domain-level policy ensure that the domain-level policy is not blocked.

Loopback Processing

Loopback Processing is a Group Policy setting that will cause the computer Group Policy settings to take precedence over the user settings. Normally, the order in which GPOs are applied is as follows:

1. Computer turns on and computer GPOs are applied.

2. User logs on and user GPOs are applied.

Because the user logs on after the computer starts, the user settings are applied last and the user settings take precedence. However, loopback processing allows this behavior to be reversed. In other words, you can use the Loopback Processing setting to have the computer settings take precedence over the user settings.

Figure 10.14 shows the User Group Policy Loopback Processing Mode setting. The Loopback Processing setting is in the Computer Configuration ➢ Policies ➢ Administrative Templates ➢ System ➢ Group Policy node.

When configuring loopback processing, you have the choice of using Replace or Merge.

Replace The computer settings defined in the computer's GPOs completely replace the settings that would normally apply to the user.

Merge The computer settings defined in the computer's GPOs are combined with the user settings that apply to the user. If there are any conflicts, the computer settings in the computer's GPOs take precedence.

FIGURE 10.14   Configuring loopback processing

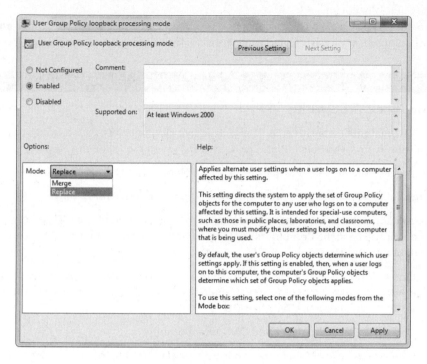

Exercise 10.4 demonstrates the default behavior of Group Policy and then shows how this can be reversed with loopback processing. In this exercise, you'll perform the following big-picture steps.

- Create two test OUs named TestComputer and TestUser.

- Place a computer in the TestComputer OU and a user in the TestUser OU.

- Create a GPO to remove the Games link and link it to the TestComputer OU using the settings in the Computer Configuration node.

- Log on to the computer, and verify that the Games link is still there.

- Move the user account to the TestComputer OU, and verify that the GPO removes the Games link.

- Move the user account back to the TestUser OU, and verify that the Games link returned.

- Enable loopback processing on the GPO applied to the TestComputer OU. Verify that the Games link is removed.

Note that this exercise uses only one simple setting—Remove Games Link From Start Menu. However, by moving the accounts so that they move in or out of the scope of the GPO, you can see how the GPO applies. In addition, this shows the subtlety of how the User Configuration and Computer Configuration settings apply to users or computers in the scope of the GPO, as discussed earlier. Last, it shows how loopback processing can modify the default behavior.

You can complete this exercise in the virtual environment of a domain controller and a Windows 7 computer that was created in Chapter 9, "Managing Windows 7 in a Domain."

EXERCISE 10.4

Using Loopback Processing

1. Log on to the domain controller, and launch Active Directory Users and Computers via the Administrative Tools menu. Create two OUs with the following steps:

    a. Right-click the domain and click New ➢ OU. Name the OU **TestComputer**.

    b. Right-click the domain and click New ➢ OU. Name the OU **TestUser**.

    c. Locate the Windows 7 computer account of the computer you'll use. The computer account will be in the Computers container unless it has been moved. Drag and drop it into the TestComputer OU.

    d. Locate a Windows 7 user account you'll use to log on to the computer. You can use Administrator account for the domain if you're using a virtual environment. Drag and drop it into the TestUser OU.

    e. Keep Active Directory Users and Computers open.

2. Launch the Group Policy Management console via the Administrative Tools menu. Create a GPO named RemoveGames linked to the TestComputer OU with the following steps:

    a. Browse to the Test Computer OU. Right-click the TestComputer OU, and select Create A GPO In This Domain And Link It Here. Name the GPO **TestRemoveGames**.

    b. Expand TestComputer. Right-click the TestRemoveGames GPO and select Edit.

    c. Browse to the User Configuration Policies Administrative Templates Start Menu And Taskbar node.

    d. Double-click Remove Games Link From Start Menu. Select Enabled and click OK.

    e. Leave the GPO open to modify later in this exercise.

3. Log on to the Windows 7 computer using the test account. Click Start, and you'll see that the Games link still appears.

    The GPO applied to the computer in the TestComputer OU doesn't affect the user because the user account isn't in the scope of the GPO.

4. Return to the domain controller. Drag and drop the user account from the TestUser OU to the TestComputer OU.

5. Return to the Windows 7 system and launch a command prompt. Enter **GPUpdate /Force** to force Group Policy to be updated now (instead of waiting for the 90–120 minutes refresh cycle). When it completes, click Start.

    You'll see that the Games link has disappeared. Because the user account is now in the scope of the GPO, the user settings from the GPO apply.

6. Return to the domain controller. Drag and drop the user account from the TestComputers OU back into the TestUsers OU.

7. Return to the Windows 7 system and access the command line. Enter **GPUpdate /Force** again to update Group Policy. When it completes, click Start and verify that the Games link has returned.

8. Modify the TestRemoveGames GPO to use loopback processing with the following steps:

    a. Return to the domain controller, and access the Group Policy Management Editor with the TestRemoveGames GPO open.

    b. Browse to the Computer Configuration ➢ Policies ➢ Administrative Templates ➢ System ➢ Group Policy node. Double-click the User Group Policy Loopback Processing Mode setting. Select Enabled and select Merge. Click OK.

9. Return to the Windows 7 system and access the command line. Enter **GPUpdate /Force** again to force Group Policy. When it completes, click Start and verify that the Games link is no longer there.

10. Access Active Directory Users and Computers on the domain controller, and return the user and computer accounts to their original locations. If you're using the virtual environment, the Administrator account should be returned to the Users container, and the Windows 7 account should be returned to the Computers container.

Filtering

GPOs normally apply to all users in the Authenticated Users group within the scope of the GPO. When users log in to a domain and are authenticated, they are automatically added to the Authenticated Users group, and the settings from the Default Domain Policy will apply to all users.

GPO filtering allows you to change the default behavior so that the GPO applies only to a specific group of users. Figure 10.15 shows the permissions for a Group Policy. The two most important permissions to understand are Read and Apply Group Policy, and you can see that these permissions apply to the Authenticated Users group.

FIGURE 10.15   Group Policy permissions

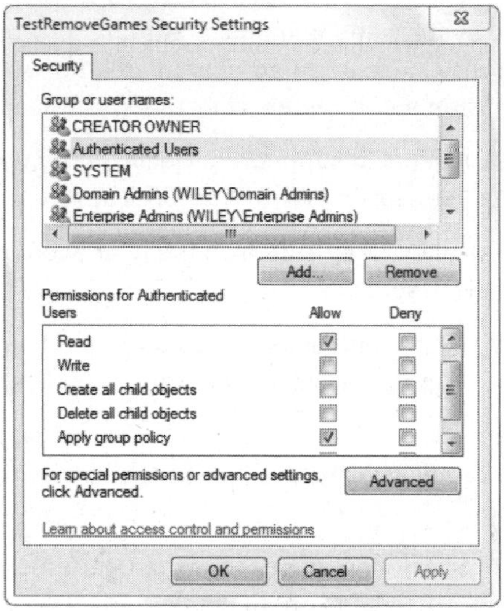

You can access the Security page with the following steps.

1. Select the GPO in Group Policy Management.

2. Select the Delegation tab.

3. Click Advanced.

4. Select Authenticated Users.

Read   This permission allows the settings in the GPO to be read. If only Read permission is applied, the GPO can be read but it won't be applied.

Apply Group Policy   This permission allows the settings in the GPO to be applied as long as the Read permission is also applied. If this setting is set to Deny for a group, the GPO will not apply to the group.

Other groups, such as the Domain Admins and Enterprise Admins, are granted other permissions that allow members to manage the GPO. These groups aren't assigned Apply Group Policy directly. However, since members of these groups become a member of the Authenticated Users group when they log on, GPOs will also apply to users in these groups.

What if you don't want a GPO to apply to a specific group, such as members of the Domain Admins group? You can then assign Deny Apply Group Policy to this group. Just as Deny takes precedence in NTFS, Deny takes precedence with GPO permissions.

On the other hand, you may want the GPO to apply only to a specific group. You can remove the Authenticated Users group, add another group, and assign the Read and Apply Group Policy permissions for the target group.

For example, if you want a GPO to apply only to a G_ITAdmins group that you've created, you would remove the Authenticated Users group and add the G_ITAdmins group.

Instead of adding groups from the permissions screen, you can also add groups from the Delegation tab. When adding groups to this tab, you're prompted to assign one of three permissions:

Read   Only Read permission is assigned. Apply Group Policy is not assigned.

Edit Settings   Read, Create All Child Objects, Delete All Child Objects, and some special permissions are assigned.

Edit Settings, Delete, Modify Security   Read, Create All Child Objects, Delete All Child Objects, and some special permissions that allow users to modify permissions are assigned.

It's important to note that none of the selections from the Delegation tab will automatically assign both Read and Apply Group Policy. If you use this tab, you'll also need to modify the permissions from the Security page shown earlier in Figure 10.15.

You can also use the Scope tab of a Group Policy to modify the security filtering. Figure 10.16 shows the Scope tab selected for a GPO. Notice in the Security Filtering section that the Authenticated Users group is shown.

FIGURE 10.16   Group Policy Management Scope tab used for filtering a GPO

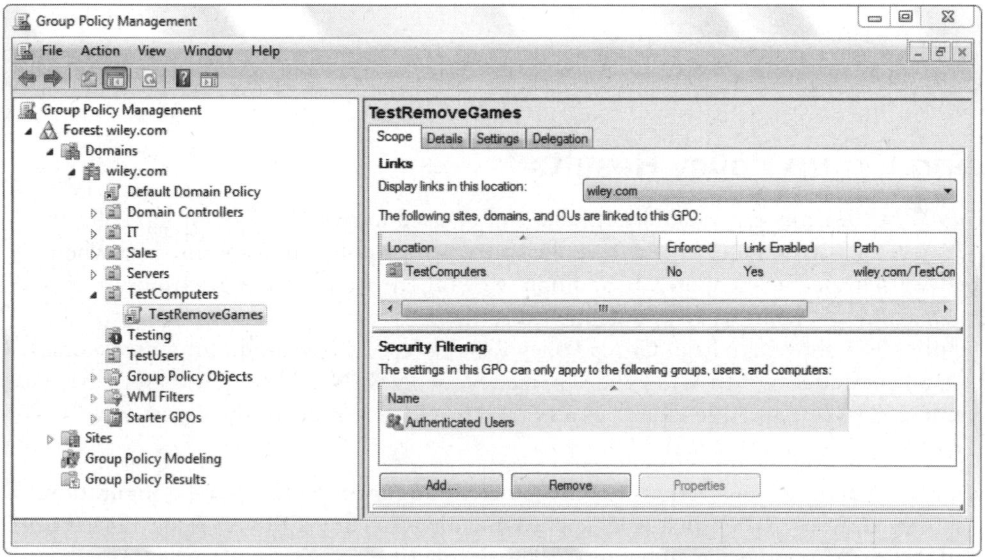

To filter a GPO using Security Filtering, you would remove the Authenticated Users group by selecting it and clicking Remove and add another group by clicking Add. The Read and Apply Group Policy permissions will be applied to any group you add here.

WMI Filtering

Any GPO can have a single Windows Management Instrumentation (WMI) filter applied to it. A WMI filter can be used first to inspect the system to check for a condition, and if the condition is met, the GPO can be applied.

As an example, you may want to deploy a GPO only to Windows XP computers but not to Windows 7 computers. A WMI filter could be created and linked to the GPO. Before the settings are applied, the WMI filter determines whether the system is running Windows XP and applies the GPO settings for only the XP computers.

WMI filters use WMI Query Language (WQL), which is beyond the scope of this book. However, you can usually find a sample WQL script to include in a WMI filter if needed. The most important thing to remember is that the scope of the GPO can be modified by linking the WMI filter to the GPO.

Here are some examples of what a WMI filter is used to check:

- The version of the operating system
- How much space is available on a disk drive
- Specific services running on a system
- The time zone of a system
- The existence of a specific hot fix
- The existence of specific software
- The make or model of the computer

Using Group Policy Results

Group Policy Results is a valuable tool that can be used to troubleshoot Group Policy. It allows you easily to determine what policies are being applied to a specific user when logged on to a specific computer. In addition, when there are conflicting settings, it helps you determine the winning GPO and applied setting.

Figure 10.17 shows a partial Group Policy Results report. It was run for a user named Sally on a computer named Win7 and is named Sally on WIN7. The report is formatted as a dynamic HTML page, allowing you to expand or hide elements of the report.

The report includes three tabs:

Summary   This page has sections for Computer Configuration and User Configuration. It identifies all of the GPOs that were applied and also lists any GPOs that may have been denied. A GPO could be denied because of Block Inheritance.

Settings   This tab lists all of the settings that are being applied. Details include the policy setting and the winning GPO that is applying the setting.

Policy Events   Group Policy–related events are listed here. These are the same events that can be viewed using Event Viewer but are filtered to show only Group Policy–related events.

FIGURE 10.17   Group Policy Results report

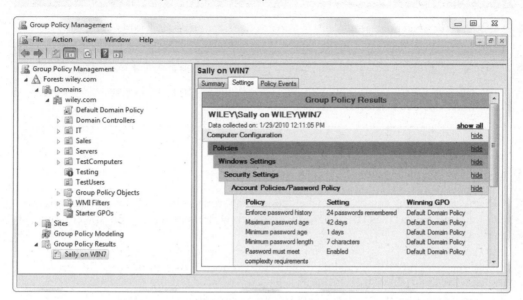

You should be aware of a few restrictions when running Group Policy Results:

- The computer must be a member of the domain and currently reachable on the network. WMI is used to query the computer, and if it is down or unreachable, you can't create a report.

- Only users who have logged on to the computer and have profiles on the computer can be included. WMI is used to identify who these users are, and you can select one of the users from a list.

Exercise 10.5 shows you how to create and view a Group Policy Results report. Make sure that both the Windows 7 computer and a domain controller are running.

EXERCISE 10.5

Using Group Policy Results

1. Launch the Group Policy Management console from the Administrative Tools menu.

2. Right-click Group Policy Results, and select Group Policy Results Wizard.

3. Review the information on the Welcome screen and click Next.

4. On the Computer Selection screen, you can select either This Computer or Another Computer. If you select Another Computer, ensure that it is a member of the domain and reachable on the network. Click Next.

EXERCISE 10.5   *(continued)*

5.   On the User Selection screen, select Current User or one of the listed users. Only users who have previously logged on to this computer will be listed. Click Next.

6.   Review the information on the Summary Of Selections page and click Next. Click Finish.

7.   You can now browse through the report. Note that this report will be saved on the computer and can be viewed at a later time if desired.

Using Group Policy Modeling

Group Policy Modeling can be used when designing Group Policy. It helps domain administrators determine what the effect might be if a specific user logs on to a specific computer in different situations.

For example, you may be considering moving users or computers to different OUs. You could use the Group Policy Modeling tool to run a report to determine what the effective GPOs and GPO settings will be if this change is made.

You can also simulate the effect of the following situations:

- Loopback processing is enabled.

- Users or computers are in different security groups.

- A WMI filter is applied.

- A user logs on with a slow network connection.

Group Policy Settings

As I mentioned earlier in this chapter, there are thousands of Group Policy settings that can be configured for users and computers. There's no way that we'll cover them all, and that's not the goal in this section.

One of the goals of this book is to cover the objectives in the 70-685 and 70-686 exams. Thus, in this section I've used these objectives as a guide to help determine what Group Policy settings to include. The settings included in this section are

- Managing Profiles

- Logon And Startup Scripts

- Deploying An Application

In addition to the settings in this chapter, some of the Group Policy settings are mentioned in other chapters when relevant. For example, in Chapter 11, several Group Policy settings related to security are discussed.

Managing User Profiles with Group Policy

Chapter 9 covered the different types of profiles that can be used. If you want to implement roaming profiles, you can use Group Policy to automate the setting or modify the default behavior.

As a reminder, a local profile is created on a system when a user logs on. Normally the profile is created from the Default Users profile, and then, as the user makes changes to the environment, the user's profile is modified to retain these changes.

If a roaming profile is used, the profile is retrieved from a server and copied down to the client's computer. Changes are copied back to the server when the user logs off unless the profile is configured as a mandatory profile. When a mandatory profile is used, changes can be made locally, but the changes are not copied back to the server, and the next time the user logs on, the local profile is again overwritten by the mandatory profile.

Figure 10.18 shows the User Profiles node, which includes several settings that can modify the default behavior of user profiles. You can access these settings from Computer Configuration ➢ Policies ➢ Administrative Templates ➢ System ➢ User Profiles.

FIGURE 10.18   Group Policy User Profiles node

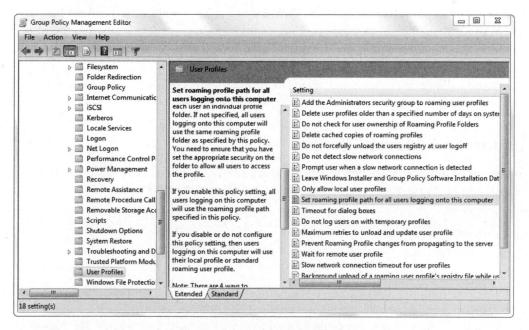

These are some of the key User Profile settings in this node:

Delete User Profiles Older Than A Specified Number Of Days On System   This can be useful to reclaim space consumed by older profiles. If this setting isn't enabled, older profiles will remain on the system until they're manually deleted by an administrator.

Delete Cached Copies Of Roaming Profiles   Roaming profiles are downloaded to the local system each time a user logs on. When a user logs off, the changes are uploaded. This setting will cause the local version of the profile to be deleted each time the user logs off.

Only Allow Local User Profiles   This can be used to prevent the use of roaming profiles on specific computers.

Set Roaming Profile Path For All Users Logging Onto This Computer   This allows you to set the roaming profile path for all users logging onto the computer. This is much more efficient than setting the roaming profile on a per-user basis using Active Directory Users and Computers.

Prevent Roaming Profile Changes From Propagating To The Server   This setting is similar to creating a mandatory profile because the profile cannot be changed. When a user logs off, changes to the profile are not merged to the server, so when the user logs on again, they have the same profile each time.

Some of the User Profiles settings in the User Configuration node can also be used to modify the default behavior. These are located in the User Configuration ➢ Policies ➢ Administrative Templates ➢ System ➢ User Profiles node.

Exclude Directories In Roaming Profile   When this setting is enabled, you can list the directories that should not be included in the roaming profile. This can be used to limit the size of the profile and the amount of bandwidth needed to download it.

Limit Profile Size   Because the profile includes the Documents folders, it can become large. This setting allows you to set a maximum size of either local profiles or roaming profiles. You can include a custom message to the user when the maximum size has been exceeded.

Logon and Startup Scripts

You can use Group Policy to run scripts automatically on computers. You have the option of configuring the scripts to run during one of the following four events:

- User logon
- User logoff
- Computer startup
- Computer shutdown

One of the common ways a script is used is to show a logon banner. Logon banners are often used to remind users of acceptable usage policies or other security-related policies. As an example, the following script could be used to show a message box when a user logs on:

```
msgbox "Usage of this computer is subject to monitoring at all times."
 & vbcrlf & vbcrlf &
"If you aren't an employee of Acme corporation you shouldn't be using
this computer. Log off now.", vbExclamation, "Usage Policy"
```

You can create this script in Notepad. You should enter it as a single line with no carriage returns and save it with a .vbs extension. The msgbox Visual Basic script command creates a message box, and this script creates the message box shown in Figure 10.19.

FIGURE 10.19　Script result

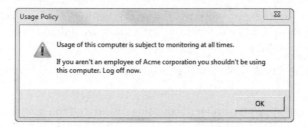

The first set of text (up to Log off now) identifies what will be displayed as the text. The & vbcrlf string represents a carriage return and line feed to start a new line; vbExclamation indicates that the warning triangle with an exclamation point icon should be included. The last set of text, Usage Policy, is used as the title of the message box.

> You can also configure messages that will be presented when users attempt to log on with the Interactive Logon: Message Text For Users Attempting To Log On and Interactive Logon: Message Title For Users Attempting To Log On Group Policy settings. These are available in the Computer Configuration ➤ Windows Settings ➤ Security Settings ➤ Security Options node.

Exercise 10.6 shows how to configure a logon script.

EXERCISE 10.6

Configuring a Logon Script

1. Launch Notepad by clicking Start, typing in **Notepad**, and pressing Enter.

2. Enter the following text in Notepad:

   msgbox "Usage of this computer is subject to monitoring.", vbInformation, Time

   vbInformation will display an information icon, and Time is a variable that will display the current time.

   (If you cut and paste this from the book's PDF file, the copied quote characters will cause this to fail. Delete the quotes and retype them within the Notepad document.)

3. Press Ctrl+S to save the file. Browse to a location on your hard drive where you can save the file. You can name it whatever you like but you must save it with the `.vbs` extension.

4. Launch Windows Explorer and browse to the location of the script you created. Double-click it to ensure it runs, and correct the script if there are any typos preventing it from running successfully.

5. Right-click the script and select Copy. You will paste this into another folder in a later step.

6. Launch the Group Policy Management console and expand the domain.

7. Right-click the Default Domain Policy and select Edit.

8. Browse to the User Configuration ➢ Policies ➢ Windows Settings ➢ Scripts (Logon/Logoff) node.

9. Right-click Logon and select Properties. Click Show Files. Right-click within the Windows Explorer window, and click Paste to paste your script into this folder. Close Windows Explorer.

10. Click Add. Click Browse. Select the script you pasted into this folder and click Open. Click OK, and your display will look similar to the following graphic.

11. Click OK and close all open windows. At this point, each time a user logs on to the domain, this script will run and display the message box.

Although this exercise showed how a basic script can be created and configured to run when a user logs on, you can use the same procedure to configure any scripts to run. Chapter 3, "Using the Command Prompt and PowerShell," covered some basic scripting techniques, but it really only scratched the surface. When it comes to scripting, there are almost no limitations. If you can't accomplish a task another way, you can almost always accomplish it with a script.

It is possible to have more than one script configured to run for any of the four events (logon, logoff, startup, and shutdown). By default, multiple logon and logoff scripts will run simultaneously, though you can change this with Group Policy.

In contrast, multiple startup and shutdown scripts are configured to run asynchronously by default, but you can also change this. When scripts are configured to run asynchronously, a script will not start until the previous script has completed.

In addition, with Windows 7 and Windows Server 2008 R2, you can include PowerShell scripts with Group Policy. Figure 10.20 shows the GPMC with the Logon Properties page and the PowerShell scripts selected. This looks the same in the Logon, Logoff, Startup, and Shutdown Group Policy Properties pages.

FIGURE 10.20   Configuring PowerShell scripts via Group Policy

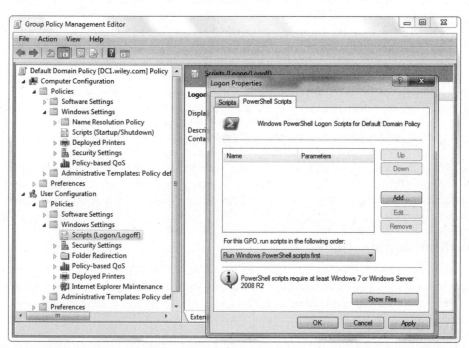

One difference with PowerShell scripts is that you can configure whether PowerShell scripts should be run first or last. This can be useful if multiple scripts are running and they conflict with one another.

Deploying an Application via Group Policy

You can also use Group Policy to deploy applications. For small-to-medium-size enterprises, this can be very useful to deploy, update, and maintain applications on multiple computers in a network.

Any application that is installed with a Microsoft installer (.msi) package can be deployed via Group Policy. The application is first copied to a share on a server that is available to clients in the network, and then the GPO is configured to deploy the application.

Applications are either assigned or published.

Assigning Applications

An application can be assigned to a computer or a user. When assigned to a computer, it is installed on the next startup cycle. When assigned to a user, it is advertised on the Start menu and installed when the user starts the program.

In addition, the application will be installed if the user attempts to open a file that requires it. For example, if Microsoft Excel is assigned to a user, it will be installed if the user double-clicks a document with an .xls or .xlsx extension.

In many environments, users have a single computer that they use all the time. If you want these users to have a specific application, assigning it to the computer is often the best method. You can force a reboot during nonworking hours so that you have a little control of when the application is deployed over the network.

> If you need more control over when an application is deployed, you can use advanced server products such as System Center Configuration Manager (SCCM). SCCM is a Microsoft server product that can be purchased, and it allows you to schedule deployments of applications and also deploy images of systems, deploy updates, and more.

If you expect few users to need the application at the same time, you can assign it to the users so that it's available on the Start menu. Because users will need it at different times, the actual deployment will be staggered.

Publishing Applications

Applications can be published to users but not to computers. When published to a user, an application is available to be installed via Control Panel by clicking the Get Programs link under Programs. The application will also be installed if the user attempts to open a file that requires it. Figure 10.21 shows how a program appears in Control Panel when it is published.

Publishing an application to a user can be useful if you want the application to be widely available but expect only a limited number of users to install it. Since it isn't advertised on the Start menu, a limited number of users will see it.

FIGURE 10.21   A published application available to a user from Control Panel

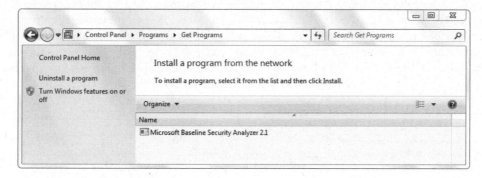

Configuring Software Installation

The Group Policy settings to deploy applications are located in the Computer Configuration ➤ Policies ➤ Software Settings ➤ Software Installation node for computers and the User Configuration ➤ Policies ➤ Software Settings ➤ Software Installation node for users.

If you want to deploy an application to users or computers in your network, you should take the following steps:

1. Stage the application. Create a share on a server and copy the .msi file to the share. The share should be available using a UNC path.

2. Decide if you want to deploy it to computers or users. This can vary depending on how many licenses you've purchased for the application and how the users use applications in your network.

3. If it will be deployed to users, decide whether you want to assign it or publish it. If it will be deployed to computers, it can only be assigned.

4. Create a GPO and link it to a site, domain, or OU based on the desired scope of the GPO.

5. Browse to the Software Installation node. Right-click the node, select New ➤ Package, and point to the package using the UNC path.

6. Select Assigned or Published.

AppLocker

AppLocker can be used to specify which users or groups can run particular applications. AppLocker uses rules that specifically allow or deny applications from running. It is intended to be an improvement over Software Restriction policies available before Windows 7 and Server 2008 R2.

You can access the AppLocker Group Policy settings in the Computer Configuration ➢ Policies ➢ Windows Settings ➢ Security Settings ➢ Application Control Polices node.

Figure 10.22 shows the AppLocker node in Group Policy. When you first configure a rule, you'll be prompted to create rules. These default rules are intended to ensure that normal operation of the system isn't negatively impacted by the rule. In the figure, the default rules are on the top and labeled Allow, and the one rule on the bottom labeled Deny is the rule created specifically to deny a script for users in the scope of the GPO.

FIGURE 10.22 AppLocker script rules

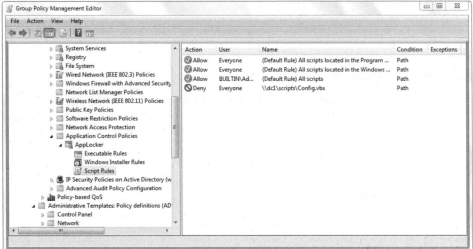

Three types of rules can be implemented:

- Executable Rules include files with the `.exe` and `.com` extensions.
- Windows Installer Rules include files with the `.msi` and `.msp` extensions.

Script Rules include files with the `.ps1`, `.bat`, `.cmd`, `.vbs`, and `.js` extensions.

It's also possible to configure DLL rules to restrict execution of `.dll` and `.ocx` files. However, using DLL rules will impact the performance of the system because each DLL that is accessed must be checked to see if it is allowed.

Two of the significant improvements of AppLocker over Software Restriction policies are as follows:

Per User and Per Group rules These are Software Restriction policies applied to all users within the scope of the GPO. AppLocker allows you to specify which users or groups should be granted or denied access.

Audit-only mode This is new and allows you to test the rules before they're deployed. The rules aren't enforced, but activity is logged.

Searching Group Policy

One of the strengths of Group Policy also becomes one of its weaknesses. Just about anything you want to manage or restrict for users and computers in a domain can be done with Group Policy. However, locating the setting that you need can be a challenge.

Thankfully, the GPMC that comes with Windows Server 2008 and newer versions includes a search feature. You can use this to search through the Administrative Templates node. As a reminder, the Administrative Templates node includes settings that will modify the Registry. This node is frequently used to control the user desktop and environment.

You can filter Administrative Template Group Policy settings based on properties, keywords, or requirements. Figure 10.23 shows the search screen. You can access this screen by right-clicking Administrative Templates in the Group Policy Object Editor and selecting Filter Options.

FIGURE 10.23   Group Policy Filter Options

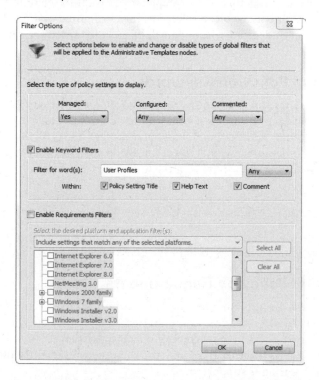

You can remove the filter by right-clicking Administrative Templates and selecting Filter On. The Filter On selection can be toggled on or off and will have a checkmark when enabled.

Searching Group Policy on Properties

You can filter the viewable Group Policy settings based on one of three properties. Each of these settings allows you to choose Yes, No, or Any:

Managed   When you select Yes, only managed settings are shown. Most Group Policy settings are managed, so this doesn't have much effect. An unmanaged Group Policy setting is typically used to set preferences for an operating system component.

Configured   Selecting Yes for this setting allows you to filter the view based on Group Policy settings that are set to Enabled or Disabled. If the Group Policy setting is set to Not Configured, it is not shown when the setting is set to Yes.

Commented   Administrators can add comments to any GPOs. These comments can be useful in the future if you're trying to remember why you configured a specific setting six months earlier. Selecting Yes for Commented shows only the GPOs that have comments.

These filters can be used together. For example, if you want to see only the configured settings that include comments, you can select Yes for Configured and Yes for Commented. Only the settings that include both selections will be included when the settings are combined.

Searching Group Policy on Keywords

The Keyword Filter allows you to enter any text to search for a relevant Group Policy. This is very useful if you have an idea of what you want to do but just can't find the setting.

As an example, you may want to manipulate user profiles but can't find the settings. You can enter *User Profiles* as the words to search. By default, the filter will search for any occurrence of your search word or phrase in the following:

- Policy Setting Title
- Help Text
- Comments

You can deselect any of these choices to limit the search.

Searching Group Policy on Requirements

The explanation of each Group Policy setting in the Administrative Templates node includes a Supported On section. Some are supported on Windows 2000 and above, some only on Windows 7, and others on a mixture of operating systems. Some settings apply only to applications such as Internet Explorer, and these settings identify the version of the application where the setting is supported.

You can use the Requirements Filters to search based on the different operating systems or applications. Filters are provided for the following:

Windows 2000 family   You can choose Windows 2000 without a service pack or with SP1, SP2, SP3, or SP4.

Windows XP   You can choose Windows XP without a service pack or with SP1 or SP2.

Windows Vista   You can choose Windows Vista without a service pack or with SP1.

Windows 7 family   Currently, only Windows 7 is available, but as service packs are released, these will likely be included if the Administrative Templates are updated.

Windows Server 2003   You can choose Windows Server 2003 without a service pack or with SP1 or SP2. You can also choose Windows Server 2003 R2.

Windows Server 2008   This includes the options of Windows Server 2008 and Windows Server 2008 R2.

BITS   Background Intelligent Transfer Service (BITS) versions 1.5, 2.0, and 3.5 can be selected.

Internet Explorer   Versions 3.0, 4.0, 5.0, 6.0, 7.0, and 8.0 can be selected.

Net Meeting   Version 3.0 is included.

Windows Installer   Versions 2.0, 3.0, and 4.0 can be selected.

Windows Media Player   Windows Media Player 8, 9, 10, and 11 can all be selected.

Figure 10.24 shows the Group Policy Management Editor with a filter enabled for Internet Explorer 8.0 settings. Many of the nodes that normally appear under Administrative Templates are not showing because they don't match the filter. You can also see an icon of a filter on the Administrative Templates nodes, which indicates that the filter is on.

FIGURE 10.24   Group Policy Management Editor with a filter enabled

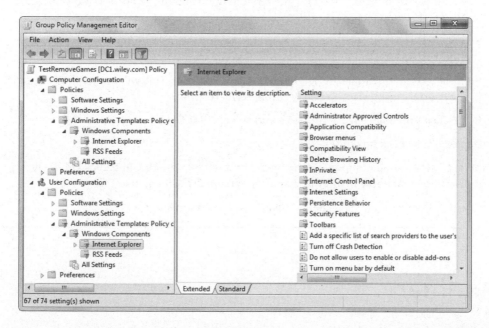

When searching with the Requirements Filters, you can choose to include settings that match *any* of the selected platforms or those that match *all* of the selected platforms. For

example, if you want to view only the settings that apply to Windows Vista or Windows 7, you can select these two families as the requirement and select Include Settings That Match Any Of The Selected Platforms.

You can use the Exercise 10.7 to see how to use these filters to locate settings. The exercise uses the Local Group Policy Editor, but it will work the same way on any GPO.

EXERCISE 10.7

Using a Filter to Locate Group Policy Settings

1. Launch the Local Group Policy Editor by clicking Start, typing in **Group**, and selecting Edit Group Policy.

2. Browse to the Computer Configuration ➤ Administrative Templates node. When you select the Administrative Templates node, an icon that looks like a funnel will appear on the editor's toolbar. This is the Filter icon. Also notice that there are five nodes within Administrative Templates (six if you count the All Settings node).

3. Right-click Administrative Templates, and select Filter Options.

4. Select Enable Keyword Filters. Ensure that Policy Setting Title, Help Text, and Comment are all checked. Type in **Profiles** and click OK.

5. The filter will be enabled, and only the System node and the Windows Components nodes will be showing.

6. Select each of the nodes to see the available settings. Only settings with the word *Profiles* in the settings title, help text, or comment sections are included.

7. Right-click Administrative Templates and select Filter On. This will toggle the filter so that it is off. All of the Group Policy settings will reappear.

8. Right-click Administrative Templates, and select Filter Options.

9. Deselect the check box for Enable Keyword Filters.

10. Select Enable Requirements Filters. Select Internet Explorer 8.0 and click OK. Only the settings that apply to Internet Explorer version 8.0 will appear.

11. Click the filter icon on the toolbar. The filter will be removed.

Summary

Group Policy is a powerful tool that can be used to manage user and computer objects within a domain. You can create and link a GPO to a site, a domain, or an OU. When multiple GPOs are applied, all of the settings are merged and applied. If there are any conflicts, the last GPO applied wins, and the order in which GPOs are applied is local, site, domain, and OU.

RSAT can be installed on Windows 7 computers to manage roles and features on servers in the domain. It includes multiple tools including the GPMC. In addition to learning the default behavior of Group Policy, you learned some of the advanced settings, including Block Inheritance, Enforced, Loopback Processing, and Filtering, and how to configure these settings using RSAT.

Several Group Policy settings were presented that can be used to manage objects in a domain. You saw how to configure user profiles, configure scripts, deploy applications, and implement AppLocker. Last, you saw how to search Group Policy Administrative Templates for specific Group Policy settings.

Chapter Essentials

Group Policy and the GPMC   Understand what Group Policy objects are and how they are used in a domain. Be aware that you can link GPOs to a site, a domain, or an OU, and understand that where you link the GPO determines its scope. Be able to identify the winning GPO based on the GPO precedence. Know how to install RSAT and use the Group Policy Management console.

Understand the effect of the advanced Group Policy settings. Block Inheritance will block all parent GPOs unless the GPO has Enforced set. Enforced will ensure that all settings in the GPO will apply even if there are conflicts and even if the Block Inheritance is enabled. Loopback processing allows the Group Policy settings for the computer to take precedence over the Group Policy settings for the user. Filtering can be used to cause a GPO to only apply to specific groups within the scope of the GPO.

Group Policy settings   Be aware of some commonly used Group Policy settings. Understand how to configure a logon or startup script. Know how to deploy applications to computers or users with Group Policy. Understand how AppLocker can be used to restrict applications on a per-user or per-group basis.

Chapter

11

Managing Security in Windows 7

TOPICS COVERED IN THIS CHAPTER INCLUDE

- ✓ User Account Control
- ✓ Security Policies
- ✓ Designing BitLocker Support
- ✓ Windows Firewall

Security is an integral part of any administrator's job. The number of possible attacks on any computer within a network continues to increase. Similarly, the amount of money and data lost because of attacks also continues to rise.

User Account Control (UAC) has been improved since it was first introduced in Windows Vista. It is an important tool that can be used to limit stealth malware attacks. A wide assortment of security settings is available in Group Policy. These can be used to configure password requirements, lockout policies, rights assignments, and much more. Windows Firewall can be another line of defense for a system. It can be used to control and limit unwanted network traffic and mitigate attacks on your Windows 7 computers.

User Account Control

User Account Control (UAC) provides an added layer of security to ensure that you are notified if changes to your system are attempted. UAC is intertwined with much of the underlying operations of Windows 7, but the core goal is to limit the capabilities of malicious software.

Chapter 8, "Accessing Resources on a Network," covered SIDs and DACLs. As a reminder, when a regular user logs on, an access token is created that includes the user's SID and the SIDs of any groups where the user is a member.

In earlier Windows systems, a significant risk was present if a user logged on with administrative permissions. If a system was infected with malware while a user was logged on with administrative permissions, the malware had administrative permissions and was able to do significant damage.

Corporate environments often implemented policies requiring administrators to use two accounts. One account was for regular usage. If administrative access was needed to perform tasks, only the administrative account was used, but only for the time needed to perform the task.

In Windows XP and Windows Server 2003, administrators were able to log on as a regular user and then use the Run As feature to run individual applications with administrative permissions. This reduced the risk of malware taking over the administrative account.

Windows Vista introduced UAC, and Windows 7 has improved on the functionality of UAC. The core goal remains to protect the system from malware that tries to modify settings. UAC requires any attempts to modify the system settings by an application to be approved.

The default UAC setting in Windows 7 separates the actions taken by the user from the actions taken by applications. In other words, if a user makes the change, they aren't prompted by UAC. If an application attempts to make a change, UAC does prompt for approval. This prevents malware from making unauthorized changes while reducing the number of UAC pop-ups when a user is making changes.

In Windows Vista, UAC prompted the user every time an action needed administrative privileges. This included every time an application tried to make a change and every time the user tried to make a change. This resulted in a significant number of UAC prompts and was one of the criticisms of Windows Vista.

UAC works by implementing something called Admin Approval Mode. Admin Approval Mode uses two access tokens when a user logs on to Windows 7 with an administrative account. One is for regular use, and the second is used only when administrative permissions are needed.

Standard user access token This is the token used for most regular work, such as launching and using applications. This token does not have any administrative privileges.

Administrator access token If an action requires administrative privileges, this token is used. UAC usually prompts the user to use this access token before the token is used.

Figure 11.1 shows the UAC screen that appears when the administrator access token is needed. The program name identifies the program that is requiring the elevated permissions. In the figure, the command prompt is being launched with administrative permissions.

FIGURE 11.1   User Account Control settings screen

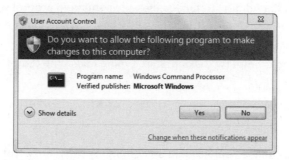

Control Panel includes an icon of a shield for any activity that requires UAC permissions. When you click one of these links, the UAC prompt will appear unless the default behavior has been modified.

A useful tool that shows you the different privileges that are available when the administrative token is used is the whoami command-line command. It can be used to get user name and group information along with assigned privileges or rights.

> The whoami command is also a quick way to determine the logon context of a user. When entered without a switch, it identifies the user in the format of computer\username or domain\username.

As an example, if a regular user account is used, whoami will show that only the following privileges are assigned:

- SeShutdownPrivilege shuts down the system.
- SeChangeNotifyPrivilege bypasses traverse checking.
- SeUndockPrivilege removes the computer from the docking station.
- SeIncreaseWorkingSetPrivilege increases a process working set.
- SeTimeZonePrivilege changes the time zone.

If the administrative account is used, there are over 20 privileges granted.

Exercise 11.1 shows how to use whoami and, more specifically, allows you easily to see the difference in the privileges assigned to the regular user and the administrator accounts.

EXERCISE 11.1

Using Whoami to View Privileges

1. Log on to Windows 7 with an account that has administrative permissions but is not the Administrator account.

   (If you log on with the Administrator account, the command prompt will always be launched with administrative privileges and you won't be able to see the differences.)

2. Launch a command prompt by clicking Start, typing **cmd** in the Start Search box, and pressing Enter.

3. Enter the following command:

   Whoami /all

   You can see details on the user account and group memberships. Notice that the BUILTIN\Administrators account is included, but the attribute specifies that this account is being used for Deny Only. In other words, rights and permissions are not being granted for this group. View the list of privileges listed at the end of the output. Leave this command-prompt window open.

4. Launch a command prompt with elevated permissions. Click Start, type **cmd** in the Start Search box, right-click cmd, and select Run As Administrator. If prompted by UAC, click Yes.

5. Enter the following command:

   Whoami /all

   Compare this output to that generated by whoami for the regular user account. The Administrator group isn't being restricted to Deny Only, and the list of privileges is extensive.

UAC Settings

Although the default setting for UAC provides good protection, you can modify the default behavior. You can access the UAC settings screen by clicking Start, entering UAC in the Start Search box, and pressing Enter. You can also access it by clicking Start ➢ Control Panel ➢ System And Security ➢ Action Center ➢ Change User Account Control Settings.

Figure 11.2 shows the User Account Control Settings screen with the default settings selected.

FIGURE 11.2   User Account Control Settings screen

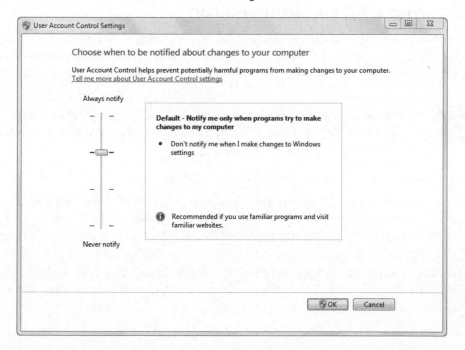

Always Notify   This is the way that UAC works in Windows Vista. UAC will notify you anytime you make changes to a Windows setting or a program tries to install software or make changes. This level of notification was annoying to many Windows Vista users and was one of the more common complaints. However, for users who routinely install new software and visit unfamiliar websites, it is recommended.

Default – Notify Me Only When Programs Try To Make Changes To My Computer   This setting will still notify you if an application makes changes to your system, but it doesn't notify you when you make changes to Windows settings. This is recommended if you use familiar programs and visit familiar websites.

Notify Me Only When Programs Try To Make Changes To My Computer (Do Not Dim My Desktop)   This setting is similar to the default setting, but it does add some risk. Normally the desktop is dimmed, preventing any action other than addressing the prompt. This setting doesn't dim the desktop. It may allow malware to interfere or dismiss the UAC prompt. This is not recommended.

Never Notify   This setting disables UAC. It is not recommended and is only included for programs that must run in Windows 7 but do not support User Account Control.

The dimmed desktop is also referred to as the secure desktop. When the desktop is dimmed, UAC doesn't allow any other actions except for a response to the UAC.

Configuring UAC via Group Policy

Group Policy includes several settings that you can use to modify the default behavior of UAC. The primary settings you'll modify are located in the Computer Configuration ➢ Policies ➢ Windows Settings ➢ Security Settings ➢ Local Policies ➢ Security Options node.

These settings can also be found in the Local Computer Policy in the Computer Configuration ➢ Windows Settings ➢ Security Settings ➢ Local Policies ➢ Security Options node.

The following list explains some of these Group Policy settings:

User Account Control: Run All Administrators In Admin Approval Mode   This setting turns on Admin Approval Mode for all administrators including the Built-in Administrator account. When this setting is disabled, all UAC policy settings are disabled for administrators.

User Account Control: Admin Approval Mode For The Built-in Administrator Account
This setting affects only users logged on using the built-in Administrator account, not users

in the Administrators group. When it is enabled, users who log in using the Administrator account will be prompted by UAC. This setting is disabled by default, meaning that anyone logged in with the local Administrator account will not be prompted by UAC. The administrator access token will be used by default whenever it is needed.

User Account Control: Behavior Of The Elevation For Administrators In Admin Approval Mode   This setting affects any user in the local Administrators group when Admin Approval Mode is enabled. When enabled it has several possible settings:

- Elevate Without Prompting
- Prompt For Credentials On The Secure Desktop
- Prompt For Consent On The Secure Desktop
- Prompt For Credentials
- Prompt For Consent
- Prompt For Consent For Non-Windows Binaries (Default)

User Account Control: Behavior Of The Elevation Prompt For Standard Users   If users are logged on with standard user accounts (non-administrator accounts), you can use this setting to control what happens if they try to do something that requires elevated permissions. The three choices are as follows:

- Prompt For Credentials On The Secure Desktop (Default)
- Prompt For Credentials
- Automatically Deny Elevation Requests

User Account Control: Switch To The Secure Desktop When Prompting For Elevation   If enabled, this setting overrides other settings and ensures that all UAC requests dim the desktop for administrators and standard users.

User Account Control: Detect Application Installations And Prompt For Elevation This setting is disabled by default for computers joined to a domain. When disabled, it allows applications to be deployed via Group Policy or advanced tools such as Systems Management Server (SMS) or Systems Center Configuration Manager (SCCM).

User Account Control: Only Elevate Executables That Are Signed And Validated   When this setting is enabled, only files that are signed with a certificate and can be verified via a certification authority are permitted to run. This setting is disabled by default.

User Account Control: Virtualize File And Registry Write Failures To Per-User Locations This setting allows some legacy applications still to operate in Windows 7. UAC prevents applications from writing data to protected locations and the application fails. However, enabling this setting allows the write failures to be redirected to user locations when the application runs. The application can still operate, but the data is stored in the user profile instead of modifying the system.

Security Policies

Chapter 10, "Managing Windows 7 with Group Policy," covered Group Policy in depth. Group Policy has numerous settings, and we certainly didn't cover them all in Chapter 10. Several of the important settings are related to security, and Group Policy has its own node for security.

Figure 11.3 shows the Security Settings node of Group Policy for the Default Domain Policy. As you can see, many security settings can be manipulated. Other security settings are found in the Administrative Templates node.

FIGURE 11.3   Group Policy Security Settings

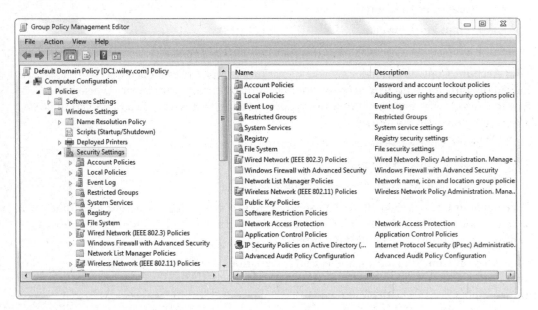

Similar settings can be found in the Local Computer Policy in the Computer Configuration ➢ Windows Settings ➢ Security Settings node. You can also access many of these settings for a single computer using Local Security Policy via the Administrative Tools menu.

The focus in this section is on the following nodes:

- Account Policies
- Local Policies
- System Services
- Removable Storage Access Policy

Local Security Policy vs. Group Policy

Group Policy can be configured via Local Computer Policy and via Group Policy objects linked to a site, domain, or OU. Instead of accessing the full Local Computer Policy and browsing to the Security Settings node, you can also access the Local Security Policy via the Administrative Tools menu. Only the Security Settings node is included in the Local Security Policy.

Figure 11.4 shows the Local Security Policy. It includes most of the same settings that are included in the Security Settings node of the Group Policy object shown earlier. The primary difference is that the Local Security Policy applies only to the local system, just as the Local Computer Policy applies only locally.

FIGURE 11.4 Local Security Policy MMC

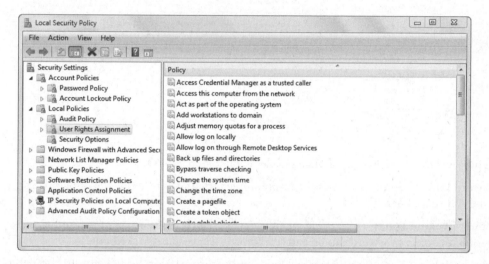

If you compare Figure 11.4 with Figure 11.3 shown earlier, it helps to see that the Security settings are just a small portion of the overall Group Policy.

The primary reason to use the Local Security Policy in a domain is when you're creating a reference computer that will be used as a source image. After creating the reference computer, you can use Windows Deployment Services to capture the image and deploy it to computers in your domain.

You would first install Windows 7 and any desired applications on the system. You could then use Local Security Policy to implement a baseline of security settings. Then each computer would start off with this baseline. Once the computer joins the domain, additional settings will be applied with Group Policy.

Account Policies

The *Account Policies* node includes three nodes that can be used to configure different settings. Figure 11.5 shows the Account Policies node with the Password Policy node selected.

FIGURE 11.5   Account Policies

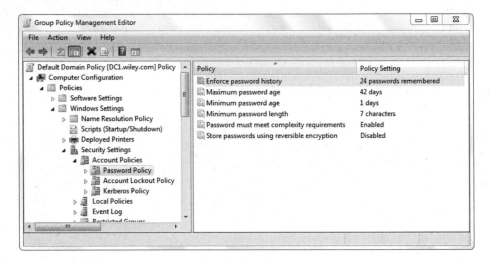

These are the three Account Policies nodes available in a GPO:

Password Policy   Settings such as the minimum length and maximum age of passwords can be configured here.

Account Lockout Policy   This node includes settings such as the maximum number of times an incorrect password can be entered before an account is locked out.

Kerberos Policy   Kerberos settings include time synchronization for tickets and computers.

The *Password Policy* and *Account Lockout Policy* are available in the Local Security Policy and a Group Policy object within a domain. However, the Kerberos Policy is available only in a GPO within a domain.

If you look closely at Figure 11.5, you'll notice a difference in the icons for all three Account Policies nodes from the icons for other Security Settings policies. The icon includes two servers and a script. However, the Local Policies and Event Log policies are just a single server and a script.

The different icon is a subtle indication that these settings are different than other settings. The difference is that these Account Policies settings apply only at the domain level. In other words, if you created a GPO with these settings and linked it at the site or OU level, these settings would not apply. They are applied only when linked at the domain level. It's common to configure these settings in the Default Domain Policy.

Windows Server 2008 introduced a new feature that allows administrators to create Password Settings objects (PSOs) that can be used to configure Account Policies settings for specific groups. The GPO settings will be applied only at the domain level, but a PSO can be applied to a group.

The Password Policy and Account Lockout Policy settings can both be applied in the Local Security Settings. These settings will still apply to the local computer unless the computer is a member of a domain and a domain-level GPO modifies the settings.

Password Policy

The longer a user continues to use the same password, the more susceptible it becomes to compromise. Similarly, if users don't use complex passwords, they are easier to crack. However, the importance of password security isn't always understood by users.

As an example, a recent study discovered that approximately 70 percent of users commonly use the same password for their banking accounts as they do for other accounts. In other words, a user could be using the same account for Google mail as they do for banking. If an attacker discovers the Google mail password, they can then use it to log in to the banking account and transfer funds to an untraceable overseas account.

Luckily, the Password Policy node can be used to configure requirements for passwords and force users to follow some basic password security practices. The password settings available are as follows:

Enforce Password History   Past passwords are remembered, preventing the user from using the same password over and over. As an example, if 24 passwords are remembered, the user won't be able to reuse a password until they have used 24 other passwords. When using this setting, you should also configure the Minimum Password Age setting to at least 1 day.

Maximum Password Age   This identifies when a password must be changed. When set to 42 days, it prompts the user to change the password as the 42nd day approaches. Once the maximum password age is reached, the user won't be able to log on until the password is changed.

Minimum Password Age   This identifies the minimum period of time in days that a password must be used before it can be changed again. It prevents a user from changing their password right back to what it was previously. If Password History is set to 24 and this setting is set to 1, it would take the user 25 days to get their original password back. This essentially makes it too difficult for a user to circumvent security.

Minimum Password Length   This identifies the minimum number of characters required. The fewer characters used, the easier it is to crack a password. While the default is set at 7, it's generally recommended to have a password of at least 8 characters.

Password Must Meet Complexity Requirements   A complex password must be at least six characters and include characters from three of the following four categories: uppercase letters, lowercase letters, numbers, and special characters. It also cannot contain any portion of the user's full name that exceeds two consecutive characters.

Store Passwords Using Reversible Encryption   This setting is normally disabled. When enabled, the password is stored using reversible encryption, which is similar to storing the password in clear text. An attacker can easily discover it. It's needed in some older applications but should be avoided. For example, this is required when using Challenge Handshake Authentication Protocol (CHAP) for remote access or when using Digest Authentication with Internet Information Services (IIS). More secure authentications are available that don't need reversible encryption.

When you change the Password Policy, many of the settings don't take effect immediately. For example, if you change Minimum Password Length from 7 to 8, users won't be required to change their passwords until the next time they log on. Instead, the policy will be enforced for any new passwords or passwords that are changed.

Account Lockout Policy

Attackers sometimes try to guess the password of accounts. If they are given an unlimited number of tries, they have a better chance of success. The Account Lockout Policy can be used to limit the number of bad password attempts and lock out an account if the limit is exceeded.

Figure 11.6 shows the Account Lockout Policy configured to lock out an account indefinitely after five failed attempts.

FIGURE 11.6   Account Lockout Policy

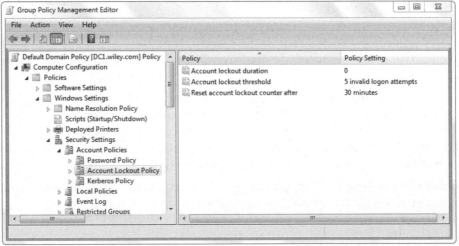

The settings that can be configured are as follows:

Account Lockout Duration   This identifies how many minutes an account will be locked out if the lockout threshold is set. For example, if the number was 45, the account would be locked out for 45 minutes and then be automatically unlocked. A setting of 0 indicates that it will be locked out until an administrator unlocks it.

Account Lockout Threshold   The threshold indicates how many failed attempts are allowed before the account is locked out. For example, if it's set to 5, a user can enter the wrong password four times and the account won't be locked out. However, on the fifth bad password, the account is locked for the duration specified in the Account Lockout Duration setting.

Reset Account Lockout Counter After   This setting resets the bad password count after a period of time. Imagine that this setting is set to 30 and the Account Lockout Threshold is set to 5. A user can enter the wrong password four times and the account won't be locked out. If the user waits 30 minutes, the count will be reset to zero. The user will have five more attempts before being locked out.

The Administrator account cannot be locked out even if an Account Lockout Policy is configured. This gives an attacker an unlimited number of guesses. This is one of the reasons why the Administrator account is often renamed on a system. When it's renamed and the new Administrator account name is unknown, an attacker can't try to guess the password.

Exercise 11.2 shows you how to modify settings in the Account Policies node in the Default Domain Policy.

EXERCISE 11.2

Modifying Account Policies

1. Launch Group Policy Management console via the Administrative Tools menu. You can launch the GPMC from a Windows 7 computer with Remote Server Administration Tools installed or on a domain controller.

2. Expand the domain and access the Default Domain Policy.

3. Right-click Default Domain Policy and select Edit. The Default Domain Policy will open in the Group Policy Management Editor window.

4. Expand Computer Configuration ➢ Policies ➢ Windows Settings ➢ Security Settings ➢ Account Policies ➢ Password Policy. You can view the current settings of the Password Policy in the main window.

5. Double-click each of the settings to view its current settings. Notice that each setting also has an Explain tab. If any of the settings are unclear, you can read more information on the Explain tab. You can modify any of these settings as needed.

6. Select the Account Lockout Policy. These settings are not configured by default. If they aren't configured, you can follow these steps to configure them.

    a. Double-click the Account Lockout Duration setting. Select the Define This Policy Setting check box. Change the minutes from 30 to **0**. Notice that this changes the description to indicate that the account will be locked out until an administrator unlocks it.

    b. Click OK. A dialog box will appear indicating the recommended settings for the other Account Lockout Policy settings. Review the changes and then click OK. Click OK again.

    c. You can return these settings to Not Defined or leave them as they are.

7. Select the Kerberos Policy. Double-click each of the settings to view its status. It's best to leave these settings as they are unless you have a specific reason to change them.

Kerberos Policy

Kerberos is the authentication protocol used in Active Directory. A domain controller acts as a Key Distribution Center (KDC) and issues tickets. These tickets are then used to access resources.

Tickets will expire after a period of time, which helps prevent replay attacks within an Active Directory domain. The five settings in this node are as follows:

Enforce User Logon Restrictions   This is enabled by default. It ensures that the KDC validates every request for a session ticket against the user rights policy of the user account. If the network is slow, this setting can be disabled to improve performance.

Maximum Lifetime For User Ticket   Users are granted a ticket-granting ticket (TGT) when they log on. This TGT is used to request service tickets when a resource is accessed. You can specify the lifetime of the TGT with this setting. It is defined in hours, and the default is 10 hours.

Maximum Lifetime For Service Ticket   This setting identifies the lifetime for a ticket used to access a resource. This setting is defined in minutes, and the default is 600 minutes (10 hours).

Maximum Lifetime For User Ticket Renewal   TGTs can be renewed when they expire. This setting identifies the maximum lifetime of ticket. The default is 7 days, meaning that a TGT can be renewed multiple times, but once 7 days have passed a new TGT must be requested.

Maximum Tolerance For Computer Clock Synchronization   This identifies the maximum amount of time that a computer can be out of sync with other computers on the network. The default is 5 minutes. If a computer is out of synchronization, it will no longer have access to network resources. When a computer reboots, it will receive the time from a domain controller and be synchronized again.

Local Policies

The Local Policies node includes three nodes that contain several security settings:

- Audit Policy
- User Rights Assignment
- Security Options

 There isn't room in this chapter to review in depth all of the settings in each of these nodes. Instead, the focus in this section is on some of the settings alluded to in the objectives of the 70-685 and 70-686 exams.

Audit Policies

Audit Policies can be set to ensure that different categories of auditable events are logged. When they are configured, these events are logged in the Security log of Event Viewer.

Figure 11.7 shows the Audit Policy node with the Audit Object Access setting opened. Notice that for any of these settings, you can select Success, Failure, or both. Each of the Audit Policy settings has a detailed explanation that can be viewed in the Explain tab.

FIGURE 11.7   Configuring success and failure auditing for object access events

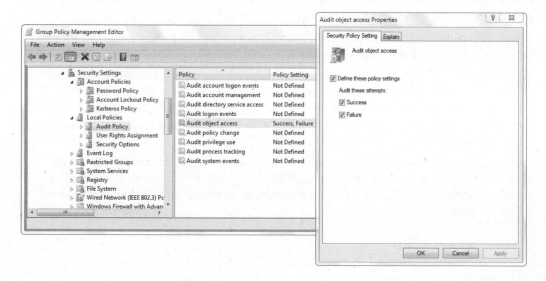

More advanced auditing is available in Windows 7 and Windows Server 2008 R2. If you're interested in these advanced capabilities, check out this TechNet article: http://technet.microsoft.com/library/dd772712.aspx.

You can modify the Audit Policy to log events in the following categories:

Audit Account Logon Events   When enabled, this setting logs each time a computer validates an account's credentials. The accounts can be validated using Active Directory in a domain or the local Security Accounts Manager on a local computer.

Audit Account Management   Enable this setting if you want to log any time a user account or group is created, changed, or deleted. It will also log if a user account is renamed, disabled, or enabled. Last, it will log when passwords are set or changed.

Audit Directory Service Access   This setting applies only to Active Directory objects. When enabled, it allows auditing to occur for any objects, such as OUs, users, groups, computers, and more.

Audit Logon Events   Each time a user attempts to log on or log off a computer, a logon event can be generated.

Audit Policy Change   When this setting is enabled, any changes to the user rights assignment policy, audit policy, account policy, or trust policy can be logged. As with all the settings, both success and failure events can be selected.

Audit Privilege Use   When a user executes a right, it is also referred to as using a privilege. This setting triggers log entries for the use of most user rights. However, a few commonly used rights aren't logged by default to avoid filling up the Security log. If you want to log all events, you can modify the Registry, as described in the Explain tab of this setting.

Audit Process Tracking   Software developers may sometimes use this to track process-related events. It can be useful during the debugging process of a new application.

Audit System Events   System events include changing the system time, startups and shutdowns, loss of audited events because of an auditing system failure, and when the Security log exceeds the configured warning threshold.

Audit Object Access   When this setting is enabled, auditing can be enabled for access to any non–Active Directory objects such as files, folders, and printers. It's important to realize that just enabling this setting will not turn on auditing for all files, folders, and printers within the scope of the policy. Instead, you must also go to the object and enable auditing. This is demonstrated in Exercise 11.3.

As an example of object access, assume that you want to audit anytime anyone deletes or even tries to delete a file in a folder named Data. You would first enable Audit Object Access as part of the Audit Policy. You would then go to the Data folder and enable auditing on the folder.

Figure 11.8 shows the Auditing tab on a folder named `Data`. When Audit Object Access is enabled, and auditing is also enabled on the object as shown in the figure, then auditing will occur for objects in the folder.

FIGURE 11.8   Configuring auditing for a folder

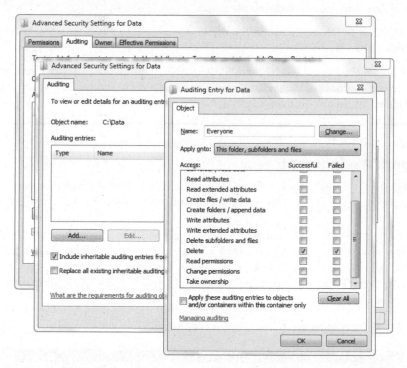

Notice that only successful and failed attempts to delete objects in the folder are selected. You can select all possible actions, but you should enable auditing only for what you need.

Exercise 11.3 shows how to enable auditing on individual folders. As a reminder, these settings have an impact only if Audit Object Access has been enabled in the Audit Policy. If Audit Object Access isn't enabled, the settings in the exercise will not apply.

EXERCISE 11.3

Enabling Audit Object Access on a Resource

1. Launch Windows Explorer by clicking Start ➢ Computer.

2. Browse to the C: drive, and right-click a folder that you want to audit.

3. Select the Security tab. Click Advanced.

EXERCISE 11.3 *(continued)*

4. Select the Auditing tab. If prompted by UAC to view the auditing properties, click Continue.

5. When the Auditing screen appears, click Add.

6. Add the user or group that you want to audit. If you want to audit all users, enter **Everyone**. Click OK.

7. Select the accesses you want to audit. For example, if you want to audit all successful and failed attempts to delete files, click Successful and Failed for Delete. Click OK four times to return to Windows Explorer.

User Rights Assignment

The *User Rights Assignment* node includes several Group Policy settings that you can use to control rights and privileges of different users. This node is within the Local Policies node.

Because rights are assigned to users or groups, these settings are configured a little differently. When a setting is enabled, you must add the groups that will be assigned the right.

Figure 11.9 shows the Group Policy Management Editor with the Allow Log On Locally right setting opened. This right has been defined and granted to the Administrators group and the G_ITAdmins group.

FIGURE 11.9 Granting the Allow Log On Locally right

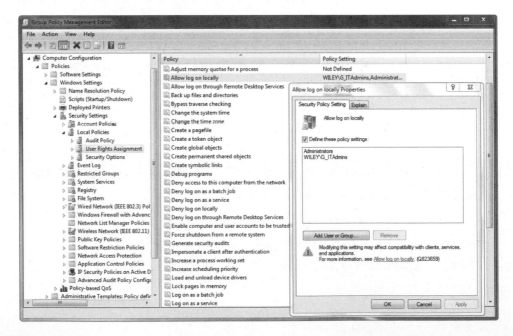

By default, a regular user in the domain is allowed to log on to any computer in the domain except for domain controllers. When this setting is configured as shown, only users in the defined groups will be able to log on to systems within the scope of the GPO.

Here are some other rights that can be assigned via this node:

Access This Computer From The Network   Normally, any user (accept the Guest account) can access a computer over the network. This right allows you to restrict network access to specific users or groups.

> Several elements must be in place to allow users to access resources over the network. For example, in order for a user to access a share, the share must have been created and the user must have permissions. Any existing firewalls must be configured to allow the access. Last, the user right must be granted.

Add Workstations To Domain   Regular users are allowed to add up to 10 computer accounts to a domain. This right can be granted to allow a user to add an unlimited number of accounts. For example, if a technician regularly sets up computers for end users, you can grant this right. Since accounts are created in Active Directory, which is located on a domain controller, this setting must be configured on a GPO that applies to domain controllers, such as the Default Domain Controllers policy.

Allow Log On Through Remote Desktop Services   This right is normally granted to the Administrators group and the Remote Desktop Users group. You would normally add users to the Remote Desktop Users group to grant this right, but you can also modify this setting.

Change The System Time   This right is granted only to users in the Administrators group. As a reminder, Kerberos requires all computers to be within five minutes of each other, and a computer will synchronize with a domain controller when it authenticates. If this right is granted, users have the potential to change the time, preventing them from accessing any domain resources.

Change The Time Zone   This right is granted to any regular user. If a user changes the time zone, it will affect the time displayed to the user but it doesn't affect the system time. In other words, if a user accidentally changes the time zone, it won't affect his access to domain resources.

Deny Access To This Computer From The Network   This right is assigned to the Guest account by default. It overrides the Access This Computer From The Network policy. In other words, you can use this policy to restrict users or groups from accessing a computer without modifying the Access This Computer From The Network policy.

Manage Auditing And Security Log   This right is assigned to administrators by default. It allows the granted user the ability to enable auditing on any objects (such as files and folders) and also to view, clear, and manipulate the Security log.

Take Ownership Of Files Or Other Objects   This right is assigned to administrators by default. It allows an administrator to take ownership of an object. The owner can modify the permissions and grant access to any other users.

Shut Down The System   Regular users are granted this right for workstations. Only the Administrators and Backup Operators groups are granted the right for servers. On domain controllers, this right is granted to the Administrators, Backup Operators, Server Operators, and Print Operators groups.

Security Options

The Security Options node includes several settings directly related to security. This node includes the User Account Control settings that were mentioned earlier in this chapter.

Some of the miscellaneous settings are as follows:

Accounts: Administrator Account Status   This setting can be used to disable the local Administrator account. This can prevent an attacker from accessing this account. Other domain groups can be added to the local Administrators group for administrative access.

Accounts: Rename Administrator Account   This can used to change the name of the Administrator account for all computers in the scope of the GPO. This can make it more difficult for attackers to guess the password. However, it does not change the SID of the Administrator account, which is widely known by attackers.

Devices: Allowed To Format And Eject Removable Media   You can enable this so that only administrators, administrators and power users, or administrators and interactive users are allowed to format and eject removable media. An interactive user is any user who is currently logged on.

 If you want to control the use of removable media, you have much more flexibility with the Removable Storage Access policy covered later in this chapter.

Shutdown: Clear Virtual Memory Pagefile   In some situations, sensitive data can be saved in the pagefile. If the system is booted using another operating system, data in the pagefile may be viewed. This setting can be used to ensure the pagefile is cleared and that sensitive data isn't saved and available.

Several additional settings in the Security Options node are associated with changes in NTLM and changes in Kerberos. These settings are covered in the following subsections.

Changes in NTLM Authentication Security Settings in Windows 7

New Technology LAN Manager (NTLM) and NTLMv2 are authentication protocols used within Microsoft networks. NTLMv2 can be used with the Security Support Provider (SSP) to increase the security in Windows 7 and Windows Server 2008 R2. It can also be used with 128-bit encryption.

Although NTLMv2 has been supported since NT 4.0 SP4, 128-bit support is newer. It has been more common to use 40-bit or 56-bit encryption. New installations of Windows 7 use 128-bit encryption by default. If Windows 7 is upgraded from an earlier Windows version, it will use the existing setting.

Because 128-bit security is the default for new installations of Windows 7, some client or server applications may not work for new installations if they're using 40-bit or 56-bit encryption for NTLM. Two new settings within the Security Options node can be used to assist in this scenario:

- Network Security: Minimum Session Security For NTLM SSP Based (Including Secure RPC) Clients

- Network Security: Minimum Session Security For NTLM SSP Based (Including Secure RPC) Servers

Figure 11.10 shows the choices for both of these settings. When configured as shown in Figure 11.10, connections can be refused if the other connection can't negotiate both NTLMv2 session security and 128-bit encryption. The same settings are available for both client and server applications.

FIGURE 11.10   Network Security: Minimum Session Security For NTLM SSP

If you need to support older applications using weaker encryption with 40 or 56 bits, you can deselect Require 128-bit Encryption. Windows 7 will then negotiate the weaker encryption used by the application.

Changes in Kerberos Authentication in Windows 7

Data Encryption Standard (DES) cryptography has been largely replaced with the newer Advanced Encryption Standard (AES) in most applications that use cryptography. It isn't just that Microsoft has replaced DES with AES, but it's the case anywhere cryptography is used. DES has been cracked, and AES is a strong, efficient standard.

In Windows 7, the older DES cipher suites are disabled by default. These two suites are DES-CBC-MD5 and DES-CBC-CRC. The following stronger cipher suites are enabled by default:

- AES256-CTS-HMAC-SHA1-96
- AES128-CTS-HMAC-SHA1-96
- RC4-HMAC

However, if you need to enable DES support for Windows 7 clients, you can do so. The setting that needs to be modified is Network Security: Configure Encryption Types Allowed For Kerberos.

The most common reason to enable DES is for interoperability with UNIX or Linux systems using DES.

Figure 11.11 shows this setting. When you define the policy settings, you can enable all of the encryption types that you want to allow.

FIGURE 11.11   Configure Encryption Types Allowed For Kerberos

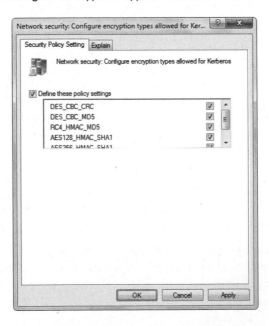

Windows 7 also supports elliptic curve cryptography (ECC) for smart cards that use X.509 certificates. Nothing needs to be changed in Windows 7 to use ECC with smart cards. As long as the smart cards and the smart card readers support ECC, they will work with Windows 7.

System Services

The Security Settings ➤ System Services node can be used to enforce the startup mode and permissions for any service. Startup modes can be configured as Automatic, Manual, or Disabled through this node. The newer Automatic (Delayed Start) startup mode is not available through the System Services node.

 Services were discussed in greater depth in Chapter 5, "Maintaining and Troubleshooting Windows 7."

The benefit of using the System Services node is that you can control the startup mode of services and which accounts can start services. For example, your organization may decide that they don't want most users to use the Encrypting File System (EFS).

Figure 11.12 shows how this can be modified. When Disabled is selected, the service will not be able to start.

FIGURE 11.12 Configuring the startup mode and permissions for a service

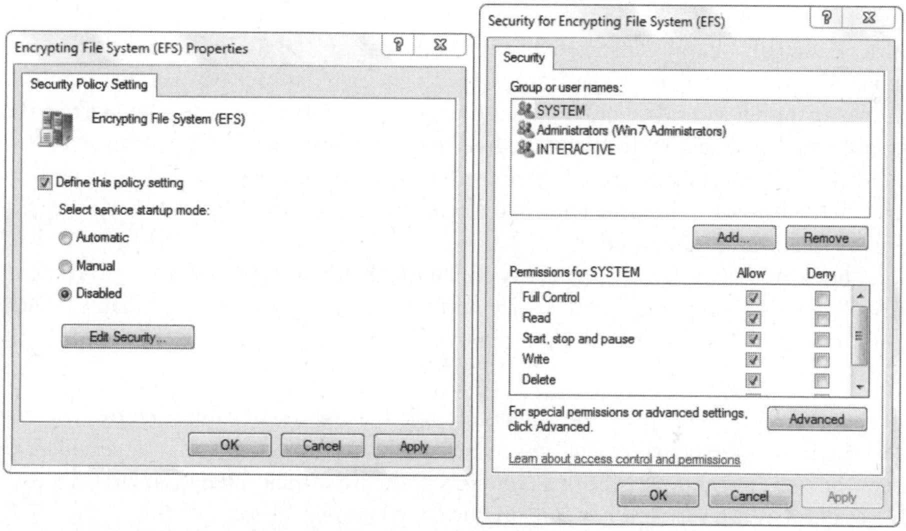

It's also possible to configure it to Manual and then configure permissions so that only users in specific groups can manipulate the service. If you click the Edit Security button, you can manipulate the permissions.

Real World Scenario

Hardening Systems

Hardening a system means that you are making it more secure than the default installation. Although Windows 7 starts out more secure than previous operating systems, it can still be tweaked to make it even more secure for your organization.

Many organizations identify the services that aren't needed and take steps to disable them. If the service is disabled in the Default Domain Policy, it will be disabled for all systems in the domain.

By disabling unneeded services, you are reducing the attack surface of a system. If malware is programmed to attack a specific service, but the service is disabled, the malware cannot attack. Disabling unneeded services makes you less susceptible to possible attacks.

Removable Storage Access Policy

Removable storage devices such as USB flash drives represent a significant risk within a corporate environment. It's very easy for employees to transport malware unknowingly from their home computer to their work computer with flash drives. In addition, with a USB drive, users can easily copy a significant amount of data in a short period of time.

Because of the risks, many organizations restrict the use of USB flash drives and other removable media. You can use a *Removable Storage Access policy* to enforce this corporate policy.

Windows includes several Group Policy settings that can be configured to restrict the use of removable media. These settings are located in the Computer Configuration ➢ Policies ➢ Administrative Templates ➢ System ➢ Removable Storage Access node.

Figure 11.13 shows the Removal Storage Access node with the Removal Disks: Deny Read Access selection highlighted.

Notice that you can configure an access policy for different types of devices. You can also deny all access to any removable device with the All Removal Storage Classes: Deny All Access setting. Each of the individual removable devices has three access rights that can be denied:

Deny Execute Access   This prevents any executable files from running directly from the device. Many malware programs attempt to run as soon as the device is plugged in. This setting can be used to help prevent this common malware attack. Deny Execute Access is available only on Windows 7. It is not available on Windows Vista.

Deny Read Access   This prevents data from being read from the device. Deny Read Access is available on Windows Vista and Windows 7 computers.

Deny Write Access   This prevents data from being written to the device. Deny Write Access is available on Windows Vista and Windows 7 computers.

FIGURE 11.13   Removal Storage Access policy node

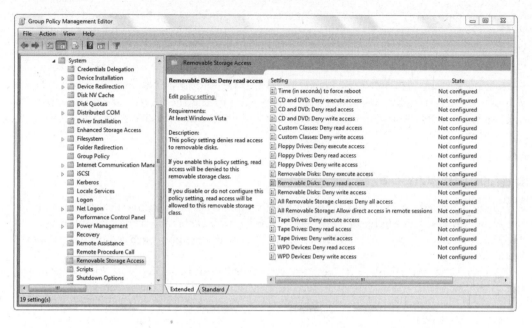

 WPD devices are listed in the Removable Storage Access policy. WPD is short for Windows Portable Devices. These can include media players, cell phones, and other small portable devices.

If any of these access rights are changed, they will not take effect until the system is restarted. The Time (In Seconds) To Force Reboot setting can be configured to force a system to reboot if any of these rights are changed.

Designing BitLocker Support

BitLocker encryption was introduced with Windows Vista and Windows Server 2008. Unlike EFS, which can be used to encrypt files and folders, BitLocker can be used to encrypt the entire hard drive. *BitLocker Drive Encryption* is used for internal hard drives and *BitLocker To Go* is used to encrypt external or USB flash drives.

 The 70-680 exam covers the configuration of BitLocker and BitLocker To Go. The 70-685 and 70-686 exams include objectives related to troubleshooting and designing encryption issues but never directly mention BitLocker. This section provides a review of BitLocker, but it does not attempt to teach all of the details of BitLocker Drive encryption. The most important topics for the MCITP Pro exams relate to recovery keys.

You can use BitLocker to protect the data on the drive or protect the system.

Protect the data   Any data drive (non–operating system drive) can be encrypted with BitLocker to protect against unauthorized access. BitLocker can be configured to unlock the data with a password, a smart card, or automatically each time you log on to the computer.

Protect the system   If you use BitLocker to protect the operating system drive, BitLocker will check the system for suspicious events before unlocking the drive. For example, if hardware components are modified, BitLocker will not unlock the drive until a recovery key is used.

BitLocker with a TPM

A *Trusted Platform Module (TPM)* is a microchip that is located on the motherboard of the system. If your system has a TPM, you can fully protect the operating system's drive and the critical startup process. TPM version 1.2 and BIOS support are required to support BitLocker fully.

When a TPM is available, the operating system drive can be locked with BitLocker using the TPM. Each time the system is turned on, TPM will verify that the system hasn't been tampered with before unlocking the drive. BitLocker can use any of the following methods to unlock the drive:

TPM only   No user interaction is required. As long as TPM doesn't detect anything suspicious, the drive is unlocked automatically.

TPM with startup key   An encryption key is stored on a USB flash drive. This USB flash drive with the encryption key is referred to as a startup key. As long as TPM doesn't detect anything suspicious and the startup key is inserted, the system will start.

TPM with PIN   A personal identification number (PIN) can also be used with TPM. The system uses TPM, and the user must also enter the PIN to unlock the volume.

TPM with startup key and PIN   TPM can also be used with both a startup key and a PIN. This provides multifactor protection. An attacker must have the startup key and know the PIN to gain access to the drive.

Authentication can be based one or more of three factors: something you know, such as a password or PIN; something you have, such as a smart card or startup key; and something you are identified with—biometrics. Requiring both a startup key and a PIN uses two factors: something you have and something you know. Any authentication method that uses more than one factor is referred to as multifactor authentication.

BitLocker without TPM

It's also possible to lock the operating system drives on systems without a TPM. For systems without a TPM, the only option available is the use of a startup key.

The encryption data is stored on a USB flash drive. This USB flash drive is then referred to as a startup key. The flash drive must be inserted in the system for the computer to start. A startup key doesn't provide full protection over the system's boot process.

BitLocker and Data Drives

BitLocker can be used to protect data drives. A data drive is any drive that doesn't hold operating system files. This can be an internal fixed drive, an external hard drive, or a USB flash drive. When using BitLocker to protect the data drives, you can use one of three options:

Password   Users will be required to enter the correct password before the drive is unlocked.

Smartcard   A smart card is a small credit card–sized card that has one or more embedded certificates. A certificate is used to lock the drive, and the smart card must be inserted to unlock the drive. Many organizations require the use of smart cards to log on. This same smart card could have a certificate to unlock the drive.

Automatically Unlock With Logon   It's possible to configure the drives to unlock automatically when the user logs on to Windows. This option is available for any removable drives. It can be used with internal fixed data drives only if the operating system is also protected with BitLocker.

BitLocker Recovery Keys

One of the challenges with using BitLocker is that legitimate users can be locked out of their data. This can occur if one of the following events occurs:

- The protected drive is moved to a different system.
- The TPM is modified. This includes replacing the motherboard or flashing the BIOS.
- The startup key is lost or destroyed.
- The smart card is lost or destroyed.
- The PIN is forgotten.

Depending on the value of the data protected by BitLocker, the loss could be substantial. BitLocker will either enter BitLocker recovery mode or simply remain locked.

BitLocker allows you to use one of several methods to recover the data. It's important to realize that you must implement a plan to use these methods before a failure occurs. If a BitLocker drive enters recovery mode and a recovery method wasn't implemented earlier, it's too late. The data will remain locked.

The following methods are available to recover data using recovery keys.

Recovery key or recovery password   If the smart card is not available or the user has forgotten the password, a 48-digit recovery password can be used to unlock the drive. A recovery key can also be used in place of a password. This key is stored on removable media, such as a USB flash drive. It can also be printed out and stored in a secure location.

Data recovery agent   A data recovery agent (DRA) can be configured in Group Policy using the Computer Configuration ➤ Policies ➤ Windows Settings ➤ Security Settings ➤ Public Key Policies ➤ BitLocker Drive Encryption node. When a DRA is designated, the DRA can recover the drive. The following link shows the process to create certificates for the DRA and designate a DRA: technet.microsoft.com/library/ee424312.aspx.

Backup of keys in Active Directory Domain Services   For systems in a domain, you can store recovery keys in Active Directory Domain Services (AD DS). This is configured via Group Policy in the Computer Configuration ➤ Policies ➤ Administrative Templates ➤ System ➤ Trusted Platform Module Services node. The setting is Turn On TPM Backup To Active Directory Domain Services, as shown in Figure 11.14.

FIGURE 11.14   Configuring TPM data to be stored in AD DS

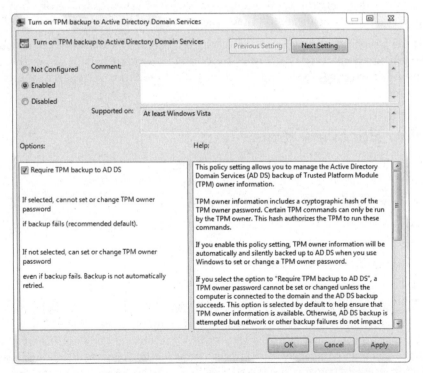

Before you can store BitLocker recovery data in AD DS, you'll need to ensure that some prerequisites have been met.

Storing BitLocker Recovery Data in AD DS

If the domain is using Windows Server 2008 domain controllers, you'll automatically be able to store the BitLocker recovery data in AD DS. However, if you have domain controllers running earlier operating systems, or upgraded from earlier operating systems, you'll need to take a few extra steps.

> The details to prepare to store the BitLocker recovery data in AD DS are extensive. This TechNet article will lead you through the process: `http://technet.microsoft.com/library/cc766015.aspx`

These are the overall steps to prepare your domain:

- Make sure that all domain controllers are running at least Windows Server 2003 SP1.
- Modify the AD DS schema.
- Modify permissions at the domain level.

BitLocker Active Directory Recovery Password Viewer Tool

Another feature that is available is the BitLocker Active Directory Recovery Password Viewer Tool. If BitLocker keys are stored in AD DS, you can use this tool to retrieve them. When this tool is installed, you can access the properties of a computer in Active Directory Users and Computers. Select the BitLocker Recovery tab, as shown in Figure 11.15.

FIGURE 11.15   The BitLocker Recovery tab for a computer account

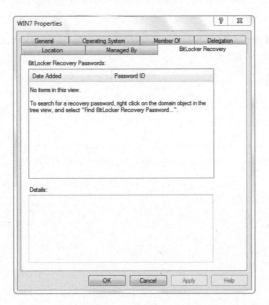

After adding the Active Directory Recovery Password Viewer Tool, you also need to extend Active Directory Domain Services. This is done by running the following command using an account with Enterprise Admins permissions: regsvr32 bdeaducext.dll. This will enable the Bit-Locker Drive Encryption (BDE) extensions for Active Directory Users and Computers.

Exercise 11.4 shows how to configure BitLocker recovery data to be stored in Active Directory and how to add the *BitLocker Active Directory Recovery Password Viewer Tool*. This activity can be done in the test bed created in Chapter 9, "Managing Windows 7 in a Domain." It assumes the Remote Server Administration Tools have been installed, as shown in Chapter 10. You can use the same procedures in an active environment that includes these elements.

EXERCISE 11.4

Adding the BitLocker Active Directory Recovery Password Viewer Tool

1. Log on to the Windows 7 computer, and launch the GPMC via the Administrative Tools menu.

2. Browse to the Default Domain Policy. Right-click the Default Domain Policy and select Edit.

3. Browse to the Computer Configuration ➤ Policies ➤ Administrative Templates ➤ System ➤ Trusted Platform Module Services node.

4. Double-click the Turn On TPM Backup To Active Directory Domain Services setting. Select Enabled. Ensure that Require TPM Backup To AD DS is selected and click OK.

5. Launch a command prompt with administrative permissions. Execute the following command to refresh Group Policy:

   Gpupdate /force

6. Click Start ➤ Control Panel. Type **Features** in the Search Control Panel box. Click Turn Windows Features On Or Off.

7. Expand Remote Server Administration Tools and Feature Administration Tools. Select BitLocker Password Recovery Viewer, as shown in the following graphic.

8. Scroll down to the Role Administration Tools. Expand Role Administration Tools ➢ AD DS ➢ AD LDS Tools ➢ AD DS Tools. Select AD DS Snap-ins And Command-line Tools. Click OK. This will install Active Directory Users and Computers and some other management consoles.

9. Log on to the domain controller using an account with administrative permissions. Launch a command prompt with administrative permissions and execute the following command:

   `regsvr32 bdeaducext.dll`

10. Return to Windows 7. Launch Active Directory Users and Computers via the Administrative Tools menu.

11. Browse to the location of a computer object. Right-click the computer object and select Properties. The BitLocker Recovery Password tab will now be present.

Windows Firewall

Windows Firewall has been standard since Windows XP. In Windows XP SP2, it was enabled by default, and it has steadily improved over the years.

A firewall is designed to protect a computer or network by controlling inbound and outbound traffic. Most firewalls operate with an implicit deny philosophy. In other words, all traffic is blocked (implicit deny) unless there is a rule that explicitly allows the traffic.

Windows Firewall on Windows 7 also uses an implicit deny philosophy. The only traffic that is allowed is the following:

- Traffic that is explicitly allowed by an exception or a rule. Both inbound and outbound rules can be configured.

- Return traffic that has been requested. For example, if a user requests a web page from a website, the web page is allowed as return traffic.

Windows Firewall works as both a packet-filtering firewall and a stateful firewall.

Packet-filtering firewall A packet-filtering firewall can filter traffic based on IP addresses, ports, and some protocols. The firewall examines packets individually. Packets can be allowed or blocked based only on what is in each packet. A packet-filtering firewall can't evaluate packets based on the entire communication.

Stateful firewall A stateful firewall can monitor the state of a connection. In other words, instead of examining each packet individually, it evaluates the packets in the conversation. This allows a stateful firewall to detect and block many attacks.

As a stateful firewall, it can inspect and filter all IPv4 and IPv6 traffic.

Checking the Firewall Status

If you suspect problems with the firewall, one of the first things you should check is the status. You can check it via the Control Panel. Type in **Firewall** in the Search Control Panel box, and click Check Firewall Status. Figure 11.16 shows the firewall status screen.

FIGURE 11.16   Windows Firewall status

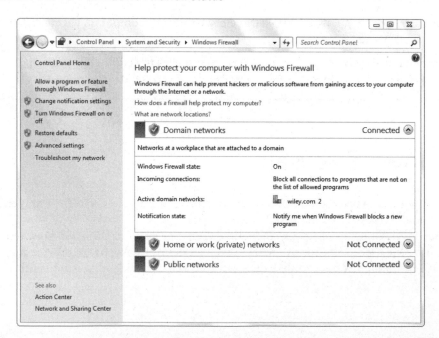

Notice that it shows the firewall is controlled using the Domain Networks settings. The firewall has detected that the system is connected to the domain. This figure also shows both the Home Or Work (Private) Networks and Public Networks as Not Connected. If the system was connected to a public network, the Public Networks would appear as Connected, and the firewall would be controlled with the Public Networks settings.

This display shows that the firewall is on and configured to block all connections that aren't on the list of allowed programs. It is also configured to provide a notification when Windows Firewall blocks a program.

Determining Whether a Port or a Protocol Needs to Be Enabled

Some applications require that certain ports be opened or traffic using certain protocols be allowed. If the traffic is blocked, the application won't work. When configuring newly installed applications that aren't working, you should consider the possibility that an exception needs to be created in the firewall.

The top link on the left of the Windows Firewall status screen is labeled Allow A Program Or Feature Through Windows Firewall. You can see this link on Figure 11.16.

If you click this link, you'll see the display shown in Figure 11.17. This can be used to create an exception for different applications. When an exception is enabled, traffic will be allowed.

FIGURE 11.17   Modifying Windows Firewall to allow different programs or features

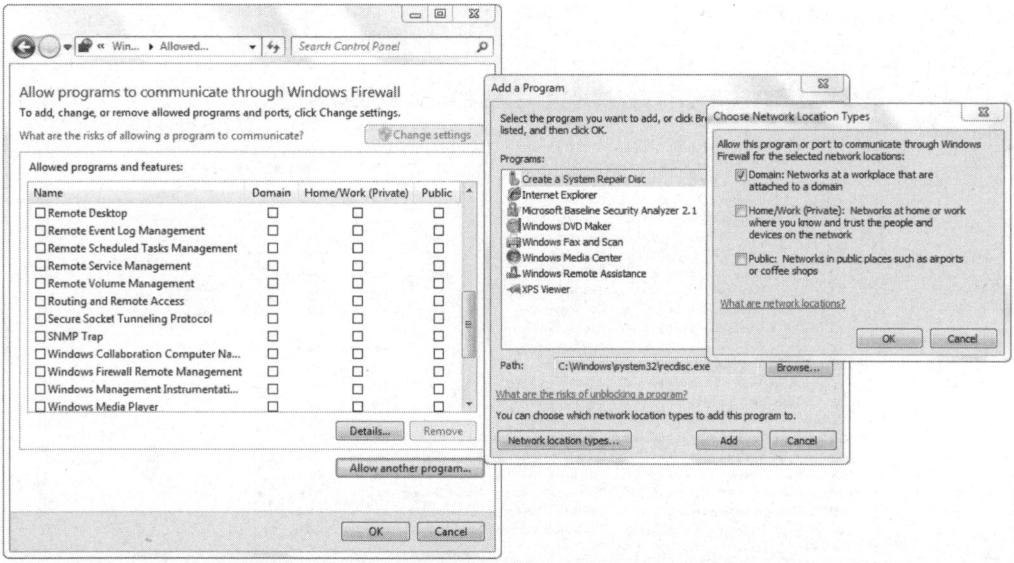

To create an exception, you can check the box for any of the features listed. You can create an exception for an application by clicking the Allow Another Program button. Most installed programs will automatically appear in this list, but you can also click Browse to locate the application.

Chapter 7, "Networking with Windows 7," covered network locations, including both public and private locations. These locations are associated with profiles. When creating exceptions, you have the ability to create them for any single profile or all profiles. When the computer is connected to the domain, three profiles can be selected: Domain, Home/Work (Private), and Public.

Designing Firewall Rules

You can create firewall rules from the Windows Firewall Advanced Settings screen. You can modify preexisting rules or create your own rules.

New rules can be created to allow traffic based on the following:

- A program
- One or more TCP or UDP ports
- A custom rule

Custom rules allow you to specify traffic for specific protocols, protocol numbers, and ports.

Figure 11.18 shows a partial list of the predefined rules. Settings that are enabled are shown with a check mark in a green circle. Any of these settings can be enabled or disabled by right-clicking and selecting Enable Rule or Disable Rule.

FIGURE 11.18 Windows Firewall with Advanced Security

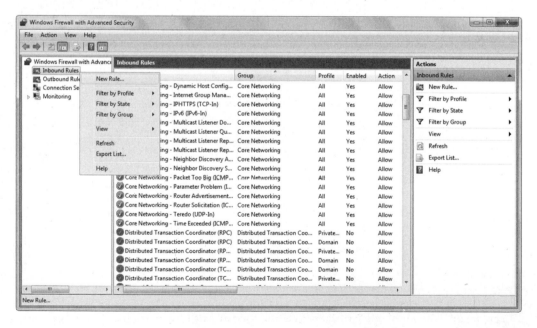

Most of the properties in the predefined rules can't be modified. However, you can re-create any rule to meet specific requirements.

You can also create rules in Group Policy. The Computer Configuration ➢ Policies ➢ Windows Settings ➢ Security Settings ➢ Windows Firewall with Advanced Security node can be used to create new inbound rules, outbound rules, or connection security rules. Although none of the predefined rules are shown by default, they can be selected when creating a new rule.

You can follow the steps in Exercise 11.5 to create a new rule. You can use these steps to create a new rule on an individual computer. Likewise, you can access the Windows Firewall with Advanced Security node in Group Policy and create the rule within a GPO.

EXERCISE 11.5

Creating a New Rule to Allow Traffic Based on Ports

1. Launch the Windows Firewall Advanced Settings screen. Click Start ➢ Control Panel. Type **Firewall** and select Windows Firewall. Click Advanced Settings.

2. Select Inbound Rules. Right-click Inbound Rules and select New Rule.

3. On the Select Rule Type page, you can select Program, Port, Predefined, or Custom. Select Port and click Next.

4. Select either TCP or UDP based on the traffic you want to allow. Enter the port numbers you want to allow. Click Next.

5. On the Action page, notice that you can select one of three settings: Allow The Connection, Allow The Connection If It Is Secure, or Block The Connection. Select Allow The Connection and click Next.

6. The Profile page appears. You can have this rule apply to the Domain, Private, and/or the Public network profiles. They are all checked by default. Click Next.

7. Name your rule and enter a description if desired. Click Finish, and it is created.

Summary

Security is an important concern for any computer, including Windows 7 computers. Thankfully, you have a wealth of tools you can use to enhance security in Windows 7 computers.

User Account Control provides a significant improvement in security by separating the actions requiring administrative permissions from actions requiring regular user permissions. It helps prevent malware from making unapproved changes to a system computer and can be controlled with Group Policy.

Group Policy also provides a wealth of security settings that can be used to control the behavior of Windows 7 systems within a domain. Some of the settings are the same as they have been in previous operating systems. Some, like the settings in NTLM and Kerberos authentication and some of the settings in the Removable Storage Access policies, are new to Windows 7.

Last, Windows Firewall provides protection to Windows 7 systems from network attacks. Although the added security is worthwhile, it does sometimes require additional troubleshooting to ensure that your applications work.

Chapter Essentials

User Account Control   Understand how UAC works and how the settings can be manipulated. You should be aware that Windows 7 uses both the standard user token and the administrator token and only prompts the user when the administrator token needs to be used. Be aware of the Group Policy settings that can modify the default behavior.

Security policies   Understand the different between the Local Security Policy and policies applied through Group Policy. Know how to manipulate the Password Policy and the Account Lockout Policy. Know what the Audit Policies and User Rights Assignment settings can do. Be aware of the changes in NTLM and Kerberos Authentication. Understand how removable devices can be controlled with a Removable Storage Access policy

Designing BitLocker Support   Understand that BitLocker can be used to protect entire hard drives. Know that it provides the best protection with TPM but can be used without TPM. BitLocker recovery keys can be used to recover drives, and you can store BitLocker recovery data in Activity Directory.

Windows Firewall   Know that the Windows Firewall provides an added layer of protection for Windows 7 clients. It acts as both a packet filtering firewall and a stateful firewall. You can also add additional rules to allow any traffic based on the port, the protocol, or the application.

Chapter

12

Supporting Mobile Windows 7 Users

TOPICS COVERED IN THIS CHAPTER INCLUDE

- ✓ Configuring and troubleshooting wireless connectivity
- ✓ Configuring and troubleshooting remote access
- ✓ Understanding DirectAccess
- ✓ Using BranchCache

Today, more and more workers need to be mobile. Mobile computers help them perform as well away from the office as at the office. Although Windows 7 performs just as well on a mobile computer as it does on a desktop, there are some extra steps involved in administering mobile computers.

Wireless networks are very popular today, not just in homes and public locations but also in corporate networks. They reduce the need to run expensive cable. However, you should be aware of how to configure wireless security on a Windows 7 client.

Mobile users often need to be able to connect to the internal network. The primary way this is done is with remote access servers hosting either dial-up or VPN connections. If you support mobile users, you'll want to know how these work.

A newer method of connecting remote users is with DirectAccess. It's available only for Windows 7 clients connecting to Windows Server 2008 R2 servers, but it has some great benefits. Authorized users with Internet access will be able to access internal servers over the Internet without requiring a VPN.

Finally, if your network includes branch or remote offices, you may be interested in BranchCache. BranchCache allows files to be cached in the branch offices. This reduces the bandwidth needed for WAN links and also improves the performance for users in these branch offices.

All of these topics are covered in this chapter.

Configuring and Troubleshooting Wireless Connectivity

One of the great strengths of mobile computers is their ability to connect to wireless networks. Today, most mobile computers come with built-in wireless capabilities, and you can connect to wireless networks within the company and in public places.

Windows 7 supports all the standard wireless protocols. If your wireless devices and wireless NICs support it, so does Windows 7. This includes 802.11a, 802.11b, 802.11g, and 802.11n. Windows 7 also supports the newer WPA2 authentication options that significantly improve wireless network security. In this section, you'll learn about

- Using wireless security
- Configuring wireless on Windows 7

- Connecting to a wireless network
- Troubleshooting wireless connections

Using Wireless Security

When wireless networks were first designed, the primary goal was ease of use. The designers wanted to make it easy to discover, connect to, and use wireless networks. They did a great job. However, security was more of an afterthought.

They came up with *Wired Equivalent Privacy (WEP)* to provide the same level of privacy for a wireless network as you'd have in a wired network. Unfortunately, WEP had significant problems and was later cracked. Attackers could download software from the Internet and easily crack WEP-protected networks.

Wi-Fi Protected Access (WPA) is the first improvement over WEP. One of the primary benefits of WPA is that it is compatible with most of the same hardware that used WEP. WPA was intended to be an interim fix for WEP until a more permanent solution was identified. Although WPA is more secure than WEP, attackers have cracked it.

Wi-Fi Protected Access 2 (WPA2) is the permanent fix for WEP. It is also known as 802.11i. If you have a choice among WEP, WPA, and WPA2, use WPA2. WPA2 provides the strongest security.

> WEP is not recommended for use today. You should use at least WPA, but use WPA2 whenever possible. WEP is easy to crack. Even though WPA has vulnerabilities, it isn't as vulnerable as WEP.

When configuring Windows 7 to connect to a wireless network, you should have an understanding of the security types and encryption types available. First, it's important to understand what each of these is doing:

Security type   The security type identifies the type of authentication used. Authentication is used to verify a client prior to allowing access.

Encryption type   After the client connects, the data can be encrypted. This provides confidentiality by preventing others from being able to read the data. Advanced Encryption Standard (AES) is a strong, efficient encryption algorithm. WEP can also be selected as an encryption type for some security types. However, WEP is the weakest.

Consider Figure 12.1. It shows the security settings for a wireless profile named WileyNetwork. As you can see, it is using the WPA2-Enterprise security type and AES as the encryption type. These are the strongest settings available.

FIGURE 12.1 Wireless profile security settings

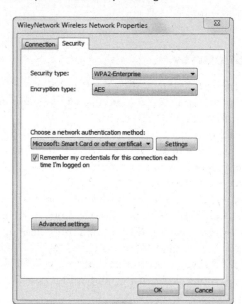

This figure also shows the Choose A Network Authentication Method drop-down box. These selections are available only for the WPA-Enterprise and WPA2-Enterprise security types. The Microsoft: Smart Card Or Other Certificate option (selected in the figure) is the strongest authentication method available. You can also choose the Microsoft: Protected EAP (PEAP) authentication method.

It's important to realize that you must match these settings to the wireless network. In other words, if your network is using a wireless access point with WPA2-Personal, you must configure Windows 7 to use WPA2-Personal. Otherwise, the Windows 7 system won't connect.

Windows 7 supports the following security types:

No Authentication (Open) This uses no authentication. It is not recommended for use in a production environment but can be used for testing.

You can select either WEP or None for encryption. If you select WEP, you also need to enter a pre-shared key (PSK). This is also known as a password or passphrase. You need to enter the same PSK on the Windows 7 system as is used on the wireless device.

Shared Shared uses a PSK for authentication and WEP for encryption. WEP uses the same PSK that you enter for authentication. Shared is not recommended for use in a production environment but can be used for testing. It is marginally better than No Authentication (Open) but can be easily cracked.

WPA-Personal *WPA-Personal* uses a pre-shared key for authentication. This PSK provides limited authentication.

You can select either Advanced Encryption Standard (AES) or Temporal Key Integrity Protocol (TKIP) for encryption. TKIP is compatible with older hardware, but AES is preferred if your hardware supports it.

WPA-Enterprise   *WPA-Enterprise* is similar to WPA except that it uses an 802.1x server for authentication. The 802.1x server will distribute the keys to each client instead of the clients using a PSK. It can also use either smart cards or Protected Extensible Authorization Protocol (PEAP) for authentication. Smart cards provide better security, but they also require more resources on your network. For example, you must have a Public Key Infrastructure (PKI) to issue certificates for the smart cards.

You can select either AES or TKIP for encryption. AES is preferred.

WPA2-Personal   *WPA2-Personal* is similar to WPA-Personal except it uses the stronger WPA2 authentication instead of WPA. WPA2-Personal uses a PSK. You enter the same PSK on the Windows 7 system and the wireless devices.

You can select either AES or TKIP for encryption. AES is preferred.

WPA2-Enterprise   *WPA2-Enterprise* is the strongest security type available with Windows 7. It uses an 802.1x server for authentication just as WPA-Enterprise does. It can use either smart cards or PEAP for authentication. Smart cards provide the best authentication.

You can select either AES or TKIP for encryption. AES is preferred.

802.1x   The 802.1x security type was intended to provide better protection for WEP by providing a better authentication mechanism when WEP was used. With WEP no longer recommended, this is also not recommended.

802.1x uses WEP for encryption.

There's an important distinction when using 802.1x servers. The 802.1x security type is not recommended because it uses WEP, and WEP is not secure. However, WPA-Enterprise and WPA2-Enterprise both use 802.1x servers. WPA2-Enterprise provides the best security, and it is recommended for use in enterprise environments.

Both WPA and WPA2 can use either Personal or Enterprise mode. When Personal is used (as in WPA-Personal or WPA2-Personal), it uses a pre-shared key (PSK). This PSK can be a password or passphrase. When Enterprise is used (as in WPA-Enterprise or WPA2-Enterprise), an 802.1x server is used.

Configuring Wireless on Windows 7

You can configure a Windows 7 computer to work with three different wireless configurations. You can connect to wireless access point or a wireless router in a network. You can also configure a Windows 7 system to connect to an ad hoc network.

Wireless Access Point

A *wireless access point (WAP)* can be used to provide access from a wireless device to a wired network. WAPs are commonly used in larger networks to provide this access.

Figure 12.2 shows how a Windows 7 system can connect to a WAP in a network. Once the Windows 7 system is connected, it can access resources in the network just as if it were a wired computer.

FIGURE 12.2   Wireless access point in a network

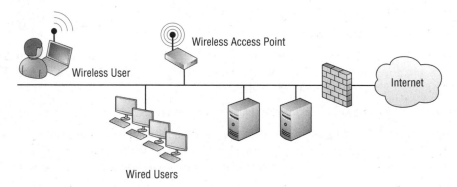

The wireless client will be able to connect to servers in the network. If other clients have Internet access, the wireless client will also have Internet access.

Wireless Routers

A *wireless router* is a WAP with additional capabilities. Many small offices, home offices (SOHOs) and home users commonly use a wireless router. Figure 12.3 shows how a wireless router can be used to provide connectivity for users in a network.

FIGURE 12.3   Wireless router in a network

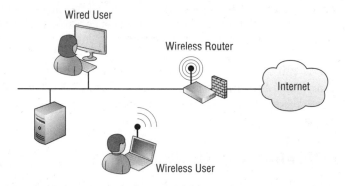

The wireless client is able to connect to the wireless router and have access to the same resources as the wired user. Notice how the router has connectivity with the Internet. On the Internet side, it would have a public IP address issued from the Internet service provider. On the internal network side, it would have a private IP address. In addition to being a router, it would also have network address translation (NAT) capabilities to translate the internal private IP addresses to external public IP addresses.

Most wireless routers also have DHCP capabilities. DHCP is used to issue TCP/IP configuration to internal clients. This includes IP addresses, subnet masks, default gateway addresses, DNS addresses, and more.

 Real World Scenario

Wireless Networks Common in SOHOs

It is very common for SOHOs to use wireless networks. The hardware is relatively inexpensive, and the technology is not that difficult to configure.

You can purchase a single wireless router and connect it to the Internet. This wireless router can then be used to provide connectivity to multiple systems. The systems can be mobile computers or desktop PCs with wireless NICs. Most wireless routers also have connections for some wired computers.

The biggest benefit is that you don't need to run cables to all the computers. Still, the biggest concern is ensuring that adequate security is used. It is possible to create a wireless network that is wide open, allowing attackers to capture important data.

Ad Hoc Network

Ad hoc is a Latin phrase that essentially means "as needed." An ad hoc network is a wireless network without a wireless access point or wireless router. Imagine that you and a friend or two want to connect your computers to share some data or even play a game. If all three of your computers have wireless capabilities, you can create an ad hoc network.

Figure 12.4 shows three wireless users configured in an ad hoc wireless network. One of the computers creates the ad hoc network, and the other two computers connect to it.

An ad hoc network is created for a specific purpose but is usually destroyed when users disconnect. However, it is possible to save the network profile for later use.

Figure 12.5 shows the screen used to create the ad hoc network. You need to give the network a name. In the figure, I've called it TempAdHoc. You also need to identify the security type and the security key that will be used. The security key is a pre-shared key such as a password or passphrase. All participants in the ad hoc network need to use the same security type and PSK.

FIGURE 12.4   A wireless ad hoc network

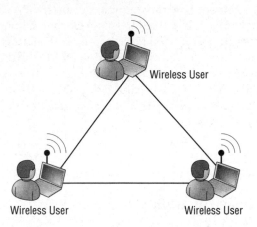

FIGURE 12.5   Creating a wireless ad hoc network

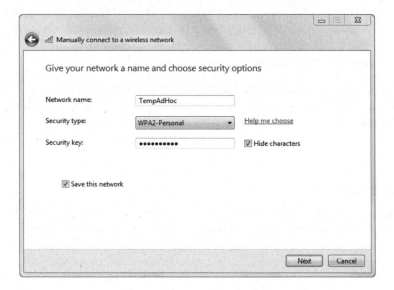

You can get to the screen shown in Figure 12.5 by clicking Control Panel ➤ Network And Internet ➤ Network And Sharing Center. You can also get to the Network and Sharing Center by entering Network in the Control Panel Search box and selecting Network And Sharing Center. From there, click Manage Wireless Networks. Click Add and select Create An Ad Hoc Network.

The Manage Wireless Networks screen will appear only on clients that have wireless NICs. If your system doesn't have a wireless NIC installed, you will not see this choice.

Ad hoc networks support three security types:

No Authentication (Open) Data is sent in the clear. Generally, this is not recommended. However, gamers may choose this for better performance over a wireless network.

WEP If older computers support only WEP, you can use this. It has known vulnerabilities but is better than nothing to secure the connection.

WPA2-Personal WPA2-Personal provides the best security. An ad hoc network does not support WPA2-Enterprise.

WPA-Personal is not available as a choice for ad hoc networks. WPA Enterprise and WPA2 Enterprise aren't available as choices either, because you are connected only between peers. Enterprise choices require a separate 802.1x server to be used for authentication.

The security key is a shared secret. Each user will need to enter the same security key in their wireless profile to connect to the ad hoc network.

Last, if you want to save the ad hoc network for later use, you can check the Save This Network box, as shown in Figure 12.5 earlier. It will save this as an ad hoc profile that can be used later.

Only the first computer needs to create the ad hoc network. Once it's created, other computers can connect to it as if it was a wireless network connection.

Connecting to a Wireless Network

If you're running Windows 7 and want to connect to a wireless network, you'll need to create a wireless profile. First, ensure you have the correct information on the wireless network. You'll need to know the following:

- The name of the wireless network
- The security type used by the wireless network
- The encryption type used by the wireless network
- The security key if one is used

The name of the wireless network is also called the Service Set Identifier (SSID). Wireless devices come with default names such as Linksys. However, it's common for administrators to rename the SSID.

Figure 12.6 shows the screen used to create a wireless profile. For this figure, the network name is WileyNetwork. It is using WPA2-Personal and AES. The PSK is IL0veWindows7.

FIGURE 12.6 Creating a wireless profile

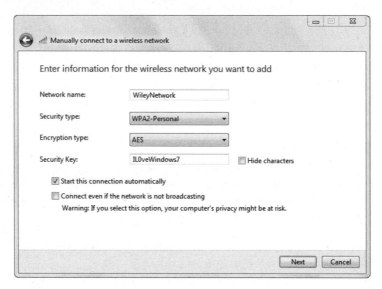

Notice in the figure that the Start This Connection Automatically box is checked. This will ensure that Windows 7 will connect to this wireless network when it is in range. If WileyNetwork is configured to broadcast the SSID, the Windows 7 system will detect the broadcast and automatically connect.

You can get to the screen shown in Figure 12.6 by clicking Control Panel ➢ Network And Internet ➢ Network And Sharing Center. Click Manage Wireless Networks. Click Add and select Manually Create A Network Profile.

 **Real World Scenario**

Don't Disable SSID Broadcasts

In the past, it was commonly recommended to disable SSID broadcasting for a wireless network. The idea was that this hides the wireless network and makes it more difficult for an attacker to locate it.

However, Microsoft does not recommend this practice. Instead, they suggest that SSID broadcasting should be left enabled. Even though the WAP doesn't broadcast the SSID, clients must transmit the SSID to connect to it. Moreover, if the client is configured to connect to a hidden network (one where the SSID is not broadcasting), the client is constantly transmitting the SSID even when it isn't in range.

Attackers who know what traffic to look for can intercept the client's transmissions. This allows an attacker to learn the names of the SSIDs that a client is configured to use. For example, when an employee takes their laptop to a coffee shop, the computer doesn't know it's in a coffee shop, so it continues to transmit the SSID of the wireless network at work.

Because of this, Microsoft recommends that SSID broadcasting be enabled on wireless access points and wireless routers. You can read more about this here: `http://technet .microsoft.com/en-us/library/bb726942.aspx`.

Once you have created the wireless profile, you can access it from the Network and Sharing Center. Figure 12.7 shows the Network and Sharing Center with a computer named DRG connected to a wireless network named HomeSweetHome.

FIGURE 12.7   Network and Sharing Center

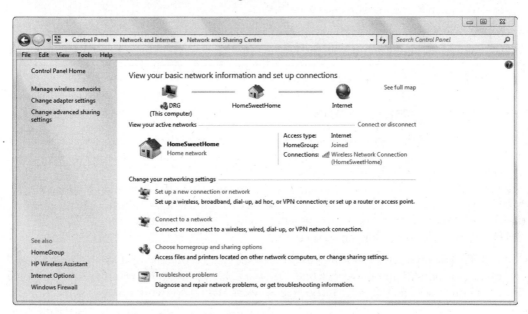

You can click the Connect Or Disconnect link to connect to another wireless network. If the system wasn't connected, this link would be labeled Connect To A Network. You can also click the Connect To A Network link in the Change Your Networking Settings section.

As a reminder, the extra menu item in the left pane, Manage Wireless Networks, will appear only if the computer has a wireless adapter installed. If your computer doesn't have a wireless adapter, you won't see it. Exercise 12.1 shows how to create a network profile.

EXERCISE 12.1

Creating a Network Profile

1. Launch the Network and Sharing Center. Click Start ➢ Control Panel ➢ Network And Internet ➢ Network And Sharing Center.

2. Click Manage Wireless Networks.

3. Click Add. Click Manually Create A Network Profile.

4. Enter the name of the wireless network (SSID) in the Network Name text box.

5. Select the security type used by the wireless network. This can be WEP, WPA-Personal, WPA-Enterprise, WPA2-Personal, WPA2-Enterprise, or 802.1x.

6. Select the encryption type. This is also dependent on the wireless network settings.

7. If the security type requires a security key, enter it in the Security Key text box. This is also known as the pre-shared key, or PSK.

8. If you want to connect to this network whenever it is in range, ensure that Start This Connection Automatically is checked.

Setting Up Connections

The Network and Sharing Center includes other tools to make the setup and connection of wireless networks easy. You can click Set Up A New Connection Or Network in the Change Your Networking Settings section.

Figure 12.8 shows this screen. You can use this to launch several different wizards for different types of connectivity. Some of these wizards are for wireless connections. Some are for remote access connections, which will be covered later in the chapter.

This screen gives the following choices:

Connect To The Internet   You would use this to set up a broadband or dial-up connection. Broadband includes digital subscriber line (DSL) or cable connections. Dial-up includes traditional phone lines and the faster Integrated Services Digital Network (ISDN) connections.

Set Up A New Network   You can use this to configure some wireless routers or access points. While this may work, you'll probably have better luck following the directions of the manufacturer for the wireless device.

Manually Connect To A Wireless Network   You can use this to connect to a hidden network, connect to an ad hoc network, or create a new wireless profile. A hidden network is one where the SSID is not broadcasting. You saw this screen earlier in Figure 12.6. This is just a different path to get to the same place. After you enter the network name, the security type, encryption type, and security key (if used), you'll be able to connect.

Connect To A Workplace   You can use this to create a connection to a remote access server. It allows you to create either a dial-up connection to your workplace or a VPN connection. Remote access connections are explored later in this chapter.

Set Up A Dial-up Connection   You can use this to create a dial-up connection to your Internet service provider. You'll need to have the phone number and credentials provided by the ISP. Although most urban areas have high-speed Internet access, many rural areas are still using dial-up.

Set Up A Wireless Ad Hoc (Computer-To-Computer) Network   You can use this option to create the ad hoc network from this wizard, and then other users can connect using the Manually Connect To A Wireless Network option. This choice is not shown in the figure but can be viewed by scrolling down.

FIGURE 12.8   Creating connections

Troubleshooting Wireless Connections

Occasionally, things don't work as planned. There are a few things you can check to trouble-shoot the connection:

- Signal strength
- Security settings
- Network diagnostics

Signal Strength

If the signal strength of the wireless network is low, your computer may not be able to connect to it. If you're unable to connect, you can easily check the signal strength.

As background, wireless technologies often advertise specific speeds. For example, 802.11g advertises speeds of 54 Mbps. However, this is not the guaranteed speed. Instead, this is the fastest speed it can achieve without errors.

When a wireless system connects with the wireless device, it attempts to connect at the fastest speed without errors. If the WAP and the wireless client are close, they may use the maximum speed. However, if distance and barriers such as walls separate the two devices, the speed may be substantially slower.

> Hobbyists and attackers have played around with methods to increase the range of wireless networks for a long time. One well-known method uses a directional Pringles potato chip can. A wire is attached to the base of an empty Pringles can and then to the wireless NIC. The Pringles can is then pointed to the wireless network. Some people have reported getting a signal from more than a mile away using this method.

At some point, the devices will determine that the signal is just not strong enough and they can't connect. You can check the signal strength by clicking Connect To A Network from the Network and Sharing Center. You can hover your mouse over any of the connections to see additional details. Figure 12.9 shows the display.

FIGURE 12.9   Checking signal strength

Although not apparent in a black-and-white picture, the strength is shown by colored bars. The more colored bars, the better the signal strength. If the signal is not readable, it will be listed as No Signal.

In the figure, I've hovered over the HomeSweetHome connection. It shows Signal Strength as Excellent. Notice that it also shows Security Type, Radio Type, and SSID.

Security Settings

In addition to checking the signal, you can also verify the security settings of the wireless profile. We covered all of these settings previously in this chapter. The simplest thing to do is double-check the settings.

You can access the settings for a wireless profile after clicking Manage Wireless Networks from the Network and Sharing Center. You can also access these profiles by launching Control Panel, entering Wireless in the Control Panel Search box, and selecting Manage Wireless Networks. Right-click any profile and select Properties.

Double-check the following settings:

- Network Name
- Security Type
- Encryption Type
- Security Key

A common problem you may see with mobile computers is that the wireless capability is turned off. Some mobile computers do this automatically to save power. You can usually turn it on from a switch somewhere on the laptop. For example, my HP Pavilion laptop has a touch switch. When I touch it, it turns orange indicating it's off. If I touch it again, it turns blue indicating it's on.

Network Diagnostics

Network Diagnostics in Windows 7 can identify and resolve many problems with network connections. This includes both wired and wireless connectivity issues.

Some of the troubleshooting wizards in earlier Windows versions didn't always provide real help for professional administrators. They may have been useful for basic users but not for the professionals. However, the Network Diagnostics tool is clearly valuable to both basic users and advanced troubleshooters.

Microsoft mentions that the Network Diagnostics tool can diagnose more than 180 different issues. I'm stressing this because you may think of the older wizards and overlook this tool. This and other troubleshooting wizards are truly valuable.

You can also launch Network Diagnostics from the Network and Sharing Center. Click the Troubleshoot Problems link in the Change Your Network Settings section.

Network Diagnostics works best with native Wi-Fi drivers. You can check to ensure that your system is using native drivers with the following command prompt command: `netsh wlan show drivers`. The type should be listed as Native Wi-Fi Driver. If it is listed as Legacy Wi-Fi Driver, you should update the driver to get the best performance from the diagnostics.

Exercise 12.2 shows how to run Network Diagnostics on a Windows 7 system with a wireless adapter.

EXERCISE 12.2

Running Network Diagnostics on a Wireless Connector

1. Launch the Network and Sharing Center. Click Start ➢ Control Panel ➢ Network And Internet ➢ Network And Sharing Center.

2. Click Change Adapter Settings. Select your wireless connection. Your display will look something like the following graphic. Note that the commands available on the toolbar change based on the connection you select.

3. Select Diagnose This Connection. This will run a wide range of diagnostics and lead you through the steps needed to resolve the problem.

4. If you're unable to resolve the problem with the diagnostics, check the System log in Event Viewer. The Network Diagnostics Wizard logs events with a source of Diagnostics – Networking.

Troubleshooting Remote Access Issues

Mobile users often need to have access to an internal network even when they aren't at the company. Many companies use different types of remote access solutions to support them.

Whereas the administrators are responsible for designing, implementing, and maintaining the remote access servers, desktop administrators are required to support the end users. If you're the desktop administrator, you'll want to have a good understanding of all the pieces. This section covers the following topics:

- Remote access overview
- Creating a dial-up connection
- Creating a VPN connection
- Adding a certificate
- Troubleshooting a VPN client
- A few words about Teredo

Remote Access Overview

Remote access allows users to connect to the company's internal network while they are away from the network. They can be traveling, working at a remote customer's site, or working from home. Users can connect with a dial-up connection or a virtual private network connection.

A VPN connection allows a user to connect to a private network over a public network. The majority of the time, the public network is the Internet. Some VPN connections that connect offices use leased lines instead of the Internet as the public network.

Consider Figure 12.10. This shows two types of remote access connections. At the top left, the user is connecting to the remote access server using dial-up. The client needs to have a modem and access to phone lines. Similarly, the remote access server has a modem and access to phone lines.

The second mobile user (at the bottom left) is connecting using a VPN. The client first connects to the Internet. Once connected to the Internet, the client can then connect to the remote access server. The remote access server must have a public IP address and a connection to the Internet.

The terms *remote access server* and *VPN server* are sometimes confusing. *Remote access server* is generic, indicating that it provides remote access. However, *VPN server* is specific, indicating that remote access is provided using a VPN connection. In other words, a VPN server may also be called a remote access server. However, a remote access server that provides only dial-up access isn't a VPN server.

FIGURE 12.10   Dial-up and VPN user connections

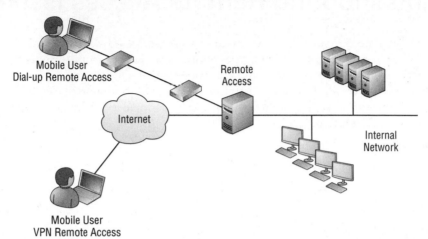

VPN connections use tunneling protocols. These tunneling protocols include encryption and provide additional protection for the connection. Windows 7 supports the following four tunneling protocols:

Internet Key Exchange version 2 (IKEv2)   IKEv2 is the newest tunneling protocol and was introduced with Windows 7 and Windows Server 2008 R2. It can also go through a NAT server and provides an additional choice over PPTP. Windows Vista, Windows Server 2008 servers, or older versions do not support IKEv2.

Secure Shell Tunneling Protocol (SSTP)   SSTP was introduced with Windows Vista and Windows Server 2008. It uses SSL to encrypt the traffic as HTTPS traffic. It can go through a NAT server, providing an additional choice if your VPN server is located behind a NAT server. SSTP provides better security than PPTP and supports both IPv4 and IPv6. You can use SSTP with clients running Microsoft Windows Vista, Windows Server 2008, or later versions.

Layer 2 Tunneling Protocol (L2TP)   L2TP was developed by combining the strengths of Microsoft's PPTP with the strengths of Cisco's Layer 2 Forwarding (L2F) protocol. It encrypts data using IPSec (and is shown as L2TP/IPSec) and supports both IPv4 and IPv6. The only drawback is that IPSec can't go through a network address translation server. If the VPN had to go through a NAT, the previous recommendation was to use PPTP. You can use L2TP/IPSec with clients running Microsoft Windows 2000 or later versions.

Point-to-Point Tunneling Protocol (PPTP)   PPTP is the oldest of the four protocols. It encrypts data using Microsoft Point-to-Point Encryption (MPPE). PPTP is not supported on IPv6. While PPTP is still used, you can expect it to be used less often in the future. You can use PPTP with clients running Microsoft Windows 2000 or later versions.

When taking the exams, remember that PPTP does not support IPv6. If your clients must go over IPv6, you will not be able to use PPTP. IKEv2 is the most likely choice for Windows 7 clients connecting to a Windows Server 2008 R2 server.

IKEv2, L2TP/IPSec, and SSTP provide several important security protections:

- Data confidentiality by encrypting the data
- Data integrity (ensures the data hasn't been modified)
- Data authentication (verifies the hosts)

IKEv2 and SSTP both require the use of a Public Key Infrastructure to issue certificates. IPSec will work without a certificate using a pre-shared key, but the use of a certificate is highly recommended.

When you create a VPN connection, it will default to Automatic for the tunneling protocol. In other words, you don't have to choose which tunneling protocol the server is using. Windows 7 will attempt to connect to a VPN server using the different tunneling protocols in the following order:

- IKEv2
- SSTP
- PPTP
- L2TP

Windows 7 also supports a neat feature with IKEv2 connections called MOBIKE, or VPN Reconnect. MOBIKE allows clients to reconnect easily a broken VPN connection without user interaction.

This can be very useful for mobile clients that have unreliable connections. When they reconnect, the original security association is retained instead of creating a new one. This requires only about a tenth of the traffic and results in a quick reconnection for the clients.

Creating a Dial-up Connection

You saw how to create different types of connections earlier in this chapter. The Set Up A New Connection Or Network choice on the Network and Sharing Center includes several wizards to create connections.

One choice is Connect To A Workplace. You can use this wizard to create either a dial-up or a VPN connection. When you select this choice, you'll be prompted either to use your Internet connection to connect via a VPN or to dial directly.

If you choose to dial directly, you'll be prompted to pick a modem (if you have more than one), and then you'll see a screen similar to Figure 12.11. You enter the phone number of the remote access server and the name of the connection on this screen.

If your company requires the use of a smart card, you can check the Use A Smart Card check box. You can also select the Allow Other People To Use This Connection check box. This will make the profile available for all users who can log on to the computer.

The Dialing Rules link allows you to configure rules that may be required. For example, you may need to dial 9 to get an outside line or use specific carrier codes for long-distance or international calls.

FIGURE 12.11 Creating a dial-up connection

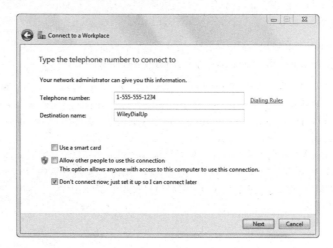

Exercise 12.3 shows how to create a dial-up connection for remote access. This exercise assumes you have a modem in your system.

EXERCISE 12.3

Creating a Remote Access Dial-up Connection

1. Launch the Network and Sharing Center. Click Start ➤ Control Panel ➤ Network and Internet ➤ Network and Sharing Center.

2. Click Set Up A New Connection Or Network.

3. Select Connect To A Workplace. Click Next.

4. If you have existing connections, you'll be prompted to use one of them or create a new one. Select No, Create A New Connection, and click Next.

5. Select Dial Directly. If you have more than one modem, you will see a list of modem choices. Select a modem.

6. Type the telephone number and the connection name in the Telephone Number and Destination Name text boxes.

7. Select Don't Connect Now; Just Set It Up So I Can Connect Later. Click Next.

8. Enter your user name and password in the User Name and Password text boxes. If your network is using a domain, enter the domain name. Your display will look something like the following graphic.

EXERCISE 12.3 (continued)

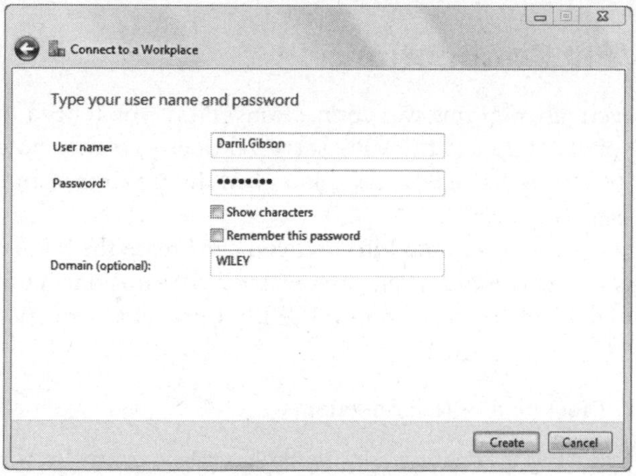

9. Click Create to create the connection. You can then click Connect Now to test it or click Close.

After you create a dial-up connection, it will show up in several places. Two links are available directly from the Network and Sharing Center.

Connect To A Network You can select the dial-up connection from here and click Connect to connect to the remote access server.

Change Adapter Settings You can select the dial-up connection from here and select Start This Connection to connect to the remote access server.

Figure 12.12 shows the screen you'll see when you choose either of these methods.

FIGURE 12.12 Connecting to a dial-up connection

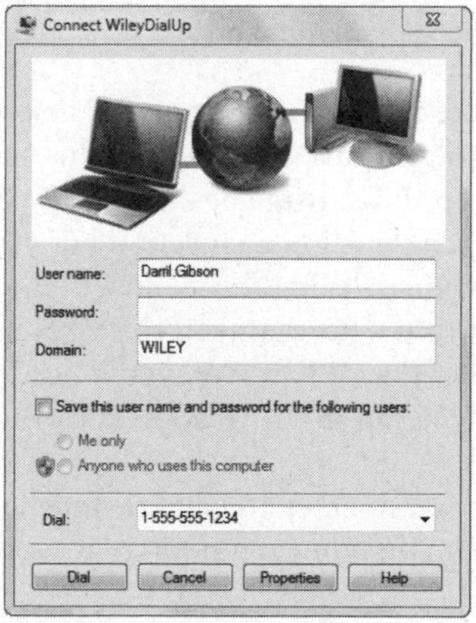

If you didn't save the password, you can enter it and then click Dial. You can also access advanced properties for the connection by clicking the Properties button.

Creating a VPN Connection

A VPN connection actually requires two connections. First, you'll need to connect to the Internet, and then you'll connect to the VPN server. It doesn't matter how you connect to the Internet. It can be over a dial-up connection, a DSL line, a broadband connection, or even through a wireless router.

After creating the connection to the Internet, you can create the VPN connection. You follow the first steps just as you did when you created a dial-up connection. However, instead of choosing Dial Directly, you choose Use My Internet Connection (VPN), as shown in Figure 12.13.

FIGURE 12.13 Creating a VPN connection

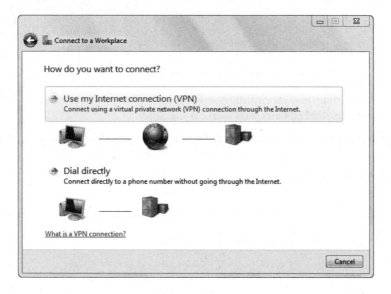

If you aren't currently connected to the Internet, you'll be prompted to identify how you want to connect to the Internet. Figure 12.14 shows this screen. You can choose from one of the connections in the drop-down list. The Always Use This Connection check box is selected by default. If you launch the VPN connection but you're not connected to the Internet, you'll be prompted to connect using this connection.

You then enter the IP address or the hostname of the VPN server and a name for the connection. If you use the name of the VPN server, you'll need to ensure that it is resolvable from an Internet DNS server. If you put in the IP address directly, you'll bypass the DNS name-resolution step.

The wizard will then prompt you to enter credentials for the VPN server. These include the user name, password, and domain name if a domain is used.

FIGURE 12.14   Identifying Internet access for the VPN

Exercise 12.4 shows how to create a VPN connection for remote access. This exercise assumes you have a connection created for Internet access.

EXERCISE 12.4

Creating a Remote Access VPN Connection

1. Launch the Network and Sharing Center. Click Start ➤ Control Panel ➤ Network And Internet ➤ Network And Sharing Center.

2. Click Set Up A New Connection Or Network.

3. Select Connect To A Workplace. Click Next.

4. Ensure that No, Create A New Connection is selected. Click Next.

5. Select Use My Internet Connection (VPN).

6. On the Type The Internet Address page, enter the IP address or the name of the VPN server in the Internet Address text box. Enter a name for the VPN connection in the Destination Name text box.

7. Select Don't Connect Now; Just Set It Up So I Can Connect Later. Click Next.

8. Enter your user name, password, and domain (if needed). Click Create.

At this point, the connection is ready to use. While a lot of the connection activity is automatic, you may need to troubleshoot some connections.

Add a Certificate

If you're using IKEv2 or SSTP, a certificate is required for the connection. If you're using L2TP/IPSec, a certificate is recommended. The VPN server passes the certificate to the client during the connection process. However, the client won't necessarily trust this certificate.

Chapter 6, "Configuring and Troubleshooting Application Issues," discussed trusted certificate authorities (CAs) and the trust chain. As long as the certificate is issued from a trusted CA, the certificate is trusted. However, if the certificate is not issued from a trusted CA, the certificate won't be trusted and the user will see a warning.

Consider these two scenarios:

1. Your company purchases a certificate from a public CA such as VeriSign. This certificate is installed on the VPN server and sent to the clients. Because Windows 7 clients have a certificate from VeriSign in their Trusted Root Certification Authorities store, they trust the certificate from the VPN server. They will not receive a warning.

2. Your company chooses not to pay for the certificate. Instead, administrators create an internal CA. This internal CA issues a certificate to the VPN server. Because Windows 7 clients don't have a certificate from the internal CA in their Trusted Root Certification Authorities store, they do not trust the certificate from the VPN server. They will receive a warning.

The second scenario is cheaper, but the warning can be confusing to users. Users can ignore the warning, but with security as challenging as it is already, you probably don't want to train your users to ignore warnings. The solution is to add the certificate from the internal CA to the Windows 7 Trusted Root Certification Authorities store.

You can use Exercise 12.5 to add a certificate to a Windows 7 client. You'll need to obtain a certificate from the administrator of the internal CA. Copy this certificate to a location on the computer.

EXERCISE 12.5

Add a Certificate to a Windows 7 Client

1. Click Start and type **MMC** in the Start Search box. If prompted by UAC, click Yes to continue.

2. Select File ➢ Add/Remove Snap-in.

3. Select Certificates and click Add. Select Computer Account and click Next. Ensure Local Computer is selected and click Finish. Click OK.

4. Expand Certificates ➢ Trusted Root Certification Authorities ➢ Certificates.

5. Right-click Certificates and select Import. The Certificate Import Wizard will launch. Review the Welcome screen and click Next.

6. Click Browse and go to the location of the certificate file. Click Open. Click Next.

7.   On the Certificate Store page, ensure that Place All Certificates In The Following Store is selected and the Certificate Store is listed as Trusted Root Certification Authorities. Your display will look similar to the following graphic. Click Next.

8.   Click Next.

9.   Review the information on the Completion screen and click Finish. A dialog box will appear indicating the import was successful. Click OK.

Once the certificate has been imported, the clients will no longer receive the warnings for certificates issues from the CA.

It's also possible to publish these certificates to internal clients using Group Policy. Certificates are deployed using the Computer Configuration ➤ Policies ➤ Windows Settings ➤ Security Settings ➤ Public Key Policies ➤ Trusted Root Certification Authority Store node.

You can right-click the Trusted Root Certification Authority node and select Import. It uses a similar wizard to import the certificate. After the certificate is imported, Group Policy will deploy the certificate to all computers in the scope of the GPO.

Troubleshooting a VPN Client

If everything goes well, you'll be able to connect to the VPN server right after you create the connection. However, not everything always goes well. Instead, you may need to do a little troubleshooting.

Figure 12.15 shows the error screen you'll probably see if you can't connect. By default, it will try to redial or reconnect three times. However, if it didn't work the first time, it probably won't work the second or third time.

FIGURE 12.15   VPN connection error

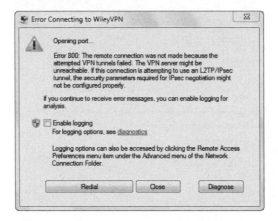

There are a few important steps you can take. First, make sure you have Internet access. Without Internet access, the VPN connection won't work. However, this is the easiest problem to solve because the VPN connection will let you know and prompt you to connect to the Internet.

If you have Internet access but still can't connect, you can try these extra steps.

- Check the settings.
- Enable logging.
- Run diagnostics.

Check Settings

The logical first step is to double-check the settings. Often the problem is just a simple issue of entering the wrong IP address. You can do this by checking the properties of the connection. If your VPN server has more specific settings, you'll be able to configure them from these property pages.

You can access the VPN connection properties with the following steps. Launch the Network and Sharing Center. Click Change Adapter Settings. Right-click the VPN connection and select Properties.

There are five tabs, and we explore four of them in the following sections. The Sharing tab is more important for home users than for enterprise users. It can be used to enable Internet Connection Sharing (ICS). In other words, it can be used to share its Internet connection.

VPN General Tab

You can access the General tab to change some of the basic properties you set when you created the connection. Figure 12.16 shows properties available on the General tab. The obvious thing to check here is to ensure you have entered the correct IP address.

FIGURE 12.16   The General tab of the VPN connection properties

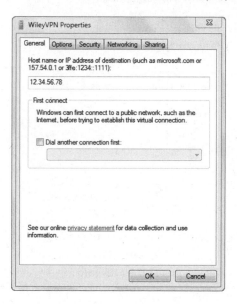

You can also reconfigure how the VPN connects to the Internet. This should be configured if the system isn't normally connected to the Internet. You can select the Dial Another Connection First check box, and then select one of the connections from the drop-down list box.

VPN Options Tab

The Options tab allows you to set the options for the connection. Even though these options are labeled as Dialing Options and Redialing Options, they also refer to the VPN connection. In other words, even if you're using a broadband connection and not dialing at all, these settings apply.

Figure 12.17 shows the Options tab with the default settings. If the system can't connect on the first try, it will automatically attempt to retry three more times. This gives the VPN server time to recover if multiple clients are connected at the same time, stretching its resources.

FIGURE 12.17   The Options tab of the VPN connection properties

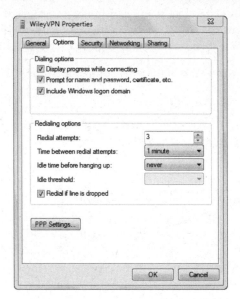

If you click the PPP Settings button, you'll have the option of setting three advanced options. These may be needed for some VPN servers:

- Enable LCP Extensions. This is enabled by default.
- Enable Software Compression.
- Negotiate Multi-Link For Single-Link Connections.

VPN Security Tab

The Security tab has several important settings that you may need to configure. At the very least, you should be aware of what can be configured here. Figure 12.18 shows the choices.

Type Of VPN refers to the tunneling protocol used. As a reminder, Windows 7 supports IKEv2, SSTP, PPTP, and L2TP. When it is set to Automatic (as shown), it will try each of these protocols until it connects.

You can also select the tunneling protocol to match what the VPN server is using. This will save time on the connection. In addition, it will make the configuration easier. For example, if you select IKEv2, it limits the authentication choices to only the more advanced type of authentication needed by IKEv2.

The Data Encryption setting allows you to specify how the data is encrypted. This includes four choices. The first choice is the default.

- Require Encryption (Disconnect If Server Declines)
- Maximum Strength Encryption (Disconnect If Server Declines)
- Optional Encryption (Connect Even If No Encryption)
- No Encryption Allowed (Server Will Disconnect If It Requires Encryption)

FIGURE 12.18 The Security tab of the VPN connection properties

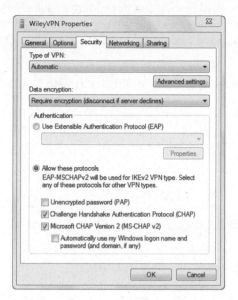

 If the VPN is connecting over the Internet, it's highly recommended that you use either Require Encryption or Maximum Strength Encryption. This ensures that any data transmitted over the VPN tunnel is protected from interception.

The bottom of the screen shows the authentication protocols that you can select. As a reminder, you use authentication to prove who you are. This is commonly done with either a user name and password or a smart card.

If you're using a user name and password, you should use Challenge Handshake Authentication Protocol (CHAP) or Microsoft CHAP Version 2 (MS-CHAP v2). Password Authentication Protocol (PAP) sends the credentials in clear text and should be avoided. Again, your choice will depend on what the VPN server expects. If multiple choices are selected on the client, Windows 7 will attempt the more secure protocols first and continue down the list until the connection completes.

If the VPN server is configured to require smart cards or another stronger protocol, you would select Use Extensible Authentication Protocol (EAP). This drop-down list includes three Microsoft choices and several AuthorID choices for third-party solutions. The three Microsoft choices are

- Microsoft: Smart Card Or Other Certificate (Encryption Enabled)
- Microsoft: Secured Password (EAP-MSCHAP v2) (Encryption Enabled)
- Microsoft: Protected EAP (PEAP) (Encryption Enabled)

When you select any of these settings, you can also click the Properties button. The Properties page that appears will be different depending on what is selected. For example, if you have selected Microsoft: Smart Card Or Other Certificate, you'll see the screen shown in Figure 12.19. If you've selected Microsoft: Protected EAP (PEAP), you'll see a different screen.

FIGURE 12.19   Advanced properties for the Smart Card Or Other Certificate setting

Notice that you can configure this to use a smart card. You can also configure it to use a certificate if needed by the VPN server.

VPN Networking Tab

The Networking tab allows you to select or deselect protocols and services available to the VPN connection. These include the protocols needed to connect to the VPN server and the protocols needed after you connect.

Figure 12.20 shows the Networking tab with the default selections.

At least IPv4 or IPv6 is needed for connectivity. Both are selected by default, which allows IPv6 to be used when it's available and IPv4 to be used when IPv6 isn't available. It's possible to have an IPv6 connection over the Internet and then use an IPv4 connection on the internal network.

FIGURE 12.20   The Networking tab of the VPN connection properties

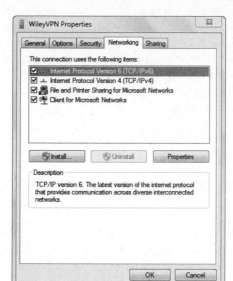

 You can enable both IPv4 and IPv6. IPv6 will be used when available (such as on the Internet), and IPv4 will be used when IPv6 is not available.

File And Printer Sharing For Microsoft Networks allows other computers in the network to access resources on your computer. The Client For Microsoft Networks client is needed to access resources on other computers.

Enable Logging

If you're unable to get the VPN connection working by double-checking and reconfiguring the settings, you can enable logging. Select the Enable Logging check box (shown in Figure 12.15 earlier) and try to connect again. This will create logs that you can read to reveal more details on the problem.

 The RAS logs can take up extra resources and may impact the performance of your system if you leave them running. Think of these as debugging logs. Turn them on when you need them. However, remember to turn them off once you've resolved the problem.

When you enable logging, log files are created in the %windir%\tracing directory. If the tracing directory doesn't exist yet, it will be created when you enable logging. There will also be additional entries enabled in the Security Event log available from the Event Viewer.

Instead of selecting the Enable Logging check box from the error page, you can use the netsh command to enable or disable logging. These commands need to be run from an administrative command prompt to work completely. If you don't run them with administrative permissions, all of the logs won't be enabled.

This command will enable logging:

```
netsh ras diag set tracefacilities enable
```

This command will disable logging:

```
netsh ras diag set tracefacilities disable
```

Run Diagnostics

On the error page for the connection (shown earlier in Figure 12.15), you can click the Diagnostics link. This will bring you to the Remote Access Preferences dialog box with the Diagnostics tab selected, as shown in Figure 12.21.

FIGURE 12.21 Run diagnostics from the Remote Access Preferences screen.

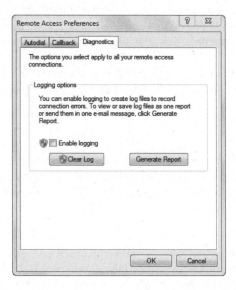

You can click the Generate Report button to run detailed diagnostics on your system. This will take a few minutes to complete. When it does complete, it will open the report in Internet Explorer.

This report is quite extensive. It retrieves data from more than 40 logs and puts them into an HTML file. It performs several installation information checks, performs several configuration checks, and records all of the results in the file.

The data in this report is rather deep. However, if you're troubleshooting a problem that is eluding your best efforts, this report may give you exactly what you need.

A Few Words about Teredo

Windows 7 supports *Teredo*, and Teredo becomes very apparent when you are working with VPNs. Teredo is a tunneling protocol that encapsulates IPv6 packets within IPv4. It is intended to be a temporary bridge as all networks transition from IPv4 to IPv6.

Teredo uses Teredo clients and Teredo servers. In this context, Windows 7 will be the client. Windows 7 clients use the server located at teredo.ipv6.microsoft.com as their Teredo server.

The server is used to detect what type of NAT is between the client and the server so that Teredo can determine how to encapsulate the packets.

Teredo can be in one of four possible states in Windows 7:

Qualified state   IPv6 traffic is able to flow into and out of the system over Teredo.

Dormant state   Teredo is enabled but not active. Applications that need to use IPv6 traffic can activate Teredo. IPv6 traffic isn't sent while in the Dormant state.

Probe state   When Teredo is transitioning between the Dormant state and the Qualified state, it will be listed as in the Probe state. During this time, it attempts to contact a Teredo server. If it can't connect to a Teredo server, it will enter the Offline state; but if it can connect, it will enter the Qualified state.

Offline state   This indicates that Teredo is not working. It could be placed in the Offline state by a command such as `netsh int teredo set state disabled`. It will go into this state if it detects a domain controller indicating it's in a managed environment (unless the state is set to enterprise client). It can also go into this state if it is unable to transition from a Dormant state to a Qualified state.

> The state of Teredo in Windows 7 isn't dependent on whether the system is joined to a domain. It is dependent on whether it can detect a domain controller. If a workgroup computer is in a network with a DC, Teredo will be in Offline state once it detects the DC. On the other hand, if a user takes a domain-joined laptop home, Teredo won't be able to detect the DC and the state will change to Dormant.

You can use the `netsh` command to manage the state of Teredo. The following commands may be useful when you're working or troubleshooting issues with Teredo.

You can use this command to view the state of Teredo:

```
netsh int teredo show state
```

You'll see output similar to Listing 12.1.

Listing 12.1: Output of the `netsh int teredo show state` command

```
C:\>netsh int teredo show state
Teredo Parameters
--------------------------------------------
Type                      : client
Server Name               : teredo.ipv6.microsoft.com.
Client Refresh Interval   : 30 seconds
Client Port               : unspecified
State                     : dormant
```

You can use this command to disable Teredo:

```
netsh int teredo set state disabled
```

You can use this command to enable Teredo:

```
netsh int teredo set state enabled
```

You can use this command to enable Teredo even when a domain controller is present:

```
netsh int teredo set state enterpriseclient
```

Understanding DirectAccess

DirectAccess is a new feature available with Windows 7 and Windows Server 2008 R2. It allows clients to access internal resources using Internet access but without creating a VPN.

You can think of DirectAccess as a virtual tunnel. It uses IPv6 over IPSec to secure the traffic. Once it is configured, remote clients can access servers on the internal network over the Internet, just as if they were on the internal network. In other words, as long as the clients have access to the Internet, they can access servers on the internal network.

In order to take advantage of DirectAccess, you must meet several requirements:

Clients   Clients must be running Windows 7 Enterprise or Ultimate edition. The clients must also be members of the same domain hosting the DirectAccess servers.

Servers   Servers must be running Windows Server 2008 R2 or later. These servers have two NICs. One NIC is connected to the internal network, and one NIC is connected to the Internet.

IPv6   Both the client and server must be running IPv6. This includes DNSv6 and DHCPv6 if DHCP is being used.

Network resources The servers must be in a Windows domain. Domain controllers and DNS servers must be running at least Windows Server 2008 SP2 or Windows Server 2008 R2. The network must also have a Public Key Infrastructure to issue certificates.

> If you want to dig deeper into DirectAccess, Microsoft has several resources to help you configure the pieces. This website is a great starting place:
> http://technet.microsoft.com/network/dd420463.aspx.

Using BranchCache

BranchCache is another new feature available only for Windows 7 and Server 2008 R2 servers. It doesn't apply to mobile computers but instead applies to remote offices. You can use BranchCache to improve performance for users in remote offices.

The primary benefit of BranchCache is to reduce the amount of traffic over a WAN link. It also improves the response time for users in the remote office because they are able to retrieve data quicker.

Consider Figure 12.22. It shows a company with a main office and a branch office. The two offices are connected via a wide area network. Clients in the branch office have access to servers in the main office. However, because they have to traverse the WAN link, it is slower.

Imagine that Sally and Bob both work in the branch office. Sally needs to access a project file in the main office, so she retrieves it over the WAN link. A few minutes later, Bob needs to access the same file. He would also retrieve the file over the WAN link.

FIGURE 12.22 Multiple-site company

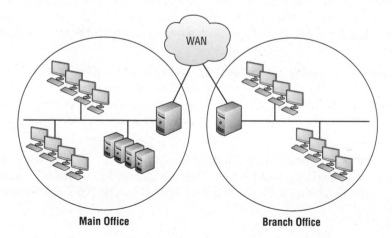

Main Office   **Branch Office**

However, if BranchCache is used, the file is cached on a computer in the branch office. When Bob needs to access the file, his system is able to retrieve the cached file stored in the branch office. The WAN link is used less, and the performance for users is improved.

BranchCache Modes

BranchCache uses two modes. The mode you select largely depends on whether you have a Windows Server 2008 R2 server in the branch office. The two modes are as follows:

Hosted cache mode   Files are stored on a Windows Server 2008 R2 server located in the remote office. The server can be doing other functions, but it needs to have the BranchCache feature enabled.

Distributed cache mode   Windows 7 clients cache content using a peer-to-peer architecture. Distributed cache mode doesn't require a Windows Server 2008 R2 server in the branch office. The first client that retrieves the file caches it. Other clients in the branch office can then retrieve the file from the first client. Clients can automatically detect the existence of BranchCache files stored on Windows 7 computers in the same subnet. If the remote office has more than one subnet, clients on different subnets can cache the same content.

BranchCache Requirements

BranchCache has several specific requirements that must be met. These primarily focus on ensuring that you have the right operating systems and that they are configured to use BranchCache. The requirements are as follows:

Windows 7 clients must be configured.   Only Windows 7 clients can cache or access files used with BranchCache. In addition, the clients must be configured using either Group Policy or the `netsh` command. For example, you can use this command from an administrative command prompt to configure clients to use distributed caching: `netsh branchcache set service distributed`. This command will configure the firewall and service settings. You can disable it with this command: `netsh branchcache set service disabled`.

Source servers must be running Server 2008 R2.   The server hosting content that will be cached must be running Windows Server 2008 R2, and the BranchCache For Network Files role service must be added as part of the File Services role. Also, shares must be configured to support BranchCache. Some servers, such as web servers, require additional configuration.

Remote office servers must be running Windows Server 2008 R2.   If hosted cache mode is used, you must enable the BranchCache feature on a Windows Server 2008 R2 server in the remote office. If you don't have a Windows Server 2008 R2 server, you can use distributed cache mode instead.

If you want to dig deeper into BranchCache, Microsoft has several resources to help you implement it. This website is a great starting place: http://technet.microsoft.com/network/dd425028.aspx.

Summary

In this chapter, you learned about several issues related to mobile or remote users. Topics included wireless users, mobile connectivity, DirectAccess, and BranchCache.

Wireless is very valuable today. While it has had some problems with security in the past, it is possible to implement a secure wireless solution. You learned about the different types of security that can be implemented and how to troubleshoot wireless connections. Stay away from WEP. WPA2-Enterprise provides the best security. Of course, you must match the Windows 7 client settings with the wireless devices used in your network.

Mobile users need to be able to connect to the internal network while they are away. Many companies implement remote access servers to allow the clients to dial in or use VPN connections. When things don't work, double-check the settings, enable logging, or run detailed diagnostics. VPN connections use tunneling protocols. IKEv2 is the most secure and will work with Windows 7 and Windows Server 2008 R2 servers. Other tunneling protocols are SSTP, PPTP, and L2TP/IPSec. IKEv2 and SSTP require certificates (and certificates are recommended with IPSec). To prevent users from seeing warnings related to these certificates, you can install root certificates on the Windows 7 computer.

DirectAccess is a new feature available only with Windows 7 and Windows Server 2008 R2. It can be used as an alternative to VPNs, allowing clients to connect to a server over the Internet. Several key requirements must be met. For example, the clients and servers must be running IPv6 and must be part of a Windows domain.

BranchCache can be used to support clients in branch offices. Clients in the branch office may regularly retrieve files from servers in the main office over a slow WAN link. You can enable BranchCache to allow these files to be cached on computers in the branch office. Clients must be running Windows 7, and servers must be running Windows Server 2008 R2.

Chapter Essentials

Configuring and troubleshooting wireless connectivity   Understand that wireless connection settings on the Windows 7 computer must match those on the wireless devices. Security is very important with wireless. Windows 7 supports WEP, WPA, and WPA2. WEP should be avoided. WPA2 is the strongest. WPA-Personal and WPA2-Personal use a pre-shared key. WPA-Enterprise and WPA2-Enterprise use an 802.1x server for authentication. WPA2-Enterprise with smart card authentication provides the best protection.

Configuring and troubleshooting remote access   Be aware that Windows 7 supports multiple tunneling protocols. When set to Automatic, it will try to connect in this order: IKEv2, SSTP, PPTP, and L2TP. IKEv2 is supported only with Windows 7 and Windows Server 2008 R2 servers. When troubleshooting, check the settings first to ensure the client matches the server. You can also enable logging and run diagnostics.

Understanding DirectAccess   Understand how DirectAccess can be used instead of a VPN. It is supported by only Windows 7 and Windows Server 2008 R2 servers. These computers must be running IPv6 and be joined to the same Windows domain. When DirectAccess is configured, Windows 7 users can connect to the Windows Server 2008 R2 servers over the Internet to access resources without a VPN.

Using BranchCache   Know that BranchCache can improve performance for clients who need to access resources over a WAN link. It reduces the bandwidth required over the WAN link by caching files on systems in the remote office. BranchCache can be used by only Windows 7 and Windows Server 2008 R2 servers.

Chapter

13

Administering Internet Explorer

TOPICS COVERED IN THIS CHAPTER INCLUDE

✓ Managing Windows Internet Explorer settings

✓ Understanding advanced settings

✓ Troubleshooting Internet Explorer issues

The Internet is an important resource for almost any enterprise. Users regularly perform research on the Internet and interact with both customers and vendors using the Internet. The primary web browser most enterprises use is Windows Internet Explorer. It's an important tool for any administrator to know how to manage and troubleshoot.

Internet Explorer (IE) version 8 supports many of the basic settings supported in older versions. It also includes several new settings and capabilities such as InPrivate Browsing, InPrivate Filtering, and the SmartScreen Filter.

Administrators often need to check and troubleshoot advanced settings of IE. In addition to checking this manually, you also can configure more than 1,200 Group Policy settings.

When things don't work as expected, you need to start troubleshooting. It's always a good idea to start with basic connectivity issues. However, because of the ability to extend IE capabilities with plug-ins and add-ons, you may find that these need to be checked and troubleshot as well.

This chapter covers all of these topics.

Managing Windows Internet Explorer Settings

Windows Internet Explorer 8 is a built-in application in Windows 7. On the surface, it's a web browser used to surf the Internet. However, it has many extra capabilities you should understand.

 Internet Explorer version 8 is installed by default with Windows 7. Windows Vista included Internet Explorer version 7, and Windows XP included Internet Explorer version 6. It is possible to install Internet Explorer version 8 on older operating systems.

Because it's a built-in application, it's important to understand Internet Explorer settings and capabilities. Knowing how to manipulate these settings will help you support your enterprise Window 7 users. This section covers the following settings and capabilities:

- Managing cache
- InPrivate Browsing

- InPrivate Filtering
- SmartScreen Filter
- Security zones
- Protected Mode

Because this book is intended for IT professionals, this chapter does not cover the basic features of IE. Instead, it focuses on the relevant objectives for the 70-685 and 70-686 exams.

Managing Cache

Windows Internet Explorer maintains different types of information for each web page you visit. Much of this stored data is used to make your next visit quicker. The data is stored in a location commonly called *cache*.

Cache can be either hardware cache or software cache. For example, a hard drive includes memory used to cache data to improve performance. Cache on a hard drive is hardware cache. Cache used by IE is software cache. IE stores these files in a location on the hard drive so that it doesn't have to retrieve them over the Internet. Retrieving the files from the local cache is much more efficient than retrieving them from the Internet.

Data stored in cache includes

- List of web pages by URL
- Copies of web pages
- Cookies
- Images such as .jpeg and .gif
- Media files such as music or video files
- Style sheets including cascading style sheets (CSS) and Extensible Stylesheet Language (XSL) style sheets
- Script files
- Any data that is typed into forms if AutoComplete settings are enabled
- Any saved passwords that are automatically filled in when you sign on to a website
- Some installation applications that were downloaded for immediate installation

Forms data and passwords that are saved depend on how IE is configured. Figure 13.1 shows the settings page you can use to enable or disable the data entered into web page forms. You can access this page via Internet Options by clicking Tools ➢ Internet Options from any open IE window.

FIGURE 13.1   IE AutoComplete settings

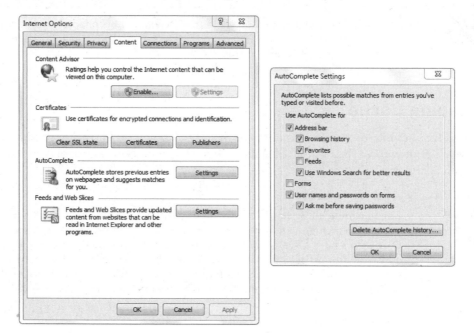

Viewing Cache Contents

You can view the files stored in cache. Similarly, if someone else has access to your system, they can view the files stored in cache.

The default cache location for IE is `C:\Users\%username%\AppData\Local\Microsoft\Windows\Temporary Internet Files`.

`AppData` is a hidden folder, so it probably won't show up unless you've already changed the settings. You can cause hidden files to appear in Windows Explorer by clicking Organize and then choosing Folder And Search Options, selecting the View tab, and picking Show Hidden Files, Folders, And Drives.

The Organize drop-down menu is on the left of the Windows Explorer toolbar.

You will then be able to browse to `C:\Users\%username%\AppData\Local\Microsoft\Windows`.

However, the `Temporary Internet Files` folder is a system folder. You need to enable the display of protected operating system files before you'll see it. You can do this from the same View tab that allows you to enable viewing of hidden files and folders. Deselect Hide Protected Operating System Files (Recommended).

The display will look similar to Figure 13.2. The two arrows show the settings needed to display the contents of cache.

FIGURE 13.2   Configuring Windows Explorer settings to show hidden and system files

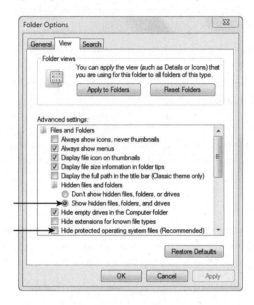

Cookies are simple text files that are written to your hard drive by many websites. Cookies are used to track user activity and provide targeted advertising. When you visit a website, cookies are written to the system. When you visit the website or related sites again, additional data is gathered on your activities. When you return to the website, the cookie is read, and it provides the website with information about you.

As an example, if you've ever purchased something online, a cookie was probably written to your system that could identify you when you return to that site. When you return, the cookie is read, and the website knows who you are.

Cookies are stored in the `\Users\%username%\AppData\Roaming\Microsoft\Windows\Cookies` folder.

History data includes all the sites a user has visited. It is stored in the `\Users\%username%\AppData\Local\Microsoft\Windows\History` folder. You can also click the Favorites button on the toolbar in the browser and select the History tab to view this data.

When a web page prompts a user to download a file, the file is stored in the `Windows\Downloaded Program Files` folder.

The Registry also holds some data related to IE usage. Although this requires you to dig a little deeper, you may need access to this information at some point. It's certainly important to realize how easy it is for an attacker to gain access to this information if they have unrestricted physical access to the computer. The three relevant IE keys are as follows:

IE Typed URLs   This key shows URLs that a user typed, as opposed to links that a user clicked. You can access this from the `HKEY_Current_User\Software\Microsoft\Internet Explorer\TypedURLs` node.

IE Forms AutoComplete   This key includes information stored by AutoComplete. Although the information isn't in clear text, there are tools available that can read the data. You can access this key from the `HKEY_Current_User\Software\Microsoft\Internet Explorer\IntelliForms\Storage1` node.

IE Password AutoComplete   This key includes stored passwords used by AutoComplete. Although the information isn't in clear text, there are tools available that can read the data. You can access this key from the `HKEY_Current_User\Software\Microsoft\Internet Explorer\IntelliForms\Storage2` node.

The contents of these folders depend on the settings for IE. For example, if Forms is deselected in AutoComplete, there won't be a Storage1 node.

Clearing Cache

You can clear cache by manipulating the Internet Options page. Figure 13.3 shows the page you can use to delete browsing history. You can get to this page by clicking Tools ➢ Internet Options, and clicking the Delete button in the Browsing History area.

FIGURE 13.3   Deleting browsing history

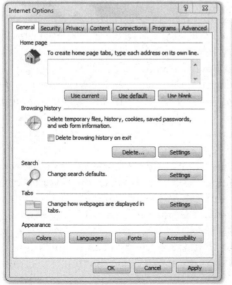
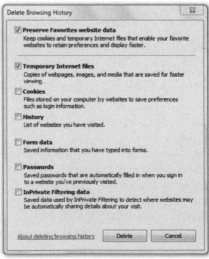

Notice that you can choose what data to delete. Exercise 13.1 shows you how to view the current contents of cache and then clear it.

EXERCISE 13.1

Viewing and Clearing Cache

1. Click Start ➢ Computer to start Windows Explorer.

2. Browse to the C:\Users*username* folder, where *username* is the name of the account you used to log on. If you're not sure what user account you're logged on with, open a command prompt and type in **whoami**.

3. Click Organize ➢ Folder And Search Options. Select the View tab.

4. Select Show Hidden Files, Folders, Or Drives.

5. Deselect Hide Protected Operating Files (Recommended).

6. Browse to the C:\Users\%username%\AppData\Local\Microsoft\Windows\ Temporary Internet Files folder. At this point, you can look around to see the files stored in cache.

    -   View the cookies in this folder: \Users\%username%\AppData\Roaming\ Microsoft\Windows\Cookies.

    -   View the history data in this folder: \Users\%username%\AppData\Local\ Microsoft\Windows\History.

    -   View downloaded files in this folder: Windows\Downloaded Program Files.

7. Open Internet Explorer. Select Tools ➢ Internet Options. The General tab should be selected.

8. Click the Delete button.

9. Select the browsing history that you want to delete, and click Delete.

Several Group Policy settings allow you to manipulate what a user can delete. Settings exist in both the User Configuration and Computer Configuration nodes. The settings are located in the Administrative Templates ➢ Windows Components ➢ Internet Explorer ➢ Delete Browsing History node.

The following settings apply to at least IE version 8.0 in Windows 7:

-   Prevent Deleting Cookies
-   Prevent Deleting Web Sites That The User Has Visited
-   Configure Delete Browsing History In Exit
-   Prevent Deleting Temporary Internet Files
-   Prevent Deleting Favorites Site Data

Some settings were introduced with Windows Vista and require at least IE version 7.0:

- Turn Off "Delete Browsing History" Functionality
- Prevent Deleting Form Data
- Prevent Deleting Passwords

InPrivate Browsing

When IE caches all the data from your browsing sessions, it can improve performance. However, there are times when you or another user may want to surf the Internet but not leave any traces. You can do so with *InPrivate Browsing*.

Any data collected during an In-Private Browsing session is deleted as soon as the browser session is closed. You can start an InPrivate Browsing session in one of several ways.

If you create a new tab by clicking a blank tab or pressing Ctrl+T, you'll see a screen similar to the one shown in Figure 13.4. You can then click either Browse With InPrivate or Open An InPrivate Browsing Window. This will open a new IE Windows session in InPrivate mode.

FIGURE 13.4 Default new tab

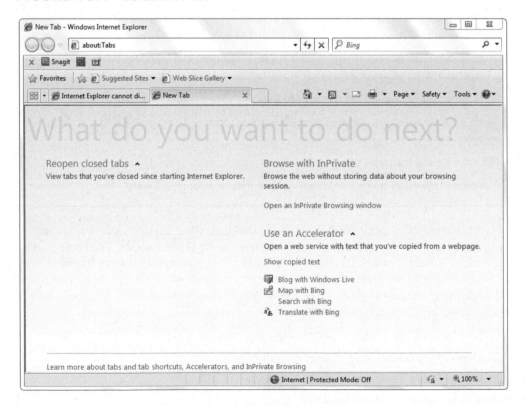

If you have modified the default installation of IE by adding plug-ins or add-ons, the screen shown in Figure 13.4 may not display.

You can also launch an InPrivate browser window using one of the following methods:

- Select Safety ➢ InPrivate Browsing.
- Press Ctrl+Shift+P.

Figure 13.5 shows an InPrivate Browsing window. Notice the InPrivate icon at the beginning of the URL address bar.

FIGURE 13.5   InPrivate Browsing window

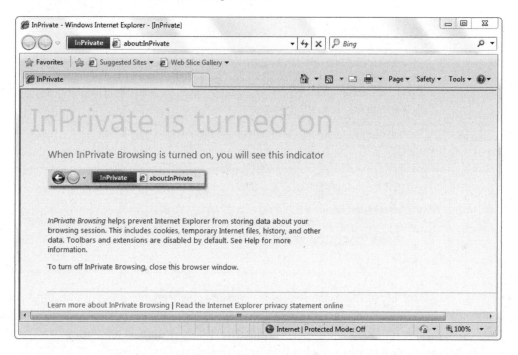

You can browse the Internet using the InPrivate window just as you would normally. The only difference is that all of the data from the session is deleted as soon as you close the browser.

If you want to prevent users from using InPrivate Browsing, you can do so with Group Policy. Settings exist in both the User Configuration and Computer Configuration nodes. The settings are located in Administrative Templates ➢ Windows Components ➢ Internet Explorer ➢ InPrivate Node. The primary setting is Turn Off InPrivate Browsing.

You can also configure Group Policy to disable toolbars and extensions when InPrivate Browsing starts.

InPrivate Filtering

The primary purpose of *InPrivate Filtering* is to improve your privacy by blocking ads, images, and other tracking content.

Many web pages use content from other websites (referred to as third-party websites). When a third-party website hosts content on different sites that you visit, this third-party website can track your activity.

By default, these third-party websites can track a user's session across 10 different websites. You can change this threshold to any value between 3 and 30. This is based on the default InPrivate threshold setting of 10, shown in Figure 13.6.

FIGURE 13.6   InPrivate Filtering window

InPrivate Filtering logs data from content providers. It can then determine through how many sites a content provider can track a user by analyzing these logs.

If you want to disable InPrivate Filtering, you can do so with Group Policy. Settings exist in both the User Configuration and Computer Configuration nodes. The settings are located in the Administrative Templates ➤ Windows Components ➤ Internet Explorer ➤ InPrivate node. The primary setting is Turn Off InPrivate Filtering.

Several other Group Policy settings exist for InPrivate Filtering:

- Do Not Collect InPrivate Filtering Data

- Disable Toolbars And Extensions When InPrivate

- InPrivate Filtering Threshold

SmartScreen Filter

The SmartScreen Filter in IE 8 provides an added layer of protection against phishing sites. Phishing is a form of social engineering whereby users are tricked into going to a malicious website.

The SmartScreen Filter replaces the Phishing filter used in Windows Vista.

When a user goes to a malicious website, they are encouraged to reveal sensitive information such as usernames and passwords or banking account information. Other phishing attempts encourage a user to download and install malware on their computer.

However, the SmartScreen Filter works in real time to protect users. It runs in the background and sends web addresses to the Microsoft SmartScreen service. If the visited website is a known phishing or malware site, IE will display a blocking web page and the address bar will appear in red. Users can still choose to ignore the warning and visit the website.

Figure 13.7 shows how you can access the SmartScreen Filter tools from the Safety drop-down menu.

FIGURE 13.7   Accessing the SmartScreen Filter tools

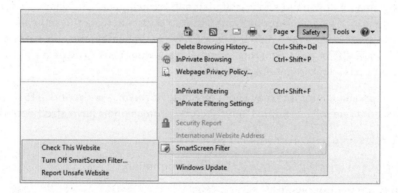

This menu offers three choices:

Check This Website   Select this to check any website you visit. When the SmartScreen Filter is enabled, it automatically checks the website.

Turn Off SmartScreen Filter   This setting toggles back and forth between Turn Off SmartScreen Filter when it is on and Turn On SmartScreen Filter when it is off. Figure 13.7 shows that this setting is on because the selection allows you to turn it off by selecting Turn Off SmartScreen Filter.

Report Unsafe Website   If you suspect a site is malicious, you can report it via this selection. Microsoft will investigate the site and verify that it is malicious before adding it as a malicious website.

Real World Scenario

Phishing In Action

Phishing attempts continue to rise. The classic example goes like this: You receive an email letting you know that your account (email, banking, investment, PayPal, or other account) is being reviewed. It further states something along the lines of "You need to validate your information as soon as possible. If you don't, your account will be locked."

It then provides a link. If you click the link, it will take you to a site that looks like the real thing. It's not difficult for a thief to copy the graphics and reproduce the look and feel of an actual site. If you provide the information, you are often redirected to the live site and prompted to log in normally. Sometimes, simply clicking the link and visiting the malicious site allows malware to be downloaded onto your system.

These emails often include a call to action and a sense of urgency. The call to action is to get you to click the link and provide the information. The sense of urgency indicates that if you do nothing, you'll lose access to your account.

A slight modification to this is a Windows pop-up that indicates that malware has been discovered on your system with an offer to fix it. If you choose Yes to fix it, you're actually giving approval to download and install their software application, which is itself malware. Some attackers have reprogrammed the No button to work the same as the Yes button. In other words, even when the user clicks No, indicating they do not want to install the software, the pop-up attempts to install it anyway. The only way out is to click the X in the pop-up or close the entire IE session.

On the surface, phishing attempts may seem obvious. However, they continue to thrive because users continue to bite. Some IT and security professionals have also been tricked.

Some simple rules help to protect you and your users:

- Be suspicious of unsolicited requests for any information.

- Never give out your password.

- If you want to go to a website, go directly to the website. Don't click the link in an email. For example, if you receive an email that looks like it's from your bank, don't click the link. Instead, type in the URL directly.

- Pay attention to the URL of a website. Attackers may include a partial URL in the path to fool you. The actual URL is www.yourbank.com, but they use a URL like this: www.yourbank.com.hacker.com.

- Install and update antivirus software.

- Take advantage of anti-phishing features offered in email clients and web browsers.

Security Zones

Internet Explorer includes four security zones. Each zone has different levels of security enabled based on the trust level of the zone. You can access the security zones property page by clicking Tools ➢ Internet Options and selecting the Security tab.

Figure 13.8 shows the four security zones with the Internet security zone selected. Each of these zones has default security settings. You can click the Custom Level button and view the individual settings.

FIGURE 13.8   IE security zones

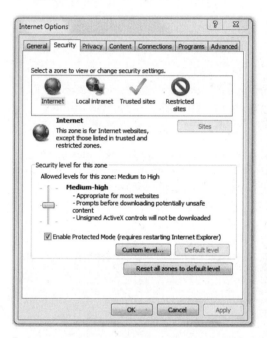

The four zones are as follows:

Internet   This includes all Internet-based websites that aren't in either the local intranet zone or the trusted sites zone. This zone has a higher level of security than all other zones except the restricted sites zone.

Security is set to Medium-High for this zone by default.

Local Intranet   Sites from web servers in the local intranet are automatically identified. Because the pages are hosted from an internal web server, they are trusted and security isn't as strict. You can also add websites to this zone.

Security is set to Medium-Low for this zone by default.

Trusted Sites You can add websites to this zone if you're sure they are safe and you need to do so to ensure all the functions of the website work. Security is relaxed in this zone, adding additional risk, so you should add only sites you trust. By default, the trusted sites zone does not include any sites.

Security is set to Medium for this zone by default.

Restricted Sites You can add websites to this zone that you need to visit but have known risks. The restricted sites zone adds a higher level of security. It helps protect you when visiting known malicious websites. By default, the restricted sites zone does not include any sites.

Security is set to High for this zone by default.

Protected Mode

Protected Mode was introduced in IE 7 on Windows Vista. It's also supported on IE 8 in Windows 7. Protected Mode runs IE in a restricted privilege mode to help protect against different types of malware. It makes it harder for malware to be installed on your computer.

By default, Protected Mode is enabled for the Internet and restricted sites zones but not for the local intranet or trusted sites zones. Figure 13.9 shows how you can easily tell what zone IE is in and the status of protected mode. They are both displayed on the bottom status bar.

FIGURE 13.9 IE security zones

In the figure, the bottom status bar is labeled Internet | Protected Mode: On. This indicates the website is in the Internet zone and Protected Mode is On.

If you trust a website and want to disable Protected Mode without adding the site to the trusted sites zone, you can do so. Figure 13.8, shown earlier, has a picture of the Internet Options Security tab. The Enable Protected Mode check box can be checked or unchecked. If you modify this setting, you need to close IE and restart it for the change to take effect.

You can ensure that Protected Mode is enabled for any specific zone using Group Policy. Settings exist in both the User Configuration and Computer Configuration nodes. The settings are located in the Administrative Templates ≻ Windows Components ≻ Internet Explorer ≻ Internet Control Panel ≻ Security Page node. Each of the following nodes includes the Turn On Protected Mode setting:

- Internet Zone

- Intranet Zone

- Local Machine Zone

- Locked-down Internet Zone

- Locked-down Intranet Zone

- Locked-down Local Machine Zone

- Locked-down Restricted Sites Zone

- Locked-down Trusted Sites Zone

- Restricted Sites Zone

- Trusted Sites Zone

When Protected Mode is enabled for the zone, users will be unable to modify the setting.

Understanding Advanced Settings

Internet Explorer includes several advanced settings that you can manipulate to control how IE functions. These settings are located in the Advanced tab of the Internet Options screen.

The Security category is the most important section on the Advanced tab. Figure 13.10 shows the Advanced tab with the Security section showing.

FIGURE 13.10 IE Advanced settings

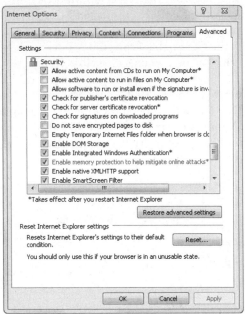

Several categories of settings exist on the Advanced tab:

Accessibility   These settings can be manipulated to make the web pages user friendly for people with disabilities.

Browsing   These settings can be modified to affect how pages are displayed. This category also includes settings for some new features such as Suggested Sites and the Accelerator button.

HTTP 1.1 Settings   These setting are used to indicate that HTTP 1.1 will be used over HTTP 1.0. HTTP 1.1 was widely adopted in 1996.

International   These settings allow you to manipulate how internationalized domain names (IDNs) are used. IDNs can be used to support different character sets. You can also use the Unicode Transformation Format - 8 (UTF-8) display set.

Multimedia   These settings allow you to manipulate how multimedia elements such as pictures, animations, and sounds are treated. You can enable or disable any of the elements.

Printing   Only a single setting is included here. It allows you to choose to print background colors and images.

Search From The Address Bar   This controls what information is sent to the search provider and how the results are displayed.

Security   This is the one of the most important sections from an enterprise administrator's perspective. You can control many of the important security settings from this screen. Several of these settings are explored in more depth in the following sections.

Certificate Settings

The Security tab includes several settings related to certificates. Before covering these settings, it's worthwhile understanding how certificates are used with IE.

Chapter 6, "Configuring and Troubleshooting Application Issues," presented information on certificates and certificate authorities (CAs). The focus in Chapter 6 was on how a certificate can be used to sign software applications.

Certificates are used on the Internet to establish secure sessions using HTTPS. Consider Figure 13.11. A client starts an HTTPS session by clicking a link. The web server then returns a certificate that includes a public key. The public key is matched to a private key on the web server. The client and the web server use the public/private keys to establish a secure SSL session.

FIGURE 13.11   IE receiving and verifying a certificate

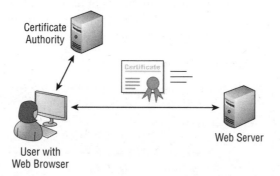

However, there's more to the story. The client makes several checks to ensure that the certificate passed from the web server is to be trusted.

The first check ensures that the certificate that was sent matches the server that sent it. Certificates are issued to specific servers. If someone tries to use the certificate on another server, this check will fail and the user will see an error.

The next check ensures that the certificate from the web server was issued from a CA in the Trusted Root Certification Authorities store. Most e-commerce websites purchase certificates from well-known CAs. These CAs have agreements with Microsoft to place the certificates in the Trusted Root Certification Authorities store.

You can view the Trusted Root Certification Authorities store by clicking Tools ➢ Internet Options, selecting the Content tab, clicking Certificates, and selecting Trusted Root Certification Authorities store. If the web server purchased a certificate from one of these CAs, the check will not return an error.

On the other hand, if the web server uses a certificate that was created from a CA that is not in the Trusted Root Certification Authorities store, the user will see an error. The error indicates that the certificate is not trusted and encourages the user to not continue.

The second check is to ensure that the certificate is still valid. Certificates expire, but sometimes the certificate becomes compromised and the CA will revoke it. Every certificate has a serial number, and this serial number uniquely identifies it. When a CA revokes a certificate, it publishes the serial number on a Certificate Revocation List (CRL, pronounced "crill").

There are two ways a certificate is checked to see if it's been revoked:

Check the CRL   The client can request a copy of the CRL. The client then checks to see if the serial number of the certificate is on the CRL. If it is, it's been revoked and the client receives an error encouraging the client not to use it.

Use OCSP   The Online Certificate Status Protocol (OCSP) can also be used to check the certificate. The client uses OCSP to send the serial number of the certificate to the CA. The CA then answers by indicating the certificate is healthy, not healthy (revoked), or unknown (indicating it's an invalid serial number).

There are two ways to verify that you have a secure connection. HTTPS (instead of just HTTP) shows in the address bar, and a lock icon appears at the end of the address bar.

You can view the web server's certificate anytime you have established a secure connection using one of two methods. Figure 13.12 shows what appears if you click the lock icon. You can click the View Certificates link to view the certificate.

FIGURE 13.12   Viewing website information in IE

    If the certificate isn't valid, the Website Identification section will appear with a warning, and the address bar will have a red background.

You can also select Page ➢ Properties and click the Certificates button. Whether you click the Certificates button from the Page Properties screen or click the View Certificates link from the lock icon, you'll see the same certificate details as shown in Figure 13.13.

FIGURE 13.13   Viewing certificate details in IE

With this background information, the certificate-related settings in the Advanced tab are easier to explain. The following certificate settings are available:

Check For Publisher's Certificate Revocation   When this is checked, the CA's certificate is examined to see if it has been revoked. This setting is checked by default.

Check For Server Certificate Revocation   When this is checked, IE examines the certificate from the web server to see if it has been revoked. This setting is checked by default.

Use SSL 2.0 and Use SSL 3.0   SSL is used to establish HTTPS sessions. Both SSL 2.0 and SSL 3.0 are supported in IE 8. This setting is checked by default.

Warn About Certificate Mismatch   If the certificate presented by the server doesn't match the server, this setting will ensure that an error is presented to the user. This sometimes occurs when the website operator changes the name of the server. This setting is checked by default.

Check For Signatures On Downloaded Programs   When this is checked, IE checks signatures for any programs that have been downloaded. This setting is checked by default.

Allow Software To Run Or Install Even If The Signature Is Invalid   When this is unchecked, software with invalid signatures will not be installed. This is useful because malware will either not be signed or not have a valid signature. This setting is not checked by default.

Active Content

The Security tab includes two settings related to active content. Active content is content that includes scripts or ActiveX controls. Although active content can be useful, it can also contain malware.

By default, the following two settings are unchecked. This prevents active content from running from within IE.

- Allow Active Content From CDs To Run On My Computer
- Allow Active Content To Run In Files On My Computer

Branding Internet Explorer

You can brand IE 8 by adding custom graphics and text to Internet Explorer. The Internet Explorer Administration Kit 8 (IEAK 8) can be used to customize the appearance of IE. IEAK 8 allows you create an installation package to complete a full installation of IE 8 or just modify the settings.

The objectives for the 70-686 exam specifically mention branding of IE. You should be aware that the IEAK can accomplish branding and much more.

Some of the branding capabilities available with IEAK 8 are these:

- Use custom graphics in IE such as a company logo.
- Customize the browser toolbar button.
- Add icons for the Favorites list.
- Modify the Autorun splash screen when IE is installed.

You can also modify many of the other settings for Internet Explorer. Figure 13.14 shows the Feature Selection screen from the IE Customization Wizard 8.

FIGURE 13.14 IE Customization Wizard 8 Feature Selection screen

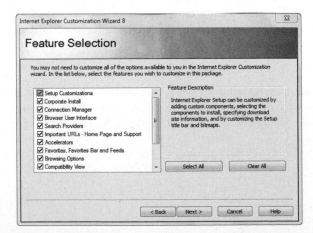

Once you start digging into the capabilities of the IEAK, you'll soon realize you can do just about anything that may be needed or desired in corporate network.

This section provided only a high-level overview of the branding capabilities by using IEAK 8. For more in-depth details, you can check out full documentation for IEAK 8 at http://technet.microsoft.com/library/cc817437.aspx.

Group Policy Settings

Chapter 10, "Managing Windows 7 with Group Policy," covered Group Policy settings in much greater depth. This included how Group Policy settings are applied and how to determine the scope and precedence of a GPO. This section provides an overview of some of the relevant Group Policy settings that apply to IE.

Many Group Policy settings have already been presented earlier in this chapter. These include settings to delete browsing history, prevent users from using InPrivate Browsing, manage InPrivate Filtering, and ensure Protected Mode is enabled for any zone.

One of the great strengths of Internet Explorer browsers over other browsers is that you can manage them using Group Policy. If you add third-party browsers to your network, you lose a significant amount of management capability. It becomes very difficult to lock down any of the settings and ensure they stay locked down.

Both the Computer Configuration and User Configuration nodes have IE settings. Between the two nodes, there are over 1,200 individual settings for IE. Obviously, this chapter will not cover them all.

Figure 13.15 shows the settings for the Computer Configuration node, and Figure 13.16 shows the settings for the User Configuration node. Many of the settings are the same, but you can see that a few of the settings are different. For example, the Computer Configuration node includes Corporate Settings.

FIGURE 13.15   Computer Configuration node Group Policy settings used to manage IE

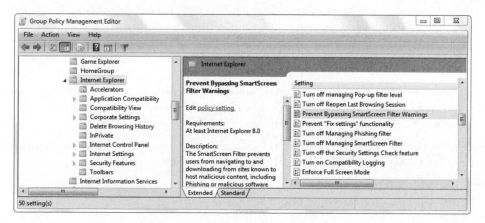

FIGURE 13.16 User Configuration node Group Policy settings used to manage IE

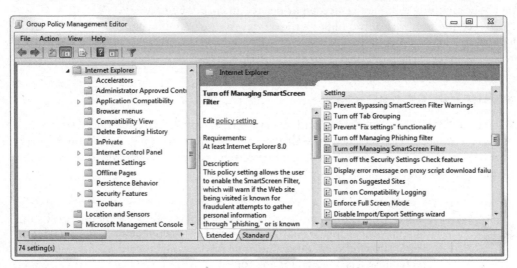

 Chapter 10 covered the filtering capability available in newer Group Policy Management Editors. If you can't easily find the setting you're looking for, right-click any node in Administrative Templates and select Filter Options. Enter a keyword or key phrase such as "crash detection" and click OK. Only the settings that match the search term will appear.

You can access these settings via Administrative Templates ➢ Windows Components ➢ Internet Explorer.

The full path for the Computer Configuration node is Computer Configuration ➢ Policies ➢ Administrative Templates ➢ Windows Components ➢ Internet Explorer. The full path for the User Configuration node is User Configuration ➢ Policies ➢ Administrative Templates ➢ Windows Components ➢ Internet Explorer.

On a local user system, you can use local Group Policy, which can be accessed by clicking Start, typing Group, and selecting Edit Group Policy. Use this path: Computer Configuration ➢ Administrative Templates ➢ Windows Components ➢ Internet Explorer or User Configuration ➢ Administrative Templates ➢ Windows Components ➢ Internet Explorer.

Many of these settings apply to earlier versions of IE. However, some of them apply only to IE 7 and IE 8, which came out with Windows Vista and Windows 7, respectively.

Some of the more notable settings are these:

Delete Browsing History You can use this node to control whether users can delete different types of data. Settings that apply to at least IE 8 are as follows:

- Prevent Deleting Cookies
- Prevent Deleting Web Sites That The User Has Visited

- Prevent Deleting InPrivate Filtering Data
- Prevent Deleting Temporary Internet Files
- Prevent Deleting Favorites Site Data
- Configure Delete Browsing On Exit

Settings that apply to at least IE 7 are these:

- Turn Off "Delete Browsing History" Functionality
- Prevent Deleting Forms Data
- Prevent Deleting Passwords

InPrivate   As discussed earlier in the chapter, InPrivate mode is new to Windows 7 and IE 8. All of the settings only apply to IE 8. The following settings are available:

- Turn Off InPrivate Filtering
- Turn Off InPrivate Browsing
- Do Not Collect InPrivate Filtering Data
- Disable Toolbars And Extensions When InPrivate Browsing Starts
- InPrivate Filtering Threshold

Internet Settings / AutoComplete   This node includes one setting that applies to at least IE 8: Turn Off Windows Search AutoComplete. AutoComplete is used to fill in the URL for users.

Internet Control Panel   This node includes two additional nodes: Advanced Page and Security Page. These settings allow you to configure a significant number of settings for IE.

Security Features   This node includes several other nodes that allow you to manage additional security settings for IE with Group Policy. Combined with the Internet Control Panel settings, you can configure just about all (if not all) of the security settings needed for IE.

Troubleshooting Internet Explorer Issues

Occasionally, IE doesn't work as you'd expect. There are several steps you can take to check and troubleshoot different issues:

- Check network and proxy settings.
- Troubleshoot plug-ins and add-ons.
- Restore IE original settings.
- Disable Add-on Crash Detection.
- Enable Compatibility View.

Check Network and Proxy Settings

Chapter 7, "Networking with Windows 7," discussed networking and proxy servers. It also included an exercise on how to configure IE to use a proxy server.

If a user is unable to reach any Internet sites, you should start with the basics. Make sure that the client is able to reach other network resources. However, if you can ping other network resources but can't access Internet resources with IE, you should check the proxy settings.

You can access these settings from Tools ➤ Internet Options. Select the Connections tab, and click the LAN Settings button. If a proxy server is used in your network, ensure that the correct address and port are configured. Figure 13.17 shows these settings.

FIGURE 13.17   Configuring proxy server settings

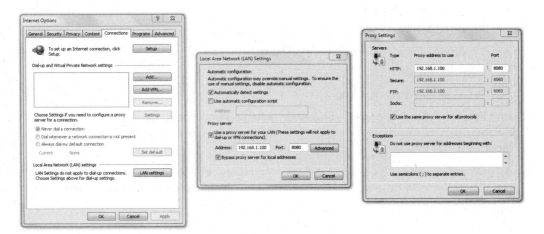

If you have different proxy servers for different protocols, you can click the Advanced button and configure different IP addresses for the different proxy servers. However, it's common for a single proxy server to handle all the protocols.

Troubleshoot Plug-ins and Add-ons

One of the strengths of IE is that it can be extended with plug-ins and add-ons. These can add significant capabilities to IE. However, unreliable plug-ins and add-ons can make IE unstable.

IE supports four types of add-ons:

- Toolbars and extensions
- Search providers
- Accelerators
- InPrivate Filtering

If you suspect that an add-on is causing instability problems with IE, you can launch IE without any add-ons. If it's stable, you'll have verified that the problem is caused by the add-on. Now, the challenge is determining which add-on is causing the problem. You can do this with the Manage Add-ons screen.

Figure 13.18 shows the Manage Add-ons screen with Toolbars And Extensions selected. You can select any of the add-ons and select Disable.

FIGURE 13.18   Managing add-ons

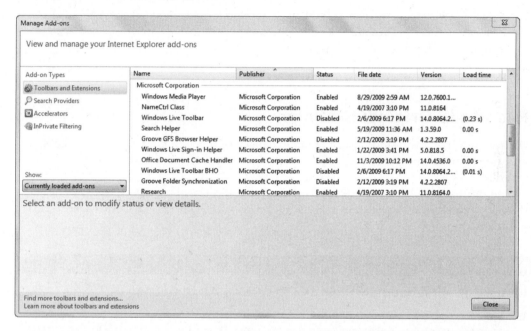

This display shows another valuable piece of information. On the far right is the Load Time column. If an add-on is causing problems, it will likely have a long load time. Unfortunately, only the Toolbars And Extensions screen includes the Load Time column.

Exercise 13.2 shows how to launch IE without add-ons and how to access the Manage Add-ons screen.

EXERCISE 13.2

Disable and Manage Add-ons

1. You can launch an instance of IE in No Add-ons mode. Click Start ➢ All Programs ➢ Accessories ➢ System Tools ➢ Internet Explorer (No Add-ons). This will launch a page with text indicating that Internet Explorer is running without add-ons.

2. Launch a regular instance of IE.

3. Select Tools ➤ Manage Add-ons. By default, the Toolbars And Extensions add-ons are shown. You can select any of the add-ons and select Disable.

4. Select Search Providers. This screen shows the search providers that have been added to IE. You can choose any of these and select Remove to remove it completely. You can select one to be the default provider.

5. Select Accelerators. You can view all of the accelerators that have been added to IE, disable them, or remove them. If any of the categories includes more than one accelerator, you can also set one as the default.

Restore IE Original Settings

Occasionally, the settings for IE can become changed so much that it is no longer reliable or secure. This can be due either to a user experimenting with IE or to modifications from malware.

You can completely reset all of the IE settings and add-ons. This is a drastic step, but if IE has become unreliable, it can be very useful. Exercise 13.3 shows how to view and reset IE settings.

Viewing IE Advanced Settings and Resetting All IE Settings

1. Start Internet Explorer.

2. Select Tools ➤ Internet Options.

3. Click the Advanced tab.

4. Scroll through the settings. The last category of settings is Security. Notice that some settings are marked with an asterisk (*). If you change these settings, they will take effect only after you restart IE.

5. If you want to restore all of the Advanced settings to what they were when IE was first installed, click Restore Advanced Settings.

6. Click the Reset button. Your display will look similar to the following graphic.

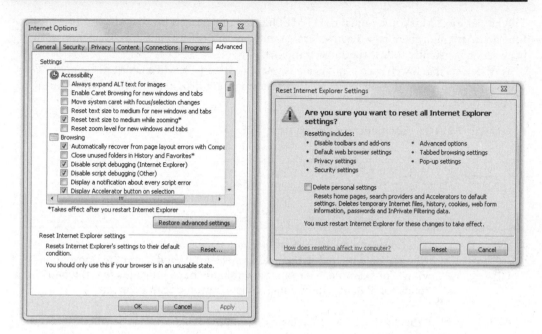

Notice that you can use this to reset all IE settings. If you select the Delete Personal Settings check box, IE will be returned exactly to how it was when it was first installed. This is a drastic step but can be used if IE is no longer running reliably.

7. Click Cancel.

Disable Add-on Crash Detection

By default, IE will detect problematic add-ons and automatically disable them. However, there may be times when you need the add-on to remain functional. This could be for testing or until a solution is discovered.

If you want to ensure that the add-on is not disabled, you can modify the following Group Policy setting: Administrative Templates ➢ Windows Components ➢ Internet Explorer ➢ Turn Off Crash Detection. This setting is available in both the User Configuration and the Computer Configuration nodes.

Enable Compatibility View

The Hyper Text Markup Language (HTML) has evolved quite a bit over the lifetime of the Internet. Although there have been several standards published, not all websites and even browsers consistently follow the same standards.

If IE detects that a web page is not being displayed correctly, it will enable the *Compatibility View* button on the Address bar. Figure 13.19 shows where the Compatibility View button appears in IE.

FIGURE 13.19   Compatibility View button in IE

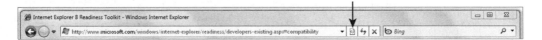

    The Compatibility View button is not always available. It appears only when IE detects that the display may be improved using the Compatibility View. For example, if a metatag within the page indicates that the page is ready for IE 8, the Compatibility View button doesn't appear.

When you click the button, IE will display using compatibility settings. It will also add the site to the Compatibility View Settings list. You can add and remove sites from this list by manipulating the Compatibility View Settings. With IE started, click Tools ➢ Compatibility View Settings or Page ➢ Compatibility View Settings.

Summary

In this chapter, you learned about Internet Explorer version 8. IE 8 caches a lot of data to optimize the user's experience, but sometimes you may want to manipulate this data. You learned what is cached and where it is cached. You learned about many of the new capabilities of IE 8 including InPrivate Browsing, InPrivate Filtering, and the SmartScreen Filter. This chapter covered the traditional security zones used by IE 8 and how they are used to provided added security when users browse different locations.

Several advanced settings are available in IE 8. Many of these are the same as they were in previous versions such as IE 6 and IE 7, but there are additional choices. This chapter covered many of these settings and also many of the Group Policy settings that can be used to control them.

Chapter Essentials

Managing Windows Internet Explorer settings   Know how to view and manage cache. Know the location where cache is stored. Understand the new features such as InPrivate Browsing, InPrivate Filtering, and the SmartScreen Filter. Know how the security zones are used and how Protected Mode can protect clients from malicious websites.

Understanding advanced settings   Understand how to access, view, and manipulate the advanced settings. Know how to verify certificates and how to ensure that active content cannot run. Know that IEAK is used to brand Internet Explorer. Be aware of some of the new Group Policy settings. Know how these settings can be used to control the behavior of IE 8.

Troubleshooting Internet Explorer issues   Know how to check the proxy server settings for IE. Understand that many problems can arise after installing plug-ins and add-ons but that these can be controlled from the Manage Add-ons screen. Know how to disable Add-on Crash Detection and how to enable Compatibility View.

Appendix A

Objective Mapping to Chapter Titles

In addition to being a real-world guide for administrators on the job, this book is intended to be a supplementary study guide for those preparing for the 70-685 and 70-686 exams. Objectives for both of these exams are covered throughout the book.

Table A.1 and Table A.2 show the chapters and sections where the 70-685 and 70-686 exams are covered. The primary location where the objectives are covered is listed first and in bold. When objectives have content that is covered elsewhere in the book, the additional chapters and sections are also listed.

TABLE A.1   70-685 Objectives Mapped to Chapter Sections

Exam Objective	Chapter and Section
Identifying Cause of and Resolving Desktop Application Issues	
Identify and resolve new software installation issues. This objective may include but is not limited to: installation permissions; local administrator requirement; licensing restrictions; digital signing	**Ch. 6, "Installing and Configuring Software"**
Identify and resolve software configuration issues. This objective may include but is not limited to: enabling and disabling features; advanced settings; pointing to a network resource; changing the default settings on the image	**Ch. 6, "Identifying and Resolving Software Failure Issues"** Ch. 2, "Imaging with the Windows Automated Installation Kit" Ch. 7, "Understanding Network Connectivity in an Enterprise," "Resolving Names to IP Addresses," "Troubleshooting Network Connectivity Problems" Ch. 8, "Accessing Network Resources"
Identify cause of and resolve software failure issues. This objective may include but is not limited to: checking the logs; checking whether the application runs in Safe mode; running the application in a previous version of Windows; repairing the installation; checking recently added programs; restoring or reimaging the system	**Ch. 6, "Identifying and Resolving Software Failure Issues"** Ch. 1, "Virtualization Considerations" Ch. 2, "Imaging with the Windows Automated Installation Kit," "Deploying Images with Windows Deployment Services" Ch. 5, "Identifying and Resolving Performance Issues," "Troubleshooting Boot Issues"

TABLE A.1   70-685 Objectives Mapped to Chapter Sections *(continued)*

Exam Objective	Chapter and Section
Identifying Cause of and Resolving Networking Issues	
Identify and resolve logon issues. This objective may include but is not limited to: hardware vs. network; password expiration; trust relationships with machine accounts; determining logon context; logon hours compliance	**Ch. 9, "Authentication vs. Authorization," "Identifying and Resolving Logon Issues"** Ch. 7, "Understanding Network Connectivity in an Enterprise," "Resolving Names to IP Addresses," "Troubleshooting Network Connectivity Problems"
Identify and resolve network connectivity issues. This objective may include but is not limited to: determining scope of issue; determining whether it's a PC or a network connectivity issue; TCP/IP; hardware and cabling; proxies; default gateway	**Ch. 7, "Understanding Network Connectivity in an Enterprise," "Resolving Names to IP Addresses," "Troubleshooting Network Connectivity Problems"** Ch. 3, "Using the Windows Command Prompt," Using Windows PowerShell and the PowerShell ISE"
Identify and resolve names resolution issues. This objective may include but is not limited to: checking which DNS is assigned; flushing the DNS cache; nslookup to DNS server; checking the DHCP scopes	**Ch. 7, "Understanding Network Connectivity in an Enterprise," "Resolving Names to IP Addresses," "Troubleshooting Network Connectivity Problems"** Ch. 3, "Using the Windows Command Prompt"
Identify and resolve network printer issues. This objective may include but is not limited to: hardware failure; server issues; printer failure; network issues; driver issues	**Ch. 8, "Accessing Network Resources," "Identifying and Resolving Network Printer Issues"** Ch. 7, "Understanding Network Connectivity in an Enterprise," "Troubleshooting Network Connectivity Problems"
Managing and Maintaining Systems That Run Windows 7 Client	
Identify and resolve performance issues. This objective may include but is not limited to: analyzing system and application logs; analyzing started services; setting power management; checking hard drive space; optimizing virtual memory	**Ch. 5, "Identifying and Resolving Performance Issues," "Managing Hardware in Windows 7," "Troubleshooting Boot Issues"** Ch. 3, "Using the Windows Command Prompt," "Using Windows PowerShell and the PowerShell ISE"

TABLE A.1 70-685 Objectives Mapped to Chapter Sections *(continued)*

Exam Objective	Chapter and Section
Identify and resolve hardware failure issues. This objective may include but is not limited to: identifying bad sectors; diagnosing memory issues; recommending replacement hardware; updating the BIOS; determining which component is broken	**Ch. 5, "Identifying and Resolving Performance Issues," "Managing Hardware in Windows 7," "Troubleshooting Boot Issues"**

Supporting Mobile Users

Identify and resolve wireless connectivity issues. This objective may include but is not limited to: signal strength; encryption types; encryption keys; wireless profiles; mobile devices	**Ch. 12, "Configuring and Troubleshooting Wireless Connectivity"**
Identify and resolve remote access issues. This objective may include but is not limited to: VPN client not connecting; IPv6 support; access and authentication to network resources	**Ch. 12, "Troubleshooting Remote Access Issues"** Ch. 7, "Understanding Network Connectivity in an Enterprise," "Resolving Names to IP Addresses," "Troubleshooting Network Connectivity Problems" Ch. 8, "Understanding Permissions," "Accessing Network Resources" Ch. 9, "Authentication vs. Authorization"

Identifying Cause of and Resolving Security Issues

Identify and resolve Windows Internet Explorer security issues. This objective may include but is not limited to: adding trusted sites; advanced settings; installing plugins; identifying group policy restrictions; certificates	**Ch. 13, "Managing Windows Internet Explorer Settings," "Understanding Advanced Settings," "Troubleshooting Internet Explorer Issues"**
Identify and resolve issues due to malicious software. This objective may include but is not limited to: analyzing services; analyzing programs; analyzing processes; analyzing browser helper add-ons; user account control	**Ch. 9, "Anti-malware Software"** Ch. 3, "Using the Windows Command Prompt," "Using Windows PowerShell and the PowerShell ISE" Ch. 5, "Configuring Services" Ch. 6, "Identifying and Resolving Software Failure Issues" Ch. 11, "User Account Control," "Security Policies" Ch. 13, "Troubleshooting Internet Explorer Issues"

TABLE A.1   70-685 Objectives Mapped to Chapter Sections *(continued)*

Exam Objective	Chapter and Section
Identify and resolve encryption issues. This objective may include but is not limited to: requirements for installing; recovering encryption keys; key management	**Ch. 11, "Designing BitLocker Support"**
Identify and resolve software update issues. This objective may include but is not limited to: identifying software update level; checking whether client is receiving regularly scheduled updates; identifying incompatibility of update with other applications	**Ch. 4, "Keeping Windows Up to Date," "Choosing an Update Tool," "Using MBSA for Security Audits," "Using Windows Server Update Services"** Ch. 3, "Using the Windows Command Prompt" Ch. 6, "Designing a Deployment Strategy," "Identifying and Resolving Software Failure Issues"

TABLE A.2   70-686 Objectives Mapped to Chapter Sections

Exam Objective	Chapter and Section
Planning and Managing a Client Life Cycle Strategy	
Plan and manage client licensing and activation. This objective may include but is not limited to: applications and operating systems; activation method; KMS vs. MAK; prerequisites; choosing a SKU; licensing infrastructure; licensing compliance audits; inventory audits; virtualization licensing considerations; making recommendations for licensing strategy and compliance	**Ch. 1, "Planning and Managing Client Licensing and Activation"**
Plan and manage software updates. This objective may include but is not limited to: application updates and operating system updates; evaluating and approving software updates; enterprise applications; designing an update strategy; choosing an update tool; planning and deploying a service pack; schedule considerations; network considerations; test updates; auditing for security compliance	**Ch. 4, "Keeping Windows Up to Date," "Choosing an Update Tool," "Using MBSA for Security Audits," "Using Windows Server Update Services"** Ch. 3, "Using the Windows Command Prompt"

TABLE A.2   70-686 Objectives Mapped to Chapter Sections *(continued)*

Exam Objective	Chapter and Section
Plan and manage a physical hardware and virtualization strategy. This objective may include but is not limited to: analyzing existing hardware environment; determining which systems meet minimum requirements; tradeoffs of physical vs. VDI environment; network load considerations; disk space; direct connection vs. brokered connection; determining a VHD strategy; choosing 32 bit vs. 64 bit	**Ch. 1, "Virtualization Considerations"**

Designing a Standard Image

Design an image creation strategy. This objective may include but is not limited to: identifying operating system and enterprise applications that will be included with the standard image; thick, thin, or hybrid; role-based or geographic-based images vs. single core image; image localization	**Ch. 2, "Understanding and Designing Images," "Choosing a Deployment Strategy"**
Design a custom image. This objective may include but is not limited to: identifying applications to be installed; identifying features and components to be enabled or disabled; testing the customized image	**Ch. 2, "Understanding and Designing Images," "Imaging with the Windows Automated Installation Kit," "Deploying Images with Windows Deployment Services"**
Define an image update strategy. This objective may include but is not limited to: performance optimization; security considerations; efficiency; offline servicing vs. online or post-image updates; re-creating; recapturing	**Ch. 2, "Understanding and Designing Images," "Imaging with the Windows Automated Installation Kit," "Deploying Images with Windows Deployment Services"**

Designing Client Configurations

Design standard system settings. This objective may include but is not limited to: choosing methods, including logon scripts, startup scripts, and Group Policy; designing profiles; designing error reporting; designing audit policy	**Ch. 5, "Identifying and Resolving Performance Issues," "Managing Hardware in Windows 7"** Ch. 3, "Using the Windows Command Prompt" Ch. 9, "Understanding User Profiles" Ch. 10, "Group Policy and the GPMC," "Group Policy Settings"

TABLE A.2   70-686 Objectives Mapped to Chapter Sections *(continued)*

Exam Objective	Chapter and Section
Define client security standards. This objective may include but is not limited to: application control policies; encryption; stopping unnecessary services; designing firewall rules; defining anti-malware settings; changes to Kerberos and NTLM; configuring user rights; defining UAC policy; designing a security template for system lockdown; defining account policies; designing security standards for removable storage	**Ch. 11, "User Account Control," "Security Policies," "Designing BitLocker Support"** Ch. 9, "Anti-malware Software" Ch. 10, "Group Policy and the GPMC," "Group Policy Settings" Ch. 11, "Windows Firewall"
Define Windows Internet Explorer settings. This objective may include but is not limited to: defining security zones; cache location; branding; in-private mode; restricting or allowing plug-ins; add-ons; privacy policy; browser protected mode	**Ch. 13, "Managing Windows Internet Explorer Settings," "Understanding Advanced Settings," "Troubleshooting Internet Explorer Issues"**

Designing a Windows 7 Client Deployment

Analyze the environment and choose appropriate deployment methods. This objective may include but is not limited to: building the infrastructure; advantages of lite-touch vs. zero-touch vs. local install; capacity and scale considerations; determining required changes to the infrastructure	**Ch. 2, "Understanding and Designing Images," "Choosing a Deployment Strategy"**
Design a lite-touch deployment strategy. This objective may include but is not limited to: unicast vs. multicast; auto-cast vs. scheduled-cast; staggered deployment; scheduling considerations; network load considerations; choosing a client boot method for deployment; unattended answer files; restricting who can receive images; choosing a delivery mechanism	**Ch. 2, "Deploying Images with Windows Deployment Services"**
Design a zero-touch deployment strategy. This objective may include but is not limited to: designing and configuring task sequencing; unattended answer files; scheduling considerations; staggered deployment; network load considerations; restricting who can receive images	**Ch. 2, "Using the Microsoft Deployment Toolkit 2010"**

TABLE A.2 70-686 Objectives Mapped to Chapter Sections *(continued)*

Exam Objective	Chapter and Section
Design a user state migration strategy. This objective may include but is not limited to: determining which user data and settings to preserve; local vs. remote storage considerations; determining mitigation plan for non-migrated applications; securing migrated data; testing designed strategy; wipe-and-load migration vs. side-by-side migration	**Ch. 1, "Designing User State Migration"**

Designing Application Packages for Deployment

Design a delivery or deployment strategy. This objective may include but is not limited to: auditing for prerequisites and minimum requirements; choosing a deployment method such as virtualized, Remote Desktop Services, Group Policy, or software distribution; server-based or client-based install; scheduling considerations; staggered deployment; network considerations; package creation standards	**Ch. 6, "Installing and Configuring Software," "Designing a Delivery Strategy," "Designing a Deployment Strategy," "Identifying and Resolving Software Failure Issues"** Ch. 10, "Group Policy and the GPMC," "Group Policy Settings"
Manage application compatibility. This objective may include but is not limited to: testing incompatibility; choosing a method for resolving incompatibility, such as upgrading, Remote Desktop Services, shim, or VDI; auditing incompatible software	**Ch. 6, "Designing a Deployment Strategy," "Identifying and Resolving Software Failure Issues"** Ch. 5, "Analyzing Logs with Event Viewer"

Identifying and Resolving Deployment and Client Configuration Issues

Identify and resolve Internet Explorer issues. This objective may include but is not limited to: security zones; Web applications; advanced settings; Group Policy restrictions; certificates	**Ch. 13, "Managing Windows Internet Explorer Settings," "Understanding Advanced Settings," "Troubleshooting Internet Explorer Issues"**
Identify and resolve Group Policy issues. This objective may include but is not limited to: delegation; inheritance; policies are not effective; blocking; permissions; loopback processing; user vs. computer settings; filtering; performance	**Ch. 10, "Group Policy and the GPMC"**

TABLE A.2   70-686 Objectives Mapped to Chapter Sections *(continued)*

Exam Objective	Chapter and Section
Identify and resolve networking issues. This objective may include but is not limited to: wireless; remote access; VPN; certificates; performance; IP communication; Windows Firewall	**Ch. 7, "Understanding Network Connectivity in an Enterprise," "Resolving Names to IP Addresses," "Using the Network and Sharing Center," "Troubleshooting Network Connectivity Problems"**
	Ch. 11, "Windows Firewall"
	Ch. 12, "Configuring and Troubleshooting Wireless Connectivity," "Troubleshooting Remote Access Issues"
Identify and resolve authentication and authorization issues. This objective may include but is not limited to: user rights; distinguishing between client-based and server-based issues; time synchronization (Kerberos)	**Ch. 9, "Authentication vs. Authorization"**
	Ch. 8, "Accessing Network Resources," "Identifying and Resolving Network Printer Issues"
	Ch. 11, "User Account Control," "Security Policies"

Appendix
B

About the Companion CD

IN THIS APPENDIX:

- What you'll find on the CD
- System requirements
- Using the CD
- Troubleshooting

What You'll Find on the CD

The following sections are arranged by category and summarize the software and other goodies you'll find on the CD. If you need help with installing the items provided on the CD, refer to the installation instructions in the "Using the CD" section of this appendix.

Video Walkthroughs

The CD contains about 40 minutes of video walkthroughs from author Darril Gibson. Darril shows readers how to perform some of the more difficult tasks readers can expect to encounter on the job.

Sybex Test Engine

The CD contains the Sybex test engine, which includes the two bonus exams, one each for Exam 70-685 and Exam 70-686.

Electronic Flashcards

These handy electronic flashcards are just what they sound like. One side contains a question or fill-in-the-blank question, and the other side shows the answer.

PDF of the Book

We have included an electronic version of the text in .pdf format. You can view the electronic version of the book with Adobe Reader.

Adobe Reader

We've also included a copy of Adobe Reader so you can view PDF files that accompany the book's content. For more information on Adobe Reader or to check for a newer version, visit Adobe's website at www.adobe.com/products/reader/.

System Requirements

Make sure your computer meets the minimum system requirements shown in the following list. If your computer doesn't match up to most of these requirements, you may have problems using the software and files on the companion CD. For the latest and greatest information, please refer to the ReadMe file located at the root of the CD-ROM.

- A PC running Microsoft Windows 98, Windows 2000, Windows NT4 (with SP4 or later), Windows Me, Windows XP, Windows Vista, or Windows 7

- An Internet connection

- A CD-ROM drive

Using the CD

To install the items from the CD to your hard drive, follow these steps:

1. Insert the CD into your computer's CD-ROM drive. The license agreement appears.

 Windows users: The interface won't launch if you have autorun disabled. In that case, click Start ➤ Run (for Windows Vista or Windows 7, Start ➤ All Programs ➤ Accessories ➤ Run). In the dialog box that appears, type **D:\Start.exe**. (Replace *D* with the proper letter if your CD drive uses a different letter. If you don't know the letter, see how your CD drive is listed under My Computer.) Click OK.

2. Read the license agreement, and then click the Accept button if you want to use the CD.

The CD interface appears. The interface allows you to access the content with just one or two clicks.

Troubleshooting

Wiley has attempted to provide programs that work on most computers with the minimum system requirements. Alas, your computer may differ, and some programs may not work properly for some reason.

The two likeliest problems are that you don't have enough memory (RAM) for the programs you want to use or you have other programs running that are affecting installation or running of a program. If you get an error message such as "Not enough memory" or "Setup cannot continue," try one or more of the following suggestions and then try using the software again:

Turn off any antivirus software running on your computer. Installation programs sometimes mimic virus activity and may make your computer incorrectly believe that it's being infected by a virus.

Close all running programs. The more programs you have running, the less memory is available to other programs. Installation programs typically update files and programs; if you keep other programs running, installation may not work properly.

Have your local computer store add more RAM to your computer. This is, admittedly, a drastic and somewhat expensive step. However, adding more memory can really help the speed of your computer and allow more programs to run at the same time.

Customer Care

If you have trouble with the book's companion CD-ROM, please call the Wiley Product Technical Support phone number at (800) 762-2974.

Glossary

A

Access Control Entry (ACE)   An entry in a security descriptor for an object such as a file or folder on an NTFS drive. It includes the SID of a user or group and the permissions assigned to the user or group. A group of ACEs on a system is referred to as an access control list, and when used on an NTFS drive, it's referred to as a Discretionary Access Control List (DACL).

Account Lockout Policy   Group Policy settings that can control the maximum number of times an incorrect password can be entered before an account is locked out.

Account Policies   Three Group Policy nodes that can be used to control different security settings. The three nodes are Password Policy, Account Lockout Policy, and Kerberos Policy.

Action Center   A central location to view alerts and take actions. Messages in the Action Center provide insight into the system's security, reliability, and stability. When the Action Center has issues that can be resolved by taking specific actions, a little white flag appears in the notification area of Windows 7.

activation   A process used to help thwart counterfeiting. Windows 7 uses a product key and an activation process. The product key is paired with the computer in the activation process. Windows 7 has a grace period of 30 days before it needs to be activated.

Active Directory Domain Services   The service hosted on a domain controller in a Windows domain. Active Directory Domain Services is a database of objects in the domain. Objects include users, computers, printers, and more.

Administrators   A group that is preassigned rights and permissions. The local Administrators group grants members rights and permissions to do anything on the local system. The domain Administrators group grants members rights and permissions to do anything on any computers in the domain.

Advanced Boot Options   A screen accessible by pressing the F8 key when Windows 7 is booting. You can select options such as Repair Your Computer and one of the different safe modes from this screen.

alias   Another name for a PowerShell cmdlet. Many command-prompt commands have been rewritten as PowerShell commands, and the original command-prompt command is recognized as an alias.

All Users profile   The All Users profile holds settings that affect all users. As an example, when you install an application, you are often prompted to choose to allow all users access to the program. When you select All Users, the application modifies the All Users profile, ensuring the application is available to any user who logs on to the system.

anti-spyware software   Software designed to protect against spyware. Spyware is software that can install itself or run on your computer without your knowledge or consent. It often is used to monitor your online activities, collect personally identifiable information, and report this back to the attacker.

antivirus software   Software intended to protect against viruses, worms, Trojan horses, rootkits, and other malware. Many current antivirus software products also protect against spyware.

Application Compatibility mode   A Windows 7 feature that allows applications to run using settings from previous operating systems such as Windows XP.

AppLocker   A new feature used to specify which users or groups can run particular applications. AppLocker uses rules that specifically allow or deny applications from running. It is intended to be an improvement over Software Restriction policies available before Windows 7 and Server 2008 R2.

Audit Policies   Group Policy settings that can be used to enable different categories of auditable events. Events are logged in the Security log of Event Viewer.

authentication   Used to prove a user's identity. In general, there are three factors of authentication: something you know, something you have, and something you are.

authorization   Used to control access of the user after the user has been authenticated. Authorization grants users rights and permissions.

auto-cast transmission   A type of image transmission from Windows Deployment Services. Auto-cast transmissions start as soon as the WDS client connects.

Automatic Private IP Addressing (APIPA)   A range of addresses from 169.254.0.1 through 169.245.255.254, with a subnet mask of 255.255.0.0. APIPA is used to configure DHCP clients with addresses when a DHCP server doesn't respond.

Automatic Update   A method of keeping systems up to date. Clients can be configured to connect automatically to the Microsoft Update site, download updates that apply to them, and install them.

B

batch file   A list of one or more command-line commands in a text file. A batch file ends with the .bat extension and can be executed. Batch files can also be scheduled.

BCDEdit   A command-line tool used to make modifications to the boot configuration data (BCD) store.

BitLocker Active Directory Recovery Password Viewer Tool   A free download that allows you to view BitLocker Recovery keys if they are stored in Active Directory Domain Services.

BitLocker Drive Encryption   A technology used to encrypt the entire hard drive. *BitLocker Drive Encryption* is used for internal hard drives. It works best with a Trusted Platform Module (TPM) but can be used without a TPM.

BitLocker to Go   A technology used to encrypt external or USB flash drives.

Block Inheritance   A GPO setting that blocks the inheritance of all GPOs for an OU. You can enable the Block Inheritance setting on an OU, not a GPO. When enabled, all GPOs are blocked. You can't choose which GPO to block.

boot configuration data (BCD)   Information used by Windows 7 during the boot process. It identifies the location of the operating system files on the system. This replaces the boot.ini file used in Windows XP and older operating systems. It can be modified with the BCDEdit command-line tool.

boot image   A type of image used with Windows 7 installations. The boot image installs the Windows Preinstallation Environment (Windows PE). The full install image can be installed from the Windows PE.

BranchCache   A new feature available only for Windows 7 and Server 2008 R2 servers. BranchCache can improve performance for users in remote offices by caching data on computers in the remote office. The primary benefit of BranchCache is to reduce the amount of traffic over a WAN link. It also improves the response time for users in the remote office because they are able to retrieve data quicker.

C

cached credentials   Credentials of the last 10 users who have logged on to a system are stored in an encrypted format in a secure area of the Registry. They can be used by Windows 7 if a domain controller is not available to authenticate a user.

Change Permissions   An NTFS permission that allows the user to change other NTFS permissions. By default, users have Change Permissions for all objects they own.

cmdlets   PowerShell built-in commands. They work as mini-programs and are tightly integrated with Microsoft's .NET Framework, giving them many more capabilities than command-line commands.

command prompt   A text screen that allows you to execute commands by typing them in instead of using the point-and-click interface.

Compatibility View   A feature of IE 8 that allows web pages to be displayed using settings from previous browsers. If IE detects that a web page is not being displayed correctly, it will enable the Compatibility View button. Users can then click this button to view the web page using older browser settings.

D

Default Domain Controllers Policy   A default GPO created when the domain is created. It is linked to the Domain Controllers Organizational Unit (OU) and affects all objects in the Domain Controllers OU. By default, only domain controllers are on the Domain Controllers OU.

Default Domain Policy   A default GPO created when the domain is created. It is linked at the domain level and affects all users and computers in the domain.

default gateway   The address of the NIC on the near side of the router. It is used to define the default path out of the subnet for clients. Clients must have the correct default gateway configured to ensure they can access the Internet or any clients on different subnets.

Default User profile   The profile used when a user first logs on to a system. Windows 7 will copy the Default User profile to a new folder named with the user's logon name. This new profile is used to store settings and then re-create the same environment for the user each time the user logs on.

Deployment Image Servicing and Management (DISM)   A command-line tool included with the Windows Automated Installation Kit that can be used to mount and modify images.

Device Manager   The primary application used to install, manage, and troubleshoot devices and device drivers. It can be used to check on the status of devices installed on the system, update device drivers, and roll back drivers.

Devices and Printers   The primary tool used to manage printers, faxes, and miscellaneous devices on Windows 7. It's accessible via the Start menu below the Control Panel.

DHCP scope   A range of IP addresses within a subnet where a DHCP server issues IP addresses. For example, a subnet could be designated as 192.168.1.0/24 (with addresses between 192.168.1.1 and 192.168.1.254). A DHCP scope could be created on a DHCP server to issue addresses from 192.168.1.10 through 192.168.1.254. A single DHCP scope could include all of the addresses of a subnet, but it's more common to have the scope include only a subset of the addresses.

digitally signed software   Software published with a certificate. The certificate provides verification that the software has been published by a specific company and that it has not been modified.

DirectAccess　A new feature available with Windows 7 and Windows Server 2008 R2. It allows clients to access internal resources using Internet access but without creating a VPN. DirectAccess creates a virtual tunnel using IPv6 over IPSec to secure the traffic.

Discretionary Access Control List (DACL)　A list of Access Control Entries within a security descriptor. A security descriptor is included in NTFS files and folders and used to determine who will have access. When a user tries to access an object, the object's DACL is compared to the user's token to determine whether the user should be granted access.

Disk Defragmenter　A tool that runs in the background to defragment hard drives. The Disk Defragmenter is scheduled to run in the Task Scheduler.

DiskPart　A command-line tool that can be used to manage hard disks. DiskPart has some added capabilities that aren't available via the Disk Management graphical user interface.

distribution group　A group used for email only. It cannot be assigned permissions. Another type of group is a security group. The security group can be assigned permissions and can also be used for email.

Domain Admins　A group in the domain. Users in this group can do anything in the domain. This group is automatically added to the local Administrators group for every computer in the domain.

domain local groups　A group used to assign permissions to specific resources. A domain local group typically contains one or more global groups and can also contain universal groups.

Domain Name System (DNS)　A service hosted on a server that provides name resolution for host names. In other words, the DNS server is queried with a name and it provides an IP address. DNS servers are required in a Windows domain. The DNS server in the domain includes SRV records used to locate domain controllers in addition to regular name-resolution services.

DOSKEY　A built-in utility with the command-prompt. It allows you easily to retrieve previously issued commands by pressing the up and down arrows. It can be very useful, especially when entering long commands that have typos. Instead of entering the entire command again, you can retrieve the previous command with the up arrow and then use the right and left arrows to position the cursor where you want to make a correction.

downstream server　A WSUS server that receives its updates from an upstream WSUS server instead of from the Microsoft Update site.

driver store　The location where drivers are staged. The driver store is located at `%systemroot%\ system32\DriverStore`. Drivers are installed from the driver store and if a driver ever becomes corrupt, the original can be retrieved from the driver store.

Dynamic Host Configuration Protocol (DHCP)　A service hosted on a server to provide TCP/IP configuration information to DHCP clients. TCP/IP configuration information commonly includes an IP address, subnet mask, default gateway, and address of a DNS server.

E

Enforced   An option that can be applied to a GPO. It will ensure that all the settings of the GPO are not overwritten or blocked. Normally, the last GPO applied wins, but you can use the Enforced setting to override this default behavior. In addition, if any OUs have the Block Inheritance setting enabled, the GPO configured with the Enforced setting will not be blocked.

Enterprise Admins   A group in the forest. Users in this group can do anything in the forest. This group is a member of the domain Administrators group for every domain in the forest.

Event Viewer   A built-in tool that allows you to view several logs on Windows 7 and other operating systems. You can view the System log, the Application log, the Security log, the Setup log, and much more with the Event Viewer.

F

firewall   A tool used to filter traffic so that only specific traffic is allowed into or out of a network or into or out of a specific system. Network-based firewalls filter traffic into or out of a network and are usually a combination of hardware and software. A host-based firewall filters traffic into or out of a specific system and is software based.

function   A type of command that can be executed with PowerShell or PowerShell scripts. A PowerShell function will accept parameters and return values.

G

global groups   A type of group used to organize users (such as all the users in the Sales department with a group named G_Sales). Global groups can also contain other global groups.

GPO filtering   A technique that allows you to change the default behavior so that the GPO applies only to a specific group of users. You can remove the Apply Group Policy permission for the Authenticated Users group and instead apply this permission to another group. Or, you could set the Deny Apply Group Policy permission for any group that you don't want to be affected by the policy.

GPO scope   Where a GPO is applied. Where a GPO is linked determines which users and computers will have the GPO settings applied. Any users or computers within the scope of a GPO will inherit the settings of the GPO. If a user or computer is within the scope of multiple GPOs, it will inherit the settings of all the GPOs.

GPUpdate   A command-line tool used to reapply all GPO settings for the currently logged-on user and computer. `GPUpdate /force` is commonly used to reapply all computer and user Group Policy settings.

Group Policy   A management tool that can be used in domains to control multiple computers or users at the same time. Group Policy settings are configured in Group Policy objects (GPOs). GPOs can be linked to a site, domain, or Organizational Unit object, and the settings will apply to all the users and computers in the scope of the GPO. Local Group Policy can be used to manipulate the settings for the local system.

Group Policy Management console (GPMC)   A Microsoft Management Console (MMC) used to manage Group Policy objects. You can use the GPMC to create, manage, and manipulate GPOs.

Group Policy objects (GPOs)   A container that holds Group Policy settings. Once a GPO is created, it can be linked to a site, domain, or Organizational Unit (OU), and it will apply to all users and computers within the scope of the GPO.

Group Policy Results   A tool used to troubleshoot Group Policy. It allows you easily to determine what policies are being applied to a specific user when logged on to a specific computer. In addition, when there are conflicting settings, it helps you determine the winning GPO and applied setting.

H

Hibernate   A power-saving feature primarily used for laptops. It takes the entire contents of memory and stores them on the hard drive. When the data is stored on the hard drive, the system will completely power down and not use any power. When the system is turned back on, it retrieves the data from the hard drive and returns the system to the condition it was in before it powered down.

host cache   One of the methods of name resolution. When a name is resolved by DNS, the result is placed in the host cache (also called the DNS cache). The host cache also includes the contents of the Hosts file. You can view the host cache with the following command: `IPconfig /displaydns`.

hostname   The type of name used by hosts on the Internet. The hostname can be up to 255 characters. When a hostname is combined with a domain name, it becomes a fully qualified domain name (FQDN). Hostnames are primarily resolved by DNS servers.

Hosts file   A file located in the `%windir%\System32\Drivers\etc` folder used to resolve hostnames to IP addresses. Entries in the Hosts file are automatically placed into the host cache. Malware sometimes modifies the Hosts file to prevent a client from accessing specific websites. For example, a bogus entry could be placed in the file for Microsoft's update site, and the client would no longer be able to get updates.

hybrid image   A cross between a thin image and a thick image. Hybrid images use the Microsoft Deployment Toolkit to deploy applications using task sequences.

Hybrid sleep   This is similar to the hibernate mode used on laptops, but the system remains powered on. It is used on desktop PCs as an additional measure of protection. The current state of the computer is retained in memory with enough power provided to keep the memory refreshed. In addition, the contents of memory are stored on the hard drive.

I

Important updates   Updates released by Microsoft that address specific security issues. Important updates are also known as Security updates.

InPrivate Browsing   An IE browsing mode that prevents any data collected to be cached. Normally, data is cached from browsing sessions to improve performance. When an InPrivate Browsing session is started, cached data is deleted as soon as the browser session is closed.

InPrivate Filtering   A security feature that can be used within IE 8 to improve privacy. It can be used to block ads, images, and other tracking content.

install image   A type of image used with Windows 7 installations. The install image includes the full operating system. Custom install images can be fully configured operating systems with applications installed and settings configured. The install image is installed after the boot image.

Internet Key Exchange version 2 (IKEv2)   A tunneling protocol used with virtual private networks (VPNs). IKEv2 is the newest tunneling protocol and was introduced with Windows 7 and Windows Server 2008 R2. It can go through a NAT server and provides an additional choice over PPTP. Windows Vista, Windows Server 2008 servers, or older versions do not support IKEv2.

IPConfig   A command-line tool used to check and manipulate some basic TCP/IP configuration information. IPconfig /all is used to show TCP/IP configuration. IPConfig /release and IPConfig /renew can be used to release and renew DHCP leases.

K

Kerberos   The primary authentication protocol used within an Active Directory Domain Services domain. Kerberos requires all computers to be set to within five minutes of each other.

Key Management Service (KMS)   A service installed on a server for activation of clients in secure networks. The KMS server is used when the clients cannot activate over the Internet normally because they don't have access to the Internet. The KMS server can be used in any network with more than 5 servers or more than 25 clients and servers.

L

Last Known Good Configuration   One of the selections available from the Advanced Options screen after pressing F8 on bootup. When a user successfully logs on, the Last Known Good Configuration data is stored in the Registry. If changes are made to the system preventing the user from logging on again, the Last Known Good Configuration selection can be used to return the system to its condition when the user last logged on.

Layer 2 Tunneling Protocol (L2TP)   A tunneling protocol used with virtual private networks (VPNs). L2TP was developed by combining the strengths of Microsoft's PPTP and Cisco's Layer 2 Forwarding (L2F) protocol. It encrypts data using IPSec (and is known as L2TP/IPSec) and supports both IPv4 and IPv6. The only drawback is that IPSec can't go through a network address translation (NAT) server. You can use L2TP/IPSec with clients running Microsoft Windows 2000 or later versions.

link-local address   An IPv6 address with a prefix of FE80. It is used within a private network and is not recognized outside the enterprise. Link-local addresses are assigned using autoconfiguration similar to IPv4 APIPA addresses. They are used when a DHCP server is not available.

lite-touch installation (LTI)   A type of installation that requires very little interaction from administrators. LTIs commonly use Windows Deployment Services.

LoadState   One of the tools in the User State Migration Toolkit (USMT). LoadState can read files and settings from a migration store and restore them to the computer. ScanState is used to collect files and settings from a previous installation or from the `Windows.old` folder. ScanState stores these files and settings in a migration store.

Local Computer Policy   Group Policy settings that affect only the local computer. The Local Computer Policy can be configured when creating a reference computer. When the image is captured and deployed, all the computers that receive the image will have the same settings.

loopback processing   A Group Policy setting that will cause the computer Group Policy settings to take precedence over the user settings. Normally, the user Group Policy settings take precedence over the Computer Group Policy settings because they are applied last.

M

malware   Malicious software. It includes viruses, worms, Trojan horses, rootkits, and more.

managed service accounts   Managed service accounts allow administrators to create a class of domain accounts that can be used to manage and maintain services on local computers.

mandatory profile   A roaming profile that is configured as read-only. Users use this profile as a roaming profile, but any changes made by the user are not saved. The primary reason to create mandatory profiles is so that users have a consistent profile.

MBSACLI   The command-line equivalent of the MBSA. Because it works from the command line, you can create batch files and schedule the batch files with the task scheduler.

Microsoft Baseline Security Analyzer (MBSA)   A free download that can be used to check systems for compliance with security issues. It can check the security status of the local computer or multiple remote computers.

Microsoft Deployment Toolkit (MDT) 2010   A free download toolkit that can be used to automate installations of Windows 7. It includes the Deployment Workbench, which offers the ability to create deployment shares, add images, and create task sequences.

Microsoft Update   A website hosted by Microsoft that allows clients and servers to download updates. Clients can use Automatic Update to connect to Microsoft Update. Servers such as Windows Software Update Services can also connect to the Microsoft Update site to download updates.

Microsoft Virtual PC   An application that can host virtual operating systems and virtual networks within Windows 7. When used with Windows XP Mode, you can host virtual applications running within a Windows XP operating system on a Windows 7 system.

Multiple Activation Key (MAK)   A single key used to activate multiple clients. Large enterprises can purchase a MAK with a specific number of licenses. This single key can be used for an image, and activation is automatic over the Internet.

N

name resolution   A method used to resolve names to IP addresses. On the Internet, this is done with DNS. On internal networks, it can be done with DNS, WINS, the Hosts file, the LMHosts file, the host cache, the NetBIOS cache, and broadcasts.

NetBIOS name   A name used to identify systems on a Windows network. A NetBIOS name is composed of 15 readable characters, with the 16th byte identifying a service running on the system. The use of NetBIOS names has been significantly reduced in networks in favor of hostnames, but they are still being used by older applications. NetBIOS names are not supported in IPv6.

netsh   A shell command that can be accessed from the command prompt. The Net Shell (netsh) command can be used to configure many different networking settings.

Network and Sharing Center   A central tool used to manage network connectivity for Windows 7 computers. You can view basic network connections and set up new connections here.

Network Discovery   A process used to simplify configuring and connecting network-connected systems and devices. It is enabled by default in private (non-domain) networks and can be enabled in a domain network with Group Policy. It uses the Function Discovery Provider Host service and Web Services Dynamic Discovery service.

NSLookup   A command-line tool used to get specific information from a DNS server. It can be used to query DNS servers and determine if the DNS server can resolve specific names.

NTFS   New Technology File System (NTFS) is the secure filesystem used with Windows systems including Windows 7. NTFS includes permissions that can be assigned at the file and folder levels.

O

optional updates   Free additional software programs that can be downloaded and installed on a system. Optional updates aren't related to Important or Recommended updates.

P

paging file   A file on the disk that is used by Windows 7 as virtual memory. The recommended size of the paging file is 1.5 times the physical RAM.

Password Policy   Group Policy settings that can control password requirements such as the minimum length and maximum age of passwords.

permission inheritance   Permissions are inherited from parent folders to child folders. In other words, if a folder is created within another folder, the child folder inherits all of the permissions assigned to the parent folder. Inherited permissions are dimmed and can't be changed unless permission inheritance is disabled.

permissions   Used to identify the resources a user can access. Contrast this with rights, which identify what a user can do on a system.

Ping   A command-line tool used to check connectivity with other systems on the network. It sends out echo request packets and returns echo reply packets using the Internet Control Message Protocol (ICMP). It is possible for ICMP packets to be blocked.

Point-to-Point Tunneling Protocol (PPTP)   A tunneling protocol used with virtual private networks (VPNs). PPTP is an older tunneling protocol. It encrypts data using Microsoft Point-to-Point Encryption (MPPE). PPTP is not supported on IPv6. Although PPTP is still used, you can expect it to be used less often in the future. You can use PPTP with clients running Microsoft Windows 2000 or later versions.

PowerShell Execution Policy   A built-in policy that controls the execution of PowerShell scripts. The default setting is Restricted, and it prevents the execution of any PowerShell scripts. The policy can be modified with the `Set-ExecutionPolicy` command at an elevated PowerShell command prompt.

Pre-boot Execution Environment (PXE) Pronounced "pixie." A set of hardware and BIOS capabilities that allow a client to boot to the network environment without any client operating system. The F12 key is pressed on most computers to start the boot process. If a Windows Deployment Services server is available, pressing the F12 key will cause the client to connect to the Windows Deployment Services server.

Previous Versions A part of the Windows 7 System Protection feature. When Previous Versions is enabled (and it is by default), you can restore a modified file to a previous version of the file. Previous versions of files are stored on a per-drive basis.

Problem Steps Recorder A Windows 7 feature that can record the actual steps users take to run or use an application. This can be very useful for users who have trouble articulating the actions they took.

Programs and Features applet An applet within Control Panel that can be used to uninstall, change, and repair applications. It can be useful to reinstall an application that has become corrupt and no longer runs normally.

Protected Mode A feature introduced with IE 7 in Windows 7 and supported in IE 8 in Windows 7. Protected Mode runs IE in a restricted privilege mode to help protect against different types of malware. It makes it harder for malware to be installed on your computer.

proxy server A central server used by internal clients to access the Internet. When it's used in a network, all clients are configured to submit Internet requests to the proxy server, and the proxy server will then request the data from the Internet.

Public folder A folder in the `C:\Users\` folder, which is shared as `Users`. The `Users\Public` folder includes these subfolders: `Public Documents`, `Public Downloads`, `Public Music`, `Public Pictures`, `Public Recorded TV`, and `Public Videos`. When Public Folder Sharing is enabled, users can copy data they want to share directly into the related folder so that it is accessible to other users.

Public Key Infrastructure (PKI) A group of technologies used to issue and manage certificates. Certificates are issued by certification authorities. Certificates include a public key that is matched to a private key. These keys are used to encrypt and decrypt data. Certificates can be used to sign applications and drivers digitally. They are also used to create secure sessions on the Internet.

R

Recommended updates Updates that are performance related. These are designed to help improve the operation of a computer. They can include updates that will resolve bugs that cause an application to hang or crash. They can also include new drivers.

Remote Desktop Services (RDS)   A virtualization technology used to deliver applications or desktops to users. It was previously known as Terminal Services but was renamed in Windows Server 2008 R2.

Remote Server Administration Tools (RSAT)   A group of tools that can be installed on a Windows 7 computer to enable IT administrators to manage roles and features on servers in the domain. Windows Server 2003, Windows Server 2008, and Windows Server 2008 R2 servers can all be managed using RSAT.

Removable Storage Access policy   Group Policy settings that can control the use of removable storage devices such as USB flash drives. You can configure an access policy for different types of devices. You can also deny all access to any removable devices with the All Removal Storage Classes: Deny All Access setting.

rights   Used to identify what a user can do on a system. Contrast this with permissions, which identify the resources a user can access.

roaming profile   A profile that is available to a user when they log on to any computer in the domain. A roaming profile ensures the same profile is available to a user no matter which computer is used. A folder is shared on a server that is available to the user on the network, and the user's account is then configured to use this share for the profile.

S

Safe Mode   A mode used to boot a system with only the core drivers and services running. If you suspect that one of the drivers or services is causing the system to misbehave, you can access one of the safe modes and start the system without the errant driver or service. Three safe modes are available: Safe Mode, Safe Mode with Networking, and Safe Mode with Command Prompt.

ScanState   One of the tools in the User State Migration Toolkit (USMT). ScanState is used to collect files and settings from a previous installation or from the Windows.old folder. It will store these files and settings in a migration store. They can then be restored using LoadState.

scheduled-cast transmission   A type of image transmission from Windows Deployment Services. Scheduled-cast transmissions start based on three criteria: when a threshold is reached (such as five clients), when a specific time is reached, or when an administrator manually starts them.

Secure Shell Tunneling Protocol (SSTP)   A tunneling protocol used with virtual private networks (VPNs). SSTP was introduced with Windows Vista and Windows Server 2008. It uses SSL to encrypt the traffic as HTTPS traffic. It can go through a NAT server, providing an additional choice if your VPN server is located behind a NAT server. SSTP provides better security than PPTP and supports both IPv4 and IPv6. You can use SSTP with clients running Microsoft Windows Vista, Windows Server 2008, or later versions.

security group   A group that can be assigned permissions or used as a distribution group. A distribution group cannot be assigned permissions and can be used only for email.

security identifier (SID)   A string of characters used to identify objects such as users, computers, and groups in Windows domains. The SID is created when the object is created. SIDs are unique within domains and forests.

Security updates   Updates released by Microsoft that address specific security issues. Security updates are also known as Important updates.

Service Control (SC)   A command-line tool that can be used to query, start, stop, and manipulate services.

service pack (SP)   A comprehensive update to the system that includes all of the critical updates, security updates, and update rollups released since either the last service pack (SP) or the operating system was released.

Services console   A graphical user interface tool that can be used to manipulate services.

share   A folder that has been shared. Shared folders can be accessed over the network using a Universal Naming Convention of \\servername\sharename.

signed driver   A driver that has been tested by the Windows Hardware Quality Labs (WHQL). After the driver passes the tests, it is signed with a certificate and referred to as a signed driver or a trusted driver. Signed drivers are made available through the Windows Update site.

sleep   A low-power mode for a computer. When the computer is in sleep mode, most of the components do not draw any power. Power is provided to the memory to ensure that the contents of memory are not lost, and enough power is provided to the processor to check occasionally for user action such as pressing a key. When a key is pressed, the computer wakes up fully.

Startup Repair   A tool that can automatically resolve many startup problems. If the system fails to start, Windows 7 will usually boot into this tool automatically. It can also be launched manually.

super-mandatory profile   A user profile similar to a mandatory roaming user profile with one important addition: If network or server problems prevent the user from downloading the mandatory profile, the user is unable to log on.

Sysprep   A tool used to prepare reference computers prior to being imaged. Sysprep removes the unique information of the system such as the security identifier (SID) and the computer name. Windows Deployment Services cannot capture an image of a system unless Sysprep is first run.

System Center Configuration Manager (SCCM)   A Microsoft server product that can be used to assess, deploy, and update servers, client computers, and devices. It can be used with the Microsoft Deployment Toolkit for Zero Touch Installations.

System Configuration   A utility also known as MSConfig that can be used to modify different system configuration settings, boot options, and startup options.

System Restore   A tool that can be used to create restore points that can return the system to a previous state. It does not affect any documents, pictures, or other user data. It affects only system files by applying a restore point created previously.

system variables   Variables used within Windows 7 and other operating systems. These variable names can be used instead of the actual names or paths in scripts. For example, the %computername% variable will substitute the actual computer name when a script is run. The %systemroot% variable holds the location where Windows was installed (such as C:\Windows). The %username% variable holds the name of the currently logged-on user.

T

Take Ownership   An NTFS permission. Any user with the Take Ownership permission of a file or folder can take ownership of it, and then, as the owner, the user can change permissions. Administrators can always take ownership of NTFS files and folders.

Task Scheduler   A built-in program that can be used to schedule any executable program, including scripts.

task sequence   An element of the Deployment Workbench in the Microsoft Deployment Toolkit. It allows an administrator to identify the specific steps of an installation. Task sequences are an important element of Zero Touch Installations.

Teredo   Teredo is a tunneling protocol that encapsulates IPv6 packets within IPv4. It is intended to be a temporary bridge as all networks transition from IPv4 to IPv6. Teredo uses Teredo clients and Teredo servers. In this context, Windows 7 is the client. Windows 7 clients use the server located at teredo.ipv6.microsoft.com as their Teredo server. The Teredo server is used to detect what type of NAT is between the client and the destination server so that Teredo can determine how to encapsulate the packets.

thick image   A Windows installation image that is customized with applications, device drivers, and updates.

thin image   A basic Windows installation image with very little customization. The default install images available on Windows 7 installation DVDs could be considered thin images.

transforms   A file with the .mst extension used to alter the default installation of an .msi installation package. Transforms are deployed with the .msi installation file.

trusted certification authority   A certification authority (CA) that has a certificate in the Trusted Root Certification Authority store. If you trust the CA, you automatically trust any certificates issued from the CA.

Trusted Platform Module (TPM)   A microchip that is located on the motherboard of the system and can be used to store BitLocker keys. TPM version 1.2 and BIOS support are required to support BitLocker fully. TPM can be used to protect fully the operating system's drive and the critical startup process.

U

Universal Naming Convention (UNC)   A specific format used to access shared resources over the network. The Universal Naming Convention uses the format \\ServerName\Share-Name, and it is used to access both shared folders and shared printers.

Update History   A list of all updates that have been deployed to a computer. The Update History report includes the common name, the status (Successful or Failed) of the update installation, the importance (Important, Recommended, or Optional), and the date it was installed.

update rollup   A significant number of updates released since the last service pack or since the operating system was released. It is a cumulative set of critical updates, security updates, hotfixes, and other updates.

updates   Any additions or modifications to the operating system or applications released after the official release of the operating system or software.

upstream server   A WSUS server that receives its updates from the Microsoft Update site and sends updates to downstream WSUS servers.

User Account Control (UAC)   A security feature designed to ensure that changes cannot be made to the system by malware. Administrative users have two tokens when they log on: the standard user access token and the administrator access token. If an action requires administrative permission, the user is prompted before the administrator access token is used.

user profile   A set of data that is used to re-create the user's environment each time the user logs on. It includes several folders such as Contacts, Cookies, Desktop, Downloads, Favorites, and more. It also includes user-specific Registry settings.

User Rights Assignment   A Group Policy node you can use to control rights and privileges of different users. This node is within the Local Policies node.

User State Migration Toolkit (USMT)   Part of the Windows Automated Installation Kit (Windows AIK). It includes tools such as LoadState and ScanState that can migrate data and settings from previous installations and restore them to a Windows 7 installation.

V

Virtual Desktop Infrastructure (VDI)   The practice of hosting one or more virtual desktop operating systems on a host operating system. Windows 7 supports several VDI methods. These include Windows Virtual PC (VPC) and Remote Desktop Services (RDS).

virtual memory   Hard drive space used to mimic physical RAM. A processor can't access the data stored in virtual memory on the hard drive but instead must move it to physical RAM. When the system needs to access data that is stored on the drive, other data in the physical RAM is moved onto the hard drive and the requested data is swapped back to RAM.

W

Wi-Fi Protected Access (WPA)   The first improvement over WEP. One of the primary benefits of WPA is that it is compatible with most of the same hardware that used WEP. WPA was intended to be an interim fix for WEP until a more permanent solution was identified. Although WPA is more secure than WEP, attackers have cracked it. The permanent solution is WPA2.

Wi-Fi Protected Access 2 (WPA2)   The permanent fix for WEP. It is also known as 802.11i. If you have a choice among WEP, WPA, and WPA2, use WPA2. WPA2 provides the strongest security of the three.

wildcard   A character that can take the place of one or more other characters in the command line or batch files. The * character will take the place of zero or more characters. The ? character will take the place of a single character.

Windows 7 Enterprise   The edition of Windows 7 used in most enterprises. It includes additional features such as BitLocker, AppLocker, and BranchCache. Enterprises must have a Software Assurance contract with Microsoft and purchase this edition with a volume license.

Windows 7 Professional   The edition of Windows 7 intended for high-end home users and business users. It can join a domain but lacks some of the advanced features supported in Windows 7 Enterprise and Ultimate editions.

Windows 7 Ultimate   This edition of Windows 7 includes all of the features of Windows 7 Enterprise. Home users can purchase it without having a Software Assurance contract.

Windows Automated Installation Kit (Windows AIK)   A set of tools that are used to automate the installation of Windows 7. It includes the User State Migration Toolkit (USMT), ImageX, the Deployment Image Servicing and Management (DISM) tool, and Windows System Image Manager.

Windows Defender   A built-in Windows 7 application designed to protect against spyware. It's configured to run automatically in the background and protect the system against spyware.

Windows Deployment Services (WDS)   A server role that can be added to Windows Server 2008 and Windows Server 2008 R2. WDS can capture images and automate the deployment of images. WDS is commonly used with Lite Touch Installations.

Windows Error Reporting (WER)   WER is used to report issues to Microsoft from individual computers. When a problem event occurs, WER can be invoked to collect and report information on the error. WER is most commonly invoked when an unresponsive application is terminated using Task Manager.

Windows Feature   A tool used to add or remove features from Windows 7. For example, after installing the Remote Server Administration Tools (RSAT), you can use the Windows Feature tool to add and remove specific RSAT tools.

Windows Firewall   A software-based firewall built into Windows 7. It uses different rules to allow or deny traffic.

Windows Hardware Quality Labs (WHQL)   An organization sponsored by Microsoft that performs a series of compatibility tests on drivers. If the driver passes the tests, WHQL issues a certificate and associates the certificate with the driver. The certificate provides the signature for the driver and assures you that it has been tested and verified by Microsoft. Signed drivers are then made available via the Windows Update site.

Windows Internet Name Service (WINS)   A service used to resolve NetBIOS names to IP addresses. The use of NetBIOS names is significantly reduced in current Microsoft networks, but they may still be used by legacy applications. If legacy applications use NetBIOS names, a WINS server may be required in the network.

Windows Management Instrumentation (WMI)   A tool that can be used from the command line and in scripts to query systems for detailed information. WMI queries can retrieve information about local or remote computers.

Windows Memory Diagnostic   A test available from the System Recovery screen. It will check both your installed RAM and the processor cache memory. This test is the easiest and most effective way to check your memory.

Windows PowerShell   An extensible version of the command prompt. Windows 7 includes PowerShell 2.0, which is the same version that is installed on Windows Server 2008 R2. PowerShell includes many cmdlets, aliases, and functions that can be executed from the PowerShell prompt.

Windows PowerShell ISE   An integrated scripting environment built into Windows 7. You can use it to create, debug, and modify PowerShell scripts.

Windows Preinstallation Environment (WinPE)   A minimal operating system used to begin the installation for Windows 7. It provides access to the tools needed to complete the full installation.

Windows Recovery Environment (WinRE)   An extension of the Windows Preinstallation Environment (PE). It includes several tools that can be used to troubleshoot and recover a system.

Windows Software Updates Services (WSUS)   A free server product that can be used to control updates sent to clients. Instead of clients using Automatic Update to retrieve updates from the Microsoft Update site, the WSUS server can retrieve the updates from the Microsoft Update site. An administrator can approve the desired updates, and the updates will then be sent to the clients.

Windows System Image Manager   A tool available in the Windows Automated Installation Kit. It is used to create unattended answer files to automate Windows 7 installations.

Windows Update client   An application that is responsible for installing updates on Windows 7 computers. It includes the Windows Update service, which is the primary service used to detect, download, and install updates used to keep Windows 7 and other applications up to date.

Wired Equivalent Privacy (WEP)   A security protocol designed to provide the same level of privacy for a wireless network as for a wired network. Unfortunately, WEP had significant problems and was later cracked. It was replaced by WPA as an interim fix and then by WPA2 as a permanent fix.

wireless access point (WAP)   A device used to provide access from a wireless device to a wired network. WAPs are commonly used in larger networks to provide this access.

wireless router   A WAP with additional capabilities. Many small offices, home offices (SOHOs) and home users commonly use a wireless router. The wireless client is able to connect to the wireless router and have access to the same resources as wired users.

WPA-Enterprise   WPA with an 802.1x server for authentication. The 802.1x server will distribute keys to each client instead of the clients using a PSK. It can also use either smart cards or the Protected Extensible Authorization Protocol (PEAP) for authentication. Smart cards provide better security, but they also require more resources on your network. You can select either AES or TKIP for encryption. AES is preferred.

WPA-Personal   WPA with a pre-shared key (PSK) for authentication. This PSK provides limited authentication. You can select either Advanced Encryption Standard (AES) or Temporal Key Integrity Protocol (TKIP) for encryption. TKIP is compatible with older hardware, but AES is preferred if your hardware supports it.

WPA2-Enterprise   The strongest wireless security type available with Windows 7. It uses an 802.1x server for authentication—the same as is used in WPA-Enterprise. It can use either smart cards or the Protected Extensible Authorization Protocol (PEAP) for authentication.

Smart cards provide the best authentication. You can select either AES or TKIP for encryption. AES is preferred.

WPA2-Personal   Similar to WPA-Personal, except it uses the stronger WPA2 authentication instead of WPA. WPA2-Personal uses a pre-shared key (PSK). You enter the same PSK on the Windows 7 system and the wireless devices. You can select either AES or TKIP for encryption. AES is preferred.

WSUS statistics server   A single WSUS server that collects information from all WSUS-managed clients in the enterprise. If your environment has multiple WSUS servers, a central WSUS server could still be used for overall statistics in the enterprise.

Z

zero-touch installation (ZTI)   A type of installation that requires almost no interaction from administrators. ZTIs commonly use the Microsoft Deployment Toolkit and System Center Configuration Manager (SCCM).

Index

Note to the Reader: Throughout this index **boldfaced** page numbers indicate primary discussions of a topic. *Italicized* page numbers indicate illustrations.

The Perfect Companion for all Windows 7 Desktop Technicians and Administrators

Contains about 40 minutes of video walkthroughs with author Darril Gibson

- Darril walks you through some of the more difficult tasks you can expect to face as a Windows 7 Desktop Technician or Administrator.

- See firsthand how to enable and create file shares, create users and groups, perform a startup repair, and much more.

For Certification candidates, we've included practice tests for both IT Pro: Windows 7 exams

- Windows 7, Enterprise Desktop Support Technician (70-685)

- Windows 7, Enterprise Desktop Administrator (70-686)

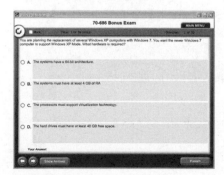

CD also includes electronic flashcards to jog your memory of topics covered in the book!

- Reinforce your understanding of key concepts with these hardcore, flashcard-style questions.

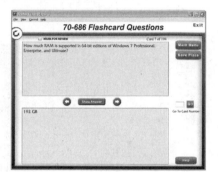

Search through the complete book in PDF!

- Access the entire *Windows 7 Desktop Support and Administration*, complete with figures and tables, in electronic format.

- Search the *Windows 7 Desktop Support and Administration* chapters to find information on any topic in seconds.

Get real!

Get *Real World Skills* from Sybex and take your career to the next level. These books not only help you on the job, they also help you prepare for your next certification exam.

Get real. Get Sybex!

For more information, go to www.sybex.com/go/realworldskills

An Imprint of ⊕WILEY
Now you know.